V&R

Refo500 Academic Studies

Edited by
Herman J. Selderhuis

Volume 97

Elisa Frei / Eleonora Rai (eds.)

Profiling Saints

Images of Modern Sanctity in a Global World

Vandenhoeck & Ruprecht

Bibliographic information published by the Deutsche Nationalbibliothek:
The Deutsche Nationalbibliothek lists this publication in the Deutsche Nationalbibliografie; detailed bibliographic data available online: https://dnb.de.

Cover design: SchwabScantechnik, Göttingen
Typesetting: le-tex publishing services, Leipzig
Printed and bound: Hubert & Co. BuchPartner, Göttingen
Printed in the EU

Vandenhoeck & Ruprecht Verlage | www.vandenhoeck-ruprecht-verlage.com

ISSN 2198-3089
ISBN 978-3-525-57356-3

Gustave Doré (1832–83), Dante and Beatrice gaze upon the highest Heaven; illustrations to the Divine Comedy, Paradiso Canto XXXI. Courtesy of Wikimedia Commons.

Contents

Acknowledgments

In the last few years, sanctity and martyrdom have been objects of interest for diverse projects with which we had the pleasure to collaborate. This book, and the online conference preceding it, has been enriched by the lively scholarly contributions from such projects. We are most grateful to the institutions promoting, financing, and hosting these projects, and to the scholars, colleagues, and friends with whom we were able to collaborate for their mentorship and generous exchange of ideas.

In particular, we thank the Research Foundation – Flanders (FWO) and KU Leuven whose project G044621N *'Knocking on Heaven's Doors'. Free will, Money, and Emotions in the Theological Systems of Leonard Lessius and Luis de Molina (late 1500s–early 1600s)* (Promoter Wim François and co-promoter Wim Decock), conducted by Eleonora Rai in 2021–2022, focused on the soteriological and moral thought of Jesuits Leonard Lessius (1554–1623) and Luis de Molina (1535–1600) while also tracing the link between Lessius's theology of salvation and his failed cause for canonization; the University of Macerata with the PRIN (Progetti di Rilevante Interesse Nazionale) project *Sacrifice in the Europe of the Religious Conflicts and in the Early Modern World: Comparisons, Interpretations, Legitimations* (PI Vincenzo Lavenia, University of Bologna) which, focusing on the idea of sacrifice in the Early Modern Age, also touched on the theme of martyrdom and thus sanctity. Elisa Frei worked on this latter project within the local unit of the University of Macerata (directed by Sabina Pavone) and explored the topic of sacrifice and self-sacrifice (i. e. martyrdom) in Asia, as viewed by Catholic missionaries; the Department of History at the University of Turin, with the MUR Young Researchers project *Jesuitization – The Jesuit Law of Canonization: Models, Aristocracy, Gender (1500s–1700s)* (with the support of the Fondazione Compagnia di San Paolo), carried out by Eleonora Rai, which analyses the key and yet underestimated Jesuit influence on the development of systematic law regulating canonization, and the creation and use of models of sanctity as means of soft power for influencing or shaping the behaviour of Early Modern Italian aristocracies; the Goethe-Universität Frankfurt am Main, Faculty of Catholic Theology, where Elisa Frei works on Church history, relations and perceptions between East and West, and the missionaries and writers of the Society of Jesus under the supervision of Christoph Nebgen; and finally, the Institute for Advanced Jesuit Studies at Boston College that hosted the online conference on its platforms.

As for the online symposium from which this book originated, the editors wish to thank those who participated as speakers or discussants but for various reasons are not represented as authors in this volume, namely: Michela Catto (University of

Turin), Leonardo Cohen (Ben-Gurion University of the Negev), Emanuele Colombo (DePaul University), Simon Ditchfield (University of York), Jean-Pascal Gay (UC Louvain), Grace Harpster (Georgia State University), Robert Aleksander Maryks (Adam Mickiewicz University in Poznań), Camilla Russell (Sapienza University/ Newcastle University, AU), and Steffen Zierholz (University of Tübingen). They have our deepest gratitude for having enriched the online symposium with their brilliant contributions.

Elisa Frei, Eleonora Rai

Fantastic Saints and Where to Find Them: Why does Sanctity Matter?

Preface to *Profiling Saints*

When we began, during the pandemics, to reflect on the possibility of organizing an online, international conference on Early Modern and Modern Christian sanctity and saints – which we had the pleasure to host in December 2021 – we were confronted with a pressing question: why do these themes still matter today? Communicating the reasons for researching sanctity – and upstream, why do we spend our lives studying what we do? – is of the utmost importance for developing our understanding of a phenomenon that has characterized Christian history since the very beginning, although its meanings, features, and images have changed according to different times and places, over the course of two millennia.

To begin with, Early Modern and Modern saints are not at all *fantastic*, and readers are thus invited to forgive the cinema-inspired joke behind our title. There is a clear distinction between ancient or Medieval saints, who were more creatively imagined than historically framed, and the saints as understood and represented from the 1500s onwards. Modern sanctity required both historical investigations and compliance with a juridical and judicial system that did not exist in earlier eras. Hagiography was born as an attempt to elaborate a science of saints and canonization law developed between the 1600s and 1700s, especially through Urban VIII (1568–1644) and Prospero Lambertini's (future Benedict XIV, 1675–1758) legal reorganization of the cult of the dead and canonization. Modern sanctity is meant to be unassailable: through the centralization and normalization of canonization procedures, the Roman Church responded to the need to regulate local communities and powers as well as the cult of the dead, the latter representing a key factor in the life of Catholics. No *fantastic saints* will be found in this book, but it does sketch many different images of sanctity and saints in a world that, through geographical expansion, religious renovation, and the unravelling of modernity, was relentlessly changing – and sanctity changed along with it. We can read sanctity through a set of lenses that offer us different perspectives and try to integrate these various views for a more comprehensive understanding.

First of all, saints embody imitable models of behaviour of Christian perfection. Starting in the Early Modern Age, such models were identified as heroic; that is to say, saints practiced virtues to a heroic degree but, being only human, through their example offered not only the guidelines needed for other human beings to follow their lead, but also the hope that Christian perfection is within reach. Throughout the centuries, these behavioural models have changed depending on both the cultural benchmarks of the areas where they were promoted and the strategies of those who postulated for the candidates to sanctity's canonization: in other words, sanctity can be understood as a phenomenon orchestrated "from above", directed by the upper echelons of the Church and its institutions (just think of the religious orders, for example, and their efforts to canonize their own members) and, at the same time, growing up "from below", as a product of the sensibilities of the societies practicing devotion to the dead.

When we observe sanctity as a strategic site of communication, we cannot but notice that hagiographical models launch specific messages, as intended by the postulators of the cause. As such, they constitute powerful means of soft power influencing the societies in question. To illustrate this point, take for example the promotion of the martyrial model in the 1800s, after the revolutionary period and rise of a series of anti-Catholic or anti-Roman cultural and political movements, when the Church aimed to foster the image of a suffering, besieged body. Or the success of the female sanctity model of the good mother fostered in the 1900s. Gianna Beretta Molla (1922–62), the first example that comes to mind, met the Church's need to offer an imitable example of Christian perfection to the lay world in the context of increasingly important Catholic associationism and was deeply caught up with contemporary ongoing discussions about the family and abortion.

On the other hand, when we look at sanctity as a changing phenomenon nourished by the places in which it surfaces, we can better understand not only the devotional side of it – there is no sanctity without devotion – but also how local communities have influenced canonization attempts. Local veneration of the dead is particularly stressed, for example, in cases of missionaries who spent their lives in specific geographical or social contexts. Some popular missionaries were considered living saints by the faithful among whom they preached: the case of Jesuit Francesco De Geronimo (1642–1716) is self-explanatory given that, after his death, devotees dismantled his confessional to take pieces home, and even fed the sick with it begging for miracles through a sort of relic-eating practice. Another example is missionaries who evangelized far-away lands in the age of geographical expansion: to cite another Jesuit, Matteo Ricci (1552–1610), the evangelizer of China, was proclaimed *venerable* quite recently.

Keeping in mind that every canonization entails a degree of strategy, some cases in particular allow us to analyse how the local communities in which devotion arose considered the candidates to sainthood: what features mattered in the place and time when devotion developed? Which raises the correlated question: what was fundamental for the communities of the faithful, what were their needs, and what did they value as characteristics of holiness? De Geronimo, to clarify with an example, was considered a living saint for many reasons among which his alleged ability to provoke rain or heal crops, acts that were key necessities in the rural areas where he preached.

In the Catholic panorama, saints, along with the tangible relics of their bodies, provide a connection between this world and the other. Saints have the ability to intercede before God for those who pray to them: they are mediators, they bridge healings and miracles. They are a "hook" pointing upwards, towards Heaven, and give hope to the faithful in need. It is thus no surprise that the culture of sanctity is still key in the Catholic world, that ceremonies of canonization attract waves of pilgrims to Rome, and that devotion towards the saints occupies a seminal place in the life of billions of Catholics around the world. Saints, along with their relics, also have eschatological meaning, as already outlined by Gregory of Tours (539–94): they preview the final times, the last moment, when the saints and others who are saved will stand with God in Heaven. Canonizing a candidate to sainthood means, first and foremost, announcing to the world that he or she is undoubtedly in Heaven.

Sanctity is an ongoing historical, anthropological, legal, social, cultural, liturgical, gendered, emotional, and artistic phenomenon. As such, it deserves to be fully explored from a variety of angles and has attracted the interest of scholars ranging from cultural, legal, and Church historians to experts in liturgical studies or art historians, to name just a few. *Profiling Saints* attempts to offer diverse images and representations of a phenomenon as multifaceted as Modern sanctity, in a global perspective that mirrors the times when it developed, between Europe and overseas.

Exploring sanctity and canonization records, rich with witnesses' depositions, thus offers a chance to observe the development of an amazingly wide array of ideas and practices – from the cult of the dead and their relics to the shaping of behavioural models and the culture of martyrdom, from social, emotional, and gendered practices of sanctity to the artistic representation of saints. We will thus have the opportunity to explore the functioning of different societies around the world in their relationship with the promotion of canonization causes and better understand the choices of the Roman power centres. Sanctity still matters not only by virtue of the undeniable value it holds in the Catholic world, but also because it represents a surprisingly powerful prism through which to observe various facets of religious, social, and cultural history in the course of the Early Modern and Contemporary Age. This awareness was the starting point for inviting scholars from the most diverse of backgrounds to offer their competencies during the intense activities of the abovementioned online conference and now for the realization of this volume.

Fuelled by fruitful and cordial collaboration between the volume editors, the conference *Profiling Saints: Understanding the Theological and Cultural Foundations of Catholic Hagiographical Models (1500s–1900s)* was held online at the end of 2021. The event was successful in terms of participation, and the participants showed interest in publishing the proceedings – not only the speakers, but also those who attended the international workshop as scholars who have been engaging with the topic for years. Researchers working on the Early Modern Age, with different areas of expertise and academic experience, thus became the authors of this book and enriched the discussion initiated at the conference with new contributions, making the most of an interdisciplinary approach to study a heterogeneous array of topics related to sanctity.

The first and last papers of this volume offer an overview of sanctity in the Early Modern Age. The very idea of sanctity was continually scrutinized, judged, and reformed during the sixteenth and seventeenth centuries, as Franco Motta (University of Turin) explains so well in his introductory essay, *Sanctity and Modernity: Opposition or Agreement? An Introduction to Profiling Saints*; its global dimension is underlined in the insightful *Sanctity in a Global World: Continuity and Discontinuity in the Early Modern Age. Conclusions to Profiling Saints* by Sabina Pavone (University of Napoli L'Orientale).

The first section of the book sketches a portrait *Through the Saints: Understanding the Church across the Centuries*, starting from the case of *Temptation, Torture, and Truth: Philip Neri and Reforming Catholic Rome.* Tom Santa Maria (Yale University) clarifies how multiple aspects of Neri's life made him a most fitting candidate for canonization – such as having founded a new religious order, the Oratorians – and Neri thus obtained this status fairly easily and quickly, as part of the famous group of saints canonized in 1622. The timespan of this first sections allows us to appreciate the points of continuity and difference from the Medieval model of sanctity until the Modern Age, thanks also to Stefan Samerski (Ludwig-Maximilians-University Munich). Samerski asks *What about Saints of the French Revolution? Canonization and Beatification after 1789,* pointing to a fundamental date that deeply influenced the Church's canonization policies. Finally, Joris Geldhof (KU Leuven) offers an overview of the presence of *Modern Saints in the Roman Missal: An Exploration of the Proprium de Sanctis.* The author notes continuities and discontinuities over the centuries (from the sixteenth to the twentieth centuries Roman Missals), compares different categories of sainthood and their related prayers, and reflects on them statistically (religious order, gender, geographic and cultural provenance, etc.).

Art history is a marvellous lens through which to appreciate the many, hazy nuances of sanctity, and the second section of this book thus focuses on *Visualizing Sanctity and the Sacred: Images and Promotion.* The Swiss-based group GLOBECOSAL (Global Economies of Salvation) lays out the aims of their ERC- and SNF-funded research. *Promoting Sanctity by the Means of Artworks,* a collaborative paper written by Raphaèle Preisinger (PI), Hannah Friedman, Jonathan Greenwood, Wei Jiang, and Lucia Querejazu Escobari (University of Zürich), investigates the multiple functions of artwork in the process of negotiating sanctity between Rome and local areas from the 1500s to the 1700s. Rachel Miller (California State

University, Sacramento) reflects on *Imagining the World through St Francis Xavier Imagery: A Case Study in Quito.* Xavier, among the 1622 group of saints, was one of the first two Jesuit saints to be canonized – together with the founder of the order, Ignatius of Loyola. His missionary activities in Japan became famous thanks not only to his own written accounts, but also to multiple artworks depicting him very differently depending on whether they were produced in European or Latin American contexts. Antonio Gerace (Fscire/KU Leuven) and Tamara Dominici (independent researcher) focus on *De picturis et imagines sacris*, published by the theologian Johannes Molanus in 1570. In *From Book to Image. Molanus and the Netherlandish Holy Images*, the authors also highlight the importance of holy images in expressing Catholic devotion.

The third section investigates the *Hagiographical Representations in the Society of Jesus.* Among the many religious orders founded in the sixteenth century, the importance of the Jesuits cannot be overestimated, especially in the fields of pedagogy and missionizing, as well as hagiographical promotion. The names of some of the most important Jesuits – *in primis* Francis Xavier, also known as "the Apostle of the Indies" – thus resurface throughout *Profiling Saints*. Shiri Roelofs (KU Leuven) studies the case of the Jesuit *Robert Bellarmine (1542–1621), the Louvain Lectures, and Economic Thought: Image and Impact of a Saint Viewed from an Underestimated Perspective*, focusing on the evolution of Bellarmine's hagiographical model. Carlo Pelliccia (Università degli Studi Internazionali di Roma) publishes the first critical edition of *"Or voi conoscete qual sarà stata la santità del Saverio": The Panegyric by Eriprando Maria Giuliari (1728–1805)*. Both essays show how, even centuries after their death, figures such as Bellarmine and Xavier offered exemplary but extremely different and evolving models of sanctity, with the consequence that their canonizations also took place under various circumstances and in distinct times.

The development of the idea of Early Modern sanctity and hagiographical models is closely related to the history of the Society of Jesus, as the latter is intertwined with the order's Japanese missions. Jesuits were the first Catholics to establish missions in such a distant civilization and, although the first years were depicted as extremely promising by Jesuit sources, Japan was soon recognized as one of the most dangerous and hopeless of such endeavours. In the Early Modern Age, missionaries sent to faraway lands ran the risk – or had the much-hoped-for chance, from their perspective – of suffering a violent death that could be framed as martyrdom and thus trigger a canonization cause. The fourth section focuses on *Martyrs of Japan: Models, Emotions, and the Causes for Beatification and Canonization.* Carla Tronu Montané (Kansai University of Foreign Studies) outlines a complete introduction on sanctity in Japan, from the sixteenth century until recent times. Her *From 'Martyrs of Japan' to 'Japanese Martyrs'. Models of Sanctity and Diversity in the Canonization Causes for Martyrs of Japan* shows the importance of approaching such topics not only from a religious perspective, but with an in-depth analysis of all the elements involved in the bigger picture – and in light of the most recent developments in historical research, such as post-colonial and women's studies. Similarly, the chapter by Linda Zampol D'Ortia (Ca´ Foscari Venezia/Australian Catholic University) uses the promising and relatively recent methodologies of the history of emotions. In *Emotional Practices of Catholic Martyrdom in Early Modern Japan*, the author analyses numerous documents produced by Catholic missionaries to identify the practices that characterized martyrdom models in in the Japanese Catholic community, particularly struck by violent deaths. Hitomi Omata Rappo (Kyoto University) studies the most renowned and celebrated martyrs of Asia: a group of Japanese converts and missionaries whose crucifixion (1597) made a deep impression on Catholics all over the world. In *Profiling the Japanese Martyrs: The Beatification Process of the Twenty-Six Martyrs of Nagasaki (1597–1627)*, she explains why such a tragic event was endorsed with official beatification just a few decades after the event, with processes taking place on a global scale – in Asia, the Americas, and Europe.

The final section, *Vocation to Holiness: Three Case Studies from Early Modern Europe*, deals with three examples of the different possible outcomes when well-known and admired figures died in the odour of sanctity. Beatrice Saletti (University of Ferrara) describes the circumstances of the failed canonization of Lucia da Narni in her chapter *Lucia Broccadelli da Narni in Ferrara: The Short Season of a Saint, the Changing Memories of the Biographers*. The cult surrounding this female figure was sustained for political reasons, and her adventurous story involving kidnapping, faked stigmata, and thousands of pages of personal memories is of the utmost interest today. A similar "unsuccessful" saint is the focus of the chapter by Lucio Biasiori (University of Padua). *Holiness and Madness in Florence* analyses the case of the Dominican preacher Girolamo Savonarola, hanged and burned at the stake in Florence in 1498, who nonetheless became the object of intense religious devotion – and even an attempted canonization cause. And finally, Patryk Ryczkowski (University of Innsbruck) studies the life and canonization of a martyr of the Polish-Lithuanian Commonwealth. *Like the Phoenix into the Ashes: Christological and Jesuit Profile of Uniate Martyrdom in Andrzej Młodzianowski's Emblematic Vita (1675) of Josaphat Kuntsevych (1580–1623)* once again testifies to the complexity and heterogeneity of factors involved in beatifications and canonizations, and shows how they may be pursued via different kinds of agency.

As these chapters clearly show, each author has contributed to the wide array of possible answers to the question at the heart of *Profiling Saints*: What brought certain men and women to the end of the path to sanctity, while others were excluded from it for decades, centuries, or even forever? Many of the "holy" men and women studied in *Profiling Saints*, despite living in the Early Modern Age, were not canonized until recent or very recent times, between the nineteenth and twentieth centuries: multiple elements converge in advancing or delaying a cause for canonization, and numerous changes can occur – including in the hagiographical models of sainthood candidates – in the span of time from their death to the first hagiographical descriptions to their (possible) canonization.

The road to sainthood can be long and tortuous, models of sanctity highly diverse, and the elements determining the success or failure of canonization causes widely disparate. What do saints tell us? They set a path, that is the path of Christian perfection, which in turn entails a set of imitable, heroic moral standards. After all, *Profiling Saints* means understanding how and why the Church, both as an institution (including all of its bodies such as the religious orders or dioceses) and as the ensemble of the faithful, fosters accepts, and venerates specific behavioural models with a view to the salvation of the soul. History (in all its facets), hagiography, art, and liturgy: all of these fields of research aid us in grasping the importance of exploring sanctity not only as a religious matter but also – and especially – as a socio-cultural element that has contributed so extensively to making the history of Early Modern Christianity. *Profiling Saints* thus aims to reveal at least part of the amazingly rich sphere of Early Modern and Modern sanctity, complete with many of its representations and images in an ever-changing global world.

Franco Motta

Sanctity and Modernity: Opposition or Agreement?

An Introduction to *Profiling Saints*

The cult of saints and the development of the Modern world appear to have coexisted in quite a problematic way. Even if we leave to one side the Weberian concept of modernity as a process of 'disenchantment of the world' (*Wissenschaft als Beruf*, 1919), we cannot deny that many of the political and cultural phenomena that have shaped our reality have brought with them a deep aversion to the traditional Christian conception of the sacred, materialized in the form of sanctity, in the form of holy places and relics, for example.[1]

Just to mention a few historical examples, we can remember the iconoclastic moment that characterized the radical fringe of the supporters of the Spanish Republic in the 1930s, with several episodes of the public display of the bodies of saints and ordinary monks and nuns and the destruction of holy images, or mock processions like that of the image of Nuestra Señora de la Consolación near Madrid in 1936. A well-known victim of this was St. Francis Borja, the third general of the Society of Jesus, whose body was destroyed during the fire in the Jesuits' residence in the Spanish capital, set alight by the supporters of the Republic in May 1931.

A few years earlier, a similar iconoclastic campaign had been organized in Russia and Belarus in the wake of the Bolshevik Revolution. This was not a consequence of popular rage against the Church or the anticlerical program of the anarchist movement and the trade unions, as it was in Spain, but was, rather, the political strategy of the soviet Ministry of Justice, then named the Peoples' Commissariat to Justice, intended to unmask and eradicate all superstitious belief in the power of the relics of the saints, as part of a process to modernize the country.[2]

Between 1919 and 1921 the bodies of about 58 saints, all of them, with one exception, belonging to the Orthodox Church, were displayed in public ceremonies

---

1 The concept of a 'disenchantment of the world' has been more recently developed by Marcel Gauchet in his controversial book *The Disenchantment of the World. A Political History of Religion* (Princeton, Princeton University Press, 1999 [French original 1985]. As for the idea of secularization in general see, among others, H. Blumenberg, *The Legitimacy of the Modern Age* (Boston: Mit Press, 1985 [German original 1966]); J. Casanova, *Public Religions in the Modern World* (Chicago: The University of Chicago Press, 1994); *Die Säkularisation im Prozess der Säkularisierung Europas*, ed. P. Blickle – R. Schlögl (Epfendorf: Bibliotheca Academica, 2005).

2 S. A. Smith, *Bones of Contention: Bolsheviks and the Struggle against Relics 1918–1930*, «Past and Present», 204 (2009), 155–94.

Fig. 1 A l'aspect de la Verité le Prêtre se depouille et abjure le mensonge (A mock procession of the Holy Lady with the phrygian cap), ca. 1793.

and translated to local museums, in order to demonstrate the falsehoods the people had been exposed to for centuries: they were not only relics of monks and churchmen, but also of princes and aristocrats who had been venerated as saints – we must remember that Nicholas II, the last Tsar of Russia, has also figured among the Russian saints since 2000. Relics were examined by official commissions made up of representatives of the local soviets, members of the clergy, and coroners: the commission charged with investigating the relics of prince Mikhail Yaroslavich in the cathedral of Tver, in Central European Russia, consisted of 24 members, and performed its task before an audience of more than three hundred onlookers.[3] These rites of exposition had the overall aim of desacralizing the relics, but not desecrating them, as was later to happen in republican Spain.

If we take a further step backwards of about 130 years, to the French Revolution, we can find the archetype of the clash between modernity and the Christian sacred sphere (Fig. 1). In August 1793 the entire symbolic construct of the alliance between sanctity and power that had supported the monarchy of the *Ancien Régime* was merrily demolished with the destruction of the royal graves in Saint-Denis in Paris,

3 Smith, *Bones of Contention*, 168.

including those of the dynasties of the Valois and the Bourbons, and the dispersion of the royal relics they preserved.[4]

Now, none of the historical events I have just summarized should of course be taken as evidence of a supposedly 'natural' opposition between sanctity and modern political culture. Each of them must be interpreted and placed within its proper historical context. From this viewpoint, we can see that modern political discourse has always created a holy dimension in its own terms, both as a reaction to contrary ideas and systems, and as a simple substitution of symbols and references.

To go back to the examples I have just mentioned, it is enough to recall that the experience of the secularized Spanish Republic came to a tragic end with the creation of the clerical fascist regime of Francisco Franco, which asserted an alliance between the State and the Catholic Church as a pillar of the re-established traditional order. This is well illustrated by the construction of the sanctuary of the 'Valle de los caídos', the 'Valley of the Fallen', the monumental graveyard of those who had died for the cause of nationalist Spain, embedded into a Benedictine abbey, and the consecration of the country to the Sacred Heart of Jesus, the same Sacred Heart whose monument had been 'executed' in August 1936.

At a different level, the 'war against relics' in the Soviet Union ended with the proclamation of the program of the New Economic Policy in 1921, and was soon converted into the sacralization of the Soviet regime with the embalming of the corpse of its founder, Vladimir Ilic' Lenin in 1923, and its public exhibition outside the Kremlin's walls, where it is still visible today.[5] Going back further, the de-Christianization program launched by the French Convention led, as we know, to the proclamation of the cult of the Supreme Being, while in that same August 1793 the revolutionary officials tasked with supervising the demolition of the royal tombs in Saint-Denis gave care and attention to the corpses, noting those that appeared to be more or less intact, taking a death mask of Henry IV and sketching the mummy of general Turenne, a renowned hero of French wars under Louis XIV. Among these events, the desacralization of Christian symbols was accompanied by lay miracles intended to legitimize the new secular order established by the Revolution (Fig. 2).[6]

---

4 P. Boutry – Dominique Julia, *Reliques et Révolution française*, in *Religione cultura e politica nell'Europa dell'età moderna. Studi offerti a Mario Rosa dagli amici*, eds. C. Ossola – M. Verga – M.A. Visceglia (Firenze: Leo S. Olschki, 2003), 337–52.

5 N. Tumarkin, *Lenin Lives! The Lenin-Cult in Soviet Russia* (Cambridge, Ma: Harvard University Press, 1983). The case of the cult of Lenin in the Soviet Union is one example among many of what historians call 'political religion': see, on this topic, D. Herbert, *Religion and Civil Society. Rethinking Public Religion in the Contemporary World* (Ashgate: Aldershot, 2003), and several essays by E. Gentile, like his short synthesis *Political Religions in the 20th Century*, in *Die Säkularisation im Prozess der Säkularisierung Europas*, 551–62.

6 A general framing of this topic in N. Aston, *Religion and Revolution in France, 1780–1804* (London: MacMillan, 2000), 259–330.

Fig. 2 Truth appearing before a priest, convincing him to reject his clerical status (detail of Sans-culottes parade through Paris ridiculing Christianity and the Church, 1793).

Finally, when we come to more recent phenomena, we must not forget that the massive irruption of the Christian faith in the public sphere during the late 1900s was decisively promoted by the large-scale canonization policy of John Paul II, who himself canonized 482 saints, more than half the number of all the saints that have been proclaimed since the founding of the Congregation of Rites (now the Congregation for the Causes of the saints) in 1588.

Now, if we move from a consideration of the political dimension of holiness in the Modern world to its cultural and philosophical premises, we cannot underestimate the meaning of the process of secularization in Modern Europe. This statement requires us to move to a deeper cultural level, stepping back to the 17th and 18th centuries, to find the roots of a larger process that involved an overall criticism of the very concepts of sanctity and the supernatural.

Leaving aside the harsh critiques of the idea of the possibility of miracles by rationalist thinkers of the late 17th century such as Spinoza and Pierre Bayle, it will be enough to look at a couple of the most celebrated expressions of the mainstream Enlightenment thought of the mid-18th century. If we read the entry *Miracles* in Voltaire's *Dictionnaire philosophique* (1764), which enjoyed an enormous clandestine success all over Europe, we can see the very idea of miracles radically demolished both at a physical and a moral level: on one hand, writes Voltaire, "a miracle is the violation of laws which are deemed to be mathematical, divine, unchangeable, and eternal. According to this definition, a miracle is a contradiction in its own terms. A law cannot be unchangeable and violated at the same time"; on the other, "Why should God perform a miracle? To accomplish a design concerning some living being. [...] But this would be an admission of God's weakness, not of His power".[7] We can easily grasp why Voltaire's work was prohibited by the Paris Parliament and condemned in Rome as well as in Geneva.

A more moderate, but nevertheless still radical criticism of the cult of the saints, based on historical grounds, can be found in the pages of Diderot and D'Alembert's *Encyclopédie*. Here sanctity is described as a cultural phenomenon not exclusive to Christianity, but common to the different religions of humanity, starting from the ancient pagan religions whose cults and feasts had been simply adopted and renamed by the Christians.[8]

From this viewpoint, it cannot be denied that biblical criticism and the widespread adoption of philological and historical methods by scholars held a key role in the 18th century in reshaping the Western attitude toward religion and the sacred. Despite this, it cannot be denied that saints continued to be proclaimed, and, with even greater frequency since the pontificate of Pius IX in the second half of the 19th century, their images continued to be offered prayers and precious objects, and miracles continued to be performed, even with the direct involvement of physicians and scientists in the beatification and canonization processes.

This simple fact should induce us to adopt a different meaning of 'modernity' when dealing with sanctity and, more broadly, with the historical development of Christianity in the Modern world. On the one hand, it cannot be disputed that the formation of modernity has been aided and shaped by phenomena like the Scientific revolution, the growth of capitalism and the rise of an economic and scientific rationality. Yet, on the other, if we take early modern European history as a set of processes, such as the geographical discoveries, the rising of colonialism,

---

7 *Dictionnaire philosophique*, in *Oeuvres complètes de Voltaire*, vol. 36 (Paris: Thomin et Fortic, 1821), 499–519, 499–500.

8 *Encyclopédie, ou dictionnaire raisonné des sciences, des arts et des métiers*, ed. R. Morrissey – G. Roe (University of Chicago: ARTFL Encyclopédie Project [Autumn 2022 Edition]), vol. 14, 522, https://encyclopedie.uchicago.edu. Accessed on 28 December, 2022.

the Reformation and so on, that marked a profound discontinuity with the reality that preceded it, and took place mainly in the period between the mid-15th and the mid-17th century, then there can be no doubt that sanctity in the West, both in the way it was conceived and in the way it was practised, underwent a rapid and important change in the decades that followed the Council of Trent, becoming something very different from what it had been in the late Middle Ages.

Such a change was mostly, but not exclusively, prompted by two main elements, which exerted a deep influence on the Catholic Church: the need to respond to the spread of the Protestant rejection of the saints and the power of their relics and images on one hand, and, on the other, the strategy of pursuing a new cultural and moral hegemony over believers through the resources offered by the cult of the saints, and the performance of miraculous healings in the first place.

These two elements define what can be considered as Counter-Reformation sanctity, which according to its different aspects has been extensively investigated, by scholars like Simon Ditchfield, Jean-Michel Sallmann, Stefan Samerski, Angelo Turchini and Miguel Gotor among others. In my opinion, these elements converged into what can be viewed as a true 'system of sanctity': it was a system in the sense that it had an aim, to reaffirm the power of saints, their relics and the prayers addressed to them; an object, holy men and women who had lived not only in the past, but also, and mostly, in the present-day Church, and who largely belonged to the institutional hierarchy; and a method, the tools used to assess the reality of their acts and their supernatural powers.

In the decades between 1588 (the foundation of the Congregation of Rites by Sixtus V) and the decrees of Urban VIII, issued between 1625 and 1634, sanctity underwent a strong process of centralization in the hands of the Roman curia, since the proclamation of saints became strictly linked to the office of the pope and to his infallibility, thus acquiring the profile of an outstanding theological and political matter. Moreover, a transition took place from the traditional pattern of legitimation of the holiness of a man or a woman, largely based on their fame, shared memory and legends, and the importance of his or her local cult, to a judicial model administered by the professional figures of skilled theologians and canonists like the *promotor fidei* and the *consultores*, the advisers of the congregation.[9]

Those events can also be seen as evidence of a tension between a surging demand for the supernatural springing from society, fostered and controlled by bishops, religious orders, local Churches and local powers on the one hand, and the rising bureaucratic attitude of the Apostolic See, always keen to underscore its supreme privilege of surveillance and judgment, on the other. We have a revealing example

9 M. Gotor, *I beati del papa. Santità, Inquisizione e obbedienza in età moderna* (Firenze: Leo S. Olschki, 2002).

of this in the overwhelming rise of the figure of Charles Borromeo (d. 1584), a bishop and symbol of the Counter-Reformation, whose celebrations held in 1602 and 1603 summoned tens of thousands of faithful to Milan, forcing Rome to rapidly canonize him, on the 1st of November of 1610, just twenty-six years after his death. On the other hand, we must remember the interventions of Clement VIII and the Spanish Inquisition to arrest any manifestation of devotion – such as altars, *ex voto*, unauthorized pictures and biographies – toward Ignatius of Loyola, effectively promoted as an 'informal saint' by the Society of Jesus since the 1570s.

Such a redefinition of sanctity heavily relied on the resources granted by the new holy figures that lived and acted in the years corresponding to and following the Council of Trent. These were the new characters who responded to a rising need for the supernatural - the blessed, the *beati*, those men and women whose acts, bodies and relics performed miracles and healings during their lives, or immediately after their deaths, but whose cult still needed to be verified and guided by the officers of the Roman curia.

These holy people were forceful instruments of the divine power conveyed on the Catholic Church. Paul V paved the way, beatifying twelve men and women between 1605 and 1619. Just two of them, Margherita da Città di Castello and Isidro Labrador, had lived in previous centuries (respectively, in the 14th and the 12th century); all the others had died between 1552 and 1595, meaning that many of them were more or less contemporaries of the pope himself (who was born in 1552, the same year as the death of Francis Xavier). Some of them, specifically Ignatius of Loyola, Teresa of Ávila, Francis Xavier, Filippo Neri and Isidro Labrador, to whom we must add Charles Borromeo who was never formally beatified, were canonized in the following years. None of them was a martyr, unlike many of the blessed and the saints who were to be celebrated as martyrs by the Church between the late 17th and the 20th centuries. Most of them belonged to religious orders and showed their charisma among their contemporaries through miracles and the holiness of their life, meaning that institutional bodies of the Church, like regular orders and congregations, played a role as key actors in controlling and promoting popular devotion, facilitating miracles, and mediating the supernatural.

The generations of Churchmen and simple Catholic believers living in these decades shared the idea of belonging to a new age of sanctity, maybe not too dissimilar to what had been early Christianity. A new age of sanctity that was thought to foreshadow the final triumph of the Church over heresy and, at the same time, its future conquest of the whole world, as symbolized in the famous frontispiece of the volume of Daniello Bartoli's *Historia della Compagnia di Gesù*, the history of the Society of Jesus (1659), where the supernatural light shed by the holy father Ignatius illuminates a world depicted in its cartographical reality (Fig. 3).

Fig. 3 Daniello Bartoli, *Historia della Compagnia di Gesù*, vol. I (Roma: Nella stamperia d'Ignatio Lazzari, 1659), frontispiece.

We can argue this not only on the basis of evidence like the multiplication of holy graves and sanctuaries and the huge flow of people to the funerals of the servants of God, but also from a higher testimony like that of cardinal Bellarmine – later himself a saint, canonized in1930 – as mentioned in the foreword to the first volume of the *Acta sanctorum* of the Bollandists, published in 1643: "We have been told that cardinal Bellarmine used to say that this century in which we live is a century of saints, because God seems to have communicated His gifts, and the most clear reasons to display sanctity more largely than in the previous ages; so we can agree in saying that never before have the acts of the saints been demonstrated as they are now".[10]

10 *De actis sanctorum Ioannis Bollandi praefatio*, in *Acta sanctorum*, ed. I. Bollandus (Venetiis: apud Sebastianum Coleti et Io. Baptistam Albrizzi, 1734 [1st ed. 1643], vol. 1, *Ianuarius*, I–LII, XI.

Fig. 4 *Acta sanctorum*, ed. I. Bollandus (Venetiis: apud Sebastianum Coleti et Io. Baptistam Albrizzi, 1734 [1st ed. 1643]), vol. 1, Ianuarius, frontispiece.

Of course, this reference to cardinal Bellarmine, the prominent Jesuit controversialist, must not be considered as accidental, since his fame derived from the great effort he made to prove the truth of Catholic faith – including the belief in the saints – on theological and historical grounds. Indeed, the Bollandists' *Acta sanctorum* were precisely conceived to collect and organize the saints' lives in order to prove their truth and reliability. The question of truth, along with that of the method, was central in the Counter-Reformation system of sanctity, as shown by the inscriptions on the monumental base engraved in the architectural frontispiece of the first volume of the work: *veritas*, on the right side, and *eruditio*, that is historical method, on the left (Fig. 4).

We must remember that the *Acta sanctorum* were not really the first attempt to establish a new method in assessing the reliability of the collections of saints' lives: they were preceded by the *Vitae sanctorum priscorum Patrum*, the 'Lives of the first

Fig. 5 Marco d'Agrate, *St. Bartholomew* (1562), Cathedral of Milan. Courtesy of Wikimedia Commons.

holy Fathers of the Church' published by Luigi Lippomani from 1551, and by the *De probatis sanctorum historiis*, 'The proven histories of saints' by Laurentius Surius, published between 1570 and 1575, the most prominent collection of hagiographies before the Bollandists.

Lippomani was also the author of the *De ritibus sepeliendi mortuos apud veteres Christianos*, 'On the burial rites of the ancient Christians', the first archaeological work on the catacombs of Rome, followed by the renowned *Roma subterranea* of Antonio Bosio, printed in 1629. We are here clearly dealing with the problem of creating a foundation of historical evidence of the Christian tradition in the face of the criticism issued by the Reformation: it was the same problem that, as I have noted, was then being dealt with by Bellarmine in his *De controversiis Christianae fidei adversus huius temporis haereticos*, 'On the disputed matters of Christian faith, against the heretics of our time' (1586–93), with regard to Catholic doctrine, and by cardinal Baronius in his *Annales ecclesiastici* (1588–1607), with regard to Church history. The 'heretics of our time' and 'the saints of our time' were, from this point of view, the opposite sides of the same coin.

However, in my opinion, these considerations do not fully complete the true meaning of the modern 'system of sanctity' I have tried to sketch: together with the apologetic aim suggested by the struggle against the Reformation, I think we should consider another side of the problem, which is equally linked to the question of truth.

The search for a true representation of history, nature, and the body was undoubtedly one of the key elements that shaped early modern culture, science, and the arts: be it in Machiavelli's account of the mechanisms ruling political power; in the formalization of the physical laws presiding over the motion of the earth and the skies by Kepler and Galileo; in the representation of the human body in Andreas Vesalius' *De humani corporis fabrica*; or in the illustration of the reality of the pains suffered by martyrs, as in the case of the well-known statue of St. Bartholomew by Marco d'Agrate in 1562 (Fig. 5), shown in the Duomo of Milan, which certainly owes much to Vesalius' iconography, we are actually dealing with a sort of 'quest for truth' which appears to have been shared by many disciplines.

What is more, D'Agrate's statue should be paired with a later interest in martyrdom which found expressions in the treatise by Antonio Gallonio on the tortures suffered by the ancient martyrs, the *Trattato degli instrumenti di martirio* printed in 1591, and with the opening pages of Pedro Ribadenyra's hagiographic collection, the *Flos sanctorum* of 1599, devoted to the ancient instruments of martyrdom, to show us that the relationship between sanctity, modernity, and truth, which in these cases appears to be mediated by the evidence given by suffering, should not be placed in the background.

Section 1
Through the Saints: Understanding the Church across the Centuries

Thomas Santa Maria

Temptation, Torture, and Truth

Philip Neri and Reforming Catholic Rome[1]

Introduction

In recent years, the stakes for understanding early modernity have continued to rise. Scholars have traced the origins of today's racial division, globalism, and even the rise of far-right populist movements and competing truth claims to early modernity.[2] For the better part of the twentieth century, following the work of Max Weber, modernization, seen as a positive force, was a product of the Protestant Reformations.[3] More recently, scholars turning to the history of Catholicism, and especially Jesuit studies, credit Catholicism with the birth of modernity. They point to Catholic missions as foundational, if albeit oftentimes tragic, moments of cross-cultural encounter that shaped the global world today.[4] Furthermore, they have questioned many of the myths surrounding the era of Reformations that praise

---

1 This article is one of three projects in which I analyze the sanctity of Philip Neri to commemorate the 400th anniversary of his canonization. By necessity, much of the material in question is based on similar sources (canonization processes and hagiographies); however, I approach these texts with three distinct angles. Here I focus on the importance of the use and custody of the senses in Early Modern Catholicism, and its relationship to belief and truth. I argue that Neri's hagiographers identified him as an exemplary practitioner of this complex phenomenon. I am grateful to Elisa Frei and Eleonora Rai for inviting me to contribute to their volume on profiling sanctity.

2 For example, see, B.S. Gregory, *Rebel in the Ranks: Martin Luther, the Reformation, and the Conflicts that Continue to Shape Our World* (New York: Harper One, 2017). To some degree, *Rebel in the Ranks* popularized some of the argumentation from Gregory's earlier work, see B.S. Gregory, *The Unintended Reformation: How a Religious Revolution Secularized Society* (Cambridge: Belknap Press, 2012). Ethan Shagan has challenged some of Gregory's ideas in his monograph on the ways in which religious belief has had ramifications for the present all while maintaining that Early Modern ideas and movements have shaped our world, see E.H. Shagan, *The Birth of Modern Belief: Faith and Judgment from the Middle Ages to the Enlightenment* (Princeton: Princeton University Press, 2021). Perhaps the most well-known example is the New York Times *1619 Project*, see N. Hannah-Jones, *The 1619 Project: A New Origin Story* (New York: Random House, 2021).

3 See M. Weber, *The Protestant Ethic and the Spirit of Capitalism*, trans. Talcott Parsons (New York: Charles Scribner's Sons, 1958).

4 See for example the Brill's series which links Jesuit Studies and modernity, *Jesuit Studies: Modernity through the Prism of Jesuit History* (Boston: Brill, 2013–), and R. Po-Chia Hsia, ed., *A Companion to Early Modern Catholic Global Missions*, Companion to the Christian Tradition, 80 (Boston: Brill, 2018).

the Protestant Reformation as a movement marked by reason and literacy, and denounce Catholicism, especially in its reactionary modality as "counter-reformation" meaning stagnant and regressive. In this model, Protestantism became the religion of the word and the book, whereas Catholicism became the religion of superstition and sensuality. In the reductionistic brevity of the inter-confessional polemics: Protestants championed the pulpit and Catholics the "smells and bells."

To be sure, the caricature of the lay Catholic as oppressed and stultified by Church hierarchy has been debunked over the last few decades by many studies that reveal the vibrance of Early Modern Catholicism and its lay participation.[5] This new interpretation of Early Modern Catholicism has depended on studying its cultural, devotional, intellectual, and spiritual elements. To this end, examining sanctity has reigned supreme. As Peter Burke notes in his oft-cited study, saints reflect the values of the culture that reveres them.[6] The problem is that the Early Modern Catholic Church raised relatively few holy people to sainthood, especially in the century following the German reformer Martin Luther's excommunication. For that reason, the 1622 canonization in which Gregory XV canonized five people at once, Ignatius Loyola, Francis Xavier, Teresa of Avila, Isidore the Laborer, and Philip Neri has stood out as a particularly important and unique event for investigating Early Modern Catholicism.[7] For some, the event has been hailed as the canonization of the Catholic Reformation.[8] In itself, that begs some questions. What does that mean? Can the canonization of this group of holy people elucidate some aspect of that movement, or at least how the Catholic Church understood itself? In short what does sanctity reveal about Catholicism in the age of reformations, after Trent?

There has already been enormous interest in these five saints, especially the Jesuit saints. So far, much of the scholarship on this canonization event has emphasized the political process of saint-making; that is, the ways in which various entities, institutions, and monarchies supported the canonizations of particular candidates.[9] Some scholars have suggested that each of these saints represents a certain aspect of

---

5 This process began in large part thanks to the work of Eamon Duffy, who examined the vibrancy of religion in late medieval England, see E. Duffy, *The Stripping of the Altars: Traditional Religion in England, c. 1400–c. 1580* (New Haven: Yale University Press, 1992).

6 P. Burke, "How to be a Counter-Reformation Saint," in *The Historical Anthropology of Early Modern Italy: Essays on Perception and Communication* (New York: Cambridge University Press, 1987), 48.

7 Indeed, this was the first time five people were canonized together in one ceremony, see F. La Barga, "1622 o la canonización Católica," *Anuario de historia de la Iglesia* 29 (2020): 74.

8 See La Barga, "la canonización Católica."

9 C. Copeland, "Sanctity," in *The Ashgate Research Companion to the Counter-Reformation* ed. Alexandra Bamji et al. (Burlington: Ashgate, 2013), 233; Simon Ditchfield, "'Coping with the *Beati Moderni*:' Canonization Procedure in the Aftermath of the Council of Trent," in *Ite Inflammate Omnia: Selected Historical Papers from conferences held at Loyola and Rome in 2006*, ed. Thomas McCoog (Rome: Institutum Historicum Societatis Jesu, 2010), 413–440.

the Catholic Reformation whereby Isidore signifies the role of lay people; Ignatius, the new orders; Francis, the missionaries, Teresa of Avila; the reform of the ancient orders; and, Neri, the reformation of Rome, the very heart of the Catholic Church.[10] But there remains a notable absence from this group. It does not contain a significant or important theologian of the era. Albeit, this was not rare in canonizations from the period. If one were to consider other notable canonizations of the seventeenth century, such as that of Carlo Borromeo, the pattern of eschewing theologians becomes even more evident. To be sure, theological controversy was an important feature of the Catholic Reformation and shaped many of the contemporary political and military events. Theological controversy was not significant for salvation alone, but also for the affairs of the world. Suffice it to say that heterodoxy was important, and so much so that people gave their lives as martyrs for the cause.[11] It is perhaps for that reason that scholars have carefully parsed the thought of the major figures of the reformation. At the same time, the Catholic Reformation, especially after Trent, was not exclusively about theological disputations with Protestants. In fact, we must note that by the seventeenth century Catholics were debating as much amongst themselves as they were with other faith traditions.[12]

Furthermore, the fact remains that few if any of the men and women canonized in the decades following the Council of Trent were theologians. What is more, Ignatius, Teresa, and Philip were even interrogated by the Spanish and Roman Inquisitions or at least censured in part for their lack of theological training. Indeed, the most notable theologian of the Catholic Reformation, Robert Bellarmine, who personally promoted the causes of at least three of the saints canonized in 1622, Ignatius, Francis, and Philip, was canonized, but only in 1930.[13] But even Bellarmine seemed to hold his own theological works in relatively low esteem. When he was reflecting on his own life in his *Autobiography* and his other works, he highlighted

---

10 La Barga, "la canonización Católica," 119. La Barga discusses other possible representations, and geographic and symbolic meanings, see La Barga, "la canonización Católica," 109–120.

11 See B.S. Gregory, *Salvation at Stake: Christian Martyrdom in Early Modern Europe* (Cambridge: Harvard University Press, 1999).

12 The Jesuits were often either the victims or perpetrators of these internecine theological squabbles. Largely these were based on issues in moral theology and debates over the role of free will and grace in salvation. On the origins of Jesuit moral probabilism, see R. A. Maryks, *Saint Cicero and the Jesuits: The Influence of the Liberal Arts on the Adoption of Moral Probabilism* (Burlington: Ashgate, 2008).

13 Bellarmine had hoped for a triple canonization of Carlo Borromeo, Ignatius, and Philip, see La Barga, "la canonización Católica," 120. Furthermore, he ultimately collaborated with Federico Borromeo, Cesare Baronio, and Antonio Gallonio to promote Neri, see R.S. Noyes, *Peter Paul Rubens and the Counter-Reformation Crisis of the Beati Moderni*, Sanctity in Global Perspective (New York: Routledge, 2018), 11.

his successes as a pastor, preacher, and author of devotional texts, rarely mentioning his career as a controversial theologian.[14]

How can these canonizations explain the relationship between Early Modern Catholicism, sanctity, and theology? In this paper, I explore this question by examining the life and canonization of Philip Neri. I argue that Neri's life and activity in Rome closely reflected key aspects of the Catholic Reformation: a tension between history and innovation in both piety and intellectual pursuits. It is perhaps this close relationship between Neri's mission and religious expression with the Catholic Church's that explains Roman aphorism repeated throughout his canonization day "today we canonize four Spaniards and one saint."[15] At the core of these tensions was the Catholic search for truth, meaning true practice of Christianity and uncovering true belief.[16] Defending pious practices, the Church drew on historical examples, and yet these were ever evolving. That is, Catholic worship became undeniably more sensuous, and simultaneously more wary of the senses. Both of these elements were longstanding parts of Catholic tradition, a point which Catholic Reformers referred to as part of their renewed interest in history. Philip Neri and his brand of piety embraced this sensuous paradox, which was rooted in his reading, teaching, and patronage of history. Neri was not a theologian but important tenets of Catholicism's claims on truth were at the root of his ministry.

This paper begins by exploring Philip Neri's piety and devotional practices emphasizing the ways in which the adhered to the dominant sensuous paradox of Early Modern Catholicism: using the senses for spiritual benefit and practicing careful custody over them to avoid temptation. By way of conclusion, I try to explain how and why Early Modern Catholicism developed a special relationship to this paradox, which was a reaction to theological currents of the day and rooted in the obsession with historical study.

---

14 See R. Bellarmine, *The Autobiography of St. Robert Bellarmine*, trans. Gerald F. Giblin, S.J. (Woodstock: Woodstock College Press, 1960). Giblin called Bellarmine's considerations of his major theological work, the *Controversies* an "afterthought," see in Bellarmine, *The Autobiography*, 5. Similarly, in his devotional text, on the *Mind's Ascent to God* he wrote "I do not know how others will judge this book, but I have found it very useful compared to my other smaller works. I do not read my other books unless I am forced to; this one I have already gladly read three or four times, and I have resolved to reread it frequently in the future. Perhaps I am more fond of it, not because of its merits, because I love it as a child, a second Benjamin, which I produced in my extreme old age," in *Robert Bellarmine: Spiritual Writings*, ed. J.P. Donnelly (New York: Paulist Press, 1988), 20.

15 M. Gotor, "'Han canonizado a cuatro españoles y un santo:' La propuesta hagiográfica del oratoriano Felipe Neri entre 'el esplendor de Iberia' y 'la gloriosa memoria de Enrique IV,'" *Anuario de Historia de la Iglesia* 29 (2020), 261.

16 See S. Tutino, *Shadows of Doubt: Language and Truth in Post-Reformation Catholic Culture* (New York: Oxford University Press, 2014 and S. Tutino, *The Many Faces of Credulitas: Credibility, Credulity, and Belief in Post-Reformation Catholicism* (New York: Oxford University Press, 2022).

Piety and Paradox

This "paradox of the senses" requires some unpacking.[17] As derisive as the "smells and bells" interpretation of Catholicism may be, it is not without some truth. The defense and intensification of the sensuous dynamics of Catholicism after Trent cannot be questioned. The twenty-fifth session of the Council upheld the cult of the saints, images, and relics. The fifth session reaffirmed the Catholic commitment to teaching doctrine and morals through preaching. Church building and decorating exploded. Sacred art employed the innovations of renaissance perspective to bring realism to art, which critics and moralists sometimes decried as all too real. Music resounded through Churches, processions marched through cities for all to see, and the ritual activities of the mass engaged, or exploited, all the senses. So pervasive was Catholicism's sensuousness that it even infiltrated the interior life, as Ignatius's *Spiritual Exercises* indicate. Ignatius' fifth contemplation, on the incarnation and the nativity, urges retreatant to use all five senses in imaginatively composing a biblical scene: "see the persons…listen to what they are saying…smell the fragrance and taste the infinite sweetness of the Divinity…Using the sense of touch, I will, so to speak, embrace and kiss the places where the persons walk or sit."[18] Advocating such practices has earned Ignatius the reputation of being "sensorially sympathetic."[19]

Exploring the sensuous dynamics of Catholicism only reveals one side of the coin. As moral literature indicates there was also an intensification of the opposite dynamic, the custody of the senses. While the faithful could exploit the senses in an effort to raise the mind to lofty meditation of God, the senses were also the "gates of sin," according to medieval tradition. Think for example of the rites of confession and extreme unction. Since the Middle Ages formulas for confession guided penitents to confess with each of the five senses in mind.[20] Similarly, as Robert Bellarmine relates in his *Art of Dying Well*, in extreme unction

> all the parts of the body are anointed, in which reside the five senses of the body, and it is said with reference to each, 'May God pardon you whatever sins you may have committed through sight,' and so of the rest of the senses. We gather from this that the five senses are

---

17 See T.J. Santa Maria, "Aesthetics and Asceticism: The Paradox of the Bodily Senses in the Catholic Reformation," Ph.D. Diss., (Yale University, 2022).

18 Ignatius of Loyola, *Spiritual Exercises* in *Ignatius of Loyola: Spiritual Exercises and Selected Works*, ed. George E. Ganss, S.J. (New York: Paulist Press, 1991), 121–126. (The numbers used here are not page numbers, but refer to paragraphs in the *Spiritual Exercises*).

19 M.M. Smith, *Sensing the Past: Seeing, Hearing, Smelling, Tasting, and Touching in History* (Berkeley: University of California Press, 2007), 78.

20 C. Casagrande, "Sistema dei sensi e classificazione dei peccati (secolo XII–XIII)," *Micrologus* X (2002): 33–34.

> the gates through which sins of all kinds enter into the soul. So if anyone carefully guards these gates, he will easily avoid a great number of sins, and thus he will live well and die happily.[21]

By highlighting the pitfalls of the senses Bellarmine was following an Ignatian precedent. For example, in the *Spiritual Exercises*' "second method of praying" Ignatius writes that the retreatant "should keep the eyes closed or intent on one place, and not allow them to wander."[22] Ignatius' most thorough treatment of the senses comes from the third part of the *Constitutions* on "The Preservation and Progress of those who enter the Society." Here he decrees: "All should take special care to guard with great diligence the gates of their senses (especially the eyes, ears, and tongue) from all disorder, to preserve themselves in peace and true humility of their souls…"[23]

This ambivalence to the senses was not new to Catholicism in the Early Modern Period, but pervasive in western culture in a variety of iterations from Plato's concept of the ideal, to Paul's notion of the antagonism between *sarx* and *pneuma*. Catholicism inherited this ambivalence embracing both the use of the senses for spiritual and epistemological benefit, and the custody of the senses as a means to ward off temptation. The prevalence of this paradox in Early Modern Catholicism suggests that it is mistaken to view Catholicism as merely a sensuous religion. Instead, it is better to think of Catholicism offering a paradigm that included a range of appropriate sensory behaviors. For Catholics the world remained enchanted, and the senses were the mediators that harnessed its power for spiritual benefit or corruption.

Embracing the Sensuous and Ecstatic Bliss

Neri's hagiographers and the testimonials in his canonization trials indicate how the saint embraced this paradox in his life and works. It is appropriate to begin by considering the ways in which Neri embraced the sensuous aesthetics of Catholicism. This dynamic was fundamental to holiness as a key element of the ministry of Jesus Christ as related in the Gospels. His works of power and teachings demonstrated a centrality of the human body.[24] Jesus fed the hungry, healed the sick by touch,

21 Bellarmine, *Art of Dying*, 303.

22 Ignatius, *Spiritual Exercises*, 252.

23 Ignatius Loyola, *The Constitutions of the Society of Jesus*, ed. John W. Padberg, S.J. (St. Louis: The Institute of Jesuit Sources, 1996), 250. The number given here is a paragraph number, not a page number.

24 See Santa Maria, "Aesthetics and Asceticism," 45.

turned water into exceptional wine, and dined with friends. The parameters for final judgment, according to Jesus, even depended on the charitable care of the body of others "when I was hungry, you gave me food; when thirsty, you gave me drink" (Mt. 25:34–5). He even restores afflicted persons' sensuous capabilities by giving sight to the blind (Jn. 9:1–13). In his earthly ministry and through his thaumaturgic interventions, Jesus outlined the vital sensuousness of Christianity.

Therefore, a clear model existed for saints like Philip Neri to embrace sensuousness in their religious expression and charitable endeavors. To be clear, Philip did embrace sensuousness in all the Oratory's spiritual and corporal ministries. This penchant is evident from Philip's earliest efforts in Rome's hospitals. Neri insisted that his followers work with the sick and dying. Indeed, much of his fame throughout Rome sprouted from stories of his miraculous ability to heal the sick. His healings, like those of Jesus, frequently involved a haptic element. Take for example, his healings of one Sebastiano, Prospero Crivelli, a certain Ambrogio, Giovan Francesco Anerio, and the youth Paolo Massimo. Sebastiano, according to Gallonio, was a "spiritual son" of Neri, who fell grievously ill, and became a victim of demonic assault on his sick bed.[25] His local parish priest visited him and "said all the right things to the sick man but with no effect." It appears that the words appealing to the auditory sense were not enough. When Philip arrived in the front hall of the house, he cried out:

> 'What's the matter?' Then he came into the bedroom and took Sebastian gently by the hand. At his touch the sick man was immediately raised from the deepest despair and depression to a great peace of mind … He began to call out aloud, 'Father Philip is driving the devils away – look, the demons flee from Philip! O how powerful Philip is! Long live Christ, long live Philip, who has helped me to escape the jaws of hell! Long live the Oratory! Long live my father Philip! I owe him so much – may he live forever!'

Through sensuous activity, Philip showed his power over both the natural and supernatural world, eviscerating demons with his voice, and healing Sebastiano with his touch.

Similarly, Philip intervened at the sick bed of the Milanese nobleman, Prospero Crivelli, showcasing his power over nature and his proximity to the divine.[26] As the story goes, Neri rushed to the bedside of Crivelli to accost him when he discovered that the nobleman had made Neri his heir. Philip offered himself as a sacrifice to

---

25 This anecdote comes from Gallonio, 75–76.

26 Find the story of Crivelli's healing in Gallonio, *The Life*, 34, though all the testimonies regarding this story can be found in *Il primo processo per san Fillipo Neri nel Codice Vaticano Latino 3798 e in altri esemplari dell' Archivio dell'Oratorio di Roma*, vols. 1–4, ed. Giovanni Incisa della Rochetta and Nello Vian (Vatican City: Biblioteca Apostolica Vaticana (1957–1963), IV, 285.

God in Crivelli's face, tearfully prayed at his bedside, and then laid his hands on the afflicted man, who immediately fell asleep.[27] Once Crivelli was sleeping, Neri rushed to Saint Peter's to pray for his health. To the astonishment of Crivelli's physicians, who had been certain he would die, and to the priests, who had administered the last rites to him, Crivelli arose about fifteen minutes after Philip departed feeling much better. Philip's intercessory prayers, healing touch, and Christ-like self-sacrifice had cured him. The likenesses between Christ's healing ability and Neri's do not stop with Crivelli. In fact, two stories from Gallonio's hagiography mimic some of the more astounding Gospel stories. Neri's healing of Ambrogio mimics Christ's healing of the lame man (Jn. 5:8).[28] In this story, Neri entered the house of Ambrogio, a servant of Pietro Spadaro, a priest of Saint Jerome of Arezzo, where he found the man weak and bedridden. Neri commanded Ambrogio to "get up at once" and so he arose immediately.

Neri's most notable healing intervention, the resurrection of Giovan Francesco Anerio, also displayed his Christ-like power over illness in an anecdote that echoes both Jesus' raising of Lazarus (Jn. 11:38–44) and Jesus' miraculous healing of Jairus's daughter (Mk. 5:21–43).[29] When Neri learned that the boy was ill, motionless, corpselike, and unable to eat for a period of seventeen days, he visited his sickbed. Resting his hands on the boy's forehead he encouraged everyone present to pray the Our Father and Hail Mary. Once again, he laid his hands on the boy's forehead, this time scolding his mother for starving her child. Thereafter he moistened the boys' lips with wine, and a few days later he rose. Through touch, hearing, and taste, Neri cured the sick boy. The efficacious nature of Neri's thaumaturgic power, reached its apogee in his miraculous resurrection of the young boy, Paolo Massimo.[30] Neri had frequently visited Paolo's bedside throughout the duration of a monthslong illness, and urged those caring for Paolo to alert him in the event that his health should deteriorate. Unfortunately, word of his worsening health did not reach Neri in time as he was saying mass when the boy died. Philip rushed to his bedside, laid hands on him, embraced him, brought the boy close to his chest — famous for its strong and irregular heartbeat — prayed, invoked the boy's name, and sprinkled

---

27 J. Touber, *Law, Medicine, and Engineering in the cult of the Saints in Counter-Reformation Rome: The Hagiographical works of Antonio Gallonio, 1556–1605*, Studies in Medieval and Reformation Traditions 178 (Boston: Brill, 2014), 161.

28 For the full accounting, see Gallonio, *The Life*, 103. Likely, Gallonio's source was the testimony of Giuliano Fuscherio, a chaplain from San Givolamo della Carità, see *Processo*, I, 301.

29 See Gallonio, *The Life*, 130. Francesco della Molara, someone personally healed by Neri, attests to this story, see *Processo*, I, 7–11.

30 For the story, see Gallonio, *The Life*, 125. Ponelle and Bordet note that multiple eyewitnesses attested to this story in the *Processo*, see Louis Ponnelle and Louis Bordet, *St. Philip Neri and the Roman Oratory of his Times*, trans. Ralph Francis Kerr (London: Sheed & Ward, 1932), 163–164.

him with holy water. Thus, the boy rose from death, and enjoyed Philip's counsel. Following their conversation, and perhaps a confession, Neri asked the boy if he would prefer to die in order to enjoy the blessedness of heaven. The boy said he wished to die and moments later he did.[31] From these healings, not only does the relationship between the senses and the efficacy of divine power become evident, but so too does Neri's interest in and care for the body.

Neri's other ministries, even if they were decidedly more spiritually oriented, were no less centered on the body and its senses. Building on his ministry to the hospitals and the sick, Philip was also eager to care for the ill and pilgrims visiting Rome. For this reason, he founded the Confraternity of the Holy Trinity in 1548. For those who visited the Confraternity in the church of San Salvatore in Campo, Philip would frequently preach moving his listeners to greater piety.[32] Furthermore, he promoted the *quarante'ore* devotion, a form of eucharistic devotion that included vigils before the blessed sacrament. The aural and visual elements of these pious activities were clear and became the bedrock for the sensuous devotions adopted and promoted by Philip as the founder of the Oratory. Through the customs of the Oratory, Neri exploited Catholicism's sensuous dynamics insofar as meetings included singing, praying, preaching, and holy readings.[33] The Oratory, like all Catholic devotions, relied on transmitting Catholic doctrine through the senses as a vehicle for moving audiences to adopt Christian ideals.

In his personal ministry, Philip was known as a tireless confessor. As Gallonio relates, "He was so eager to summon wandering souls back to their senses, that merely being seated in the chair which he used to hear confessions gave him the greatest refreshment and delight. You would not believe how many people, and what great ones, he enabled to bring forth ample fruit from the manure of their sins..."[34] The sacrament of confession, by its very nature relied on oral and aural sensation, and yet here too Gallonio notes a haptic and spatial dimension as well insofar as the mere act of sitting moved Philip. All the more interesting, is the special connection between Philip's olfactory sense and his career as a confessor. As a general principle, Gallonio claims that Neri "could detect virginity and other

31 There was a healthy dose of skepticism regarding this story, see Ponelle and Bordet, 164. Furthermore, Only Paolo's sister, Vittoria de'Massimi suggested that the boy had confessed to Neri. Nevertheless, Benedict XIV used her testimony to authenticate the miracle, see Ponnelle and Bordet, 164, fn. 5.

32 Gallonio, *The Life*, 15.

33 P. M. Jones, "Celebrating New Saints in Rome and across the Globe," in *A Companion to Early Modern Rome, 1492–1692*, eds. Pamela M. Jones, Barbara Wisch, and Simon Ditchfield (Boston: Brill, 2019), 166.

34 Gallonio, *The Life*, 26.

virtues by their scent, just as he detected impurity and all that sort of thing by its stench."[35] Gallonio recounts how sins of the flesh offended Neri's nostrils:

> when hearing the confessions of men involved in these kinds of sin, he was so affected by the foul and pestilential stench which emanated from their unclean desires that he would put his hand or his handkerchief before his nose, and have to turn slightly away, though he did this with great subtlety to prevent anyone noticing. He used to say that he detected such an unpleasant smell arising from this vice that he could think of no other to be compared with it.[36]

Philip even mobilized his sense of smell to enhance his ability as a confessor and caretaker of souls.

Embracing the senses was also a fundamental aspect of Philip's personal devotion Neri's sensory reception of artworks manifested within him ecstatic and mystical experiences that were a major part of his "personal devotion and the governance of his congregation."[37] Take one example, according to the testimony of Giacomo Crescenzi, from when Neri was still a layman attending lectures at San Marco, "the devotion that he gave the crucifix that was in that place, where it was hanging, was so deep that he was not able to pay attention to the lectures but was continually shedding tears."[38] The most famous example of Neri's ecstatic raptures at the sight of images came from his biographer, Pietro Giacomo Bacci, who discusses Neri's interaction with Barocci's altarpiece of the *Visitation* in the Chiesa Nuova, "another time he was in the chapel of the Visitation, where he liked to stay since he loved Barocci's painting, and when seated as he was used to, in a small chair, he was overcome by rapturous ecstasy...Some penitents were there and shook him in order to wake him up..."[39] In using his senses for meditation when viewing sacred art, Neri surrendered them to ecstatic rapture. It appears that these episodes inspired

35 Gallonio, *The Life*, 39. Gallonio also relates that many patristic saints including Euthemius, Pachomius, Hilarion, Antony, and Birgitta also shared this special ability.

36 Gallonio, *The Life*, 39.

37 Franco Mormando, "Gian Paolo Oliva: The Forgotten Celebrity of Baroque Rome," in *The Holy Name: The Art of the Gesù, Bernini and his Age*, Linda Wolk-Simon, ed., (Philadelphia: St. Joseph's University Press, 2018).

38 *Processo*, II, 207 makes up part of Crescenzi's testimony from July 7, 1598. For a lucid discussion of Neri's mysticism and its relationship to visual art, see Costanza Barbieri, "'To be in Heaven' St. Phillip Neri Between Aesthetic Emotion and Mystical Ecstasy," in *The Sensuous in the Counter-Reformation Church*, ed. Marcia B. Hall and Tracy E. Cooper (New York: Cambridge University Press, 2013), 207–208.

39 In Barbieri, "Neri Between Aesthetic Emotion and Mystical Ecstasy," 207–208.

Guido Reni's official portrait of the saint in ecstasy before an image of the Madonna and child.[40]

Some of Philip's most famous ecstasies; however, occurred while he was saying mass. It was common knowledge that Neri spent hours saying the mass reveling in his proximity to Christ in the form of the Eucharist. It is evident that the physical proximity with the eucharist through sight, touch, and taste deeply affected Neri, as Gallonio observes:

> I must say something about the delight he had in drinking the Blood of Christ, and in eating His Body. Those who stayed close to his side believed that he was able to perceive the actual flavour of the Blood and the Body, as if he were tasting simple flesh and simple blood. He used to lick his lips most eagerly, and we could see that he brought the Chalice to his mouth again and again, although he would not allow anyone present to stand too close to the altar, or to be in such a position that they could see his face. When he was consuming the Precious Blood, you could hear a sound from his throat which made you think he was tasting something so thick and glutinous that it stuck to the priest's palate...He was so taken by delight in the divine Sacrament that he would retain the sweet flesh of Christ and His most precious Blood in his mouth, not swallowing it at once but letting it pass slowly, drop by drop, into his stomach.[41]

For his disciples witnessing his spiritual fervor, Neri's intimate eucharistic experiences revealed Catholic doctrine regarding the real presence through the senses. The visceral account exposes just how sensuous the mass and reception of the eucharist were to Early Modern Catholics. The senses served not only as a means to captivate Catholic audiences and move them, but also to expose truth.

Custody of the Senses and Ascetic Rigor

For all the importance of and reliance on the sensuous, it is vital to underscore that Catholicism urged the faithful toward asceticism, that is denial of the body and its senses. Of course, custody of the senses also had a significant role in Catholic devotional life starting with the example of Jesus Christ, who accomplished incredible feats of fasting (Mt. 4:13), frequently, spurned the world and worldly riches, and even declared that it was better to gouge out one's eye or cut off one's hand rather than sin (Mt. 5:29–30). This was clearly a high bar, but one that many saints attempted to surpass. Philip Neri was one of them.

---

40 For more on this image, see below.

41 Gallonio, *The Life*, 25.

Neri's program of sensuous abstemious was thorough. Each sense that he used for his spiritual benefit and that of his neighbors, he also guarded to resist temptation and sin. If taste was a key element of his eucharistic adoration, then it was also a pivotal part of his program of self-abnegation. Like so many other saints, Neri followed a strict diet, almost to the point of inedia.[42] According to Gallonio, from Neri's earliest days in Rome:

> he lived almost like a hermit, refreshing himself more with tears than food... For his meals he took ordinary bread with some olives, vegetables or fruit, and he drank plain water. This frugal and simple regime lasted with him until the very end of his life. Once he had become a priest, he used to have a light breakfast, and a simple supper in the evening to sustain his body, with a little wine, much diluted, or frequently just water to drink. Supper consisted of a couple of soft-boiled eggs, or broth, or vegetables, followed by a salad with salt and vinegar; he hardly ever allowed any more dishes to be brought to his table. He very rarely admitted meat to his diet, and he was never greedy for any food even if he had been fasting for three days. All his life he tasted neither milk nor anything made from milk; fish he consumed very occasionally polenta never.[43]

As Ruth Noyes has indicated Neri's contemporaries celebrated him for custody over his sense of taste "his death masks manifested extreme emaciation. His likenesses emphasized the sunken cheeks and prominent, protruding bone structure of his face as signs of his spiritual martyrdom."[44] His command over his appetite was a sign of his denial of the world and embrace of the spiritual life.

Similarly, Neri, despite his use, promotion, and personal involvement with the arts, even to the point that he is credited with the planning the Oratorian Church, the Santa Maria in Vallicelli, he was also wary of art.[45] He urged his disciples not to look at images too much and "'advised his spiritual sons that when he was orating they should not stare at an image or a crucifix obsessively, that could create its own risks to the mind.'"[46] This mistrust of art was a common and pervasive part of

---

42 Hagiographers seemed to delight in sharing information about the diets of their subject. See, for example, Fuligatti's explanation of Bellarmine's diet: Giacomo Fuligatti, *Vita del cardinale Roberto Bellarmino della compagnia di Gesù* (Rome: Bartolomeo Zanetti, 1623), 140–1. Caroline Walker Bynum also discussed the role of diet in the lives of medieval holy women, see Caroline Walker Bynum, *Holy Feast and Holy Fast: The Religious Significance of Food to Medieval Women* (Berkeley: University of California Press, 1987).

43 Gallonio, *The Life*, 9.

44 Noyes, *Crisis of the Beati Moderni*, 186.

45 For Neri's role in the construction of the Vallicella, see Ponnelle and Bordet, *St. Philip Neri*, 340; Mormando, "Forgotten Celebrity," 195.

46 In Barbiere, "Neri Between Aesthetic Emotion and Mystical Ecstasy," 226, fn. 4.

Catholic art theory following Trent. Above all, churchmen and art theorists were concerned that lascivious sacred art could move a viewer to lust.[47] This sentiment reflects Neri's aspirations as a custodian of his senses, insofar as he was careful to protect his chastity and his followers ardently publicized his lifelong virginity.

The image of Neri as a virginal mystic was concretized by Reni's portrait of him, which hangs above his tomb in the Vallicella. Reni's image emphasizes Neri's chastity and virginity by placing lilies at his feet and highlighting his closeness with the Virgin Mary, who appears to him in the upper corner of the painting. In his life, Neri was careful to protect his chastity by guarding his senses a habit that his hagiographers widely publicized. As a confessor he shielded his ears to wanton talk from ladies as Gallonio reports:

> he was more ready to hear the sins of men than of women, and as far as he could, avoided hearing the faults of the latter. Cautious of any threat to his virginal purity... I will add that he was so strict and vigilant in guarding his modesty that if he was obliged to hear womens' confessions, he would receive them in church, speakingabruptly rather than gently, and from time to time showing his annoyance in his looks.[48]

Neri's approach to confessing women, which may seem prudish at first, likely reflected the wider cultural criticisms regarding confession and penance, which had been ridiculed in late medieval literary figures and by Protestant detractors alike. Indeed, Bocaccio's *Decameron* is replete with stories of abusing the sacrament.[49] As Stephen Haliczer has noted, sexual tensions in confession, where priests likely heard the about sins of flesh, were very high.[50] It was for this reason that Carlo Borromeo, the saintly cardinal archbishop of Milan, implementer of the Council of Trent, and admirer of Philip Neri, fashioned the confessional box, which maintained the privay of the sacrament while exposing it to witnesses.[51] The confessional permitted auditory transmission of information and established oversight of the sacrament, while foreclosing the possibility of sensual contact.

To his hagiographers the careful custody of the senses that Neri practiced in the confessional to defend his chastity was evidence of his virginal heroism. Chastity

47 For an in-depth discussion of the place of art, the sense of sight, and lust in Catholic devotional life, see Santa Maria, "Aesthetics and Asceticism," 193–240.

48 Gallonio, *The Life*, 27.

49 See G. Boccaccio, *The Decameron*, G. H. McWilliam (New York: Penguin, 2003), III, 3; III, 4; VII, 5 (numbers refer to "day" and story, not pagination).

50 See Stephen Haliczer, *Sexuality in the Confessional: A Sacrament Profaned* (New York: Oxford University Press, 1996).

51 W. de Boer, *Conquest of the Soul: Confession, Discipline, and Public Order in Counter-Reformation Milan* (Boston: Brill, 2011), 95.

and virginity had been long established aspects, nearly requirements, for sanctity.[52] To this point, Cardinal Francesco Maria Tarugi dug into Neri's past insisting that his boyhood nickname, "Pippo Buono" signified he was a virgin as a youth.[53] In addition, Cardinal Cesare Baronio emphasized this fact when he disclosed Neri's confession to him about his perpetual chastity.[54] To bolster these claims, Baronio revealed that Neri was free from "natural pollutions," and Gallonio added that Philip's bed was "always unspotted."[55] What is more, Neri's hagiographers always present him as a model of resisting temptation via custody of the senses:

> Philip guarded this precious treasure [his virginity] so well from his youth up to his death with the greatest diligence. He was not content to hide under the ashes of humility alone, and to maintain vigilance over the custody of his heart, but he also had exact care of all his exterior senses. From his mouth there was never heard a word that had the least shade of dishonesty. So great was the manner of the custody of his eyes that one of the most beautiful women, living in Rome at that time, who confessed to him for nearly thirty years, affirmed that in that great space of time she had never observed that Philip had looked at her even once.[56]

At the same time, his hagiographers note numerous times that the devil tempted him for the purpose of "staining the whiteness of his purity."[57] Of course, most of these anecdotes underscore Neri's ability to withstand temptation. Some stories are particularly illustrative. In the first of these examples, Gallonio explains that Neri encountered a naked beggar on his route to the Lateran Basilica and as a result, "an impure thought crossed his mind…he was quite convinced that the beggar was indeed a demon, not a man, even though it presented itself to him under the attractive form of a man…"[58] Nevertheless, according to Gallonio, "he took refuge in prayer, and the temptation ceased at once."[59] Gallonio adds another story in which Neri, as a layman, was tempted by a group of men, "He was travelling one day, and met some characters of very dubious morality. Prompted by an evil spirit, and

---

52 Donald Weinstein and Rudolph M. Bell, *Saints and Society: The Two Worlds of Western Christendom, 1000–1700* (Chicago: University of Chicago Press, 1982), 73. Their study indicates statistically just how important chastity was to the establishment of heroic virtue.

53 *Processo*, III, 379.

54 *Processo*, I, 138

55 *Processo*, 1, 138; *Processo*, I, 159–160.

56 P.G. Bacci, *Vita del B. Filippo Neri* (Rome: Brugiotti, 1622), 112 (my translation).

57 Bacci, *Vita*, 113.

58 Gallonio, *The Life*, 11. For Robinson these anecdotes about sexual temptation worked to humanize the saint, see Jonathan Robinson, *In No Strange Land: The Embodied Mysticism of Saint Philip Neri* (Kettering: Angelico Press, 2015), 79.

59 Gallonio, *The Life*, 11.

perhaps attracted by his good looks, they cast modesty aside and invited him, chaste youth that he was, to join them in sin."[60] Though it is difficult to read these stories today without some consideration of Neri's sexuality, it is anachronistic and not altogether helpful to do so. Still, the suggestion of homoeroticism likely prompted Gallonio to remind the reader that similar temptations befell the venerable Saint Bernardino of Siena.[61]

Nevertheless, the stories speak more to Neri withstanding temptation than to his sexuality insofar as his hagiographers also report similar encounters with women. In one instance, while he was travelling, men hired "women of ill repute" to enter his room, bolting it from the outside. With no other option, Philip prayed so fervently that the women did not even dare to speak and left him alone.[62] In another instance, an "immodest woman," Cesaria, boasted and wagered that she could convince Neri to sin. She duped him into visiting by feigning a desire to confess her sins. On these grounds Philip hurried to her home, but when he "climbed the stairs before the woman that instrument of the devil, cast off all modesty and shame, and exposed herself to him naked, save for a veil drifting across her body, hoping it would fall off attractively in front of him and so achieve her object."[63] According to Gallonio, Philip detected the assault on his chastity, and maintained custody of his senses by fleeing the scene altogether.[64] These stories demonstrate how Bacci and Gallonio understood Neri's heroic virtue, his sanctity.

Add to this a program of self-mortification, and Neri's heroic virtue became undeniable altogether. Despite his jocularity, and reputation for moderation, Philip was an ascetic, and his hagiographers reminded their audiences of that fact. In general terms, Neri, according to Gallonio was, "glad to be harsh with his own body."[65] He "often slept on the bare ground," and "every day he flogged himself briskly."[66] Moreover, he urged others to follow in these practices. He pressed his Oratorians to "lash themselves with ropes three times per week."[67] Gallonio was personally committed to these feats of self-mortification.[68] They spurred people to greater humility and to hold all worldly honors in low-esteem thereby centralizing

---

60 Gallonio, *The Life*, 4.

61 Gallonio, *The Life*, 4.

62 Bacci, *Vita*, 113. Gallonio shares this same story noting how it is reminiscent of the famous saints, Vincent Ferrer and Bernard of Clairvaux, see Gallonio, *The Life*, 11.

63 Gallonio, *The Life*, 36.

64 Gallonio, *The Life*, 36.

65 Gallonio, *The Life*, 7.

66 Gallonio, *The Life*, 9.

67 Touber, *The Hagiographical Works of Antonio Gallonio*, 158.

68 Touber, *The Hagiographical Works of Antonio Gallonio*, 37.

devotion.[69] In his reflections on religious life written for his niece Neri suggested that the purpose of the rigor of cloistered life was to "die to the world, as if in a strapped tomb."[70] Neri reminds her that it is through the flesh that people sin, and therefore tells her to "be attentive...to how the soul has such ugly skin, and therefore to how it is necessary to use the knife of holy discipline to amputate it."[71] If the monastic project was about removing oneself from temptation and the occasion of sin through heroic solitude, then saintliness for Early Modern Catholicism was about withstanding exposure to temptation with custody of the senses and taming of the flesh.

Neri as a Sensuous Object

Not only did Neri practice careful custody of the senses, and encourage others to do the same, but he modeled that behavior for others. As Gallonio reports: "Whether he was well or ill he never allowed anyone to see his chaste limbs, his bare flesh."[72] In this way, throughout his life, Neri because a sensuous object. That only became more true in his death. Like so many living saints of the period, huge crowds of the faithful flocked to the Chiesa Nuova, to see and touch the saint's corpse. Many of these even stripped his clothes, touched his body with rose petals, and ripped his fingernails. Some women slid their rings on and off his fingers.[73] Others approached Neri's body hoping for a cure. Agostino and Margarita de Magistris both visited the holy corpse and placed Neri's hands on their body so that they could be cured of ulcers by his touch.[74] All of these activities reflected the longstanding beliefs about the efficacy of saints's relics as well as the growing consensus that living a life of virtue manifested itself in the bodies of saints. For this reason, as Bradford Bouley has shown, autopsies of holy people became much more

69 In this vein, Neri was famous for his practical jokes, which he played especially on Baronio and Gallonio. Saint Ignatius was also harsh in his efforts to humiliate his most ardent followers. He once commanded the man who penned his so-called "Autobiography," Luís Gonçalves da Camara, to attach bells to his ears so that whenever he opened his mouth they would ring, and he would be remained to maintain monastic silence, see Alexander Eaglestone and Joseph A. Munitz, eds., *Remembering Inigo: Glimpses of the Life of Saint Ignatius of Loyola the Memoriale of Luis Gonçalves da Camara* (Saint Lous: Institute of Jesuit Sources, 2004), 291 (numeral here referring to paragraph number).

70 *Gli Scritti e le Massime*, 68 (translation mine).

71 *Gli Scritti e le Massime*, 68.

72 Gallonio, *The Life*, 38.

73 Bacci, *Vita*, 240–248.

74 Gallonio, *The Life*, 187. For the testimonies to these events, see *Processo* I, 32–35 40, 209–10; III, 219, 294; IV, 404.

common in the Early Modern Period as Catholics endeavored to prove the truth of sanctity. During his autopsy it appears that Neri continued to model modesty as the records indicate, "the physicians who opened Filippo Neri's body, for example, noted only that Neri supernaturally moved to cover his sexual organs after his death, a sign of his modesty and virginity."[75] Together these two supernatural signs truly demonstrated Neri's heroic virtue which depended on exploiting the sensuous aesthetics of Catholicism to encourage spiritual awakening and on custody of the senses to thwart temptation. The sensuous interaction with Neri's body was fundamental to the self-understanding of Early Modern Catholicism. Such practices boldly reasserted the legitimacy of the sensuous dynamic of Catholic worship, and reveal the deep desire Catholics had to use the senses as a means to verify their beliefs.

Conclusion

Much of what undergirded Catholic belief and devotional practice was an intellectual commitment to conserving history. Neri was at the forefront of that movement. On a personal level he was devoted to Christian history. When he arrived in Rome, he famously wandered around the catacombs, and he frequently read the lives of the saints and desert fathers. He bequeathed the Oratory with some 500 books at the time of his death.[76] What is more, he promoted those studies as a fundamental part of the works of the Oratory. The gatherings always included readings from Christian history. Furthermore, his effort to enliven those historical lectures led to his sponsorship of Baronio's *Annales Ecclesiastici*, one of the most celebrated works of sacred history of the era.[77] His hagiographers, Antonio Gallonio chief among them, were also notable contributors to the Catholic effort to harness history as a means to understand not only the theological tenets of the Catholic faith, but their relationship to the proper practice of it. Sanctity, ecclesiastical history, and Christian ethics were a daily part of the Oratorian's lives as producers and consumers of knowledge.[78]

Baronio and other Oratorian historians began to develop an understanding of the nature of history as cyclical, and indeed even understood their Oratory as a

75 B. Bouley, *Pious Postmortems: Anatomy, Sanctity, and the Catholic Church in Early Modern Europe* (Philadelphia: University of Pennsylvania Press, 2017), 122.

76 Touber, *The Hagiographical Works of Antonio Gallonio*, 35.

77 Pamela M. Jones, "Celebrating New Saints in Rome and across the Globe," in *A Companion to Early Modern Rome, 1492–1692*, eds. Pamela M. Jones, Barbara Wisch, and Simon Ditchfield (Boston: Brill, 2019), 158.

78 Touber, *The Hagiographical Works of Antonio Gallonio*, 45.

recapitulation of Saint Paul's meetings mentioned in the letters to the Corinthians.[79] Given this broad understanding of history, the ways in which the Oratorians became critical interpreters of Catholic life are increasingly evident. Seeing themselves in the mold of the apostolic communities they sought to live holy lives and share their knowledge with their adherents. Through reading the lives of the saints they identified longstanding currents that resurfaced throughout Catholic devotion: the custody and the use of the senses. In their own time, this manifested itself in a particular way. Oratorians, with Philip Neri as their guide, patronized the arts and valued artwork in their spiritual lives. They attended to the sacraments in all their sensuous ritualism. Finally, in keeping with movements in early modern science, they used the sensuous aspects of Catholic worship as a tool of verification. The Early Modern Catholic life, which relied on an embrace of the senses came with certain risks and temptations. In fact, it could be argued that Early Modern Sanctity required saints to withstand and resist temptation throughout their ministry in the world. For this Oratorians turned again to Christian history as a way to validate their behaviors, and find examples from the past on how to deal with temptation. Very often that answer was self-torture. In Philip Neri, the Church found a holy person they could canonize who embodied these tenets. Neri lived in and of the world, and clearly practiced Catholicism in its new sensuous dynamics. He also clung to traditional teachings in morality through self-abnegation. All of these he undergirded with history. From this view, truth was on the side of the balancing act between the body, temptation, and torture.

79 Touber, *The Hagiographical Works of Antonio Gallonio*, 93.

Stefan Samerski

What about the Saints of the French Revolution?

Canonization and Beatification after 1789

The Pope of the French Revolution, Pius VI (r. 1775–1799), responded to the spirit of his times with a large number of beatifications. Although there had been no canonisations since 1767, Pius VI beatified nine candidates during his long tenure (five after the storm on the Bastille) – that was more than his two predecessors.[1] In the times of the Enlightenment, beatification and canonisation *per se* were bound to meet with fierce resistance from the rationalist and anti-clerical mainstream[2] – how much more so because of the multitude of cultish approbations imposed by Pius VI.[3] During the French Revolution, the images and relics of the saints had not only been destroyed, but they had also been desecrated and subjected to popular ridicule. In November 1793, for example, the citizens brought the church treasures in a procession from St. Denis to Paris, where they were destroyed as a "republican sacrifice".[4]

Pius VI resisted in Rome, first by increasing the number of canonisations and beatifications and then by facilitating the proceedings.[5] To achieve this, he had simplified the procedure and the methods of payment. He clearly understood these two cultish approbations as an "instrument of ecclesiastical politics".[6] Added to this were the contrasting messages that the new blessed presented to the public. In his beatification decrees, for instance, the Pope repeatedly spoke of the "secularisation and effeminacy of the times"[7], which required a multiple corrective by the new blessed with their specific messages. In his beatifications, the ideas of humility, virginity and priestly zeal for the soul are repeatedly emphasised, which in those

---

1 J. Evenou, „Liturgia e culto dei santi (1815–1915)", in E. Fattorini (ed.), *Santi, culti, simboli nell èta della secolarizzazione (1815–1915)* (Torino: Mondadori, 1997) 43–65, esp. pp. 44, 53–55.

2 A. Angenendt, *Heilige und Reliquien. Die Geschichte ihres Kultes vom frühen Christentum bis zur Gegenwart* (München: Beck, ^{2}1997), 261–70.

3 St. Samerski, *Wie im Himmel, so auf Erden? Selig- und Heiligsprechung in der Katholischen Kirche 1740 bis 1870* (Stuttgart: Kohlhammer, 2002), 129.

4 Angenendt, *Heilige und Reliquien*, 271; D. Gaborit-Chopin (ed.), *Le trésor de Saint-Denis. Musée du Louvre, Paris, 12 mars – 17 juin 1991* (Paris: Equipe, 1992).

5 Samerski, *Wie im Himmel, so auf Erden*, 131–3.

6 Samerski, *Wie im Himmel, so auf Erden*, 133.

7 L. von Pastor, *Geschichte der Päpste im Zeitalter des fürstlichen Absolutismus von der Wahl Benedikts XIV. bis zum Tode Pius' VI. (1740–1799), vol. 3: Pius VI. (1775–1799)* (Freiburg/Br.: Herder, 1933), 246.

years of the Revolution – and even before – did not enjoy social prestige at all.[8] It is therefore not surprising that Pius VI promoted mainly members of severe orders such as those from the Franciscan family or the Carmelites to the honour of the altars. One of the best examples is the Franciscan Father Leonardo da Porto Maurizio (1676–1751), who was spectacularly canonised just 40 years after his death, in 1796.[9] Leonardo was the first promoter of devotions to the Stations of the Cross and had established some 500 Ways of the Cross for this purpose. Pius VI had also promoted such figures as the Passionist founder Paul of the Cross (1694–1775)[10] and Juan de Ribera (1533–1611)[11], who rejected the advantages of their noble birth and led exemplary ascetic and austere lives.

In the decree of the beatification of Catalina Tomàs (1531–1574) from Mallorca, who was beatified in 1792, the Pope put it in a nutshell: "Errors, turmoil, and discord were rushing in her time to a great extent against the little ship of St. Peter; if there were not the *Providentia Divina*, one would have to fear that the floods of hell would swallow it whole. Heresies that had been condemned long ago were now reappearing and the ideals of Christianity were being dragged through the mud. It is precisely for this reason, that it is a work of Providence, that the image of virginity is once again clearly visible".[12] Is all this not a contemporary description of the specific Roman Curia perspective, which act against the condemned heresie of Jansenism? But this will be discussed later. This Breve shows the early reaction of the Roman Church only with few words but clearly and succinctly.

One of the first reactions of the Curia was the beatification of Barbe Acarie (1566–1618) in 1791.[13] She had been married and had children. After the death of her husband, with the help of Cardinal Pierre de Berulle (1575–1629), she led the first Discalced Carmelites from Spain to France in October 1604 and was thus considered the first French Carmelite. Immediately after her death, devotion began; miracles occurred so that investigations were conducted. Due to the decrees of

8 Samerski, *Wie im Himmel, so auf Erden*, 130.

9 R. Haas, „Leonardo da Porto Maurizio", in Lexikon der Heiligen und Heiligenverehrung, vol. 2 (Freiburg/Br.: Herder, 2003) 946–7.

10 E. Zoffoli, *S. Paolo della Croce*, 3 vol. (Roma: Paoline, 1962–1968); A. Calabrese, *Maestro e mistico. San Paolo della Croce* (Roma: Feltrinelli, 1993); E. Zoffoli, *I Passionisti. Spiritualità, Apostolato* (Roma: Casa Editrice Vaticana, 1955); R. Mercurio, *The Passionists* (Religious Order Series 7; Collegeville, Min.: University Press, 1991); M. Bialas, *Im Zeichen des Kreuzes. Leben und Werk des heiligen Paul vom Kreuz, des Gründers der Passionisten* (Leutesdorf: Selbstverlag, ^{2}1989).

11 Ribera was Archbishop of Valencia and was beatified in 1796.

12 Breve of the Beatification quoted by: Pastor, *Geschichte der Päpste*, 246.

13 *Kurze Lebensbeschreibung der seligen Schwester Maria von der Menschwerdung, Stifterin der Barfüßer...* (Augsburg: St. Ulrich-Verlag, 1792); Ph. Bonnichon, *Madame Acarie. Une petite voie à l'aube du grand siècle* (Paris: ecole catholic, 2002); B. Sese, *Madame Acarie. Petite vie* (Paris: ecole catholic, 2005).

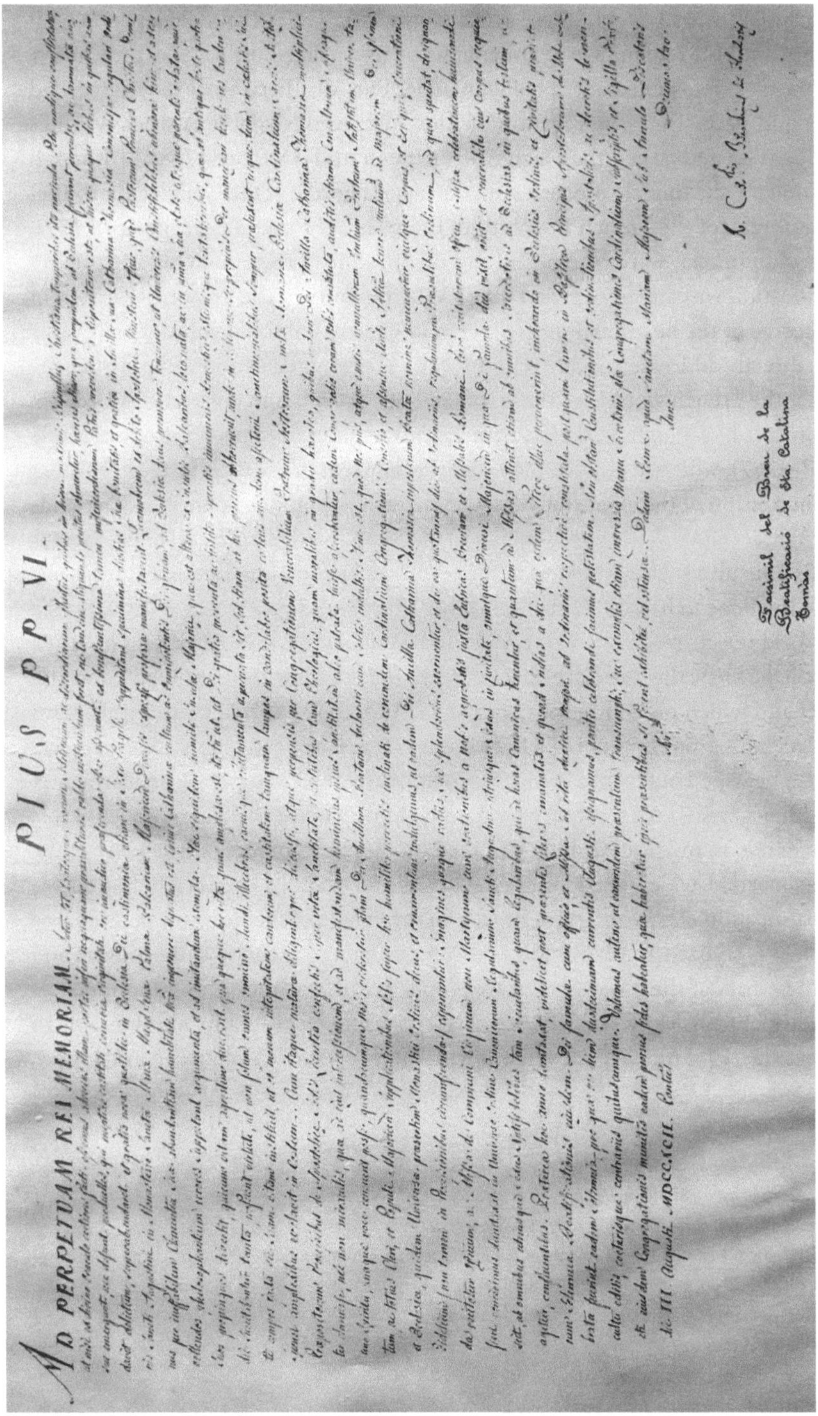
PIUS PP. VI.

AD PERPETUAM REI MEMORIAM.

... Die III. Augusti. MDCCXCII. ...

Facsimil del Breu de la Beatificació de Sta Catalina Tomàs

Breve of the Beatification of Catalina Tomás; Valldemossa; Photo: Samerski

Urban VIII (r. 1623–1644), these proceedings had been put on hold since 1634. It was not until 1781, in the age of Enlightenment and massive criticism of the Church, that the files were pulled out of oblivion under Pius VI. Then things moved forward at a rapid pace. The Congregation of Rites approved Madame Acarie's writings in May 1785 and issued the Degree of Virtue in mid–October 1788.[14] Although traditionally the miracle processes are the biggest hurdle at the Congregation, after the outbreak of the French Revolution, things moved even faster: in April 1791, three old miracles were recognised and on 5th June of the same year, the solemn beatification was already carried out.[15] Why the hurry? The answer is written in the decree of the beatification itself: Here the horros of the revolutionary events were directly addressed and Madame Acarie is presented as an example of virtue so that the French would see the errors of their actions and convert.[16] Moreover, the process had a high protector, namely the daughter of Louis XV, Louise–Marie (1737–1787), who had entered the Carmelite convent in St Denis in 1771.[17] Under the impression of the expulsion of her fellow sisters from the Spanish Netherlands after 1783, Louise–Marie wrote to Pius VI that she trusted in the Heart of the Saviour in this difficult situation. In view of the secular attacks on the Carmelite Order, she asked the Pope to beatify Madame Acarie: "That would be a triumph for us, while the world rejects us!"[18] she wrote. Pius VI was only too happy to pick up on this – after all, he knew that the Carmelites were the only order whose spirituality was still intact and which had numerous vocations. And Louise–Marie's letter must have seemed like a prophecy after 1789, for it was precisely the contemplative orders that were to be wiped out by the French Revolution. In September 1792, 16 Carmelites in Compiegne suffered a brutal execution and this marked the end of Robespierre's reign of terror. In any case, Pius VI called the Acarie a "model of true piety of the virgin, married, widow and cloistered status"[19] and beatified her in 1791. The decree of beatification clearly referred directly to the events of the Revolution: Madame Acarie was stylized as an example of virtue so that the French would convert and see the errors of their ways.[20] For the Pope, Acarie was the second foundress of the Carmelite order, which had preserved its original spirituality and was able to oppose the revolutionary movement with intact austerity, asceticism and prayer.

---

14 *Kurze Lebensbeschreibung der seligen Schwester*, 96–7.

15 *Kurze Lebensbeschreibung der seligen Schwester*, 97.

16 G. Pelletier, *A new mission for Mary of the Incarnation…* (Internet: https://www.madame-acarie.org/beatification-de-madame-acarie/ (28.06.2022).

17 *Kurze Lebensbeschreibung der seligen Schwester*, 96.

18 Pelletier, *A new mission for Mary.*

19 *Kurze Lebensbeschreibung der seligen Schwester*, 97.

20 Pelletier, *A new mission for Mary.*

Severe Franciscan and Carmelite spirituality was thus the first 'blessed answer' to the French Revolution.

The next beatifications built on this message and expanded it. I would like to single out Catalina Tomás (1531–1574), who was and is completely unknown even on the Italian peninsula and in Western Europe.[21] She was beatified in August 1792 – also after a long process (200 years) during which it had lain dormant for many years. At that very time, religious communities in France were being massively persecuted and the monarchy was being abolished. Clerics who did not want to take the oath to the new Constitution were deported. Many fled to Britain and the Papal States, where the first refugees arrived as early as December 1791.[22] There they drew attention to the terror and anti-clerical measures with writings and petitions to the Roman Curia. As a first reaction, between the end of 1791 and September 1792, the Holy See had established relief measures for the approximately 1800 French clerics who had fled to the Papal States.[23] Already the first circular letters in the Patrimonium Petri spoke of the "horror with which the persecution had recently raged cruelly in Paris and in the province. These events caused the number of highly deserving Confessors of Our Holy Religion to grow, as did the number of martyrs in France."[24]

Already in 1791, even before the flow of refugees began, the Italian ex-Jesuit Alfonso Muzzarelli (1749–1813) had published a pamphlet in Foligno warning against the poison, the "colera of the infidels and libertines"[25], and calling the refusers of the oath to the Constitution heroes of the faith. It had been shown that it was not resistance to state authority which caused the rejection of the oath but the spirit of obedience to the Supreme Universal Power. Thus, he said, there was a persecution of the Faith going on in France, similar to that which had taken place in the first centuries of Christianity.[26] In this sense, the Spanish Father Francesco Gusta (1744–1816) also spoke in 1794 of the many illustrious and precious heroes of the Church in France and the "holocaust"[27] of the French clergy. Gusta saw the main

---

21 G. Carrió e Vives, *El carro triunfal, manifestacions populars al'entorn de santa Caterina Tomás* (Palma de Mallorca: Monasteres, 2006); P. Riutort, *Santa Catalina Tomás, la santa payesa* (Barcelona: empresa catalunia, 2006).

22 M. Tosti, „Gli ‚atleti della fede': Emigrazione e Controrivoluzione dello Stato della Chiesa (1792–1799)", in D. Menozzi (ed.), *Chiesa italiana e Rivoluzione Francese* (Bologna: EDB, 1990), 233–85, on pp. 235–8.

23 Tosti, „Gli atleti della fede", 239.

24 Tosti, „Gli atleti della fede", 240.

25 Tosti, „Gli atleti della fede", 245.

26 Tosti, „Gli atleti della fede", 245–6.

27 Tosti, „Gli atleti della fede", 247.

evil and the deeper cause of the persecution of the Church in Jansenism.[28] Loyalty to the Church of Rome and to the symbols of the Faith, such as the veneration of the Sacred Heart, were the real motives for the French church haters to act brutally.[29] From the beginning, the cult of the Sacred Heart was the shorthand message for God's love and man's necessary atonement for wrongs committed. The Jansenists had tried with success in the 18th century to stop the veneration of the first great Sacred Heart promoter, Marguérite-Marie Alacoque (1647–1690).[30] And indeed, during the Revolutionary Wars, the fledgling cult of the Sacred Heart became an anti-revolutionary and legitimistic symbol of resistance.[31] For already Louis XVI (r. 1774–1793), in prison, had consecrated the French nation to the Heart of Jesus in case of his liberation. Thus, the image of the Sacred Heart became a symbol of the monarchist counter-revolution. The peasants of the Vendeé, for example, wore an emblem of the Sacred Heart as a sign of their loyalty to the king and the Church when they undertook an uprising against the revolutionary regime. As a result, the government banned both the cult and the display. In Nantes, for example, a family that had the Sacred Heart image distributed was then executed by guilloutine. Sacred Heart worship also came into play in the assassination of Jean Paul Marat (1743–1793) in 1793. Also the revolt of Andreas Hofer (1767–1810) in Tyrol in June 1796 began with a vow to the Sacred Heart. Thus, since the Battle of Spinges, this cult became a moment of identification for the Ancien regime, for the Church and the monarchy.[32]

It was a compatriot who rediscovered Catalina Tomás in the 18th century, the later Cardinal Antonio Despuig y Dameto (1745–1813).[33] Like Catalina, Despuig

---

28 D.K. van Kley, *Jansenists and the Expulsion of the Jesuits from France, 1757-65* (Leiden: Brill, 1975); Chr. Vogel, „Von Voltaire zu Le Paige – Die französische Aufklärung und der Jansenismus", in *Geschichte und Gesellschaft. Sonderheft 23: Die Aufklärung und ihre Weltwirkung* (Göttingen: Vandenhoeck, 2010), 77–99; D. Burkhard/T. Thanner (ed.), *Der Jansenismus – eine ‚katholische Häresie'? Das Ringen um Gnade, Rechtfertigung und die Autorität Augustins in der frühen Neuzeit* (Münster: Aschendorff, 2014).

29 Fr. Gusta, *Dell'influenza die giansenisti nella rivoluzione di Francia aggiuntevi alcune notizie...* (Ferrara: Montori: [2]1794), 209–11.

30 Samerski, *Wie im Himmel, so auf Erden*, 274–5.

31 J. Le Brun, „Politica e spiritualità: la devozione al Sacro Cuore nell'epoca moderna", in *Concilium* 7 (1971) 41–57; M. Rosa, „Regalità e „douceur" nell'Europa del'700: la contrastata devozione a Sacro Cuore", in F. Traniello (ed.), *Dai Quaccheri a Gandhi. Studi di storia religiosa in onore di Ettore Passerin d'Estrèves* (Bologna: il mulino, 1988) 71–98; D. Menozzi, „Devozione al Sacro Cuore e instaurazione del Regno sociale di Cristo: la politicizzazione del culto nella chiesa ottocentesca", in Fattorini, *Santi, culti, simboli*, 161–94, on pp. 174–5.

32 R. Kampling, „Metapher und Symbol. Zur Herz-Jesu-Frömmigkeit im Katholizismus", in *Wissenschaftsmagazin in der FU-Berlin*, Heft 1 (Berlin: Academie, 2000), 18–26, on pp. 24–5.

33 J. Salvá, *El Cardenal Despuig* (Palma de Mallorca: mallpress 1964); *Dictionnaire biographique des cardinaux du XIXe siècle* (Montréal: unipress, 2007), 302–4 (Jean LeBlanc).

Birthplace of Catalina Tomás at Valldemossa/Mallorca, today Oratory; Photo: Samerski

came from Mallorca and had made her beatification his life's work. He himself wrote a life story about the Augustinian sister, which was published in 1816.[34] She became the first blessed of the island in 1792. Despuig became Canon of the cathedral chapter in Palma de Mallorca in 1774, Rector of the university of the island in 1783, and Auditor of the Sacred Roman Rota in May 1785. In this capacity, he promoted the beatification proceedings of Catalina directly at the Roman Curia until 1791. Despuig then became Archbishop of Valencia in 1794, Archbishop of Seville in 1795, and returned to Rome in the revolutionary turmoil the following year. He was strictly anti-revolutionary and loyal to the Pope: When Pius VI was captured by the French and forced into exile in 1798, Despuig went with him and financed his living expenses and his funeral. The sick old Pope endured his exile with an

34 A. Despuig, *Vida de la Beata Catalina Thomás, religiosa profesa en el Monasterio de Santa Maria Magdalena de la ciudad de Palma* (Palma de Mallorca: Arbués, 1816).

Popular tile with the image of Calatina Tomàs in heaven, Vallde-mossa; Photo: Samerski

unbreakable faith in the future victory of the enslaved Church and in sacrificial humility – and thus embodied the programme of the revolutionary saints in person. Despuig demonstratively stayed away from the wedding of Napoleon with the Austrian emperor's daughter Marie–Louise in 1810 and was therefore forced to take off his red cardinal's robe.

Catalina Tomás fitted the bill of a Revolution Saint perfectly. Even as a young girl, Catalina devoted herself to prayer at an altar she had built herself in an open field. At the age of 20, the penniless orphan entered the convent of the Augustinian nuns in Palma de Mallorca, where she died in 1574. Her life in the convent was marked by asceticism and visions but also inner temptations and the suspicion of her fellow sisters. She endured everything in patience and godly humility. Her monastic life thus had many parallels with the great Spanish Mystic Teresa of Avila (1515–1582), the founder of the Discalced Carmelites. Contemplative humility and asceticism, renunciation of the world as well as prophetic visions – these were the elements of the early Revolution Saints of the Roman Curia.

After 1798, beatifications and canonisations were understandably out of the question. After the death of Pius VI in 1799, even the institution of the papacy was at stake. It was not until 1806 that another beatification became possible, namely that of a Jesuit of Naples: Francesco de Gerolamo (1642–1716).[35] Francesco had called the faithful in the city to repentance and conversion in homilies lasting three to four hours and had thus brought a large number of believers to penitence and conversion – according to the *Positio* of 1806.[36] This was also the great message of the new Jesuit saint in view of the Revolutionary atrocities and overthrows, which the Roman Curia had to experience at first hand as well.

The process of the beatification, sustained by the intense piety of southern Italy and the Bourbon monarchs, was extremely slow after 1747 and has made no progress since 1767. Until the end of 1804, the Causa of Gerolamo rested completely.[37] Then, however, things moved very quickly. The reason for this was the new possibility for the former dissolved Jesuit Order to take over colleges in the south of Italy again from July 1804 and to exercise pastoral care there.[38] Letters of postulation now arrived again in immense numbers in the Roman Curia. In addition, the already mentioned ex-Jesuit Alfonso Muzzarelli, had held the position of Postulator of the Causa Gerolamo since the end of 1804. Muzzarelli was the right man for this job in the eyes of the Curia: Pius VI had summoned him from Parma to Rome in 1803, where he worked as a theologian at the Poenitentiary. The renowned ascetic writer was a great promoter of the devotion to the Sacred Heart.[39] He managed to complete the beatification process in less than 15 months.[40]

Despite Pius VI's concession at Napoleon's coronation in 1804 and the Concordat with France in 1801, Roman disappointment was great when Napoleon's anti-ecclesiastical policies continued and the treaty was broken. In this period of disappointment with the development of revolutionary France, the process of the beatification of Gerolamo was resumed and completed. The Roman Curia did not have much time for this. In April 1805 a first meeting was held at the Congregation of Rites, and in February 1806 the miracles were recognized so that in the same month the proceedings at the Congregation could be completed. The corresponding

35 E. Papa, „Francesco de Geronimo“, in *Biblioteca Sanctorum, vol. 5* (Roma, Ediz. Vaticana, 1967) 1201–4.

36 Samerski, *Wie im Himmel, so auf Erden*, 318.

37 Samerski, *Wie im Himmel, so auf Erden*, 263–4.

38 M. Volpe, I Gesuiti nel Napoletano. Note ed appunti di storia contemporanea da documenti inediti e con larghe illustrazioni 1814–1914, *vol. 1* (Napoli: Caffiero, 1914), 36–7.

39 L. Koch, *Jesuiten-Lexikon. Die Gesellschaft Jesu einst und Jetzt* (Paderborn: Bonifatius, 1934), 1262–3.

40 Samerski, *Wie im Himmel, so auf Erden*, 265.

decrees were promulgated in March and May so that the solemn beatification could be held in St. Peter's on 11th of May.[41] Already in the *Positio* of 1806, Gerolamo is described as an intrepid popular preacher who had led the erring in great numbers along the path of virtue and brought them back to the Church.[42] His very long sermons would have called the people of Naples to repentance and brought them to conversion at that time. And this was exactly what was needed in 1800, in the extreme crisis situation of the papacy and the Church, from the point of view of the Curia. Gerolamo was thus stylized as a kind of apostle of repentance whose message still included a certain hope for improvement of the ecclesiastical situation. A demonization of the opponent was still avoided on the part of the Curia. Rome thus never left its genuine functions: theology, pastoral care and ecclesiastical life, even when it came to beatification and canonisation. Direct interference in politics was not an element of the Curia's beatifications or canonizations at that time. A second disaster for the papacy did not seem to have been anticipated in 1806. However, this occurred only a few months later: French troops entered Rome on 2nd February 1808 and deported the Pope to France in July 1809. This put an end to any regular administration of the Curia until 1814.[43]

The beatification of the stylised apostle of the penitent Francesco, however, had another effect: the hope of the general readmission of the Jesuit order, which had been dissolved by Clement XIV (r. 1769–1774) in 1773 – under French pressure. In the Kingdom of Naples, however, Francesco's homeland, the Society of Jesus was already readmitted in 1804. The *Positio on Miracles* of 1805 expressed this clearly: Just as the Jesuits had saved the Catholic Church from ruin after the Lutheran Reformation, so too – around 1800 – the Curia hoped that the readmitted Jesuits could to rescue them from the anti-clerical revolutionary events.[44] Penitance, contrition and conversion were thus the abundantly clear messages of the new blessed, without directly naming the French Emperor and his European vassals. Like the Carmelites, the old Jesuits were considered a religious order loyal to the Pope, propagating a strict ecclesiasticism and firm morals. Thus, these orders were already considered anti-revolutionary per se. And many of them had been persecuted, exiled and martyred in several parts of Europe since about 1760.[45]

It becomes clear, however, that the personal profile of the new blessed took on ever sharper contours: Whereas in 1791 they were still ascetic nuns in strict enclosure by the late nineties and 1806 they were beatified public popular preachers who had proclaimed the harsh message of penitence and atonement loud and clear.

---

41 Samerski, *Wie im Himmel, so auf Erden*, 266–7.

42 Samerski, *Wie im Himmel, so auf Erden*, 318.

43 Samerski, *Wie im Himmel, so auf Erden*, 323–5.

44 Samerski, *Wie im Himmel, so auf Erden*, 318.

45 P.C. Hartmann, *Die Jesuiten* (München: Beck, 2001), 87–91.

However, the idea of an effective fighting-force like that of the Jesuits in the Counter-Reformation had caught on. While the Society of Jesus was readmitted worldwide in 1815, and then only gradually rose to its former importance, there was now a new order called the 'little Jesuits': the Redemptorist order, founded in 1732 by Alfonso de Liguori (1696–1787).[46] This order was also characterised by its closeness to the people, its educational function and its strict moral standards. Its spread was international and rapid. Liguori's writings were translated into 90 languages during his lifetime and received 402 editions.[47] Decisive for the Curia in those years was not only the strict moral teaching but also the anti-Jansenist character of Liguori's writings.[48]

His beatification process began in Rome in July 1794 – not even ten years after his death.[49] This was only possible because Pius VI had granted dispensations of all kinds. It was necessary, because Liguori was known to bequeath an infinite amount of writings (already as bishop of S. Agata dei Goti) that had to be soundly examined. Indeed, the Pope did even more: He set up a *Congregatio particularis* in 1795, which could effectively face the mass of opposition, doubts and contradictions.[50] Pius VI even imposed a *Silentium Perpetuum* on new accusations concerning Liguori's episcopal term at S. Agata dei Goti. Why this special interest of the Pope? In the list of Liguori's main works at the time, there was a booklet entitled: *La fedeltà de' vasalli verso Dio li rende fedeli al loro principe.*[51] If the title of the booklet already speaks volumes, the remark of the Congregation of Rites speaks even more: "This work is written for the benefit of the princes"[52], meaning: an apologetic defence of the *Ancien Régime*. In Liguori's work, therefore, direct political implications stand out, which are quite understandable at the moment of the extreme danger for the papacy: A few months later, in February 1798, as we know, the time had come: The Papal States were occupied, the Pope was deposed as secular ruler and deported to France. Despite the end of the administration of the Curia, the process continued abroad, albeit delayed. The new Pope Pius VII (r. 1800–1823) granted new dispensations in early 1802 and approved all ten disputed episcopol-processes in September 1803, so that all (!) sittings of the Congregation of Rites on Virtues

46 F.M. Jones, *Alphonso de Liguori* (Dublin: St. Patricks-Press, 1992); Th. Rey-Mermet, *Il santo del secolo dei lumi: Alfonso de Liguori (1696–1787)* (Rom: Paoline [2]1987).

47 Extensive and detailed: *La Recezione del pensiero Alfonsiano nella Chiesa. Atti del congresso in occasione del terzo centenario della nascita di S. Alfonso Maria de Liguori, Roma 5–7 marzo 1997* (Roma: Alfonsiano, 1998); O. Weiß, *Deutsche oder römische Moral?* (Regensburg: Pustet, 2001).

48 Jones, *Alphonso de Liguori*, 291–5.

49 Samerski, *Wie im Himmel, so auf Erden*, 320.

50 Samerski, *Wie im Himmel, so auf Erden*, 321.

51 Samerski, *Wie im Himmel, so auf Erden*, 321.

52 Samerski, *Wie im Himmel, so auf Erden*, 321.

and Miracles could be held between June 1806 and 1815.[53] For most of this period, the Pope was in exile in France again. But a report of the Congregation in 1809 spoke of the "merit of the question"[54], so that Liguori could be beatified in record time in 1816. The Breve then also sketched the image of the *ecclesia militans*, for which the new blessed stood: in writing and action, he had given a militant witness to discipline and bravery.[55] Liguori had shown the erring the way to reach the goal in the night of the century. This was an entirely new, aggressive message on the revolutionary scene, brimming with activity and political expressiveness. The supporters of the Causa were not without reason arch-conservative cardinals and monsignori as well as a multitude of European monarchs.[56] Blessed Liguori was thus stylised into a monarchistic fighting type. The visionary element was completely missing here.

Lastly, I would like to present Benoît-Joseph Labré (1748–1783)[57], who – because he had no lobby – was not beatified until 1860. Nevertheless, his beatification process must be considered a Revolution Causa.[58] From 1770, the Frenchman Labré led the life of a homeless pilgrim, wandering anonymously, praying, begging and mocking half of Europe, seeking out the most important places of pilgrimage and finally settling in Rome in 1777. Atonement and contemplation were his way of life, not *caritas* or practical activity. This was contrary to the philosophical and social mainstream of his times. Already shortly after his death, Labré's veneration took off, and the first informative processes began in 1785.[59] After 1789, due to his poverty and self-denial, at Rome he was considered an antipode of the revolutionary Enlightenment and was even regarded by the French as a patron saint against the revolutionary evils.[60] The reason for this also lay in his visions: Labré had confided to his confessor that "he had seen a place or a homestead burst into flames"[61]. "Certainly I did not understand at the time, but later, after the Revolution had raged in the kingdom of France, I thought that these visions must be ascribed to divine illumination"[62], he said to his Confessor. The figure of Labré now took on a prophetic focus during his beatification process: as a preview of the great upheavals

53 Samerski, *Wie im Himmel, so auf Erden*, 322–6.

54 Samerski, *Wie im Himmel, so auf Erden*, 324.

55 Samerski, *Wie im Himmel, so auf Erden*, 326.

56 Samerski, *Wie im Himmel, so auf Erden*, 326–7.

57 Y.-M. Hilaire, *Benoît Labré* (Paris: Ecole des chartes, 1984); Samerski, *Wie im Himmel, so auf Erden*, 314–5.

58 M. Caffiero, *La politica della santità. Nascita di un culto nell'età dei Lumi* (Roma: Rosenberg & Sellier, 1996).

59 Samerski, *Wie im Himmel, so auf Erden*, 315–6.

60 Samerski, *Wie im Himmel, so auf Erden*, 316.

61 Samerski, *Wie im Himmel, so auf Erden*, 316.

62 Samerski, *Wie im Himmel, so auf Erden*, 316.

of Europe and as a punishment for the sins of an entire epoch. The beatification, which took place only in 1860, had then also the following indirect and already known message: conversion, return to the faith and loyality to the Church and the Pope.[63] Labré was functionalised into an anti-revolutionary symbolic figure, which of course came much too late in 1860. Already after 1824, the Curia's interest in Labré had clearly diminished.[64] As is well known, as a layman he had no lobby; perhaps his message was too sophisticated to spread far and wide and inspire the masses after 1815. With him, however, the visionary was clearly in the foreground. The retrospective defence of the *Ancien Régime* was only indirectly revealed by his life and his visions. Any case of activity is clearly secondary in this figure.

Let us briefly summarise: The Revolution Causae all began before 1789 as philosophical-spiritual responses to the anti-clerical Late Enlightenment. They gained very significant momentum after 1789 and were then functionalised into a Roman response to the brutal events of the French Revolution. The first new blessed had no direct political meaningfulness, but they did have apocalyptic features. Their messages were those of the strict orders: contemplative humility, asceticism, penitance and conversion. It was only when the Pope had to go into the French exile, that the Causae became clearly more political, and organizational countermeasures were considered – such as the promotion of the Jesuits or the Redemptorists.

63 Samerski, *Wie im Himmel, so auf Erden*, 317.

64 Samerski, *Wie im Himmel, so auf Erden*, 317.

Joris Geldhof

Modern Saints in the Roman Missal

An Exploration of the *Proprium de Sanctis*

Introduction

Even if often neglected, the *proprium missarum de sanctis* or *proprium sanctorum* is a constitutive part of the Missale Romanum as much as the *ordinarium missarum de tempore* or *proprium de tempore*. In particular, the sanctoral cycle of the Roman missal is a crucial reference for the study of the veneration of the saints.[1] It is the place where one finds the prayers to be prayed and the readings to be read in the masses celebrated on the feasts commemorating the saints. Interestingly, however, upon issuing the missal in 1570 in the immediate aftermath of the Council of Trent, pope Pius V decreed that henceforth not the slightest change or addition be made to it.[2] Quite ironically, however, that is precisely what happened slowly but surely, and actually quite naturally, in the liturgical register of the 'proper of the saints'.

In the present contribution the changes and additions made to the universal calendar of the Missale Romanum between 1570 and 1962 will be carefully mapped and studied.[3] The reason for this start and end date is that they mark the first and the last version of the Roman missal in the timespan between the Council

1 Even if there is a lot of scholarship about the history of the veneration of the saints (mostly individual saints or martyrs) and hagiographical studies, theological and liturgical literature about the *sanctorale* is actually quite scarce. In general commentaries on the history and composition of the liturgical year, for instance, if at all it is discussed, it usually occupies a minor chapter at the end of the volume. See e. g. the classical study of A. Adam, *Das Kirchenjahr mitfeiern: Seine Geschichte und seine Bedeutung nach der Liturgieerneuerung* (Freiburg – Basel – Wien: Herder, 1979), 162–205; and, more recently, M. Augé, *L'anno liturgico: È Cristo stesso presente nella sua chiesa* (Città del Vaticano: Libreria Editrice Vaticana, 2011), 227–84, where a threefold distinction is made between devotional feasts, Marian feasts and feasts of the saints.

2 The pope said so much in the bull "Quo Primum" with which the Missale Romanum was issued in 1570. For an edition, translation and commentary of that striking document, see M. Klöckener, "Die Bulle 'Quo Primum' Papst Pius' V. vom 14. Juli 1570 zur Promulgation des nachtridentinischen Missale Romanum. Liturgische Quellentexte lateinisch-deutsch 2," in *Archiv für Liturgiewissenschaft* 48 (2006) 41–51.

3 Reference will be made to the following editions: *Missale Romanum: Editio Princeps (1570)*, ed. Manlio Sodi – Achille Maria Triacca, Monumenta liturgica Concilii Tridentini, vol. 2, 2nd ed. (Città del Vaticano: Libreria Editrice Vaticana, 2012); *Missale Romanum: Editio typica 1962*, ed. Manlio Sodi – Alessandro Toniolo, Monumenta liturgica Piana, vol. 1 (Città del Vaticano: Libreria Editrice Vaticana, 2007). Henceforth MR 1570 and MR 1962, respectively.

of Trent and the Second Vatican Council.[4] The basis for the present survey is the calendar as it appears on the first pages introducing the missal itself.[5] The hypothesis undergirding this investigation is that one can learn a great deal from the liturgical profile of the saints whose celebration was inserted from roughly the late sixteenth until the second half of the twentieth century. It reveals a lot about the evolution of religious mentalities and sensitivities in the Roman Catholic Church in the modern era.

Accordingly, the concrete question to which this paper seeks an answer is: which patterns and evolutions can one observe with respect to the veneration of the saints in Roman Catholicism between the late 16th and mid-20th century, if one takes the Roman missal as a sole point of reference? The advantage to exclusively highlight the Roman missal, is that it contains the universal saints, whose commemoration is allowed, sometimes even encouraged, to be celebrated all over the world, i. e. in every diocese, and by every religious order, on the set date. Moreover, this perspective makes it possible to make certain comparisons between different contexts, both geographically and historically. This approach additionally allows to focus on the Roman rite,[6] which has been the dominant liturgical tradition in Western Christianity for at least about one millennium. Over the centuries one can observe a certain development from a focus on the city of Rome itself, with the many martyrs locally venerated, to a focus on Rome as the center of ecclesial power, as the place from where the official recognition of a saint being a saint is granted.[7] The fact that,

---

4 For some studies on the development of the Roman missal, see D. McCarthy, "Seeing a Reflection, Considering Appearances: The History, Theology and Literary Composition of the Missale Romanum in a Time of Vernacular Reflection," in *Questions Liturgiques* 94 (2013), 109–43; P. Sorci, "Il Messale Romano come strumento della tradizione celebrativa," in C. Giraudo (red.), *Il Messale Romano: Tradizione, traduzione, adattamento*, Biblioteca 'Ephemerides Liturgicae' 'Subsidia', vol. 125 (Roma: Edizioni Liturgiche, 2003), 37–78.

5 MR 1570, 39–50; MR 1962, 45–53.

6 Other liturgical families such as the Byzantine, Armenian, Coptic and several (other) oriental traditions also know a veneration of the saints and a sanctoral cycle of the liturgical year. In many cases, however, the specific dates on which a common saint is commemorated or a feast celebrated often differs. In addition, these traditions do not have the same selection of saints and ranking system. While henceforth no references will be made to these traditions, it is interesting to note in passing that especially modern saints (i. e. saints recognized as such since the 16th century) have increased the differences. Besides, also the Anglican and Lutheran churches commemorate saints, but they obviously deal with them in an entirely different way. Many of the ancient and medieval saints which the Roman Catholic Church also has, were kept, often on the original dates, but obscure martyrs were canceled and, in modern times, different emphases were laid, often including holy and learned people from their own ecclesial tradition.

7 R. Gribble, "Saints in the Christian Tradition: Unraveling the Canonization Process," in *Studies in Christian-Jewish Relations* 6 (2011) 1–18; Giulio Sodano, "El nuevo proceso de canonización de la edad moderna," in *Anuario de historia de la Iglesia* 29 (2020) 53–72; D.S. Prudlo, *Certain Sainthood:*

eventually, a whole procedure of beatification and canonization was elaborated, which still exists and is applied nowadays, is in a way typical of a church having adapted itself to modern culture.

The Universal Calendars in MR 1570 and MR 1962

The universal calendars inserted in MR 1570 and MR 1962 show both continuity and discontinuity. The most robust element of continuity is the placing of the celebration of most feasts and saints on the same dates, especially the most important ones, such as the Assumption of Mary, the feasts of the apostles, and Saint Lawrence, to name but a few. The sanctoral cycle is structured in the 12 months of the Gregorian calendar still known and universally used today, thus beginning with January 1 and ending with December 31. The vast majority of saints mentioned in MR 1570 were kept in MR 1962, even if the origins of their veneration are obscure and known to be obscure.

Almost everything else is different, from formal characteristics like the lay-out and the font to the classification system which organizes the importance of individual feasts in different ranks. With respect to the latter, MR 1570 had developed categories including 'first class', 'duplex', 'semi-duplex', etc., which ceased to exist in MR 1962.[8] Many celebrations of saints from antiquity, among which the feasts of many martyrs about whom very little is known beyond legends and scarce references in inscriptions, had become *commemorationes*, which means that their feast day became optional. All these *commemorationes* are consistently put in italics in MR 1962, and if they collide with the feast of one or several other saints, the latter have precedence.

MR 1962 had discontinued still two other emphatic elements of the universal calendar. First, it cut out all the octaves, with the noteworthy exception of Christmas. Octaves are the eight days following a feast, whereby the conclusion of the feast's aftermath on the eighth day was marked with a particular reference to the feast in question. As the table below shows, MR 1570 had 11 feasts with octaves, which led to quite complex situations, especially around the end of the (civil) year.

Canonization and the Origins of Papal Infallibility in the Medieval Church (Ithaca and London: Cornell University Press, 2015); P. Delooz, "Pour une étude sociologique de la sainteté canonisée dans l'église catholique," in *Archives de sociologie des religions* 7 (1962) 17–43.

8 The details of how these systems worked fall out of the scope of the present contribution. But what was common to them was that some feasts were optional whereas other ones were mandatory.

Table 1: Feasts with octaves in MR 1570

Feast	Date	Start Octave	End Octave
Epiphany	6/1	7/1	13/1
Nativity of John the Baptist	24/6	25/6	1/7
Peter and Paul	29/6	30/6	6/7
Saint Lawrence	10/8	11/8	17/8
Assumption	15/8	16/8	22/8
Nativity of the Virgin	8/9	9/9	15/9
All saints	1/11	2/11	8/11
Christmas	25/12	26/12	1/1
Saint Stephen	26/12	27/12	2/1
Saint John	27/12	28/12	3/1
Holy Innocents	28/12	29/12	4/1

The complexity consisted in particular in the overlap of octaves either with the octave of other feasts or of the celebration of other saints' feasts. An example of the latter was the case with the feast of the Exaltation of the Cross (14/9), which fell in the octave of the Nativity of the Virgin (8/9). The former was the case with Peter and Paul, which fell in the octave of the Nativity of John the Baptist (24/6), and with the Assumption of Mary (15/8), which fell in the octave of Saint Lawrence (10/8). In practice, this meant that the last day of the octave of the Nativity of John the Baptist was the first day of the octave of Peter and Paul, and that on August 16th, e. g., both the octave of Saint-Lawrence and the octave of the Assumption were scheduled. Particularly in the period after Christmas, however, the situation was notoriously complicated, with four octaves colliding for four consecutive days from December 29 till January 1, namely the ones of Christmas itself, of Saint Stephen, of Saint John, and of Holy Innocents.

A second reduction of complexity concerns vigils on the eve of certain feasts. MR 1962 only took over the vigils of Christmas, the Nativity of John the Baptist and Peter and Paul. This is interesting from a symbolic point of view, because the first two are connected with the cosmic rhythm of the winter and the summer solstices (in the northern hemisphere). MR 1570 additionally had vigils for the feasts of Epiphany, the Assumption, Saint Lawrence, All saints, and all the apostles' feasts. Not all the apostles were celebrated on separate days, however. In addition to Peter and Paul (29/6), Philip and Jacob Minor (1/5) and Simon the Zealot and Judas Thaddeus (28/10) are celebrated on the same day.

Furthermore, one needs to know that Pius X deemed it important to restore the importance of Sundays for pastoral reasons. As a consequence, some feasts that had been assigned to one or another Sunday under the reign of one of his predecessors, were now removed to a fixed date in the calendar.

A next important factor in describing the universal calendars in MR 1570 and MR 1962 is the difference between feast days and saints' feast days, for in addition to feasts dedicated to one saint or group of saints the sanctoral cycle also knows Marian feasts and so-called devotional or thematic feasts. It is difficult, however, to subsume these feasts under one fitting common denominator, since they have divergent origins and meanings. Therefore, labelling them in one or another way always betrays theological interpretations. The table below shows the Latin names of the feasts appearing in MR 1570 and MR 1962. In the course of four centuries, some feasts were cancelled or put together, others were added. Many of them remained stable. All in all, however, there has been an increase of feasts. In MR 1570 there are 25 of them, in MR 1962 31.

Among the feasts that have remained stable are, of course, Epiphany (6/1), Christmas (25/12), Saint Paul's conversion (25/1), the Nativity of Saint John the Baptist (24/6), Saints Peter and Paul (29/6), the Transfiguration of the Lord (6/8), the Exaltation of the Cross (14/9), All Saints and All Souls (1–2/11), the commemorations of the dedication of the four major basilicas at Rome (Santa Maria Maggiore,[9] Saint John of Lateran,[10] Saint Peter's and Saint Paul Outside the Walls), and the four central Marian feasts of the Purification or Candlemas (2/2), the Annunciation (25/3), the Assumption (15/8), and the Immaculate Conception (8/12).

Table 2: The feasts in MR 1570 and MR 1962

Date	MR 1570		MR 1962
1/1	Circumcisio Domini	≠	/
6/1	Epiphania Domini	=	In Epiphania Domini
18/1	Cathedrae Sancti Petri Romae	≠	/
25/1	Conversio Sancti Pauli	=	In Conversione S. Pauli
2/2	Purificatio beatae Mariae	=	In Purificatione B. Mariae Virg.
11/2	/	≠	In Apparitione B. Mariae Virg. Immaculatae
22/2	Cathedrae Sancti Petri Antiochiae	≈	Cathedrae S. Petri Ap. + Commemoratio S. Pauli Ap.

9 In Latin it says "S. Mariae ad Nives" in MR 1570 and MR 1962, *nives* meaning 'snow'. This refers to a popular and widespread medieval legend that in the midst of the summer once snow had fallen on the Esquiline hill. This miracle was interpreted as an indication that on that very spot a church in honor of our Lady be built.

10 The official name in MR 1570 and MR 1962 does not refer to Saint John but to the Savior (*Salvator*), to whom the basilica is indeed dedicated. It is in the course of the middle ages that the church was additionally dedicated to Saint John the Baptist first and to Saint John the Evangelist later, too. 'Lateran' refers to the Lateran palace, where the popes had resided since the reign of the emperor Constantine until the middle of the 15th century, when they moved to the Vatican. The basilica of Saint John in Lateran was in fact the first cathedral of Rome.

Date	MR 1570		MR 1962
25/3	Annuntiatio beatae Mariae	=	Annuntiatio B. Mariae Virg.
3/5	Inventio sancti Crucis	≠	/
6/5	Ioannis ante portam Latinam	≠	/
8/5	Apparitio s. Michaelis	≠	/
24/6	Nativitas S. Ioannis Baptistae	=	In Nativitate S. Ioannis Baptistae
29/6	Petri, & Pauli Apostolorum	=	SS. Petri et Pauli App.
30/6	Commemoratio S. Pauli Apostoli	≈	In commemoratione S. Pauli Ap. + Commemoratio S. Petri Ap.
1/7	/	≠	Pretiosissimi Sanguinis D. N. I. C.
2/7	Visitatio beatae Mariae	=	In Commemoratione B. Mariae Virg.
16/7	/	≠	Commemoratio B. Mariae Virg. de Monte Carmelo
1/8	Petri ad vincula	≠	/
3/8	Inventio s. Stephani protomartyris	≠	/
5/8	Dedicatio s. Mariae ad Nives	=	In Dedicatione S. Mariae ad Nives
6/8	Transfiguratio Domini	=	In Transfiguratione D. N. I. C.
15/8	Assumptio beatae Marie virg.	=	In Assumptione B. Mariae Virg.
22/8	/	≠	Immaculati Cordis B. Mariae Virg.
12/9	/	≠	Sanctissimi Nominis B. Mariae Virg.
14/9	Exaltatio s. Crucis	=	In Exaltatione S. Crucis
15/9	/	≠	Septem Dolorum B. Mariae Virg.
17/9	/	≠	Commemoratio Impress. Ss. Stigmatum S. Francisci Conf.
24/9	/	≠	Commemoratio B. Mariae Virg. a Mercede
2/10	/	≠	S. Angelorum Custodum
7/10	/	≠	B. Mariae Virg. a Rosario
11/10	/	≠	Maternitatis B. Mariae Virg.
1/11	Festum omnium Sanctorum	=	Omnium Sanctorum
2/11	Commemoratio omnium fidelium defunctorum	=	In commemoratione omnium fidelium defunctorum
9/11	Dedicatio basilicae Salvatoris	=	In Dedicatione Archibasilicae Ss.mi Salvatoris
18/11	Dedicatio Basilicarum Petri et Pauli	=	In Dedicatione Basilicarum Ss. Petri et Pauli App.
21/11	/	≠	In Praesentatione B. Mariae Virg.
8/12	Conceptio beatae Mariae	=	In conceptione Immaculata B. Mariae Virg.
25/12	Nativitas Domini nostri Iesu Christi	=	In Nativitate Domini

Some feasts with a clearly legendary dimension were removed from the calendar between the 16th and the 20th century: the finding of the holy cross near Jerusalem

(3/5),[11] Saint John at the Latin gate (6/5),[12] the apparition of Saint Michael the archangel (8/5),[13] all of which took place in early May, the liberation of Saint Peter from prison (1/8),[14] and the finding of the remains of Saint Stephen (3/8).[15] Also removed was the commemoration of the Lord's circumcision celebrated on January 1, as the completion of the octave of Christmas. Feasts that were taken together are related to Saint Peter and Saint Paul, where a certain rationalization seems to have been a priority: the feasts commemorating Saint Peter's taking the episcopal seat at Antioch and at Rome were merged (22/2), as was a commemoration of Saint Paul on those dates. It seems that an equilibrium in feasts connected with Saints Peter and Paul was a preoccupation. In that context one could additionally refer to the double commemoration on June 30, the day after their big feast.

Feasts which were added to the universal calendar of MR 1962 include first and foremost Marian feasts: Our Lady of Mount Carmel (16/7), the Immaculate Heart of Mary (22/8) one week after the Assumption, Mary's Holy Name (12/9), Our Lady of Sorrows (15/9) on the day after the Exaltation of the Cross, Our Lady of Mercy (24/9), Our Lady of the Rosary (7/10), Mary the Mother of God (11/10), and the Presentation of Mary in the temple (21/11), as a clear parallel with the presentation of her Son on February 2. Also added were a feast dedicated to Jesus' Precious Blood (2/7), a feast commemorating Saint Francis' reception of the stigmata (17/9),[16] and a feast in honor of the guardian angels (2/10), a category of angels distinct from the archangels.

Finally, something should be said about 'empty' days in MR 1570 and MR 1962. By 'empty' I mean that there is no mention of anything 'special' on these days, neither a feast, nor a saint, a commemoration or even an octave. Whereas MR 1570 has 154 empty days on a sum total of 366 (42%), this number has gone down drastically in MR 1962 to 90/366 (24,6%). As table 3 below shows, January is the only month which has more empty days in MR 1570 than MR 1962, which has everything to do

11 This feast goes back to the legend that Saint Helena, Constantine's mother, while on a pilgrimage to the Holy Land, found the physical remnants of the cross on which Jesus had hung and died.

12 This feast remembers the miracle whereby Saint John, captivated at Ephesus, was brought to Rome, where he was tortured in a huge cauldron filled with boiling oil. This did not injure him, however, instead he came out as if he had been refreshed by a wonderful bath.

13 Apparently, it has not only been Mary who appeared to certain faithful in the history of the Church, but also the archangel Michael.

14 This feast is probably better known as Saint Peter-in-chains, and goes back to the story in the Acts of the Apostles (12:6–11) where the imprisoned Peter is visited by an angel who breaks his chains and leads him out of the prison.

15 Also in the Acts of the Apostles (8:2) it is said that, after he was stoned, Saint Stephen was buried.

16 It was taken for granted that this was the first time in history that the stigmata appeared on a human body. Therefore, the feast was not only, or not even primarily, an extra feast for Saint Francis, but a thankful commemoration of God's mysterious interventions in history.

with the four octaves running after Christmas and the one after Epiphany. December is the month with the least modifications, which is indicative of the stability of Advent and the Christmas season. July and August are the most occupied months, whereas March and April proportionally have the smallest number of occupied days, probably because Lent and the Easter season in the temporal cycle run concurrently.

Table 3: Empty days in MR 1570 and MR 1962

Empty days	**MR 1570**	**MR 1962**
January	3	8
February	16	9
March	25	16
April	22	13
May	15	6
June	12	5
July	8	4
August	2	1
September	12	5
October	19	6
November	8	6
December	12	11
SUM TOTAL	**154**	**90**

A Profile of the Saints in MR 1570 and MR 1962

In what follows the details of the additions and changes to the saints' feasts between 1570 and 1962 are mapped. After a discussion of the sex and nationality of the saints, they are discussed along the lines of a classical classification referring to their role and function in the Church. The focus is on the saints added in modern times, which means that the many martyrs from ancient times will not be highlighted.[17]

Women and Men

A first important consideration concerns the number of women and men among the saints. On the basis of general knowledge about gender distinctions in European history in general and in the history of Catholicism in particular, one would expect that men significantly outnumber women when it comes to canonized persons, and that is actually the case. While the overall number of saints in the universal calendar

17 There are no less than 92 *commemorationes* of martyrs in MR 1962; 29 martyr feasts are not a *commemoratio*. On most of these days, other saints are remembered as well.

significantly increased from MR 1570 (226) to MR 1962 (344), the proportion of 1 woman for 5 men more or less remained the same, as the table below shows. Counted are those men and women whose name is mentioned explicitly, e. g. not the "seven sons" or "forty martyrs".

Table 4: Women and men in the sanctoral cycle of MR 1570 and MR 1962

Months	**MR 1570**		**MR 1962**	
	Men	*Women*	*Men*	*Women*
January	17	5	23	6
February	6	4	13	4
March	4	2	11	3
April	12	0	21	1
May	19	3	33	4
June	23	1	32	4
July	22	8	32	11
August	25	4	34	5
September	16	4	25	4
October	17	2	25	7
November	15	4	23	6
December	10	3	13	4
SUM TOTAL	**186**	**40**	**285**	**59**

When looking into these data somewhat more precisely, one can make a couple of interesting observations. In January, for instance, one actually has one female saint celebrated twice in MR 1570, Saint Agnes (21/1 and 28/1), a duplicate that was remarkably preserved in MR 1962. The one woman that was added in the month of April, where there was no female saint at all in MR 1570, is Saint Catherine of Siena (30/4). In August, similarly, the one woman that was added is Rosa of Lima (30/8). Moreover, if one does not take into account the rare figures coming from outside of the Mediterranean basin in the first centuries, and whether or not one attaches great weight to making a difference between the Roman province of Africa and the contemporary continent in this respect, Rosa of Lima is the only non-European saint in the MR 1962 universal calendar. Finally, all the holy women in MR 1962 are either widows or virgins; often, they had been martyrs, too. None of them was married at the time of their death, but that is actually true for lay men as well. As a matter of fact, neither MR 1570 nor MR 1962 contains any married lay persons, with the exception of Anne and Joachim, Jesus's grandparents (cf. infra).

The table below shows the female saints, who were not martyrs in the first five centuries. The only ones from that era, then, are Saint Martha of Bethany (29/7) and Saint Monica (4/5), Saint Augustine's mother. Together with Clare of Assisi (12/8), these are the only ones in MR 1570. In MR 1962 another 12 female saints were inserted in the universal calendar. Many of them are notorious mystics: Teresa of Lisieux (3/10), Birgitta of Sweden (8/10), Teresa of Avila (15/10), Marguerite-Marie Alacoque (17/10) – October, as it happens, being a particularly fruitful month in that respect – and Gertrude 'the Great' of Helfta (16/11); or royals who resigned their privileges: Margaret of Scotland (10/6), Elisabeth of Portugal (8/7), Hedwig of Silesia (16/10), and Elisabeth of Hungary (19/11); or founders of religious congregations for women: Angela de Merici, who founded the Ursulines; Birgitta of Sweden, the Birgittines; Jane de Chantal, the Visitandines, and Teresa of Avila, who profoundly reformed the Carmelite order. Many of them also had a peculiar relationship with a male saint: Saint Scholastica was Saint Benedict's sister, Saint Monica was Saint Augustine's mother, and some maintained a special spiritual friendship: Saint Clare of Assisi with Saint Francis, Saint Jeanne de Chantal with Saint Francis of Sales, and Saint Teresa of Avila with Saint John of the Cross.

Table 5: Female saints not martyrs in MR 1570 and MR 1962

Name	Category	Century	MR 1570	MR 1962
Scholastica	Virg.	6	–	10/2
Monica	Vid.	4	4/5	4/5
Angela de Merici	Virg.	16	–	1/6
Margaret of Scotland	Vid.	11	–	10/6
Elisabeth of Portugal	Vid.	14	–	8/7
Martha	Virg.	1	29/7	29/7
Clare of Assisi	Virg.	13	12/8	12/8
Jeanne de Chantal	Vid.	17	–	21/8
Rosa of Lima	Virg.	17	–	30/8
Teresa of Lisieux	Virg.	19	–	3/10
Birgitta of Sweden	Vid.	14	–	8/10
Teresa of Avila	Virg.	16	–	15/10
Hedwig of Silesia	Vid.	14	–	16/10
Marguerite-Marie Alacoque	Virg.	17	–	17/10
Gertrude of Helfta	Virg.	14	–	16/11
Elisabeth of Hungary	Vid.	13	–	19/11

Country and Century of Origin

In terms of nationality, it is difficult to avoid anachronisms, of course, for the borders between nation states have changed over the centuries. Moreover, there are saints in the calendar who have lived (long) before there were nation states, but are recognized as belonging to a certain nation. These histories and connections are interesting in themselves, but for the sake of clarity no saints from the first millennium have been taken up in the table below. Instead the table focuses on those countries who have one or more saints in the sanctoral cycle of the missal.

The dominance of Italy strikes one immediately. Almost half of the saints from the 11th till the 19th century in MR 1962 are Italian, and Italy is the only nation with more than one saint in every century.[18] Even if one were to reduce the number of Italian saints from the 13th century from 13 to 7 – something which was not done because the seven founders in question are known and revered by their individual name as well –, and thus count the seven founders of the Order of the Servants of Mary as one, a remarkable disproportion is obvious.

Table 6: Saints per nationality and per century in MR 1962

Country	Number	11th	12th	13th	14th	15th	16th	17th	18th	19th
Spain	15	0	0	4	0	3	6	1	0	1
France	10	0	0	2	0	0	0	5	1	2
Italy	48	4	2	13	3	4	10	8	2	2
Poland	5	1	0	2	0	2	0	0	0	0
Portugal	3	0	0	1	1	0	1	0	0	0
England	3	1	2	0	0	0	0	0	0	0
Germany	5	2	0	1[19]	0	0	1	1	0	0
Scotland	1	1	0	0	0	0	0	0	0	0
Peru	1	0	0	0	0	0	0	1	0	0
Hungary	2	1	0	1	0	0	0	0	0	0
Sweden	1	0	0	0	1	0	0	0	0	0
TOTAL	**94**	**10**	**4**	**24**	**5**	**9**	**18**	**16**	**3**	**5**

When one looks closer into saints from other countries, one can derive a couple of interesting conclusions. Spain is strongly represented with saints from the 16th century, France with saints from the 17th century. Poland, Scotland, Hungary, Sweden, and England, do not have a saint from later than the middle ages. France, Spain and Italy are the only nations with a saint from the 19th century.

What strikes one, too, in this table is the relative importance of the 13th, the 16th and the 17th century in terms of the total amount of saints. Taken together, these three centuries count for more than 60% of the total amount of saints from the second millennium in MR 1962. By contrast, the 12th and the 18th century seem a bit underrepresented, and one may wonder why that is the case.

18 A saint is assigned to a century on the basis of the year in which he or she died. If a saint passed away in 1101, as did Saint Bruno of Cologne, he is subsumed under the 12th century, even if most of his life and activity are to be situated in the 11th century. This is also true for other tables in this paper.

19 Elisabeth of Thüringen/Hungary is the only saint counted twice in this table. So she is not only part of the selection for 'Germany' but also the second saint from Hungary.

Archangels, Apostles, Evangelists, New Testament and Apocryphal Saints

As one may expect, there is quite some continuity and stability in these categories of saints, if only because their number cannot increase anymore. Nevertheless, there are some interesting details to point at. In MR 1570 Michael was the only archangel who had a feast of himself; in MR 1962 Gabriel and Raphael received one, too. Gabriel's feast is scheduled on March 24, the day before the feast of the Annunciation.

Table 7: Feasts of the archangels in MR 1570 and MR 1962

Name	MR 1570	MR 1962
Gabriel	–	24/3
Michael	29/9	29/9
Raphael	–	24/10

As to the apostles, things remained virtually the same, if one makes abstraction from the fact that vigils were removed (cf. supra). There is, however, one noteworthy exception. In 1955 the feast of the apostles Philip and Jacob was moved from May 1 to May 11, so as to create space for the second feast of Saint Joseph 'the worker' on that particular date. This shows how important the cult of Saint Joseph was for Catholicism in the time span roughly between Vatican I and Vatican II.[20] Moreover, one needs to realize that not only 'the twelve' are celebrated as apostles, but also Barnabas, Saint Paul's companion, that Matthias had replaced Judas after the latter's betrayal and death (cf. Acts 1:26), and that both Saint John and Saint Matthew are recognized and venerated as authors of a gospel, in addition to being an apostle, even if that is historically untrue.

Table 8: Feasts of the apostles in MR 1570 and MR 1962

Name	MR 1570	MR 1962
Matthias	24/2	24/2
Philip and Jacob (minor)	1/5	11/5
Barnabas	11/6	11/6
Peter and Paul	29/9	29/6
Jacob (maior)	25/7	25/7
Bartholomew	24/8	24/8
Matthew	21/9	21/9

20 Saint Joseph had been made patron saint of the universal church by pope Pius IX in 1870. Pope John XXIII put the Second Vatican Council under Saint Joseph's protection precisely in that capacity.

Name	MR 1570	MR 1962
Simon and Judas Thaddeus	28/10	28/10
Andrew	30/11	30/11
Thomas	21/12	21/12
John	27/12	27/12

With respect to the four evangelists, there are no changes in the universal calendars of MR 1570 and MR 1962. This is by no means a surprise, since this category of saints is outstandingly stable in the Christian tradition.

Table 9: Feasts of the evangelists in MR 1570 and MR 1962

Name	MR 1570	MR 1962
Mark	25/4	25/4
Matthew (also apostle – cf. table 7)	21/9	21/9
Luke	18/10	18/10
John (also apostle – cf. table 7)	27/12	27/12

In terms of other figures from the New Testament and apocryphal sources, there are a couple of additions, not changes. Anna and Joachim, Mary's parents and Jesus' grandparents, have each received a special feast day.[21] Titus, another companion of Saint Paul, was added. And Saint Joseph (cf. supra) has received a second feast day fixed on May 1. The feasts of Timothy (24/1), Joseph (29/3), Mary Magdalene (22/7), Martha of Bethany (29/7), Stephen the first martyr (26/12) and the innocent children who died as a consequence of Herod's rage (28/12) have been part of the sanctoral cycle for centuries. An interesting detail is that Mary Magdalene is the only saint in MR 1962 to receive the extra qualification of "penitent" (*paenitentis*).

Table 10: Feasts of New Testament saints and saints from apocryphal sources in MR 1570 and MR 1962

Name	MR 1570	MR 1962
Timothy	24/1	24/1
Titus	–	6/2
Joseph	19/3 –	19/3 1/5
Mary Magdalene	22/7	22/7
Martha (of Bethany)	29/7	29/7

21 While Saint Anne had been a very popular saint already in the middle ages, the insertion of a feast for Saint Joachim dates only from the late 16th century. Originally it was placed on the Sunday after the octave of the Assumption, but later fixed on the very day after that feast. Today Saints Anne and Joachim are celebrated together on July 26, the day assigned to Saint Anne in MR 1962.

Name	MR 1570	MR 1962
Anne (Mary's mother)	–	26/7
Joachim (Mary's father)	–	16/8
Stephen, the protomartyr	26/12	26/12
Holy Innocents	28/12	28/12

Popes

The popes constitute an interesting group in the context of this contribution. Many popes from the first centuries have been commemorated and venerated as saints for centuries. With the exception of Alexander I, Sixtus I and Anterus all of the first twenty popes have been inserted in the universal calendars of both MR 1570 and MR 1962. Almost 75% of the popes with a mention in the universal calendar were martyrs, even if serious doubts can be raised whether at all they had been martyred (such is the case with, e. g. Caius and Urban I); the others are remembered as confessors. On some feast days more than one pope is commemorated, but there is not always a logical explanation why they have been taken together, as they stem from different times and are appreciated for very different accomplishments. That is the case, e. g., with popes Soter (2nd century) and Caius (3rd century), who are celebrated on 22/4, or with Victor I (2nd century) and Innocentius I (5th century), whose feast is on 28/7.

In comparison to other categories of saints, the popes are quite numerous. MR 1962 has 35 holy popes, of which only five were added after the publication of MR 1570: Telesphorus (5/1), Gregory VII (25/5), Celestine (19/5), Pius V (5/5) and Pius X (3/9). This is interesting, because Telesphorus', Gregory VII's and Celestine's life date from long before the promulgation of MR 1570. This shows that for a saint to be inserted in the sanctoral cycle of the Church's liturgy, it does not matter when one has lived neither when the canonization has taken place. In a way these are different lines of development. Telesphorus, for instance, a pope from the first half of the second century, was particularly revered by Carmelites, who depict him as a hermit on Mount Carmel and strongly promoted the saint being inserted in the universal calendar.

The table below shows the dates on which holy popes are celebrated as they appear in the MR 1570 and MR 1962 universal calendars. In addition, the table indicates their rank in the succession of Saint Peter, the years of their papacy and the century in which they were active.[22] The vast majority among them date from the first five centuries, but there are also several from the 6th and the 7th century. The abovementioned saints who were added in MR 1962 are even the only ones

22 For the details pertaining to the popes in the table below, an appeal was made to H. Wortelboer, *De Rooms-Katholieke Kerk: Het complete handbook* (Kampen: Kok, 2005).

dating from medieval and modern times. Celestine is a special case; he occupied the seat of Rome only for a couple of months in 1294, when he was already very old. He is the only one in many centuries who voluntarily resigned the office of the supreme pontiff.

Table 11: Holy popes in MR 1570 and MR 1962

Name & category	Rank	Reign	Century	MR 1570	MR 1962
Telesphorus (mart.)	8	125?-136?	2		5/1
Hyginus (mart.)	9	136?-140?	2	11/1	11/1
Marcellus I (mart.)	30	308-309	4	16/1	16/1
Fabian (mart.)	20	236-250	3	20/1	20/1
Gregory I 'the Great' (conf.)	64	590-604	7	12/3	12/3
Leo I 'the Great' (conf.)	45	440-461	5	11/4	11/4
Anicetus (mart.)	10	155?-166?	2	17/4	17/4
Soter (mart.) Caius (mart.)	12 28	166?-175? 283-296	2 3	22/4 Id.	22/4 Id.
Cletus (mart.) Marcellinus (mart.)	3 29	76?-88 or 92 296-304	1 3	26/4 Id.	26/4 Id.
Pius V (conf.)	223	1566-1572	16	–	5/5
Peter Celestine (conf.)	190	1294	13	–	19/5
Gregory VII (conf.) Urban I (mart.)	155 17	1073-1085 222-230	11 3	– 25/5	25/5 25/5
Eleutherius (mart.)	13	175?-189	2	26/5	26/5
John I (mart.)	53	523-526	6	27/5	27/5
Felix I (mart.)	26	269-274	3	30/5	30/5
Silverius[23] (mart.)	58	536-537	6	20/6	20/6
Pius I (mart.)	10	140?-155?	2	11/7	11/7
Victor I (mart.) Innocent I (conf.)	14 40	189-199? 401-417	2 5	28/7 Id.	28/7 Id.
Stephen I (mart.)	23	254-257	3	2/8	2/8
Xystus II (mart.) [also Sixtus II]	24	257-258	3	6/8	6/8
Zephyrinus (mart.)	15	198?-217	3	26/8	26/8
Pius X (conf.)	255	1903-1914	20	–	3/9
Cornelius (mart.)	21	251-253	3	16/9	16/9
Linus (mart.)	2	68?-76?	1	23/9	23/9
Marcus (conf.)	34	336 (9m)	4	7/10	7/10
Callistus (mart.)	16	217-222	3	14/10	14/10
Evaristus (mart.)	5	99?-107?	2	26/10	26/10
Martin I (mart.)	74	649-654	7	12/11	12/11
Pontian (mart.)	18	230-235	3	19/11	19/11

23 In MR 1962 it confusingly says "Silvestri," but pope Silvester is actually the one celebrated on 31/12. MR 1570 instead has "Siluerii."

Name & category	Rank	Reign	Century	MR 1570	MR 1962
Clement I (mart.)	4	88 or 92–97?	1	23/11	23/11
Melchiades (mart.) [also Milti-ades]	32	311–314	4	10/12	10/12
Damasus I (conf.)	37	366–384	4	11/12	11/12
Silvester I (conf.)	33	314–335	4	31/12	31/12

Bishops

Like the qualification "papa," "ep." or *episcopus*, bishop,[24] is usually combined with "conf." or "mart." and, where applicable, "Eccl. Doct." Many holy bishops have indeed been martyrs or else confessors. As the table below shows, there are bishops from every century in MR 1962, with the exception of the 6th and the 10th. Together, the holy bishops from the 4th and the 5th centuries make out 40% of the total amount of saints with the qualification of bishop.[25] Other than the popes, there are many more holy bishops in MR 1962 than there were in MR 1570: 31 out of 53 (or 58%) are new. Some of them are well known, whereas others are virtually unknown.

Table 12: Holy bishops MR 1570 and MR 1962

Name	Diocese	Cent.	MR 1570	MR 1962
Hilary	Poitiers	4	14/1	14/1
Timothy	Ephesus	1	24/1	24/1
Polycarp	Smyrna	2	26/1	26/1
John Chrystostom	Constantinople	5	27/1	27/1
Ignatius	Antioch	2	1/2	1/2
Blaise	Sebaste	4	3/2	3/2
Andreas Corsini	Fiesole	14	–	4/2
Titus	Crete	2	–	6/2
Cyril	Alexandria	5	–	9/2
Simeon	Jerusalem	2	–	18/2
Peter Damian	Faenza	11	–	23/2
Patrick	Armagh	5	–	17/3
Cyril	Jerusalem	4	–	18/3
Isidore	Seville	7	–	4/4
Anselm	Canterbury	12	–	21/4

24 A difference between a bishop and an archbishop is not made in the universal calendar. Neither is there any mention of a person having been a cardinal, even if some them were one. In rare cases one does find "pont." or *pontifex*, literally a bridgebuilder, instead of "ep." for a bishop. This is the case e. g. for Bonaventure (14/7) in MR 1570; in MR 1962 this is adapted and made into "ep."

25 There are 43 holy bishops – i. e. saints with the qualification of "*episcopus*" in the MR 1962 universal calendar. Fifteen of them date from the 4th century, 6 from the 5th.

Name	Diocese	Cent.	MR 1570	MR 1962
Athanasius	Alexandria	4	2/5	2/5
Iuvenalis	Narni	4	3/5	3/5
Stanislas	Krakow	11	–	7/5
Gregory	Nazianze	4	–	9/5
Antonine	Firenze	15	–	10/5
Robert Bellarmine	Capua	17	–	13/5
Ubaldus (Theobald)	Gubbio	12	–	16/5
Augustine	Canterbury	7	–	28/5
Boniface	Fulda	8	–	5/6
Norbert	Magdeburg	12	–	6/6
Basil the Great	Caesarea	4	14/6	14/6
Gregorio Barbarigo	Bergamo, Padova	17	–	17/6
Paulinus	Nola	5	22/6	22/6
Ireneus	Lyon	3	–	3/7
Cyril & Methodius	?	9	–	7/7
Bonaventura	Albano	13	14/7	14/7
Apollinaris	Ravenna	2	23/7	23/7
Liborius	Le Mans	4	–	23/7
Alphonsus de Liguori	Agatha de' Goti	18	–	2/8
Donatus	Arezzo	4	7/8	7/8
Augustine	Hippo	5	28/8	28/8
Lorenzo Giustiniani	Venice	15	–	5/9
Cyprian	Carthage	3	16/9	16/9
Ianuarius (Gennaro)	Naples, Benevento	4	–	19/9
Thomas of Villanova	Valencia	16	–	22/9
Anthony Mary Claret	Santiago de Cuba	19	–	23/10
Charles Borromeo	Milan	16	–	4/11
Martin	Tours	4	11/11	11/11
Josaphat (Kuntsevych)	Polotsk	17	–	14/11
Albert the Great	Regensburg	13	–	15/11
Gregory Thaumaturgus	Neocesarea (Pontus)	3	17/11	17/11
Peter Alexandrinus	Alexandria	4	26/11	26/11
Peter Chrysologus	Ravenna	5	–	4/12
Nicholas	Myra	4	6/12	6/12
Ambrose	Milan	4	7/12	7/12
Eusebius	Vercelli	4	–	16/12
Thomas Becket	Canterbury	12	28/12	28/12

When looking more closely at where the seats of the canonized bishops are located, one observes that the four patriarchates of the East, Jerusalem, Antioch, Alexandria, and Constantinople, are represented. There are also some other episcopal sees from the Christian East, like Smyrna, Epheses or indeed Sebaste in Armenia. However, as was the case with the nationality of most of the modern saints, which was Italian, the majority of dioceses in the above table is situated on the Italian peninsula. Some smaller cities, like Nola in the south or Vercelli in the north can claim a very old episcopal tradition. Milan figures prominently in the above list with Ambrose and Carolo Borromeo, as does Ravenna with Apollinaris and Peter Chrysologus. A city in a complete different geographical and cultural environment is Canterbury, connected with even three saints, Augustine, Anselm and Thomas Becket. Interestingly, however, particularly in comparison to cities in the Mediterranean area, there aren't that many cities represented from other parts of northern Europe, with the exception of a couple of episcopal sees in German-speaking lands, like Fulda, Magdeburg and Regensburg, and Armagh in Ireland, although the concept of city there is open for interpretation. France, not Spain, is the 'country' that has the second most sees in the list, with Poitiers, Le Mans, Lyon, and Tours. Two other saints in this list deserve a quick highlighting: Anthony Mary Claret (19th c.), because he is connected with the only episcopal see of the 'new world', Santiago de Cuba, and Josaphat Kuntsevych (17th c.), because he is the only Catholic from an Eastern rite in the universal calendar, if one does not take in to account the patristic age.

Priests and Deacons

When paralleled to popes and bishops it is absolutely striking how few priests and deacons are taken up in the universal calendar. The qualification "presb." (the abbreviation of *presbyter* or priest) is used thrice, and "diaconi" only once, in the case of Saint Ephrem the Syrian, and all of them apply to persons from the patristic period. This is all the more striking because there are certainly more priests in the calendar than the ones followed by the indication "presb." A fitting example here is Saint John Vianney, the infamous "curé d'Ars" and even a patron saint of parish priests (8/8), who receives the simple qualification "conf." As to deacons, saints Stephen (26/12) and Lawrence (10/8) are commemorated, and iconographically imagined as deacons, but this is not evident from the classification they receive in the missal's universal calendar. The three saints with the mention "presb." are Felix, Valentine and Jerome, the first two of whom also carry the qualification of martyr. Saint Ephrem and Saint Jerome are also doctors of the church (cf. infra).

Table 13: Saints with the qualification "presb." or "diaconus" in MR 1570 and MR 1962

Name	Category	Century	MR 1570	MR 1962
Felix (of Nola)	Presb. + mart.	3	14/1	14/1
Valentine	Presb. + mart.	3	14/2	14/2
Ephrem	Diaconi + Eccl. Doct.	4	–	18/6
Jerome	Presb. + Eccl. Doct.	5	30/9	30/9

Abbots and Hermits

The qualification of "abb.," referring to abbots, is a relatively rare category in the universal calendar, which, intriguingly, also comprises hermits such as Saints Anthony, Giles, Hilarion of Gaza and Sabbas, who thus do not belong to a particular religious congregation. In MR 1962 the category of *abbas* is actually used only twelve times, in MR 1570 eight times. The four holy "abbots" added to the universal calendars in four centuries are founders of medieval, not modern, movements which intended to reform monastic life. Saint Giovanni Gualberto (11th c.) founded the Vallambrosians, Saint Sylvester Gozzolini (13th c.) the Sylvestrines, but both congregations can be considered to have close ties with the Benedictines. Saints Romuald and William founded orders with an even more remote profile, the Camaldolese and the Williamites – the latter of which ceased to exist in the course of the 19th century. Another saint whom one might expect in this context, is Bruno of Cologne, the founder of the Carthusians. However, he does not receive the qualification "abb." in the universal calendar. Neither is there any woman indicated with this category, although some of them, to mention only Saint Birgitta of Sweden, have been in charge of monasteries and even founded them. Finally, the hagiographies of some of the figures in the table below were written by other saints: Saint Athanasius wrote about Saint Anthony's life, Saint Jerome about Saint Hilarion.

Table 14: Holy abbots and hermits in MR 1570 and MR 1962

Name	Congregation	Century	MR 1570	MR 1962
Paul of Thebes, the first hermit	/	4	15/1	15/1
Maurus	Benedictines	6	15/1	15/1
Anthony	/	4	17/1	17/1
Romuald	Camaldolese	11	–	7/2
Benedict of Nursia	Benedictines	6	21/3	21/3
William of Maleval, "the Hermit"	Williamites	12	–	25/6
Giovanni Gualberto	Vallombrosians	11	–	12/7
Bernard of Clairvaux	Cistercians	12	20/8	20/8
Giles (Lat. Aegidius), hermit	/	8	1/9	1/9
Hilarion (of Gaza), hermit	/	4	21/10	21/10
Sylvester Gozzolini	Sylvestrines	13	–	26/11
Sabbas the Sanctified (or Mar Saba)	/	6	5/12	5/12

Kings, Queens and Dukes

There were no kings or queens or any other political rulers in the MR 1570 universal calendar.[26] Their insertion clearly is a modern phenomenon. Interestingly, all the queens, kings and dukes who were added to the calendar are exclusively medieval figures. They come from all over Europe and lived short and longer lives between the 10th until the 15th century. What is common in their profile is that they courageously defended and/or spread Christianity in contexts in which this was by no means evident or even dangerous. Also, they are venerated for their personal piety and the high moral standards according to which they decided to live in spite of their social and financial privileges. It is also remarkable that these saints are connected to countries which are to some extent underrepresented among other categories of saints such as the popes and the bishops. There are no Spanish or Italian kings in the list.

Table 15: Holy kings and queens in MR 1570 and MR 1962

Name	Country	Role	Century	MR 1570	MR 1962
Canute (Knud) IV, "the Holy"	Denmark	King	11	–	19/1
Casimir	Poland	King	15	–	4/3
Margaret	Scotland	Queen	11	–	10/6
Elisabeth	Portugal	Queen	14	–	8/7
Henry II, "the Exuberant"	Germany	Emperor	11	–	15/7
Louis IX, "the Saint"	France	King	13	–	25/8
Stephen I	Hungary	King	11	–	2/9
Wenceslaus I (Vaclav)	Bohemia	Duke	10	–	28/9
Edward, "the Confessor"	England	King	11	–	13/10
Jadwiga (Hedwig)	Poland	Queen	14	–	16/10
Elisabeth	Hungary/Thüringen	Queen	13	–	19/11

Religious and Founders of Religious Congregations

Among founders and members of religious congregations one probably finds the most differences between the MR 1570 and MR 1962 universal calendars. In terms of founders, the only ones that are mentioned in MR 1570 are Saint Benedict, Saint Francis and Saint Dominic, who founded the orders which carry their names, the Benedictines, the Franciscans, and the Dominicans. As the table below demonstrates, the picture in MR 1962 is quite different. No less than 31 additional orders

26 MR 1962 occasionally uses the abbreviation "Reg." for genitive forms *Reginae* (queen) or *Regis* (king) or else the full word. Henry (15/7) is explicitly called "Imperatoris" and Wenceslaus (28/9) "Ducis."

or congregations saw their founder(s) canonized. Four of them are female and put in italics in the list. Most of the congregations mentioned still exist, but some of them don't (e. g. the Celestines or Williamites).

Table 16: Founders of religious congregations in MR 1962

Congregation – Order	**Founder(s)**	**MR 1962**
Mercedarians – Order of the Blessed Virgin Mary of Mercy	Peter Nolasco	28/1
Camaldolese* – Hermits of Mount Corona	Romuald	7/2
Servites – Order of Servants of Mary	7 founders	12/2
Trinitarians* – Order of the Most Holy Trinity (and of the Captives)	John of Matha & Felix of Valois	8/2 20/11
Brothers Hospitallers of Saint John of God*	John of God	8/3
Benedictines – Order of Saint Benedict	Benedict of Nursia	21/3
Minims* – Order of Minims	Francis of Paola	2/4
Passionists – Congregation of the Passion of Jesus Christ	Paul of the Cross	28/4
Brothers of the Christian Schools* – De La Salle Brothers	Jean-Baptiste de La Salle	15/5
Celestines*	Peter Celestine (Celestine V)	19/5
Oratorians* – Oratory of Saint Philip Neri	Philip Neri	26/5
Ursulines* – Order of Saint Ursula	*Angela de Merici*	1/6
Caracciolini Fathers* – Clerics Regular Minor	Francis Caracciolo (et al.)	4/6
Norbertines* – Order of Canons Regular of Prémontré	Norbert of Xanten	6/6
Mantellite Sisters – Third Order of Servites	*Juliana Falconieri*	19/6
Williamites* – Congregation of Monte Vergine	William of Montevergine	25/6
Barnabites* – Clerics Regular of Saint Paul	Anthony Mary Zaccaria	5/7
Vallombrosians*	John Gualbert	12/7
Camillians* – Clerics Regular Ministers to the Sick	Camillus de Lellis	18/7
Lazarists* – Congregation of the Mission	Vincent de Paul	19/7
Somascan Fathers* – Clerics Regular of Somasca	Gerolamo (Jerome) Emiliani	20/7
Jesuits – Society of Jesus	Ignatius of Loyola	31/7
Redemptorists* – Congregation of the Most Holy Redeemer	Alphonsus Liguori	2/8
Dominicans – Order of Preachers	Dominic de Guzman	4/8
Theatines – Congregation of Clerics Regular	Cajetan (dei Conti di Thiene)	7/8
Eudists* – Congregation of Jesus and Mary	Jean Eudes	19/8
Visitandines* – Order of the Visitation of Holy Mary	*Jeanne de Chantal*	21/8
Piarists* – Order of Poor Clerics Regular of the Mother of God of the Pious Schools	Joseph Calasanz	27/8
Franciscans – Order of Friars Minor	Francis of Assisi	4/10

Congregation – Order	Founder(s)	MR 1962
Carthusians* – Order of Carthusians	Bruno of Cologne	6/10
Bridgettines* – Order of the Most Holy Savior	*Birgitta of Sweden*	8/10
Clerics Regular of the Mother of God*	John Leonardi	9/10
Claretians* – Congregation of Missionaries, Sons of the Immaculate Heart of the Blessed Virgin Mary	Anthony Mary Claret	23/10
Sylvestrines*	Sylvester Gozzolini	26/11

Among the religious orders and congregations in the above table, many of them have only their founder in the universal calendar. They are indicated with an asterisk. Others – the Mercedarians, the Servites, the Benedictines, the Passionists, the Jesuits, the Dominicans, the Theatines, and the Franciscans – each have more than one saint from within their ranks. Still others – the Augustinians,[27] the Carmelites, and the Cistercians – do not have their founders among the saints in the universal calendar but do nonetheless have more than one saint belonging to their order. Moreover, as the table below shows, there were only very few 'ordinary', i. e. non-founders, members of religious congregations in MR 1570, but the ones that were already there in 1570 are arguably among the most famous ones. The Dominicans had Saint Thomas Aquinas (7/3), the Benedictines Saint Maurus (15/1), who was Saint Benedict's first disciple, and Saint Gregory the Great (12/3), and the Franciscans Clare of Assisi (12/8).

Table 17: Members of religious congregations in MR 1570 and MR 1962

Order	Name	Century	MR 1570	MR 1962
Dominicans (10 [2])	Raymond of Penyafort	13	–	23/1
	Thomas Aquinas	13	7/3	7/3
	Vincent Ferrer	15	–	5/4
	Peter of Verona (the Martyr)	13	–	29/4
	Catharine of Siena (3rd order)	14	–	30/4
	Pius V	16	–	5/5
	Antoninus of Florence	15	–	10/5
	*Dominic Guzman	13	4/8	4/8
	Hyacynth of Poland	13	–	17/8
	Rosa of Lima (3rd order)	17	–	30/8
Mercedarians (2 [0])	*Peter Nolasco	13	–	28/1
	Raymond Nonnatus	13	–	31/8
Carmelites & Discalced Carmelites (5 [3])	Andrew Corsini	14	–	4/2
	Mary Magdalene de' Pazzi	17	–	29/5
	Thérèse of Lisieux	19	–	3/10
	Teresa of Ávila	16	–	15/10
	John of the Cross	16	–	24/11

27 Of course, Augustine of Hippo (28/8) is a prominent saint in the universal calendar, but since there is no continuity between the community he founded and the religious order(s) making use of the rule he put together, he is not counted here among the founders of religious congregations.

Order	Name	Century	MR 1570	MR 1962
Servites (9 [1])	*Seven founders	13	–	12/2
	Juliana Falconieri	14	–	19/6
	Philippus Benizi	13	–	23/8
Benedictines (8 [0])	Maurus	6	15/1	15/1
	Peter Damian	11	–	21/2
	Gregory the Great	7	12/3	12/3
	*Benedict of Nursia	6	21/3	21/3
	Bede the Venerable	8	–	27/5
	Anselm of Canterbury	12	–	28/5
	Emperor Henry II (oblate)	11	–	15/7
	Placid	6	–	5/10
Passionists (2 [0])	Gabriel of Our Lady of Sorrows	19	–	27/2
	*Paul of the Cross	18	–	28/4
Franciscans & Capuchins (13 [2])	John of Capistrano	15	–	28/3
	Fidelis of Sigmaringen	17	–	24/4
	Paschal Baylón	16	–	17/5
	Bernardino of Siena	15	–	20/5
	Anthony of Padua	13	–	13/9
	Elisabeth of Portugal (3rd order)	14	–	8/7
	Bonaventure	13	–	14/7
	Lawrence of Brindisi	17	–	21/7
	Clare of Assisi	13	12/8	12/8
	Joseph of Cupertino	17	–	18/9
	*Francis of Assisi	13	4/10	4/10
	Peter of Alcántara	16	–	19/10
	Didacus of Alcalá	15	–	13/11
Jesuits (6 [0])	Peter Canisius	16	–	27/4
	Robert Bellarmine	17	–	13/5
	Aloysius Gonzaga	16	–	21/6
	Francis Borgia	16	–	10/10
	*Ignatius of Loyola	16	–	31/7
	Francis Xavier	16	–	3/12
Augustinians (4 [0])	John of Sahagún	15	–	12/6
	Lawrence Justinian	15	–	5/9
	Nicholas of Tolentino	14	–	10/9
	Thomas of Villanova	16	–	22/9
Theatines (2 [0])	*Cajetan (Gaetano dei Conti di Thiene)	16	–	10/11
	Andrew Avellino	17	–	7/8
Cistercians (2 [1])	Bernard of Clairvaux	12	–	20/8
	Gertrude "the Great" of Helfta	14		16/11

Not all the orders have female saints, since some of them like the Jesuits and the Mercedarians simply do not have a female branch. Others do include female saints (whose numbers are in square brackets in the left column), such as the Cistercians, the Servites and the Discalced Carmelites, who are much appreciated for their mystic visions. The orders which have been most 'successful' in terms of saints in the universal calendar are the Dominican and the Franciscan families, with ten and thirteen saints respectively, two of which in the two cases are women. In terms of different nationalities, the Mercedarians with Catalonians and the Servites, the Theatines and the Passionists, all with Italians, are the only ones who do not have at least two nationalities among their saints in the universal calendar of MR 1962. By contrast, orders such as the Dominicans, the Franciscans and the Jesuits have been very international since their very inception. Many of their members, including ones that were eventually canonized, traveled a lot during their lifetime. These three orders, moreover, in addition to other ones, are known to have developed an impressive missionary zeal beyond Europe in modern times. Saint Francis Xavier (3/12) is a name that comes to mind first in this context.

Doctors of the Church

A final category of saints which should definitely be looked at in the context of the present contribution is the doctors of the Church (*doctores ecclesiae*).[28] The first four to receive that honorary title were Saints Ambrose of Milan, Jerome, Augustine of Hippo, and Gregory the Great, the four 'pillars' of Latin or Western Christianity. That happened already in 1298 under the papacy of pope Boniface VIII. In the later part of the 16th century this category was used again, when in 1568 pope Pius V declared another four, now learned and prolific saints from Eastern Christianity, doctors of the church as well: Saints Basil the Great, Gregory Nazianzen, Athanasius of Alexandria and John Chrysostom. Just one year before, in 1567, Pius V, notably a Dominican, had also declared Thomas Aquinas a doctor of the Church – probably just too early to allow him that title in the records of the MR 1570 universal calendar. It seems, moreover, that this emphatic move by Pius V had somehow to be compensated, because a couple of years later, in 1588, Aquinas' contemporary Bonaventure, from the Franciscan order, was promoted doctor of the Church as well, by pope Sixtus V, notably a Franciscan.

In the 17th century, no saint received the additional quality of doctor of the Church. In the 18th century there were again four: Saints Anselm of Canterbury (1720), Isidore of Seville (1722), Peter Chrysologus (1729), and Leo the Great (1754). In every century since then, many more saints with different origins and diverse profiles have been made doctors of the Church. One finds not only scholars and theologians among them, but equally spiritual masters. Not surprisingly, saints from the great religious congregations have become well represented in this category. There is a Cistercian, a Discalced Carmelite, and a Redemptorist, and there are several Benedictines, Dominicans, Franciscans, and Jesuits. Especially the last ones are noteworthy, inasmuch as they are among the very few who were declared doctors of the Church within months after their canonization. Both in the case of Peter Canisius (1925) and Robert Bellarmine (1931), it was pope Pius XI who

---

28 Christopher Rengers – Matthew Bunson, *The 35 Doctors of the Church*, rev. ed. (Charlotte, NC: TAN Books, 2014).

commanded a surprisingly rapid procedure, since it usually takes decades or even centuries between the year of canonization and the year of becoming a doctor of the Church. The only other such case is Albert the Great, a Dominican, who was, again by Pius XI, canonized and promoted a doctor of the Church within one year (1931).

The table below lists the doctors of the Church as recognized in that capacity in MR 1570 and MR 1962. The table additionally indicates in which century these special saints died, when they were canonized,[29] and when their promotion of doctor of the Church followed. If indicated with an asterisk, that means that the saint in question was already there in the MR 1570 universal calendar, but not yet with the title of doctor of the Church. In all these cases, the saints kept the date of their feast day.

Table 18: Doctors of the Church in MR 1570 and MR 1962

Name (+ congregation)	Century	Canonized	Doct.	MR 1570	MR 1962
Hilary of Poitiers*	4	bop	1851	14/1	14/1
John Chrysostom*	4	bop	1568	27/1	27/1
Francis de Sales	17	1622	1877	–	29/1
Cyril of Alexandria	5	bop	1883	–	9/2
Peter Damian (OSB)	11	nok	1828	–	23/2
Thomas Aquinas* (OP)	13	1323	1567	7/3	7/3
Gregory the Great (OSB)	6	bop	1298	12/3	12/3
Cyril of Jerusalem	4	bop	1883	–	18/3
John of Damascus	8	bop	1890	–	27/3
Isidore of Seville	7	bop	1722	–	4/4
Leo the Great*	5	bop	1754	11/4	11/4
Anselm of Canterbury (OSB)	11	1163	1720	–	21/4
Peter Canisius (SJ)	16	1925	1925	–	27/4
Athanasius of Alexandria*	4	bop	1568	2/5	2/5
Gregory Nazianzen	4	bop	1568	9/5	9/5
Robert Bellarmine (SJ)	17	1930	1931	–	13/5
Bede the Venerable (OSB)	8	bop	1899	–	27/5
Anthony of Padua (OFM)	13	1232	1946	–	13/6
Basil the Great*	4	bop	1568	14/6	14/6
Ephrem the Syrian	4	bop	1920	–	18/6

29 In the case of saints from the first millennium, it is not known with exactitude when they were canonized, because no records of that remain and because it was usually done by the simple fact that they were venerated by the people as well as acclaimed and appealed to. The code 'BOP' here thus means 'before there was an official procedure'. 'NOK', in the case of Peter Damian only, means that it is 'not officially known' whether and, if so, when he was actually canonized.

Name (+ congregation)	Century	Canonized	Doct.	MR 1570	MR 1962
Bonaventure* (OFM)	13	1482	1588	14/7	14/7
Lawrence of Brindisi (OFM Cap)	17	1881	1959	–	21/7
Alphonsus Liguori (CSsR)	18	1839	1871	–	2/8
Bernard of Clairvaux* (O. Cist.)	12	1174	1830	20/8	20/8
Augustine of Hippo	5	bop	1298	28/8	28/8
Jerome	5	bop	1298	30/9	30/9
Albert the Great (OP)	13	1931	1931	–	15/11
John of the Cross (OCD)	16	1726	1931	–	24/11
Peter Chrysologus	5	bop	1729	–	4/12
Ambrose of Milan	4	bop	1298	7/12	7/12

An additional comment to the above table could point to the fact that none of the saints who became a doctor of the Church in the timespan under consideration was a woman. That first happened in 1970, when pope John Paul II declared Catherine of Siena and Teresa of Ávila *doctores ecclesiae*. Moreover, there are no saints from the first three centuries in this category, whereas the fourth and fifth centuries seem to have been particularly productive. The 13th century brought forth two Dominicans (Saints Thomas Aquinas and Albert the Great) and two Franciscans (Saints Bonaventure and Anthony of Padua). The 17th century is represented with Saints Francis de Sales, Robert Bellarmine, and Lawrence of Brindisi, spearheading central preoccupations of the Church at the time, namely piety, polemics, and predication. The most recent doctor of the Church in the MR 1962 list is Saint Alphonsus Liguori.

Comments and Conclusions

In the present conclusion I confine myself to two series of comments. The first one circles around the overall picture of saints in the modern era which the above investigations have delivered. I see four clear patterns. The first one is the strong continuity between the universal calendars of MR 1570 and MR 1962. Even if there are many micro differences between the universal calendars in the two missals, one cannot but conclude that there are very few changes with respect to those components which occur in both missals. There is hardly any change of date or name or even title. What was there in MR 1570 is, by and large, still there in MR 1962. What does differ – and that is at once the second point – is the huge amount of additions. As a matter of fact, especially if one makes abstraction from the feasts and if one focuses on the saints, changes between the MR 1570 and MR 1962 universal calendars are very few, but there a lot of additions. These additions, thirdly, are to be situated in a small selection of categories of saints. They are not to be found among the apostles, the evangelists, the saints from the New Testaments or even among the popes. Moreover, the additions in the categories of the archangels and the apocryphal saints or even the abbots (including the hermits) are, all in all, minor and rather to be seen as refinements than as transformations. The major additions, which one could argue bring about a transformation of the respective categories of saints are, fourthly, to be located chiefly among the among earthly rulers – none of which was mentioned in MR 1570 –, and among the founders and the members of religious congregations. In the same vein, one should also point at the increasing use that popes made, particularly since the 19th century, of promoting a saint to *doctor ecclesiae*.

A second series of comments pertains to future scholarly work which could be done on the basis of the data here gathered. In particular, I see three promising avenues for further research. First, the contribution of liturgical sources including the euchology of the *proprium de sanctis* in missals as well as in the Divine Office could be explored, analyzed and discussed. Comparisons could be made between different categories of saints as well as between saints sharing the same categories. What do the prayers and other liturgical material reveal in terms of the peculiar characters of the saints and the ways in which the Church commemorates and venerates them?

Second, specific connections between individual saints could be scrutinized. One can think of different kinds of connections, including a common martyrdom like Saints Cyprian of Carthage and Pope Cornelius (16/9), a hagiography like Saint Bonaventure about Saint Francis or Saint Athanasius about Saint Anthony, a spiritual kinship like the one between Jane de Chantal and Francis de Sales or Giuliana Falconieri and her uncle Alessio Falconieri (one of founders of the Servants of Mary), or just saints belonging to the same congregation but stemming from different countries and periods.

Third, one can think of pursuing critical theological thinking on the basis of the data mapped above. One can ask (very) critical questions about the mechanisms which have determined the canonizations of individual saints, about saints of the same order and balances between different orders, about male and female saints and the manifest inequality between them, about saints from under- and overrepresented areas, about centuries from which there are hardly any saints, about selection criteria and the many ways in which they are subjected to sheer power games of various kinds and intensity, and about many other possible blind spots in the selection of saints as it stands. In sum, the present article simply scratched the surface and is no more than an exploration of the *proprium de sanctis*. Much more interdisciplinary work crossing borders between the history of the Church, the study of spirituality and liturgical theology needs to be done to uncover the unsuspected riches of the Church's tradition of venerating the saints, commemorating them, and celebrating them.

Section 2
Visualizing Sanctity and the Sacred: Images and Promotion

Raphaèle Preisinger, Hannah Joy Friedman, Jonathan E. Greenwood, Wei Jiang, Lucía Querejazu Escobari

Promoting Sanctity by the Means of Artworks

The GLOBECOSAL Project

Looking Behind the Theatre of Authority

On 12 April 1671, five new saints were elevated to the altars by Pope Clement X (r. 1670–1676), whose proclamation of their universal cults occurred in an opulent canonisation ceremony in the Roman basilica of Saint Peter. An etching (Fig. 1) by the graphic artist Giovanni Battista Falda (1643–1678) emphasises the canonisation *teatro*'s magnificence: the full half-metre of the print's width opens onto a bird's-eye view of the immense crossing of the basilica, showing the cavernous space between the floor before the high altar and the base of the dome with a profusion of ornamental detail as well as an airy, atmospheric impression of the transept, 140 metres deep and 46 metres high.[1] The print conveys the celebration's lavishness

---

1 This publication is part of a project that has received funding from the European Research Council (ERC) under the European Union's Horizon 2020 research and innovation programme (grant agreement No 949836). Views and opinions expressed are however those of the authors only and do not necessarily reflect those of the European Union or the European Research Council Executive Agency. Neither the European Union nor the granting authority can be held responsible for them. This project was also funded by a Swiss National Science Foundation PRIMA grant.

For the interior dimensions of Saint Peter's basilica, see https://www.vaticanstate.va/it/monumenti/basilica-di-san-pietro/interno.html (accessed 7 July 2022). On Falda, see P. Bellini/W. Strauss/A. von Bartsch, *The Illustrated Bartsch* 47, part 2 (New York: Abaris Books, 1993); A. Margiotta/S. Tozzi, "FALDA, Giovanni Battista", in *Dizionario Biografico degli Italiani* 44 (1994), https://www.treccani.it/enciclopedia/giovanni-battista-falda_(Dizionario-Biografico) (accessed 15 July 2022); and F. Consagra, "De Rossi and Falda: A Successful Collaboration in the Print Industry of Seventeenth-Century Rome", in A. Ladis/C. Wood (ed.), *The Craft of Art: Originality and Industry in the Italian Renaissance and Baroque Workshop* (Athens, GA: University of Georgia Press, 1995) 187–203. On canonisation *teatri*, see especially M. Fagiolo dell'Arco, *La festa barocca* (Rome: De Luca, 1997); A. Anselmi,

Fig. 1 Giovanni Battista Falda. *Canonisation ceremony in St. Peter's Basilica for Gaetano Thiene, Francis Borgia, Louis Beltrán, Rose of Lima, and Philip Benizi*, 1677. Etching, 35.8 x 50 cm. Rijksmuseum, Amsterdam. Photo courtesy of the Rijksmuseum, Rijksstudio http://hdl.handle.net/10934/RM0001.COLLECT.108963

in word and image: starting with the pope himself, the ecclesiastical and secular dignitaries in attendance are identified in groups using numbered captions in the print's margins, describing even the pebble-like multitude filling the basilica's floor as both Roman and foreign "Cavalieri, e Nobili". The print goes to great lengths to suggest both the event's splendour and the colossal expense involved in producing it, as for instance the last caption claims that there were "over two thousand candles of eight *libre* each, of white wax" ("due mila e più fiaccole di libre otto l'una, di cera biancha") that stood along the cornice at the bases of the

"Theaters for the Canonization of Saints", in W. Tronzo (ed.), *St. Peter's in the Vatican* (New York: Cambridge University Press, 2005) 244–69; V. Casale, *L'Arte per le canonizzazioni. L'attività artistica intorno alle canonizzazioni e alle beatificazioni del Seicento* (Turin: Umberto Allemandi, 2011); V. Casale, "La basilica di S. Pietro nelle cerimonie di beatificazione e di canonizzazione del Seicento", in G. Morello (ed.), *La Basilica di San Pietro. Fortuna e immagine* (Rome: Gangemi, 2012) 445–54, and M. Fagiolo dell'Arco, "Il 'Gran teatro barocco' della santità ibero-americana", in F. Quiles García/J.J. García Bernal/P. Broggio/M. Fagiolo dell'Arco (ed.), *A la luz de Roma: Santos y santidad en el barroco iberoamericano*, (3 vols; Seville: EnredARS/Universidad Pablo de Olavide, 2020) 1.19–42.

vault and of the dome, on gilt candelabras.[2] For purposes of comparison, consider that a Patrician funeral in Renaissance Florence might warrant the lavish expense (over double an artisan's annual salary) required for 500 *libre* of wax;[3] Falda's pains in specifying the use of over 16,000 *libre* of the costliest white wax is intended to stagger, reinforcing the canonisation *teatro*'s commonalities with the coronation of a monarch. Massive banners with images of the new saints flutter aloft, giving their elevation to sainthood the most literal form possible.[4] By framing the images of the newly canonised saints within the overwhelming ceremonial pomp of the canonisation itself, Falda's print gives persuasive form to the papacy's ever more vehement account of its powers and prerogatives in pronouncing on sainthood.[5]

The tightening of the bureaucratic process leading up to canonisation in the successive reforms of Sixtus V (r. 1585–1590) and Urban VIII (r. 1623–1644) has deservedly attracted a wealth of scholarship on Rome's increasingly urgent efforts to retain control of an ever more diverse and far-flung set of liturgical practices.[6] Within the global spread of Catholicism over the course of the sixteenth and seventeenth centuries, the multifarious ways in which saints' cults became sites of adaptation, resistance, and experiment are confirmed *a contrario* in the increasingly

2 On this and other powerful multisensory effects produced within canonisation ceremonies, see Casale, *L'arte per le canonizzazioni*, 39.

3 Based on estimates pertaining to wax prices in Florence at the turn of the sixteenth century in J. Shaw/ E. Welch, *Making and Marketing Medicine in Renaissance Florence* (Amsterdam: Rodopi, 2011), 168–9.

4 On the banners' miraculous origins and multiple celestial meanings, see Casale, *L'arte per le canonizzazioni*, 38–9.

5 Casale, *L'arte per le canonizzazioni*, 30–2.

6 Fundamental studies, with further bibliography, are G. Papa, *Le cause di canonizzazione nel primo periodo della Congregazione dei Riti (1588–1634)* (Rome: Urbaniana University Press, 2001); S. Ditchfield, *Liturgy, Sanctity, and History in Tridentine Italy. Pietro Maria Campi and the Preservation of the Particular* (New York: Cambridge University Press, 1995); and M. Gotor, *I beati del papa: Santità, Inquisizione e obbedienza in età moderna* (Florence: Leo Olschki, 2002). Among numerous more recent case studies, see especially A. Rubial García, *La santidad controvertida. Hagiografía y conciencia criolla alrededor de los venerables no canonizados de Nueva España* (Mexico City: Universidad Nacional Autónoma de México, 1999); R. Millar Carvacho, *Santidad, falsa santidad y posesiones demoníacas en Perú y Chile: Siglos XVI y XVII* (Santiago: Universidad Católica de Chile, 2009); J. Duffin, *Medical Miracles: Doctors, Saints, and Healing in the Modern World* (New York: Oxford University Press, 2009); C. Cussen, *Black Saint of the Americas: The Life and Afterlife of Martín de Porres* (New York: Cambridge University Press, 2016); C. Copeland, *Maria Maddalena de' Pazzi. The Making of a Counter-Reformation Saint* (New York: Oxford University Press, 2016); B.A. Bouley, *Pious Postmortems: Anatomy, Sanctity, and the Catholic Church in Early Modern Europe* (Philadelphia: University of Pennsylvania Press, 2017); R.S. Noyes, *Peter Paul Rubens and the Counter-Reformation Crisis of the Beati moderni* (London: Routledge, 2018); C. Conover, *Pious Imperialism: Spanish Rule and the Cult of Saints in Mexico City* (Albuquerque: University of New Mexico Press, 2019); and S. Tutino, *A Fake Saint and the True Church: The Story of a Forgery in Seventeenth-Century Naples* (New York: Oxford University Press, 2021).

loud assertions of top-down authority that Falda's print so adroitly exemplifies. On the one hand, such ceremonies for the official conferral of sainthood forged a repertoire of official imagery for the new saint: the iconography on display during the *cerimonie*, which was often shown for the first time then, may be termed 'official' insofar as it was approved by the Curia, generally considered canonical throughout the Catholic world, and corresponded to the way in which a saint was characterised in the bull of canonisation.[7] The saint's imagery was disseminated through prints commemorating the festivities in Rome and spread as far as Catholicism reached, including those geographical areas in which veneration had first taken root. On the other hand, the official iconography of a saint was only one of many sets of images in circulation, as images were not only a *sine qua non* of the campaigns leading to sainthood, but were the very backbone of a saint's actual cult, prompting their veneration and invocation, circulating their likenesses, deeds, and virtues, and often acting as their most ready-to-hand instruments for miraculous intervention.[8]

Falda's etching fictionalises a degree of papal authority over the process of canonisation that scholars such as Alessandra Anselmi have rightly qualified by pointing to the way sanctity reflected international diplomacy and influence-trading, acting as a barometer for geopolitical allegiances and ascendancies.[9] For instance, the political preponderance of Spain is reflected in the high number of blesseds and saints from the Spanish empire in the seventeenth century.[10] Both the canonisation ceremonies themselves and the images that commemorated and advertised them could establish hierarchies among the new saints, as for instance Falda's print places a recognisable likeness of Gaetano da Thiene (1480–1547), shown holding lilies and

---

7 Casale, *L'arte per le canonizzazioni*, 36. This was observed earlier in the pathbreaking 1932 study by Emile Mâle, whose focus on official imagery has been complemented by broader perspectives in more recent literature. E. Mâle, *L'art religieux de la fin du XVIe siècle, du XVIIe siècle et du XVIIIe siècle. Étude sur l'iconographie après le concile de Trente. Italie – France – Espagne – Flandres* (Paris: 2nd rev. edn Armand Colin, 1951 [orig. 1932]), 98–100.

8 Among the many studies that bear this out with specific regard to images' role in canonisation campaigns, see for instance S. Ditchfield, "How Not to Be a Counter-Reformation Saint: The Attempted Canonization of Pope Gregory X, 1622–45", *Papers of the British School at Rome* 60 (1992) 379–422; C. Gerken, *Entstehung und Funktion von Heiligenbildern im nachtridentinischen Italien (1588–1622)* (Munich: Michael Imhof, 2016); K. Burzer, *San Carlo Borromeo. Konstruktion und Inszenierung eines Heiligenbildes im Spannungsfeld zwischen Mailand und Rom* (Berlin: Deutscher Kunstverlag, 2011); F. Quiles García, "Cerca del cielo. La creación de los santos y su imagen en la América hispana", *SEMATA, Ciencias Sociais e Humanidades* 24 (2012) 89–109; L.L. Vargas Murcia, "Construcción, circulación y uso de una imagen. El caso de la Azucena de Quito", in M.P. López/F. Quiles García (ed.), *Visiones renovadas del Barroco iberoamericano* (Seville: Universo Barroco Iberoamericano, 2016) 1.134–45; and Noyes, *Crisis of the Beati moderni*.

9 Anselmi, "Canonization of Saints", 251–55; Fagiolo dell'Arco, *Festa barocca*, 47.

10 P. Burke, "How to Become a Counter-Reformation Saint", in D. Luebke (ed.), *The Counter-Reformation: the Essential Readings* (Malden, MA: Blackwell, 1999) 130–42, on p. 141.

Fig. 2 Jean-Baptiste Barbé, *Benedicta Rosa de Sancta Maria*, before 1650. Engraving, 12 x 7.2 cm. Image from Ramón Mujica Pinilla, *Rosa limensis. Mística, política e iconografía en torno a la patrona de América* (2nd edn, Mexico City: Instituto Francés de Estudios Andinos, Centro Francés de Estudios Mexicanos y Centroamericanos, Fondo de Cultura Económica, 2005), fig. no. 91, p. 339.

an open book, directly above Bernini's *baldacchino* at the top centre of the image. Of the five saints canonised, only the Theatine founder and Rose of Lima, shown kneeling in prayer on a banner at the top right of the print, can be distinguished on the large banners hanging from the base of the dome, leaving much smaller and more obscure images-within-the-image to bear the likenesses of Francis Borgia, Louis Beltrán, and Philip Benizi. The noticeable presence in Falda's etching of Saint Rose of Lima (1586–1617), one of the new saints whose canonisation the print commemorates, might suggest to the print's audience that both the cult of Saint Rose and the Spanish political and spiritual influence behind her were subordinate to the authority of the Roman Curia, as well as being secondary to the fame of Italian saints (and their backers) such as the more prominently depicted Gaetano da Thiene. This at any rate could be one reading of the effect produced by the etching, regardless of the political and spiritual realities beyond it. As Anselmi notes, such prints should not be read too literally as *reportage* on the events they depict.[11] Yet images like Falda's bear eloquent witness to a view of the entire process of canonisation that insists so vehemently on papal authority as to beg the question of what other potential perspectives it might contradict.

11 Anselmi, "Canonization of Saints", 260–1.

Thus, if one begins to read Falda's print against the grain of its own centralising narrative, the entire etching becomes a prompt to investigate further the rich questions pertaining to saints' images, and particularly to those whose veneration first took root outside of Europe. Returning to the example of Rose of Lima, one might understand Falda's print as exemplifying – or at any rate, effectively advertising – the role of official recognition in forging and distributing a saint's image. Yet (as was not unusual) Rose of Lima's likeness was already in wide circulation well before she was even beatified, let alone canonised.[12] One of her earliest-known images, an engraving by the Antwerp-based printmaker and publisher Jean-Baptiste Barbé (Fig. 2), shows not only the currency of her likeness well before her beatification (Barbé died in 1649, nineteen years prior to Rose's beatification in 1668) but also how much her representation lent itself to emphasis on her role as protector of her native city of Lima, which she is often shown holding atop an anchor of hope.[13] As Barbé's print attests, a potential saint's image was significantly coined and popularised long before there was any officially sanctioned imagery, particularly through the illustrations that accompanied the published hagiographies used to promote the cause for sainthood. Hagiographic imagery that preceded a saint's formal recognition by the Curia was a crucial battleground in clashes between the papacy's increasingly aggressive centralising initiatives and the actual lived practices of veneration and intercession that were often conducted at the margins of Rome's control, even within the papal city itself, as scholars such as Ruth Noyes have ably demonstrated.[14] Especially in the case of saints whose veneration sprang up in newly Christianised territories, the role of images in this negotiation between local veneration and official recognition (and regulation) of sainthood merits further investigation.[15] The impressive view that Falda opens onto the transept of Saint

12 V. Casale (ed.), *La primera flor de santidad de América latina: Santa Rosa de Lima* (Lima: Casa de Ejercicios Espirituales de Santa Rosa, 2011); R. Mujica Pinilla, *Rosa limensis: Mística, política e iconografía en torno a la patrona de América* (rev. edn Mexico City: Centro de estudios mexicanos y centroamericanos, 2004).

13 Mujica Pinilla, *Rosa limensis*, 209–60.

14 Noyes, *Crisis of the Beati moderni*; see also Burzer, *San Carlo Borromeo*; and Gerken, *Entstehung und Funktion von Heiligenbildern*.

15 Building on a fast-growing body of scholarship, among which see especially Rubial García, *Santidad controvertida*; G.A. Bailey, *Art on the Jesuit Missions in Asia and Latin America, 1542–1773* (Toronto: University of Toronto Press, 1999); A. Greer/J. Bilinkoff (ed.), *Colonial Saints: Discovering the Holy in the Americas, 1500–1800* (London: Routledge, 2003); S. Morishita, *L'art des missions catholiques au Japon (XVIe–XVIIe siècle)* (Paris: Editions du Cerf, 2020); H. Omata Rappo, *Des Indes lointaines aux scènes des collèges. Les reflets des martyrs de la mission japonaise en Europe (XVIe–XVIIIe siècle)* (Munster: Aschendorff Verlag, 2020); F. Quiles García/J.J. García Bernal/P. Broggio/M. Fagiolo dell'Arco (ed.), *A la luz de Roma: Santos y santidad en el barroco iberoamericano* (3 vols; Seville: EnredARS/Universidad Pablo de Olavide, 2020); C.H. Lee, *Saints of Resistance: Devotions in the Philippines Under Early Spanish Rule* (New York: Oxford University Press, 2021); Conover, *Pious*

Fig. 3 Anonymous sculptor, Philippines. *Saint Rose of Lima*, seventeenth century. Ivory, h. 31.5 cm. Museo de América, Madrid. Photo: Joaquin Otero. CER.es (http://ceres.mcu.es), Ministerio de Cultura y Deporte, España.

Peter's on the day of Rose's canonisation stands to benefit from a reconsideration as one perspective among a wider constellation of images, texts, and viewpoints, ranging from the sculptors fashioning Rose's likeness on the lateral façade of the cathedral of Oaxaca to the Chinese émigré artists producing ivory cult statues of Rose in the Philippines (Fig. 3).[16]

Between Rose's death in 1617 and her beatification fifty years later, papal efforts to police the veneration of pre-beatification *servorum Dei* made images of these unofficial saints a focus of regulation.[17] In the wake of Urban VIII's reforms, promoters of causes for beatification and canonisation thus found themselves in the equivocal position of having simultaneously to prove the vigour of the would-be

---

Imperialism; and R. Miller, "From 'Apostle of Japan' to 'Apostle of All the Christian World': The Iconography of St. Francis Xavier and the Global Catholic Church", *Journal of Jesuit Studies* 9.3 (2022) 415–37.

16 E. González León, "La representación de Santa Rosa de Lima en la Nueva España. Ejemplos de las catedrales de Puebla, México y Oaxaca", in E.M. Torres Torres (ed.), *Arte y hagiografía, siglos XVI–XX* (Bogotá: Universidad Santo Tomás, 2019) 143–66, on pp. 158–61; S. Porras, "Locating Hispano-Philippine Ivories", *Colonial Latin American Review* 29.2 (2020) 256–91.

17 R.S. Noyes, "On the Fringes of Center: Disputed Hagiographic Imagery and the Crisis over the *Beati moderni* in Rome ca. 1600", *Renaissance Quarterly* 64.3 (2011) 800–46; Gotor, *I beati del papa*.

saint's cult and that it never overstepped the tight boundaries imposed by Rome.[18] The obligation to fulfil new requirements of *non cultu* focused in particular on the absence of publicly venerated images, even as images continued to be the primary channels through which the prospective saint's intercession could result in miracles and their *fama sanctitatis* could circulate and take shape. While in some situations, images depicting the would-be saint with an unsanctioned halo could threaten their cause, their likenesses appear far more often as positive evidence for sainthood: ancient pictures with halos could verify the antiquity of a cult, the sheer volume of images in existence could attest to a holy reputation, and of course new images would not only accompany hagiographies but would be commissioned as gifts to grease the wheels of the ponderous bureaucratic machinery leading up to beatification and canonisation.[19]

In Falda's print, the images of the five new saints of 1671 appear as minor and interchangeable details in an essentially secular display of princely *magnificenza* on the part of the pope. Ostensibly, the etching showcases an exceptional event focused on five exceptional people. Yet the very terms in which this event is presented make the new saints secondary at best to the theatre of authority in which their sainthood is recognised.[20] The recycled nature of Falda's print is a further hint that the real subject is neither this group of saints nor even this particular ceremony, but the papal power that is supposedly there to celebrate them. While the etching appears at first glance to emphasise the particularity of this one canonisation ceremony, the print expeditiously repurposes Falda's own depictions of earlier canonisations (a fact betrayed by the Chigi heraldic devices that still remain on the pilasters for a *teatro* celebrated by the then-reigning Altieri pope Clement X). The main modifications are of the captions and the banners, on which Falda has inserted the newly canonised saints of 1671 over the burnished-out likenesses of Peter of Alcántara and Maria Maddalena de' Pazzi. Their canonisation *teatro* two years earlier, on 28 April 1669, was commemorated with an earlier state of the same print (Fig. 4), which was itself based on a mirror-reversed image of Falda's design celebrating the 1665 canonisation of Francis de Sales.[21]

---

18 Gotor, *I beati del papa.*

19 See for instance Noyes, "Fringes of Center"; Casale, *L'arte per le canonizzazioni*, 48–87; Ditchfield, "How Not to Be a Counter-Reformation Saint", 392, 399–400, 407; Vargas Murcia, "Construcción, circulación y uso de una imagen"; Quiles García, "Cerca del cielo".

20 As Casale notes, "Se dapprima l'apparato era piuttosto contenuto e il papa era sentito come un semplice 'ministro', con il tempo l'addobbo diverrà sempre più fastoso e il pontefice acquisterà un rilievo crescente fin quasi a gareggiare con il canonizzando." Casale, *L'arte per le canonizzazioni*, 37.

21 Bellini et al. *Illustrated Bartsch*, 45, cat. 4725. 083 [B.77 (250)]; on the reversed earlier version, see Fagiolo dell'Arco, *Festa barocca*, 426–7.

Fig. 4 Giovanni Battista Falda. *Canonisation ceremony in Saint Peter's Basilica for Peter of Alcántara and Maria Maddalena de' Pazzi*, Etching, 32.7 x 43.7 cm. Image from Paolo Bellini, Walter Strauss, and Adam von Bartsch, *The Illustrated Bartsch* 47, part 2 (New York: Abaris Books, 1993), cat. no. 4725.083 S1[B.77 (250)], p. 44.

The story told by all of these versions is that the images of the saints – and their public veneration – are in a basic sense inventions or by-products of the papal authority that exercised increasingly stringent protocols in sanctioning them. Yet a noteworthy aspect of Falda's etching is precisely the set of circumstances that the image belies: that images of saints commanded veneration long before and far beyond the recognition of official sainthood by Rome, that even *servorum Dei* who did not successfully overcome the bureaucratic hurdles on the path to canonisation had immense power to shape people's lived experience of Catholicism, and that the papacy itself was not the sole agent in control of bestowing sanctity but was only one among several participants in a complex process of negotiation. A closer understanding of sainthood as the result of a process of negotiation, and of the multifarious realities that find echoes and refractions in an image like Falda's, demands further research. What are the many other stories that can be told from the diverse vantage points outside of Rome? And how do images of saints in the increasingly global Catholic world of the early modern period dislodge the idea of a controlling centre and a reactive periphery and enrich our understanding of the period as a whole? What is the view from backstage at the *teatro*, and how can we situate an image such as Falda's as a responsive (and even reactive) perspective in dynamic interplay within an increasingly global and varied landscape of saints' images?

Art and the Negotiation of Sanctity

The ERC- and SNSF-funded project "Global Economies of Salvation: Art and the Negotiation of Sanctity in the Early Modern Period" (hereinafter "GLOBECOSAL"), led by Raphaèle Preisinger and hosted by the University of Zurich, undertakes a sustained investigation of the functions of artworks in the process of negotiating sanctity with the Roman Curia in the age of Iberian hegemony. The specific negotiation of sanctity that it addresses pertains to individuals first venerated in newly Christianised territories around the globe. The project thus builds simultaneously upon the interdisciplinary study of circulations in the early modern era and on the art historical study of Catholic post-Tridentine hagiographic imagery, while also increasing and valorising the connectivity between these fields of study. Over the last twenty years, interdisciplinary historical research has focused increasingly on the growing connectivity between the continents that characterised the early modern period, with a recent interest in the period's intensified circulation of objects in particular.[22] Serge Gruzinski, in addressing the question of whether it is "possible to

22 From this immense and fast-growing body of scholarship, key studies include P.H. Smith/P. Findlen (ed.), *Merchants and Marvels. Commerce, Science, and Art in Early Modern Europe* (New York: Routledge, 2002); J. Anderson (ed.), *Crossing Cultures: Conflict, Migration and Convergence. The Proceedings of the 32nd International Congress in the History of Art* (Melbourne: Miegunyah Press, 2008); M.D. Sheriff (ed.), *Cultural Contact and the Making of European Art Since the Age of Exploration* (Chapel Hill: University of North Carolina Press, 2010); C.H. Parker, *Global Interactions in the Early Modern Age* (New York: Cambridge University Press, 2010); L. Roberts (ed.), *Centres and Cycles of Accumulation in and Around the Netherlands during the Early Modern Period* (Zurich: Lit Verlag, 2011); R.M. San Juan, *Vertiginous Mirrors: The Animation of the Visual Image and Early Modern Travel* (Manchester: Manchester University Press, 2011); A. Gerritsen/G. Riello (ed.), *The Global Lives of Things. The Material Culture of Connections in the Early Modern World* (London: Routledge, 2016); S. Burghartz/L. Burkart/C. Göttler (ed.), *Sites of Mediation: Connected Histories of Places, Processes, and Objects in Europe and Beyond, 1450–1650* (Leiden: Brill, 2016); T. DaCosta Kaufmann/C. Dossin/B. Joyeux-Prunel (ed.), *Circulations in the Global History of Art* (New York: Routledge, 2015); A. Romano, *Impressions de Chine: L'Europe et l'englobement du monde* (Paris: Fayard, 2016); D. Bleichmar/M. Martin (ed.), *Objects in Motion in the Early Modern World* (Oxford: Wiley-Blackwell, 2016); C. Göttler/M. Mochizuki (ed.), *The Nomadic Object. The Challenge of World for Early Modern Religious Art* (Leiden: Brill, 2017); P.H. Smith (ed.), *Entangled Itineraries: Materials, Practices, and Knowledges across Eurasia* (Pittsburgh: University of Pittsburgh Press, 2019); P. Findlen (ed.), *Early Modern Things: Objects and Their Histories, 1500–1800* (London: Routledge, [2]2021);

define the circulation processes of the arts as observed between the late Middle Ages and the beginnings of modernity as the expression of cultural exchanges alone", sets out a challenge to the field of art history to better grasp the power issues at work in the early modern circulation of artworks, in particular with regard to the period marked by the hegemony of the Iberian empires.[23] The GLOBECOSAL project seizes Gruzinski's challenge by studying the negotiation of sanctity by the means of artworks in the post-Tridentine era. The vital necessity in the Iberian imperial context of using the conversion of non-Christians as the ideological justification for conquest accentuates how tightly the religious and political spheres were interwoven.[24] In such an imperial context, on the one hand, saints conferred both religious and political legitimacy on the ranks from which they arose and on those who appropriated them as local patrons.[25] On the other hand, the veneration of saints was a hotly contested borderland between spontaneous appropriations of Catholic cult practices and imposition of religious compliance as a tool of conquest. Works of art depicting both recognised and would-be saints map out a shifting terrain, cultivated and fought over by an evolving roster of constituencies ranging from the most humble recent converts to Catholicism to the Pope, from religious orders and institutions to the individuals both within and beyond their confines.

The GLOBECOSAL project undertakes a study of the crucial body of evidence formed by saints' images on a global scale, combining perspectives taken from art historical analysis of hagiographic imagery with those from studies of early

---

H. Madar (ed.), *Prints as Agents of Global Exchange, 1500–1800* (Amsterdam: Amsterdam University Press, 2021); and Porras, "Hispano-Philippine Ivories".

23 S. Gruzinski, "Art History and Iberian Worldwide Diffusion: Westernization / Globalization / Americanization", in T. DaCosta Kaufmann/C. Dossin/B. Joyeux-Prunel (ed.), *Circulations in the Global History of Art* (New York: Routledge, 2016) 47–58, on p. 47.

24 See especially S. Gruzinski, *La colonisation de l'imaginaire: sociétés indigènes et occidentalisation dans le Mexique espagnol: XVIe–XVIIIe siècle* (Paris: Gallimard, 1988); S. MacCormack, *Religion in the Andes: Vision and Imagination in Early Colonial Peru* (Princeton: Princeton University Press, 1991); K. Mills, *Idolatry and Its Enemies: Colonial Andean Religion and Extirpation, 1640–1750* (Princeton: Princeton University Press, 1997); C. Dean, *Inka Bodies and the Body of Christ: Corpus Christi in Colonial Cuzco, Peru* (Durham: Duke University Press, 1999); J.C. Estenssoro Fuchs, *Del paganismo a la santidad. La incorporación de los indios del Perú al catolicismo, 1532–1750* (Lima: Pontificia Universidad Católica del Peru, 2003); C. Brosseder, *The Power of Huacas: Change and Resistance in the Andean World of Colonial Peru* (Austin: University of Texas Press, 2014); for a broader recent overview with further bibliography, see V. Lavenia/S. Pastore/S. Pavone/C. Petrolini (ed.), *Compel People to Come In: Violence and Catholic Conversion in the non-European World* (Rome: Viella, 2018).

25 T. Hampe Martínez, *Santidad e identidad criolla. Estudio del proceso de canonización de Santa Rosa* (Cusco: Centro Bartolomé de las Casas, 1998); Rubial García, *Santidad controvertida*; R.J. Morgan, *Spanish American Saints and the Rhetoric of Identity, 1600–1810* (Tucson: University of Arizona Press, 2002); Greer/Bilinkoff, *Colonial Saints*; Conover, *Pious Imperialism*.

modern circulations. This project contributes to a vibrant and growing body of scholarship from across disciplines, considering the role of artworks in the process of negotiating the status of candidates for sainthood in the context of early European expansion, i. e. relating to prospective saints whose campaigns were launched in newly Christianised territories or whose veneration first arose there. In addressing this issue, the project considers, as a hypothesis, to what extent such artworks might reveal an underlying negotiation of non-European Catholic communities' spiritual status within universal Catholicism. As the spreading of Catholicism served as the ideological justification for European expansion under Iberian rule, to what extent did negotiation of an individual's saintly status also shape the status awarded to newly evangelised societies within the order established by the Iberian colonial and mercantile empires? If official recognition of the saintly status of a local patron conferred increased legitimacy on the society that had appropriated him or her as its own, what was the extent and nature of such legitimacy, and what were its limitations, quirks, or exceptions across rapidly evolving global contexts? Taking as a point of departure the sociological concept that the constructed image of a saint reflects a society's ideals, this project views the process by which a saint's canonisation was promoted as a form of self-manifestation occurring within the broader framework of social identity formation.[26]

To examine the negotiation of sanctity by the means of artworks, the GLOBECOSAL project adopts a strategy founded upon the historiographic concept of *histoire croisée*, emphasising the reflexive and dynamic mutual interplay and shifting viewpoints among interconnected institutions, contexts, and individuals.[27] Furthermore, the project traces the circulation of material objects and iconographies within and among global networks of knowledge transmission, and combines this approach with a hypothetical global market of symbolic values developed on the basis of concepts taken from critical sociology.[28] The early modern religious fields considered in the GLOBECOSAL project competed with one another with regard to the "capital" represented by sanctity, which conferred religious legitimacy on the corresponding field as a whole. The Roman Curia was the authority that granted access to the "symbolic capital" of sanctity.

To describe the construction of identity relating to a saint's portrayal in artworks, the GLOBECOSAL project expands on a Panofskyan concept of iconology relying

26 P. Brown "The Rise and Function of the Holy Man in Late Antiquity", *Journal of Roman Studies* 61 (1971) 80–101.

27 M. Werner/B. Zimmermann, "Vergleich, Transfer, Verflechtung. Der Ansatz der Histoire Croisée und die Herausforderung des Transnationalen", *Geschichte und Gesellschaft* 28.4 (2002) 607–36.

28 P. Bourdieu, *Das Religiöse Feld. Texte zur Ökonomie des Heilsgeschehens* (Constance: Édition discours, 2000).

on textual and visual sources by availing itself of the full range of methods connected with *Bildwissenschaft* or Visual Studies.[29] The supple approach to images afforded by *Bildwissenschaft*, combined with iconology's refined apparatus for articulating the interactions between visual material and cultural history, make it possible to consider not only "traditional" textual and iconographic sources such as hagiographic literature, but also to consider specific visual media and their material properties, pictorial practices, local traditions of figuration, and the technical and aesthetic characteristics of a wide range of objects including paintings, prints, sculpture, medals, drawings, liturgical objects, and architecture.

Interlocking Arenas of Study

Articulating the transition between a global study and its necessarily local nodes of evidence is a perpetual *vexata quaestio*, one which the GLOBECOSAL project tackles by emphasising complementarity and connectivity among a wide-ranging set of themes. These are selected, on the one hand, for their capacity to speak to each other. On the other hand, the research topics collectively have been chosen for their differences and for the breadth of the entire study thus achieved, each bringing to the fore a distinct arena in which the project's central questions apply with different inflections and emphases. Thus, the project's overarching concern with sanctity across the Iberian global sphere of influence includes geographical settings and cults that range from the far-flung (such as the cult of Francis Xavier) to the highly localised (such as that of Mariana de Jesús Paredes y Flores), and from centres of imperial power, such as Lima, to settings that never came under European rule at all, like Japan. At the level of individual case studies, the strands of study together include both successful and unsuccessful candidates for sainthood, men and women, and high-profile as well as recondite cases. Chronologically, the cases considered are grouped around a relatively tight temporal framework that largely fits both within the post-1588 Congregational era of increased papal regulation of sanctity, and also within the age of Iberian hegemony prior to the War of the Spanish

29 On iconology, the foundational text is E. Panofsky, *Studies in Iconology: Humanistic Themes in the Art of the Renaissance* (New York: Harper & Row, 1972); on *Bildwissenschaft*, key texts include H. Belting, *Bild-Anthropologie: Entwürfe für eine Bildwissenschaft* (Munich: W. Fink, 2001); H. Bredekamp, "A Neglected Tradition? Art History as Bildwissenschaft", *Critical Inquiry* 29 (2003) 418–28; H. Belting (ed.), *Bilderfragen. Die Bildwissenschaften im Aufbruch* (Munich: W. Fink, 2007); G. Boehm (ed.), *Ikonologie der Gegenwart* (Munich: W. Fink, 2009); D. Hornuff, *Bildwissenschaft im Widerstreit: Belting, Boehm, Bredekamp, Burda* (Munich: W. Fink, 2012); M. Rimmele/K. Sachs-Hombach/B. Stiegler (ed.), *Bildwissenschaft und Visual Culture* (Bielefeld: Transcript, 2014); and A.J. Lehmann/P. Ursprung (ed.), *Bild und Raum. Klassische Texte zu Spatial Turn und Bildwissenschaft* (Bielefeld: Transcript, 2016).

Succession. The five research avenues described below, pursued respectively by Jonathan Greenwood, Wei Jiang, Lucía Querejazu Escobari, Hannah Joy Friedman, and Raphaèle Preisinger, thus offer together a de-centred perspective on early modern sainthood that is simultaneously global in its reach and fine-grained in its handling of evidence. The topics cover: the martyrs of the Japan mission, among whom were the first blesseds originating from territories encountered by European polities in the early modern period; Saint Francis Xavier, the pioneer of the Society of Jesus in India and of Christian missions in Asia more broadly; and the patron saint of the American continent, Saint Rose of Lima; in addition to several unsuccessful candidates for sainthood whose veneration was based in Spanish territories outside of Europe, such as Viceregal Peru and the Philippines.

Jonathan Greenwood. From Shangchuan to Saint: Images of Francis Xavier and the Growth of his Global Cult, 1552–1640

Francis Xavier (1506–1552) was the exemplary missionary of the Society of Jesus sent to Asia in 1540 soon after the papal confirmation of the religious order. The scholarship on his cultic images focuses primarily on the Lusophone world since Portuguese intervention was vital to his canonisation that culminated in the processes held in Lisbon and throughout Asia during the 1610s. The two processes in Lisbon that examined the life, virtues, and miracles of Xavier (1614–1616) were held at the Professed House of São Roque, later home to the painted cycle by André Reinoso (ca. 1610–ca. 1650) that gave visual form to what was expressed by witnesses.[30] Goa, the epicentre of the Estado da Índia, is well known as the home of his body with its tomb and decoration receiving extensive scholarly attention for its religious and visual import.[31] While the iconography has been examined at length, the global dimensions of the veneration of Xavier, especially through his

30 V. Serrão, *A lenda de São Francisco Xavier pelo Pintor André Reinoso* (Lisbon: Casa da Misericórdia de Lisboa, 1993); V. Serrão, "André Reinoso (c. 1590–pós 1650), um «pintor de fama» para a fama de São Francisco Xavier", in M.M. Montenegro (ed.), *Missão, espiritualidade e arte em São Francisco Xavier* (Lisbon: Edições Santa Casa Misericórdia de Lisboa, 2020) 50–91; and J.M. Simões, "O ciclo pictórico dedicado a São Francisco Javier na sacristia da igreja de São Roque de Lisboa: iconologia, ideologia imagética e política no contexto da União Ibérica (1580–1640)", in M.M. Montenegro (ed.), *Missão, espiritualidade e arte em São Francisco Xavier* (Lisbon: Edições Santa Casa Misericórdia de Lisboa, 2020) 92–133. An inventory of all the processes for Xavier's cause is found in L.J. Fortún Pérez de Ciriza, "Los procesos para la canonización de San Francisco Javier", *Anuario de historia de la iglesia* 29 (2020) 220–7.

31 I.G. Županov, *Missionary Tropics: The Catholic Frontier in India (16th–17th Centuries)* (Ann Arbor: University of Michigan Press, 2005), 35–86: L.M. Brockey, "The Cruelest Honor: The Relics of Francis Xavier in Early Modern Asia", *Catholic Historical Review* 101.1 (2015) 41–64; P. Gupta, *The*

Fig. 5 Attributed to Pedro Kano, *Portrait of Francis Xavier*, early seventeenth century. Watercolor on paper, 60 x 50 cm. Kobe City Museum, Kobe, Japan. Image courtesy of the Kobe City Museum, Kobe, Japan.

likeness, have only just begun with Rachel Miller leading the vanguard.[32] How and where did the devout interact with representations of the missionary throughout the early modern world? What were the negotiations between local and universal

---

Relic State: St. Francis Xavier and the Politics of Ritual in Portuguese India (Manchester: Manchester University Press, 2014).

32 F. García Gutiérrez, *San Francisco Javier en el arte de España y Oriente* (Seville: Guadalquivir ediciones, 2005); M.C. Osswald, "Cultos e iconografías jesuíticas en Goa durante los siglos XVI y XVII: El culto e iconografía de San Francisco Javier", in R. Fernández Gracia (ed.), *San Francisco Javier en las artes: el poder de la imagen* (Pamplona: Gobierno de Navarra y Fundación Caja Navarra, 2006) 235–53; E. Morales Solchaga, "Iconografía de San Francisco Javier en la portada del libro barroco", in R. Fernández Gracia (ed.), *San Francisco Javier en las artes: el poder de la imagen* (Pamplona: Gobierno de Navarra y Fundación Caja Navarra, 2006) 254–83; M.G. Torres Olleta, *Redes iconográficas: San Francisco Javier en la cultura visual del barroco* (Madrid: Iberoamericana, 2009); Miller, "Iconography of St. Francis Xavier".

in the visual aspects of a saint's cult? The result will reveal the broader geography of the visual cult of the new "Apostle of the East" (Fig. 5).

This part of the project examines the making and movement of likenesses of Xavier in the development of his cult both before and after his canonisation in 1622. Problems often arise due to the lack of surviving images with scholars overly reliant on biographies prepared amid his cause. Fortunately, Jesuit annual letters, news sheets, mission histories, and documents from the canonisation processes abound in discussion on images and their place in believers' lives. These findings can supplement the extant images, allowing for the reconstruction of the networks that traded, circulated, and used these objects. This part of the GLOBECOSAL project begins by considering the incipient cult that emanated from Goa after Xavier's death in 1552, which included the relocation of his body from Shangchuan to Goa via Malacca and the commencement of the informative process of his canonisation. Held between 1556 and 1557, processes in Goa, Vasai, Kochi, and Malacca had witnesses questioned on matters related to the sanctity of the Jesuit missionary.[33] It was a fallow period of canonisations, but this dearth ended with the foundation of the Congregation of Sacred Rites in 1588 as an entity to oversee canonisations.

In the case of Xavier, devotees worked to craft representations of the missionary in the form of lives, biographies prepared for saints that followed the Gospels, and images. These formed the basis of the likenesses found throughout Europe by 1600. These prints formed part of a larger strategy by the Society and other religious orders to promote their candidates for sainthood, such as the Oratorians with Filippo Neri (1515–1595).[34] I use these printed works to assess the first phase of the visual culture, wherein biographies and engravings converged to illustrate the famed missionary for viewers decades after his death with an iconography hailing from Goa.

Finally, this research arena considers global case studies on the representations of Xavier between 1600 and 1625. Throughout this period, mentions and discussions of images can be found in the annual letters from the Jesuit provinces along with the news sheets about the celebrations of both the beatification and canonisation of Xavier, sources that have had scant use by scholars working on his visual culture. Although not without their problems, these documents frequently reference setting, use, cost, and other details about the representations, which are indispensable to their understanding, particularly if the images themselves have been lost over the centuries. These documents also direct us toward local interests in a saint's cult and how Xavier featured within the religious landscape of a community. Reverence

33 Fortún Pérez de Ciriza, "Los procesos de san Francisco Javier", 220–3.

34 As studied at length by Noyes, *Crisis of the Beati moderni*. The key work on Jesuit founder Ignatius Loyola remains U. König-Nordhoff, *Ignatius von Loyola: Studien zur Entwicklung einer neuen Heiligen-Ikonographie im Rahmen einer Kanonisationskampagne um 1600* (Berlin: Mann, 1982).

for the Jesuit in Goa is well documented, especially as the site of his tomb, but the affinity for the saint among the Paravars – Tamil speakers of southeastern India and Sri Lanka – for example, gets overlooked.[35] The fixation on Xavier as a saint of India remained, yet this notion was recontextualised in the disparate regions where devotions can be located. The project concludes with the post-canonisation era (1622–circa 1655), which encompassed the end of what Giovanni Papa called the "first period of the Congregation" (1588–1634).[36] Amid political, imperial, and religious change, the transoceanic cult of Xavier and its images continued to be recontextualised for local needs despite his sainthood being confirmed. Rather than fixate on early modern Portugal and its pluricontinentalism, the focus is on wherever the crafting of the imagery of Xavier took place during his canonisation cause and afterwards. These case studies challenge long-standing trends in the field by globalising the networks in which images negotiated with local religious cultures.

Wei Jiang. Ex Oriente Sanctitas? Images and Unsuccessful Beatification Causes from Iberian Asia

Even though the history of art and material culture in the early modern Catholic missions to Asia is a thriving field, studies dedicated to sanctity and iconography are rather limited, with the exception of one specific subject.[37] This concerns Saint Francis Xavier, whose artistic representations have received ever growing attention, including the GLOBECOSAL project, ever since Georg Schurhammer published seminal works in the context of his life-long scholarly endeavours devoted to the first and foremost Jesuit saint in Asia.[38] In contrast to Latin America, the Catholic Church in Asia has by no means been characterised as productive in the promotion of local sanctity. On the one side, there was a relatively small number of local candidates laying claim to universal sanctity, and on the other side, Saint Francis Xavier and the 26 martyrs of the Japan mission, the latter being the largest group of *beati* in the early modern era, became globally influential and artistically inspiring.

35 S. Bayly, *Saints, Goddesses, and Kings: Muslims and Christians in South Indian Society, 1700–1900* (Cambridge: Cambridge University Press, 1989), 378–81.

36 Papa, *Le cause di canonizzazione.*

37 Published in 1970, D.F. Lach's volume, *Asia in the Making of Europe, Volume II: A Century of Wonder. Book 1: The Visual Arts* (Chicago: University of Chicago Press, 1970) is still a useful reference. Most recent studies include Lee, *Saints of Resistance*; and E.E. Benay, *Italy by Way of India: Translating Art and Devotion in the Early Modern World* (Turnhout: Harvey Miller Publishers, 2021).

38 G. Schurhammer, *Gesammelte Studien* (5 vols; Lisbon: Centro de estudios históricos ultramarinos, 1962–1965).

The remaining candidates from the early modern Catholic Church in Asia whose *processūs* reached the Congregation of Rites were much less well known. They are: Rodolfo Acquaviva, S.J. and the other Martyrs of Cuncolim († 1583, beat. 1898); Jerónima de la Asunción, O.S.C. († 1630); Dénis de la Nativité, O.C.D. (Pierre Berthelot) and Redento da Crus, O.C.D. (Tomás Rodrigues da Cunha; both † 1638, beat. 1900); Marcello Mastrilli, S.J. († 1637); Andrea from Phu Yen († 1644, beat. 2000); Francisco Fernández de Capillas, O.P. († 1648, beat. 1909, canon. 2000); and João de Brito († 1693, beat. 1853, canon. 1947). While the processes of Mastrilli and Mother Jerónima have not yet succeeded to this day, many other potential martyrs and saints did not even manage to reach Rome throughout the early modern era.[39] "Ex oriente sanctitas?" is focused on these unsuccessful candidates.

Inspired by Simon Ditchfield's work on the processes of Pope Gregory V and by Ronald C. Finucane's book on contested canonisations in late medieval Europe, this portion of the project explores the obstacles and the vicissitudes that occurred in the beatification processes, deriving from the Spanish Philippines, Portuguese Goa, and the East Asian Christian communities, which did not reach completion by the end of the eighteenth century.[40] Adding to the textual analysis employed in previous studies, "Ex oriente sanctitas?" offers a visual arts angle to historical reconstructions, while stressing a non-European dimension in the saint-making processes. The first case under study examines the beatification process of Jerónima de la Asunción, dividing the visual materials about her cult into two types, namely ephemeral emblems and effigies. At least 42 emblems designed by the Cathedral chapter and noble families of Manila are known to have been utilised at the funeral rites of Jerónima, so as to keep an enduring memory of the Clarissan nun in the multi-ethnic and religiously hybrid Philippines. Emblems were not only a Spanish cultural form, but also a device that safeguarded the growth of Jerónima's cult without trespassing the *non cultu* rules newly imposed by Rome to fight "feigned sanctity".

Lucía Querejazu Escobari. Portraying the American Rose: The Evolution of Peruvian Saints' Images Between Lima and Rome

This part of the GLOBECOSAL project investigates the role of images in three successful canonisation campaigns of saints initiated in the Viceroyalty of Peru. The focus is primarily on Santa Rosa de Santa Maria, better known as Santa Rosa

39 This project excludes the figures who received local veneration but without a cause, such as Candida Xu (1607–1680) in China and Joseph Vaz (1651–1711) in Ceylon.

40 Ditchfield, *Liturgy, Sanctity, and History*; R.C. Finucane, *Contested Canonizations: The Last Medieval Saints, 1482–1523* (Washington, D.C.: The Catholic University of America Press, 2011).

de Lima (1586–1617). She was beatified in 1668 and canonised in 1671, becoming the first saint of the New World. A comparative approach is chosen, which allows to also examine the causes of the archbishop of Lima Santo Toribio de Mogrovejo (1538–1606) beatified in 1679 and canonised in 1726, and the Franciscan San Francisco Solano (1549–1610), beatified in 1675 and canonised in 1726 as well. The latter two saints lived earlier than Rosa and were born in Spain, however they are considered here as Peruvian saints, for it is the Andean colonial society, in its complexities, that set the stage for them to live heroic lives. Through these three cases, this study examines the colonial society that for more than six decades witnessed and shaped the sainthood of these figures.

In the Viceroyalty of Peru, the time frame marked by the lives of these three saints, between 1538 and 1617, corresponds to the settlement, complex as it was, of the invasion turning into the violent period of the Civil Wars between *conquistadores* (1537–1554), and slowly moving to a pacified settlement full of difficulties and challenges, but also with immense potential for wealth, fame and – notoriously – for sanctity.[41] These troubled settings had much need for men such as Toribio de Mogrovejo and Francisco Solano, who would bravely and tirelessly walk the newly created provinces trying to seed the land with the new faith. Such efforts were longed for by a young Rosa de Santa Maria, enclosed in her garden in Lima/Los Reyes, ardently searching for God in the smallest things, wishing she could also have the opportunity to face the infidels and take part in the fight against idolatry and heresy. Thus it is not difficult to think of the three in the paradigmatic roles of a pious mystic, a shepherd, and an apostle/missionary. But we must also take into account that in the same time period two other saints lived, San Juan Macías and San Martín de Porres, and many other cases were considered worthy of pursuing an apostolic cause. However, here the focus is on the three that were officially recognised by Rome within the seventeenth century (at least as *beatos*).[42]

Our analysis stems from the early accounts of their lives, with the first engravings or drawings portraying their most significant characteristics, the portraits designated as *vera efigie*, in order to examine the process of construction of the *persona*.

---

41 These conflicts are often referred to as the war between *pizarristas* and *almagristas* and the Rebellion of Gonzalo Pizarro. The fact is that it was an internal conflict that delayed the settling of the administration in the viceroyalty of Peru and marked the beginning of colonial rule. A well-documented and clear explanation of events can be found in A.M. Lorandi, *Ni Ley, ni Rey, ni Hombre Virtuoso. Guerra y Sociedad en el Virreynato del Perú Siglos XVI y XVII* (Buenos Aires: Gedisa, 2002). An introduction to Lima and its historical development can be found in E.A. Engel (ed.), *A Companion to Early Modern Lima* (Leiden: Brill, 2019).

42 R. Sánchez-Concha Barrios, *Santos y santidad en el Perú virreinal* (Lima: Vida y espiritualidad, 2003) gives a thorough account of these saints and virtuous men and women in colonial Peru and in the period of our interest, and there are 27 saints, *beatos, siervos de Dios* and candidates for canonisation in that timeframe.

Once created, this *persona*, carefully assembled from the information of the processes, was then sent to Rome for thorough examination following Urban VIII's new regulations, and thus begins a negotiation between what Lima proposes as saints and what Rome is looking for (accepting) as such. In that sense, the comparative approach to these three cases, negotiated during the seventeenth century, allows us to understand the different paths this process could take, given the complexities and expense of each one.

As stated previously, the main focus rests on the cause of Saint Rosa de Santa Maria, for it was the first to be successful. In this case we find solid scholarship both on her *proceso apostólico*, on her iconography, and on her life (Mujica Pinilla, Grazziano, Hart, Arias Cuba).[43] From that scholarly foundation we go looking into the specific role of images, particularly from the early years leading to her beatification in 1668, the role of the Dominican order in the commissioning of specific iconographies, and after that, the appropriation of her image by the devout. Thus, in view of the abundance of images produced after her beatification, and even more after her canonisation in 1671, we also propose to analyse the evolution of how she was portrayed for different audiences. An accurate determination of how this saint was depicted is particularly significant because she would become the example presented to be admired, but the question also arises of how and to what extent she was also intended to be imitated.

The same approach will also apply to Mogrovejo and Solano, pursuing the dynamics between the causes and the "end result" but taking into consideration the differences in each case, for instance the gender aspect and their belonging to either the regular or secular clergy. The image strategies in both Mogrovejo's and Solano's cases vary significantly from Rosa's and also between one another; however, by asking the same questions of the corpus of images and their uses, we aim to disentangle the role of images, as noted, both in Lima – among their communities – and in Rome, among the ecclesiastical hierarchy.

---

43 Mujica Pinilla, *Rosa limensis*; F. Grazziano, *Wounds of Love: The Mystical Marriage of Saint Rose of Lima* (Oxford: Oxford University Press, 2004); S.M. Hart, *Edición critica del Proceso Apostólico de Santa Rosa de Lima (1630–1632). Congr. Riti Processus 1573, Archivum Secretum Vaticanum* (Lima: Editorial Ċatedra Vallejo, 2017); Y. Arias Cuba, *Integración de un sistema devocional indiano en la Monarquía Hispana. El culto de santa Rosa de Santa María en las ciudades de Lima y México, 1668–1737* (PhD Thesis, Mexico City: Colegio de México, 2019).

Hannah Joy Friedman. Exemplarity and Experimentation: Images in Unsuccessful Canonisation Campaigns from the Viceroyalty of Peru

The vast and diverse set of nations and territories that came, more or less effectively, under Spanish rule as the Viceroyalty of Peru were fertile ground for candidates for sainthood in the long seventeenth century. Exemplary figures who established international saintly reputations arose from the ranks of Iberian-born missionaries, of the Andeans whom they evangelised, and of the *criollo* (American-born but of Spanish parentage) urban elites in various parts of the Viceroyalty. Alongside the successful campaigns that quickly brought Rose of Lima first to beatification and then to canonisation, many other causes for beatification were initiated on behalf of candidates who were either born or active in the Viceroyalty, and whose *fama sanctitatis* had taken root there.[44] While Rose of Lima's high-profile success story vindicated both the faith of the Peruvian church and the Spanish imperial project that led to its establishment, many unsuccessful causes for sainthood complete and qualify this picture in vital ways. The veneration of saints, both those who had received official recognition and those aspiring to it, was among the most fundamental and immediate arenas of practicing Catholicism, and was thus a strategic arena for promoting, resisting, and adapting a wide range of social, spiritual, and political causes.[45] Complementing the study of successful cases such as Rose of Lima's, this study of images relating to the veneration of unsuccessful candidates for sainthood (or whose success came long after the early modern period) reconsiders the very categories of success and failure, with the aim of reaching a fuller understanding of what might separate the official recognition of sainthood from a de facto saintly status in another context.

One case study that vividly complements the example of Rose of Lima is that of Mariana de Jesús Paredes y Flores (1618–1645). Generationally and biographically an immediate successor of Rose, Mariana's honorific designation as the Lily of Quito indicates how explicitly the promoters of her cult saw her as representing, for the smaller seat of the Real Audiencia de Quito, what Rose stood for in the more populous and powerful Viceregal capital of Lima.[46] While Ronald Morgan has ably argued that Mariana's hagiographies strategically framed her cult within a promo-

44 R. Vargas Ugarte, *Historia de la iglesia en el Perú* (5 vols; Lima: Imprenta Santa Maria, 1953–1963), on 2.454–92, 3.417–44; Estenssoro Fuchs, *Del paganismo a la santidad*; Sánchez-Concha Barrios, *Santos y Santidad*; Millar Carvacho, *Santidad, falsa santidad, y posesiones*; Cussen, *Black Saint*; N.E. Van Deusen, *Embodying the Sacred: Women Mystics in Seventeenth-Century Lima* (Durham: Duke University Press, 2018).

45 Estenssoro Fuchs, *Del paganismo a la santidad*; Mujica Pinilla, *Rosa limensis*; Cussen, *Black Saint*.

46 As argued by R.J. Morgan, "Just like Rosa: History and Metaphor in the *Life* of a Seventeenth-Century Peruvian Saint", *Biography* 21.3 (1998) 275–310.

tion of *criollo* spiritual and political clout and of the *patria chica* of Quito, Mariana's evolving imagery, especially within the wider context of the Viceroyalty, has only recently become the subject of art historical scholarship.[47] Within Mariana's surviving iconography, prior to the recognition of her heroic virtue by Pius VI in 1776, a dominant type emerges that presents absolutely minimal distinctions between Mariana and the exemplars of sanctity on whom she directly modelled her behaviour, particularly Catherine of Siena. This image type is best exemplified by an early painting attributed to the Panamanian artist Hernando de la Cruz, S.J. (c. 1592–1646) (Fig. 6).[48] While the later prints show Mariana framed by the memorable narrative of her propitiatory self-sacrifice to save her hometown of Quito from plagues and earthquakes, the sparse economy of the earlier imagery appears more indebted to prior models of female hagiographic imagery. Thus Mariana's images act out many of the specific and gendered ways in which sainthood itself, particularly in a colonial context, occupied a tight space between adherence to and departure from established models, summoning questions of emulation that remain central to postcolonial studies, colonial Latin American art history, and early modern art history more broadly.[49] A first task is to reconsider Mariana's early iconography with a view to challenging the superficial contrast between simple and imitative productions for an American

---

47 Morgan, *Spanish American Saints*, 99–118; on Mariana's iconography, see M.A. Fernández Valle, "De Roma a las Indias: Religiosidad y circulación de estampas de la Azucena de Quito", in I. Rodríguez Moya/M.A. Fernández Valle/C. López Calderón (ed.), *Arte y patrimonio en Iberoamérica: tráficos transoceánicos* (Castelló de la Plana: Universitat Jaume I, 2016) 135–56; Vargas Murcia, "Construcción, circulación y uso de una imagen"; C. de Tena Ramírez, "Mortificación y martirio. La espiritualidad de los jesuitas en la imagen de santa Mariana de Jesús, Azucena de Quito", in F. Quiles García/J.J. García Bernal/P. Broggio/M. Fagiolo dell'Arco (ed.), *A la luz de Roma: Santos y santidad en el barocco iberoamericano*, (3 vols; Seville: EnredARS/Universidad Pablo de Olavide, 2020) 2.291–312; and E. Manchado Rodríguez, "Dibujar con buril y pluma: la iconografía textual y visual de Mariana de Jesús Paredes y Flores (1618–1645) y su circulación transatlántica (siglos XVII–XVIII)", *Hipogrifo* 9.1 (2021) 639–56.

48 On Hernando de la Cruz, see S. Verdi Webster, *Lettered Artists and the Language of Empire. Painters and the Profession in Early Colonial Quito* (Austin: University of Texas Press, 2017), 161–2, with further bibliography.

49 The topic looms too large to give thorough references here, but see for example H.K. Bhabha, *The Location of Culture* (London: Routledge, 1994); B. Ashcroft/G. Griffiths/H. Tiffin, *Post-Colonial Studies: The Key Concepts* (London: Routledge, ^{2}2007); M.H. Loh, *Titian Remade: Repetition and the Transformation of Early Modern Art* (Los Angeles: Getty Research Institute, 2007); R.T. Neer, "Poussin and the Ethics of Imitation", *Memoirs of the American Academy in Rome* 51/52 (2007) 297–344; G.A. Bailey, *The Andean Hybrid Baroque: Convergent Cultures in the Churches of Colonial Peru* (Notre Dame: University of Notre Dame Press, 2010); A.W.A. Boschloo (ed.), *Aemulatio: Imitation, Emulation, and Invention in Netherlandish Art from 1500 to 1800; Essays in Honor of Eric Jan Sluijter* (Zwolle: Waanders, 2011); D. Mayernik, *The Challenge of Emulation in Art and Architecture* (Farnham: Ashgate, 2013); and A.M. Hyman, *Rubens in Repeat: The Logic of the Copy in Colonial Latin America* (Los Angeles: Getty Research Institute, 2021).

Fig. 6 Attributed to Hernando de la Cruz, *Mariana de Jesús Paredes y Flores*, 1645–1646. Oil on canvas, 128 x 99 cm. Museo del Carmen Alto, Quito. Photo: Hannah Friedman.

audience and more distinctive ones for an "official" Roman audience. The very notions of failure and delay that appear to confine Mariana's images to a supposed spiritual and geographic periphery also hold great potential as analytical tools for the complex work carried out by images of early modern candidates for sainthood.

A dynamic counterpoint to the case of Mariana de Jesús, a woman from a *criollo* family whose activities took place in a tight sphere between home and church, is the case of the active and socially mobile urban artisan Nicolás Ayllón (1632–1677), also called Nicolás de Dios. Born in Chiclayo to a family of Indigenous *caciques* (local leaders), Nicolás at a young age entered the service of the Franciscan father Juan de Ayllón, who brought his *indio* servant-protégé with him to Lima.[50] Having

50 R. Vargas Ugarte, *Vida del siervo de Dios, Nicolás Ayllón: o por otro nombre, Nicolás de Dios, natural de Chiclayo* (Buenos Aires: Imprimería Lopez, 1964), 17–24.

Fig 7. Anonymous, *Nicolás de Ayllón*, published in Bernardo Sartolo, *Vida admirable y muerte prodigiosa de Nicolas de Ayllon, y con renombre mas glorioso Nicolas de Dios, natural de Chiclayo en las Indias del Peru* (Madrid: Juan Garcia Infançon, 1684). Etching and engraving, 17.3 x 12.4 cm. Image from the collections of the Biblioteca de la Universidad Complutense de Madrid

trained as a tailor, Nicolás as an adult married María Jacinta Montoya, and the two of them together came not only to co-found and operate charitable institutions (notably a *beaterio* for at-risk young women) but also to occupy key roles in the intense urban spiritual centre of Lima.[51] The earliest surviving image of Nicolás, an anonymous print included as an illustration in his biography by the Jesuit Bernardo Sartolo (Fig. 7), gestures towards this participation in a specific stage of the city's spiritual life, as it makes reference to a vision of Nicolás recounted by his and María Jacinta's friend Ángela Carranza, a high-profile visionary and unorthodox spiritual

51 Vargas Ugarte, *Vida*; Estenssoro Fuchs, *Del paganismo a la santidad*, 468–98.

lay-leader whose eventual trial by the Inquisition was probably the deciding factor in (at least temporarily) derailing Nicolás's cause for beatification.[52] Building on the pioneering work of historians such as Juan Carlos Estenssoro Fuchs and Nancy van Deusen, this work aims at an in-depth analysis of the engraved portrait of Nicolás accompanying Sartolo's biography. Thus I look more closely at the dynamic ways in which both the hagiographic text and the image, in handling the socially groundbreaking subject of an Indigenous Peruvian saint, experiment with imagery that aspirationally conveys a status still in the process of negotiation, as Nicolás's cause for beatification is still open.

Raphaèle Preisinger. The Global Itineraries of the Martyrs of Japan: Early Modern Religious Networks and the Circulation of Images across Asia, Europe, and the Americas

This strand of research spotlights the visual representations of the victims of Christian persecution in Japan. The missionary enterprise on the archipelago started when the Jesuit Saint Francis Xavier reached the shores of Kagoshima on August 15, 1549. Christian evangelism in Japan lasted until 1614 and produced thousands of martyrs. Among them, the 26 Christians who fell victim to the first great martyrdom in Japan stand out. The Japanese ruler Hideyoshi had sentenced a group of Christians to death by crucifixion at Nagasaki, accusing them of violating the law of the realm and disturbing the public peace. On February 5th, 1597, 26 Christians – six Franciscan missionaries and seventeen of their acolytes, as well as three Japanese Jesuit lay brothers who were included by mistake – were crucified in Japanese fashion at Nagasaki. They were beatified in 1627 and would remain the only victims of Christian persecution in Japan to be beatified before the nineteenth century.[53]

52 Vargas Ugarte, *Vida*, 89–107; Estenssoro Fuchs, *Del paganismo a la santidad*, 473–98; C.A. Espinoza Rua, "Un indio camino a los altares: santidad e influencia inquisitorial en el caso del 'siervo de Dios' Nicolás de Ayllón", *Histórica* 36.1 (2012) 135–180; Van Deusen, *Embodying the Sacred*, 71–94, 117–42.

53 The fast-growing bibliography on the victims of Christian persecution in Japan includes: C.R. Boxer, *The Christian Century in Japan 1549–1650* (Berkeley: University of California Press, 1951); K. Koshi, "Die 26 Märtyrer von Japan in der Kunst: ein Werkkatalog", *Bulletin annuel du musée national d'art occidental* 8 (1974) 16–72; J. Ruiz-de-Medina *El martirologio del Japón, 1558–1873* (Rome: Institutum Historicum S.I., 1999); M.M. Mochizuki, "Shock Value. The Jesuit Martyrs of Japan and the Ethics of Sight", in S.M. Promey (ed.), *Sensational Religion. Sensory Cultures in Material Practice* (New Haven: Yale University Press, 2014) 375–97; R.H. Hesselink, *The Dream of Christian Nagasaki. World Trade and the Clash of Cultures, 1560–1640* (Jefferson, NC: McFarland & Company, 2016); H. Vu Thanh, *Devenir japonais. La mission jésuite au Japon (1549–1614)* (Paris: Presses de l'université Paris-Sorbonne, 2016); Conover, *Pious Imperialism*; Omata Rappo, *Des Indes lointaines aux scènes*

This portion of the GLOBECOSAL project examines the negotiation of the martyrs' saintly status by visual means, concentrating on the most important globally circulating artworks and iconographies. This requires taking into account the evolving discourse on martyrdom in post-Tridentine Catholic Europe, one formed by heavy conflicts with Protestant reformers, who produced their own martyrs, and the rediscovery of the Roman catacombs in the late sixteenth century. The latter led to a revival of the early Christian cult of the martyrs in Catholic Europe, a tradition in which the veneration of new martyrs came to be understood.[54] A particular focus is on the rivalry between religious orders involved in the missionary enterprise in Japan, which mirrored the conflict between the Iberian kingdoms over the lucrative China-Japan trade and which is also reflected in the iconography of the victims of persecution by the Japanese authorities.

Fig. 8 Lázaro Pardo de Lago, *The Franciscan Martyrs of Japan of 1597*, 1630. Convento Franciscano de La Recoleta, Cusco, Peru. Image from J.J. Rishel/S.L. Stratton-Pruitt (ed.), *The Arts in Latin America 1492–1820* (Philadelphia: Philadelphia Museum of Art, 2006), cat. no. VI-71, p. 419.

des collèges; and R. Roldán-Figueroa, *The Martyrs of Japan. Publication History and Catholic Missions in the Spanish World (Spain, New Spain, and the Philippines, 1597–1700)* (Leiden: Brill, 2021).

54 On early modern martyrdom, the foundational text is B.S. Gregory, *Salvation at Stake. Christian Martyrdom in Early Modern Europe* (Cambridge, MA: Harvard University Press, 1999). Many more recent publications have since been authored or edited by the participants of the "Profiling Saints" conference in particular.

Most of the 26 Christians crucified at Nagasaki in 1597 were of Asian descent. These martyrs were the first blesseds originating from territories encountered by European polities in the early modern period, which is why they became the object of complex processes of appropriation across the continents. This can be observed in the two paintings on display in the church of the Franciscan convent of the Recoleta in Cusco (Fig. 8), which were executed by Lázaro Pardo de Lago (active in Cusco 1630–1669) in 1630. They were commissioned by the Franciscan monastery of La Recoleta for the festivities in Peru celebrating the beatification of the Franciscan martyrs of 1597. These paintings attest to a very local interest in the faraway event they feature: surrounding the Franciscan missionaries shown prominently in the foreground, the Asian victims are depicted according to the artistic conventions of the day to represent Mestizos or members of the Christianised Indigenous population.[55] This local appropriation of the Japan martyrs hints at how these figures helped establish and propagate a new ideal of sanctity tightly bound to the early modern missionary enterprise. The Peruvian adoption of the Japan martyrs is also evidence for how this ideal opened up opportunities for inclusion to the newly Christianised populations hitherto excluded from the institutionally governed access to the ranks of sanctity.

This subproject brackets all the other research topics included in the GLOBECOSAL project both geographically and conceptually. Geographically, because it reaches across the oceans to examine the devotion to these martyrs in Asia, the Americas, and Europe: its focal points are located in East Asia, where the martyrs' veneration, first revolving around relics, began; in the Americas, as a great number of artworks depicting the Japan martyrs were created there; and in Rome, because this is where many of the artworks were destined, executed, and commissioned. The topic of the Japan martyrs embraces the other strands of research also conceptually, as it is ambiguously located between "success" and "failure": the 26 beatified martyrs were "successful" candidates for sainthood, as they were the only ones among the myriad victims of the missionary enterprise in Japan to obtain partial papal recognition of sainthood in the early modern period, but they were also "unsuccessful", as their canonisation did not occur until the nineteenth century. The visual representations of these martyrs are thus key in uncovering the factors contributing to "success" or "failure" in early modern saint-making.

55 On the Cusco paintings, see J.J. Rishel/S.L. Stratton-Pruitt (ed.), *The Arts in Latin America 1492–1820* (Philadelphia: Philadelphia Museum of Art, 2006), 419, with further bibliography.

Conclusion: Prospects for Global Approaches Across Disciplines

While the project's core is art historical, GLOBECOSAL seeks to contribute to lively ongoing discussions across several sub-disciplines of early modern studies that share an investment in finding useful ways of discussing the global dimensions of the pre-modern world without impoverishing the study of particular contexts. Investigating the negotiation of sanctity between Rome and geographically distant areas participates in globalising the history of early modern art. As the spreading of Catholicism served as the ideological justification for European expansion under Iberian rule, negotiation of an individual's saintly status amounted to a negotiation of the status awarded to the "new" Catholic societies within the order established by the Iberian colonial and mercantile empires. Because this process attests to the claims and aspirations of Christian societies around the globe beginning at an early stage of European expansion, it calls into question the dynamics of desire and demand generally associated with its economic aspects. Such an investigation is therefore qualified to challenge established perspectives on Roman Catholicism, colonialism, and the early modern world at large, impacting not only art history, but historical research at its broadest and most interdisciplinary.

Rachel Miller

Imagining the World through St Francis Xavier Imagery

A Case Study in Quito

Introduction

After his 1656 conversion to Catholicism, Baldassare Loyola (1631–67) had a dream in which an enormous tree with branches laden with beautiful blossoms appeared to him. Loyola had been born a prince of Fez and a Muslim and, at the time of the dream, was deciding which Catholic religious order to join. As he gazed at the tree, he noticed that some of the branches had more flowers than others:

> God… helped me to understand the meaning of this image: the tree is the world, and the flowering branches are the religious orders spread in the world; some of them produce more fruits than the others, and the flowering top of the tree is the Society of Jesus.[1]

This vision demonstrated to Loyola that among all the Catholic orders, the Jesuits had been most effective in propagating Catholicism throughout the world and solidified his decision to join the Society of Jesus. This is far from the only instance in which arboreal imagery came to represent the Jesuits' global missionary work and education efforts. Ignatius of Loyola (1491–1556), the founder of the Jesuit order, was likely the first to take the word "seminary," a horticultural term for a seedling nursery, and use it to describe a school for priests.[2] For early modern Jesuits, these education efforts were completely intertwined with their missionary work. Once these Jesuit seedlings matured, they went out into the world, bore fruit by converting souls, and thus became part of a network that encompassed the globe. Images of trees were often used to visualise and diagram this interconnected web of provinces,

1 This dream is described in Loyola's unpublished autobiography, now in the archive of the Gregorian University Rome (APUG). See APUG 1060 I–II. The excerpt above is quoted and translated in E. Colombo, "A Muslim Turned Jesuit: Baldassarre Loyola Mandes (1631–1667)," *Journal of Early Modern History* 17 (2013) 479–504, on p. 489.

2 L. Rice, "'Pomis Sua Nomina Servant:' The Emblematic Thesis Prints of the Roman Seminary," *Journal of the Warburg and Courtauld Institutes* 70 (2007) 195–246, on p. 201. J.W. O'Malley, *The First Jesuits* (Cambridge, MA: Harvard University Press, 1993), 237–8. The emblem of the Jesuit Roman seminary, devised between 1600 and 1610, was a bunch of seedlings, sprouting from the soil within a walled garden, accompanied by the Virgilian motto, *POMIS SUA NOMINA SERVANT*, or "They preserve their fame with their fruit."

missions, colleges, and residences. One example is a print created around the year 1620 in Cologne titled *Societatis Iesu Initia Progressus et Viri Illustres*, which depicts a huge tree sprouting from the reclining body of Ignatius of Loyola. The lower, thicker branches are labeled with the names of European provinces like Italia and Hispania, while the upper, new branches represent the areas of the world that the Jesuits had more recently evangelised such as Goa, Peru, and Mexico. Surrounding this vignette are representations of the fruit produced by the Company, including examples of particularly illustrious Jesuits such as cardinals, famous missionaries, and martyrs who were killed for their faith on the overseas missions.[3]

Fig. 1 *Horoscopium Catholicum Societatis Iesu*, from *Ars magna lucis et umbrae* by Athanasius Kircher, engraving, 1646. Wikimedia Commons

3 J. Chipps Smith, *Sensuous Worship: Jesuits and the Art of the Early Catholic Reformation in Germany* (Princeton: Princeton University Press, 2002), 3–4.

Arboreal maps such as these are useful not just for documenting the remarkable reach of the Society of Jesus in the early modern world, but also for thinking through issues related to the geography of art,[4] in particular the transmission of artistic influence from place to place. This paper will examine one such arboreal model in detail, an engraving titled *Horoscopium Catholicum Societatis Iesu* (Fig. 1). This diagram demonstrates how early modern Jesuits conceived and visualised their own global enterprise, while providing art historians a means to conceptualise the transmission of artistic ideas within Jesuit networks in a way that subverts the problematic notions of center and periphery that are often embedded in the discipline of art history. Such arboreal imagery reveals the interconnected nature of Jesuit activities in places that are far removed from each other geographically and makes it possible to envision the routes of transmission that facilitated artistic interactions among artists patronized by Jesuits globally. One result of these connections is that Jesuit works of art often exhibit interwoven influences from various centres of culture, a phenomenon that this paper will explore through an examination of a series of paintings depicting the life and miracles of St Francis Xavier (1506–52), created in Quito in the mid-eighteenth century.

Arboreal Imagery as a Model for Jesuit Artistic Transmission

Beginning with Giorgio Vasari (1511–74), art historians have traditionally argued that artistic innovations take place in culturally influential centers, which then spread to peripheral areas, resulting in art that was often described as derivative or retrograde.[5] Kenneth Clark's 1962 comments on provincialism embody this view:

> The history of European art has been, to a large extent, the history of a series of centres, from each of which radiated a style. For a shorter or longer period that style dominated the art of the time, became in fact an international style, which was metropolitan at its centre and became more and more provincial as it reached the periphery. A style does not grow up simultaneously over a large area. It is the creation of a centre, a single energizing unit...[6]

4 T. DaCosta Kaufmann, *Toward a Geography of Art* (Chicago: University of Chicago Press, 2004).

5 For notions of provincialism in Vasari, see Carlo Ginzburg and Enrico Castelnuovo, "Centre and Periphery," in E. Bianchini and C. Dorey (eds.), *History of Italian Art* (Cambridge: Polity Press, 1994), 54–60.

6 K. Clark, "Provincialism," in *English Association Lecture* (Oxford: Oxford University Press, 1962). Quoted in Ginzburg and Castelnuovo, "Centre and Periphery," 29–30.

Over the decades, the assumptions of this model have been repeatedly challenged, first by Carlo Ginzburg and Enrico Castelnuovo in their foundational essay "Centro e periferia," published in 1979,[7] and then by a myriad of art historians studying global and transnational topics. However, as scholars like Piotr Piotrowski and Béatrice Joyeux-Prunel have pointed out, the notion of centre to periphery artistic transmission is still very much present in art historical discourse and pedagogy.[8] One solution to these problems has been to focus on the idea of transnationality.[9] Joyeux-Prunel advises "focusing on circulations between so-called peripheries and so-called centers" as a way to "get out of questions of hierarchies and values."[10]

The *Horoscopium Catholicum Societatis Iesu* maps out such transnational circulations, functioning as a network visualization. Such diagrams are useful because they "have the potential to translate messy archival work into clouds of connection, maps of relations that can reveal hidden agents or nodes of production."[11] The print was originally included in *Ars magna lucis et umbrae*, a treatise on optics written by the Jesuit polymath and mathematics professor Athanasius Kircher (1602–80) in 1646. Here, we see St Ignatius of Loyola kneeling in front of a seascape filled with ships destined for far-off places, eyes cast heavenwards and holding a copy of the Jesuit *Constitutions*. Like the print from Cologne described above, a tree sprouts from Ignatius of Loyola; however, this trunk is explicitly identified as "Roma" and

---

7 C. Ginzburg and E. Castelnuovo, "Centro e periferia," in Giovanni Previtali (ed.), *Storia dell'arte italiana. Parte prima: Materiali e problemi* (Torino: Giulio Einaudi, 1979).

8 Piotrowski critiques the 2004 textbook *Art Since 1900* for its failure to "deconstruct the relations between center and the margins in the world history of modern art." P. Piotrowski, "Toward a Horizontal History of the European Avant-Garde," in *Europa! Europa? The Avant-Garde, Modernism and the Fate of a Continent* (Berlin: De Gruyter, 2009), 49–50, on p. 50. H. Foster et al., *Art Since 1900: Modernism, Antimodernism, Postmodernism* (London: Thames and Hudson, 2004). Joyeux-Prunel criticizes the state of global art history: "Maintaining a center-periphery logic – even one in which the periphery is now valued equally or even more than the center – produces and keeps the traditional hierarchical canon of art history, preserving the subaltern position of the artistic production of the peripheries while including them in a barely-altered canon…" Béatrice Joyeux-Prunel, "The Uses and Abuses of Peripheries in Art History," *Artl@s Bulletin* 3 (2014) 4–7, on p. 4.

9 See Piotrowski's concept of the "horizontal art history," which resists a hierarchical model of artistic transmission that privileges centres over peripheries. Piotrowski, "Toward a Horizontal History," 50.

10 Joyeux-Prunel, "Uses and Abuses," 6.

11 S. Porras, "Keeping Our Eyes Open: Visualizing Networks and Art History," *Atl@s Bulletin* 6, no. 3 (2017) 42–9, on p. 42. In this essay, Porras is discussing contemporary network visualisations made by art historians from archival data. She cautions that such images "must also be understood as artifacts of contemporary visual culture, laded with the biases and limits of both past and present knowledge systems." Using a visualisation created by Jesuits in the seventeenth century to describe the movement of Jesuit missionaries and artistic and cultural ideas avoids some of these issues; however, it remains true that the image must be analysed with the "biases and limits" of early modern Jesuits, the Catholic Church, and the colonial power structures in which the Jesuits operated in mind.

the network being visualised is more complex. The branches support semicircular nodes, each containing the name of a Jesuit province. Leaves inscribed with the names of individual missions form clusters around each provincial label. In the top portion of the print, a Habsburg double-headed eagle superimposed with a compass needle surmounts the trunk and a dove with an olive branch in its beak, the emblem of Pope Innocent X Pamphilj (p. 1644–55), flies above the entire scene. These two symbols thus represent the papacy and the Habsburg empire, embodiments of sacred and secular Catholic power in the early modern world and the global institutions that gave the Jesuits the means and authority to operate their mission for much of their early modern history. While all of the provinces on the print are oriented around the centralising axis formed by the trunk, the eagle, and the dove, they are also not completely circumscribed by the influence of these authorities.

At the same time, the *Horoscopium Catholicum Societatis Iesu* gives evidence that Jesuits viewed all of these various provincial nodes as part of a universal schema, united by worship of Christ's name and devotion to Jesuit saints such as Ignatius of Loyola and Francis Xavier.[12] The print itself can actually function as a sundial that tells the time simultaneously in all Jesuit provinces.[13] The user is meant to hang the print up on the wall and place a pin in each provincial node. There are different groupings of numbers in each of the semicircles that bear the names of the provinces, and the pins would cast shadows onto the correct time for each province. Additionally, the arrangement of the branches was carefully designed so that the shadows cast by the pins would merge together to form the letters IHS, Christ's monogram and the symbol of the Society of Jesus.[14] As Michael John Gorman writes, one can imagine this IHS monogram as "[walking] over the world with the passage of time, like the synchronized, uniformly trained members of the Jesuit order."[15] Taking such a broad view of the Jesuit missionary efforts addresses Luke Clossey's critique that scholarship on early-modern Catholic missions often fails to seriously consider the macrohistorical nature of the enterprise. Instead of imagining "the Jesuit project as a disjointed collection of homomorphic regional missions

12 The print is framed by the phrase, "From East to West, praiseworthy is the name of our Lord" translated into thirty-four of the languages that Jesuits used on the missions, underlining the global nature of this evangelical initiative and the universality of Catholic truth.

13 M.J. Gorman, "The Angel and the Compass: Athanasius Kircher's Magnetic Geography," in Paula Findlen (ed.) *Athanasius Kircher: The Last Man Who Knew Everything* Findlen (New York: Routledge 2004), 239–59, on pp. 248–50.

14 The IHS monogram has several possible origins. It could be considered a Latinized version of the letters iota, eta, and sigma, the first three letters of Jesus's name in Greek (ΙΗΣΟΥΣ) or an acronym standing for the Latin phrase *Iesus Hominum Salvator*, or "Jesus, Savior of Man." Jesuits also give an alternative meaning to the acronym, *Jesum Habemus Socium* or "We have Jesus for our companion." Smith, *Sensuous Worship*, 3.

15 Gorman, "The Angel and the Compass," 250.

directed and supported from centres of power in Rome, Madrid, and Lisbon," the *Horoscopium Catholicum Societatis Iesu* world map appropriately envisions Jesuit missions as "a single world-spanning enterprise."[16]

At the same time, the interconnectedness of the nodes allows us to loosely map possible transmissions of art objects and ideas as they moved through Jesuit networks. Innovations in Jesuit iconography and devotional images regularly developed as responses to local circumstances in the provincial nodes depicted in the *Horoscopium Catholicum Societatis Iesu*. These new visual forms could take root in a province and flourish in the immediate surrounding area, while also making larger geographic leaps along the major branches, either towards or away from the Roman trunk around which all provinces are oriented. The close proximity of one branch's leaves to another demonstrates that artistic transmission could bypass Rome altogether. Some branches defy geography, with Brazil placed next to Japan and the Philippines next to Chile. Instead of replicating the actual locations of these places in the world, they are grouped according to imperial relationships. The Portuguese province is placed at the end of the branch that contains Goa, Malabar, China, Japan, and Brazil, while Spanish colonies similarly shoot off the branch that represents the Spanish provinces. These colonial relationships and accompanying mercantile connections between metropole and colony could greatly facilitate the movement of Jesuits and the art they often carried with them.[17]

St Francis Xavier: His Life and Image

As Jesuits established residences and missions throughout the world, they would foster devotions and cults that that were particular to the Society. This is nowhere more evident than with Jesuits' promotion of their own saints, such as Sts Ignatius of Loyola, Francis Xavier, Francis Borgia, Aloysius Gonzaga, and Stanislaus Kostka. The cult of St Francis Xavier proved to be exceptionally successful. Born in 1506 to Basque nobles in the kingdom of Navarre, Xavier met Ignatius of Loyola as a student at the University of Paris, inspiring his conversion to a more pious life.[18]

---

16 L. Clossey, *Salvation and Globalization in the Early Jesuit Missions* (Cambridge: Cambridge University Press, 2008), 3.

17 The power structures inherent in the *Horoscopium Catholicum Societatis Iesu* diagram disqualify it from being considered a rhizome, as described by Gilles Deleuze and Félix Guattari. Deleuze and Guattari posit the "arborescent" as the antithesis of the rhizomatic, functioning as "hierarchical systems with centers of significance and subjectification." Gilles Deleuze and Félix Guattari, *A Thousand Plateaus* (New York: Continuum, 2004), 7 and 16.

18 For the most comprehensive modern biography of Xavier, see G. Schurhammer, *Francis Xavier: His Life, His Times* (Rome: Jesuit Historical Institute, 1973–82).

Loyola and Xavier, along with their other companions, travelled to Rome where they met with Pope Paul III (p. 1534–49) to get their new order approved. However, even before official status of the Society was officially confirmed, King João III of Portugal (r. 1521–57) urged the Jesuit companions to come to Lisbon in order to become missionaries in Portuguese territories overseas.[19] On April 7, 1541, Xavier departed for India from Lisbon on board the *Santiago* and arrived in Goa a year later, on May 6, 1542, where he stayed for four months before beginning his mission on the Pearl Fishery Coast. Over the next ten years, Xavier preached the Gospel throughout Portuguese Asia, including Malacca, the Maluku Islands, and Japan. By January 1552, Xavier had returned to India and was preparing for an attempt to secretly enter Ming China; however, on the way there, he stopped on the island of Shangchuan, where his peregrinations came to an end. He died of a fever on December 3, 1552, and was initially buried on the beach of the island. His incorrupt body was exhumed two months later and taken to Malacca, where it stayed for less than a year before being sent to Goa.

While Xavier was still alive, he began to acquire saintly renown throughout Portuguese Asia and in Europe, as rumors of his miracles began trickling back to Rome and Lisbon.[20] When news of Xavier's death finally reached Europe in 1555, authorities immediately expressed interest in conducting investigations into the missionary's miraculous deeds for the purpose of beginning a canonisation campaign.[21] King João III of Portugal wrote to Pedro de Mascarenhas, the newly appointed viceroy to India, instructing him to begin documenting Xavier's miracles, a process that involved interviewing witnesses in Malacca, Bassein, Cochin, and Goa.[22] Devotion to Xavier on the part of non-European rulers also contributed to this drive for sanctification with the Japanese daimyō of Bungo, Ôtomo Yoshishige (1530–87), writing that he would like Xavier to be canonised so that "we can build

19 Schurhammer, *Francis Xavier*, I: 542.

20 For example, in 1548, Xavier was delayed in his return to Goa. According to a letter sent back to Lisbon from Goa, a rumor spread that Xavier had died in Cape Comorin and his supporters immediately began to gather evidence of his miracles to begin a canonisation campaign. J.A. Hardon, "The Miracles of St Francis Xavier," *American Ecclesiastical Review* 127 (1952) 248–63, on pp. 251–2. *Selectae Indiarum Epistolae* (Florence: Ex Typographia a SS. Conceptione, 1887), 54.

21 M.C. Osswald, "The Iconography and Cult of Francis Xavier," *Archivum historicum Societatis Iesu* 71, no. 142 (2002) 259–77, on pp. 260–3. Franco Mormando, "The Making of the Second Jesuit Saint: The Campaign for the Canonization of Francis Xavier, 1555–1622," in Franco Mormando and Jill G. Thomas (eds.), *Francis Xavier and the Jesuit Missions in the Far East: An Anniversary Exhibition of Early Printed Works from the Jesuitana Collection of the John H. Burns Library, Boston College* (Boston: Jesuit Institute, 2006) 9–23.

22 Osswald, "The Iconography and Cult," 260. Josef Wicki and John Gomes, eds., *Documenta Indica*, 4 vols., vol. 70–3, Monumenta historica Societatis Iesu (Rome: Monumenta Historica Soc. Iesu, 1948), III: 470–1.

churches and altars to him, set up images of him, celebrate his Mass, and pray daily for his intercession."[23]

The Jesuits' ceaseless promotion of the cult of Francis Xavier, involving the global dispersal of hagiographic texts, images, and relics, eventually came to fruition with his official beatification in 1619 and his canonisation in 1622. After he officially became a saint, the number of churches and chapels dedicated to Xavier worldwide increased dramatically, necessitating a concurrent increase in the number of visual representations of him. On Jesuit missions both within and outside of Europe, Xaverian images had the ability to perform vital "cultural work," to borrow a phrase from Simon Ditchfield.[24] In the border zones of Roman Catholicism and the territories of Iberian empires, these visual representations had the agency to shape worldviews, advance imperial ideologies, and engender conversion.[25] Jesuits and Iberian colonial officials worldwide used paintings, prints, and sculptures depicting St Francis Xavier for a variety of purposes, from sanctifying spaces that had previously been non-Christian to propagandising a global vision of the Church that included peoples from all known continents. Jesuits continued to utilise the power of Xaverian representations in the border zones of Catholicism within and outside of Europe throughout the seventeenth century. As the years progressed, the images representing this missionary saint became more complex, chapels commemorating Xavier became even grander, and cycles of his life and miracles began to contain dozens of paintings or prints. By the beginning of the eighteenth century, artists were able to draw upon more than a century of iconographic development to create large eclectic printed and painted series. Retracing the sources, motifs, and inspirations upon which these artists drew allows us to reconstruct the world-spanning nature of the Jesuit network, envisioning the transcontinental connections that existed between their far-flung provinces.

The Xaverian Series of Quito: Its History and Sources

Returning to the *Horoscopium Catholicum Societatis Iesu*, among the leaves that sprout from the province "Nova Granata" is one labeled Quito, one of the most important Jesuit centres in South America. Jesuits arrived in the city in 1572 and had opened a college there by 1586. By 1700, the Jesuits ran a university, five colleges, a seminary, and a novitiate in Quito, a city that many of these missionaries came to

23 Quoted in Mormando, "The Making of the Second Jesuit Saint," 10.

24 S. Ditchfield, "Thinking with the Saints: Sanctity and Society in the Early Modern World," *Critical Inquiry* 35 (2009) 555–84, on p. 555.

25 R. Miller, "Patron Saint of a World in Crisis: Early Modern Representations of St Francis Xavier in Europe and Asia" (PhD diss., University of Pittsburgh 2016).

view as "a new Rome, spreading civility to the margins and leading the spiritual conquest of its own periphery."[26] Construction had begun on their magnificent church, known as La Compañia, in 1605 and during the eighteenth century, artists were hard at work decorating the façade and manufacturing the sumptuous gilded *retablos* that would adorn each chapel of the church.[27] The Jesuits in Quito were economically prosperous in the mid-eighteenth century and the years leading up to their expulsion from Spanish territories in 1767 were some of their most profitable, leaving them with more than enough income to finance lavish works of art.[28]

One example is a series of thirty paintings depicting the life and miracles of St Francis Xavier, dated to sometime between 1750 and 1767.[29] This is one of the few complete Xaverian series anywhere in the world to survive the Jesuit expulsion intact; many other cycles were broken up or outright destroyed.[30] It is unknown which Jesuit institution in Quito commissioned these paintings, but they were acquired by the Mercedarians after 1767, either through purchase at auction or as a gift from the government after the confiscation of Jesuit possessions following the suppression. Art historians have detected the presence of multiple hands in this large painted series, likely a master and his assistants. However, the name of

---

26 C. Fernández-Salvador, "Jesuit Missionary Work in the Imperial Frontier: Mapping the Amazon in Seventeenth-Century Quito," in Stephanie Kirk and Sarah Rivett (eds.), *Religious Transformations in the Early Modern Americas* (Philadelphia: University of Pennsylvania Press, 2014), 205–28, on p. 209.

27 A. Kennedy Troya, ed. *Arte de la Real Audiencia de Quito, siglos XVII–XIX* (Hondarribia: Nerea, 2002), 91.

28 While some of the *retablos* in La Compañía were financed through alms, a report sent to Rome in 1752 specifically mentions that incomes from Jesuit estates were enough to pay for the gilded *retablos* dedicated to St Ignatius of Loyola and St Francis Xavier, as well as to gild half of the church. Troya, *Arte de la Real Audiencia*, 91. For Jesuit estates and profits in the eighteenth century, see K. Andrien, *The Kingdom of Quito, 1690–1830: The State and Regional Development* (Cambridge: Cambridge University Press, 2002), 102–6. On the Jesuit expulsion from Spanish territories, see M. Mörner, "The Expulsion of the Jesuits from Spain and Spanish America in 1767 in Light of Eighteenth-Century Regalism," *The Americas* 23, no. 2 (1966) 156–64.

29 S.L. Stratton-Pruitt, ed. *The Art of Painting in Colonial Quito* (Philadelphia: Saint Joseph's University Press, 2012), 165–76. M.G. Torres Olleta, *Redes iconográficas: San Francisco Javier en la cultura visual del barroco* (Navarre: Universidad de Navarra, 2009), 238–58. A. Rodríguez G. De Ceballos, "Las pinturas de la vida de San Francisco Javier del convento de la Merced de Quito," *Anales de Museo de América* XV (2007). *Filipinas: Puerta de oriente de Legazpi a Malaspina* (Madrid: Sociedad Estatal para la Acción Cultural Exterior, 2003) 89–101, on pp. 151–4. Photographs of the entire series can be found in Torres Olleta, *Redes iconográficas*, 672–707.

30 C. Fernández-Salvador, "The Life of St Francis Xavier" in Suzanne L. Stratton-Pruitt (ed.) *The Art of Painting in Colonial Quito* (Philadelphia: Saint Joseph's University Press, 2012), 165–76, on pp. 165–6. Rodríguez G. De Ceballos, "Las pinturas de la vida," 89.

this master painter remains unknown.[31] Traditionally, these paintings had been attributed to Fernando de Ribera, an artist born to a Sevillian family in Panama. He trained as an artist and joined the Jesuit order as a lay brother, taking the name Hernando de la Cruz.[32] However, this artist died in 1644 and the Quito series has been convincingly dated to the mid-eighteenth century based on an analysis of its iconographic and visual sources. Many of the figures in paintings wear eighteenth-century costumes and some of the miracles illustrated in the series took place in the 1730s and 1740s. Furthermore, several of the European print sources utilised by the artists were created in the mid-eighteenth century, making a seventeenth-century date impossible.[33]

The lack of certain information about the artist responsible for this series creates challenges for its interpretation and contextualisation. However, the question of authorship in a Jesuit context is almost always a complicated one, even when the artist is known. Evonne Levy has noted that one of the factors that led to nineteenth- and twentieth-century art historians' denigration of Jesuit art was the perception that the Jesuit corporate institution often subsumed the individual creativity of the artist. Levy refers to this as the *Jesuit-Ur Author* theory, which "rests on the assumption that the Society of Jesus was the 'author' of all its productions.... collapsing any distinction between the Society (which had its own internal rules), external patrons (who had their own taste), and artist."[34] Levy rightly asks, "Who is the 'author' of a Jesuit building paid for by an external patron, guided by the Society's advisors, and designed by a Jesuit or, for that matter, a non-Jesuit artist?"[35] In another essay, titled "Che cos'è un autore/architetto gesuita?" Levi explores these ideas further.[36] Basing her argument on Michel Foucault's "Qu'est-ce qu'un auteur?" (1969) and Roland Barthes's "La mort de l'auteur" (1967), Levy demonstrates that it is almost impossible to discuss the intentions of the artist when analysing Jesuit works of art due to the multitude of actors involved in the commissions. Instead, it is more useful to follow the methodology of Barthes and consider these projects to be products not of a single author or even multiple authors, but a weaving together of multiple "centres of culture."

---

31 X. Carcelén, "San Francisco Javier convierte a la fe a muchos pueblos de África y Oriente" in *Filipinas: Puerta de oriente de Legazpi a Malaspina* (Madrid: Sociedad Estatal para la Acción Cultural Exterior, 2003), 251–52, on p. 251. Torres Olleta, *Redes iconográficas*, 239.

32 R.G. De Ceballos, "Las pinturas de la vida," 91.

33 R.G. De Ceballos, "Las pinturas de la vida," 91.

34 E. Levy, *Propaganda and the Jesuit Baroque* (Berkeley: University of California Press, 2004), 32–3.

35 Levy, *Propaganda and the Jesuit Baroque*, 33.

36 E. Levy, "Che cos'è un autore/architetto gesuita?," in Alberta Battists (ed.), *Andrea Pozzo* (Milan: Luni, 1996).

Taking inspiration from this methodology, it is possible to also think of the Quito series as a product of various "centres of culture," including the Society of Jesus (at both the corporate and local level), the artist (who may or may not have also been a Jesuit), and perhaps an external patron who represented the elite Creole culture of eighteenth-century Quito. The eclectic nature of the visual and textual sources accessed by the artist further complicate these pictures, meaning that we must also consider the cultural influence of the print centres of Europe, like Antwerp and Augsburg, on this series. In turn, not all of the European prints used as a source by the Quito artist are actually original compositions: several of them copy paintings created for Jesuit churches in places like Antwerp and Rome. Finally, it is vital to consider the subject matter of the Xaverian cycle itself. For the most part, these paintings represent scenes that took place in Portuguese Asia in the mid-sixteenth century, a "centre of culture" far removed from that of eighteenth-century Quito. The artist's ability to imagine this different world was conditioned by the visual material to which he had access, which included European prints with compositions filled with Asian stereotypes and generically exotic figures and locations. The artist may also have been familiar with Asian luxury goods imported to the Americas via the Manila Galleon trade route.[37]

As Alfonso Rodríguez G. de Ceballos and María Torres Olleta have noted, the artist and his Jesuit advisors did not copy a complete series of prints depicting the life and miracles of St Francis Xavier. Instead, they drew from a wide-ranging collection of various sources, demonstrating that they must have had access to an extensive library.[38] The sources used by the artist can be grouped into several different categories. The most common group consists of prints that were copies of famous European paintings representing St Francis Xavier. Many of these are compositions that could be described as having "gone viral,"[39] meaning images that have reached the point where they are "copied on a large scale by different

---

37 K.H. Corrigan, "Asian Luxury Exports to Colonial America," in Dennis A. Carr and Gauvin Alexander Bailey (eds.), *Made in the Americas: The New World Discovers Asia* (Boston: Museum of Fine Arts 2015), 39–52. G. Alexander Bailey, *Art of Colonial Latin America* (London: Phaidon Press, 2014), 65.

38 Rodríguez G. De Ceballos, "Las pinturas de la vida," 91. Torres Olleta, *Redes iconográficas*, 245. Both Rodríguez G. de Ceballos and Torres Olleta, as well as Ricardo Fernández Gracia, have been successful at identifying many of the print sources described below. R. Fernández Gracia, *El fondo iconográfico del P. Schurhammer: La memoria de Javier en imágenes* (Pamplona: Cátedra de Patrimonio y Arte Navarro, 2006). These sources are also documented in the Project on the Engraved Sources of Colonial Art (PESSCA), University of California, Davis.

39 Stephanie Porras has applied the concept of "virality" to early modern compositions like Maerten de Vos's *St Michael the Archangel*, which circulated throughout Europe, Asia, and the Americas, being copied innumerable times and in various ways. S. Porras, "Going Viral? Maerten de Vos's *St Michel the Arcangel*," *Nederlands Kunsthistorisch Jaarboech* 66, no. 1 (2016).

groups within [a] short period of time."[40] Although these viral compositions often began with a single creator, these designs took on a life of their own after they were copied in print and disseminated along multidirectional networks like that of the Jesuits, being constantly reinterpreted in each location where they were copied yet again. One salient example in the Quito series is the painting that represents Francis Xavier as a generic miracle worker. There is nothing about the painting that can be tied to any one particular prodigious act, and the inscription on the frame of the painting is actually completely unrelated to the scene.[41] The original version of this composition, however, is one of the most famous paintings of Francis Xavier, the *Miracles of St Francis Xavier* altarpiece, created in 1617–18 by Peter Paul Rubens (1577–1640) for the Jesuit Church of Antwerp (Fig. 2).[42] Created before Xavier's official beautification and canonisation, Rubens's altarpiece helped to inspire devotion to Xavier in Antwerp in the years of the canonisation campaign and also played a fundamental role in the development of a nascent iconography for this venerable missionary who was not yet a saint.[43] In the 1630s, the composition, which depicts a variety of the miracles performed by Xavier during his mission to Asia, was engraved by Marinus Robyn van der Goes (ca. 1599–ca. 1639) and went on to have a profound effect on works of art representing the preaching, baptisms, or miracles of St Francis Xavier. In the mid-seventeenth century, a relic

---

40 Porras, "Going Viral?," 59.

41 See image 1500B in the PESSCA database (https://colonialart.org/archives/subjects/saints/individual-saints/francis-xavier/1500a-1500b). It describes a time when Xavier encountered a Portuguese sailor who had not been to confession in eighteen years. The saint took his confession and, despite the fact that the man had committed many sins, gave the sailor a penance of only one "Our Father" and one "Hail Mary." Later, the sailor encountered Xavier in a grove of trees flagellating himself and he realized that the saint had taken on the punishment for his sins. O. Torsellino, *De vita Francisci Xaverii. Qui primus e Societate Iesu in Indiam & Iaponiam evangelium invexit.* (Rome: Luigi Zannetti, 1596), 134–6. Torres Olleta, *Redes iconográficas*, 247. María Torres Olleta suggests that the original painting representing the penitent sailor may have been lost and its frame used on a different painting, or that the artist and his Jesuit advisors changed their minds about the subject after the frame was completed but before the painting was made. Torres Olleta, *Redes iconográficas*, 238.

42 There is an extensive bibliography on this painting. The foundational study is Graham Smith, "Rubens' Altargemälde des hl. Ignatius von Loyola und des hl. Franz Xaver für die Jesuitenkircher in Antwerpen," *Jahrbuch der Kunsthistorischen Sammlungen in Wien* 29 (1969). More recent studies include Anna Knaap, "*The Miracles of Francis Xavier* and the Visual Tradition of Broken Idols," in C. van Eck (ed.), *Idols and Museum Pieces: The Nature of Sculpture, Its Historiography and Exhibition History, 1640–1880* (Boston: De Gruyter, 2017) 65–84. B. Uppenkamp, "'Indian' Motifs in Peter Paul Rubens's *The Martyrdom of St Thomas* and *The Miracles of St Francis Xavier*," *Nederlands Kunsthistorisch Jaarboech* 66, no. 1 (2016) 112–41; W. Sauerländer, *The Catholic Rubens: Saints and Martyrs* (Los Angeles: Getty Research Institute, 2014).

43 C.M. Boeckl, "Plague Imagery as Metaphor for Heresy in Rubens' The Miracles of Saint Francis Xavier," *Sixteenth Century Journal* 27, no. 4 (1996) 979–995, on p. 982.

of the missionary saint's arm arrived in Mechelen, a Flemish city close to Antwerp, and immediately, a windfall of miracles took place in the saint's name. Various printmakers, including Peeter Clouwet (1629–70) and Matthäus Küsel (1629– ca. 1681), took the Rubens composition, subtracted the Asian figures that Rubens provided, and added the specific miracles that took place in Mechelen.[44] These prints also had a vibrant afterlife and were used as sources by artists like Peter Sion (died in 1695), a Flemish painter who received commissions from Jesuits in Pamplona.[45] It is likely that the Quito painting is based on one of these so-called "Miracles of Mechelen" prints.

Another category of sources used by the painter in Quito includes prints of famous European paintings that originally had nothing to do with St Francis Xavier. For example, one image in the Quiteño cycle represents an incident that took place during Xavier's journey from Rome to Lisbon in the company of Pedro Mascarenhas (1470–1555), the Portuguese ambassador to the Holy See and later viceroy of India. While crossing the Alps, Francis Xavier saved the life of the ambassador's secretary after this man fell from his horse into a snow bank among some slippery craggy rocks. The secretary was in danger of falling even further down the cliff into a dangerous river, but Francis Xavier quickly dismounted from his horse and pulled him to safety.[46] The painter of the Quito cycle has selected to copy the motif of the man falling from the horse from Peter Paul Rubens's *The Conversion of St Paul* in the Courtauld Gallery, London (1610–12), which had been engraved by Schelte Bolswert.[47] St Paul has become the ambassador's secretary and the man who leans down to aid the temporarily blinded apostle in Rubens's painting has been transformed into St Francis Xavier. The artist in Quito also adapted two prints from an illustrated life of St Ignatius of Loyola, engraved by Jean Baptiste Barbé (ca. 1578–1649) after designs by Rubens.[48] The original prints depicted St Ignatius of Loyola studying at grammar school in Barcelona and then exorcising demons. In Quito, these prints became sources for paintings of St Francis Xavier teaching a philosophy course at the University of Paris and then performing exorcisms, an act

44 These miracles are described in G. Grumsel, *Mechlinia illustrata luce miraculum S. Francisci Xaverii* (Mechelen: Linstsii, 1666). The text, however, postdates some of the prints. R. Fernández Gracia, "San Francisco Javier patrono: Imágenes para el taumaturgo de ambos mundos," in R. Fernández Gracia (ed.), *San Francisco Javier en las artes: El poder de la imagen* (Pamplona: Fundación Caja Navarra, 2006), 155–99, on p. 174.

45 R. Fernández Gracia, ed. *San Francisco Javier en las artes: El poder de la imagen* (Pamplona: Fundación Caja Navarra, 2006), 372–3.

46 Torsellino, *De vita Francisci Xaverii*, 29.

47 Torres Olleta, *Redes iconográficas*, 244–5.

48 Torres Olleta, *Redes iconográficas*, 242 and 251.

Fig. 2 Peter Paul Rubens, *The Miracles of St. Francis Xavier,* oil on canvas, 1617–1618, Kunshistorisches Museum, Vienna, Austria, Wikimedia Commons.

that is not usually considered to be one of Xavier's most famous miracles and is not tied to any one particular incident.

The Xaverian painter in Quito also utilised book illustrations from printed histories of the Society and Jesuit thesis prints. The thesis prints generally date to the mid-eighteenth century and were, for the most part, printed in Augsburg. Their elaborate Rococo decorative elements and complicated allegories provided the Quito painter with more artistically current source material, as compared to the seventeenth-century designs that were used for most of the other images. As described by Louise Rice, thesis prints were complex broadsheets commissioned by doctoral students on the occasion of their defences and played an important role in the pageantry of such events. The broadsheets would summarize the student's thesis and the image would usually be extremely erudite in order to show off the candidate's learning and taste.[49] The Quito paintings that are based off of the thesis prints tend to be the most complicated for this reason. In keeping with the nature of the thesis prints, these images are also the more allegorical of the series, rather than being concrete depictions of exact events pulled from Xaverian hagiography. The painting depicting the calling of St Francis Xavier to his vocation as a missionary is a particularly good example.[50] Based on a thesis print by Gottlieb Heiss, printed in Augsburg in 1739 for a student's defence at Charles University in Prague, this iconography is unusual.[51] It shows an abstract representation of Xavier's conversion to a more pious life after meeting St Ignatius of Loyola, who is not actually pictured in the scene. Instead, we only see a piece of paper near Xavier with the words, QUID PRODEST HOMINI, the first three words of the famous phrase from Matthew 16:26 that Ignatius spoke to Xavier in order to convince him to give up his quest for worldly and ecclesiastical glory: "What good will it be for a man to gain the whole world, yet forfeit his soul?" The sphere above Xavier represents secular power, which the future missionary renounces, but also the world that he will later help win over to Catholicism and the true faith. On the ground at his feet are symbols of military and intellectual triumph, representing accomplishments he will no longer pursue. In the background, there is a seascape with a ship and an exotic regal figure, wearing the stereotypical Amerindian feather headdress and skirt, symbolising the kings of the Indies that Xavier will become famous for having converted to Christianity.[52]

Scholars like María Gabriela Torres Olleta, Alfonso Rodríguez G. de Ceballos, and researchers working on the Project on the Engraved Sources of Colonial Art (PESSCA) database have uncovered many of the immediate print sources utilised by the artist responsible for the Quito Xaverian series. However, it is vital to acknowledge that these prints were only the most immediate sources for the Quiteño artist and were rarely the ultimate origin point for particular Xaverian motifs and themes. Tracing these visual ideas back through their various iterations reveals the global connections that were engendered by Jesuit travel and missionary work in the early modern world.

---

49 Rice, "'Pomis Sua Nomina Servant,'" 197 and 203–5.

50 See image 2211B in the PESSCA database, https://colonialart.org/archives/subjects/saints/individual-saints/francis-xavier#c2211a-2211b.

51 The correspondence between the Quito painting and the Heiss print is noted in the PESSCA database. See image 2211A, https://colonialart.org/archives/subjects/saints/individual-saints/francis-xavier#c2211a-2211b.

52 Although royal baptisms are some of the acts most commonly celebrated in visual representations of Xavier, there is no evidence that he actually performed any during his mission to Asia. He certainly never converted any Amerindian kings.

A True Likeness Transmitted Across the World

Moving away from Quito on the *Horoscopium Catholicum Societatis Iesu*, back down the trunk towards the Roman root, we pause in the Neapolitan province and find the leaf labelled *Napoli*. In Naples in 1634, a young Jesuit named Marcello Mastrilli (1603–37) had been helping to construct some decorations to celebrate the Feast of the Immaculate Conception in the Jesuit college there.[53] He was gravely injured when a hammer fell from some scaffolding and struck him on the head. It seemed as if Mastrilli would die, until he gazed upon a painting of St Francis Xavier that was hung on the wall of the infirmary. Suddenly, the painted representation walked off of its surface and began to speak to Mastrilli, asking, "So what's going on? Do you want to die or go to India?"[54] The young Jesuit chose the latter and made a vow that if he were healed, he would go to spread the word of God in Asia. Mastrilli recovered and went to Goa and later, Japan, where he was martyred in 1637.

In Quito, the painter of the Xaverian series included a representation of this event. Mastrilli is in bed, with his head wrapped in a bandage, as Xavier stands by his side, reaching out to him. The other Jesuits in the room who are attending to Mastrilli do not see the saint. This image includes a picture within a picture, as the painting of Xavier that inspired Mastrilli's vision can be seen hung on the wall. This half-length portrait of Xavier is an example of one of the oldest and most common ways of representing the saint. This image operates within the tradition of the *vera effigie*, or true likeness, and can be traced back to one of the first documented images of Francis Xavier, created several decades after his death in 1552.

On December 31, 1583, Alessandro Valignano (1539–1606), the Visitor of Missions in the Indies, wrote to Claudio Acquaviva, the superior general of the Jesuit order from 1581 to 1615, and explained that he had commissioned an artist in Goa to paint a portrait of the deceased Francis Xavier. Thirty years after the missionary's incorrupt corpse had arrived in Goa, the body was supposedly so perfectly preserved that the artist was able to use it as a model. Valignano went on to explain that he was concerned that this image be as accurate as possible, so he asked Jesuits

53 I.G. Županov, "Passage to India: Jesuit Spiritual Economy between Martyrdom and Profit in the Seventeenth Century," *Journal of Early Modern History* 16 (2012) 1–39. For contemporary accounts of this miracle, see *Relacam de HVM prodigioso milagre: que o glorioso S. Francisco Xauier, Apostolo do Oriente, obrou na cidade de Napeles no anno de 1634*, (Lisbon: Biblioteca Nacional 1989). Leonardo Cinami, *Vita e Morte del Padre Marcello Francisco Mastrilli della Compagnia di Giesù* (Viterbo: [n.p], 1645).

54 "E bem, que se fas? Quereis morrer ou ir para a India?" The *Relacam* states that Xavier was speaking to the young Jesuit in Mastrilli's own Italian tongue, but provides only a Portuguese translation. *Relacam de HVM prodigioso milagre*, 8v. See also Županov, "Passage to India," 129–31.

in Goa who had known Xavier in life to confirm its truthfulness. Along with this letter, Valignano included a copy of the painting.[55] This copy of the first portrait of Xavier, originating in the periphery of the Catholic world, was then used as a source for a variety of prints, including many of the frontispieces of the earliest Xaverian hagiographies printed in Europe. In turn, these images also circulated throughout the world via networks established by Jesuit missionaries, thus moving back to the periphery and serving as sources for non-European works of art, such as the so-called Kobe Portrait of Francis Xavier, painted by an anonymous Japanese artist in the early seventeenth century.[56]

Neither the original kept in Goa nor the copy sent to Rome survive; however, this initial depiction informed the way that Francis Xavier was represented from that point onwards, at least in terms of the saint's appearance. Valignano's care to create an accurate *vera effigie* gave this work of art an aura of authority, resulting in the saint's physical characteristics being relatively the same in almost every Xaverian image created in the early modern period. Early copies of the image Valignano sent to Rome are now preserved in the Collegio Romano and the Jesuit *casa professa* in Rome.[57] In both of these paintings, we see an image of Francis Xavier that would be repeated over and over again throughout the centuries, including in the eighteenth-century paintings created in Quito: straight black hair with bangs, cut long enough on the sides to touch or cover his ears, a short beard and moustache, light complexion, and dark eyes lifted to heaven.[58] This generally conforms to depictions of his appearance written by his earliest biographers. Manuel Teixeira (1536–90), who had worked alongside Xavier in India when he was only sixteen years old, described him as follows:

> Father Francis was taller than he was short. His face was well proportioned, white and rosy, happy and full of grace. His eyes were between brown and black, his forehead was large, his hair and beard black. He wore a poor, clean, and loose robe, without cape or any

55 This letter is summarized in G. Schurhammer, "Das Wahre Bild des hl. Franz Xaver?," in *Gesammelte Studien: Varia* (Lisbon: Centro de Estudos Historicos Ultramarinos, 1965), 213–16, on p. 214. See also P. Andueza Unanua, "La vera effigies de San Francisco Javier: la creación de una imagen postridentina," in R. Fernández (ed.), *San Francisco Javier en las artes: El poder de la imagen*, Gracia (Pamplona: Fundación Caja Navarra, 2006), 96–119, on p.101.

56 G. Vlam, "The Portrait of S. Francis Xavier in Kobe," *Zeitschrift für Kunstgeschichte* 42, no. 1 (1979) 48–60.

57 Andueza Unanua, "La vera effigies," 101.

58 J.K. Cadogan et al., *Wadsworth Atheneum Paintings II: Italy and Spain* (Hartford, CT: Wadsworth Atheneum 1991), 303–4.

other covering because that was how poor priests of India dressed. When he walked, he lifted his robe a little with both hands. He almost always had his eyes set on heaven…[59]

Xavier is never shown in visual representations dressed in the manner of Indian priests; however, Teixeira's description of the missionary lifting his robe with both hands would become quite common in early images of Xavier. The bust-length copy of Valignano's image that is now in the Roman *casa professa* shows a variation upon this motif, in which Xavier is opening his cassock. According to letters written in Goa by those who knew him, Xavier was accustomed to doing this in order to cool the burning of his heart that resulted from his great love of God.[60] In Quito, almost two centuries after Valignano first commissioned an artist in Goa to create a *vera effigie* from Xavier's corpse, we see a similar bust-length image of St Francis Xavier pasted on the wall behind Marcello Mastrilli's sick bed: a dark-haired man with dark eyes and a light complexion, opening his robe to cool the inflamed passion of his heart.

Preaching to the Four Continents

Almost as soon as Francis Xavier was canonised, images of him preaching to or baptising large crowds of extra-Europeans became some of the most common representations of the new saint. In Rome, the ephemeral decorations that accompanied the festivities celebrating the 1622 canonisation were influential on further iconographic development. Although these images do not survive, their subjects were documented in a 1622 description by Giovanni Briccio and most of their compositions were copied by a French (or Flemish) printmaker named Valérien Regnard (active ca. 1622–50) in his *Sancti Francisci Xaverii Indiarum Apostoli Societatis…*[61] Both Briccio's text and Regnard's pamphlet contain multiple references

59 Teixeira's account is the first biography of Francis Xavier, written in 1575 to record his personal experiences with the missionary, as well as the memories of others in Goa who had had direct interactions with him. Although well-known in Jesuit circles and often used as a source by later biographers, a Spanish translation of Teixeira's manuscript was not published until 1912 (the original Portuguese text is lost). Mariano Lecina, ed. *Monumenta Xaveriana: Scripta varia de sancto Francisco Xaverio*, vol. 43, Monumenta historica Societatis Iesu (Matriti: Typis Augustini Avrial, 1912), 815–918. See also Andueza Unanua, "La vera effigies," 100. F. García Gutiérrez, "Iconografia de San Francisco Javier en Oriente," *Archivum historicum Societatis Iesu* 71, no. 142 (2002) 279–301, on pp. 281–2.

60 See the letter from António de Quadros to Tiago Mirón, written in Goa and dated December 8, 1555. Lecina, *Monumenta Xaveriana: Scripta varia*, 950. Osswald, "The Iconography and Cult," 268.

61 Giovanni Briccio, *Relatione della solenne processione fatta in Roma nella trasportatione de' Stendardi de' Gloriosi Santi* (Rome: Giacomo Mascardi, 1622). P. Tacchi Venturi, "La canonizzazione e la processione dei cinque Santi negli scritti e nei disegni di due contemporanei (Giovanni Bricci, Paolo

to Xavier's activities preaching and baptising. One of the most famous incidents was the so-called "miracle of the languages," in which Xavier was once preaching to a crowd in Asia filled with people from "diverse nations" and miraculously, all of them could hear Xavier speaking their own native tongues.[62] This miraculous acquisition of foreign languages clearly casts the Jesuit missionary saint as a new Apostle, filled with Pentecostal zeal to spread the word of God and the power to transcend language barriers and speak to all people of the world. Briccio wrote that a painting of this subject was hung on the left-hand side of the façade of the Gesù in Rome, and Regnard included a copy of that painting in his pamphlet that shows Xavier preaching to a crowd filled with figures wearing generically exotic headgear.

These images of Xavier among crowds of extra-Europeans are another example of viral Xaverian images. It is virtually impossible to trace which prints influenced which paintings and vice versa due to the sheer numbers of copies and variations made in an enormous variety of places throughout the Jesuit network. The members of the crowd, however, often vary dramatically from artwork to artwork. In some, like Francesco Curradi's *St Francis Xavier Preaching*, commissioned for the Jesuit church of the *casa professa* in Florence (now San Giovannino degli Scolopi) around the year 1622, the assembly of people includes individuals who are clearly intended to be allegories of the four continents: Europe, Asia, Africa, and the Americas. The inclusion of these allegories in scenes of Xavier preaching successfully positions him as a universal saint working to unite the four continents of the world in Christianity and bring about the ultimate triumph of the Catholic Church. Other artists, however, created crowds that are more geographically confusing, where there are markers of otherness but they are combined in strange ways (for example, African figures wearing feathers to identify them as Amerindians, as is seen in Godfried Maes's *St Francis Xavier Preaching*, commissioned for the Chapel of the Castillo de Javier, 1692). Yet other images contain people wearing a hodgepodge of generically exotic clothing and headgear that seems to have no basis in reality.

The painter in Quito has chosen yet another strategy for his representation of Xavier preaching on the Pearl Fishery Coast in India. Instead of a realistically

---

Guidotti Borghese)," in *La canonizzazione dei Santi Ignazio di Loiola e Francesco Saverio* (Roma: Grafia, S.A.I. Industrie Grafiche, 1922), 70. Valérien Regnard, *S. Francisci Xaverii Ind: apli Societ: Iesv: qvædã miracvla* (Rome: n.p., 1622). Not many copies of this pamphlet survive. I consulted the copy in the John J. Burns Library, Boston College and there is another in the Biblioteca del Sanctuario de Loyola, Azpeitia (Guipúzcoa, Spain). Massimo Leone, *Saints and Signs: A Semiotic Reading of Conversion in Early Modern Catholicism* (Berlin: De Gruyter, 2010), 433–46.

62 This is described in the canonisation bull issued by Pope Urban VIII on August 6, 1623. Lecina, *Monumenta Xaveriana: Scripta varia*, 709–10. For another account of the "miracle of the languages," see F. García, *Vida y milagros de San Francisco Xavier de la Compañia de Jesús, Apóstol de las Indias* (Madrid: Marcos Alvarez de Arellano, 1672), 67.

Indian crowd or a fantastical multicultural crowd representing the inhabitants of the entire world, the artist has decided to depict a homogenous crowd of people wearing feathered skirts and headdresses, which by the early seventeenth century had become the signifier *par excellence* for Amerindians.[63] It may seem surprising that an artist actually living in the colonial Americas would make a choice to perpetuate such stereotypes; however, throughout the eighteenth century, artists in Central and South America often utilized feathers to depict non-Christian, non-Europeanized indigenous Americans as a comment on their perceived barbarism. This is often evident in series of *casta* paintings where the artists, having exhaustively categorized all the various racial identities present in the hybrid societies in which they lived, dedicated the last painting to semi-nude figures, wearing only feathers, walking through an untamed jungle (Andrés de Islas's 1774 series, now in the Museo de América, Madrid, is a representative example). For an artist living in a colonial metropolis like Mexico City or Quito, indigenous Americans were considered to be uncivilised others, and were marked as such through the use of feathers. In the Quito painting, Xavier has not begun baptising the crowd; their feathers therefore symbolise the fact that they have not yet officially converted.

Since Francis Xavier never actually stepped foot in the Americas, it is indeed curious that the Quito artist has chosen to depict him converting Amerindians. Throughout the seventeenth century, there had been a concentrated effort among Jesuits in the New World and beyond to cast Xavier as the apostle not only to the East Indies, but also to the West. The key connection here was in Xavier's reputation as a new St Thomas. After Christ's resurrection, the Apostles were filled with the Holy Spirit and given the power to speak the languages of the world; they dispersed and, according to tradition, St Thomas went to India where he died as a martyr in Mylapore, now a district of the city of Chennai.[64] His supposed tomb is still located there and was a pilgrimage destination for European Catholics throughout the Middle Ages. In 1545, Xavier himself went on a pilgrimage to visit the tomb of the apostle.[65] According to Pedro de Ribadeneira, Francis Xavier spent every night for three months in the shrine of Thomas's tomb, praying and supplicating God with tears, asking for a small fraction of the evangelising spirit of St Thomas, whom Xavier desired to imitate. In the morning, Xavier took Thomas as his protector and

---

63 See Chapter 4 in Hugh Honour, *The New Golden Land: European Images of America from the Discoveries to the Present Time* (New York: Pantheon Books, 1975).

64 L. Fernando and G. Gispert-Sauch, *Christianity in India: Two Thousand Years of Faith* (New Delhi: Viking, 2004), 59–60.

65 Schurhammer, *Francis Xavier*, 557–92.

vowed to "renew the old seed that had already been sown."[66] In the early modern period, the idea that St Thomas also went to the New World began to develop.[67] Authors such as Bartolomé de las Casas (ca. 1484–1566) and Antonio de la Calancha (1584–1684) advanced the idea that Thomas had gone to the Americas at some point in his ministry and converted some of the inhabitants to Christianity. Antonio Ruiz de Montoya wrote that the inhabitants of Paraguay converted so willingly that they must have had some memory of the Christian God, a remnant of the faith brought to them by St Thomas, who was the "apostle of the most humble people in the whole world, the blacks and the Indians."[68] Since Francis Xavier was seen as a new St Thomas, it made sense to also argue that he had played a pivotal role in the Christianisation of the Americas. Xavier's hagiographers were happy to admit that he had never touched American soil; however, they were also eager to make the case for his patronage of the New World, as well as the Old. The Spanish edition of Orazio Torsellino's Xaverian biography explained that while Xavier had never touched the land of the Americas, he had

> touched their seas because those who sail to India, fearful of the Cape of Good Hope, swing close to Brazil, the land of America. Also, [Xavier] sailed the sea that is between the Moluccas and New Spain, which some count as being part of America, according to the division of Pope Alexander VI.[69]

The Quito series is, of course, not the only instance in which an artist in Spanish America selected to depict the saint's ministry in the New World. In the baptistery attached to the Capilla de Curahuara de Carangas in the town of Curahuara de Carangas, Boliva, an anonymous Andean artist painted Xavier baptising a group of regal Incans, wearing feather headdresses and chequered tunics. Elisa Vargas Lugo has described this type of image as "contravening history,"[70] relocating Francis Xavier in time and space with the intention of "Americanizing" him.[71] In the Franz Mayer Museum in Mexico City, a painting by Juan Rodríguez Juarez (1675–1728)

66 J. Cuadriello, "Xavier Indiano o los indios sin apóstol," in Ricardo Fernández Gracia (ed.), *San Francisco Javier en las artes: El poder de la imagen* (Pamplona: Fundación Caja Navarra, 2006), 200–33, on p. 203.

67 D.A. Brading, *The First America: The Spanish Monarchy, Creole Patriots, and the Liberal State, 1492–1867* (Cambridge, UK and New York: Cambridge University Press, 1991), 172–4.

68 Quoted and translated in Brading, *The First America*, 174.

69 Quoted in Fernández Gracia, "San Francisco Javier patrono," 164.

70 E. Vargas Lugo, "San Francisco Javier bautizando a un cacique mexica," in *Catálogo: Obras maestras del arte colonial* (Mexico City: UNAM, 1990), 13.

71 R. Ruiz Gomar, "San Francisco Xavier en la pintura de la Nueva España," in Ignacio Arellano, Alejandro González Acosta, and Arnulfo Herrera (eds.), *San Francisco Javier entre dos continentes* (Madrid: Iberamericana, 2007), 222.

similarly depicts Xavier in the midst of baptizing a Mexica chief or king.[72] These images were intended to strengthen community ties between European Catholic priests, indigenous nobility, and commoners in the socially complex environment of the colonial Americas, helping to cement the loyalty of new converts by including representatives of their own on the walls and altars of Christian spaces of worship.[73]

Enemies of the Faith: Fucarandono and the Idols of Japan

Following along the Portuguese branch of the *Horoscopium Catholicum Societatis Iesu*, one passes through Brazil before arriving in Japan. Created in 1646, the print's inclusion of Japan as a Jesuit province represents the Society's wishful thinking. Christianity had been outlawed in Japan since 1614 and the borders of the country officially closed to foreigners since 1638. The Jesuit province of Japan still existed, but was administered from Macao and was a community in exile, with sporadic, mostly unsuccessful, attempts to secretly go back to the Japanese islands. Image cycles depicting the life of St Francis Xavier usually included a significant number of scenes set in Japan. Since Xavier was the first Catholic to ever proselytise there, Japan was important to his image as an intrepid missionary, willing to go to lands that were almost completely unknown to Europeans. Although short-lived, the Japanese mission field also represented one of Xavier's greatest successes; when Xavier first arrived in Japan, there were no Christians there and within a few decades of his departure, there were approximately 200,000. When the Jesuits were expelled, a large community of the faithful was left behind, orphaned without priests to care for their souls. Recapturing Japan for Christendom was a goal that Jesuits continuously hoped to accomplish throughout the early modern era, and visual representations of St Francis Xavier in Japan should be interpreted with this context in mind.

The Quito series contains two Japanese scenes, including a depiction of St Francis Xavier's disputation with Fucarandono, a Buddhist priest, at the court of the daimyō of Bungo, based upon a thesis print by Johann Daniel Herz published in Augsburg before 1748.[74] In the scene, Xavier stands in the midst of a large crowd, gazing upwards at a crucifix. To the right is a group of older bearded men wearing woven

---

72 Some scholars anachronistically identify this figure with Moctezuma. Torres Olleta, *Redes iconográficas*, 232. According to Jaime Cuadriello, the figure in this painting is reminiscent of the costuming used by actors playing Moctezuma in Jesuit plays, particularly in the 1623 festivities celebrating the canonisation of St Francis Xavier in Puebla, Mexico. Cuadriello, "Xavier Indiano," 222.

73 Cuadriello, "Xavier Indiano."

74 See images 2539A and 2539B in the PESSCA database, https://colonialart.org/archives/subjects/saints/individual-saints/francis-xavier#c2539a-2539b.

hats, perhaps references to the *takuhatsugasa* worn by Buddhist monks when traveling or begging for alms, but more likely a stereotypical reference to any manner of conical Asian hats. These "bonzes," as they are called in inscription on the frame, wave around bound books, presumably Buddhist texts that they hope to use to prove Xavier wrong. To the left are people wearing a variety of exotic costumes including turbans and robes made of beautifully-patterned Asian textiles. Several of these figures kneel and also look up at the cross, as if they have just been converted. Other figures wear necklaces decorated with demonic figures, toying with them as if they are preparing to cast their old gods aside. In the background, four semi-nude men with feather headdresses attack a similarly be-feathered idol. This statue looks nothing like a Japanese Buddhist sculpture and instead resembles the classical figure Midas with the ears of an ass.

The conception of Buddhism put forth by this work of art is common in Jesuit texts and images. Even Francis Xavier himself, who had spent years in Japan, misconstrued the religion, equating figures like Amida, the Buddha of the Pure Land, and Shakyamuni, the historical Buddha, with demonic idols.[75] As Makoto Harris Takao notes, Xavier's letters often refer to these figures as "pure inventions of the demons" and dismiss Buddhas as just "men of ancient times."[76] In the painting, the Quito artist similarly reduced Buddhism to an idolatrous religion, echoing the famous *Miracles of St Francis Xavier* altarpiece by Peter Paul Rubens, which includes the detail of a Hindu idol being destroyed through the intercessory power of Xavier. The feathered headdresses worn by the god oddly marks him as being an Amerindian idol, not an Asian Buddha. Pre-conquest, feathers of various types had been used in the Inca Empire as markers of royalty and divinity,[77] and for a Europeanised, Christianised American viewer of the eighteenth century, this headdress might still have evoked the idea of an indigenous deity, now recast as an idol, the sinful nature of which had been thoroughly explained by Jesuits such as José de Acosta.[78] The feathers worn by the iconoclasts function similarly to those worn by the soon-to-be Christian converts in the scene of Xavier preaching described above,

75 M. Harris Takao, "Francis Xavier at the Court of Ôtomo Yoshishige: Representations of Religious Disputation between Jesuits and Buddhits in *La conversione all santa fede del re Bungo gioponese*," *Journal of Jesuit Studies* 3, no. 3 (2016) 451–474, on p. 468.

76 Harris Takao, "Francis Xavier at the Court of Ôtomo Yoshishige," 468. See Saint Francis Xavier, *The Letters and Instructions of Francis Xavier* (St Louis: The Institute of Jesuit Sources, 1992), 298 and 337.

77 The feathers worn by the Buddha in the Quiteño painting are not the gently arcing ostrich feathers that sometimes adorn the Virgin Mary in colonial South American paintings, but instead are "stiff and pointed," which are more common in stereotypical images of Amerindians made for European or Europeanized audiences. Maya Stanfield-Mazzi, *Object and Apparition: Envisioning the Christian Divine in the Colonial Andes* (Tucson: University of Arizona Press, 2013), 154.

78 José de Acosta, *Natural and Moral History of the Indies* (Durham, NC: Duke University Press, 2002).

marking them as not fully assimilated to Christian European culture. Here, these men have only just been persuaded by Xavier of the divine truth of Christianity and, in their zeal for their new faith, have picked up weapons to smash their old god. This interpretation is underscored by the fact that the Quiteño artist has included an additional Amerindian figure who was not a part of Herz's original thesis print. This man had been wearing a necklace adorned with an image of this so-called Buddha, but now that he has heard Xavier's arguments for the Catholic faith, is removing the idol from his neck and presumably will dash it to the ground in the next instant.

Both the Quito painting and its thesis print sources portray this event in Bungo as an unequivocal triumph for Francis Xavier. The Buddhists seem to be giving up and walking out of the frame of the painting to the right, while multiple figures are on the verge of conversion to Christianity.[79] The hagiographies that describe Xavier's encounter with Fucarandono are far more ambiguous. Torsellino wrote that while Xavier won the debate, the king (properly, daimyō) of Bungo, Ōtomo Yoshishige, did not convert to Christianity and instead was inclined to just treat Xavier favourably, which caused the Buddhist priests to be filled with rage.[80] Fernão Mendes Pinto, who was actually present in Bungo at the time, reiterates this, while Dominique Bouhours straightforwardly stated that no one converted as a result of the debate.[81] Instead of depicting the disputation with the Buddhists as being rather anticlimactic, like these texts did, the triumphal eighteenth-century visual representations of the event could be interpreted as an alternative history where Xavier successfully rid Japan of its idols, causing its leaders to embrace the true faith and become the bastion of Asian Christendom that Xavier had hoped it would be.

Conclusion: An Imagined Community of Xaverian Devotees

As we have travelled back and forth through the limbs of the *Horoscopium Catholicum Societatis Iesu*, encountering the various centres of cultures that were interwoven to create a remarkably eclectic series of paintings, we can see how

79 The print upon which this painting is based is extremely triumphal, from its label, "Philosophia triumphata," to the fact that Xavier's defeat of the Buddhists is equated with a scene of the rebel angels being cast out of heaven at the top of the print.

80 Torsellino, *De vita Francisci Xaverii*, 189–91.

81 F. Mendes Pinto, *The Travels of Mendes Pinto* (Chicago: University of Chicago Press, 1989), 489. D. Bouhours, *The Life of St Francis Xavier, of the Society of Jesus, Apostle of India* (Philadelphia: E. Cummiskey, 1841), 314. Ôtomo Yoshishige did eventually convert to Christianity, but it was more than two decades after Xavier's time in Japan. However, out of affection for the Jesuit missionary, Ôtomo took the Christian name Francis at his baptism.

Jesuits and their followers perceived the world. The artist has depicted a vision of an "imaginary community," a Catholic global community created through St Francis Xavier's missionary efforts and, two hundred years after his death, sustained and given cohesion by devotion to the saint and his visual representations. Benedict Anderson was primarily concerned with the concept of nations in his *Imagined Communities* (1983); however, the second chapter of the book discusses the religious communities that he believes preceded the rise of nationalism. Although Anderson primarily understands the pre-modern world's religions as communities "imaginable largely through the medium of a sacred language and written script,"[82] scholars such as Thomas DaCosta Kaufmann and Christopher Nygren have begun linking Anderson's ideas to early modern Catholic devotional networks and asking whether or not such communities can be imagined via images as well.[83] Nygren states, "the imagined community of viewership lay at the heart of the reproducible Christian cult image"[84] and indeed, it was the dissemination and reuse of certain compositions and motifs via global networks like the Jesuits' that helped a Christian in Quito imagine that they were united with Japanese and Indian Christians in the communion of saints, "the spiritual solidarity which binds together the faithful on earth, the souls in purgatory, and the saints in heaven in the organic unity of the same mystical body…."[85] The imagined community envisioned by this Xaverian cycle was created though an amalgamation of ideas that came to Quito by way of Goa, Naples, Antwerp, Japan, Augsburg, and Rome and like the network mapped out in the *Horoscopium Catholicum Societatis Iesu,* is characterized as world-spanning and universal, "coterminous with mankind" itself.[86]

---

82 B. Anderson, *Imagined Communities: Reflections on the Origin and Spread of Nationalism* (New York: Verso, 2016), 13.

83 Kaufmann has written that an imagined community can be "expressed through the veneration of particular saints and their representation in the arts." Kaufmann, *Toward a Geography of Art*, 150–51. Nygren, in his dissertation on icons painted by Titian, examines a similar phenomenon, discussing various copies of Titian's *Ecce Homo* paintings. Nygren writes that in disseminating these copies, Titian created a "devotional network" or "a community of faith united by a common source of devotional inspiration." C. Nygren, "Vibrant Icons: Titian's Art and the Tradition of Christian Image-Making" (PhD diss., Johns Hopkins, 2011), 266–85. I thank Christopher Nygren for pointing me towards this line of thinking.

84 Nygren, "Vibrant Icons," 284–5.

85 J. Sollier, "The Communion of Saints," in *The Catholic Encyclopedia* (New York: Robert Appleton Company, 1908).

86 Anderson, *Imagined Communities*, 7.

Tamara Dominici, Antonio Gerace

From Book to Image

Molanus and the Netherlandish Holy Images

Introduction[1]

The development of the *Devotio moderna* in the second half of the 14th century, spread across both the Francophone and Germanophone world,[2] brought about a re-thinking of faith as an intimate process, which lay people could approach thanks to both a common life and the vernacular reading of the Bible.[3] The lack of a solid education for priests – as Johannes Trithemius (1462–1516), for instance, had denounced in his *Institutio vitae sacerdotalis* (1486) – lay access to religious books in the vernacular – not only the Bible or its parts, but above all the *Imitatio Christi* – and the arrival of humanism in the Low Countries intensified the need for a reform of customs, as Erasmus of Rotterdam (1466–1536) highlighted in his *Moriae Encomium* (1508) and in the *Enchiridion militis Christiani* (1515). The ideas contained therein soon became visually represented by Netherlandish artists, such as Quentin Metsys (1466–1530), who painted a society in moral decline, deformed by the ugliness of sins, thanks to their magnificent capability to thoroughly depict the world in all its elements while hiding symbolic meanings.[4]

When the Reformation arrived, the Low Countries were therefore open to the new Christian doctrines rising in the Holy Roman Empire and in the Old Swiss Confederacy. Protestant churches came into the Netherlands in various confessional 'waves': Lutheranism, Sacramentism (1520s), Anabaptism (1530s), and Calvin-

---

1 This section is authored by Tamara Dominici and Antonio Gerace.

2 M. von Habsburg, *Catholic and Protestant Translations of the* Imitatio Christi, *1425–1650. From Late Medieval Classic to Early Modern Bestseller* (Farnham: Ashgate, 2011) 53. See also W. Scheepsma/ G. van Vliet/G. Warnar (ed.), *Friends of God. Vernacular Literature and Religious Elites in the Rhineland and the Low Countries (1300–1500)* (Rome: Edizioni di Storia e Letteratura, 2018).

3 W. François, "Vernacular Bible Reading and Censorship in Early Sixteenth Century. The Position of the Louvain Theologians", in A. den Hollander/M. Lamberigts (ed.), *Lay Bibles in Europe. 1450–1800* (Louvain: Peeters, 2006) 69–96.

4 T. Dominici, "Erasmus of Rotterdam and Quentin Metsys: a Reassessment", in P. Foresta/F. Meloni (ed.), *Arts, Portraits and Representation in the Reformation Era* (Göttingen: V&R, 2019) 109–22; L. Silver, "Prayer and Laughter: Erasmian Elements in Two Late Metsys Panels", *Erasmus in English* 9 (1978) 17–23; C. Limentani Virdis, "Moralismo e satira nella tarda produzione di Quentin Metsys", *Storia dell'arte* 20 (1974) 19–24.

ism (1560s).[5] The last harshly criticised the Catholic worship of sacred images. Jean Calvin (1509–64) himself in his *Institution de la religion chrétienne* maintained that the production of statues or paintings representing God dishonours his majesty.[6] In 1561,[7] the *Confessio Belgica* by Calvin's disciple Guy de Bray (1522–67), stated at the end of the 29th article that the "false Church" – namely the Roman Catholic one – is infected by two errors: avarice and idolatry.[8] In the Low Countries, the obvious consequences of Reformed preaching against religious art arrived after a few years: in 1566, an iconoclastic fury, known as the *Beeldenstorm*, crossed the region from South to North, bringing about the loss of many works of art, especially in churches.[9] That event was a shock for Catholics, who saw in it the fingerprint of

---

5 G.H. Williams, *The Radical Reformation* (Kirksville: Truman State University Press, 1997) 97. See also A. Duke, *Dissident Identities in the Early Modern Low Countries* (London: Routledge, 2009) 16–27; W. Estep, *The Anabaptist Story: An Introduction to Sixteenth-Century Anabaptism* (Grand Rapids: Eerdmans, 1996) 152; G.K. Waite "The Anabaptist Movement in Amsterdam and the Netherlands, 1531–1535: An Initial Investigation into its Genesis and Social Dynamics", *SCJ* 18 (1987) 249–65. Actually, the first Calvinist minister arrived in the Netherlands in 1544, cf. Ph.M. Crew, *Calvinist Preaching and Iconoclasm in the Netherlands 1544–1569* (Cambridge: Cambridge University Press, 1978) 6.

6 J. Calvin, *Institution de la religion chrétienne*, lib. I, c. 12 (3 vol.; Genève: Labor et Fides, 1955–57) 71–3.

7 C. Kooi, *Calvinists and Catholics during Holland's Golden Age: Heretics and Idolaters* (Cambridge: Cambridge University Press, 2012) 65.

8 E. Busch, "Confessio Belgica von 1561", art. 29, in E. Busch/E. Campi/H. Faulenbach (ed.), *Reformierte Bekenntnisschriften* (4 vol.; Neukirchen-Vluyn: Neukirchener, 2003–22) 2/1.338, l. 5–12; 1.362, l. 24–31.

9 There is extensive literature on Calvinism in the Low Countries, the *Beeldenstorm*, and the Dutch Revolt. Amongst others, see the monographic issue A.-L. van Bruaene/K. Jonckheere/R. Suykerbuyk (ed.), *Beeldenstorm*, *BMGN* 131 (2016); G. Janssen, *The Dutch Revolt and Catholic Exile Reformation in Europe* (Cambridge: Cambridge University Press, 2014); S. Deyon/A. Lottin, *Les casseurs de l'été 1566: L'iconoclasme dans le Nord* (Villeneuve d'Ascq: Presses Universitaires du Septentrion, 2013); V. Soen, "Reconquista and Reconciliation in the Dutch Revolt: The Campaign of Governor-General Alexander Farnese (1578–1592)", *JEMH* 16 (2012) 1–22; K. Jonckheere/R. Suykerbuyk (ed.), *Art after Iconoclasm: Painting in the Netherlands between 1566 and 1585* (Turnhout: Brepols, 2012); K. Jonckheere, *Antwerp Art after Iconoclasm: Experiments in* Decorum *1566–1585* (Brussels/New Haven: Mercatorfonds/Yale University Press, 2012); P. Arnade, *Beggars, Iconoclasts, and Civic Patriots. The Political Culture of the Dutch Revolt* (Ithaca: Cornell University Press, 2008); J. Dillenberger, *Images and Relics: Theological Perceptions and Visual Images in Sixteenth-Century Europe* (Oxford: Oxford University Press, 1999); M. van Gelderen, *The Political Thought of the Dutch Revolt 1555–1590* (Cambridge: Cambridge University Press, 1993); D. Freedberg, *Iconoclasm and Painting in the Revolt of the Netherlands 1566–1609* (New York: Garland, 1988); D. Freedberg, "Art and iconoclasm, 1525–1580, The Case of the Netherlands", in *Kunst voor de Beeldenstorm [Cat. Exhib., Amsterdam, Rijksmuseum]*, J.P. Filedt Kok *et al.* (ed.) (Amsterdam: Rijksmuseum, 1986) 69–84; D. Freedberg, "The Hidden God: Image And Interdiction in The Netherlands in the Sixteenth Century", *Art History* 5 (1982) 133–53; Crew, *Calvinist Preaching and Iconoclasm*; D. Freedberg, "The Representation of Martyrdom during the

the Devil.[10] Two years later, in 1568, the confessional strife assumed the form of a civil revolution against the Catholic Spanish Crown: this marked the beginning of the Dutch Revolt (1568–1648), also known as the Eighty Years' War. Yet the iconoclastic fury in the Netherlands was not temporally limited to 1566. On the contrary, it "remained endemic in the Low Countries. Religious buildings came under attack again in the 1570s and early 1580s, during the first and most intensive phase of the Dutch Revolt, when both in the North and the South of the Low Countries Calvinist civic regimes were installed".[11]

Meanwhile, in its 25th and last session (3rd–4th December 1563), the Council of Trent decreed "On the invocation, veneration and relics, of saints, and on sacred images", declaring the lawfulness of the Catholic worship, which was addressed not to the objects themselves – such as statues and paintings – but to the 'prototypes' which they represented: namely God, Jesus, the Virgin Mary and the saints. In sum, any accusation of idolatry was false. Moreover, the Council expressly asked to teach the flock on this specific matter.[12] Being on the front lines of a confessional war, the Louvain Faculty of Theology answered Trent's call by writing treatises to stem the advance of Calvinism and its aggression against sacred images. This essay aims to compare the Louvain theological reflection on religious art with the Netherlandish production. It is divided into two main sections. In the first, Antonio Gerace analyses a few writings published in Louvain at the beginning of the Dutch Revolt against iconoclasm and the abuses of the images, in particular those of Johannes Molanus and Nicholas Sanders; in the second, Tamara Dominici analyses the Marian iconographies that Molanus proposed in his book *De Historia*

Early Counter-Reformation in Antwerp", *The Burlington Magazine* 118 (1976) 128–38; D. Freedberg, "The problem of Images in Northern Europe and Its Repercussion in the Netherlands", in *Hafnia Copenhagen Papers in the History of Art. Proceedings of the 7th International Colloquium in the History of Art* (Copenhagen: University of Copenhagen, 1976) 25–45; D. Freedberg, "Johannes Molanus on Provocative Paintings. *De Historia Sanctarum Imaginum et Picturarum*, Book II, Chapter 42", *Journal of the Warburg and Courtauld Institutes* 34 (1971), 229–45.

10 "Anno vero sexagesimo sexto, cum huiusmodi rebellio tanto furore plerisque locis erumperet, quod ipse Satanas solutus videretur, non scio vel unum ex hac Schola a Catholica fide defecisse, vel in ea nutasse, aut etiam eam dissimulasse … Unde cum haereticorum furor et clamor insaniret contra Lovanium, studiorum piam matrem non solum Lovanium, sed nec ullam circumcirca adiacentem Ecclesiam, attingit violenta illa et Satanica Ichonomacarum rabies", J. Molanus, *De historia sacrarum imaginum et picturarum, pro vero earum usu contra abusus. Libri IV* (Louvain: Typis Academicis, 1771) XIII. In order to harmonise the various Latin sources quoted in the footnote, <&> is rendered as <et> and j is <i>.

11 Van Bruaene/Jonckheere/Suykerbuyk (ed.), *Beeldenstorm*, 9. For instance, in Antwerp in 1581, see Freedberg, "The Representation of Martyrdom", 128.

12 "Concilium Tridentinum", s. 25, in G. Alberigo/K. Ganzer/A. Melloni (ed.), *Conciliorum Oecumenicorum Generaliumque Decreta Editio Critica* (Turnhout: Brepols, 2010) 149–51.

Sacrarum Imaginum et Picturarum (1594), comparing them with some examples of the artistic production both before and after this book.

Louvain in Defence of the Holy Images[13]

In the very same year that marked the beginning of the Dutch revolt (1568), the very famous theologian Johannes Molanus (1533–85)[14] gave a lecture at the Louvain Faculty of Arts, with a view to explaining the Tridentine position regarding the use of holy images. He focused his talk on two main topics: 1. The defence of the legitimate use of religious art against "the perfidy of iconoclasts" (*perfidia iconomachorum*); and 2. The abuse of images which may occur due to either the "incompetence" (*imperitia*) or the "negligence" (*negligentia*) of Catholics.[15] To develop his lecture, he divided it into three arguments: 1. Iconoclasm had its origin in the Eastern Roman Empire – and that's the reason why the Greek word 'iconomachia' is used to define this phenomenon; 2. The Roman Church had refused this Byzantine

---

13 This section is authored by Antonio Gerace.

14 Born at Lille in 1533, Molanus was a priest and canon of St. Peter's Church in Louvain, where he died. He was Professor of Theology and Rector from 1578 of the Louvain University, where he had studied. Many of his works were published, also after his death in 1585: 1. *Usuardi martyrologium* (Louvain, 1568); 2. *Calendarium ecclesiasticum ad usum breviarii Romani* (Antwerp, 1569); 3. *De Picturis et Imaginibus Sacris* (Louvain, 1570); 4. *Indiculus Sanctorum Belgii* (Louvain, 1573); 5. *Erotemata scholastica, de rudimentis Christianae pietatis* (Bremen, 1573); 6. *Anni M D LXXXI Conclusiones impertinentes* (Louvain, 1581); 7. *Conferentiarum conclusiones* (Louvain, 1581); 8. *De fide haereticis servanda libri tres* (Cologne, 1584); 9. *Liber de piis testamentis* (Cologne, 1585); 10. *Theologiae Practicae Compendium* (Cologne, 1585); 11. *De Canonicis libri tres* (Cologne, 1587); 12. *Militia sacra ducum et principum Brabantiae* (Antwerp, 1592); 13. *De historia sacrarum imaginum et picturarum* (Louvain, 1594); 14. *Natales sanctorum Belgii et eorundem chronica recapitulatio* (Antwerp, 1595); 15. *Medicorum ecclesiasticum diarium* (Louvain, 1595); 16. *Libri quinque: in quibus praeter antiquitatem et veterem historiam urbis Antwerpiae* (Leiden, 1605), 17. *Bibliotheca materiarum theologica* (Cologne, 1618). To these books, another must be added: *Historia Lovaniensium libri XIV*, P. F. X. De Ram (ed.) (Brussels: M. Hayez, 1861), where in the introductory part a synopsis of Molanus' works is provided, see pp. XCIX. De Ram was not aware of a few of Molanus' publications, which are now accessible through the *Universal Short Title Catalogue* – though this does not include all of Molanus' works. There are also a number of manuscripts which have never been published. See De Ram's introduction to *Historia Lovaniensium*.

15 "Quod autem attinet ad quaestionem praesentem, utrum sacrarum imaginum usus legitimus sit retinendus, multa in eius decisionem adferenda forent, si pro amplitudine sua absolvenda esset. Complectitur enim duas partes … Una est, contra iconomachorum perfidiam, De legitimo sacrarum imaginum usu retinendo. Altera vero, est contra Catholicorum quorundam imperitiam aut negligentiam, De vitando abusu, sive illegitimo usu, earundem. Utriusque enim curam diligentem haberi voluit sacrosancta Synodus Tridentina", Molanus, *De historia sacrarum imaginum et picturarum*, 2.

doctrine, which was then abandoned also by Orthodox Church; and 3. There is a legitimate use for sacred images.[16]

Perhaps influenced by Molanus' lecture, in 1569 an English Catholic living in Louvain, Nicholas Sanders (1530–81), published the *De typica et honoraria sacrarum imaginum adoratione*, dedicated to the Duke of Alva, Fernando Álvarez de Toledo y Pimentel (1507–82), the successor of Margaret of Parma (1522–86) as Spanish Governor of the Low Countries. In the prefatory epistle, the Englishman points out the programmatic intent of his work: to counter the Calvinist reproof of the Catholic veneration of images, showing that it must not be conceived as an idolatry, a calumny that Reformers sustain because of their ignorance. Indeed, the Catholic Church admits only a "certain veneration" (*aliqua veneratio*) – addressed not to the artefacts, but to those whom they represent – while rejecting an "absolute veneration" (*summa veneratio*) – since this might be considered as idolatry. The ignorant Calvinist position must therefore be countered, to avoid any attempt on the unity of the Church. Sanders underlines that the *casus belli* of the Dutch revolt was indeed the demolition of religious pieces of art, showing once again the importance of the policy of images in the context of the Eighty Years' War.[17] Furthermore, Sanders claims that the conservation of religious artistic heritage during wartime is something that must be put on the agenda, and this is what the Duke of Alva actually did, even at his own risk.[18] As Andrew Spicer shows, since the very beginning of the confessional revolt, the Spanish authorities sought for the conservation and restoration of religious places, to make them once again worthy of being spaces of worship.[19] Sanders considers his work to be in some way in synergy with the Spanish military and political enterprise, and furnishes the theological arguments

16 Molanus, *De historia sacrarum imaginum et picturarum*, 3.

17 "Cum igitur nec veritas fidei Catholicae deferenda sit (quae non quidem summam, sed tamen aliquam venerationem Sacris Imaginibus deferendam statuit) nec rursus ab illis ad unitatem Ecclesiae revocandis, qui per ignorantiam erraverunt, cessare unquam debeamus: faciendum putavi, ut operam aliquam tum in depellenda idolatriae calumnia, tum in asserenda Catholica fide, his praesertim diebus, ponerem et collocarem. Etenim si magna Germaniae pars (initio tanti tumultus non nisi ab imaginum sacrarum deiectione primum petito) in bellum postea gravissimum exarsit", N. Sanders, *De typica et honoraria sacrarum imaginum adoratione libri duo: quorum prior in adorandis Sanctorum imaginibus nullum esse idolatriae periculum: posterior docet, figuralem quadam adorationem illis deberi, et Naturali, et Gentium et Divino, et Ecclesiastico iure* (Louvain: Foulerus, 1569) IIV.

18 "Si Dux Albanus ab Hispaniis usque, ex Catholici Regis mandato cum exercitu profectus, auctis etiam in his regionibus copiis, non sine valetudinis, atque adeo vitae ingenti periculo, Templorum, Altarium, Sacrarumque imaginum defensionem contra Iconomachos intrepide suscepit: nonne interim decuit nos, qui sub ipsius tutela secure egimus, quique per ipsius arma pace fruebamur, eadem causam et precibus apud Deum, et itam verbis quam scriptis apud proximum agere?" Sanders, *De typica et honoraria sacrarum imaginum*, IIV–IIIr.

19 A. Spicer, "After Iconoclasm: Reconciliation and Resacralization in the Southern Netherlands, ca. 1566–85." *The Sixteenth Century Journal* 44 (2013) 411–33. See also V. Soen, "The Beeldenstorm and

capable of justifying the Catholic view on religious art. Sanders divided his volume into two books: the former shows that there is no idolatry in the worship of the images of the saints, while the latter explains that a "figurative worship" (*figuralis adoratio*) of the images follows from natural, 'international', divine and canon law (*naturale, gentium, divinum, ecclesiasticum ius*).[20] In his analysis, he points out the two crimes of the iconoclasts: 1. Having distanced themselves from the Gospel; and 2. Having dislodged the holy images without having the legitimate authority to do so.[21] Moreover, Sanders stresses the importance of religious images, since they are a means to explain the difficult content of faith to unlearned people (*rudes*).[22] In his treatise, Sanders felt the need to rebut the strongest Reformers' theological argument against the use of religious art: God's prohibition against making images, as expressed in the Decalogue, "Thou shalt not make to thyself a graven thing, nor the likeness of any thing that is in heaven above, or in the earth beneath, nor of those things that are in the waters under the earth" (Ex 20:4). Sanders maintains that God's prohibition is addressed only to those artefacts which are against the natural law.[23] He further maintains that God's commandment was against the images of false deities, with which the Jews were familiar during their time in Egypt. The images of a pagan pantheon are of course to be regarded as idols, but the same principle is not applicable to the images of saints, for two reasons: 1. Pagan gods are false, while saints were real; and 2. Saints are not conceived as divine entities.

---

the Spanish Habsburg Response (1566–1570)", *BMGN* 131 (2016) 99–120. On Alexander Farnese, see Freedberg, "The Representation of Martyrdom", 128.

20 See above the full title, n. 17.

21 "Hoc ergo primum crimen Iconoclastorum est, quod sua temeraria devastatione proximos ab eo Evangelio, quod ipsi verum iudicant, alienores reddiderunt. Alterum vero crimen est, quod imagines absque legitimate potestatis iussu deturbarunt", Sanders, *De typica et honoraria sacrarum imaginum*, 9r.

22 "Cum enim scripturae a spiritu Sancto promanarint, eaque prout homines capere possunt, invisibilia Dei expresserint, si nos idem commendamus oculis rudium per picturas, hoc est per literas vulgares et plebeias, quod scripturae doctorum oculis per secretiores et misticas literas commendarunt: nihil aliud fecisse intelligimur, quam ut, quod scripturae commemorant, quam significantissime proponamus, quod sane ingratum Deo esse non potest. Illud ergo Idolum est, quod nullum omnino exemplar in Dei operibus habet", Sanders, *De typica et honoraria sacrarum imaginum*, 16v.

23 "Qui puntant eam Sacram imaginum adorationem, qua Catholici defendunt, iure divino prohiberi, ad Decalogum ante omnia confugiunt, ibique mandatum esse clamant, ne ulla prosus imago aut similitudo adoretur. Atqui cum inter nos conveniat, Decalogum (excepta sabbati caerimonia) non nisi legis naturae veram ac perspicuam declarationem esse: iam autem declaratum sit, imaginum fabricationem (in iis quidem rebus, quae aut corporae sunt, aut divina quapiam ratione corporeis sensibus exhibentur) secundum naturam esse, ac propterea Deo qui auctor naturae est, displicere ulla ex parte non posse: necesse est, ut si quae imagines in Decalogo aut fieri, aut coli prohibeantur, id intelligatur de tali fabricatione, ac tali cultu, qui omnino secundum naturam non sit", Sanders, *De typica et honoraria sacrarum imaginum*, 48v.

The two sets – pagan gods and saints – have nothing in common.[24] Therefore, that divine commandment does not forbid the production of sacred images by either natural or divine law.[25] Moreover, these images are to be regarded as holy, not because of the matter of which they are made – e. g. stone, wood, ivory etc. – or the artistic craft used to make them – e. g. sculpture and painting – since in this sense they are no different from profane works, but rather in their use: they are signs imitating the signifiers to which they refer,[26] namely Christ, the Virgin Mary, and the saints.

Sanders' work shows once again the complexity and the importance that this topic had among Catholics, who fiercely defended their traditional worship of religious artefacts, even though they were aware of its possible abuses. This was the context in which Molanus worked, and his analysis of the holy images was heavily influenced by the harsh opposition between the two contenders, Catholics and Calvinists; hence its clear references to the iconoclastic fury.[27] Just one year after Sanders' work, in 1570, Molanus published his famous *De picturis et imaginibus sacris liber unus* in Louvain. Not by coincidence, the Flemish theologian here shows his appreciation of Sanders' book; and indeed, shortly after the *Index capitum*, Molanus inserts a very short synopsis of the Englishman's treatise, reporting the ten reasons why sacred images are useful: for (1) doctrine, (2) the remembrance of specific issues, and (3) the confession of faith. Moreover, they are (4) signs of charity towards Christ, they are a means for the (5) imitation, (6) invocation and (7) honouring of God, and for the (8) rejection of heretics' statements against holy images. Finally, they serve (9) to train the faithful in churches and (10) to represent the afterlife – either in hell or in paradise.

---

24 "Nam illa adoratio tantum prohibita est, quae idolis atque iis similitudinibus quae pro diis colebantur, solebat exhiberi. Sanctorum vero imagines non sunt idola, quoniam res quae vere ita se habent, repraesentant, nec velut deorum similitudines habentur, quia palam profitemur tum ipsos sanctos non esse Deos, tum eorum similitudines non ad alium finem reverenter a nobis tractari, quam ut unius Dei fides et cultus ea ratione melius moveatur", Sanders, *De typica et honoraria sacrarum imaginum*, 54v.

25 "Non autem ita vetamur iure naturali aut divino, ullas omnino creaturarum similitudines vel cogitare, vel facere", Sanders, *De typica et honoraria sacrarum imaginum*, 55v.

26 "Quotiens enim certus est, res vere sacras esse quae pinguntur aut sculpuntur: mox id quod pingitur et sculpitur ex prophano fit sacrum, non secundum materiam aut artem, sed secundum usum et significationem. Signa enim quatenus signa sunt, earum rerum conditionem imitantur, quibus significandis constituta sunt", Sanders, *De typica et honoraria sacrarum imaginum*, 102v. Cf. C. Hecht, *Katholische Bildertheologie im Zeitalter von Gegenreformation und Barock: Studien zu Traktaten von Johannes Molanus, Gabriele Paleotti und anderen Autoren* (Berlin: Gebr. Mann, 1997) 58 n. 279.

27 "Unde cum haereticorum furor et clamor insaniret contra Lovanium, studiorum piam matrem, non solum Lovanium, sed nec ullam circumcirca adiacentiem ecclesiam attigit violentia illa et satanica ichonomacorum rabies", J. Molanus, *De picturis et imaginibus sacris liber unus tractans de vitandis circa eas abusibus et de earundem significationibus* (Louvain: Wellaeus, 1570) A3v–A4r.

The literature has already paid attention to Molanus' *De picturis et imaginibus sacris*, as well as to the updated and much expanded version,[28] posthumously issued in Louvain in 1594 by Jean Bogard (died c. 1624) as *De historia sacrarum imaginum et picturarum, pro vero earum usu contra abusus. Libri IV*. Here our theologian furnishes a systematic analysis of the use of images in Christianity, with specific focus on the iconoclastic movements that arose in the Church over the course of its history. The volume was edited by Henri van Cuyk (1546–1609), then vicar for the Archbishopric of Malines, which was vacant in those years (1589–95) – who addressed his prefatory epistle to Jacques de Marquais, Abbot of the St. Martin's Monastery in Tournai. The editor undertakes a close comparison between the Byzantine iconoclasm during the emperorship of Leo III the Isaurian, Constantine V Copronymus, Leo IV the Khazar, and his present time,[29] as Molanus himself does in his work, as shown below.

De historia sacrarum imaginum et picturarum is divided into four books. The first consists of the abovementioned public talk given at the Louvain Faculty of Arts in 1568; the second provides clear insights into the uses and abuses of images, while also furnishing the allegorical and sometime obscure meanings which lay behind certain elements of the paintings; the third is a calendar in which he provides the iconographies of the feasts and saints; and the fourth and last furnishes additional instructions on moveable feasts and other elements on the saints.[30] As Molanus points out, iconoclasm had its birth in the Eastern Roman Empire, as a consequence of a failed political strategy to make the Constantinopolitan Patriarchy the new Universal See, replacing Rome both as the only political centre of the Roman Empire

---

28 The very first monumental study on Netherlandish art during the Counter-Reformation is J.B. Knipping, *De iconografie van de Contra-Reformatie in de Nederlanden* (2 vol.; Hilversum: N.V. Paul Brand's Uitgeversbedrijf, 1939); E. Mâle, *L'art religieux de la fin du XVIe siècle, du XVIIe siècle et du XVIIIe siècle: étude sur l'iconographie après le Concile de Trente, Italie-France-Espagne-Flandres* (Paris: A. Colin, 1951); Freedberg, "Johannes Molanus on Provocative Paintings". As Freedberg reports, Molanus' work had many editions: Antwerp 1617, Cologne 1617, Lyons 1619, Antwerp 1626 and Louvain 1771. In this contribution, all quotations are taken from the final 1771 Louvain issue.

29 "Graeci primum Imperatores, tertius et quartus Leones, et quintus Constantinus in controversiam vocaverunt … Illis e medio sublatis, cum Iconomachicum illud bellum paulisper deferbuisset, Episcopi pletique paenitentes, qui nefando concilio interfuerunt errorem illum suum in posterioris Nicaenae Synodi Actione prima abiurasse describuntur. Et hos cineres dudum sepulti erroris, nostrae aetatis sectarii denuo excitaverunt; qui in Gallias primum tum in hoc nostrum infelix et attritum Belgium Iconomachiam nuper invexerunt, innumera alia damna ac veluti lernam quandam malorum secum trahentem", Molanus, *De historia sacrarum imaginum et picturarum*, XVI.

30 "Liber primus est oratio contra iconomachos, dicta Lovanii in Scholis Artium, Anno 1568. Liber II. est instructio quaedam Catholicorum de vitandis abusibus, ubi significationes etiam obscuriores explicantur. Libro III. idem particulatim agitur, discurrendo per XII. anni menses, et natales Sanctorum. Libro IV. quaedam notantur circa festa mobilia, et communia Sanctorum", Molanus, *De historia sacrarum imaginum et picturarum*, XVIII.

and as the only head religious seat, in order to provide the New City with the full status of Capital by housing both the Emperor and the Pontifex Maximus. The development of Monothelitism gave the Eastern emperor the key to obtain these ends; however, the attempt failed thanks to the Third Council of Constantinople (680–81), which rejected the new doctrine. Molanus considers that attempt as a prodrome of the Iconoclastic movement in Byzantium and the beginning of its ruin; indeed, a vast and Christian Empire was destroyed, and its lands became subject to Saracens and Turks.[31] There is therefore an implicit but very clear comparison between the Eastern Roman Empire and the Spanish Kingdom: both of them are Christian powers, affected by heretical ideas – Monothelitism and Reform movements respectively – and Spain as a Catholic empire must learn a lesson from Byzantine history: estrangement from the 'true' faith leads inevitably to the fall of the constituted social order, a doom that Molanus was experiencing in his lifetime. Furthermore, even though Molanus does not clearly state it, by referring to the political strategy behind the rise of Byzantine Iconoclasm, he seems even to suggest that the *Beeldenstorm* has a political dimension, offering a way for Calvinists to distance themselves from both the Catholic Church and the Spanish Crown, similarly to the attempt of the Byzantine emperor to take religious affairs into his own hands by imposing a heresy as the official religion. At least, it seems quite clear that for Molanus, religious affairs are inextricably linked to politics.

As the Louvain theologian maintained in another book, the *Militia sacra ducum et principum Brabantiae*, posthumously published in 1592, Catholic rulers in the Netherlands had always countered the attacks of pagans, Muslims and heretics, since the Frankish Clovis, fighting against the Arian Visigoths with a "holy army" (*sacra militia*).[32] To Molanus, also Philip II was fighting his "holy wars" (*sacra bella*)

---

31 "Iconomachia originem suam habet ab amplissimo et florentissimo Orientis imperio. Id enim, cum ad supremum dignitatis fastigium devenisset, non diu permansit in eo quem habebat fulgore, sed sensim inclinatum est diuturna illa ambitione, qua se contra Romanam Ecclesiam, aliarum omnium matrem, erexit. Voluit enim patriarcham suum Constantinopolis (quae tunc nova quoque Roma dicebatur) universalis patriarchae titulo insigniri: voluit novae Romae Patriarcham eiusdem omnino potestatis esse cum veteris Romae Pontifice maximo. Quam ob rem cum moneretur, et doceretur a Leone ter sancto, Gregorio Magno, aliisque plurimis clarissimis urbis Romae Pontificibus, nec manifestissimae veritati caecum suum superbumque iudicium, atque typhum submitteret, ex pertinacissimae ambitionis malo natus est error Monothelitarum: quem sexta Synodus oecumenica refutavit. Atque ex hisce initiis mox prodiit iconoclastarum furor in sacras imagines. Qui non solum fidem imperii, sed (quod filii huius saeculi maius iudicant) ipsum quod; tam vastum imperium, ambitione inclinatum et fractum, non modo perdidit, non modo exstinxit, sed etiam ex Christi regno quondam Christianissimo, regnum fecit Antichristi, regnum Saracenorum et Turcarum, qui in feritate sua adversus Christi nomen confidunt, et pro capite habent capitalem et iuratum omnium nostrum hostem", Molanus, *De historia sacrarum imaginum et picturarum*, 3–4.

32 J. Molanus, *Militia sacra ducum et principum Brabantiae* (Antwerp: Plantin, 1594) 1.

against many enemies of the faith, including the Turks in the Mediterranean Basin and the heretics in the Low Countries.[33] Therefore, to the Louvain theologian, the Dutch Revolt is not to be conceived as a civil war between the central power and the rebels, but rather as a 'holy war' between the 'true' faith and heresy. In effect, according to Molanus, no pact and/or friendship can be made with heretics (for heretics have abandoned the faith), nor can the Spanish Crown permit them any freedom of religion/confession.[34] This argument is the foundation upon which the Louvain theologian builds his ideas of religious art, a perspective in which Catholic faith is challenged by heretics, who cannot be trusted and tolerated, and who put the very stability of the Low Countries in danger, as the rise of iconoclastic movements has shown. Precisely for this specific reason, Molanus feels the need to explain the legitimate use of images, to counter the deceitfulness of heretics. However, he is simultaneously aware of the possible abuses that may occur in Catholic worship of holy images – as evidenced by the Council of Trent – because of the negligence or ignorance of people, whose errors must be corrected.[35] *De historia sacrarum imaginum et picturatum* reminds us that in its 25th Session (1563) the Council of Trent decreed against the abuse of the images while recognizing their pedagogical value, since through them even unlearned people are given the ability to grasp elements of the faith. On the other hand, argues Molanus, since images are a kind of 'painted scripture', censorship shall be applied to them, as it is applied to writings.[36] It would seem that, similarly to the *Index librorum prohibitorum* which Louvain theologians first published in 1546,[37] Molanus is proposing the publication of a kind of *Index imaginum prohibitarum* (although he does not use such an expression),

33 Molanus, *Militia sacra*, 127–33.

34 J. Molanus, *Libri V. De fide haereticis servanda III. de fide rebellibus servanda liber unus qui est quartus, item unicus de fide et iuramento quae a Tyranno exiguntur, qui est quintus* (Cologne: Godfried van Kempen, 1584) 33–43.

35 "De sacris imaginibus atque picturis duo potissimum tractanda esse, primo libro praefati sumus. Earum enim legitimus usus contra iconomachorum, sive iconoclastarum perfidiam, defendendus est et retinendus. Earundem quoque usus illegitimus, sive abusus, contra Catholicorum quorundam negligentiam, vel ignorantiam, corrigendus est et vitandus", Molanus, *De historia sacrarum imaginum et picturarum*, 29.

36 "Non est autem mirandum quod sanctum Concilium dicat se vehementer cupere abusus istos imaginum prorsus aboleri, praesertim si attendimus, quanta diligentia mater nostra Ecclesia omnes malos libros e filiorum suorum manibus eripere conetur. Quid enim differunt picturae a scripturis? Quid est aliud pictura quam picta scriptura? Quam picta historia? Unde etiam Graece ζωγραφία, hoc est, viva scriptura, vocatur, Caput sicut annotat Beda in libro de templo Salomonis. Picturae dicuntur laicorum et idiotarum libri: quod doctis sunt libri, hoc legere non valentibus sunt picturae. Quod legentibus scriptura, Gregorius hoc idiotis praestat pictura cernentibus, quia in ipsa etiam ignorantes vident, quod sequi debeant, in ipsa legunt qui litteras nesciunt. Quod igitur in libris prohibetur in picturis quoque est prohibendum", Molanus, *De historia sacrarum imaginum et picturarum*, 31.

37 François, "Vernacular Bible Reading", 89.

and his book may indeed be considered as a canon to be strictly followed so as not to fall into errors, even heretical ones, while producing works of art.

In the same years, another theologian, the Archbishop of Bologna Gabriele Paleotti (1522–97), followed a very similar approach, as shown by his well-known *Discorso intorno alle immagini sacre e profane* (1582) – a work that was very probably influenced by Molanus' book. Carlo Borromeo (1538–84) sent a private letter to Paleotti in April 1579 to inform him that he had found a copy of the *De picturis et imaginibus sacris*, so there was no need for the Bishop of Bologna to send him his own – clear evidence that Paleotti had Molanus' work in his hands before issuing his book.[38] With Molanus' ideas in his mind, and possibly because of them, in 1596 in his *De tollendis imaginibus abusibus novissima consideratio*, Paleotti asks "the supreme ecclesiastical authority for universal precepts, and even a species of *Index imaginum prohibitarum*".[39]

It is important to stress here that another systematic work on religious images was posthumously published in the Spanish Low Countries in 1593: the *Evangelicae Historiae Imagines*, by the Jesuit Jeronimo Nadal (1507–80). This work consists of 153 woodcuts representing scenes from the Gospels, following the liturgical calendar, made by Netherlandish artists. Molanus and Nadal could not have influenced each other, since the engravings were prepared in Rome in the middle of the 16th century, but it seems that most of them are related to the *Iesu Christi Vita*, a Gospel harmony by Willem van Branteghem published in Antwerp in 1537.[40] It is therefore possible that the Louvain theologian, while rejecting or accepting some iconographies, was also looking at the *Iesu Christi Vita* – which therefore might have influenced both Molanus and Nadal. In any case, if Molanus wrote the theoretical treatise on religious images, Nadal is the author of a kind of visual handbook

---

38 "Ho ritrovato il Molano *de picturis*: onde non accadrà che ella più si scomodi di mandarmi il suo", Carlo Borromeo to Gabriele Paleotti, 22 April 1579, in Biblioteca Ambrosiana, *Carteggi di San Carlo*, F. 74, inf., f. 496. Quotation taken from P. Prodi, *Ricerche sulla teorica delle arti figurative nella Riforma Cattolica* (Rome: Edizioni di Storia e Letteratura, 1962), 137, n. 4. On Paleotti, see P. Prodi, *Il cardinale Gabriele Paleotti (1522–1597)* (2 vol.; Rome: Edizioni di Storia e Letteratura, 1959–67).

39 P. Prodi, "Introduction", in G. Paleotti, *Discourse on the sacred and profane images* (Los Angeles: Getty Research Institute, 2012) 1–42, on p. 25.

40 P.-A. Fabre, "*Evangelicae Historiae Imagines* as a Paradigm of the Tridentine's Image (16th–17th centuries)", in G. Capriotti/P.-A. Fabre/S. Pavone (ed.), *Eloquent Images, Evangelisation, Conversion and Propaganda in the Global World of the Early Modern Period* (Leuven: Leuven University Press, 2022) 31–48; J.M. Massing, "Jerome Nadal's *Evangelicae Historiae Imagines* and the Birth of Global Imagery", *Journal of the Warburg and Courtauld Institutes* 80 (2017) 161–220, on p. 162; M. Wadell, "The *Evangelicae Historiae Imagines*: The Designs and their Artists", *Quaerendo*, 10 (1980) 279–91; J. Nadal, *Evangelicae Historiae Imagines* (Antwerp: Plantin, 1594); W. van Branteghem, *Iesu Christi vita iuxta quatuor Evangelistarum narrationes, artificio graphices perque eleganter picta* (Antwerp: Cromme, 1537).

for artists willing to strictly follow Trent's decree. Hence, the two works are the expression of the need felt by the Church to standardise Catholicism throughout the world, an exigency shown for instance by the issuance of the Roman Catechism (1566), the Roman Breviary (1568), the Sixto-Clementine (1592), and other texts.[41] On the other hand, the rigour of the images was not institutionally addressed, since Rome has never published an official treatise on artistic production, or an index of prohibited images; the question was therefore analysed by theologians like Molanus.

Among the images to be rejected, the Louvain theologian points out that obscene and lascivious images must be avoided, as well as portraits of the heresiarchs, just as indecent and heretical books cannot be read.[42] Sacred images, in contrast, have a clear pedagogical value, which Molanus stresses several times: for example, they may induce believers to hate sins. Molanus even refers to the Roman Catechism (1566) when he invites parish priests to show images to the faithful, in order to encourage them to venerate these images and thereby to learn proper Christian behaviour.[43] On the other hand, some representations might be difficult to understand, as for instance Jesus' name abbreviated in the initials IHS encircled within sunrays – an image that the theologian does not reject, but which he is aware that unlearned people may not understand; so if a parish priest realises that the name of Jesus is

---

41 J. Geldhof, "Trent and the Production of Liturgical Books in its Aftermath", in W. François/V. Soen (ed.), *The Council of Trent: Reform and Controversy in Europe and Beyond (1545–1700)* (3 vol.; Göttingen: V&R, 2017) 1.175–89.

42 "Imo, ne in prophanis quidem picturis quidlibet audendum est a pictoribus. Quis enim nesciat obscoenas imagines iure naturae perinde prohibitas esse atque libros sive haereticos sive obscoenos? Quare eiuscemodi imagines et sculpturae venum propositae, rectissime per saecularem magistratum omnes auferuntur et abolentur, dignae quae cum libris obscoenis pereant: de quibus Patres a Synodo Tridentina deputati Regula dixerunt, Libri qui res lascivas, seu obscaenas ex professo tractant, narrant, aut docent (eum non solum fidei, sed et morum, qui huiusmodi librorum lectione facile corrumpi solent, ratio habenda sit) omnino prohibentur; &, qui eos habuerint, severe ab Episcopis puniantur. Hoc praeterea adiicio, non mihi videri nimium fore disciplinae ecclesiasticae rigorem, si etiam effigies haeresiarcharum, ut, Lutheri, Melancthonis ac similium, haberi prohibeantur. Sic enim proxime accederetur ad id, quod deputatio Tridentinae Synodi habet, Haeresiarcharum libri, tam eorum qui post annum Domini M. D. XV. haereses invenerunt, vel suscitarunt, Regula quam qui haereticorum capita aut duces sunt vel fuerunt, cuiuscunque nominis, tituli aut argumenti existant, omnino prohibentur", Molanus, *De historia sacrarum imaginum et picturarum*, 31–2. About the provocative paintings in Molanus, see Freedberg, "Johannes Molanus on Provocative Paintings".

43 "Hoc insuper ex veneranda Antiquitate adiicio, tunc temporis frequentes fuisse eas imagines, quae sui inspectione nostras affectiones a peccatis abstrahunt: imo ecclesiam solere eas indicare laborantibus avaritia, turpi amore, fastu, aut alia peccati specie, ut ex earum iugi contemplatione se a peccatis suis abstraherent. Quod et nunc faciendum est, dicente Parochorum Catechismo: *Sanctorum quoque imagines in templis demonstrabit* (Parochus) *ut et colantur et exemplo moniti, ad eorum vitae et mores nos ipsos conformemus*", Molanus, *De historia sacrarum imaginum et picturarum*, 60. See *Catechismus, ex decreto Concilii Tridentini, ad parochos* (Rome: Manutio, 1566) 231.

not worshipped, he should not admit such an image into his church.[44] Actually, this was a very widespread Catholic icon, which even became the Seal of the Jesuits.

In order to implement the pedagogical value of the images, it can sometimes be useful to 'adapt' the paintings by including events or elements which are absent in the Gospels, if their presence allows a better comprehension of the biblical passages the painter represents. For instance, the Virgin Mary is never described in the act of kneeling down before the Archangel Gabriel (Luke 1:26–38), but it is right to depict her in this way, as it is very probable that this is what happened. Similarly, the Flight into Egypt (Matthew 2:13–23) must be depicted by adding elements which are absent in the Gospels: the youth of the Virgin, who was carrying the little Jesus, and the vastness of the space they are to traverse. Another example is the actual presence of stones while Jesus was tempted by the Devil (Matt 4:3; Mark 1:13; Luke 4:3), or the arbitrary decision to put the Penitent Thief to Jesus' right (Luke 23:39–43), because the right is the side of the good, or to add a horse while depicting the conversion of Paul (there is no mention of a horse in Acts [9,1–9; 22,6–16; 26,12–18], but its presence seems highly probable, given Paul's social status).[45]

Similarly, the Church has never approved pagan representations of God, such as the Egyptian Eye of Horus.[46] Molanus then lists those religious images which have been used in the Church since its beginning, like those representing Christ, the Cross, the Holy Spirit, the Virgin Mary, the Angels, John the Baptist, the Patriarchs, the Apostles, and the Martyrs, furnishing some examples of their representations, as handed down by the Church Fathers.[47] Concerning the depictions of the saints, first of all they should not be placed on the floor, as bas-relief, as may happen in monasteries;[48] yet images of saints could be legitimately shown along streets – and in any public place – as already stated in the Second Nicene Council (787), under

---

44 "Exordium igitur sumendum est a suavissimo nomine Iesu, quod Salvatori nostro Kalendis Ianuariis impositum est. Atque is ipse est servi sui calamum dirigere dignetur. Videri itaque posset inconvenienter Nomen Iesu pingi in radiis solaribus … Non est igitur improbanda predicta picturae ratio: sed, si qui e rudiori plebicula, quae litterarum ignara est, haec non satis assequatur, cum picturae libri sint idiotarum, Parochi erit eos instruere, aut, si ita videbitur, non admittere picturam nomini Iesu inter radios solares, sed ipsius Iesu, qui *in sole posuit tabernaculum suum*", Molanus, *De historia sacrarum imaginum et picturarum*, 231; 235.

45 Molanus, *De historia sacrarum imaginum et picturarum*, 63–6.

46 "Numquam item Ecclesia approbavit Aegyptorum morem, qui pro Deo pingebant Oculum in Sceptro", Molanus, *De historia sacrarum imaginum et picturarum*, 38.

47 Molanus, *De historia sacrarum imaginum et picturarum*, 40–56.

48 "Honestas autem exiguit et loci ratio in collocandis imaginibus habeatur. Quare nec in pavimento sunt historiae Sanctorum sculpendae, quamvis istud videatur quandoque usitatum fuisse in monasteriis quibusdam", Molanus, *De historia sacrarum imaginum et picturarum*, 129.

the emperorship of Irene, between the two Byzantine Iconoclastic periods.[49] Some works of art can also have an intermediate status between holy and profane: these are images of the devil, death, hell and similar things. In the corresponding footnote to this sentence, however, Molanus points out that only those elements are to be considered holy which appear in the *Quattuor novissima*, a treatise on the 'four last things' – death, last judgement, hell or paradise – by a 14th-century Netherlandish theologian based in Utrecht, Gerardus de Vliederhoven, attached to the *Devotio moderna*. Of course, in churches, images of the devil, death and hell cannot contain anything satirical, obscene and/or taken from the pagans.[50] This might be a criticism of Hieronymus Bosch (1453–1516), in particular of his depictions of the afterlife, although Bosch's pertinent works – *The Last Judgement* (1482) and *The Garden of Earthly Delights* (1490–1510) were not intended for churches. It is no coincidence that, at the beginning of the Dutch Revolt, the Spanish Inquisition considered the satirical elements of the latter painting to have heretical nuances, even though this reprimand was not universally shared by the Spaniards; for instance, Philip II (1527–98) greatly appreciated the work in question.[51]

Other sets of images between holy and profane include some "signs" (*signa*) which always refer to specific events or status, like the banner with the Cross, the halo, the palm in saints' hands, the papal mitre, or the bishops' crosier.[52] Among this kind of image, Molanus mentions the ex-votos, for instance reproductions of arms or legs made of wax or silver: these artefacts have full right to be placed in churches, since they have the function of showing the recovery of a limb thanks to an act of divine intervention. These objects indeed have a very long tradition: not only were they used by pagans, but Theodoret of Cyrrhus (c. 393–458/66) in his *De Graecarum affectionum curatione* also shows that such ex-votos were indeed used in

---

49 "Rectissime autem in viis publicis eriguntur Crucis signa et Sanctorum imagines, iuxta definitionem secundae Nicenae Synodi", Molanus, *De historia sacrarum imaginum et picturarum*, 31.

50 "Sunt rursus et alia, quae etiam observanda sunt, ne male pingantur; quae si non inter sacras Imagines collocetur, saltem negari non potest, quin medium locum obitneant inter sacras et prophanas. Tales sunt enim Imagines Diaboli, Mortis, Inferni, ac similium (Y)"; "(Y) In Sacris imaginibus possunt omnino censeri, quae Quattuor Novissima exprimunt: et in locis sacris absque ulla haesitatione collocari. Cavendum tamen ne, ut aliquando factum est, Inferni, extremi Iudicii, picturis admisceantur aut Satyrica quaedam, aut lubrica, aut denique ex Gentibus Poetis hausta", Molanus, *De historia sacrarum imaginum et picturarum*, 138–39. See G. de Vliederhoven, *Quattuor novissima cum multis exemplis pulcherrimis* (Cologne: Duentell, 1506).

51 D. van Heesch, "Paulus de Kempenaer and the Political Exploitation of Hieronymus Bosch in the Dutch Revolt", *Simiolus* 41 (2019) 5–38.

52 "Huc etiam pertinet signa quaedam quae Sanctis propter significationem rei sacrae appinguntur. Qualia sunt, Vexillum cum Cruci Christi apponitur, ad significandam victoriam eius: item aureola, quae sanctorum capitibis apponitur: Palmae in manibus sanctorum, Mitra ac Baculus Pastoralis, quae episcopis dantur, ac similia", Molanus, *De historia sacrarum imaginum et picturarum*, 138–39.

Early Christianity, and "the Lord very gratefully accepts [such] gifts".[53] Furthermore, the Bible refers to 'artefacts', first and foremost the one produced by God to show what people must not do, viz. disobey his orders. This is the transformation of Lot's wife into a statue of salt (Gen 19:26), but there are other mentions of artefacts, as for instance Ezekiel's representation of the Siege of Jerusalem (Ezek 4:1–12), or Zechariah's vision of the *Imago peccatis* (Zech 5:5–11).[54] These specific biblical passages show the full lawfulness of producing images.

In his work, Molanus also addresses criticisms to Erasmus of Rotterdam (1466–1536): "even though he died in communion with the Church, he was vehemently inclined towards Luther".[55] More specifically, Molanus quotes extracts from the *Explanatio Symboli Apostolorum* (1533), in which the Dutch humanist maintains that before Jerome, no holy images – neither painted, nor sculpted, nor on textile – were brought into churches, out of an interest in avoiding falling into the anthropomorphization of God. While he recognizes the pedagogical and even emotional role that images may have for unlearned people, Erasmus specifies that a Christian believer knows that the worship is owed to those whom the image represents – Christ for instance – and not to the material itself. Furthermore, there is no specific rule that imposes the use of images in the temples, so that – Erasmus says – it might be easier to remove all the images from churches, in order to avoid any possibility of superstition, since some people preach only before a holy image.[56] While confuting Erasmus, Molanus refers to Nicholas Sanders' *De typica et honoraria sacrarum imaginum adoratione* to stress the importance of the pedagogical value of sacred images, which are capable of being impressed on the

53 "Hunc pertinet quod in Ecclesiis ad Memorias Sanctorum appendatur brachia, pedes et similia, ex cera, aut argento, aut alia materia. Cum enim haec appendantur in memoria restitutae divinitus sanitatis, merito numerantur inter Imagines, quae medium locum obtinent inter sacras et prophanas … Illustre autem pro his Donariis testimonium habemus apud Theodoretum, libro VIII … *Nam illi quidem oculorum, alii vero pedum, alii porro manum simulacra suspendunt, ex argento aurove confecta. Gradissime namque accipit eorum Dominus, qualiacumque sunt, dona*", Molanus, *De historia sacrarum imaginum et picturarum*, 139. On the *ex-votos* in Early Modern Era, see M. Holmes, "Ex-votos: Materiality, Memory and Cult", in M.W. Cole/R. Zorach (ed.), *The Idol in the Age of Art: Objects, Devotions and the Early Modern World* (Farnham: Ashgate, 2009) 167–82.

54 "Sed dum de imaginibus sacris, et quae ad eas referri possunt, agitur, non oportet silentio praeterire Statuam uxoris Loth, aut Obsidionem Jerusalem ab Ezechiele in latere descripta, aut denique Peccati imaginem, a Zacharia visam", Molanus, *De historia sacrarum imaginum et picturarum*, 141.

55 "Erasmum, etsi in Catholica communione mortuum, in partes Lutheri vehementer inclinasse, iam pridem demonstratum est", Molanus, *De historia sacrarum imaginum et picturarum*, 154, n. O.

56 Cf. Erasmus, *Explanatio Symboli Apostolorum* VI, 917–66, in *Opera Omnia Desiderii Erasmi Roterodami recognita et adnotatione critica instructa notisque illustrata*, vol. V/1 (Amsterdam-Oxford: North-Holland Publishing Company, 1977) 304–5.

minds of the faithful, and therefore can induce them to act in accordance with the commandments of God.[57]

One of the key arguments against the use of the sacred images in late antiquity was chapter 9 of the 51st letter of Epiphanius (c. 310/320–403), Bishop of Salamis, to John (c. 356–417), Bishop of Jerusalem, according to which Jerome harshly criticised the presence of a holy image in a church of Anablatha, near Jerusalem. This episode was probably behind Erasmus' claim that until Jerome, holy images were not used,[58] but the Englishman replies – referring to Erasmus' *Explanatio* – that the last chapter of Epiphanius' letter is a very recent addition, as proven by the fact that no such event was mentioned during the Second Council of Nicaea (787) during discussions concerning iconoclasm.[59] Molanus too refers to the Second Council of Nicaea while rebutting Erasmus' claim in the *Explanatio* that no rule imposes the use of images in churches: that Council hands down the most evident constitutions regarding the legitimate use of holy images.[60]

---

57 "At vero contra dicendum fuisset nullam esse in eis crassitudinem, sed multum perfectionis inesse, dum ex sacrarum imaginum utilitate multiplices concipiuntur utilitates. Perfectius enim addiscitur, quod simul per utrumque sensum, quam quod per alterum solum imbibitur: et ex frequenti imaginum intuitu vehementer confirmatur memoria in iis rebus, quas crebro pictas aut insculptas videmus. Nec parum eiusmodi monumenta conducunt ad bonos mores, dum per Sanctorum Imagines ad Sanctorum imitationem accedimur: et plerumque similes eorum esse cupimus, quorum memoriam non sine admiratione spectamus", Molanus, *De historia sacrarum imaginum et picturarum*, 157. In the margin, there is the reference to Sanders.

58 "Idem Erasmus Catechesi sexta: *Usque ad aetatem Hieronymi erant probatae religionis viri, qui in Templis nullam ferebant Imaginem, nec pictam, nec sculptam, nec textam ac ne Christi quidem, ut opinor, propter Anthropomorphitas*. Respondeo falsum esse quod assumitur. Repetitur tale quid sub fine Epistolae Epiphanii, quam Hieronymus transtulit, coque crediderunt Erasmum respexisse: sed permulti docti annotarunt narrationem illam et censuram de Imaginibus, ad fine Epistolae Epiphanii, ab Iconomacho quodam assutam fuisse, ut sub Epiphanii nomine maior haeresi conciliaretur authoritas; inter quos Dominus Sanderus, in posteriori libro de honoraria imaginum adoratione, ubi tot clarissimis rationibus comprobat falsum esse, atque falso Epiphanio imponi, ut praefactus sit oportet, ac multum durae cervicis, qui hac parte ei acquiescere nolit", Molanus, *De historia sacrarum imaginum et picturarum*, 157–8.

59 "Iam vero non tantum hoc totum est falso affixum, sed etiam est affixum nondum abhinc annis septingentis. Nihil enim tale citatum reperitur in *Secunda Synodo Nicaena* ab iis, qui nihil omiserunt quod contra Sacra imagines vel specie tenus facere videretur", Sanders, *De typica honoraria sacrarum imaginum adoratione*, 163v.

60 "Sed ulterius: *Nam ut imagines sint in templis, nulla humana praecipit constitution. Et ut facilius est, ita tutius quoque est omnes imagines e templis submovere, quam impetrare, ut nec modus praetereatur, nec admisceatur superstitio*. Tu hic, Erasme, quas Ecclesiasticas dicere debuisse, tuo loquendi more humanas appellari maluisti Constitutiones: et sic loqueris, quas nunqum orbis Christianus secondo Niceae convenisset ad retinendum sacrarum imaginum legitimum in Tremplis usum", Molanus, *De historia sacrarum imaginum et picturarum*, 161.

Another important argument of heretics against sacred images is their prohibition by the Synod of Elvira (305/6) in its 36th canon, but Molanus explains that the imposition in question was a way to safeguard Christians from persecution by Roman emperors, a measure which became useless after Christianity became a State religion and the production of holy images was increasingly widespread.[61] The Louvain theologian also shows the hypocrisy of the Protestants who claim they reject holy images, even while selling them on the market, though the images they sell do not represent saints, but heresiarchs. Molanus gleans this information from a German Lutheran theologian who converted to Catholicism, Friedrich Staphylus (1512–64), who maintains in his *Apologia* that the images representing Christ and the saints had been replaced by pictures of heretics with their wives:[62] among the most famous examples, consider Lucas Cranach the Elder's portraits of Martin Luther and Katharina von Bora (1525; 1526 and 1529), the portraits of Luther and Melanchthon (1543) and – possibly – of John Calvin's wife, Idelette de Bure, now lost but copied by Xavier Wurth in 1909. Molanus also reports that William van der Lindt, or 'Lindanus' (1525–88), has seen portraits of Luther, with the caption "Saint Martin". Indeed, in his *Apologeticum ad Germanos* (1568), the Bishop of Roermond affirms that pictures of 'saint' Luther, regarded as the fifth evangelist, are quite common in Wittenberg and elsewhere in Germany.[63]

As can be readily seen in the first two books of *De historia sacrarum imaginum et picturarum*, Molanus puts a lot of effort into rebutting the Reform reprimand

61 "*Picturas in Ecclesia esse non debere, ne, quod colitur aut adoratur, in parietibus pingetur.* Etenim (ut nec illud interim taceatur) si picturae, sacram historiam exprimentes, in parietibus ecclesiarum passim positae fuessent, cum illas imminente persecutione Christiani auferre secum, aut occultare, non potuissent … Postquam vero penitus cessavit infidelium Tyrannorum persecutio, mox in Ecclesiis positae sunt non exiguo numero Imagines et Statuae sacrae", Molanus, *De historia sacrarum imaginum et picturarum*, 146–47.

62 "Vidit etiam Antistes Lindanus Lutheri imaginem, titulo divi Martini praenotatam. Vidit et Dominus Staphylus per Germaniam Iconoclastas, pro Christi et Sanctorum Imaginibus, Haereticorum effigies reposuisse, et uxorum suarum, eleganter et amatorie depictas", Molanus, *De historia sacrarum imaginum et picturarum*, 227. Cf. F. Staphylus, *Apologia recens aucta et recognita. De Vero germanoq[ue] intellectu, De Sacrorum Bibliorum in idioma vulgare tralatione, De Luteranorum concionatorum consensione* (Cologne: Quentel/Calenium, 1562) 178v.

63 "Hac igitur in doctrina facilis sit partium consensus (de iis Confessionistarum ago, qui purum putum Lutheranismum obtinent. nam istum degenerem atque ad Calvinismum declinantem amplexantur, veri fiunt Iconoclastae) quod imagines habere legitimeque venerari liceat, cum ipsi non paucas suis in Ecclesiis Wittenbergae et alibi reverenter habeant, suumque ipsi Quintum Evangelistam Divo Sancti Martini Lutheri titulo ad vivum praelo expressum circumferant non solum magnificis encomiis ampullatisque elogiis ornatum; sed divinis etiam (si Christo placet) divorum Augustini et Ambrosii prophetiis de ipsius adventu condecoratum", W. van der Lindt, *Apologeticum ad Germanos, pro religionis catholicae pace, atque solida ecclesiarum in vero Christi Iesu evangelio concordia* (Antwerp: Plantin, 1568) 52.

of religious art, even speaking in terms of a 'holy war' against the iconoclasts in his *Militia sacra*. He also rejects the improper use of images and furnishes some examples of what is permissible. However, it is in the last two books that he focuses on specific iconographies, which is the subject of the second section of his essay.

Molanus' Canon and the Netherlandish Paintings: Rigour or Freedom?[64]

After having delineated Molanus' thoughts on iconoclasm, the use and abuse of holy images, in this section we turn to his ideas on the proper iconographies to be used in representing the key moments of the liturgical calendar, grasping elements from various parts of his book, in order to furnish a more coherent framework for our theologian's theory of artistic production. Molanus has specific examples in mind when describing the traditional and at the same time erroneous representations of religious subjects; therefore, there is need to make reference to Netherlandish paintings, from both before and after *De historia sacrarum imaginum et picturarum*, in order to see the evolution of these iconographies. Moreover, while writing his reprimand, Molanus was probably referring to woodcuts contained in certain books, such as the *Biblia pauperum*, the *Speculum humanae salvationis* or the *Iesu Christi Vita*, which were likely available to him. Since post-Tridentine theologians felt the need to defend Marian devotions from the attacks of heretics,[65] the present research focuses only on those iconographies representing the Virgin, by following the order of the Gospels' narration: the Annunciation (25th March; Luke 1:26–38), the Nativity (25th December; Luke 2:6–20), and the Epiphany (6th January; Matt 2:1–12).[66] Moreover, attention will also be paid to traditions which are not contained in the New Testament's canon: the Dormition and the Assumption (15th August).

Annunciation, Nativity and Epiphany: Many Elements to Be Rejected

One iconography liable to misinterpretation due to the arrival of the Reformation is that of the Annunciation. More specifically, possible criticism might be levelled at the presence of the so-called *corpusculum humanum*, nowadays known in literature as *Logosknabe* or Christ Child – a little human body, namely Jesus, sometimes carrying a cross, who is going to incarnate in Mary's womb, through a solar ray descending from the heavens, often departing from God and passing through the Holy

64 This section is authored by Tamara Dominici.

65 R. Fastiggi, "Mariology in the Counter Reformation", in T.C. Mauder (ed.), *The Oxford Handbook of Mary* (Oxford: Oxford University Press, 2019) 454–68, on p. 456.

66 For these iconographies see G. Schiller, *Iconography of Christian Art* (London: Lund Humphries, 1971) 1.33–52; 58–87; 94–100.

Spirit, represented as a white dove.[67] The Louvain theologian considers the Christ Child not only dangerous, but even capable of leading to heresy; for instance, the Gnostic Valentinus (c. 100–80) had maintained that Christ, in his body, descended to Earth, entering into Mary's womb through a pipe (*tubus, fistula*). Molanus quotes the Archbishop of Florence Antonino Pierozzi (1389–1459) to substantiate his reproval, noting that the Italian rejects the *corpusculum*. Interestingly, the Louvain theologian does not limit himself to the Archbishop's words on the *Logosknabe*, but also includes Pierozzi's reprimand of a three-headed body representing the Trinity.[68] Also at the beginning of his treatise, Molanus, citing Jean Gerson, links this iconography with another one similar to that of the Christ Child: a Virgin Mary with the Holy Trinity in her womb. That picture could actually mislead people's comprehension of the Three Persons, as if they were incarnated in Mary all together. In any case, this image was not as widespread as the former, and Molanus himself

67 E. Guldan, "*Et verbum caro factum est*: die Darstellung der Inkarnation Christi im Verkündigungsbild (Taf. 19–32)", *Römische Quartalschrift für christliche Altertumskunde und Kirchengeschichte* 63 (1968) 145–69; D.M. Robb, "The Iconography of the Annunciation in the Fourteenth and Fifteenth Centuries", *The Art Bulletin* 18 (1936) 480–526, specifically on the Christ Child, see pp. 523–26. See also K. Krüger, "Mute Mysteries of the Divine Logos: On the Pictorial Poetics of Incarnation", in W. Melion/L. P. Wandel (ed.) *Image and Incarnation. The Early Modern Doctrine of the Pictorial Image* (Leiden: Brill, 2015) 76–108, on pp. 82–3.

68 "Pingitur quibusdam locis, in historia annunciationis et incarnationis Domini nostri Iesu Christi, Corpusculum quoddam humanum, inter radios, quos Spiritus sanctus diffundit, descendens ad uterum beatissimae Virginis. Quae pictura videtur praebere occasionem, non periculosi solum, sed etiam haereticis erroris. Valentinus enim iam olim haereticus est habitus ab Ecclesia, quia docuit Christum corpus de coelo attulisse, et per Mariam tamquam per tubum et fistulam transiisse. Quod respiciens sanctus Antoninus hanc picturam gravi censura damnavit. *Reprehensibiles*, ait, *sunt etiam Pictores, cum pingunt ea quae sunt contra fidem: cum faciunt Trinitatis Imaginem unam personam, cum tribus capitibus; quod monstrum est in rerum natura: vel in Annunciatione beatae Virginis, parvulum Puerum formatum, scilicet Iesum, mitti in uterum virginis, quasi non esset de substantia Virginis corpus eius assumtum*", Molanus, *De historia sacrarum imaginum et picturarum*, 275. This representation of the Trinity is quite common in books such as missals, in which the three Persons are depicted as three heads or three faces on one body, an image which was blamed by some scholars, such as Jacobus Latomus (1475–1544), Johannes Hessels (1522–66), and indeed by Antonino of Florence, who considers such image a monster: "Altera vero imaginis ratio paulo notior est. Nam Typographi quidam, in Sacramentariis, sive, ut nunc usitatius loquimur, in Missalibus libris, eam praeposuerunt Officio de sancta Trinitate: pingentes videlicet Trinitatem, ac si esset unus homo, sed tribus capitis, aut saltem tribus faciebus. Quam pingendi rationem in huius libris refutarunt celebres Theologi lovanienses, pietissime memoriae Dominus Iacobus Latomus, Cambronesis, et Iohannes Hesselius, Lovaniensis: ante utrumque vero sanctus Antoninus, Florentinus Archiepiscopus, in Summa: ubi huiusmodi imaginem vocat *monstrum rerum natura*", Molanus, *De historia sacrarum imaginum et picturarum*, 37. See J. Hallebeek, "19. Papal Prohibitions Midway between Rigor and Laxity. On the Issue of Depicting the Holy Trinity", in W. van Asselt/P. van Geest/D. Müller (ed.), *Iconoclasm and Iconoclash* (Leiden: Brill, 2007) 353–83, on p. 362, where he deals with these passages by Latomus, Hessels and Antonino of Florence.

Fig. 1a and b Robert Campin (workshop), *Mérode Altarpiece,* 1427–32, particular, New York: The Metropolitan Museum. Credit: The Cloisters Collection, 1956.

must admit that he could fully comprehend what Gerson was criticising simply by visiting the Carthusian *Sint-Jansdal* monastery near Diest, in Brabant, where the Flemish theologian had been educated: the reference is to the so-called *Vierges ouvrantes* or Shrine Madonnas, often used as a tabernacle.[69]

Quite possibly, in his reflections on the *corpusculum*, Molanus had in mind the *Mérode Altarpiece* (New York, The Metropolitan Museum, c. 1427–32; Fig. 1a–1b)

---

69 "Unde earum unam improbat Iohannes Gerson, in sermone, quem Parisiis habuit de Nativitate Domini: *Cavendum est,* ait, *ne aliqua falsa pingatur historia. Hoc dico, partim propter quadam imaginem, quae est in Carmelitis, et similes, quae in ventribus earum unam habent Trinitatem, veluti si tota Trinitas in Virgine Maria carnem assumpsisset humanam. Mea sententia, nulla est pulchritudo, nec devotio: et possunt esse causa erroris, et indevotionis*: Haec Gerson. Vidi huiusmodi imaginem in Carthusia Distensi quae, quantum memini, eo allata dicebatur ex Francia tempore bellorum. Quod ideo moneo, quia huius imaginis inspectio multum iuvit me, aliosque iuvare poterit, ad plene intelligendum Gersonis citata verba", Molanus, *De historia sacrarum imaginum et picturarum*, 37. See J. Gerson, "Sermo de Nativitate Domini", in J. Gerson, *Opera omnia* (5 vol.; an. rep. Zurich: Georg Olms Verlag, 1987), 3.947. On Gerson's criticism, see J. Wirth, "Jean Gerson condamne les Vierges ouvrantes", in C. Dupeux/P. Jezler/J. Wirth (ed.), *Iconoclasme: Vie et mort de l'image médiévale: catalogue de l'exposition: Musée d'histoire de Berne, Musée de l'Œuvre Notre-Dame, Musées de Strasbourg* (Zurich: Somogy, 2001), 282–83. On the Shrine Madonnas, see C.W. Bynum, *Holy Feast and Holy Fast: The Religious Significance of Food to Medieval Women* (Berkeley: University of California Press, 1987), 268. See E. Gertsman, *Worlds Within: Opening the Medieval Shrine Madonna* (University Park: Pennsylvania Press, 2015). Concerning Mary's pregnancy in visual arts, cf. A.G. Andal, "The Maternal Body as a Space: Examining the Visuality of Marian Pregnancy in Late Medieval Europe", *Open Theology* 7 (2021), 256–70.

by the workshop of Robert Campin (c. 1378–1444),[70] or he might have had at his disposal a copy of the Haarlem *Biblia pauperum* (c. 1430–40),[71] or else he might have seen the *Annunciation* (Glasgow, The Burrell Collection) by the Antwerp master Marcellus Coffermans (c. 1520–78).[72] Indeed, he states that "our painters"[73] – meaning Netherlandish ones – maintain that there is no other way to represent Christ's soul descending into Mary's womb; nonetheless, the Christ Child may be interpreted as God's body incarnating. Hence, the Anabaptists may here find evidence of the fact that Jesus was not born of the Virgin Mary, but that his body comes directly from God's substance. Some examples of this iconography can be found among Lutherans, as shown by the woodcut representing the Annunciation in Luther's 1573 *Betbuchlinof* (New York, New York Public Library, Spencer Collection MS NYPL Spencer 108). To counter the idea that Christ did not receive his human nature from Mary, Molanus appeals to Peter Canisius (1521–97), who criticised this view in his *De Deipara Virgine Maria* (1584).[74] However, there were

70 B. Ridderbos, "Choices and Intentions in the Mérode Altarpiece", *JHNA* 14 (2022) 1–43; B. Ridderbos, "Objects and Questions", in B. Ridderbos/H. Van Veen/A. Van Buren (ed.), *Early Netherlandish Paintings: Rediscovery, Reception and Research* (Amsterdam: Amsterdam University Press, 2004) 4–170, on p. 19. See also Freedberg, "The Hidden God", 136. However, the Brussels' *Annunciation*, very similar to the *Mérode Altarpiece*, has no Christ Child; see Ridderbos, "Choices and Intentions", 3.

71 Guldan, "Et verbum caro factum est", 158–59.

72 Concerning the mystery of the creation of a human soul, the opening illustration of *Le Soliloque* of Saint Bonaventure is worth noting (*Soliloquium de quattuor mentalibus exercitiis*). This text is illuminated by Master of Edward IV (c. 1480–93) (fol. 174). Cf. T. Kren/S. McKendrick (ed.), *The Renaissance. The Triumph of Flemish Manuscript Painting in Europe* (Los Angeles: Getty Publications, 2003) 340–41 n. 97.

73 Molanus indeed proves to be aware of many Flemish artists; for instance, in his *Historia Lovaniensium*, he spends a few words on the painters that worked in the city: Rogier van der Weyden, Quentin Metsys, Dieric and Albrecht Bouts, Henri van der Heyden and Bartholomeuw van Kessel. See *Historia Lovaninsium*, lib. IX, c. 34, 609.

74 "Caeterum a Pictoribus nostris, per Corpusculum illud, in historia Incarnationis Domini, non plus significatur, quam Anima Christi, quae non potest commode aliter figurari; unde sic figurari solent Anime Latronum, qui cum Christo sunt: et Anima Lazari in sinu Abrahae. Significat igitur haec pictura Christum Dominum ab initio Conceptionis suae animatum fuisse, anima non quidem e caelo delapsa, sed a Deo infusa. Vel, si non placet Animam intelligere, significare potest Corpusculum illud, ipsum Deum, qui de Caelo descendit in uterum Virginis. Quanquam longe malim omitti, cum etiam nostro saeculo multi Sectarii, ac potissimum Anabaptistae nefarie sentiant Christi Domini Corpus humanum, non ex Maria Virgine natum, sed ex Patris substantia coelitus allatum esse. Contra quos Petrus Canisius per aliquot capita disserit lib. III de Deipara Virgine Maria", Molanus, *De historia sacrarum imaginum et picturarum*, 276. See. P. Canisius, *Commentariorum de verbi Dei corruptelis, tomi duo. Prior de venerando Christi Domini praecursore Ioanne Baptista, posterior de sacrosancta virgine Maria deipara disserit*, lib. 1, c. IX (Paris: Nivellius, 1584) 75. One very interesting perspective on the debates concerning Christ's incarnation is offered by J. Irwin, "Embryology and the Incarnation: A Sixteenth-Century Debate", *The Sixteenth Century Journal* 9 (1978) 93–104.

some individuals who possibly tried to keep the *Logosknabe* alive in one way or in another, being aware of its long-lasting tradition. In fact, in the *Evangelicae Historiae Imagines*, Nadal seems to have replaced the Christ Child carrying the cross with a little Gabriel with a lily in hand, descending through the sun's rays coming from God. Actually, Gabriel appears twice, the second time at normal size in front of the Virgin.[75]

Concerning the Nativity, Molanus furnishes useful elements in different places in his work for the realisation of the most appropriate paintings – of course according to his canon. As Christmas lies at the end of the year, he avoids repeating what he had already explained while describing, for instance, how the Virgin Mary or Saint Joseph are to be depicted; he thus makes a kind of index of matters with cross-references, to help the reader find all the elements of this iconography. First, he points out that the representation of Mary suffering while giving birth to Jesus is not acceptable: she was alone, without any obstetricians assisting her, in contrast to what is handed down in the apocryphal book *De infantia Salvatoris*. To make his point, Molanus appeals to Ambrogio Catarino Politi (1484–1553) and Henricus Luytens (16th century), who maintain that a suffering condition is not worthy of her status – that it is even an offence against Christ and his mother.[76]

Second, Molanus criticised the 'old Joseph' that artists sometimes very wrongly paint. Jesus' father looks like a "simple little man" (*simplex homuncio*), even "not very wise" (*parum cordatus*). However, there are many examples of this very long tradition which represent Mary's husband as a tired and aged man, as he appears in the left panel of *The Miraflores Altarpiece* (Berlin, Gemäldegalerie, 1435–45; Fig. 2) by Rogier van der Weyden (c. 1399–1464).[77] This work influenced – of course in different ways – the following generation of Netherlandish artists, such as Hans Memling (c. 1436–94), Petrus Christus (c. 1410/20–1475/76) and Hugo van der Goes (c. 1440–82). In contrast with this iconography, which was indeed quite common, Molanus stresses the importance of depicting Joseph as a young man, as affirmed by Jean Gerson on the basis of Isaiah 62:5: "For the young man shall dwell with the virgin, and thy children shall dwell in thee. And the bridegroom shall rejoice over the bride, and thy God shall rejoice over thee". In effect, Gerson

75 Nadal, *Imagines*, 1.

76 "Sed dum transire cupio ad eas imagines, quae errorem quidem continent, sed non periculosum, impedior nonnihil picturam Beatissimae Deiparae in puerperio decumbentis ... Cum Deipara Virgo Maria, sicut sine dolore benedictum suum filium peperit, ita nullos ex partu dolores refervaverit. Et quod obstetrices attinet, quae ex apocrypho libro, de Infantia Salvatoris desumptae sunt... Quare docti etiam viri vehementer hanc improbant Picturam; inter quos Ambrosius Catharinus et Henricus Luitenius", Molanus, *De historia sacrarum imaginum et picturarum*, 78. See also Freedberg, "The Hidden God", 136.

77 Of the same author in Berlin Gemäldegalerie, see also the central panel of *Bladelin Altarpiece*.

Fig. 2 Rogier van der Weyden, *The Altar of Mary (Miraflores Altar)*, 1435-45, Berlin: Gemäldegalerie. Credit: Staatliche Museen zu Berlin, Gemäldegaleri, photo: Volker-H. Schneider.

took part into a more developed debate among Scholastic authors discussing the nature of the marriage between Mary and Joseph, whether it was a real one - and the French theologian admits this possibility - or just a putative one. As Gerson considers the marriage real, he concludes that Joseph must have been young in order to be an effective husband.[78] Also, to Molanus, a young Joseph is more in line with the Gospels' tradition: he must have been strong enough to be a woodworker, to protect his wife in Egypt and to financially support the family thanks to his job. To make his point, the Louvain theologian refers to Tristandus de Lescaigne, who in his *Opusculum*, which is addressed to the bishop of Sens Luis de Bourbon-Vendôme (1493–1557), had clearly stated that the image of an old Joseph is completely inconceivable: Mary needed both consolation and protection from her husband, so he must have been young in order to accomplish his duty,[79] as is depicted by Geert-

78 P. Payan, "Pour retrouver un père...La promotion du culte de saint Joseph au temps de Gerson", *Cahiers de recherches médiévales* 4 (1997) 15–29.

79 "Post biduum occurrit natale Iosephi, sponsi deiparae virginis: quem pictores quidam pessime pingunt tamquam simplicem homuncionem, qui vix quinque numerare possit. Per quorum inscitiam etiam in vulgi proverbium abiit, quod hominem parum cordatum, aut industrium in agendis, Iosephum agnominent. Quasi vero talis prae omnibus aliis a Deo assumptus fuisset, ut esset custos beatissimae Virginis, et benedicti eius filii. A quibusdam etiam pingitur in historia nativitatis Domini, grandaevus senex, baculo prae senior nitens ... Verum nullo modo convenisset virum centenarium, et imbecillem senem, adhiberi Mariae custodem, cui fugiendum esset in Aegyptum, cum puero et matre eius: et inde redeundum. Nec decebat eum aliorum filiorum amore esse distractum, qui curam tantae virginis, et prolis, esset gesturus. ... Non pauciores rationes habet Tristandus de Lescaigne presbyter. Qui in libellis quos de Maria conscriptos dedicavit Ludovico Borbonio Cardinali, Archiepiscopo

Fig. 3 Geertgen tot Sint Jans, *Nativity at Night*, 1490, London: The National Gallery. Credit: © The National Gallery, London.

gen tot Sint Jans (c. 1465–c. 1495) in his *Nativity at Night* (London, The National Gallery, c. 1490; Fig. 3). However, Marteen de Vos (1532–1603) still represents Joseph as an old man in his *Nativity* (1577), preserved in the Antwerp Cathedral. According to Limentani Virdis, Molanus' book should have strongly influenced de Vos in his artistic production, but this is clear evidence that the Antwerp painter distanced himself from the Louvain theologian.[80] The same happens in the triptych

Senonensi, tractatum habet, in quo explicat omnes fere pictores delirare quod Iosephum senem decrepitum pingant", Molanus, *De historia sacrarum imaginum et picturarum*, 271.

80 C. Limentani Virdis, "Manierismo accademizzante anversese e controriforma: il caso di Martin de Vos", *Antichità viva*, 13 (1974) 9–18, on p. 10. Of course, the same passage occurs in the 1570 *De Picturis et Imaginibus Sacris*, 114v. Actually, literature is not always concordant concerning the 'Catholicity' of the Antwerp artist, even in analyses of the very same painting. Limentani Virdis for instance insists on the strong Catholic and even political value of the *Incredulity of St. Thomas*, by

Adoration of the Magi (1572–74) by Frans I Pourbus (1545–81, preserved at the *Sint-Martinuskerk* in Wezemaal), in Jan Snellinck's *Ascension triptych* (1601), in Saint Rumbold's Cathedral in Malines, and in the many adorations of the shepherds (see for instance, Florence, Uffizi, c. 1619–20; Fig. 4; Greifswald, Pomeranian State Museum, c. 1622) by Gerard van Honthorst (1592–1656), even though he clearly makes reference to tot Sint Jans' *Nativity at Night*. In contrast to this, some post-Tridentine painters begin representing Mary's husband as a young adult, like the Antwerp artist Gerard Seghers (1591–1651), one of the Northern Caravaggisti who painted the *Dream of St Joseph* (Vienna, Kunsthistorisches Museum, c. 1625–30). It even seems that the right hand upon which Joseph reclines his head in this painting is an indication of his wisdom, since, rather than sleeping, he looks like he is thinking about what is coming next and how to deal with it.[81] Also in Jeremias Mittendorff's *Adoration of the Shepherds* (1621), preserved at the *Sint-Pieterskerk* in Lo, Mary's husband "n'est plus le vieillard sénile"[82]; similarly, Pieter van Avont (1600–52) portrayed a young Joseph in the right panel of his triptych *Death of the Virgin* (Aarschot, *Onze-Lieve-Vrouwekerk*, c. 1622–55).[83] In sum, there is no consistency in representing Joseph's age, even after Molanus' book.

---

linking Isaiah 33:10–11 quoted in Netherlandish in that table as a clear reference to the Duke of Alva's military campaign against the Dutch rebels, going so far as to say that that biblical passage was "a reference that at the date of realisation of the triptych [1574] rightly forecasted, but with an optimistic anticipation, the Catholic victory that should have arrived ten years later"; Limentani Virdis, "Manierismo accademizzante", 14 (trans. from Italian is mine). On the other hand, Freedberg on the very same painting says: "In the triptych by Marteen de Vos – himself, ironically, a Lutheran – for the altar of the Furriers' Guild in Antwerp Cathedral in 1574, the Biblical text held open by the apostle is not only placed in a prominent position, as is common in those years. It is clearly written in vernacular", Freedberg, "The Problem of Images", 34. He further specifies in the corresponding footnote that "The book is opened on Isaiah 33:10–11. Of course, vernacular texts such as these do occur in other pictorial representations, in manuscripts and book illustrations, and in paintings for Protestants, or ones not intended for altarpiece", Freedberg, "The Problem of Images", 44 n. 83. Indeed, the *Insuper* decree (1546) regarded the Vulgate as the only official Bible for Catholic Church, to be used in any public occasion, even though the use of vernacular in the Low Countries was very strong even after Trent, see François, "Vernacular Bible Reading". Incidentally, the triptych was realised for a Catholic Cathedral, while the city was suffering the mutiny of the Army of Flanders, which led to the sack of the city in 1576; this was therefore a very difficult geopolitical and confessional context, in which the painter, in any case, worked at meeting the client's requests. Cf. K. De Clippel, "Smashing images. The Antwerpen nude between 1563 and 1585", in Jonckheere/Suykerbuyk (ed.), *Art after Iconoclasm*, 51–73, on p. 64.

81 However, that hand might also be a reference to Albrecht Durer's *Melancholia* (1514).

82 E. De Mol, "Le culte de la Vierge après le Concile de Trente perçu à travers trois triptyques flamands de la fin du XVIe siècle et du début du XVIIe siècle", in W. François/V. Soen (ed.), *The Council of Trent: Reform and Controversy in Europe and Beyond (1545–1700)* (3 vol.; Gottingen: V&R, 2017) 3.93–115, on p. 102.

83 De Mol, "Le culte de la Vierge", 109.

Fig 4 Gerard van Honthorst, *Adoration of the Shepherds*, c. 1619–20, Galleria delle Statue e delle Pitture degli Uffizi, inv. 1890 n. 739. Credit: Su concessione del Ministero della Cultura.

Two other elements characterise Joseph: his work and his staff. Concerning the former, Molanus accepts the apocryphal element of his being an artisan (*faber*), which is in line with Ambrose's metaphorical interpretation: as the Father is the 'maker' (*faber*) of the world, Jesus' putative father should also be an artisan (*faber*).[84] The latter idea is also handed down by the apocryphal source *De nativitate Mariae*, but in this case the representation itself is not to be blamed. Rather, its interpretation must be changed: the staff is to be intended as a sign of the virginal union between Mary and Joseph – making probable Joseph's virginity – rather than accepting the traditional meaning that painters generally apply to it, but which Molanus does not explain.[85]

84 "Sed habeat sane originem suam ex apocrypho scripto, quod hoc potius fabrile instrumentum elegerint, quam aliud ad significandum Iosephum fuisse Fabrum; non tamen inde sequitur Picturam hanc manifeste erroneam esse, aut etiam apocrypham. Securius etiam meminit Ambrosius, dum explicat, Josephum Fabrum, fuisse typum Patris Coelestis, qui etiam faber est", Molanus, *De historia sacrarum imaginum et picturarum*, 87–8.

85 "Aliquando vero in picturis corrigendae sunt non ipsae picturae, sed earum significatio. Sic, quod idem S. Iosephus, pingatur quandoque cum virente ramusculo in manu, sumpserunt Pictores ex Tractatu de Nativitate B. Mariae … Sed cum docti sciant fabulosam esse hunc Tractatum, et Hiero-

The third element is Christ's nudity: to Molanus, this must always be avoided, so that "children are not endangered by this or little ones brought to harm"[86] (cf. Matt 18:6–10; Mark 9:42–49, Luke 17:1–2). He also refers to William Durand, who in his *Rationale divinorum officiorum* maintains that Byzantine iconography never showed Jesus naked from the navel to the legs, precisely so as to prevent any possible illicit thoughts.[87] To reinforce his argument, Molanus appeals both to the Council of Trent, which rejected any lascivious image, and even to Erasmus, since "to many sick people – and hence to Reform-minded ones – Erasmus' authority and opinion is worth a lot". The reference is to both the *Christiani Matrimonii Institutio* (1526), in which the humanist states that images of nude bodies should be avoided, and the *Christiani Hominis Institutum* (1520), in which Erasmus quotes Aristotle's *Politics* (VII, 17, 1336b–1337a), where Aristotle argues that naked images induce people to corruption.[88] Not by coincidence, we find, in Mittendorff's painting *Adoration of the Shepherds*, Christ's privates covered by a white cloth and by the robes that are used with the same purpose by Pieter van Avont in his triptych in Aarschot.

---

nymo indignum, prout scriptores quidam eruditissime annotarunt, et res ipsa loquitur: dici potest per hunc Ramusculum non esse intelligendum id, quod pictores ex praedicta fabula intenderunt: sed referendum eum esse, ut significet Virginitatem Ioseph; nam, ut ex virginali coniugio virgo Filius nasceretur, etiam ipsum Ioseph semper virginem fuisse verisimile est", Molanus, *De historia sacrarum imaginum et picturarum*, 88. On Joseph's virginity, see I. Resnick, "Marriage in Medieval Culture: Consent Theory and The Case of Joseph and Mary", *Church History* 69 (2000) 350–71, on p. 354.

86 Freedberg, "Molanus on Provocative Paintings", 239.

87 "Notum est Pictores saepe Infantem Iesum nudum sculpere, aut pingere: sed ob hoc male audiunt a multis non exiguae pietatis et prudentiae viris. Quid enim in hac nuditate esse potest aedificationis? Atque utinam nulla hinc oriretur in parvulis destructio, nullum in pusillis scandalum. Viderit ergo Pictores, ne suo malo discant quid sit, quod Dominus ait *Qui scandalizaverit unum de pusillis isti, qui in me credunt, expedit ei ut suspendatur mola asinaria in collo eius, et demergatur in profundum maris … Vae homini illi per quem scandalum venit.* Certe si antiquas Picturas consulere velint, facile advertent in eis Puerum Iesum decenter et honeste depictum esse: ac sese multum a maiorum simplicitate degenerasse. His adde Gulielmus Durandus. *Graeci*, ait, *utuntur Imaginibus, pingentes illas, ut dicitur, solum ab umbilico supra, et non inferius, ut omnis stultae cogitationis occasio tollatur*", Molanus, *De historia sacrarum imaginum et picturarum*, 119–20. For the English translation of this section (book II, chapter 42) of Molanus' work, see Freedberg, "Molanus on Provocative Paintings", 239–42. See also Freedberg, "Hidden God", 135.

88 "Hoc facit et illud Erasmi, quod ex Institutione Matrimonii Christiani, quia ea a Patribus Tridentinis non abs re damnata est, citatione mea conservare cupio, eo quod apud multos infermos Erasmi authoritas et iudicium multum valeat", Molanus, *De historia sacrarum imaginum et picturarum*, 121. Then Molanus quotes Erasmus' works, cf. Erasmus, "Christiani Matrimonii Institutio", in *Opera Omnia*, V/6, 206–7. Freedberg indeed points out that "Erasmus saw the provocative element in art in the same light as Molanus"; Freedberg, "Molanus on Provocative Paintings", 234. However, Molanus "himself knew that the nakedness of the angels and of Adam and Eve could be regarded as a testimony of their innocence and sanctity", Freedberg, "Molanus on Provocative Paintings", 236.

Fig. 5 Erasmus II Quellinus, *Adoration of the Shepherds*, 1652, Munich: Alte Pinakothek. Credit © Bayerische Staatsgemäldesammlungen (https://res.cloudinary.com/tne/image/authenticated/s–eypJ9tfq–/q_80/artworks/ERASMUS-QUELLINUS_ANBETUNG-DER-HIRTEN_CC-BY-SA_BSTGS_4850.jpg accessed on 31 August 2022)

Similarly, Christ's privates are hidden in the right panel representing the Nativity in Jan Snellinck's *Ascension triptych*.[89] By contrast, in the above-mentioned Frans I Pourbus' *Adoration of the Magi*, Christ is completely naked, at the centre of the composition, as Ellénite de Mol emphases, "Jésus est associé à l'hostie, sa nudité renforçant visuellement cette relation", even though nudity was to be rejected.[90]

Another element of nakedness that might appear in these iconographies is Mary's breast, while she feeds Jesus: Molanus does not focus on this detail in this section, but he spends a few words on it in another part of the book, accepting it on the basis of Bernard of Clairvaux's authority.[91] This is a widespread iconography in the Middle

89 Freedberg "The problem of Images", 31. More specifically, the Church Visitor in Malines had asked for the removal of "certain nude figures" in Jan Snellinck's *Ascension*, cf. Freedberg "The problem of Images", 30.

90 De Mol, "Le culte de la Vierge", 99.

91 "De imagine Deiparae ostendentis Filio suo ubera desumpta est ex verbis sancti Bernardi, quae ex sermonibus frequenter citari solent: *O homo, securum habes accessum ad Deum, o homo, ubi mater ante filium, et filius ante patrem. Mater ostendit filio pectus et ubera; filius ostendit patri latus et vulnera*", Molanus, *De historia sacrarum imaginum et picturarum*, 93–4.

Ages and in the Renaissance – the so-called *Virgo lactans* or Γαλακτοτροφούσα – but some examples can still be found among post-Tridentine painters, such as Erasmus II Quellinus (1607–78), in his *Adoration of the Shepherds* (Munich, Alte Pinakothek, 1652; Fig. 5).

Fig. 6 After Hugo van der Goes, *Nativity at Night*, early 16th century, London: National Gallery. Credit: © The National Gallery, London.

Fourth, concerning the childbirth, Molanus insists on the fact that Mary received no assistance by obstetricians, even though they appear in some paintings: this fact is "against the historical truth".[92] With the single exception of its presenting a non-suffering Virgin, Campin's *Nativity* (Dijon, Musée des Beaux-Arts, c. 1420) is the sum of all these 'errors' (of course, according to Molanus' view): Jesus is

92 "Pictores quosdam, contra historicam veritatem, obstetricem divae Virginis amissis manibus pingere, cum non habuerit obstetricem", Molanus, *De historia sacrarum imaginum et picturarum*, 237.

completely naked, Joseph is old and there are indeed obstetricians.[93] Also in Hugo van der Goes' *Adoration of the Shepherds* (Berlin, Gemäldegalerie, c. 1480), Jesus is completely naked and his father is old,[94] as well as in his *Monforte Altarpiece* (Berlin, Gemäldegalerie, c. 1470). The midwives together with an aged Joseph also appear in the copy of Hugo van der Goes' *Nativity at Night* (London, National Gallery, early 16th century; Fig. 6) where Jesus' privates are covered, but by an almost transparent cloth. In the early 17th century, at least in the *Adoration of the Shepherds* (1608) by Peter Paul Rubens (1577–1640; preserved in Fermo), it seems that Molanus' canon is implemented: Jesus is covered, Joseph is not old, Mary looks painless. In the Antwerp *Sint-Pauluskerk*, there is another painting by Rubens with the same iconography (1611), with the very same characters.

Fifth, the presence of the donkey and the ox, which is not attested in the Gospels, but is accepted: once again Molanus refers to Erasmus, who included them on the basis of Isaiah 1:3, to which Molanus himself adds Hab 3:2.[95] Quoting Chrysostom describing the rich Nativity scene preserved in Constantinople, Molanus seems however to criticise the use of gold: as the Greek Church father says, Jesus was born in the dirt/mud (*lutum*), so Molanus – through Chrysostom's words – would avoid using precious metals while representing the birth of Christ, even though he cannot blame such use, since it exemplifies the reverence Catholics have for that event.[96]

Closely related to the Nativity is the Epiphany, with the arrival of the Three Wise Men. This is another iconography which was subject to different variations and which needed to be 'standardised'. Concerning the Biblical Magi, Molanus first rebuts Luther when he claims that they were not kings, and even casts doubt on their number.[97] Molanus totally rejects both claims, first declaring that they

93 Freedberg points out only the obstetricians, but Campin's painting indeed shows other elements that Molanus rejects as errors. See Freedberg, "The Hidden God", 135–36.

94 D. Ridderbos, "Die *Geburt Christi* des Hugo van der Goes. Form, Inhalt, Funktion", *Jahrbuch der Berliner Museen* 32 (1990) 137–52.

95 "De bove autem et de asino circa praesepe domini, Erasmus: *A priscis usque saeculi*, inquit, *manavit ad nos pictura, quae Iesu Praesepi addit bovem et asinum. Quod tamen in sacris litteris non est aperte proditum: sed occasio sumta videtur ex Isaiae prophetia* … Allegari etiam solet ex Abacuc iuxta Septuaginta duos interpretes … Quare ad apertam scripturam refero, quod Bonaventura scribit: *De bove et asino circa Praesepe Domini, non haberi auctoritatem, nisi antiquitatem picturae, quae vocatur scriptura laicorum*", Molanus, *De historia sacrarum imaginum et picturarum*, 237.

96 "Habuit denique Nativitas Domini nostri aureum Praesepium Constantinopoli; de quo Chrysostomus *o si mihi liceret videre illude Praesepe, in quo Dominus iacuit! Nunc nos Christiani, quasi pro honore tulimus luteum et posuimus argenteum: sed mihi pretiosus illud est quod ablatum est. Non condemno eos, qui honoris causa fecerunt. Neque enim illos condemno, qui in templo fecerunt vasa aurea: sed admiror Dominum. Qui creatorum mundi, non inter aurum et argentum, sed in luto nascitur*", Molanus, *De historia sacrarum imaginum et picturarum*, 398.

97 "Sequitur deinde solennitas Epiphaniae, seu Epiphaniorum Domini. Circa quam, si Lutherus audiendus foret, multipliciter errant pictores. Nam Magos Reges fuisse negant, et numerum eorum

are indeed kings, since they were powerful,[98] and second that the number of the Magi is probable: the Cathedral of Cologne preserves the relics of three Magi and Leo the Great maintained that there were three of them.[99] Molanus appeals to Pietro de' Natali (c. 1330–c. 1406) to describe them: in his *Catalogus sanctorum et gestorum eorum* he explains that there were three of them – Gaspar, 60 years old, Balthasar, 40 years old and finally Melchior, 20 years old. Molanus underlines that de' Natali's description is not anchored to any specific authority, and indeed the Italian himself seems to be quite dubious about it (*fertur*).[100] The Louvain theologian in the corresponding footnote to this passage also claims that the names of the Magi might be uncertain, as they are attested only from Petrus Comestor (1100–79) onwards.[101] Generally, one of them is painted as a Sub-Saharan man, even though there were examples of the Magi painted as Caucasian. The latter iconography is the one preferred by Molanus and Lindanus as well, on the basis of the central panel of the *Dombild Altarpiece* (1440–42) representing the *Adoration of the Magi* (painted by the 15th-century German artist Stefan Lochner [c. 1400/10–51], then preserved in Cologne in the Church of Saint Mary in Jerusalem, and now in the Cathedral).[102]

---

incertum facit. Nos igitur quid veritas habeat, expendamus", Molanus, *De historia sacrarum imaginum et picturarum*, 239.

98 "Recte tamen Magi isti Reges dicuntur, quoniam scilicet potentes erant", Molanus, *De historia sacrarum imaginum et picturarum*, 243.

99 "Caeterum probabile esset, quod Lutherus asserit, incertum esse numerum magorum, nisi Ecclesia Coloniensis trium Magorum corpora religiose conservaret, et a gravissimo doctore, Leone Magno, allisque auctoribus, tres fuisse memorarentur", Molanus, *De historia sacrarum imaginum et picturarum*, 245.

100 "Quod ad Magos attinet, *Fertur*, ait Petrus de Natalibus, *cum ad Christum venerunt, Gaspar fuisse annorum sexaginta: Balthazar, quadraginta, et Melchior, viginti: et ita communiter pingitur*. Sed nota in his verbis, quod dicat *fertur*, Qua voce satis subinsinuat istud apud nullum gravem autorem legi; quamvis nescio unde, nonnuliis e vulgo ita persuasum sit. Non igitur a quoquam Ecclesiae praefecto male audiet, qui hanc aetatum considerationem in Magorum delineatione negliget", Molanus, *De historia sacrarum imaginum et picturarum*, 239. See P. de Natali, *Catalogus sanctorum et gestorum eorum* (Lyon: Saccon, 1514) XXIV–XXV.

101 "Negligi etiam possunt nomina Gaspar, Melchior and Balthasar, quae nullus puto, Magis tribuit, ante Petrum Comestorem", Molanus, *De historia sacrarum imaginum et picturarum*, 239, n. L.

102 "Deinde quidam pingunt unum Magorum Nigrum, aut potius subnigrum, et fuscus, quales sunt albiores Mauritani. Quod mihi valde recens videtur. Nam in picturis vetustioribus saepius omnes tres candidos pingi observavi. Unde pulchre de hac Pictura ait *Porro quod Magis illis vulgo creditur, unum fuisse Aethiopem, eodem videlicet ad traditiones medii generis (de quibus pridem respondit Hieronymus: eadem facilitate contemni, qua dicitur) referemdi, putarim* [equidem, quod Coloniensis Ecclesias candidos pingat]", Molanus, *De historia sacrarum imaginum et picturarum*, 239–40. In square brackets I added the continuation of Lindanus' quote. See W. van der Lindt, *Panoplia Evangelica, Sive De Verbo Dei Evangelico Libri Qvinqve* (Cologne: Cholinus, 1568) 676. See also Freedberg, "The Hidden God", 136. Strangely in the corresponding footnote 28, Freedberg maintains that Molanus spent many pages to show that one of the Magi was not a Sub-Saharan man: this

Fig. 7 Peter Paul Rubens, *The Adoration of the Magi*, 1624, Antwerp: Koninklijk Museum voor Schone Kunsten, inv. no. 298. Credit: Collection KMSKA – Flemish Community (CC0) photo: Rik Klein Gotink.

A very good example of the implementation of Molanus' ideas seems to be the *Adoration of the Magi* (1629) by Hendrik de Clerck (c. 1570–1630) from Brussels. He made this work for the *Kerk van Sint-Pieters en Sint-Guido* in Anderlecht, duly covering Christ's privates. The Virgin's face is relaxed, Joseph is a young adult, the three Biblical Magi wear a crown to indicate their kingship. Their ages are clearly different; nonetheless, the younger is Sub-Saharan, contrary to Molanus' and Lindanus' ideas. Actually, early 17th-century paintings do not show consistency in depicting the younger Magus; for instance, Rubens made him Berberian in 1624

is actually not the case. Molanus spends only a few lines on the colour of the skin of the Magi, while most of his argument is addressed to another topic: their kingship, see Molanus, *De historia sacrarum imaginum et picturarum*, 241–45. Interestingly, the Magi of the *Dombild Altarpiece* are Caucasian, but one of the banners shows a Sub-Saharan man.

(Antwerp, Koninklijk Museum voor Schone Kunsten; Fig. 7), but painted the Magus as Sub-Saharan in the 1609 canvas (Madrid, Museo del Prado), as he also appears in the 1652 work (Greenville, Bob Jones University Collection) by the German-born artist Jan Boeckhorst (c. 1604–68). Moreover, in both paintings – Rubens 1609 and Boeckhorst 1652 – Joseph is old, and in the former Jesus' privates are not covered, contrary to Molanus' canon.

The Dormition and the Assumption of the Virgin

Finally, the last case study is the Assumption of Mary. To describe this iconography, Molanus appeals to the Roman Breviary.[103] The representation of the Assumption generally shows three events: the death and the burial – together with all the Apostles except Thomas – in addition to the Assumption itself. However, Molanus does not appreciate the representation of both the death and the burial: he wants to reject (*refragari velim*) this "widespread tale" (*vulgata historia*), "universally accepted by the popular piety", since the Roman Breviary demonstrates how this tradition was handed down by the apocryphal book *De Transitu Mariae*, with which already Jerome had recommended caution, stating that it was better "not to accept dubious elements as sure ones".[104]

On the other hand, the Eastern tradition does not show Mary's death, preferring the *dormitio virginis*, but Molanus does not approve this iconography on the basis of what John of Damascus, John Eck and Josse Clichtove say of it.[105] As De Mol affirms, "Malgré ce discrédit, elle continua à se maintenir au seizième siècle et au

103 "Ad medium mensis occurrit celebritas Assumtionis Sanctissimae Deiparae Virginis. In qua quod ei, dum moritur, item dum sepelitur, Apostoli omnes, praeter Thomam, adesse pingantur, referendum videtur inter eas picturas, quae populari pietate universaliter receptae sunt: non absque testimonio multorum Graecorum, et aliquot Latinorum. Cui picturae absit, ut refragari velim, cum sciam vulgatam hanc historiam, Iohannis Damasceni verbis, annue legi in restituto Romanae Ecclesiae Breviario", Molanus, *De historia sacrarum imaginum et picturarum*, 330.

104 "Sed haec videntur et putantur originem suam habere ex apocrypho scripto, de quo apud Hieronymum legitur: *Si venerit in manus vestras illud Apocryphum de Transitu Mariae, dubia pro certis non recipiatis*", Molanus, *De historia sacrarum imaginum et picturarum*, 331.

105 "Opinatur autem Iohannes Eckius Mariam obdormientem seu e vita migrantem, non esse pingendam habit morientis … Iodocus vero Clichtoveus, in libro de Assumptione Mariae, paulo ulterior progreditur. Sic enim: *Tam fuit a dolore carnis extranea, quam corruptione fuerat alien. Crediderim eam non debubuisse lecto, more aegrotantium, et qui morbo pressi claudunt hac vitam (cum venia Pictorum et Sculptorum) cum neque infirmitate vexata credi potius debet, neque debilitate prostrata: sed flexis reverenter genibus, et sublatis in caelum manibus, inter orandum, acceptissimum Deo spiritum commendasse*", Molanus, *De historia sacrarum imaginum*, 331–32. See J. Clichtove, *De puritate conceptioni beatae Mariae Virginis: libri duo, De dolore eiusdem sacrae virginis in passione filii sui: liber unus. De eiusdem iuxta crucem filii sui statione: homelia. De assumptione ispius gloriosae virginis: libri duo* (Paris: Estienne, 1513) 88v. See Freedberg, "Hidden God", 135.

Fig. 8 After Hugo van der Goes, *The Death of the Virgin*, probably after 1500. Credit: © The National Gallery, London.

début du dix-septième siècle".[106] In any case, the Virgin Mary must not be painted as a sick person, since she did not suffer while passing away, contrary to what happens for instance in the *Death of the Virgin* (Bruges, Groeningemuseum, c. 1475) by Hugo van der Goes,[107] as well as in the copy of this work preserved at the London National Gallery (Fig. 8), or in the same iconography (Amsterdam, Rijksmuseum, c. 1500) by the Master of the Amsterdam Death of the Virgin. By contrast, in the two versions of the *Death of the Virgin* (Munich, Alte Pinakothek, 1520; Cologne, Wallraf-Richartz Museum, early 16th century) by Joos van Cleve (1485–1540), Mary looks as though she were sleeping. There is a transition of the iconography with Petrus Christus' *Death of the Virgin* (San Diego CA, Timken Museum of

106 De Mol, "Le culte de la Vierge", 111. See De Mol's examples at pp. 111–12.

107 B. Ridderbos, "Hugo van Der Goes's 'Death of the Virgin' and the Modern Devotion: An Analysis of a Creative Process", *Oud Holland* 120 (2007) 1–30.

Fig. 9 Peter Paul Rubens, *Assumption of Mary*, 1626, Antwerp: *Onze-Lieve-Vrouwekathedraal*. Credit: Our Lady Cathedral Antwerp, www.art-inflanders.be, photo Hugo Maertens.

Art, Putnam Foundation, 1460–65), in which the Flemish artist shows Mary both serenely passing away and ascending to the heavens, similarly to both the *Polyptych with Death of the Virgin* (Brussels, CPAS-OCMW, 1520) by Bernard van Orley (c. 1491–1542) and the *Death and the Assumption of the Virgin* (Madrid, Museo del Prado, before 1550) by Michiel Coxcie (1499–1592), while in the *Assumption of Mary* (Antwerp, *Onze-Lieve-Vrouwekathedraal*, 1626; Fig. 9) by Rubens the focus of the painting is the Virgin Mary in the heavens.[108]

After the Assumption, Mary becomes the Queen of Heavens, as described in Rev 12:1: "A woman clothed with the sun, and the moon under her feet, and on her head a crown of twelve stars", with the privilege of the Nine Choirs of Angels, who can therefore be painted close to Mary. While describing this iconography, Molanus shows that he is informed about how it was represented outside the Low Countries. In particular, Jan van Grave had explained to him that in churches in Rome, Christ is represented together with Mary, and Molanus adds that the same thing happens in Germany.[109] The Louvain theologian chose to give a Mariological reading of

---

108 As Freedberg shows, Rubens was influenced by Nadal's book while realising his Leningrad *Assumption and Coronation of the Virgin*, see D. Freedberg, "A Source for Rubens's Modello of the *Assumption and Coronation of the Virgin*: A Case Study in the Response to Images", *The Burlington Magazine* 120 (1978) 432–41.

109 "At postquam Maria assumpta est in caelum, Regina caelorum facta, ei quoque Reginalem statuam erigendam esse putavit Ecclesia, in modum de quo scribitur in Apocalypsi, ubi divus Iohannes

Gen. 3:15,[110] and this could form a close link between the first and the last book of the Catholic Bible, Genesis and Revelation – between Eve crushing the head of the snake and a "woman clothed with the sun", interpreted as the Virgin Mary. Molanus appeals to this link, underlining that in the iconography Mary crushes the head of the Snake to remove the curse of Eve following original sin. The Snake must be painted as black and ugly, as the Prince of Darkness: it represents the heretics. The Virgin not only crushes the Serpent, but also its progeny, "universal heretical pravity".[111] Rubens shows the relation between Eve and the Queen of Heavens in his *Immaculate Conception* (Madrid, Museo del Prado, 1628–29): Mary steps on a snake with an apple in its jaws. However, he painted this during his second visit to Madrid, and a copy of it (London, British Museum, 1630/50) was printed by Cornelis Galle I (1576–1650). Similarly, Johannes Stradanus (1523–1605) engraved *Our Lady of the Immaculate Conception with the Symbols of the Laurentian Litany* (London, British Museum, after c. 1611). No other significant examples of the Immaculate Conception by 17th-century Netherlandish artists were found, even if it was 'promoted' by some theologians[112] – possible evidence that this iconography

---

vidit Reginam hanc amictam sole, et luna sub pedibus eius, in capite gestantem Coronam stellarum duodecim. Est enim coronata Maria novem Chorum Angelicorum privilegio … Nec incongure Angeli pinguntur circa effigiem superbenedictae Virginis, ubi ad caelum assumitur … Romae vero, ubi haec pictura in diversiis ecclesiis visitur, observavit, mihique communicavit, Iohannes Gravius, adiungi Christum, qui gloriosissimam Virginem Materm suam manibus defert in caelum: eam quoque pictura per Alemanniam frequentari … Addit Conradus Brunus *Eadem quoque Mater Domini, assumpta in caelum, recte ita pingetur, ut a superbenedicta Trinitate, tanquam regina caelorum coronetur*", Molanus, *De historia sacrarum imaginum et picturarum*, 332–33.

110 A. Gerace, *Biblical Scholarship in Louvain in the Golden Sixteenth Century* (Göttingen: V&R, 2019) 74–81.

111 "Huc etiam pertinet Deiparae, Virginis et Dominae nostrae, pictura, cum diabolo, aut Dracone sub pedibus. Ipsa est enim, quae Evae maledictionem abstulit et maxima gloria Diabolum vicit … Pingitur autem nigro colore, turpis, et tenebrosus, sicut decet amatorem turpitudinis, et Principem tenebrarum figurari. Dum vero eum a Deipara Virgine conteri video, in mentem revoco, quod in initio Pentateuchi habetur: *Inimicitias ponam inter te et mulierem, et sement tuum et semen illius. Ipsa conteret caput tuum* … Addit eum [viz. Richardus a Wassebourch] Ecclesiam Sanctae Mariae construxisse, in qua imaginem Beatae Mariae apposuit, in qua Serpens sub pedibus eius pingitur, significans haereticos, et adversarios eius … Quomodo autem ipsa Deipara Virgo Maria, ex sanctorum veterumque Scriptorum sententia, non tantum Serpentem, sed et semen eius, universam haereticam pravitatem, contriverit, docte et eleganter contra Sectariorum calumnias asserit Petrus Canisius, Societas Iesu Theologus, in libro quincto, de Maria", Molanus, *De historia sacrarum imaginum et picturarum*, 333–35. See Canisius, *Commentariorum de verbi Dei corruptelis, tomi duo*, 892–902.

112 The Immaculate Conception was indeed the subject of a few works in the first half of the 17th century in Louvain: A. Sander, *De conceptione B. Mariæ virginis panegyricus* (Louvain: Ph. Van Dormael, 1618); N. Vernulaeus, *De conceptione et visitatione deiparae Virginis, orationes duae habitae* (Louvain: J.Ch. Flavius, 1614); D. Walravens, *De sancta et immaculata sanctiss[imae] gloriosiss[imae] et semper*

was not taken into consideration by Flemish painters and their clients, who were perhaps more interested in the Assumption.[113]

Conclusion[114]

Post-Tridentine theologians put their efforts into furnishing a canon of religious images. Molanus', Paleotti's and Nadal's works are attempts to standardise Catholic iconographies, as a way to define what could be accepted and what must be rejected. Molanus probably felt this need more than the others, since he experienced the devastation of the holy images caused by Calvinist rebels in the Spanish Low Countries. Politics and religious affairs were inextricably linked to each other and the defence of artistic production against the iconoclasts required a clear explanation of the reasons why the sacred images were not idols. With this aim, at the beginning of the Dutch revolt, between 1569 and 1570, Sanders and Molanus published two treatises in Louvain, *De typica et honoraria sacrarum imaginum adoratione* and *De picturis et imaginibus sacris* respectively. Molanus then further elaborated his book, which was eventually posthumously published in 1594 as *De historia sacrarum imaginum et picturarum*. Molanus' intentions are clear: he wants not only to defend the Catholic use of images in a land that had suffered the loss of many works of art, but he also feels the need to educate the artists reproducing Christian iconographies. He wanted to provide a canon, which could offer a clear overview of all the possible sacred images. In so doing, he also condemned many figurations that he considered too dangerous, even heretical, like the *Logosknabe*. He based his work on the Greek and Latin Church Fathers, scholastic theologians and contemporary authors who had not necessarily written specific treatises on the images, but who had included their views in a plethora of sources, from questions to sermons, passing through exegetical commentaries. It was a tremendous amount of work.

Among the sources that Molanus draws from, references are inevitably made to apocryphal writings, toward which he reveals a twofold approach.[115] On the one

---

virginis Mariæ conceptione, annunciatione, purificatione, assumptione, carmina sacra (Louvain: J.I. Masius, 1608).

113 However, a private devotion related to the Immaculate Conception – but without elements such as the moon under the Virgin's feet and/or the snake – has been attested in the Low Countries since the beginning of the 16th century. See F. Scholten, "A Late Medieval Ivory of the Immaculate Conception from the Low Countries", in A. von Hülsen-Esch/D. Täube (ed.), *"Luft unter die Flügel" Beiträge für mittelalterlichen Kunst. Festschrift fur Hiltrud Westermann-Angerhausen* (Hildesheim: Georg Olms Verlag, 2010) 186–93.

114 This section is authored by Tamara Dominici and Antonio Gerace.

115 Freedberg, "The Hidden God", 136.

hand, he claims that they must be rejected, since they are not part of the canon of the Scriptures. This happens for instance in the representation of the *Death of the Virgin* based on *De transitu Virginis*, or the Nativity, with the presence of obstetricians as described in *De infantia Salvatoris*. On the other hand, he accepts other elements, like Joseph as *faber*, if they are substantiated by the Tradition of the Church Fathers (Ambrose in this case). At first sight, the choice to accept or refuse certain apocryphal elements might be considered idiosyncratic, but the reason behind it can be explained in these terms: if an apocryphal element might show a human weakness, as the suffering dimension of Mary's childbirth, it must be rejected. But if an element can exalt the extraordinary quality of a character, it can be accepted, as for example Joseph's staff, the symbol of virginal union with Mary. In addition, other elements that do not appear in the sources can be used, but only if they are complementary to the scene (such as the donkey and the ox in the Nativity), or if they have a narrative character, capable of attracting the flock through a visualised description of the Gospel, like a vast desert in representations of the Flight into Egypt.

What about the impact of Molanus' work? It is very hard to answer this question: in this essay we have focused only on the iconographies representing the Virgin Mary made in the Low Countries, and although we made reference to several paintings, we cannot give this question a definitive answer. An adequate study of it would indeed involve all the iconographies the Louvain theologian describes – especially those related to private devotion – and the entire Netherlandish artistic production, focusing not only on paintings, but also on sculptures and woodcuts – analysis which cannot be offered in a single essay. However, we may note that painters did not always or consistently follow Molanus' indications, at least in the iconographies here analysed. For instance, in the representation of the three Magi, the youngest is generally painted as a Sub-Saharan man, as indicated by the tradition; similarly, Joseph is shown to be an old man even in the 17th century, in both cases contrary to the Louvain theologian's indication. In this essay, we have also evidenced other examples. In conclusion, as David Freedberg points out, "Fifteenth-century works as well as contemporary ones have deliberately been chosen to illustrate the kinds of subjects which Molanus wished to proscribe. They testify not only to his awareness of the art around him – a rare enough phenomenon amongst the theological writers on art – but also to the strength of certain pictorial traditions. In this respect, as will become apparent, Molanus was tilting at windmills".[116]

116 Freedberg, "The Hidden God", 136.

Section 3
Hagiographical Representations: The Jesuits

Shiri Roelofs

Robert Bellarmine (1542–1621), the Louvain Lectures, and Economic Thought

Image and Impact of a Saint Viewed from an Underestimated Perspective

Introduction: Saint Robert Bellarmine and the Louvain lectures

The vagaries of the Brabant climate did not impede Jesuit superiors from sending Padua's most brilliant theology student to the Southern Low Countries. In fact, Robert Bellarmine's (1542–1621) delicate health, certainly less challenged under the Italian sun,[1] took no priority over the foreseen import of the student's excellent sermons in a region that was challenged by the circulation of Protestant ideas far more than the Italian peninsula was.[2] Upon this consideration, Father Juan Alfonso de Polanco (1517–1576), the celebrated secretary of the Society of Jesus, instructed the Jesuit pupil to finish his theological studies at the University of Louvain with the remit to provide his fellow students on site with Latin sermons.[3] Obeying the command, young Bellarmine – not having reached the age of 27 – left his

---

1 "... noluerunt Patres Patavini eum dimittere, et P. Generali responderunt, periculum esse, ne N. [Bellarminus] hiberno tempore frigus germanicum ferre non posset, et hoc esse etiam judicium medici." X.-M. Le Bachelet, S.J., *Bellarmin avant son cardinalat: 1542–1598: correspondance et documents* (Paris: Beauchesne, 1911), 450.

The author would like to thank Prof. Dr W. Druwé (KU Leuven) and Prof. Dr W. Decock (UCLouvain and ULiège) for their helpful comments on earlier versions of the present chapter. The contribution forms part of the doctoral research conducted by the author at the KU Leuven in the context of the @AULAM project (BOF Research Fund, project number: C14/19/012) 'Innovation Through Education: Pioneering Change in Law and Theology in Louvain's Golden Age' (https://www.kuleuven.be/lectio/research/aulam, last access: 14/11/2022). Within this project, the author's research seeks to understand how the early modern languages of law and economics enabled Robert Bellarmine to construct a normative framework of exchange dealings in his Louvain lectures.

2 See R. de le Court, S.J., 'Saint Bellarmin à Louvain (1569–1576)', *Revue d'histoire ecclésiastique* 28, no. 1 (1932) 74–83, on p. 76; L'Université Catholique de Louvain, 'Séjour de Cardinal Bellarmin à Louvain et ses rapports avec l'Université', in *Annuaire de l'Université Catholique de Louvain* (Louvain: Vanlinthout et Vandenzande, 1841) 164–75, on p. 164.

3 De le Court, 'Saint Bellarmin à Louvain', 75–6; M. Biersack, Initia Bellarminiana*: die Prädestinationslehre bei Robert Bellarmin SJ bis zu seinen Löwener Vorlesungen 1570–1576* (Stuttgart: Steiner, 1989), 42; S. Tutino, *Empire of Souls. Robert Bellarmine and the Christian Commonwealth* (Oxford: Oxford University Press, 2010), 11; Le Bachelet, *Bellarmin avant son cardinalat*, 59–60.

patria for the intellectual beating heart of the Southern Low Countries. During his stay (1569–1576) in the hinterland of the Catholic world, Bellarmine encountered many challenges that are largely recounted by Giacomo Fuligatti (1577–1653) and Daniello Bartoli (1608–1685) who wrote the first *Vitae* of Bellarmine in the decades following his death in 1621.[4] These hagiographies constituted the beginning of a campaign that was waged by the Jesuit Society for Bellarmine's elevation to sanctity. This panegyric[5] cult lasted over three centuries until the intended goal was finally achieved with the inscription of Bellarmine's name into the catalogue of the Saints in 1930.

The first attempt for Bellarmine's canonisation ran from his death until the suppression of the Jesuit Society in 1773, during which period the process was paused in 1678 and 1753 as a result of divergent views within the Congregation of Rites.[6] After the restoration of the Society of Jesus in 1814, the case was resumed under Pope Leo XII in 1827 but again held back due to several charges of fallacies against Bellarmine's doctrine.[7] In 1923, Bellarmine was finally declared 'Blessed', which paved the way not only for his canonisation as Saint seven years later but also for the Church's decision to bestow upon him the title of Doctor of the Church in 1931. The decretal letters regarding these events extol, amongst others, Bellarmine's

---

4 G. Fuligatti, *Vita del Cardinale Roberto Bellarmino della Compagnia di Giesù* (in Roma appresso l'herede di Bartolomeo Zannetti, 1624); D. Bartoli, *Della vita di Roberto Cardinal Bellarmino Arcivescovo di Capua della Compagnia di Giesù* (in Roma a spese di Nicolò Angelo Tinassi, 1678).

5 … as J.W. Parker and Son put it, see 'Cardinal Bellarmine's Autobiography', *Saturday Review of Politics, Literature, Science and Art* 36, no. 1644 (1887) 611–12, on p. 611. Besides those of Fuligatti and Bartoli, Bellarmine's hagiographic cult includes, amongst others, the following Jesuit contributions: N. Frizon, S.J., *La vie du cardinal Bellarmin, de la Compagnie de Jésus* (Nancy: P. Barbier, 1708); E. Raitz von Frentz, S.J., *Der ehrwürdige Kardinal Robert Bellarmin S.I., ein Vorkämpfer für Kirche und Papsttum, 1542–1621* (Freiburg: Herder, 1921); J. Thermes, S.J., *Le bienheureux Robert Bellarmin, 1542–1621* (Paris: Gabalda, 1923); J. Brodrick, S.J., *The Life and Work of Blessed Robert Bellarmine, S.J., 1542–1621*, vol. 2 (London: Burns and Oates, 1928); id., *Robert Bellarmine: Saint and Scholar* (London: Burns and Oates, 1961). For the state of the literature on Bellarmine that was published in the 20th century, see A. Mancia, 'Bibliografia sistematica e commentate degli studi sull'opera bellarminiana dal 1900 al 1990', in G. Galeota (ed.), *Roberto Bellarmino Arcivescovo di Capua teologo e pastore della Riforma cattolica* (Capua: Archidiocesi di Capua-Istituto superiore di scienze religiose, 1990) 805–72.

6 F. Motta/E. Rai, 'Jesuit Sanctity: Hypothesizing the Continuity of a Hagiographic Narrative of the Modern Age', *Journal of Jesuit Studies* 9 (2022) 1–14, on p. 8. See also E. Raitz von Frentz, S.J., 'Der Heiligsprechungsprozess des Kardinals Bellarmin. Zu seinem Abschluss am 29. Juni 1930,' *Stimmen der Zeit* 119, no. 5 (1930) 332–44, on pp. 333–9.

7 D.S. Schaff, 'Cardinal Bellarmine. Now Saint and Doctor of the Church', *Church History* 2, no. 1 (1933) 41–55, on p. 47. See also F. Motta, 'Il processo di canonizzazione (1622–1930)', in M. Sodi/ A. Glusiuk (ed.), *Bellarmino e i Gesuiti a Montepulciano. Studi in occasione del IV centenario della morte di San Roberto (1621–2021)* (Florence: Olschki, 2022) 35–47, on pp. 42–4; Raitz von Frentz, 'Der Heiligsprechungsprozess des Kardinals Bellarmin', 339–44.

role in the Church's combat against heresy,[8] a role whose roots mostly lie in the Saint's short-lived sojourn in the illustrious intellectual capital of the Southern Low Countries. Indeed, in Louvain, Bellarmine closely witnessed the challenges of both the Age of Reformation and intra-Catholic disputes, experiences that would contribute to the development of his anti-heretical and political framework that he would further develop in his post-Louvain life.[9]

Today, Saint Robert Bellarmine, affectionally called "*malleus haereticorum*",[10] is considered one of the pivotal theologians of post-Tridentine Catholicism. In this context, the *Controversiae* (published in three tomes between 1586 and 1593) is generally considered the most famous work amongst the Saint's writings. It embodies the thought of Thomas Aquinas (c. 1225–1274), a leading authority in the late scholastic tradition.[11] The *Controversiae* grew out of the lectures that Bellarmine gave at the *Collegium Romanum* in Rome between 1578 and 1589. These classes, commonly known under the name 'Controversies', aimed to provide students with a framework for combatting heresies.[12] These lectures, in turn, were inspired by the Saint's earlier activities in Louvain (1569–1576), where he ended

8 The opening lines of the decretal on Bellarmine's canonisation as Saint state: "Ipse [Robertus Bellarminus] enim, … [Ecclesiam Dei] a pravis machinationibus haereticorum strenuissime defendit." *Acta Apostolicae Sedis. Commentarium officiale*, annus XII, volumen XXII (Romae: typis polyglottis Vaticanis, MDCCCCXXX), 31 Decembris 1930, no. 14, *litterae decretales*, 593–604, on p. 593. See also Schaff, 'Cardinal Bellarmine. Now Saint and Doctor of the Church', 47. The first words of the relevant papal letter regarding Bellarmine's proclamation as Doctor of the Church read: "… Sanctus Robertus Bellarminus, … qui iam ab ipsis sanctissime mortis diebus 'vir eximius, theologus insignis, strenuus Fidei catholicae Defensor, haereticorum malleus' nuncupabatur, … ." *Acta Apostolicae Sedis. Commentarium officiale*, annus XIII, volumen XXIII (Romae: typis polyglottis Vaticanis, MDCCCCXXXI), 9 Novembris 1931, no. 15, *litterae apostolicae*, IV, 433–8, on p. 433. See also Motta/Rai, 'Jesuit Sanctity', 8.

9 De le Court, 'Saint Bellarmin à Louvain', 74; Biersack, *Initia Bellarminiana*, 42–74, see notably p. 72; L. Ceyssens, 'Bellarmin et Louvain (1569–1576)', in M. Lamberigts (ed.), *L'Augustinisme à l'ancienne faculté de théologie de Louvain* (Leuven: Leuven University Press, 1994) 179–205, see notably pp. 190–201; Tutino, *Empire of Souls*, 9–24.

10 Allegedly, Bellarmine was called the 'hammer of the heretics' by Benedict XIV, see *Acta Apostolicae Sedis. Commentarium officiale*, 31 Decembris 1930, 596.

11 See especially L. Lanza/M. Toste (ed.), Summistae. *The Commentary Tradition on Thomas Aquinas'* Summa Theologiae *From the 15th to the 17th Centuries* (Leuven: Leuven University Press, 2021). The influence of Aquinas's *Summa theologiae* did not decline after the 17th century, see J. Schmutz, 'From Theology to Philosophy: The Changing Status of the *Summa theologiae*, 1500–2000', in J. Hause (ed.), *Aquinas's* Summa theologiae: *A Critical Guide* (Cambridge: Cambridge University Press, 2018) 221–41.

12 Biersack, *Initia Bellarminiana*, 72–4. For overviews concerning the content and conserved sources of these teachings for each academic year, see S. Tromp, 'Conspectus chronologicus praelectionum quas habuit S. Robertus Bellarminus in Collegio S.I. Lovaniensi et Collegio Romano', *Gregorianum* 16, no. 1 (1935) 97–105, on pp. 101–5.

up teaching theology at the Jesuit College for most of his stay.[13] During these classes, Bellarmine dictated the course material that he had prepared in advance. These teachings all together form a large commentary of the *Summa theologiae*, the masterpiece of Aquinas.

The theology course that Bellarmine delivered in Louvain – today known as the 'Louvain lectures' – is not virgin territory as such. While less recent biographical studies sufficiently explored Bellarmine's occupations in the Southern Low Countries,[14] only few have delved into the content of the Louvain lectures. Baldini and Coyne, for instance, studied the teachings in relation to the Church's condemnation of Galileo Galilei's (1564–1642) theory of heliocentrism.[15] The lectures also form part of the primary sources in Galeota's analysis of Bellarmine's refutations of Michael de Bay (1513–1589), whose controversial propositions concerning the concepts of grace, predestination, and free will had initiated theological turmoil in Louvain before Bellarmine's arrival.[16] In this context, a ground-breaking study is the one conducted by Biersack, who showed how Bellarmine's lectures dealt with these issues.[17] Even after Bellarmine had returned to Italy for quite some time, his intervention in these ongoing theological debates was frequently put forward by his successor and fellow-Jesuit Leonardus Lessius (1554–1623),[18] the celebrated 'Oracle of the Low Countries'.[19]

---

13 Biersack, *Initia Bellarminiana*, 92–8.

14 See for instance Ceyssens, 'Bellarmin et Louvain (1569–1576)'; A.H.J. Cauchie, 'Bellarmin et l'Université de Louvain d'après un livre récent', *Bureau des Analectes* 37 (1911) 384–401; De le Court, 'Saint Bellarmin à Louvain'.

15 U. Baldini/G.V. Coyne, *The Louvain Lectures (*Lectiones Lovanienses*) of Bellarmine and the Autograph Copy of his 1616 Declaration to Galileo. Texts in the Original Latin (Italian) with English Translation, Introduction, Commentary and Notes* (Vatican City: Specola Vaticana, 1984). As this study also observes on p. 5, the name *lectiones Lovanienses* or *praelectiones Lovanienses* is a matter of convention; Bellarmine himself did not refer to his course in this way.

16 G. Galeota, *Bellarmino contro Baio a Lovanio. Studio e testo di un inedito Bellarminiano* (Herder-Roma: Imprimatur Paulus Savino, Vicarius Generalis, 1966).

17 Biersack, *Initia Bellarminiana*.

18 See E. Rai, '*Ex Meritis Praevisis*: Predestination, Grace, and Free Will in Intra-Jesuit Controversies (1587–1613)', *Journal of Early Modern Christianity* 7, no. 1 (2020) 111–50. Many letters between Lessius and Bellarmine have been published by Le Bachelet, *Bellarmin avant son cardinalat*. See also M. Lamberigts, 'The Dispute Between the Louvain Faculty of Theology and the Jesuits (1587–1588). '*Solus Augustus*' Versus Thomist Positions', in B. Dahlke/B. Knorn (ed.), *Eine Autorität für die Dogmatik? Thomas von Aquin in der Neuzeit. Festschrift für Leonhard Hell* (Freiburg/Basel/Wien: Herder, 2018) 32–46. Furthermore, the turmoil in Louvain between the University and the Jesuits was not confined to theological matters but was institutional in nature as well, see J. Roegiers, 'Awkward Neighbours. The Leuven Faculty of Theology and the Jesuit College (1542–1773)', in R. Faesen/L. Kenis, *The Jesuits of the Low Countries: Identity and Impact (1540–1773): Proceedings of the International Congress at the Faculty of Theology and Religious Studies, KU Leuven (3–5 December 2009)* (Leuven: Peeters, 2012) 153–75.

As testified by an eyewitness account imparted by Lessius, Bellarmine's Louvain lectures explained "difficult matters with great clarity".[20] Perhaps some of these *res difficiles* are related to the theme of business ethics, a topic that was heavily debated amongst early modern theologians.[21] Despite this unknown and hence intriguing aspect of the Saint's intellectual thought, no systematic study has seized the opening, given by Van Houdt, for further research into the manuscripts featuring the Louvain lectures that addressed, amongst others, economic topics.[22] This could be due to the simple fact that only part of Bellarmine's handwritten legacy has been published so far, an immense enterprise initiated by X.-M. Le Bachelet (1855–1925) and continued by his fellow-Jesuit S. Tromp (1889–1975).[23] Interestingly, Tromp also

19 There is a great number of biographical essays on Lessius. A select few are: W. Decock, *Le marché du mérite. Penser le droit et l'économie avec Léonard Lessius* (Bruxelles: Zones Sensibles Editions, 2019), see particularly the first chapter on pp. 13–26; T. Van Houdt, *Leonardus Lessius: traditie en vernieuwing* (Antwerpen: Marie-Elisabeth Belpaire, 2005); id., 'Leonardus Lessius', in W. Decock/ J.W. Oosterhuis (ed.), *Great Christian Jurists in the Low Countries* (Cambridge: Cambridge University Press, 2021) 64–79.

20 The full passage reads: "Magna erat opinio doctrinae P. Bellar. Lovanii, eo quod optima methodo ut magna claritate res difficiles explicaret." See the photo collection 'Louvain. Controverse des grades (1618–1623)', Archives de la Province Belge Méridionale et du Luxembourg de la Compagnie de Jésus (ABML), section IX, Fonds Photos Alfred Poncelet. See also T. Van Houdt, 'On 'Medium' and 'Message' in Late Scholastic Moral Theology. The Economic and Ethical Writings of Robert Bellarmine, 1570–1576, and Leonardus Lessius, 1605', *Lias. Sources and Documents Relating to the Early Modern History of Ideas* 21, no. 2 (1995 [1994]) 183–201, on p. 186, n. 11.

21 See for instance M. Grice-Hutchinson, *The School of Salamanca: Readings in Spanish Monetary Theory, 1544–1605* (Oxford: Clarendon Press, 1952); F. Gómez Camacho, S.J., *Economía y filosofía moral: la formación del pensamiento económico europeo en la escolástica Española* (Madrid: Editorial Síntesis, 1998); A.A. Chafuen, *Faith and Liberty: The Economic Thought of the Late Scholastics* (Lanham: Lexington Books, 2003); W. Decock, 'Spanish Scholastics on Money and Credit: Economic, Legal, and Political Aspects', in D. Fox/W. Ernst (ed.), *Money in the Western Legal Tradition: Middle Ages to Bretton Woods* (Oxford: Oxford University Press, 2016) 267–83; id., 'Law of Property and Obligations: Neoscholastic Thinking and Beyond', in H. Pihlajamäki/M.D. Dubber/M. Godfrey (ed.), *The Oxford Handbook of European Legal History* (Oxford: Oxford University Press, 2018) 611–31; O.I. Langholm, *The Legacy of Scholasticism in Economic Thought: Antecedents of Choice and Power* (Cambridge: Cambridge University Press, 1998).

22 Van Houdt, 'On 'Medium' and 'Message''. See also S. Roelofs, 'Robert Bellarmine (1542–1621) and the Law and Morality of the Market: A Brief Introduction', *Rivista Internazionale di Diritto Comune* 33 (2022) 269–279.

23 The literature produced by Le Bachelet and Tromp is quite extensive. Of the many titles that can be cited, a select few (which are mostly related to the scope of the present paper) are: Le Bachelet, *Bellarmin avant son cardinalat*; id., Auctarium Bellarminianum. *Supplément aux oeuvres du cardinal Bellarmin* (Paris: Beauchesne, 1913); Tromp, 'Conspectus chronologicus praelectionum'; id., 'De manuscriptis praelectionum Lovaniensium S. Roberti Bellarmini S.I. Chronologia et problemata annexa', *Institutum Scriptorum de Historia S.I.* 2 (1933) 185–99; id., *Auctarii auctaria II: addenda quaedam ad auctarium Bellarminianum Patris X.M. Le Bachelet* (Romae: 1934); id., 'Auctarii auctaria.

embarked on a full transcription of Bellarmine's autograph featuring the Louvain lectures but, unfortunately, these typewritten documents have never been released either.[24] Of particular interest for our scope is Mancini's observation that the reason for Tromp's work's absence from publication might be related to the content of the Louvain lectures. According to Mancini, this is illustrative of Bellarmine's manuscript collection, which remained a controversial object even after Bellarmine was canonised as Saint and proclaimed Doctor of the Church.[25]

Elaborating on this opening, the present study seeks to provide more insight into how the unprinted (or non-digitised) state of the Louvain lectures and especially the way Bellarmine is profiled in view of his elevation to sainthood contributed to the fact that his economic thought has generally been neglected in the literature. With this aim in mind, the first section seeks to better understand the relation between the impact of the Louvain lectures and Bellarmine's model of sanctity. To this end, relevant passages of early modern hagiographies and modern decretal letters will be considered in an open dialogue with the available data of manuscripts featuring the Louvain lectures.[26] The second section will delve into the lectures themselves by offering an overview of the scope of Bellarmine's assessment of commercial and financial practices. This will be based on Bellarmine's autograph that contains his preparatory lecture notes, which are currently preserved in the Roman Archives of

---

Addenda quaedam ad Auctarium Bellarminianum Patris X.M. Le Bachelet', *Institutum Scriptorum de Historia S.I.* 4 (1935) 234–52. See also the *Fondo Roberto Bellarmino*, an inventory of many documents of Bellarmine processed by Le Bachelet and Tromp (https://www.unigre.it/archivioimg/Cataloghi/Bellarmino1.htm, last access: 14/11/2022) preserved in the Archives of the Pontifical Gregorian University (APUG). Recently, several of Bellarmine's writings have been digitised by Lovaniensia and Magister Dixit, projects that aim to disclose works and manuscripts produced by members of the Old Louvain University in view of the 600th anniversary of the university (2025). These digitised versions are available through the projects' digital portals (www.lovaniensia.be, last access: 14/11/2022; www.heron-net.be/lectio, last access: 14/11/2022).

24 Tromp's typewritten volumes containing transcriptions, on the one hand, and additionally a commentary and critical apparatus, on the other, are currently preserved in the APUG under the signatures MS. 2419–2430 and MS. 2431–2440, respectively. See *Indice delle* Epistolae Bellarmini *(1599–1621)* (https://www.unigre.it/archivioimg/Cataloghi/Bellarmino1.htm, last access: 14/11/2022). See also L. Mancini, '«Piccola, ma sufficiente per li miei studi»: La biblioteca del cardinale Roberto Bellarmino. Prime ricerche e censimento degli esemplari postillato', *Bibliothecae.it* 10, no. 1 (2021) 70–174, on p. 94, n. 61.

25 Mancini, 'La biblioteca del cardinale Roberto Bellarmino', 93–4.

26 For a list of manuscripts of Bellarmine's Louvain teachings on the *Summa theologiae*, see Tromp, 'Conspectus chronologicus praelectionum', 98–101. As Van Houdt observes in 'On 'Medium' and 'Message'', 186, n. 13, Tromp missed a key manuscript with notes of part of the Louvain lectures taken by a student under direct dictation by Bellarmine, see 'Commentaria in 2am 2ae *Summae Theologicae* Sti. Thomae, sub Roberto Jesuito, scripta per Antonium Bochutum, Sabaudum', preserved in The State Archives in Belgium, Archive of the University of Louvain 1426–1797, Collegium Baiorum, MS. 3725–3731.

the Society of Jesus.[27] The final section will ponder how the unpublished state of the Louvain lectures and the construction of Bellarmine's profile might explain the uncharted state of a noteworthy chapter that forms part of the intellectual legacy of Saint Robert Bellarmine.

The impact of the Louvain lectures on the veneration of Bellarmine

In general, the decretal letters regarding Bellarmine's beatification, canonisation as Saint, and proclamation as Doctor of the Church profile Bellarmine as both a soldier in the battle against materialism and a defender of the faith.[28] It is especially at the service of the latter argument that the papal decrees mention Bellarmine's activities in the Jesuit College of Louvain. For instance,[29] according to the canonical bull,

> … in that most famous college [in Louvain], he cultivated theology, and, after he was elevated to the office of priests, taught in such way that he brought back many heretics to the uniformity of the Church.[30]

In the years following Bellarmine's death, the Louvain lectures were already referenced in support of the cause for his sanctity. The hagiographic works *Vita del Cardinale Roberto Bellarmino della Compagnia di Giesù* (1624) by Fuligatti and *Della vita di Roberto Cardinal Bellarmino Arcivescovo di Capua della Compagnia di Giesù* (1678) by Bartoli contain substantial chapters on Bellarmine's seven-year stay

---

27 These lecture texts are preserved in the form of four notebooks and listed in the inventory of *opera nostrorum* (Opp. NN.) of the Roman Archives of the Society of Jesus (ARSI) under the following titles and reference numbers: 'S.R. Bellarmino, Lectiones Lovanienses. In Primam Primae D. Thomae', ARSI, Opp. NN. 234; 'S.R. Bellarmino, Lectiones Lovanienses. In Iam IIae D. Thomae', ARSI, Opp. NN. 235; 'S.R. Bellarmino, Lectiones Lovanienses. Commentarium', ARSI, Opp. NN. 236; 'S.R. Bellarmino, Lectiones Lovanienses. Continuatio et finis', ARSI, Opp. NN. 237.

28 Motta/Rai, 'Jesuit Sanctity', 8. Even so, these aspects were not the chief elements of Bellarmine's model of sanctity at the start of the Jesuit campaign for his sanctity, see Motta, 'Il processo di canonizzazione (1622–1930)', 42.

29 See also the attempt for Bellarmine's beatification made by the University of Louvain in their *Annuaire* of 1814, which immediately connects Bellarmine's Louvain activities to his participation in the Louvain theological disputes: 'Séjour de Cardinal Bellarmin à Louvain et ses rapports avec l'Université', 164.

30 "… in celeberrimo illo colegio theologiam excoluit et, sacerdotio auctus, ita docuit, ut plurimos haereticos ad Ecclesiae unitatem reduxerit … ." *Acta Apostolicae Sedis. Commentarium officiale*, 31 Decembris 1930, 594.

in Louvain.[31] By stressing Bellarmine's refined interpersonal skills, extraordinary intellectual qualities, and unflagging commitment during this sojourn, the hagiographers aim to implicitly convey the image of a most genius, humble, respected, and hardworking Jesuit. In general, they eulogise Bellarmine as a virtuous man who was not in the least discouraged by any adverse circumstance (for instance, his poor health, recurrent pestilences, and the political clash between the Spanish crown and the Northern Low Countries).[32] As for Bellarmine's role in the Jesuit College, Fuligatti highlights the way in which Bellarmine was an exemplative Jesuit.

> … it can be truly said that the way of his interaction and life was the model of perfection and the norm of virtue to all in the [Jesuit] College [in Louvain], while they never saw in him a thing which, not even in the slightest part, flowed from outside the narrow path of divine counsel and perfect, steady observance.[33]

Amongst many other events, Fuligatti also relates that the leg of a fellow-Jesuit of the College healed, a miracle allegedly achieved through the intercession of Bellarmine.[34] While doubtful (Fuligatti does not provide any clues or evidence), this is an interesting element. It might be a sign that the fame of Bellarmine's sanctity

---

31 Fuligatti: chapter 7, 'E mandato a Lovanio in Fiandra per predicar in Latino, Dove anche legge Teologia', and chapter 8, 'Con quanto credito di virtù dimorasse in Fiandra, e del ritorno in Italia'; Bartoli: chapter 9, 'Il Santo generale Franceseo Borgia manda Roberto a predicare in latino nell' Università Lovagno. …', chapter 10, 'Gran concorso alle sue prediche in Lovagno. La fama d'esse trae molti d'Olanda, e d'Inghilterra a sencirlo. …', and chapter 11, 'Dimorato in Lovagno sette anni, e distruttagli dale grandi fatich; la sanità, n'è richiamato a Rome, ….'

32 Fuligatti, *Vita del Cardinale Roberto Bellarmino*, 51–3; Bartoli, *Della vita di Roberto Cardinal Bellarmino*, 65–7.

33 "Et in questa materia con verità si può dire che la sua conversatione, [*sic*] e vita era à tutto'l Collegio forma di perfettione, [*sic*] e norma di virtù, non vedendosi mai in lui cosa, la quale nè pur'in minima parte uscisse fuora del più stretto sentiero de'consigli divini, e della perfetta osservanza regolare." Fuligatti, *Vita del Cardinale Roberto Bellarmino*, 47.

34 "Era nel Collegio di Lovanio uno della Compagnia mentre che quivi leggeva, che molto tempo già portana [*sic*] una piaga in una ga[m]ba senza essersi mai potuta guarire per arte de'Medici, e per cura de' Cerusici; e pensando un giorno egli à questo suo male con ansietà, già quasi fatto incurabile, si pose à far riflessione, e considerare se conoscesse alcun servo di Dio, dalla cui intercessione potesse sperar la gratia [*sic*] tanto desiderata; mentre stava fisso in questo pensiero no trovò persona al suo parere, la quale fosse di maggior merito appresso l'istesso Signore del P. Bellarmino: & in questa consideratione [*sic*] si sentì ispirato, che se si confessasse, e si communicasse [*sic*] per sua mano rimarrebbe senza dubbio guarito. Con questa fese chiesta licenza da' Superiori, dopo di essersi con lui confessato, prese dall'istessa mano il corpo di Christo: & ecco, che con i stupore del Cirusico [*sic*] la gamba quasi totalmente ne divien sana, & in due, ò tre altri dì ritornando per tutto viva, e naturale la carne, non lasciò vestigio della passata infermità." Fuligatti, *Vita del Cardinale Roberto Bellarmino*, 49–50.

was spreading not only when he was still alive but also when he was very young, and it shows how the early modern hagiographic narrative aimed at promoting the idea that Bellarmine already proved his sanctity during his life.[35]

With respect to the Louvain lectures, Fuligatti and Bartoli limit their writings on the actual content to short overviews of the treated parts of the *Summa theologiae* for each school year.[36] In fact, during 1570–1571 and 1571–1572, Bellarmine commented on the *Prima pars* (metaphysical matters) of Aquinas's *Summa theologiae.* In this period, Bellarmine personally witnessed the turmoil of the borderland of the Catholic world. From August until November of the year 1572, Bellarmine had to temporarily leave Louvain for safer havens due to threats that came from the North led by the Protestant prince Willem of Orange (1533–1584). As soon as the situation calmed down, Bellarmine returned and began commenting on the *Secunda pars* (law, virtues, and ethics). During the *annus scholaris* of 1572–1573 and the first half of 1573–1574, Bellarmine's lectures constituted a commentary of the first part (*Prima secundae*). From April 1574, he started a commentary of the second part (*Secunda secundae*) of the *Secunda pars*, which he completed about two years later, in the Holy Week of 1576. In the following month of May, Bellarmine resumed the lectures and embarked upon the *Tertia pars* (Christ and Christian rites), which he only carried out until the seventh *quaestio*.[37] In the autumn of 1576, the inclement weather of the Southern Low Countries urged Bellarmine to return to Rome; his deteriorating health required a more favourable climate.[38]

In 1585, the Jesuit College of Louvain resumed the theology course led by Lessius.[39] It is not clear whether Lessius himself had ever attended Bellarmine's lectures, but he relayed a report of an eyewitness according to which Bellarmine's lectures were very successful.

---

35 Yet this alleged miracle is not mentioned in the decretal letter regarding Bellarmine's canonisation as Saint, which references two cures through posthumous interventions of Bellarmine. See *Acta Apostolicae Sedis. Commentarium officiale*, 31 Decembris 1930, 598–9. See also Schaff, 'Cardinal Bellarmine. Now Saint and Doctor of the Church', 47.

36 Bartoli, *Della vita di Roberto Cardinal Bellarmino*, 61; Fuligatti, *Vita del Cardinale Roberto Bellarmino*, 44. The passages resemble the few words that Bellarmine writes in his autobiography regarding this matter, see Le Bachelet, *Bellarmin avant son cardinalat*, 451.

37 For a (detailed) schedule of Bellarmine's lectures, see Tromp, 'Conspectus chronologicus praelectionum', 97–105; Cauchie, 'Bellarmin et l'Université de Louvain d'après un livre récent', 390–1; De le Court, 'Saint Bellarmin à Louvain', 77–8.

38 Cauchie, 'Bellarmin et l'Université de Louvain d'après un livre récent', 391; Biersack, *Initia Bellarminiana*, 71.

39 See A.M. Artola, 'El marco cronológico de las prelecciones del P. L. Lessio, de 1585 a 1600', *Scriptorium victoriense* 22, no. 1 (1975) 100–16.

> The inflow of listeners to the lectures of Bellarmine from all the colleges[40] was of such kind that the school of 50 feet long and 23 feet wide did not suffice, and that very many [listeners] stood outside next to the windows so that they could write under the open sky when the weather allowed it. This crowd did not cease during the time he taught.[41]

Indeed, the Louvain lectures were famous and well-attended, which was probably due to the fact that Bellarmine's teachings were based on the *Summa theologiae*, a textbook which was not systematically used in the lecture halls of Louvain until then.[42] The method formed part of a larger commentary tradition across Europe, which extended from the 15th until the 17th century.[43] In particular, it was at the beginning of the 16th century that Aquinas's treatise started to be commented upon in the European classrooms. This was initially done under the lead of several illustrious names within the Dominican Order, such as Thomas de Vio (1469–1534), Peter Crockaert (c. 1465–1514), Francisco de Vitoria (1483–1546), and Domingo de Soto (1494–1560), and the treatise then became further integrated with educational programs by the Jesuits.[44] From the 1540s onwards, the Jesuit Order had established new schools and universities (or taught in existing ones) in most of the academic cities of the continent, such as Padua, Rome, Valencia, Coimbra, Alcalá de Henares, Lisbon, Paris, and Cologne.[45] Soon after, the first Jesuits arrived in Louvain, but due to much local resistance at first, the College was allowed to open a school only in

---

40 For a historical background of all the colleges in early modern Louvain, see E. De Maesschalck, *Leuven en zijn colleges. Trefpunt van intellectueel leven in de Nederlanden (1425–1797)* (Gorredijk: Sterck & De Vreese, 2021).

41 "Tantus erat concursus auditorum ad lectiones [Bellarmini] ex omnibus collegiis, ut schola 50 pedes longa et 23 lata non caperet, sed plurimi starent foris ad fenestras ut scriberent sub dio quando aura permittebat; quae frequentia fuit assidua quamdiu ipse docuit." See ABML, photo collection 'Louvain. Controverse des grades (1618–1623)'. See also Van Houdt, 'On 'Medium' and 'Message'', 185, n. 10.

42 Van Houdt, 'On 'Medium' and 'Message'', 186.

43 See Lanza/Toste (ed.), Summistae. *The Commentary Tradition on Thomas Aquinas'* Summa Theologiae. The commentary tradition of Aquinas's *Summa theologiae* is inextricably connected to the theological renewal by the Spanish late scholastic movement, also known as the School of Salamanca, see J. Belda Plans, *La Escuela de Salamanca y la renovación de la teología en el siglo XVI* (Madrid: Biblioteca de autores cristianos, 2000); H.E. Braun/E. De Bom/P. Astorri (ed.), *A Companion to the Spanish Scholastics* (Leiden/Boston: Brill, 2022).

44 See M. Toste/L. Lanza, 'The Commentary Tradition on the *Summa Theologiae*', in eid. (ed.), Summistae. *The Commentary Tradition on Thomas Aquinas'* Summa Theologiae *From the 15th to the 17th Centuries* (Leuven: Leuven University Press, 2021) 3–93, on pp. 17–18, 23.

45 For a background of the establishment of Jesuit schools and universities in Europe from the 1540s until the suppression of the order, see P.F. Grendler, *Jesuit Schools and Universities in Europe, 1548–1773* (Leiden/Boston: Brill, 2019).

1569.[46] In Louvain, the College's use of the *Summa theologiae* was innovative, since the Faculty of Theology of the University of Louvain based its Chair of Scholastic Theology on Peter Lombard's (c. 1096–1160) *Sententiarum libri quatuor* (the default manual of late medieval theology teaching)[47] and would not adopt Aquinas's treatise as a textbook until 1596.[48]

It is not difficult to understand why the Louvain lectures are referenced in the papal bull that crowned Bellarmine as one of the few Doctors of the Church. To elevate Bellarmine to the level of *the* Doctor of the Church, *viz.* the very Thomas Aquinas himself, every link with the latter's thought is desirable. In fact, Aquinas was both the *modus operandi* and the conceptual foundation of Bellarmine's theology as laid down in the *Controversiae*,[49] the renowned treatise which

> … Bellarmine had prepared … during earlier times, when he had delivered lectures on the *Summa* of St Thomas for six years from the year 1570 onwards to a large audience of university students.[50]

Interestingly, the cited passage of the decretal letter stresses that the Louvain lectures attracted many students from the University as well. Yet if we may believe Fuligatti and Bartoli, the prestige gained by Bellarmine's teachings was not confined to Louvain and its surroundings but had even reached the Italian peninsula as the testimony of Cardinal Ottavio Bandini (1558–1629) reveals.[51] Fuligatti and Bartoli underline that Bellarmine had earned a good reputation within the University of

46 A. Poncelet, S.J., *Histoire de la Compagnie de Jésus dans les anciens Pays-Bas: établissement de la Compagnie de Jésus en Belgique et ses développements jusqu'à la fin du règne d'Albert et d'Isabelle* (Bruxelles: Lamertin, 1928), 34–142.

47 Initially, there was no fear of a competitive relation between the theologians of the Faculty and the Jesuits of the College, see Biersack, *Initia Bellarminiana*, 67.

48 For a background regarding the University's adoption of the *Summa theologiae*, see V. Brants, *La création de la chaire de théologie scolastique et la nomination de Malderus à l'Université en 1596* (Louvain: Impr. Smeesters, 1908); R.M. Martin, *L'introduction officielle de la* Somme *de Saint Thomas à l'ancienne Université de Louvain* (Toulouse: Imprimérie et librairie Édouard Privat, 1910).

49 Tutino, *Empire of Souls*, 15.

50 The full passage reads: "Diutorno quidem studiorum ac magisterii curriculo easdem [*Disputationes de controversiis*] Sanctus Bellarminus quodammodo paraverat cum antea Lovaniensi in Conlegio Societatis Iesu, audientibus quoque multis Universitatis alumnis, ab anno MDLXX praelectiones in *Summam* S. Thomae per sexennium habuisset, … ." *Acta Apostolicae Sedis. Commentarium officiale*, 9 Novembris 1931, 434.

51 "… e per altre assai più lontane provincie, più volentieri che ragionarne del mio, ne farò sentire il giudicio [*sic*] del gravissimo Cardinal Commendone, cui allegando, e comprovando il Cardinale Ottavio Bandini 'Dovendo io (dice) studiare teologia, il Signor Cardinal Commendone mi esortò ad andare in Lovanio (si come mi preparai l'anno 1576) per udire il P. Roberto Bellarmini, che ivi leggeva con gran fama, & era tenuto un de primi dottori di quel tempo. La qual deliberatione [*sic*]

Louvain as well. Bartoli writes that Bellarmine's appointment as the first theology teacher of the Jesuit College was happily supported by and received full consent of the board of the Faculty of Theology (who had to approve the installation of this alternative theology course in the city), and was "an honour not granted to our people [i. e. the Jesuits] by that eminent University until then".[52] Furthermore, the hagiographer refers to Bellarmine's own amazement in his old age about the extent to which he was capable to conduct a theology course in the first place, since he had not completed the course himself in the preceding years in Padua.[53]

It might be argued that Bellarmine's 'transfer' in both institutional and professional terms demonstrates his brilliant intellectual capacities: our Jesuit had not yet completed his four years of studies in theology nor professed the fourth vow, elements that were normally requested by the Jesuit order.[54] Yet the appointment of teachers who had not completed the full curriculum of the course itself was not unusual in the Jesuit world.[55] Rather, Bellarmine's reassignment served the larger mission of the Jesuit Society, which fundamentally aimed at accelerating the spread of the *vera doctrina* across the globe by both preaching and teaching. When the Jesuit College in Louvain decided to offer a theology course, Bellarmine was probably one of the few Jesuits who had some experience with Aquinas's treatise due to his previous years of study in Padua. This knowledge, however incomplete, coupled with the reputation of an excellent orator he had gained on the basis of his sermons, made Bellarmine 'the right person, at the right place, at the right time'. As a matter of fact, the word 'incomplete' employed here is an aspect that is further detailed by Fuligatti; Bellarmine was only familiar with passages of the *Prima pars* and *Tertia pars* of the *Summa theologiae* at the moment when he was invited to

volendo io porre in effetto, non potei farlo, per nuove turbolenze che successero allora in Fiandra." Bartoli, *Della vita di Roberto Cardinal Bellarmino*, 61.

52 The full passage reads: "Questa era di leggere tutto insieme Teologia scolastica: privilegio d'onore sino allora non conceduto [*sic*] a'Nostri da quella grande Università: ma su'merito del Bellarmino tanto ivistimato [*sic*], e havuto caro, speravano, … ." Bartoli, *Della vita di Roberto Cardinal Bellarmino*, 60.

53 "Egli stesso ragionandone già vecchio in Roma con un suo caro amico, non finiva di maravigliarsi, [*sic*] come non essendo stato due anni intieri scolare di Teologia in Padova, ne potesse esser maestro in Lovagno; cioè in faccia ad una delle più dotte, e perciò delle più famose università dell' Europa. Cominciò dunque coll'Octobre dell'ano 1570 a dettare le prima parte della sacra teologia, e ne compiè [*sic*] i trattati in due anni: ne'tre susseguenti, gli attenentisi alle due parti della seconda: poi l'altro, che fu il testo di quel magistero, quanto il più potè [*sic*] della terza." Bartoli, *Della vita di Roberto Cardinal Bellarmino*, 61.

54 Tutino, *Empire of Souls*, 11. The fourth vow promises special obedience to the Sovereign Pontiff regarding missionary activities.

55 See for instance the career path of the famous Spanish scholastic Martín de Azpilcueta in W. Decock, 'Martín de Azpilcueta', in R. Domingo/J. Martínez-Torrón (ed.), *Great Christian Jurists in Spanish History* (Cambridge: Cambridge University Press, 2018) 115–32.

teach the course,[56] hence a request that "would undoubtedly frighten anyone else, even the clever and quick minds".[57]

Still, the lacuna in the Thomistic thought of young Bellarmine may not be a solid argument to extol his assumption of office. A letter between Jesuit superiors demonstrates that Bellarmine was not appointed to teach the *Secunda pars* in the initial plan.[58] Rather, there may be two messages, not necessarily mutually exclusive, that Bartoli and Fuligatti seem to convey while stressing Bellarmine's deficient educational background. Obviously, alluding to the tenacious efforts Bellarmine had to make to update his framework, the hagiographers aim to praise Bellarmine's inexhaustible head for study, and curiously, Bellarmine's efforts paid off. Surviving manuscripts indicate that precisely part of his teachings that were based on the *Secunda pars*, especially the ones on the *Secunda secundae*, may have been the most successful classes of the Louvain lectures. In 1577, one year after Bellarmine's return to Rome, handwritten copies of his comments on the *Secunda pars* were being reread at the English College in Douai,[59] and from there, several handwritten

---

56 True, see the following passages from Bellarmine's autobiography: "… rogatus a Patribus ut doceret Theologiam Scholasticam, assensus est, et quamvis non audivisset nisi partem aliquam primae partis et tertiae partis [S[ti] Thomae] … ." Le Bachelet, *Bellarmin avant son cardinalat*, 451. For a background of the teachings of Thomistic theology in Padua, see M. Gaetano, 'Theology *In Via Sancti Thomae* at the University of Padua and the *Summa Theologiae*', in L. Lanza/M. Toste (ed.), *The Commentary Tradition on Thomas Aquinas'* Summa Theologiae *From the 15th to the 17th Centuries* (Leuven: Leuven University Press, 2021) 159–84.

57 The full passage reads: "Onde deliberarono i Superiori d'invitarlo dopo questo tempo à legger Teologia, ancorche [*sic*] havesse solo studiate poche materie della prima, e della terza parte di S. Tomasso. Questa richiesta haverebbe senza dubbio sbigottito qualsivoglia altro, ancorche [*sic*] di perspicace, e di pronto intelletto: ma non già si sgomentò Bellarmino, ò fosse perche [*sic*] già haveva esperienza di quello, che con la fatica, e studio poteva fare, ò perche [*sic*] non volesse romper il proposito d'eseguir senza repliche ciò, che dalla santa ubbidienza gli veniva proposto, ò perche [*sic*] si sentisse dal favor Cielo internamente animato, gittando ogni suo pensiero nel Signore Dio, il quale mai l'haveva abbandonato." Fuligatti, *Vita del Cardinale Roberto Bellarmino*, 43–4.

58 Le Bachelet, S.J., *Bellarmin avant son cardinalat*, 73.

59 Biersack, *Initia Bellarminiana*, 95; Tromp, *Auctarii auctaria II*, 247. In Douai, a seminary was founded in 1568 in view of the preparation of English Catholics to fight the hegemony of the Elizabethan Church. Queen Elizabeth was excommunicated by Pope Pius V, who considered Elizabeth's sovereignty over England illegitimate. See also Tutino, *Empire of Souls*, 10. A dairy reveals that the English College highly praised the fine and concise style of Bellarmine's teachings: "… ut alter scilicet D. Wrightus, mane hora 6[a] post sacrum in 1[am] 2[ae] D. Tho., et D. Bristous hora 8[a] in 2[am] 2[ae] commentationes reverendi P. Roberti Itali, docte, breviter et perspicue elaboratas, ac non ita pridem Lovanii praelectas nobis dictarent." T.F. Knox (ed.), *The First and Second Diaries of the English College, Douay. With an Historical Introduction* (London: Farnborough, 1969 [1878]), 117. See also Van Houdt, 'On 'Medium' and 'Message'', 186, n. 11; Brodrick, *Robert Bellarmine: Saint and Scholar*, 29; T.F. Knox, *The First and the Second Diaries of the English College, Douay and an Appendix of Unpublished Documents* (London: D. Nutt, 1878), 180 and 293.

copies of these *relectiones* were allegedly trafficked onto English soil by a priest called William Morcott.[60]

As Toste and Lanza argue, early modern theology teachers may have had a particular preference for a certain part of the *Summa theologiae*, but they usually aimed to cover all parts of Aquinas's treatise in their course.[61] This endeavour was already apparent in the teachings of Vitoria (cf. *supra*), who is commonly considered one of the seminal *summistae* (if not the first) with respect to the birth of late scholasticism on the Iberian peninsula.[62] Nonetheless, Toste and Lanza show that a comparison of the numbers of manuscripts featuring Vitoria's lectures on the *Prima pars* and *Secunda pars* indicates that the *Prima pars* might have found more attention amongst Vitoria's audience, as more manuscripts on this section survived.[63] This method can be extrapolated to the manuscripts featuring the Louvain lectures (including the *relectiones* in Douai) that are known up to the present day (cf. *supra*). This list includes relatively many manuscripts containing commentaries of the *Secunda secundae* alone, of which at least two are preserved in Belgium and three in England.[64] This indicates that Bellarmine's public (those who attended, reread, or discovered the commentaries second-hand through manuscripts) was relatively more interested in his moral reflections. Hence, perhaps already in a young stage of his life, Bellarmine was known for his moral doctrine. This is interesting, consid-

60 This is alleged by the catalogue of the Lambeth Palace Library (LAMB), a case that merits further investigation. Some of these manuscripts that found their way to England would form part of the libraries of Richard Bancroft (1544–1610) and William Sancroft (1617–1693), two succeeding Archbishops of Canterbury, according to the description in the inventory. See 'Lectures on the *Summa* of St Thomas Aquinas,' MS. 123–126 in the online catalogue of the LAMB. The manuscript is listed by Tromp, as well as another manuscript conserved in the British Library (BRIT), 'Rob. Politiani Itali, Dictata in secundam Secundae Thomae Aquinatis AD 1547 Scripta Duaci anno 1577 Liber chartaceus', Harley, MS. 3295. See also Tromp, 'Conspectus chronologicus praelectionum'.

61 See Toste/Lanza, 'The Commentary Tradition on the *Summa Theologiae*', 12.

62 For a recent biographical study on Vitoria, see A. Wagner, 'Francisco de Vitoria', in R. Domingo/J. Martínez-Torrón (ed.), *Great Christian Jurists in Spanish History* (Cambridge: Cambridge University Press, 2018) 84–96.

63 See Toste/Lanza, 'The Commentary Tradition on the *Summa Theologiae*', 12–13.

64 Manuscripts regarding the teachings on the *Secunda secundae* are hence the aforementioned 'Commentaria in 2am 2ae *Summae Theologicae* Sti. Thomae, sub Roberto Jesuito, scripta per Antonium Bochutum, Sabaudum', The State Archives in Belgium, Archive of the University of Louvain 1426–1797, Collegium Baiorum, MS. 3725–3731; 'Rob. Politiani Itali, Dictata in secundam Secundae Thomae Aquinatis AD 1547 Scripta Duaci anno 1577 Liber chartaceus', BRIT, Harley, MS. 3295; 'Lectures on the *Summa* of St. Thomas Aquinas', LAMB, MS. 125–126; 'S.R. Bellarmino, Lectiones Lovanienses. Commentarium', ARSI, Opp. NN. 236; 'S.R. Bellarmino, Lectiones Lovanienses. Continuatio et finis', ARSI, Opp. NN. 237; as well as 'Tractatus de iustitia et iure. Tractatus de pensionibus', Royal Library of Belgium (KBR), MS. 2156.

ering that someone will be canonised as a Saint when, amongst other prerequisites, he or she pursued a virtuous life.

Moving into uncharted areas of theological concern: Bellarmine's economic thought

The success of Bellarmine's teachings that were based upon the *Secunda secundae* might be related to what can be called a 'sub-commentary' tradition of Aquinas's *Summa theologiae*. The *Secunda secundae*, in particular, deals with virtues, law, and moral issues, and was a source of inspiration for the so-called *De iustitia et iure* ('On Justice and Right') treatises.[65] This moral-theological tradition – which still has influence in the modern era[66] – took off with Soto's *De iustitia et iure* (1556)[67] and was, amongst others, picked up by theologians who were active in Louvain shortly after Bellarmine's stay, such as Joannes Malderus (1563–1633), Ioannes Wiggers (1571–1639), and of course Lessius, all three of which published a *De iustitia et iure*.[68] Obviously, the impact of Bellarmine's teachings on the *Secunda secundae* of Aquinas's *Summa theologiae* may not have been part of the knowledge of the aforementioned Italian hagiographers Fuligatti and Bartoli. However, this does not necessarily exclude that, while stressing Bellarmine's lack of experience regarding the *Secunda pars*, they have tried to put these specific teachings in a

65 Van Houdt, *Leonardus Lessius: traditie en vernieuwing*, 42–3; M. Grice-Hutchinson, *Early Economic Thought in Spain 1177–1740* (Sydney: Allen and Unwin, 1978), 84–5; R. Schuessler, 'Was There a Downturn in Fifteenth-Century Scholastic Philosophy?', *Studia Neoaristotelica* 15, no. 1 (2018) 5–38, on p. 24.

66 For instance, Abbé Pottier (1849–1923) and Willem Duynstee (1886–1986) both published a *De iustitia et iure* in 1900 and 1956, respectively. See W. Decock, 'Neo-Thomism, Law and Society. A Prolegomenon to Further Study', in W. Decock/B. Raymaekers/P. Heyrman (ed.), *Neo-Thomism in Action: Law and Society Reshaped by Neo-Scholastic Philosophy 1880–1960* (Leuven: Leuven University Press, 2021) 7–24, on p. 15.

67 See W. Decock, 'Domingo de Soto: *De iustitia et iure* (1553–1554)', in S. Dauchy et al. (ed.), *The Formation and Transmission of Western Legal Culture. 150 Books that Made the Law in the Age of Printing*, vol. 7 (Heidelberg/New York: Springer International Publishing, 2017) 94–6.

68 For overviews of early modern *De iustitia et iure* publications, see W. Decock/C. Birr, *Recht und Moral in der Scholastik der frühen Neuzeit 1500–1750* (Berlin: Walter de Gruyter, 2016), 33–57. Whether Bellarmine (or anyone in the era) was aware of this sub-genre, (later) readers or copiers of manuscripts featuring the Louvain lectures might have received his comments on the *Secunda secundae* as an 'On Justice and Right' commentary. See for instance the title of the manuscript by an hitherto unknown scribe (KBR, MS. 2156): 'Tractatus de iustitia et iure'. It is likely that the text of this manuscript was not taken under direct dictation, for preliminary research indicates that parts of the content of this manuscript (in terms of vocabulary, digressions, etc.) do not coincide with Bellarmine's autograph.

certain 'low-profile' perspective, a second 'message' they might have wanted to convey (cf. *supra*). The present section will first take a look at part of Bellarmine's teachings based on the *Secunda secundae* that are intriguing and at the same time not deeply explored until the present day. The next section will further reflect upon the question how these particular teachings might have been considered delicate in view of Bellarmine's sanctity.

As preluded in the introduction, Bellarmine lived in an era when theological perspectives and moral reflections on money, economic transactions, and contractual relations underwent some fundamental changes. From the 1950s onwards, some famous economic theorists supported that the evolution towards economics as a science was in part fostered by the late medieval and early modern theologians and canon lawyers.[69] The state of the literature emphasises how these developments are pervaded with legal and moral reflections.[70] More particularly, as the first chapter of Noonan's seminal work *The Scholastic Analysis of Usury* argues, the root of the profound scholastic (1150–1750) interest in commercial and financial ethics goes back to the ecclesiastical prohibition against money-lending at interest, since this form of profit-making was considered a possible case of usury. The Church looked upon contracts and business practices as tokens that could be used to cover up a loan agreement at illicit interest, so these matters needed to be regulated by moral theology to avoid sin and thus eternal punishment. A moral code for merchants and bankers was hence one of the major practical concerns of scholastic theologians.[71]

It is generally known that the late scholastic (1450–1750) assessment of economic transactions is often found amongst writings that commented upon question 78 ('On the sin of usury, which is committed in loan agreements') of the *Secunda secundae* of Aquinas's *Summa theologiae*. This is an interesting reference point in light of the present study. As far as is known, Bellarmine has not published any substantial writing on usury, money, or economic transactions. This is in contrast to the state of the literature regarding the intellectual inheritance of Lessius, who, incidentally, was well aware of Bellarmine's classes on economic matters.[72] Indeed, Bellarmine has commented upon the *Secunda secundae*, so he must have

---

69 See for instance B.W. Dempsey, *Interest and Usury* (London: Dennis Dobson Ltd, 1948); J.A. Schumpeter, *History of Economic Analysis* (London: Routledge, 1987 [1954]).

70 See J.T. Noonan, *The Scholastic Analysis of Usury* (Cambridge, MA: Harvard University Press, 1957); T. Van Houdt/F. Monsalve, 'Usury and Interest', in H.E. Braun/E. De Bom/P. Astorri (ed.), *A Companion to the Spanish Scholastics* (Leiden/Boston: Brill, 2022) 475–97, see in particular pp. 475–7.

71 See Noonan, *The Scholastic Analysis of Usury*, 11–20.

72 Although this does not prove that Lessius attended the lectures of Bellarmine, Lessius explicitly refers to Bellarmine's economic classes in the passage on *chirographa*, discussed in *dubitatio* 8 of book 2, chapter 21, 'On buying and selling', where can be read: "Idem docuit olim doctissimus Cardinalis Bellarminus Lovanii." See L. Lessius, *De iustitia et iure* (Lovanii: ex officina Ioannis Masii, 1605), 260.

commented upon the aforementioned question 78 as well, which is confirmed by his lecture texts.[73] Somewhere between May and September of the year 1575,[74] Bellarmine discussed said question in the following order:

Q. 78 On usury
- Art. 1 Whether it is a sin to receive usury in return for money-lending
- Art. 2 Whether it is allowed to demand another advantage in return for the loan
- Art. 3 Whether profit derived from usury must be reimbursed
- Art. 4 Whether it is allowed to give usury in return for the loan[75]

Although our Jesuit teacher strictly follows the division of Aquinas's question 78,[76] Bellarmine's reflection only covers half a page. As a matter of fact, Aquinas's question 78 was often a starting point for scholastic commentators whose writings show a number of paragraphs or even large chapters on juridical-economic matters.[77] These passages are far more developed than Aquinas's reflections or deal with topics which Aquinas does not even explicitly discuss. This is a natural result of the fact that the commentators addressed topics of which the importance for their time had evolved, compared to when the source itself was written.[78] This holds true for

73 See also Roelofs, 'Robert Bellarmine (1542–1621) and the Law and Morality of the Market: A Brief Introduction'.

74 The exact dates of Bellarmine's lectures on question 78 cannot be sufficiently reconstructed based on Tromp, 'Conspectus chronologicus praelectionum', 97–101. The aforementioned unpublished notes of Bellarmine's student Bochutus preserved in The State Archives in Belgium (see notably MS. 3727, in the end of q. 64, fol. 51v: "Quae [quaestiones] hic desunt addo in carthis quas scripsi a 26 Aprilis 1575") and Bellarmine's autograph (ARSI, Opp. NN. 237, fol. 579r: "Initio Septembris 1575: finitur in medio q. 83") together suggest that Bellarmine discussed qq. 64–83 of Aquinas's *Secunda secundae* between 26 April 1575 and the beginning of the following month of September.

75 "Q. 78 De usura. Art. 1 An accipere usuram pro pecunia mutuata sit peccatum"; "Art. 2 An liceat aliam commoditatem expetere pro mutuo"; "Art. 3 An restitui debeat lucrum ex usura"; "Art. 4 An liceat dare usuras pro mutuo", ARSI, Opp. NN. 237, fol. 92v.

76 "Articulus I. Utrum accipere usuram pro pecunia mutuata sit peccatum"; "Articulus II. Utrum liceat pro pecunia mutuata aliquam aliam commoditatem expetere"; "Articulus III. Utrum quidquid de pecunia usuraria quis lucratus fuerit reddere teneatur"; "Articulus IV. Utrum liceat pecuniam accipere mutuo sub usura", T. Aquinas, *Summa theologica*, vol. 4 (Parisiis: apud Bloud et Barral, 1880 [1485]), 533–40.

77 A list of scholastic commentaries upon Aquinas's question 78 would be too extensive for the purpose of the present study. It suffices to refer to the treatises of two of the aforementioned late scholastic writers: D. de Soto, *De iustitia et iure* (Venetiis: apud Gratiosum Perchacinum, 1568 [1556]), see notably book 6, on pp. 145v–75v; Lessius, *De iustitia et iure*, see notably book 2, chapters 20–28, on pp. 225–327. Obviously, these treatises combined their commentary upon question 78 with their reflections on Aquinas's question 77 ('On buying and selling').

78 See Toste/Lanza, 'The Commentary Tradition on the *Summa Theologiae*', 4.

Bellarmine's notes that immediately follow his discussion of question 78 on usury, to wit: between his comments on the questions 78 and 79, Bellarmine inserts an independent essay that occupies a little over 60 pages divided in 9 chapters. This essay called 'Disputatio de usura' is written down in the following order:

Disputation on usury

- Cap. 1 On the noun and definition of usury
- Cap. 2 How manifold is usury
- Cap. 3 On grounds that allow to receive something beyond the principal
- Cap. 4 Whether usury is a sin
- Cap. 5 On the reimbursement of usury and the punishment of the usurer
- Cap. 6 On the ones who receive a loan at usury
- Cap. 7 On the mount of piety
- Cap. 8 On rent contracts
- Cap. 9 On exchanges[79]

In the first six chapters, Bellarmine develops a theory of usury. Whereas chapter 1 deals with the definition of the term usury and money-lending, chapter 2 dissects various manifestations of usury. In chapter 3, Bellarmine discusses the grounds based on which interest can be lawfully claimed.[80] Chapter 4 reflects on the question whether usury is a sin and consequently provides a legal-philosophical classification of arguments based on which the condemnation against usury itself is justified. Chapter 5 discusses the obligation to refund any interest that was illegitimately received as well as the punishment of the usurers. Finally, chapter 6 provides several thoughts on the accountability of the party who receives a loan under the obligation to pay usury. Subsequently, Bellarmine applies his theory of usury to three economic constructions, namely, the mount of piety (chapter 7), rent contracts (chapter 8), and exchanges (chapter 9).[81]

The mount of piety was a legitimised system of money-lending via public pawnbrokers originally devised in late medieval Italy. This institution provided underprivileged civilians with the necessary funds to escape from usurious lenders by

79 "Disputatio de usura. Cap. 1 De nomine et definitione usurae"; "Cap. 2 Quotuplex sit usura"; "Cap. 3 Quibus de causis liceat mutuanti accipere aliquid ultra sortem"; "Cap. 4 An usura sit peccatum"; "Cap. 5 De restitutione usurae, et poena usurarii"; "Cap. 6 De accipientibus mutuum ad usuram"; "Cap. 7 De monte pietatis"; "Cap. 8 De censibus"; "Cap. 9 De cambiis". See 'S.R. Bellarmino, Continuatio et finis', ARSI, Opp. NN. 237, fol. 93r–126r.

80 Late scholastic authors often refer to these justifications as 'extrinsic titles', a term Bellarmine does not employ in his 'Disputation on usury'.

81 See also Roelofs, 'Robert Bellarmine (1542–1621) and the Law and Morality of the Market: A Brief Introduction'.

paying a legitimate and moderate interest on the capital lent.[82] It is noteworthy that Bellarmine lectured on this topic, as this form of lending 'to the poor' was officially authorised in the Southern Low Countries only at the turn of the 17th century.[83] However, further research into the extent to which Bellarmine justifies this type of money-lending, like Lessius would do in his *De iustitia et iure*,[84] is needed. The rent, in turn, was a contract that initially constituted the obligation to annually pay fruits, but, as the economic circumstances developed, it turned into the obligation of recurrent payments of money. Amongst scholastic authors, the controversy consisted of the question whether this contract entailed the sale of a right to money. If it would be considered a loan agreement instead, this would mean that any profit derived from it was considered usury, which rendered the contract illicit.[85] The essence of the scholastic discussion on exchanges is about the same in nature, *viz.* whether this type of contract was a cover-up for a loan agreement charged with illicit interest or was concluded with the genuine aim to exchange money.[86]

Bellarmine transformed his expansion on his commentary of Aquinas's question 78, article 4, into an individual essay 'Disputatio de usura'. Aquinas's article deals with the question whether it is allowed to receive a loan at interest (which Aquinas himself answers negatively). Even so, the chapters of Bellarmine's 'Disputatio de usura', especially the third, suggests that Bellarmine's attitude towards the issue of article 4 is not as black and white as Aquinas's. This is illustrative of the early modern theological renewal of the usury debate, which generally reviewed and extended the usury analysis of scholastic predecessors.[87] Although much is open to further research, it can be reasoned that Bellarmine was genuinely concerned with the salvation of the businessmen's soul. He aimed to prepare the future confessors

---

82 See for instance N.L. Barile, 'Renaissance *Monti di Pietà* in Modern Scholarship: Themes, Studies, and Historiographic Trends', *Renaissance and Reformation* 35 (2012) 85–114; M.G. Muzzarelli, *Il denaro e la salvezza. L'invenzione del Monte di Pietà* (Bologne: Il Mulino, 2001); M.G. Muzzarelli, 'Pawn Broking between Theory and Practice in Observant Socio-Economic Thought', in J. Mixson/B. Roest (ed.), *A Companion to Observant Reform in the Late Middle Ages and Beyond* (Leiden: Brill, 2015) 204–29; H. Holzapfel, *Die Anfänge der* Montes Pietatis, *1462–1515* (München: Lentner, 1903). See also Decock, *Le marché du mérite*, 147–59.

83 This was a result of the intervention of the Archdukes Albert VII (1559–1621) and Isabella (1566–1633). For a detailed background, see P. Soetaert, *De Bergen van Barmhartigheid in de Spaanse, de Oostenrijkse en de Franse Nederlanden* (Brussel: Gemeentekrediet van België, 1986).

84 See L. Lessius, and N. Golvers/P. Soetaert/T. Van Houdt (ed.), *Tussen woeker en weldadigheid: Leonardus Lessius over de Bergen van Barmhartigheid* (Leuven: Acco, 1992).

85 Noonan, *The Scholastic Analysis of Usury*, 154–70 and 230–48.

86 Noonan, *The Scholastic Analysis of Usury*, 171–92 and 311–39; See also L. dalle Molle, *Il contratto di cambio nei moralisti dal secolo XIII alla metà del secolo XVII* (Roma: Storia e letteratura, 1954).

87 Noonan, *The Scholastic Analysis of Usury*, 199–362.

for the new socio-economic challenges and in more detail than Aquinas did. It is not reasonable to assume that Bellarmine's teachings had effects on (local) business practices, but the penitents Bellarmine had in mind may have concretely (but indirectly) included the businessmen who were active in Antwerp. Proof of this might be found in a letter of Bellarmine to his superiors written in June 1575, around the moment when the moral-economic lectures took place (cf. *supra*).[88] In the letter, Bellarmine elucidates how an Italian Jesuit, who was allocated in Antwerp to preach to the merchants, gave up the office (because he was poorly equipped with the right skills) and left the port city for Louvain to join Bellarmine's theology course.

The unexplored state of a noteworthy chapter in Bellarmine's thought: A result of image and reputation control?

Bellarmine had ideas on money, contracts, and business transactions. How can such peculiar thoughts of a celebrated Saint have largely remained under the radar? First of all, in the case where the economic lectures would have been generally known from the early modern period onwards, an in-depth analysis would not be within the Church's interest for Bellarmine's sanctity, since the ecclesiastical focus was on an altogether different scale. Bellarmine's canonisation as Saint and proclamation as Doctor of the Church are set against the competing powers of the Holy See and the Italian Government.[89] This political milieu was in turn inherently related to the broader context of the 19th-century socio-economic, political, and religious complexities in Europe which the Catholic elites attempted to address on the basis of Thomistic principles.[90] An illustrative example is the encyclical *Aeternis Patris*, in which Pope Leo XIII, against the background of the rise of the nation-state, firmly supported the philosophy of Aquinas as the fundamental framework of the Catholic Church.[91] The revival of Thomism, also called 'neo-Thomism' or 'neo-scholastic revival', paved the way for the reconsideration of Bellarmine's Thomistic thought. Especially after another encyclical of Pope Leo XIII, *Immortale Dei* (1885), the political ideas of Bellarmine – and those of other late scholastics, such as Martín de

---

88 Le Bachelet, *Bellarmin avant son cardinalat*, 95–6.

89 Motta/Rai, 'Jesuit Sanctity', 8–9.

90 See E. Lamberts, 'Religious, Political and Societal Settings of the Revival of Thomism, 1870–1960', in W. Decock/B. Raymaekers/P. Heyrman (ed.), *Neo-Thomism in Action: Law and Society Reshaped by Neo-Scholastic Philosophy 1880–1960* (Leuven: Leuven University Press, 2021) 29–40.

91 Decock, 'Neo-Thomism, Law and Society', 8. The true re-vitalisation of the Thomistic tradition in the Catholic realm, however, already happened years before, see p. 14.

Azpilcueta (1492–1586) and Francisco Suárez (1548–1617) – gained interest.[92] In fact, Bellarmine supported the idea of indirect papal authority (*potestas indirecta*), a political theory that, in the late 19th century, earned Bellarmine his epithet of "the early modern advocate of the jurisdictional interests of the Church".[93]

Hence it is generally known that Bellarmine's canonisation as Saint and proclamation as Doctor of the Church were of universal importance, which called for a universal image of his sanctity.[94] For some time, the academic world followed the canonical model and approached Bellarmine (including his Louvain lectures) in light of his contribution to the post-Tridentine Church's defence against heretical threats.[95] More recently, Tutino argued that Bellarmine's anti-heretical model, including its early roots found in the Louvain lectures, is to be considered in a larger context; the Saint's doctrine not only served the attempts to uniform the Christian faith against the rise of Protestantism, but also formed part of a higher purpose, *viz.* the confirmation of the Catholic Church as a political body – the *respublica Christiana*[96] – in reaction to rise of the early modern state.[97] Still, the latter view does not make any difference for (and in fact even stresses) one of the points of this final section, namely that the universal image of our Saint – the hammer of the heretics and the architect of the political body of souls – has (unintentionally) diverted attention from the very fact that Bellarmine had participated in the scholastic economic debates of his time. This is in complete contrast to the way in which

92 Decock, 'Neo-Thomism, Law and Society', 17–18.

93 Decock, 'Neo-Thomism, Law and Society', 18. Still, in his own age, Bellarmine's political theory was not warmly received by both Catholics and non-Catholics. In 1610, Bellarmine had published the *Tractatus de potestate summi pontificis in rebus temporalibus* to oppose William Barclay (1546–1608). This jurist had rejected Bellarmine's earlier work, the *Controversiae*, in which Bellarmine had already partly touched upon the theme of *potestas indirecta*, see for instance D. Taranto, 'La *plenitudo potestatis* e il cavallo di seiano. Barclay contro Bellarmine', *Il Pensiero Politico* 53, no. 2 (2020) 189–212.

94 See also 'Il processo di canonizzazione (1622–1930)', in which Motta demonstrates that the canonical process of Bellarmine and the transformation of his image during its duration exemplifies the way how the meaning of 'holiness' is inherently connected to a historical context (on pp. 39–40).

95 See for instance F. Motta, *Bellarmino. Una teologia politica della Controriforma* (Brescia: Morcelliana, 2005); T. Dietrich, *Die Theologie des Kirche bei Robert Bellarmin (1542–1621)* (Paderborn: Bonifatius Druck-Buch-Verlag, 1999); A. Richardt, *Saint Robert Bellarmin, 1542–1621: Le défenseur de la foi* (Paris: F.X. de Guibert, 2004). As for the Louvain lectures, see the aforementioned studies of Biersack, Baldini/Coyne, and Galeota.

96 This term is used by the scholastics to designate the Christian commonwealth as a body that is not subordinate to any other external superior. See H. Höpfl, 'Church and State', in H.E. Braun/E. De Bom/P. Astorri (ed.), *A Companion to the Spanish Scholastics* (Brill: Leiden/Boston, 2022) 363–89, on pp. 365–6.

97 Tutino, *Empire of Souls*, see in particular p. 14.

Lessius has been approached during the past century,[98] which started in Belgium with the model of an exemplative and saintly Thomist in the first half of the 20th century.[99] In the second half of the 20th century, this national portrait transformed into the founding father of economic sciences.[100] From the turn of the 21st century until the present day, Lessius represents the early modern Flemish Jesuit jurist and economist of international allure.[101] Perhaps the dynamic or 'open-minded' nature of Lessius's profile might be due to the fact that his future beatification (and thus elevation to sainthood) had been excluded at a certain point[102] and hence the pressure of maintaining a certain universal profile had dropped.

Yet the interest of the Church and of the academic world may not have been the only reason why Bellarmine's economic thought has not been systematically explored until now. Both the state of the literature and primary sources regarding the Louvain lectures might have fuelled this issue as well. On the one hand, some recent contributions have neglected the fact that Bellarmine was the first theology teacher who lectured on the *Summa theologiae* in the Louvain Jesuit College.[103]

---

98 Van Houdt, *Leonardus Lessius: traditie en vernieuwing*, 11–20.

99 V. Brants, 'L'économie politique et sociale dans les écrits de L. Lessius (1554–1623)', *Revue d'histoire ecclésiastique* 13, no. 1 (1912) 73–89; J.M. Bittremieux, S.J., *Lessius et le droit de guerre: contribution à l'histoire des doctrines théologiques sur la guerre* (Bruxelles: Dewit, 1920).

100 See the aforementioned studies of Dempsey, *Interest and Usury*, and Schumpeter, *History of Economic Analysis*, as well as R.A. De Roover, *Leonardus Lessius als economist* (Brussel: Koninklijke Academie, 1969). See also B. Gordon, *Economic Analysis before Adam Smith: Hesiod to Lessius* (London: Macmillan, 1975); R. Beutels, *Leonardus Lessius 1554–1623: Portret van een Zuidnederlandse laat-scholastiek econoom: een biobibliografisch essay* (Wommelgem: Den Gulden Engel, 1987).

101 The state of the literature on Lessius's juridical-economic thought owes much to the analyses of Van Houdt and Decock. Of the many titles that can be cited, a select few are the aforementioned ones, as well as W. Decock, 'Lessius and the Breakdown of the Scholastic Paradigm', *Journal of the History of Economic Thought* 31, no. 1 (2009); T. Van Houdt, 'Tradition and Renewal in Late Scholastic Economic Thought: The Case of Leonardus Lessius (1554–1623)', *Journal of Medieval and Early Modern Studies* 28, no. 1 (1998) 51–73; id., *Leonardus Lessius over lening, intrest en woeker*: De iustitia et iure, lib. 3, cap. 20, *editie, vertaling en commentaar* (Brussel: Paleis der Academiën, 1998); id., "Lack of money': A reappraisal of Lessius' contribution to the scholastic analysis of money-lending and interest-taking', *European Journal of the History of Economic Thought* 5, no. 1 (1998) 1–35.

102 … after he had lost the 'sainthood race' against Bellarmine, see E. Rai, 'The 'Odor of Sanctity'. Veneration and Politics in Leonard Lessius's Cause for Beatification (Seventeenth–Twentieth Centuries)', *Journal of Jesuit Studies* 3, no. 2 (2016) 238–58, see especially pp. 247–50.

103 For instance, in *Repertorio de moral económica (1526–1670): La Escuela de Salamanca y su proyección* (Barañáin: Eunsa, 2011), 347–8, J. Barrientos García erroneously states that Lessius was the first one who took the *Summa theologiae* as the basis for his lectures: "… [Lessio] fuese el primero que en Lovaina siguió la *Summa* de santo Tomás como texto en sus explicaciones." This also occurs in 'Lessius Leonard, SJ (1554–1623)', in T. Worcester, S.J., *The Cambridge Encyclopedia of*

On the other hand, records and primary source materials possibly contributed to the misinterpretation that Bellarmine had not commented upon the *Secunda pars* of the *Summa theologiae*, which might have weakened any expectation that Bellarmine had uttered economic ideas in the Jesuit lecture hall of Louvain. As for the first category, an example is the index of the *epistolae Bellarmini*, based on which one might erroneously infer that Bellarmine's Louvain lectures do not cover the *Secunda secundae* (and, thus, neither the economic-related question 78).[104] An example of the second category is the aforementioned letter of Franciscus Costerus (1532–1619), provincial of the Jesuits in the Low Countries, which reveals that the original plan of the Jesuit Superiors was to put Bellarmine in charge of commenting upon the *Prima pars* and *Tertia pars* alone.[105] Furthermore, as Mancini observes, 18th-century inventories of Bellarmine's autographs do not include the Louvain lectures, so knowledge of and thus interest in the manuscripts might have started relatively late.[106]

Nonetheless, it is more likely that the reasons for the unexplored territory of Bellarmine's moral-economic thought lie outside the literature. Obviously, the unavailability of a printed (or digitised) version of the Louvain lectures hampered an easy access to the content of the teachings. Even so, bearing in mind that part of the handwritten documents in Bellarmine's collection has been published (cf. *supra*), one might wonder why the Louvain lectures have never seen the printing press or a digitisation project at all. Before pondering this question, it is important to distinguish between young Bellarmine (until the 1580s) and old Bellarmine (from the 1590s onward). Today, the concept of 'Saint Bellarmine' is mostly linked to his large-scale engagements on the international scene, such as the ongoing

the Jesuits (Cambridge: Cambridge University Press, 2017) 460–1, where P. Begheyn, S.J., writes: "As professor he [Leonardus Lessius] introduced the *Summa theologiae* in the Netherlands, … ." Furthermore, other studies relate that Bellarmine lectured at the University of Louvain, see Schaff, 'Cardinal Bellarmine. Now Saint and Doctor of the Church', 43: "Bellarmine was the first Jesuit to be permitted to lecture in the renowned university." Rather, Bellarmine was permitted *by* the University of Louvain to lecture in the Jesuit College.

104 See *Indice delle* Epistolae Bellarmini *(1599–1621)* (https://www.unigre.it/archivioimg/Cataloghi/Bellarmino1.htm, last access: 14/11/2022), and, in particular, the list of MS. 2419–2430 of the APUG, which, according to the inventory, only covers the teachings on the *Prima pars*, *Prima secundae partis* and *Tertia pars* of the *Summa theologiae* due to an unfortunate type error, to wit: APUG 2424–2429 are titled "In I IIae" but should be called "In II IIae".

105 Le Bachelet, *Bellarmin avant son cardinalat*, 73. This source probably led to the misinterpretation that Bellarmine has not lectured on the *Secunda pars*, see Tutino, *Empire of Souls*, 11.

106 Mancini, 'La biblioteca del cardinale Roberto Bellarmino', 93–4, n. 59.

theological disputes in Louvain,[107] the Venetian Interdict, the Oath of Allegiance of James I, and the cases of Galileo Galilei and Martin Becanus.[108] Conversely, the Louvain lectures have been delivered by the younger spirit of Bellarmine, at that moment not yet the full-blown scholar as we commemorate him today. Bearing this in mind, it was old Bellarmine's own explicit desire that no one would make the lecture notes available in the public domain. In 1617, in response to Peter Cudsem (d. 1649), a publisher in Cologne who had asked Bellarmine's permission to publish the lecture notes,[109] Bellarmine explicitly wrote that he had asked the Holy See to excommunicate the one who would dare to release them. The notes were written by the hands of a young man who had many duties at the same time. Besides, they were incomplete and not worthy to be made public.[110] Furthermore, as Le Bachelet observes, a publication of the lectures would mainly be a repetition of the *Controversiae*, which would not be an innovation in his literary oeuvre.[111]

It has been proposed that the negative attitude of Bellarmine towards the publication of the lectures is related to the major attention that the Counter-Reformation needed, which made the *Controversiae* more relevant for publication than the Louvain lectures.[112] However, considering the fact that the teachings based on the *Secunda secundae* are not a point of attention in Bellarmine's letter to Cudsem nor form part of the *Controversiae*,[113] it is open to debate as to why Bellarmine did not

---

107 See for instance Rai, '*Ex Meritis Praevisis*'. See also Cauchie, 'Bellarmin et l'Université de Louvain d'après un livre récent', 391–401, where can be found a select overview of the letters between Bellarmine and Lessius, which have been published in Le Bachelet, *Bellarmin avant son cardinalat*.

108 For Bellarmine's participation in these events, see Tutino, *Empire of Souls*, *passim*.

109 Biersack, *Initia Bellarminiana*, 92 and 95.

110 See Le Bachelet, *Auctarium Bellarminianum*, ii, where can be found a French translation of a selected passage from an inedited letter by Bellarmine, which reads: "… ces notes sur la *Somme* de Saint Thomas sont quelque chose d'imparfait, d'incomplet et d'indigne, à mon avis, de paraître au grand jour. Elles sont imparfaites, car elles ne contiennent pas tout ce que je disais en chaire; ce n'en est qu'un résumé succinct. Elles sont incomplètes, car il y a une lacune au début de la I^{a} II^{ae} et une autre plus grande encore à la fin de la III^{a}. Elles sont indignes de paraître au grand jour, car ce sont les notes d'un jeune homme qui devait en même temps enseigner en classe et prêcher au peuple, deux offices dont chacun demanderait un homme entier. Vos paroles m'ont fait craindre qu'on ne voulût imprimer et publier, malgré moi, ce qui a été pris alors sous ma dictée; aussi je suis allé trouver le Saint Père et je lui ai demandé l'autorisation d'écrire en son nom au nonce apostolique de Cologne, pour lui enjoindre de défendre, sous peine d'excommunication, à tous les typographes colonais d'oser imprimer, à mon insu et sans ma permission, mes commentaires sur la *Somme* de Saint Thomas." See also De le Court, 'Saint Bellarmin à Louvain', 80; Van Houdt, 'On 'Medium' and 'Message'', 188.

111 Le Bachelet, *Auctarium Bellarminianum*, ii; Mancini, 'La biblioteca del cardinale Roberto Bellarmino', 94.

112 Toste/Lanza, 'The Commentary Tradition on the *Summa Theologiae*', 23.

113 Indeed, the letter reveals that only the *Prima secundae* and the uncompleted *Tertia pars* are Bellarmine's explicit targets. Le Bachelet, *Auctarium Bellarminianum*, ii.

publish at least part of his notes, to wit his commentaries on the *Secunda secundae*, as Soto had done (1553–1554) and Lessius as well (1605). This would be both an innovation regarding his collection of publications and a more feasible project in terms of revision. It is suggested that Bellarmine remained resolute precisely because of the economic dimension of part of the notes. He was not very fond of lecturing on these topics nor of preaching to the Italian businessmen in Antwerp.[114] The evidence put forward is the aforementioned letter of June 1575, which reveals that Jesuit superiors had asked Bellarmine himself to preach in Antwerp, a request he declined.[115] In fact, Le Bachelet observes that a few years before his death, Bellarmine still remembered that he did not feel suitable to deal with economic topics in front of that type of public.[116] Whether Bellarmine had a slight dislike for economic themes or wanted to avoid any confrontation with Italian merchants, it is a fact that the economic teachings form part of his commentary upon the *Secunda secundae*. According to himself and the hagiographer Fuligatti, Bellarmine was not familiar with this section of Aquinas's *Summa theologiae* when he was instructed to teach (cf. *supra*).

By explicitly mentioning the lacuna in Bellarmine's framework, Fuligatti might have wanted to subtly 'downplay' the commentaries on the *Secunda pars*. So far, it is not clear whether Fuligatti was informed of the very content of the lectures and even less of the scope of the moral-economic ones. However, it is not unlikely that his reasoning was the following: the *Secunda pars* of Aquinas's *Summa theologiae* (and in particular the *Secunda secundae*) deals with rather practical and thus earthly matters compared to the *Prima pars* and *Tertia pars* (cf. *supra*) and hence could be suspected of controversial teachings in view of the *De detrimentis Societatis*. The latter document was the result of an investigation into the spiritual condition of the Jesuit Order. Upon the reception of this report in 1606, Claudio Acquaviva (1543–1615), at that moment the Superior General of the Society, was of the opinion that the Jesuit outreach, the so-called *effusio ad exteriora*, had become too extreme: the Jesuit missionaries were too concerned with worldly matters and had moved away from the spiritual dimension of the faith.[117] Perhaps with this affair fresh in memory, Fuligatti wanted to anticipate the case where one might accuse Bellarmine of controversial teachings – which would be detrimental to the canonical process – by relativising the teachings in advance.

---

114 Van Houdt, 'On 'Medium' and 'Message'', 188; De le Court, 'Saint Bellarmin à Louvain', 80.

115 Le Bachelet, *Bellarmin avant son cardinalat*, 95–6.

116 Le Bachelet, *Bellarmin avant son cardinalat*, 90, see n. 1.

117 W. Decock, 'Towards a Jesuit Science of Law', in R. Faesen/L. Kenis (ed.), *The Jesuits of the Low Countries: Identity and Impact (1540–1773). Proceedings of the International Congress at the Faculty of Theology and Religious Studies, KU Leuven (3–5 December 2009)* (Leuven/Paris/Walpole, MA: Peeters, 2012) 17–42, on p. 17.

Bellarmine himself also might have been concerned about the image he would leave the world after his death. Perhaps he carried out a 'hagiographical self-construction', considering that the last decade of his life is marked by a number of ascetical works.[118] In 1615 he published the most famous one, *De ascensione mentis in Deum per scalas rerum creatarum*, which contains guidelines to walk in the presence of God.[119] Other writings in the same category are *De aeterna felicitate sanctorum* (1616), *De gemitu columbae sive bono lacrymarum* (1617), and *De arte bene moriendi* (1620), published one year before his death.[120] The treatises together evidence the spiritual, ecclesiological, and ascetical focus of a pastor of souls in the combat against materialism, an image that has even recently proven its relevance.[121] Bellarmine represents 'worldliness', a model that is also heavily underlined in the decretal letter concerning Bellarmine's canonisation as Saint: earthly matters left Bellarmine unmoved. As a child, Bellarmine abhorred boyish games, and from young adulthood onwards, he despised worldly honours.[122] Even money could not entice the Saint into the web of mundane matters, for

> … after he had steadfastly refused optimal payments provided by the Spanish Crown, [Bellarmine] only accepted a very modest sum of money from the Roman Pontificate necessary to maintain the dignity of the cardinalship.[123]

Passages like these may have 'condemned' Bellarmine's image to one that is sealed from the slightest doubt that the Saint had once had some theoretical affinity with money and economic matters. This portrait might have pleased our Saint, since the *effusio ad exteriora* affair could have played a role in old Bellarmine's attitude towards a publication of the Louvain lectures as well. The aforementioned letter to Cudsem, in which Bellarmine expresses his discontent for the case where the

---

118 Motta, 'Il processo di canonizzazione (1622–1930)', 44–5.

119 In the period until the year of Bellarmine's elevation to sanctity, the treatise was reprinted 57 times and translated into 14 different languages, see Pontifica Università Gregoriana, *De operibus S. Roberti Bellarmini* (Roma: Pontifica Università Gregoriana, 1930), 47.

120 For a categorised overview of these and other writings of Bellarmine, see Pontifica Università Gregoriana, *De operibus S. Roberti Bellarmini* (Roma: Pontifica Università Gregoriana, 1930).

121 See the General Audience held by Benedict XVI at Paul VI Audience Hall on Wednesday, 23 February 2011 (https://www.vatican.va/content/benedict-xvi/en/audiences/2011/documents/hf_ben-xvi_aud_20110223.html, last access: 14/11/2022).

122 "… a puerilibus ludis abhorrens … ." *Acta Apostolicae Sedis. Commentarium officiale*, 31 Decembris 1930, 593; "Decem et octo annos natus Robertus, mundo honores despiciens, … ." *Acta Apostolicae Sedis. Commentarium officiale*, 31 Decembris 1930, 594.

123 "… ac, opimis ab Hispanorum Rege exhibitis pensionibus firmiter recusatus, modicam tantum a Romano Pontifice pecuniae summam ad cardinalitiam dignitatem tuendam necessarium accepit." *Acta Apostolicae Sedis. Commentarium officiale*, 31 Decembris 1930, 595.

notes would be published, is dated 1617, hence relatively shortly after the *De detrimentis Societatis* was issued. Old Bellarmine possibly feared that the publication of some of his early-career teachings, such as the ones on money, contracts, and economic transactions, might interfere with the reputation he was gaining in the institutional sphere. In fact, from the 1590s onwards, Bellarmine started to hold different posts within the Roman Curia. He became the rector of the Roman College (1592), examiner of bishops and member of the Inquisition (1598), and cardinal (1599). Meanwhile, Bellarmine gained experience as censor for the *Index librorum prohibitorum*.[124] As is only natural, Bellarmine had to become careful with (or had to censor himself in) publications of his own and did not want to cause any new theological controverse.[125] At any rate, how would old Bellarmine feel about publishing lecture texts written decades beforehand? A revision of the Louvain lectures would be on top of the international political-theological issues that were already on his plate in the final years of his life (cf. *supra*). It is precisely the wide impact of these engagements that has played a substantial role in the establishment of his current image, a high-profile depiction that might have fundamentally overshadowed any suggestion that Saint Robert Bellarmine had once ventured into economic thought.

Conclusion

In the spirit of the universal importance of Bellarmine's elevation to sainthood, the papal acts concerning his canonisation as Saint and proclamation as Doctor of the Church present the Louvain lectures as an example of Bellarmine's anti-heretical contribution, one of the pillars of his model of sanctity. Early modern Jesuits had already largely referenced Bellarmine's activities in Louvain in their campaign for his canonisation. In doing so, they rather stressed the other pillar, Bellarmine's struggle against the world's preoccupation with material possessions, by focussing on the internal perfection and interpersonal skills of the Saint-to-be. Both the canonical and hagiographical model note the success Bellarmine's lectures gained. In this regard, surviving manuscripts including second-order ones that emerged in the aftermath of the Louvain lectures indicate that Bellarmine's commentaries of the *Secunda secundae* of Aquinas's *Summa theologiae* might have been the most impactful ones. A rudimentary exploration of these particular teachings suggests that young Bellarmine participated in the scholastic economic debates of his era.

124 See also P. Godman, *The Saint as Censor. Robert Bellarmine between Inquisition and Index* (Leiden: Brill, 2000).

125 Besides, after all theological challenges Bellarmine went through in his life, he obviously did not want to feed any new dispute, see Biersack, *Initia Bellarminiana*, 92.

By inserting a short treatise on usury which is more detailed and elaborated than the writings on this matter by his main source Aquinas, Bellarmine felt duty-bound to equip the next generation of confessors with the tools to address the socio-economic challenges of the age. Naturally, the mapping of this intriguing side of Bellarmine's thought might not alter the established profile of the Saint, although it will undoubtedly introduce a new, fascinating player into the historiography of law and economics.

In particular, this study has suggested that multiple elements related to the construction of Bellarmine's image contributed to the fact that Bellarmine's economic thought is not systematically known. This paves the way for further research into several preliminary conclusions. First, the unpublished nature of the Louvain lectures certainly has a role in this lacuna in the state of the art, but it might rather be, in part, a consequence of the hagiographical self-construction of Bellarmine. Secondly, although a link between the current underestimated state of Bellarmine's economic thought and hagiographies is less likely, Bellarmine's commentaries upon the *Secunda pars* may have been relativised in the early modern hagiographic narrative. Thirdly, the modern canonical model has primarily focussed on Bellarmine's fight against heresy and materialism. This depiction, in combination with old Bellarmine's own major interventions of international impact, may have led to a solid and universal image of the Saint that has simply absorbed attention from other intriguing, however small, aspects of his intellectual legacy. Either way, the engaging (and perhaps unexpected) scope of Bellarmine's economic thought demonstrates that research into our Saint's collection of manuscripts – and in particular those that feature the Louvain lectures – displays a considerable potential to grow.

Carlo Pelliccia

"Or voi conoscete qual sarà stata la santità del Saverio"

The Panegyric by Eriprando Maria Giuliari (1728–1805)

Francis Xavier: a missionary and a saint

This article's primary purpose is to publish the panegyric dedicated to Francis Xavier (1506–1552), one of the most famous and popular figures of the missionary church in the early modern age.

Xavier trained at the College of Saint Barbara in Paris (becoming *magister artium*), where he went in September 1525 and was one of the first members of the Society of Jesus. He made his private vows (with six companions) in Montmartre, in the chapel of Saint-Denis, on 15 August 1534, promising to undertake a pilgrimage to the Holy Land to convert "infidels". Xavier began to study theology in 1534 and two years later arrived in Venice, where he was ordained priest by the papal delegate (in his private chapel) on 24 June 1537. After a brief stay in Bologna, he went to Rome in April 1538 to join Ignatius of Loyola (1591–1556) and his confreres. There he started to preach in the French church of Saint Louis. Later he was chosen by the Spanish Founder to leave for Asia. He left Lisbon on 7 April 1541, aboard the ship *Santiago*, with three companions (one Italian and two Portuguese)[1] to set foot on the East Indies and to dedicate himself to the evangelization of the overseas countries.[2] Indeed, Xavier arrived at Goa on 6 May 1542. During the ten years of

1 J. Wicki S.J., "Liste der Jesuiten-Indienfahrer 1541–1758", *Aufsätze zur Portugiesischen Kulturgeschichte* 7 (1967): 269.

2 Francis Xavier replaced his Spanish companion Nicolás Bobadilla (1509–1590), who was indisposed, and arrived in Lisbon (separately) in June 1540 with Simão Rodrigues de Azevedo (1510–1579). He left Lisbon with the new governor Martim Afonso de Sousa (c. 1500–1564), after the publication of the papal brief (27 July 1540) which appointed him papal nuncio in the Portuguese colonies of the East Indies. Leo Magnino wrote: "portava seco due Brevi di Paolo III che lo dovevano introdurre presso i principi dell'Oriente. Uno era diretto al re Davide di Etiopia, l'altro lo raccomandava 'a tutti i principi e signori delle isole del Mar Rosso, Persico e Oceanico e di tutte le terre al di qua e al di là del Gange e al di là del Promontorio chiamato Capo di Buona Speranza ed a tutti i Paesi con questi confinanti'". L. Magnino, *Portogallo, paese atlantico* (Bologna: Pàtron, 1963), 53. Meanwhile, Rodrigues remained in Portugal by order of the monarch and later was appointed Provincial of the Portuguese Jesuit Province (the first established by the Society of Jesus) founded on 25 October 1546. For a quick approach to this topic, see: D. Mauricio, "Portugal e S. Francisco Xavier. D. João III na Projecção Apostólica Xaveriana", *Brotéria* 55/5 (1952) 455–82. On Xavier's biography, see: G. Schurhammer, S.J., *Franz Xaver. Sein Leben und seine Zeit - In 2(4) Bänden: Erster Band: Europa*

his stay in Asia, he founded some missionary stations, visiting Malacca firstly in 1545 and later in 1547 on his return from Moluccas to India, when Jorge Álvares (?–1552), a Portuguese captain, presented him Anjirō, a Japanese *wakō* (pirate), who was baptized in Goa on 20 May 1548 under the name of Paulo de Santa Fé. Finally, Xavier reached Kagoshima, on 15 August 1549, with Cosme de Torres (1510–1570) and Juan Fernández de Oviedo (1526–1567). Then he landed in Shangchuan, at the gates of China, where he died on 3 December 1552, assisted by António, a Chinese neophyte and his interpreter.

His missionary epic will soon be celebrated in various places on the Asian and European continents. The Portuguese crown decided to begin the beatification process by trasferring his body on 16 March 1554 to Goa, the political and ecclesiastical capital of the *Estado da Índia*.[3]

In this regard, Maria Cristina Osswald states:

> O poder real português e posteriormente ibérico demonstrou desde cedo um interesse especial no túmulo de Francisco Xavier. Até finais do séc. XVIII, vários vice-reis e governadores foram enterrados junto ao mesmo túmulo. Por outras palavras, a posse do corpo incorrupto de Francisco Xavier foi um aspecto importante da política real portuguesa para legitimar o seu Império.[4]

On 28 March 1556, King John III (1502–1557), of the house of Aviz, wrote a letter to his viceroy Pedro de Mascarenhas (1480–1555) to commission him the collecting of credible witnesses in all parts of India on Xavier's heroic virtues. But unfortunately, Mascarenhas died, and his successor Francisco Barreto (1520–1573) carried out the command of the sovereign. Indeed between 1556 and 1557 he collected sixty-three testimonies (one native Indian and all Portuguese) in several locations in South Asia. The first efforts by the Society were in 1575 when the Provincial Congregation held in Goa wrote a *postulatum* on this subject, addressed to the superior general Everard Mercurian (1514–1580).[5] The latter replied with a

---

1506–1541. Band I: Europa 1506–1541; Band II,1: Asien - Indien und Indonesien 1541–1547; Band II,2: Indien un Indonesien 1547–1549; II, 3: Japan und China 1549–1552 (Freiburg-Basel-Wien: Herder, 1955–1973).

3 J.P. Oliveira e Costa declared: "Na Índia meridional e nas Molucas, Francisco de Xavier, através da sua acção pastoral, colaborou nos esforços de consolidação da influência portuguesa nessas regiões nevrálgicas para os interesses de Goa". J.P. Oliveira e Costa, "D. João III e São Francisco de Xavier", *Oriente* 13 (2005) 13.

4 M.C. Osswald, "São Francisco Xavier: estratégias de constituição dum culto entre os séculos XVI e XVIII", *Revista Lusófona de Ciencia das Religiões* 7/13–14 (2008) 328.

5 However, one of the Society's immediate concerns, as stated Juan de Polanco (1517–1576), appointed secretary to Loyola in 1547, in a letter dated 21 November 1555, was the beginning of the investigation into the cause of Xavier's canonization: "eyewitness testimony of Xavier's 'heroic virtue', apostolic zeal,

request that ecclesiastical authorities continued to collect testimonies. Finally, the Fifth General Congregation (which lasted from 3 November 1593 to 18 January 1594) asked the successor Claudio Acquaviva (1543–1615) to create a petition to the Holy See to beatify Francis Xavier and the founder Ignatius of Loyola. Paul V (Camillo Borghese, r. 1605–1621) accepted this petition and thus began the various practices of re-examination and authentication of witnesses, and identification was authorized between 1608 and 1613 in Cebú, in the Philippines. However, in 1610 cardinal Girolamo Pamphili (1545–1610), became the promoter of the cause, giving it great impetus, so further enquiries were held in various cities in Europe and Asia.[6]

In addition, a request was also advanced by Ōtomo Yoshishige (Sōrin, 1530–1587), *daimyō* of Bungo and friend of Xavier,[7] who wrote a letter on 4 December 1583 addressed to Alessandro Valignano (1539–1606), who left Japan on 20 February 1582,[8] so that he could intercede (but also promote) the cause of beatification of Francis Xavier with the superior general and the pontiff. The feudal lord claimed that this event would benefit the Japanese Catholic community and increase the cult of this missionary. The following year "o rei Francisco"

holy death, and, above all, working of miracles, pre- or post-mortem, had to be gathered, scrutinized, and recorded for posterity". F. Mormando, "The Making of the Second Jesuit Saint: The *Campaign* for the Canonization of Francis Xavier" 1555–1622, in F. Mormando – J.G. Thomas (eds.), *Francis Xavier and the Jesuit Missions in the Far East* (Chestnut Hill, Massachusetts: The Jesuit Institute Boston College, 2006), 9.

6 M.C. Osswald, "The Iconography and cult of Francis Xavier, 1552–1640", *Archivum Historicum Societatis Iesu* 71/142 (2002) 260–61. In the footnotes the author reported the sources of the quoted documents, most of them printed in the *Documenta Indica*. This article was presented in an issue dedicated to Saint Francis Xavier to commemorate the 450th anniversary of his death.

7 The friendship between Xavier and Yoshishige was born in 1551. In this year Xavier was received in audience by Yoshishige and made a good impression on the young feudal lord. This latter was baptized on 28 August 1578 under the name of Francis (in honor of the European friend) by the Portuguese Jesuit Francisco Cabral (1533–1609). See G. Schurhammer, S.J., "Ein fürstlicher Gönner des hl. Franz Xaver: Ōtomo Yoshishige, König von Bungo", *Katholischen Missionen* 47 (1918) 25–9.

8 His first stay in Japan lasted from 25 July 1579 to 20 February 1582. Valignano left the archipelago with four Japanese boys, chosen from the seminary of Arima and entrusted to the Portuguese Jesuit Diogo de Mesquita (1551–1614). They arrived to Europe to pay homage to Gregory XIII (Ugo Boncompagni, r. 1572–1585) and Philip II (1527–1598). However, Valignano did not go to Europe because he was appointed Provincial of India (1583) and was replaced by Nuno Rodrigues (1539–1604), rector of the college of Saint Paul in Goa. On the first Japanese embassy to Europe (*Tenshō shōnen shisetsu*, 1582–1590) see: G. Sorge, *Il Cristianesimo in Giappone e il De Missione* (Bologna: Clueb, 1988); M. Cooper, *The Japanese Mission to Europe, 1582–1590: The Journey of four Samurai Boys through Portugal, Spain and Italy* (Kent: Global Oriental, 2005).

returned to writing on the same subject to Acquaviva and drafted an epistle, dated 20 November 1584.[9]

Francis Xavier was beatified on 25 October 1619 by Paul V with the brief *In sede principis*[10] and canonized by Gregory XV (Alessandro Ludovisi, r. 1621–1623) on 12 March 1622, three months before the official erection of the *Sacra Congregatio de Propaganda Fide*.[11] The canonized group consisted of Ignatius of Loyola, Teresa of Avila (1515–1582), a Discalced Carmelite nun, Isidore the Laborer (1080–1130), appointed patron saint of Madrid, and Philip Neri (1515–1595), founder of the Congregation of the Oratory.[12]

As a pioneer of the missions, Xavier was declared patron of the East in 1748 with the constitution *Indiarum gentibus* by Benedict XIV (Prospero Lorenzo Lambertini, r. 1740–1758), thanks to the request of the King John V (1689–1750), of the house of Braganza. In the last century he was awarded the title of patron of the Pontifical Society for the Propagation of the Faith (1904) and later that of patron of the missions (1927) together with Thérèse of Lisieux (1873–1897), a French Discalced Carmelite nun.

The popularity of Xavier and the dynamism of his missionary life gave rise to knowledge and the dissemination of his image as a man and a priest, developing primarily in literature (especially hagiography) and figurative arts (in particular painting). Beginning in the second half of the sixteenth century, thanks above all to the Society of Jesus,[13] who used his fugure as a model (albeit not simple) to

9 The quotations of the two letters are also in: C. Pelliccia, "Notas sobre a influência da cultura portuguesa no Japão (séculos XVII e XVIII): o legado dos missionários europeus", *Antíteses* 10/20 (2017) 644, ft. 43. Both epistles are kept in the Archivum Romanum Societatis Iesu (henceforth ARSI), Jap. Sin. 9 II, ff. 195–196v; Jap. Sin. 33, ff. 31–32v. In the manuscript Jap. Sin. 33 there is also an Italian translation of the first missive: ARSI, Jap. Sin. 33, f. 28.

10 Cfr. J.R. Armogathe, "La fabrique des saints: Causes espagnoles et procédures romaines d'Urbain VIII à Benoit XIV (XVIIe–XVIIIe siécle)", *Mélanges de la Casa de Velázquez* 33/2 (2003) 15–31.

11 This dicastery was canonically established with the bull *Inscrutabili divinae* (22 June 1622) by Gregory XV. See: G. Russo, *Governare le missioni, conoscere il mondo nel XVII secolo. La Congregazione pontificia De Propaganda Fide* (Viterbo: Sette Città, 2020).

12 It was canonically erected in 1575 with the bull *Copiosus in misericordia Deus* (15 July) by Gregory XIII.

13 In many Jesuit accounts there are references to the Xavier's missionary life. Only four examples. Giovanni Maracci (c. 1603–1654), an Italian Jesuit priest and procurator of the Province of Goa (appointed in 1647), composed the *Breve ragguaglio sopra le missioni della Compagnia di Giesù della Provincia Goana nell'India Orientale: appresentato all'Eminentissima Congregatione de Propaganda Fide dal Padre Giovanni Marracci della medesima Compagnia e procurator della detta Provincia, in Aprile dell'anno 1649*, which was divided into two parts. In the introduction of the second part titled *Breve Ragguaglio delle Missioni della Compagnia di Giesù della Provincia del Giappone e Cina nell'India Orientale apresentato alla Sacra Congregatione de propagande Fide*, Maracci wrote: "Questa Provincia Eminentissimi Signori, principiata ancor Lei dal glorioso Apostolo dell'Indie San Francesco

follow.[14] Xavier became an example for evangelization for the entire church. These works (especially biographies written by confreres) promoted and supported to the campaign for canonization and often inspired devotion among people of the time, increasing his popularity (*fama sanctitatis*) throughout Latin Christianity.

Saverio, et ampliata da altri Missionarii della nostra Religione per spatio di cento anni appunto tiene l'infrascritte Missioni. ARSI, Goa 34 II, f. 393v. Maracci composed another report always in Rome on 20 September 1649. This document, entitled *Breve Ragguaglio dello Stato della Provincia di Goa: con quanto di singolare è in quella accaduto nell'anno 1647*, contains some references to Francis Xavier and to the devotion that the people reserved for this Saint. In the paragraph *Casa professa di Goa* Maracci compiled: "La divotione verso il santo Apostolo dell'Indie S. Francesco Saverio, ogni giorno va più crescendo. Fra l'anno sempre v'è concorso di gente, che va a visitar quel sagro deposito; o a far novene, per ottener salute, o per render le gratie della già ottenuta. Questo concorso però è maggiore nella novena, che si fa con sollennità, innanzi al giorno della sua festa; e continua poi per tutta l'Ottava; spopolandosi l'isole vicine a quella di Goa per godere la consolatione, che appresso ricevono dal vedere il corpo del Santo, che si scuopre da' primi vespri, e così dura per tutto il giorno seguente. [...] La miracolosa cotta del Santo ha continue richieste per gl'infermi: i quali dal toccamento d'essa sperimentano effetti mirabili. Così accade ad uno fra gl'altri, che disperato da' medici, dopo haver chiesta quella sagra reliquia, hebbe col contatto la salute: con esserli quella stessa notte apparso il Santo. De quel fatto si presero autentiche informationi". ARSI, Goa 34 I, ff. 196v–197. The *Ragguaglio della Missione del Giappone: nell'isola Haynam, Camboscia, Macassar etc. Tratto dall'ultima lettera annua del 1649, scritta in lingua Portoghese*, an anonymous codex probably composed in the second half of the seventeenth century, begins in the following way: "Questo anno è stato il centesimo dell'entrata al Giappone del primo Apostolo, e Patriarca Orientale, San Francesco Saverio. Anno, si come, per questa circostanza, degnissimo di spetial celebrità: così sopra modo, infelice, per trovarsi in esso quell'un tempo per gli progressi della Fede fioritissimo Imperio, combattuto dalla più fiera persecutione, che sia stata mai per l'addietro". ARSI, Jap. Sin. 65, f. 2. On this manuscript see: C. Pelliccia, "«Ultimamente con non poco travaglio alla Cocincina si videro»: viaggiatori gesuiti in Asia orientale nel secolo XVII", in M. Graziani – L. Casetti – S. Vuelta Garcia (eds.), *Nel Segno di Magellano tra terra e cielo. Il viaggio nelle arti umanistiche e scientifiche di lingua portoghese e di altre culture europee in un'ottica interculturale* (Firenze: Firenze University Press, 2021) 222–23. Giovanni Filippo De Marini (1608–1682), an Italian Jesuit and a missionary in Tunkin (for eleven years), wrote the *Relatione del viaggio del Padre Filippo Marino della Compagnia di Gesù con suoi Compagni da Lisbona sino a Goa nell'Anno 1666* 1608–1682. It was compiled in Goa on 2 February 1667 and addressed to Giovanni Paolo Oliva (1600–1681), superior general of the Jesuit Order. De Marini wrote: "A 7 d'Aprile ci imbarcammo e fu il giorno, in cui nell'anno 1541 s'imbarcò il nostro Santo Apostolo per quest'Oriente". ARSI, Goa 35, f. 33. Cfr. A. De Marini, "Relazione del viaggio da Lisbona a Goa del padre Giovanni Filippo De Marini nell'anno 1666", in F. Surdich (ed.), *Miscellanea di Storia delle Esplorazioni Geografiche* vol. XXIX (Genova: Bozzi Editore, 2004) 107–22.

14 Xavier also became a model for the *indipeti*, who expressed the desire to be sent to overseas missions (*petebant Indias*). Indeed, there are many references to this Spanish Saint in the *litterae indipetae* which the Jesuits (even those of the New Society) sent to the superiors general. In this occasion I cite only an example taken from the epistle written by Girolamo Paradisi (1807–1873) in Naples on 7 September 1831 and addressed to Jan Philip Roothaan (1785–1853): "Quando poi dalla lettura della Vita di San Francesco Saverio conobbi, che ancora io potevo diventare uno di quelli; incominciai ad esser preso da quanto serj, altrettanto piacevoli pensieri, e fu in essi che lavorò il Signore la mia

The Portuguese Jesuit Manuel Acosta (1541–1604), professor in Coimbra, wrote a short biography of Xavier in the *Rerum a Societate Iesu in Oriente Gestarum ad annum usque a Deipara Virgine MDLXVIII*. This work was translated in Latin and augmented by Giovanni Pietro Maffei (1536–1603) when he was a novice and produced in Dillingen (Sebaldus Mayer) in 1571.[15] Pedro de Ribadeneira (1526–1611), historian and writer, composed in Latin *Vita Sancti Ignatii Loiolae, Societatis Iesu fundatoris* published before in Naples (Apud Josephum Cacchium) in 1572 and then in Spanish in Madrid (por Alonso Gómez Impresor de su Majestad) in 1583. It contains an account of Xavier's miracles with a focus on his possible canonization. Manuel Teixeira (c. 1536–1590), who met in person the protagonist of his narration, composed a biography entitled *Vida del bienaventurado padre Francisco Javier* between 1575 and 1579. He sent it to Rome in 1581, but it was printed only in 1912.[16] Indeed, this work circulated widely in manuscript form. The Italian Jesuit Orazio Torsellino (1545–1599), historian and man of letters, wrote *De Vita Francisci Xaverii qui primus è Societate Iesu in India & Iaponia Evangelium promulgavit*,[17] published in Rome (Ex typographia Gabiana) in 1594 and later translated in some European vernacular languages. João de Lucena (1549–1600), preacher and writer, drafted one of the first lives in Portuguese titled *História da Vida do Padre Francisco Xavier e do que fizerao na India os mais religiosos da*

Vocazione alla Compagnia". ARSI, AIT 1, f. 78. The letter is transcribed in https://indipetae.bc.edu/items/show/1716 (last access on 14 July 2022). This aspect emerges in a recently published article: "Un altro tratto tipico delle *indipetae* ottocentesche riguarda i modelli missionari utilizzati dai gesuiti per esprimere il proprio desiderio. Anche in questo caso è possibile individuare un'evoluzione nel corso dell'Ottocento. Nelle lettere scritte nei primi anni dopo la restaurazione compaiono numerosi riferimenti ai modelli di gesuiti illustri ricorrenti nelle *indipetae* dell'Antica Compagnia: Ignazio, alcuni martiri missionari, ma soprattutto Francesco Saverio". E. Colombo – M. Rochini, "Prima la missione. Indipetae italiane (1814–1853)", *Ricerche di storia sociale e religiosa* 88 (2016) 52.

15 The original Portuguese text (never published) was written around 1568–1570. The Latin edition was dedicated to Otto von Truchsess (1514–1573), bishop of Augsburg (1543) and cardinal of Santa Balbina (1544), as well as counselor of Charles V (1500–1558).

16 The work is published in *Monumenta Xaveriana Ex autographis vel ex antiquioribus exemplis collecta. Tomus secundus, Scripta varia de Sancto Francisco Xaverio* (Matriti: Typis Gabrielis López del Horno, 1912), 815–918. Teixeira was also the recipient of a long epistle composed by the Chinese António, in which this neophyte described Xavier's final days. This missive, with the narration of Juan Fernandez, known as the *Itinerario*, can be considered sources for the writing of his work. Mormando, *Making*, 18.

17 "Torsellino's work, oft-reprinted and translated into other languages, was the first of several biographies to follow upon the formal petition for Xavier's canonization made of the Church by the Society of Jesus in 1593, acting upon the decision of its Fifth General Congregation". Mormando, *Making*, 13. This idea was also declared by Massimo Leone: "This text must be read in the context of the initiatives taken for the beatification of Francis Xavier". M. Leone, *Saints and Signs: A Semiotic Reading of Conversion in Early Modern Catholicism* (Berlin and New York: Walter de Gruyter, 2010), 367.

Companhia de Iesu in Lisbon (Impressa per Pedro Craesbeeck) in 1600.[18] There were various editions in Portuguese, translations into some European languages (Spanish, Italian and Hungarian), a Latin edition and an adaptation in French.[19]

On the other hand Valignano, appointed Visitor of the Jesuit missions in the East Indies (*citra et ultra Gangem*) in August 1573, urged the commission of the first two portraits of Xavier in Goa in 1583. One was sent to Rome with a letter (31 December 1583) to Claudio Acquaviva.[20] But unfortunately, both were lost, even though the "Roman painting" was copied and utilised later by some painters and engravers, such as Theodor Galle (1571–1633), a Flemish artist, who used it for his engraving of Xavier for Torsellino's work.[21]

The literature of these years contains references to the life and evangelizing work of Xavier, as well as in the accounts of some historians and chroniclers of the Portuguese Empire of the East, such as João de Barros (1496–1570), Diogo do Couto (1542–1616) and also Fernão Mendes Pinto (1509–1583), who was a Jesuit

---

18 Osswald, *São Francis Xavier*, 329.

19 J.C. Monteiro, "Lucena, João de", in C. O'Neill, S.J. – J.M.a Dominguez, S.J. (eds.), *Diccionario histórico de la Compañía de Jesús biográfico-temático*, III (Roma-Madrid: Institutum Historicum SJ-Universidad Pontificia Comillas, 2001), 2435.

20 Some information and precious objects were always sent to Rome because orders arrived in Goa in autumn 1614. At the request of pope, the superior general instructed his confreres to open the casket containing Xavier's mortal remains. L.M. Brockey, "The Cruelest Honor: The Relics of Francis Xavier in Early-Modern Asia", *The Catholic Historical Review* 101/1 (2015) 41. For this reason Xavier's lower right arm was cut from his body and sent to Rome, where it is now kept in the church of the Most Holy Name of Jesus at the Argentina. A second amputation of his arm (including the shoulder blade) was made on 12 April 1619 and additional relics were distributed to some Jesuit residences: Malacca, Cochin and Macau. Unfortunately, no relics were delivered to Japan due to the persecution of the Tokugawa *bakufu* (1603–1867), which led to an isolationist policy of the country (*sakoku jidai*). It was officially launched in August 1639 by Tokugawa Iemitsu (1604–1651), *shōgun* of Japan from 1623 to his death. Cfr. P. Gupta, *The Relic State: St. Francis Xavier and the Politics of Ritual in Portuguese India* (Manchster: Manchster University Press, 2014). A few years earlier (1599), the Oratorian cardinal Cesare Baronio (1538–1607) placed an image of Loyola in the same Roman church (to promote his cult) above Ignatius' tomb. Cfr. S. Ditchfield, "Thinking with Jesuit Saints: The Canonization of Ignatius Loyola and Francis Xavier in Context", *Journal of Jesuit Studies* 9 (2022) 333. See also: J. W. O'Malley, *Saints or Devils Incarnate?: Studies in Jesuit History* (Leiden: Brill, 2013), 280.

21 M.C. Osswald, "S. Francisco Xavier no Oriente – aspectos de devoção e iconografia", in *Actas da Conferência Internacional São Francisco Xavier nos 500 anos do nascimento de São Francisco Xavier: da Europa para o Mundo 1506–2006* (Porto: Universidade do Porto, et al., 2007), 119.

for a short period,[22] in his *Peregrinaçam*. It was composed of 226 chapters and printed posthumously in Lisbon (by Pedro Craesbeeck) in 1614.

Eriprando Maria Giuliari: some biographical information and notes on his panegyric

Eriprando Maria Giuliari was born in Verona on 15 February 1728 from an important aristocratic family of the time, belonging to the city's patriciate. He completed his early education at first in his family and later at the Jesuits schools of Verona and Modena. He joined the *Provincia Veneta* of the Society of Jesus on 22 October 1748.[23] Giuliari spent the first stage of Jesuit formation at the *Domus probationis* of Saint Ignace in Bologna[24] and later he started to study philosophy. In 1751 he went to the college of Piacenza[25] and from 1752 to 1755 he thaught.[26] In 1756 Giuliari arrived at the college of Saint Lucy in Bologna, as a *magister*.[27] The following year, he began his theological studies, moving to the college of Saint Louis, also in the same city.[28] He was ordained a priest in 1759;[29] the following year he was sent to the college of the nobles of Saint Francis Xavier in Bologna[30] and in 1761 to the college of Modena, where he also engaged in some pastoral activities.[31] In 1762 Giuliari completed the formation of the third probation in the house of Bosseto with some confreres.[32] The following year he was in the college of Piacenza[33] and three years later (1766) in the college of Mantua.[34] However, the latest catologs of the Venetian Province did not report references for this Jesuit. Nevertheless, information on the last years of his life in the Society is included at the *Bibliotèque de la Compagnie de*

22 Fernão Mendes Pinto joined the Ignatian Order in Goa in April 1554, but he left two years later (in October 1556). J. Ruiz-de-Medina, "Mendes, Pinto Fernão", in C. O'Neill, S.J. – J.M.a Dominguez, S.J. (eds.), *Diccionario histórico de la Compañía de Jesús biográfico-temático*, III (Roma-Madrid: Institutum Historicum SJ-Universidad Pontificia Comillas, 2001), 2619–20.

23 ARSI, Ven. 70, f. 30v.

24 ARSI, Ven. 59, f. 199; Ven. 86, f. 183v; Ven. 87, f. 14v.

25 ARSI, Ven. 87, f. 77v.

26 ARSI, Ven. 60, f. 12; Ven. 87, f. 119.

27 ARSI, Ven. 88, f. 65.

28 ARSI, Ven. 60, f. 25; Ven. 88, f. 108.

29 ARSI, Ven. 88, f. 168.

30 ARSI, Ven. 88, f. 195v.

31 ARSI, Ven. 89, f. 12.

32 ARSI, Ven. 89, ff. 35v–36.

33 ARSI, Ven. 89, f. 71, Ven. 61, f. 239v.

34 ARSI, Ven. 89, f. 150v.

Jésus: in 1773 Giuliari was engaged in the Jesuit church of Bologna, teaching Holy Scriptures.[35]

Following the canonical suppression of the Order decreed by Clement XIV (Giovan Vincenzo Antonio Ganganelli, r. 1769–1774) with the brief *Dominus ac Redemptor* (21 July 1773), Giuliari returned to Verona and decided to live the last decades of his life as a simple abbot. He dedicated himself to preaching, his publications[36] and the collaboration with the printing house of his nephew *ex fratre* Bartolomeo. In this last activity, he put to good use the years of work as a editor (which he had done for several years) for some works of his Veronese companion and relative, Giuseppe Luigi Pellegrini (1718–1799).[37] Giuliari died in Verona on 24 November 1805.

When Giuliari came back to Verona, he showed his oratorian skills. He was engaged in composing and declaiming sacred orations, particularly during the Lenten periods, under the patronage of the Pious Society of Saint James of Galicia, of which he was a member.[38] Initially some of these compositions had to be published at the family printing house, but the Jesuit's death delayed the initiative. Indeed, only the first sheets were published with the title page and the dedication to the Mantuan Jesuit Saverio Bettinelli (1718–1808), a poet and literate.[39] Unfortunately, even in

35 C. Sommervogel, "Giuliari, Eriprand", in *Bibliothèque de la Compagnie de Jésus*, III (Bruxelles-Paris: Oscar Schepens-Alphonse Picard, 1892), 1477.

36 His most famous work was *Le donne più celebri della santa nazione. Conversazioni storico-sacro-morali* printed in Verona (Per gli Eredi di Marco Moroni) in 1782, of which were published several editions. Gian Paolo Marchi, echoing the expression of Clementino Vannetti (1754–1795), remembered Eriprando Giuliari as a Jesuit "dotto e cavalleresco", and added "autore di opere legate ad una franca difesa dell'*ancien régime*". G.P. Marchi, *La vocazione letteraria del canonico G.B.C. Giuliari*, in G.P. Marchi (ed.), *Il canonico veronese conte G. B. Carlo Giuliari, 1810–1892: religione, patria e cultura nell'Italia dell'Ottocento: Atti della giornata di studio, Verona 16 ottobre 1993* (Verona: Grafiche Fiorini, 1994), 240.

37 Pellegrini was a member of the Academy of Arcadia and a famous preacher in Venice, Piacenza and Vienna. In the latter city he gave a sermon in the presence of the Archduchess Maria Theresa of Habsburg (1717–1780). He joined the Society of Jesus on 14 April 1733 and professed his fourth vows in Piacenza on 2 February 1751 (ARSI, Ital. 30, ff. 400–401). After the canonical suppression of the Order, Pellegrini too returned to his hometown. C. Sommervogel, "Pellegrini, Joseph Aloys", in *Bibliothèque de la Compagnie de Jésus*, VI (Bruxelles-Paris: Oscar Schepens-Alphonse Picard, 1895), 446–48. See: *Al popolo veronese, orazione postuma dell'Abbate Giuseppe Conte Pellegrini* (Verona: nella Stamperia Giuliari, 1800). In the same year and in the same place it was printed a second edition *Accresciuta dell'Elogio dell'autore scritto dall'abbate Eriprando conte Giuliari* (1–39).

38 G.G. Fagioli Vercellone, "Giuliari, Eriprando Maria", in *Dizionario biografico degli Italiani*, LVI (Roma: Istituto dell'Enciclopedia Italiana, 2001), 785–86.

39 In the BCVr in the *busta 105* of the *Carteggi* collection are kept twenty-two letters dated from 26 July 1783 (Verona) to 24 September 1796 (Venice) and spent to Saverio Bettinelli and twenty-eight letters dated from 4 March 1782 (Mantova) to 24 September 1807 (Mantova) addressed to Eriprando Giuliari. Bettinelli joined the Society of Jesus in Novellara on 15 October 1736 (ARSI,

Rome it was impossible to carry out this project, and not even in Milan, when in 1830 Giovanni Silvestri (1778–1855) contacted the Giuliari family because they were interested in republishing his most prestigious work. On this occasion, the Milanese printer-publisher also wanted to know the unpublished works produced by the priest, thus arousing enthusiasm on the part of his relative Giovanni Battista Carlo Giuliari (1810–1892), who had already tried to publish some of his works two years earlier with a bookseller from Reggio. In addition, he wrote a short historical eulogy of the great-uncle Eriprando.[40]

> Volendo stampar tutto – conclude il Giuliari – crederei che potessero venire 4 buoni volumi del formato della Biblioteca scelta: se però Lei non pensasse che di far scelta allora, come lei me ne da' aviso, io potrei scegliere 10 o 12 delle migliori orazioni che sono molto eloquenti, e così formare un solo volume, che aggiunto all'altro delle *Donne celebri*, darebbe in tutto 2 soli volumi. Io l'esorto dunque a fare o nell'un modo o nell'altro questa edizione, e le assicuro che tanto qui in Roma, ove essendo stato autore gesuita, avrà molto successo, quanto in Lombardia e nel Veneto è ricercata tale opera.[41]

The panegyric dedicated to Francis Xavier falls within this sphere. It was composed in Verona and proclaimed in the church of San Lorenzo. The composition, almost certainly the original, is kept at the Biblioteca Civica di Verona (BCVr) in manuscript 1462, which consists of "Opere varie mss. dell'abate Conto Eriprando Giuliari Veronese".[42] This handwritten panegyric (found in the first volume of this codex) reports a curious note, maybe added later, which contains the following information: "durò 53 minuti e si disse spedito e però come piacque". Its corrected

---

Ven. 70, f. 25) and professed his last vows in Busseto on 15 August 1751 (ARSI, Ital. 30, ff. 418–419). On his biographical profile see: M. Zanfredini, "Bettinelli, Saverio", in C. E. O'Neill, S.J. – J.M.ª Dominguez, S.J. (eds.), *Diccionario histórico de la Compañía de Jesús biográfico-temático*, I (Roma-Madrid: Institutum Historicum SJ-Universidad Pontificia Comillas, 2001), 432. See also: I. Crotti – R. Ricorda (eds.), *Saverio Bettinelli. Un gesuita alla scuola del mondo* (Roma: Bulzoni, 1998).

40 Fagioli Vercellone, *Giuliari*, 785–786.

41 In the BCVr, *Carteggi, b. 585*, contains a *minuta* written by G.B.C. Giuliari (without date) and two missives compiled by Silvestri (dated 31 March 1830 and 26 May 1830, respectively). See: M. Girardi, *Giuliari in Tipografia*, in G.P. Marchi (ed.), *Il canonico veronese conte G. B. Carlo Giuliari, 1810–1892: religione, patria e cultura nell'Italia dell'Ottocento: Atti della giornata di studio, Verona 16 ottobre 1993* (Verona: Grafiche Fiorini, 1994), 300.

42 G. Biadego, *Catalogo descrittivo di manoscritti della biblioteca Comunale di Verona*, (Verona: G. Civelli, 1892), 178. The author described the manuscript in the following way: "Cart. in parte autografo in due volumi, il primo [Prose] di 463 carte, m.0,31x0,22, il secondo [Poesie] di 304 carte, m. 0,23x0,20. Il primo ha 42, il secondo 50 carte bianche. Legatura in mezza pelle. Dono Giuliari". This panegyric contains a review work (made by the same person) with some changes, additions and deletions.

copy is preserved at ARSI, as reported in the codex: "Corretto. Si stampi questa copia. Si stampi terzo".[43] Indeed, this manuscript *Opera Nostrorum 286*, entitled *Nota dell'opere manoscritte dell'Abate Eriprando Giuliari, date dal medesimo per stamparsi*, is made up of seventeen orations written by Giuliari.[44]

The panegyric to St. Francis Xavier: some ideas and considerations

The central theme of this panegyric, probably proclaimed on the day of the liturgical feast, is holiness, which consists in performing the actions and duties of ordinary life towards God and neighbor in an extraordinary way. In the *incipit*, Giuliari declared that Xavier's holiness stemmed from his tireless apostolate. His fruitful pastoral work in various places in Asia for ten years (1542–1552) made him a saint. Indeed, he was considered a "gift" to the universal Church and a concrete witness to the missionary church.

The whole composition is based on the analysis of three points that Giuliari defined as possible obstacles to the sanctity of Xavier. The author examined these "impediments" the Saint encountered during his life and his continuous wanderings in the East Indies. They manifested themselves as great difficulties capable of interrupting and diverting the beauty of his religious vocation. However, these obstacles did not succeed in changing his *modus vivendi, operandi et agendi*. They did not cloud his image as a minister of the Gospel and as a man committed to spreading the saving message.

Xavier was not attracted by passion (the first obstacle): both in India and in Japan, the Jesuit led a just and upright life, striving not to fall into sin, nor involve himself in bad deeds. Even during his itinerancy, Xavier showed himself to be an honorable and honest man, consistently acting in conformity with Christian and moral law. He also carried out his work in harmony with Catholic doctrine.

Xavier surrendered his excellence to God (second obstacle) without living in to his ambitions and without expressing a desire to improve his social and ecclesial position. His only concern way to spread the Catholic faith and to divulge its main and identifying characteristics. Giuliari considered his apostolate a free service

43 ARSI, Opp. Nn. 286, f. 185.

44 The codex includes: *Per le Ceneri* (ff. 3–12v); *Del culto esterno* (ff.13–28v); *Dell'Invidia* (ff. 29–42v); *Che cos'è l'uomo* (ff. 43–55v); *Felicità* (ff. 56–65v); *Fede* (ff. 66–77v); *Della Irreligione* (ff. 78–90v); *Contro allo spirito d'irreligione* (ff. 91–104v); *Abito peccaminoso* (ff. 105–117v); *Il Giusto Moribondo* (ff. 118–129v); *Il Giudicio* (ff. 130–145v); *Paradiso* (ff. 146–158v); *Incontinenza* (ff. 159–172v); *Vita oziosa, e vita troppo occupata* (ff. 173–184v); *Panegirico di San Francesco Saverio Appostolo dell'Indie* (ff. 185–198v); *Panegirico Di San Gianfrancesco Regis* (ff. 199–210v); *Panegirico di Santo Stanislao Kostka* (ff. 211–223v).

provided to the Church and not as a personal opportunity to demonstrate one's abilities.

The apostolate of Xavier became fruitful and an image of authentic holiness because he subjected his reason to God (third obstacle). He sacrificed himself in order to fully live his apostolate. Giuliari mentioned the main steps of his journey to land in China (his latest effort) and recalled his desire to reach the Middle Kingdom to evangelize the most coveted territory of the entire Asian continent, closed to foreigners.[45] The Spanish Jesuit died on the island of Shangchuan, situated off the southern coast of China, but his testimony and his love for this country inflamed the hearts of the future generations of companions. Indeed, the Society of Jesus in China was established about thirty years later with the settlement of Matteo Ricci (1552–1610) and Michele Ruggieri (1543–1607) in Zhaoping near Guangzhou (Canton) in 1583. They obtained authorization from Chinese officials to set up there and so started to study the language and promote their doctrine.[46] In 1601 Matteo Ricci arrived at Beijing, at the court of emperor Wanli (1563–1620) of the Ming dynasty, who soon won his esteem and allowed him a large work of apostolate.[47]

However, Xavier was celebrated as the promoter and initiator of the Jesuit mission in China. Nicolas Trigault (1577–1628), a Flemish confrere and procurator of

45 The Portuguese had settled in various territories of Asia starting from Goa in 1510. The first contact established with China was recorded in 1513 with the arrival of Jorge Álvares (?–1521) on Tamang Island. Cfr. L. Keil, *Jorge Álvares: o primeiro português que foi à China (1513)* (Lisboa: s.n., 1933). Some years later (in 1516), Tomé Pires (c.1465–1524/1540), author of the *Suma Oriental* (written between 1512 and 1515) left for Canton (Guangzhou) as ambassador of King Manuel I (1469–1521). He travelled in the fleet of Fernão Pires de Andrade. But, Pires was never received by the Zhengde Emperor (1491–1521). However, in 1557 the Portuguese were granted permission to establish a trading post at Macau, located on China's southern coast. Macau became an important international port for the Portuguese trade and missionary work. See V. F.S. Sit – R. D. Cremer – S.L. Wong, *Entrepreneurs and Enterprises in Macau: A Study of Industrial Development* (Hong Kong: Hong Kong University Press, 1991), 10.

46 See M. Ollé, "The Jesuit Portrayals of China between 1583–1590", *Bulletin of Portuguese/Japanese Studies* 16 (2008) 45–57. However, the Jesuits had already settled permanently in Macau in 1563 with the arrival (on 29 July) of Francisco Pérez (1515–1583), Manuel Teixeira and André Pinto, a scholastic. They established a residence near the small church of Saint Anthony in December 1564. Although, Melchior Nunes Barreto (c.1520–1571) vice-provincial of India, was the first Jesuit to pass through Macau in November 1555. Some years later Luís Fróis (1532–1597) and Giovanni Battista de Monte (1528–1587) landed in Macau in August 1562 in order to reach Yokoseura (Japan) on 6 July 1563. On Jesuits in Macau, see: J. Sebes, "Macao", in C. O'Neill, S.J. – J. M.a Dominguez S.J. (eds.), *Diccionario histórico de la Compañía de Jesús biográfico-temático*, III (Roma-Madrid: Institutum Historicum SJ-Universidad Pontificia Comillas, 2001), 2452–54.

47 See R. Po-chia Hsia, *A Jesuit in the Forbidden City: Matteo Ricci 1552–1610* (Oxford: Oxford University Press, 2010).

the Chinese mission, represented the pioneering role of Xavier and endeavored to carry out his project. Trigault arrived in Europe in 1610s at the behest of the superior Niccolò Longobardo (1565–1654), a Sicilian Jesuit, with the aim of spreading the Society's activities in the Vice-province of China, promoting the interests of the mission and obtaining further economic support for the missionaries.[48] He printed *De Christiana expeditione apud Sinas suscepta ab Societate Jesu* in Augsburg (Christoph Mangium) in 1615 and dedicated it to Paul V and intended for a European audience. In this work he published (translating from Italian into Latin)[49] Ricci's memories and chose to illustrate in the title page (with an engraving) the main personalities of the Jesuit mission in the Middle Kingdom. This engraving was prepared by Wolfgang Kilian (1581–1662), a German engraver and painter, who combined "in a harmonious way the portraits of Francis Xavier (surrounded by the nimb of holiness) and Matteo Ricci (posing in the robe of a Chinese scholar) with the map of China made by Ricci".[50]

The panegyric composed and shared by Giuliari is part of the body of writing dedicated to the Saint which mainly involves the Ignatian Order.[51] It includes bi-

---

48 See E. Lamalle, "La propagande du P. Nicolas Trigault en faveur des missions de Chine (1616)", *Archivum Historicum Societatis Iesu* 9/1 (1940) 49–120.

49 This work was reprinted several times and translated into some European languages. N. Standaert, *The Interweaving of Rituals. Funerals in the Cultural Exchange between China and Europe* (Washington: University of Washington Press, 2008), 38.

50 M. Miazek-Męczyńska, "*De Christiana expeditione apud Sinas suscepta ab Societate Iesu* – a gift for Pope Paul V from Jesuits", in M. Miazek-Męczyńska – A. W. Mikołajczak – P. Zając OMI (eds.), *Following Matteo Ricci* (Poznań: Humanistic and Interdisciplinary Research Group AMU, 2012), 131. She affirmed this work was particularly successful in Europe for the wealth of its information and for the particular missionary testimony of its authors. It was soon translated into several European languages. Miazek-Męczyńska, *De Christiana expeditione*, 130. Nicolas Standaert also recalled that the work was reprinted several times and translated into French, German, Spanish, Italian and partially into English. N. Standaert, *The Interweaving*, 38.

51 However, also secular and regular priests belonging to other Orders and Congregations dedicated compositions to Francis Xavier, sometimes on the occasion of the liturgical feast or to commemorate a particular episode. Only some examples. A panegyric was written by Giovanni Francesco Ravali (1692–1754), a conventual friar minor, and was proclaimed in the cathedral of Foligno. It was dedicated to Alessandro Zondadari (1669–1745), bishop of Siena. See G.F. Ravali, *Panegirico di San Francesco Saverio detto nel duomo di Fuligno nell'Avvento dell'anno 1722 dal P. Maestro Gio: Francesco Ravali, minor conventuale. Dedicato all'Ill.mo e Rev.mo Alessandro Zondadari arcivescovo di Siena* (Siena: nella Stamperia del Pubblico, 1722). An oration was compiled by Francesco Gandolfi (1810–1892), a priest and a *doctor in utroque iure*, then appointed titular bishop of Antipatride on 14 April 1848. Cfr. F. Gandolfi, *Orazione panegirica in lode di San Francesco Saverio recitata nella venerabile chiesa di Santa Maria della pace dal Sig. Ab. Francesco Gandolfi dottore in ambe due le leggi e Socio di varie Accademie di scienze e di lettere* (Roma: presso Giuseppe Gismondi, 1842). A panegyric was composed by Luigi di Canossa (1809–1900), bishop of Verona, who definitively left the Society of Jesus in 1847 due to health problems. It was shared in the church of the Gesù in Rome

ographies, published and translated into various vernacular languages, accounts produced on the occasion of his beatification and canonization, the story of prodigious events and miracles for his intercession, letters written in the various places of mission and references to some edifying episodes for the spiritual growth of readers.[52] Many Jesuits, called to preach in various Italian churches, proposed Francis Xavier as a model of Christian life and an example of priestly and missionary life. This panegyric is part of a Xaverian tradition that became firmly rooted in the Order and manifested itself during its suppression phase, with the celebration of the evangelizing work carried out by Xavier in the various territories of Asia as its primary purpose. In these territories, he continually spread the Gospel and devoted himself to his pastoral and educational activities, according to the foundational spirituality of his Society, and acting in harmony with some Jesuit pedagogical principles which would later be codified in the *Ratio studiorum* (1599).

Giuliari's panegyric is therefore part of this continuous stream of declamations dedicated to the Spanish Saint, given by various Jesuits with a flattering tone. It is possible to mention some examples, limiting them to the context of Italian hagiographic literature. Bartolomeo Donati (1651–1707) joined the Society in Novellara

---

in 1869. Cfr. Luigi dei Marchesi di Canossa, *Panegirico di San Francesco Saverio detto nella chiesa del Gesù in Roma nel 1869 dall'Ill.mo e Rev.mo Monsignore Luigi dei Marchesi di Canossa, Vescovo di Verona* (Torino: Tipografia di Giulio Speirani e Figli, 1870).

52 A list of works on Xavier is in: L. Pagès, *Bibliographie Japonaise ou catalogue des ouvrages relatifs au Japon, qui ont été publiés depuis le 15e siècle jusqu'à nos jours rédigé par M. Léon Pagès* (Paris: Benjamin Duprat, 1859); H. Cordier, *Bibliotheca japonica: Dictionnaire bibliographique des ouvrages relatifs à l'Empire japonais rangés par ordre chronologique jusqu'à 1870, suivi d'un appendice renfermant la liste alphabétique des principaux ouvrages parus de 1870 à 1912* (Paris: Imprimerie nationale E. Leuroux, 1912). The most famous miracle given to Xavier was that of Marcello Mastrilli (1603–1637), a Jesuit from Nola (Naples). He was miraculous in the night on 3 January 1634, when the Saint appeared to the young Jesuit and immediately healed him. So Mastrilli again asked his superiors to be sent to overseas missions. Indeed, he departed from Lisbon on 13 April 1635, aboard the ship *Santa Catarina* with many companions. He arrived in Goa on 18 December 1635, then went to Macau, landed Manila in July 1636 and finally reached Hyūga (Miyazaki) on 4 August 1637. He was martyred in Nagasaki on 17 October of the same year with the torment of the pit (*ana-tsurushi*) and then he was beheaded. Soon Mastrilli became one of the protagonists of the Jesuit hagiographic literature of the seventeenth century and an example for the *indepeti*. Emanuele Colombo declared the episode of Mastrilli represented the triumph of vocation over skepticism and the reticence of his superiors: "grazie all'intercessione di Saverio, infatti, Mastrilli aveva ottenuto di partire per le Indie che fino a quel momento gli erano state negate". E. Colombo, "*Repetita iuvant.* Le *litterae indipetae* di Metello Saccano (1612–1662) e compagni", in P. Giovannucci (ed.), *Scrivere lettere. Religiosi e pratiche epistolari tra XVI e XVIII secolo* (Padova: PUP, 2018) 77. See also: E. Colombo, "Miracoli di Francesco Saverio", in L. Andreani – A. Paravicini Bagliani (eds.), *Miracolo! Emozione, spettacolo e potere nella storia dei secoli XIII-XVI* (Firenze: Sismel-Edizioni del Galluzzo, 2019), 322. On Mastrilli, see: C. Willis, "The Martyrdom of Father Marcello Mastrilli S.J.", *Journal of the Royal Asiatic Society Hong Kong Branch* 53 (2013) 215–25.

on 30 April 1667 and professed the four vows in Busseto on 15 August 1684.[53] He dedicated two panegyrics to Francis Xavier. The *Panegirico XLVIII* and the *Panegirico XLIX* were then collected with other orations and published posthumously in two tomes in Parma in 1710 and reprinted in Venice in 1733.[54] Francesco Ercolani (1659–1731), born in Ferrara and entered the Society on 23 July 1675,[55] proclaimed a panegyric to Xavier entitled *Il Santo magnanimo* in Trento in 1711 on the occasion of his liturgical feast.[56] Giovan Pellegrino Turri (1645–1724), born in Sillicano (Lucca), joined the Jesuits on 28 June 1660.[57] He lived for many years in Rome, earning the benevolence of Clement XI (Giovanni Francesco Albani, r. 1700–1721). He wrote the panegyric entitled *L'Apostolo del Nuovo Mondo*. It was preached in Genoa in the presence of the Doge and his Senate and was printed in the second tome of *Panegirici sacri* in Venice in 1709 (presso Paolo Baglioni) and a second edition was published in 1716.[58] Francesco Saverio Vanalesti (1678–1741), preacher and professor of *humanae litterae*, who entered the Order on 10 June 1695,[59] composed the first panegyric to Xavier in his volume made up of thirty four compositions printed in Venice in 1742.[60]

However, in the manuscript Xavier juxtaposes two other examples of Jesuit holiness. The first is Jean François Régis (1597–1640), a French, who joined the Society in Toulouse on 8 December 1616. He was a rural missionary and was mainly engaged in the conversion of Calvinists. Régis was beatified on 24 May 1716 by Clement XI and canonized on 16 June 1737 by Clement XII (Lorenzo Corsini,

---

53 ARSI, *Schedario unificato Lamalle, sub nomine.*

54 See B. Donati, *La santità encomiata. Panegirici per le feste, che corrono in tutto l'anno di Nostro Signore, della Vergine, degli Apostoli, de' Dottori della Chiesa, de' Fondatori delle Religioni, e di moltissimi altri Santi. Opera del Padre Bartolomeo Donati della Compagnia di Gesù divisa in due tomi. Dedicata all'Eminentissimo, e Reverendissimo Signor Cardinale Anton-Francesco Sanvitale, Arcivescovo di Urbino, Tomo secondo* (Parma: Per Paolo Monti all'insegna della Fede, 1710): 428–38; 438–46.

55 C. Sommervogel, "Ercolani, François", in *Bibliothèque de la Compagnie de Jésus*, III (Bruxelles-Paris: Oscar Schepens-Alphonse Picard, 1892), 410.

56 F. Ercolani, *Il Santo magnanimo. Panegirico di S. Francesco Saverio detto nella sua Chiesa nuova di Trento, nel giorno della sua festa. L'anno MDCCXI. In cui tornò dalle Spagne chiamato al Trono dell'Imperio per Coronarsi in Francoforte L'Augustissimo Carlo VI* (Trento: Per Gio: Antonio Brunati, 1713).

57 C. Sommervogel, "Turri, Jean Pérégrin", in *Bibliothèque de la Compagnie de Jésus*, VIII (Bruxelles-Paris: Oscar Schepens-Alphonse Picard, 1898), 281–82.

58 Cfr. G.P. Turri, *Panegirici Sacri di Giovan Pellegrino Turri della Compagnia di Gesù, Tomo Secondo, Dedicato All'Eminentissimo e Reverendissimo Signor Cardinale Pietro Ottoboni Vicecancelliero di S. Chiesa* (Venezia: appresso Giacomo Tomasini, 1716), 96–122.

59 C. Sommervogel, "Vanalesti, Xavier", in *Bibliothèque de la Compagnie de Jésus*, VIII (Bruxelles-Paris: Oscar Schepens-Alphonse Picard, 1898), 437.

60 Cfr. F.S. Vanalesti, S.I., *Panegirici del padre Saverio Vanalesti della Compagnia di Gesù* (Venezia: Appresso Giambattista Pasquali, 1742), 1–11.

r. 1730–1740).[61] The second is Stanislao Kostka (1550–1568), a Polish novice who entered the Order in Rome on 27 October 1567. According to the literature and hagiographic tradition, he received the Eucharist from Saint Barbara while ill and decided to become a Jesuit.[62] He was beatified on 8 October 1605 by Paul V and was canonized on 31 December 1726 by Benedict XIII (Pietro Francesco Orsini, r. 1724–1730).

In this codex the *Panegirico di San Francesco Saverio Appostolo dell'Indie* deals with holiness. Indeed, Xavier is the first example of missionary and evangelical life given by the author to posthumous generations.[63] The holiness of Xavier thus declaimed by Giuliari realizes and implements the words of Paul of Tarsus. The Apostle to the Gentiles, as the Catholic tradition has labeled him, invited the community of Thessalonica to cultivate the gift of holiness because it conformed with the will of God: "*Haec est voluntas Dei: sanctificatio vestra*" (1, Ts 4:3). Sanctification requires a profound transformation of man, a profound purification of his mind, soul and heart. Alejandro Cañeque declares that "Xavier became the dominant Jesuit image of apostolic sanctity, and he greatly energized the evangelical zeal of many Jesuits, eager to missionize in distant East Asia".[64] For this reason Francisco Colín (1592–1660), a Spanish Jesuit and a missionary in the Philippines (from 1626 to his death), in his *Labor evangélica ministerios apostólicos de los obreros de la Compañia de Jesus* published posthumously in Madrid in 1663, considered Xavier as "un nuevo Pablo en su predicación, un bautista en el oficio y profecía, taumaturgo en los milagros". Indeed, the work was entirely dedicated to this Saint,

61 See G. Daubenton, *La vita del Beato Gio: Francesco Regis della Compagnia di Gesù. Scritta in Franzese dal R. P. Daubenton Confessore di Sua Maestà Cattolica tradotta dal Padre Sebastiano Maria Zefferini ambedue della medesima Compagnia dedicata all'Altezza Reale del Sereniss. Cosimo III, Granduca di Toscana* (Firenze: Nella Stamperia di S.A.R. per Gio: Gaetano Tartini e Santi Franchi, 1717).

62 This event is for example illustrated with an engraving in the biography written by Pedro de Ribadeneira. It was titled *Compendio Della Vita Del B. Stanislao Kostka, Della Compagnia Giesv: Estrato dalla Vita del Reverendiss. P. Francesco Borgia, che fu Duca di Gandia, e poi Generale di detta Compagnia di Giesv* in the Padua edition (Appresso Pietro Paolo Tozzi) printed in 1608. The inscription reads: "BEATUS STANISLAUS KOSTKA POLONUS SOCIETATIS IESU. *Ex Angelorum manibus S. Barbara assistente* SS. Eucharistiam suscipit".

63 His life and his missionary strategy became a model for the foundation and charism of some religious institutes. One of them is the Emilian Institute for Foreign Missions. It was founded in Parma in 1895 by bishop Guido Maria Conforti (1865–1931) and three years later was renamed the Pious Society of St. Francis Xavier for the Foreign Missions. It was definitively approved in 1921. Currently, the Congregation has about 700 members and works in 21 countries in four continents. Cfr. A. Luca, *Guido Maria Conforti vescovo e missionario* (Milano: Ed. Paoline, 2011).

64 A. Cañeque, "In the Shadow of Francis Xavier: Martyrdom and Colonialism in the Jesuit Asian Missions", *Journal of Jesuit Studies* 9/3 (2022) 438–58; Online: https://brill.com/view/journals/jjs/9/3/article-p438_007.xml?language=en (last access 12.07.2021).

who, before that, Colín defined him as "El Nuevo Apostol de las Indias, y primero de las islas del Iapon y otras del Oriente".[65]

Xavier lived and embodied the Society of Jesus's ideals and missionary charism. Giuliari presented the Spanish confrere as an image of the true and real missionary who placed the evangelizing mission at the center of his life and his vocational choice. The Ignatian Order, firstly expelled from some countries where it was well established (Portugal and its colonies in 1759; France in 1764 and Spain and its colonies in 1767) and then suppressed with the canonical decree of pope Clement XIV, was remembered as an "instrument" for spreading the Gospel in overseas missions, a "channel" for transmitting charity and increasing dialogue between peoples, an "opportunity" to educate to human and religious life the younger generations. Giuliari presented Xavier as the Jesuit missionary *par excellence* and "an icon for his order",[66] who fully responded to the commitment given to him by the Holy See and sponsored by the Portuguese crown. Xavier became a tangible image of "*Euntes ergo docete omnes gentes*" (Mt 28:19): the appeal that Jesus addressed to the Apostles sent to evangelize all peoples and called to constitute his Church as the universal sacrament of salvation. The Spanish Jesuit was, therefore, the most formidable expression of Catholicism within the host of saints.[67]

Conclusions

The panegyric by Eriprando Giuliari enriches the hagiographic literature written and shared about this Saint and further contributes to the knowledge of his human, religious and missionary life. Furthermore, it enhances and celebrates the dimension of holiness experienced by Xavier and cultivated by him during his life, despite the numerous difficulties and trials encountered along the way.

It is presented as a composition of religious nature that aims to spiritually build the community of faithful (the bystanders). It is a pietistic exhortation to a better life, promoting the Christian's material, spiritual and moral growth. Giuliari meant to urge every baptized person to know Xavier's evangelical courage, to appreciate his tenacity and the desire to promulgate the fundamental aspects of Catholic faith, to emulate the concreteness of his apostolic spirit to live his vocation in the Church worthily.

---

65 See F. Colín, *Labor evangélica, ministerios apostólicos de los obreros de la Compañia de Iesus, fundacion y progressos de su Provincia en las islas Filipinas* (Madrid: Imprenta de Ioseph Fernández de Buendía, 1663).

66 M. Friedrich, *The Jesuits: A History* (Princeton: Princeton University Press, 2022), 430.

67 See J. Ponzo – E. Rai, "Heroicity and Sanctity in Catholic thought from early modern to contemporary age", *Ocula Occhio semiotico sui media* 20 (2019) 2.

The author proposed Xavier as an archetype to emulate in order to become saints; as an example to encourage more missionaries because of his zeal fot the salvation of souls "*Ad maiorem Dei gloriam*" in the meeting of different peoples and cultures.

Furthermore, this panegyric also helps to understand how Xavier was presented to the Catholic community in a challenging moment for the Society of Jesus (suppression). Indeed, through the account of his biography (especially the apostolate carried out in the overseas missions), Giuliari could commemorate the history of the Order, the work of evangelization carried out since its foundation (on 27 September 1540 with the bull *Regimini militantis Ecclesiae*), and the activities undertaken by its members in the various territories of the East and West Indies, thanks to the establishment of colleges, seminaries and places of worship. Despite the adversity of some European political powers and the official decision taken by pontiff, Giuliari, through the figure of Xavier, wanted to reaffirm and praise the apostolic commitment lavished by the Order in the places where it had actively worked. Indeed, the Jesuits interpreted the spirit of post-Tridentine Catholicism and were called to make the glory the Roman Curia's glory shine, fight schisms and the promoters of heresies and show the faith and zeal of the recently evangelized peoples.

Appendix

Archivum Romanum Societatis Iesu (ARSI), Opp. Nn. 286, ff. 185–198.

[f. 185] Panegirico di San Francesco Saverio Appostolo dell'Indie[68]

[f. 186] *Praecinxit me virtute, et posuit immaculatam viam meam.*[69]

L'aver portata la luce dell'Evangelio alle nazioni barbare che d'un nuovo mondo; e ciò nel giro sol di dieci anni, e ciò con esito prodigiosissimo; quest'è, o Signori, che rese grande San Francesco Saverio davanti agli uomini, questo che meritogli il soprannome d'Appostolo; questo ch'ogni anno al ricorrerne il dì festivo, e all'udirne l'usato elogio suol empiere di maraviglia il divoto popolo ascoltatore. L'aver santificato se stesso e ciò per l'esercizio delle più eroiche virtù, e ciò fra gli ostacoli i più

68 In this corrected copy a work of *labor limae* has been carried out. Changes were made to punctuation, to some words starting with a lowercase letter and to the elimination of the double consonant in other words. These changes were reported directly in the transcription, without specifying them in the footnote. Indeed, I limited myself to pointing out (always in a footnote) only the words added in the overline and those deleted.

69 Phsalm 17: 33 was introduced in the right margin. This psalm celebrates salvation and victory. David addressed these words to the Lord because he had delivered him from the power of enemies and the hand of Saul.

malagevoli a superarsi; quest'è, o Signori, che rese grande ~~San~~ Francesco Saverio davanti a Dio, questo che meritogli il soprannome di Santo, questo che dee stamane riscuotere dal fino vostro giudicio un'insolita maraviglia. Mirabil cosa ella è certo ch'un uomo in sì breve tempo sottomettesse alla Chiesa più popoli, che non le furon rapiti da tutti insieme gli eresiarchi: che cinque idolatri Re, e assai personaggi di real sangue tra esse ad umiliar le corone e le fronti a piè della Croce; che discoresse tanti spazi di mare e di terra, quanti a circondar basterebbero quattro volte l'orbe terraqueo; che parlasse trenta linguaggi differentissimi; che battezzasse un milione e settecento mila infedeli sol di sua mano; che [f.186v] in tante Città, in tante Isole, in tanti Regni atterrasse innumerabili templi, stritolasse innumerabili simulacri, annullasse l'Iddolatria, vi stabilisce nuova religion, nuova legge, nuovi costumi: nulla dimeno più mirabile cosa ella[70] è che quest'uomo in questo suo sì mirabile appostolato santificasse se stesso. Pertanto ell'è più mirabile, quanto egli è più difficile e più pregevole l'esser grande davanti a Dio, che non l'esser grande davanti agli uomini. Potea il Saverio esser grande davanti a questi, e non esserlo davanti a quello: potea salvar molte genti, e ad un'ora perder se stesso; poteva santificare persino l'India e il Giappone, e non santificare se stesso. Fu dunque un Santo il Saverio; ma ciò non basta; fu il Saverio un gran Santo; né questo è tutto; il Saverio fu un Santo e un gran santo nel suo Appostolato; eccovi il tutto e il grande della santità del Saverio; ed eccovi ciò che nel suo sì mirabile Appostolato è più degno di maraviglia. Fu questo appostolato, e gli è vero fu mezzo di santità; fu effetto di santità; ma niente più manifesta a mio credere la santità e la grande santità del Saverio, che il considerare il suo Appostolato per quell'aspetto che esser doveva un multiplice ostacolo di santità. Poiché comunque per ostacolo di santità [f. 187] intendasi propiamente ciò che si oppone alla stessa, e che dalla stessa vien tolto, nulladimeno può intendersi ancor per ostacolo, ciò che rende difficile sommamente la santità, e quindi ciò che la stessa dee sofferire e incontrare per giugnere al più altro grado ed eroico delle virtù. Pertanto io prendo a misurar la grandezza maravigliosa della santità del Saverio dalla grandezza medesima di quest'ostacolo. Non vi sorprenda, o Signori, né pajavi strano l'assunto, poiché s'io di troppo non mi lusingo, varrà non meno d'ogni altro a dar nuovo pascolo di maraviglia e di compiacenza all'avida divozion vostra verso il Saverio. Dunque l'Appostolato ostacolo della santità del Saverio: ostacolo grande per la qualità dell'appostolato; più grande per lo successo dell'appostolato; grandissimo per lo termine dell'appostolato. Triplice ostacolo, ch'io non so s'altro santo maggior si avesse; e ostacolo contro al quale Diò circondò il nostro Santo di tal virtù, che serbò immaculate mai sempre le vie difficili del suo Appostolato. *Praecinxit.*

---

70 Ella interlinear word.

Punto Primo. Doppio è l'ostacolo di santità, che dalla qualità dovea opporsi dell'Appostolato. Veniva l'uno, o Signori, da quegli obbjetti alla propria santificazione contrarij, i quali all'uom comparendo sotto sembianza di bene le sue passioni lusingano a procur[f. 187v]rargli. Veniva l'altro da quegli obbjetti alla propria santificazion conducenti, i quali all'uom presentandosi sotto sembianze di male risvegliano le sue passioni a fuggirli. De primi non fo parole, poiché se il Saverio nell'età bionda non restò mai sedotto dalle pervertitrici lusinghe; se fra gli esempi de' condiscepoli licenziosi si tenne lungi mai sempre da ogni malfatta cosa; se datosi tutto all'acquisto dell'Evangelica perfezione, abbandonò patrimonj lautissimi; se fin sognandosi tolse a un fantasma reo con impeto sì vemente, che rotta in petto una vena ne mandò dalle fauci copioso il sangue; non è da stupire che non gli fossero ostacolo di santità né i piaceri, né le ricchezze, né gli altri lusinghevoli obbjetti, che incontrar potea non di rado nel suo vario pellegrinare. Ben è da stupire, che nulla più dell'ostacolo di questi beni potesse sopra il Saverio l'ostacolo de' mali opposti a tardarlo nel corso di santità. Mali ch'essendo ostacolo ad intraprendere e continuare l'appostolato, erano perciò stesso ostacolo di santità. Dio volea santo il Saverio, e un gran santo, non fra gli ostacoli a molti santi comuni, ma fra gli ostacoli insoliti a santi stessi. Quindi dall'Appostolato Europeo all'Appostolato chiamollo d'un nuovo mondo, dove disposta tenevagli quella [f. 188] serie di patimenti e travagli, che risvegliando le rifuggenti passioni, imprendere e continuar non potevasi l'appostolato, che col soccorso e la forza delle più eroiche virtù operatrici d'altissima santità imprendere io dico e continuare poiché vedete, o Signori, qual fu l'Appostolato del Santo, e vedete il maggiore ostacolo di santità, ch'oppor possa alcun genere d'appostolato.

E quai viaggi primieramente investe il Saverio nel primo anno seguire la vocazione divina? Qui non si tratta di divorar con piè rapido lungo ed alpestre cammino; trattasi d'affrontare per quindici mila e più miglia i mari più spaventosi e più smisurati, che circondano l'Africa e l'Asia. Trattasi d'impallidire e di palpitar di continuo tra l'infuriar de' tifoni, tra lo smaniare de' flutti: trattasi di rimirare la morte nelle sembianze più atroci avventarsi or sull'impeto delle procelle, or dall'insidie di scogli: trattasi di venir meno d'inedia e d'affanno tra le calme peggiori sovente delle procelle; trattasi di soffrir non di rado tormentissime malattie; e sempre di vivere lungo tempo tra la scostumatezza, l'indiscrezione, l'insolenza de' naviganti, de' marinari, della ciurmaglia. E quai sono i luoghi dove il Saverio principalmente si avvolge col suo Appostolato? Avvolgersi sull'arenosa vastissima costa di Pescheria tutta [f. 188] riarsa da cocentissimi soli, tutta intristita dall'aere tetro e insalubre: nell'Isola d'Amboino o disastrosa in sommo per folti boschi, e per montagne scoscesi, o esposta all'irruzioni frequenti del Saracin predatore: avvolgesi nell'Isole del Manco e dell'Ulate, e allora appunto, che nella prima infierisce universal pestilenza, e infellonisce d'attono della seconda l'ostenemica: nell'Isole tutte del Moro tremende ancora a naviganti più arditi, che solvi passan d'appresso, per gli tremuoti onde scuoton si orribilmente le rupi e scoscendono, e per l'eruzioni de' monti, che scagliano dal sen fremente dilavi di fiamme e di pietre sterminatrici: avvolgersi finalmente in Regni, in ispiagge, in isole, che troppo è lungo di noverare, pressoché tutte insoffribili e innabitabili e non di rado mortali alla delicatezza degli Europei. E quali sono quelle genti, che evangelizza? Quai sono? Ditelo voi, o Signori, che tante volte l'udiste da questo luogo, e forse alcuna volta il leggeste nella vividica storia del nostro santo; e dite insieme qual fu l'orror, che compresevi al fier racconto. E chi può non inorridire alla dissolutezza, alla superstizione, alla barbarie di popoli sì snaturati? Dissolutezza che freno più non sentendo d'erubescenza si fa una legge delle abbominazioni più infami, e la dipigne sulle pareti de' templi, ne' suoi numi l'adora. Superstizione che venera i diavoli dell'inferno, e scanna in sugli altari nefandi vittime umane. [f. 189] Barbarie che di continuo si lorda di sangue umano, e d'umana carne imbandisce le tavole scellerate. Dio immortale! E un uomo poté trovarsi che affrontasse que' mari; che si avvolgesse in que' luoghi; che a mansuefar si facesse e convertir quelle genti? Un uomo poté trovarsi, che per santificare se stesso nell'Appostolato, nel quale Dio lo voleva non meno per la conversione d'altrui, che per la santificazione sua propria, reggesse forte, costante, invincibile a un appostolato sì travaglioso? Deh che uomo sarà questo mai, divino uomo, che si fa santo abbattendo un ostacolo sì formidabile? Poiché non è egli vero, o Signori, che a tal aspetto di cose a tal serie non interrotta di patimenti e pericoli affatto insoliti dovean nell'animo del Saverio levarsi a romor le passioni, e il timore e l'odio, e l'avversione e lo sdegno, e ogn'altra passion che rifugge da' grandi mali, dovevano qual arrestarlo[71] in Europa, qual ritardarlo nell'intrapresa carriera, qual allontanarlo da' luoghi tanto calamitosi, da popoli tanto brutali? Che se il Saverio maggiore d'ogni pericolo e patimento assoggettò le passioni al voler di Dio per tal modo, che non osaron neppure di contraddirlo; se non arrestassi un momento, se proseguì la carriera sino alla fine, se compié tutto gl'ingiuntogli appostolato, e qual pensate voi, miei Signori, che dovett'essere la magnanimità, la fortezza, la mansuetudine, la costanza, l'imper[f. 189v]turbabilità, la pazienza, qual la cospirazione di tutte insiem le virtù ad intraprendere e continuare un tal genere d'Appostolato? E qual dovett'essere in fine la sua santità, se vinse sì grande ostacolo? Non parvi, ch'esser dovesse una santità grande sopra ogni dire e maravigliosa?

Ma forse alcuno m'accusa tacitamente, ch'oltre il dovere un'essageri la grandezza e la maraviglia; e forse va dicendo in suo cuore: non fu già il solo Saverio, che affrontasse que mari; quanti, né certo per merito di santità; prima di lui, e con lui si affrontarono spontaneamente? Non fu già il solo Saverio che si aggirasse in que' luoghi, tra quelle genti; quanti in processo di tempo; quanti appostolici uomini vi si aggirarono, i quali non direm certo solo per ciò sì gran santi e maravigliosi? Non fu già sol l'India barbara, incolta, sanguinolenta, che evangelizzasse il Saverio, evangelizzò ancora il Giappone colto, sociale, disciplinato? Piacemi quest'accusa, o

71 Lo interlinear word.

Signori, e le ragioni mi piacciono dell'accusa, poiché tanto esse non fanno contro di me, che anzi esse vagliano mirabilmente a mostrar sempre più la grandezza e la maraviglia della santità vincitrice di quest'ostacolo. Attendete, s'io dica il vero. Altri affrontarono spontaneamente pria del Saverio e col Saverio que' mari; ma gli affrontarono spinti della passione prepotente di straricchire, ma gli affrontarono colla certezza, che superati que' [f. 190] mari muterebbero condizione, fortuna, e stato. Che costor dunque affrontasser que' mari non manifesta che men siano que' mari da paventarsi, manifesta bensì la forza d'una passione, la qual vincendo il contrasto d'altre passioni, obbligavagli di sottoporsi a tanti pericoli e patimenti. Posto ciò, io ripiglio, qual dovett'esser la santità del Saverio, se poté quello che sol puote la forza d'una passione, d'una passione, la quale può tutto, o Signori, sul cuore umano. Altri appostolici uomini si aggirarono in que' luoghi, tra quelle genti. Il so, miei Signori, ma so altresì, che il Saverio fu il primo pressoché in ogni luogo a lor tracciare la via: il primo a rendere meno feroci e intrattabili quelle genti: e so finalmente che dove bastò un solo Saverio per tutta l'India di qua e di là dal Gange, bastaron poi molti appena per ogni Isola per ogni Regno dell'India. Se dunque il primo, se dunque solo il Saverio, bastò a tanto, che avrò dovuto soffrire? e quindi qual sarà stata la santità; che tenne forte e soffrì? Infine il Saverio non evangelizzò l'India sola, evangelizzò ancora il Giappone. Che dunque? almen nel Giappone si sarà menomata la forza di quest'ostacolo, menomandosi i patimenti fra popoli non disumani. Io son sicuro, o Signori, che niun di voi la discorre di questa guisa, niun che ricordi qual fosse l'appostolato del Santo tra Giapponesi. Né curo io già, che ricordi l'orgoglio e il fasto d'una [f. 190v] nazione superbissima, e de' forestieri dispregiatrice prosuntuosa: ricordi solo l'orrenda persecuzione che i Tundi, e i Bonzi depositari, e ministri della superstizione mossero contro al Saverio, e continuaron poi sempre con rabbia insana al veder rovinar il lor credito, le lor trufferie, le loro malvagità; ricordi questa ed aggiunga che per portarsi al Giappone dovette il Santo con altra consternazion degli amici affidarsi al navilio d'un corsaro Cinese uomo il più scellerato ed infame, che navigasse que' mari, e aggiunga che nel Giappone scorse colle fatiche apostoliche tutti i suoi regni, e poi dica se nel Giappon menomaronsi i patimenti. Parvi egli adesso, o Signori, che l'ostacolo opposto alla santità del Saverio da un tal genere d'appostolato sia grande ostacolo di santità? Parvi alla grande e maravigliosa la santità del Saverio a fronte di questo ostacolo? Santità, che non cede, non si sgomenta, che tutto imprende, che col soccorso e la forza delle più eroiche virtù assoggetta al voler di Dio le passioni, e le fa tacite, e quete alla presenza e al contrasto di tanti mali? E pure io non ho detto niente delle contraddizion che sostenne il suo Appostolato dalla prepotenza, dall'ambizione, dall'avarizia di molti Europei in Malacca e in Goa. Ho dissimulato tutto il di[72] più, che si aggiunse di

72 Di interlinear word.

patimenti nelle navigazioni dalle malattie che compresero i naviganti, a quali si fece padre [f. 191] infermiero, famiglio. Ho passato sotto silenzio tutti gl'incomodi che accompagnarono i suoi viaggi per terra dal camminar sì spesso in sulle arene inforate, e dal trovarsi sì spesso nella stremità d'ogni cosa più necessaria alla vita. Cent'altre cose ho lasciate, le quali immensamente gravando l'appostolato afforzaron l'ostacolo di santità. Potrà egli dunque, io ripiglio, potrà alcuno accusarmi, ch'io esageri, o nella grandezza di quest'ostacolo, o nella grandezza della santità vincitrice di quest'ostacolo? No, miei Signori, che niun di voi non m'accusa, anzi tutti già persuasi e convinti e dell'uno e dell'altro, a ragionar m'affrettate del secondo ostacolo molto più grande di santità, che oppose il successo medesimo dell'Appostolato, per poter riconoscere sempre più grande la Santità del Saverio.

Punto Secondo. Preparate ormai gli animi a lieti cose, ascr. riv. poiché da un Appostolato tutto fatiche, tutto pericoli, tutto[73] disastri, a rimirare io v'invito un appostolato tutto conquiste, tutto gloria, tutto prodigi; e preparatevi nel tempo stesso a comprendere, che il prodigio maggior d'ogni altro è il Saverio santo, e un gran santo infra l'ostacolo di sì gloriosi successi. L'assoggettare a Dio le passioni coll'incontrare e sostener grandi mali è malagevole impresa non può negarsi; ma molto più malagevole l'assoggettar a Dio la propria eccellenza [f. 191v] il non invanire dell'altre cose operate, il non darsene pur lievemente alcun merito, alcuna lode. Quell'ambizione, o Signori, che l'uomo riceve quasi in retaggio nascendo lo persuade a guardare con senso di compiacenza tutto ciò, che il fa crescere per qualche modo agli occhi propri e agli altrui. Che se nol reca, come già gli Angioli prevaricatori ad innalzare se stesso sopra di Dio, o come i parenti primi ad uguagliarsi con Dio, recalo nondimeno a rapire a Dio una parte di quella gloria, ch'è tutta di Dio, e ad attribuire a se stesso una parte di ciò, che è solo di Dio. Ambizione, che non è paga d'avvolgersi tra le mondane grandezze, ma penetra ne' recessi più sagri dell'umiltà a scuotere ed atterrare la santità più robusta. Che se frequenti non sono sì gran rovina, non è infrequente né medesimi santi a ritardo di santità qualche leggero e furtivo seducimento di questo dolce nemico. Davidde era un santo, e qual santo. Basta vederlo al cimento delle persecuzion, degli affronti, delle dimestiche disavventure; pure quel santo, che resse contro a travagli delle disonorate consorti, de' sudditi ribellati, de' servidoti insultanti, de' figli uccisi, non resse contro all'assalto d'una leggera ambizione, che trasselo a numerare i sudditi atti alla guerra per compiacenza d'un numero sì sterminato. Ma questo fascino seducitore, che poté fin sull'animo di Davidde, non poté giammai nulla sull'animo del Saverio. Restò sedotto [f. 192] Davidde, e compiacquesi, non restò sedotto il Saverio, né si compiacque. E di che si compiacque Davidde? E di che si compiacque il Saverio? Si compiacque Davidde de' numerosi vassali od ottenuti o serbati dal valor vittorioso delle sue

73 Tutto superscripted word.

armi. Ma quanta parte di queste conquistatrici vittorie all'accorteza dovevasi de' capitani; quanta alla generosità de' soldati; quanta alla fede de' partigiani. Non si compiacque il Saverio de' sudditi conquistati alla Croce, benché conquistati dalle sue sole fatiche, dalle sue sole sollecitudini, dal suo solo coraggio, dalla voce sua sola. Si compiacque Davidde di sudditi bellicosi e capaci di difendere coll'arme in mano le lor città, le lor terre, le lor famiglie, le vite loro. Non si compiacque il Saverio d'aver sottomessi alla legge di Gesù Cristo sudditi sì magnanimi, che per difendere questa legge soffrivano volentieri gli esilj dalle lor patrie, lo spoglio de' lor averi, l'abbandono delle loro famiglie, e trappoco difesa aurebbonda a costo di squallide prigionie, di dispietati supplici, d'orrende morti. Compiacquesi finalmente Davidde, ch'i suoi guerrier d'Israelle giugnessero al numero di ottocento mila, e di cinquecento mila quegli di Giuda. Non si compiacque il Saverio, che i Giapponesi, e gl'Indiani da se convertiti vincessero come dice il Sommo Pontefice Gregorio XV nella Bolla della Canonizzazione[74], vincessero il numero dell'arene del mare, e delle stelle del Cielo; che le Provincie [f. 192v] da se viaggiate, l'isole, le città, i villaggi, le popolazioni da se evangelizzate fossero innumerabili, e innumerabili i templi atterrati, e gl'idoli inceneriti. E pure, il ripeto, e pur Davidde era un santo e un gran santo a que' giorni, e ben ne fece indubitabile fede il largo pianto amarissimo, con cui lavò questa macchia, e la sommession perfettissima, onde accettonne il gastigo dal Signor Dio. Io già non voglio didurne, che maggior santo fosse il Saverio, io voglio solo provare quanto i gloriosi successi, le illustri imprese, le prosperevoli cose sian per se grand'ostacolo alla santità, s'anco i grandi santi talora nol superarono. Ma proseguiamo a conoscere la grandezza di quest'ostacolo.

Tornarono un giorno a Gesù Cristo i discepoli, e lieti di gaudio insolito per l'insolite cose operate nel nome del lor Maestro, Signor, gli dissero, non solamente le malattie, ma persino i demonj ci si assoggettano, e al comando nostro disgombrano da' corpi ossessi. Cotesta gioja pareva santa e innocente, se la riprensione seguita da Gesù Cristo non la mostrava macchiata di vanità. Direte tosto, o Signori, che a que' giorni i discepoli non eran anche saliti all'altezza di santità, a cui poi venner salendo, dove non invaniton più certo d'imprese tanto maggiori? Se così dite, ben dite, ed è appunto ciò ch'io volea che diceste. Dunque ripiglio io, dunque egli è d'uopo esser santo a non invanire pur leggermente in fra l'azioni gloriose, [f. 193] benché non ogni santo, come dicemmo, andò sempre esente da questa macchia. Dunque quanto saran più gloriose l'azioni, tanto sarà ancora più santo, che non né invanisce, non sen compiace, e si serba nell'abbiezion più dimessa, nell'umiltà più profonda. Or voi conoscete qual sarà stata la santità del Saverio, se andò sempre

74 Giuliari mentioned the bull *Rationi congruit* written by Gregory XV in this occasion. It was published on 6 August 1623 by his successor Urban VIII (Maffeo Vincenzo Barberini, r. 1623–1644), because Gregory XV died on 8 July of the same year.

esente da questa macchia, se fu mai sempre sì umile intanta gloria. Non solo le malattie, non i demonj soli si assoggettarono al suo comando, ma tutta quanta sarei per dire con enfasi certo ardita, non però falsa, ma tutta quanta si assoggettò la natura, e tutte infranse a suoi cenni le leggi usate. Assoggettossi il mare, e i sempre indocili flutti fece ubbidienti al Saverio: ubbidienti e calmarono cento volte le suscitate tempeste, e restituirono salvi al lido i naufraghi già ingojati, e rispettarono in lunghissimi anni seguenti le navi da lui prottete; e dove l'inesterilito sen fecondarono, dove le reti prima invan tese colmarono di copiosissimi pesci, dove addolcirono l'acque salmastre a ristoro de' naviganti. Assoggettossi l'aria, e al suo impeto purgandosi della pestilenziale infezione cessò la strage, e il totale eccidio già cominciato d'una città; e al suo impeto armandosi contro a ribelli del cielo scagliò subita grandine di macigni, piobbe fiamme divampatrici, saettò folgori rovinose, e compié la strage e lo sterminio di Tolo. Assoggettossi la morte, né solo si ritirò [f. 193v] tutto di dalle prede già quasi sue; ma più cadaveri a novella vita restituì. Maravigliose cose, o Signori, io vi dico, ed altre mille ugualmente maravigliose, a voi non ignote, io vi taccio, ed aggiungo solo essere stati sì grandi, sì universali, e sì frequenti i miracoli del Saverio operati, che Re e Reine, e ogni maniera di gente, prostavansi a piedi suoi chiedendo l'acque battesimali, e che gli'idolatri medesimi gli correvano incontro con rami in mano, e l'accompagnavan chiamandolo l'arbitro della natura, il gran Padre, il gran Dio; e gli avrebbono forse alzati templi ed alzati, se sgridandogli il santo non avesse lor ripetuto, come già Barnaba e Paolo in Listri sono uom mortal qual voi siete servo e ministro dell'unico vero Dio, che conferma la verità di sua Fede con tai prodigi. Io non pretendo, che n'inferiate la santità del Saverio dal rifiutare divini onori, poiché il non essere un empio, non è lo stesso ch'essere un santo: bensì pretendo a ragione, che l'inferiate dal non compiacersi, dal non invanirà giammai; ma che dico io dal non invanirne, dal non compiacersi? inferitela con altissima maraviglia dall'umiltà sua sto per dire più de' miracoli stessi miracolosa. Io dico miracolo d'umiltà in un uomo sì favorito dal cielo, e sì rispettabile agli uomini il calare con tanta sollecitudine gli adoperati prodigi, e il coprirsi di confusione, e rossore all'udir ricordargli: il riputarsi in degnissimo d'alcuna grazia miracolosa [f. 194] e però l'applicarsi ad imparar nuove lingue con tanta pena, benché la lunga sperienza l'assicurasse che Dio glien'infondeva al bisogno la cognizione: il pregar Dio di sospendere la larga piena delle interiori celesti consolazioni siccome di troppo indebite a un peccatore: il chiamarsi[75] ora scellerato, or ribaldo, or un abisso di colpe, or un baratto di miserie: il maravigliarsi[76], che Dio si valesse di lui a sua gloria: il tenersi per l'ultimo de' figliuoli d'Ignazio, né mai non iscrivere al suo santo Padre, che in umile atteggiamento prostrato sulle ginocchia:

75 Maravigliarsi superscripted word.

76 Chiamarsi superscripted word.

l'avvolgersi sopra le navi né ministeri più abbjetti tra la ciurmaglia; il mescolarsi tra il popolaccio più vile imitandone le disavvenenti maniere; il gioir tra le ingiurie, le contumelie, gl'insulti; ma che dilungomi inutilmente, o Signori, negli atti grandi sì certo, e continui dell'umiltà, del Saverio, quando a mostrarla affatto miracolosa basta affermare, che resse mai sempre invitta all'ostacolo esposto di tanta gloria. Umiltà che assoggettando a Dio la propria eccellenza fu al tempo stesso cagione, prova e misura di sorprendente grandissima santità.

Punto Terzo. Venghiamo in fine ascr. riv: all'ultima prova e più grande delle passate, all'ultimo e più grande ostacolo di Santità. È difficile impresa assoggetar a Dio le proprie passioni; più difficile assoggettar a Dio la propria eccellenza; ma difficilissima assoggettar a Dio la propria ragione. [f. 194v]. Il Saverio assoggettò a Dio le proprie passioni durando forte e costante in[77] un appostolato travagliosissimo; assoggettò a Dio finalmente la propria eccellenza servendosi umile a sì gran segno in un appostolato gloriosissimo; assoggettò a Dio finalmente la propria ragione sagrificando per morte un appostolato fruttuosissimo. Non ignorate, o Signori, come il Saverio all'età di soli quarantesei anni sul punto di entrar nella Cina videsi al termine della vita e dell'appostolato. Et questo termine dell'appostolato io chiamo ostacolo di santità di gran lunga maggiore de' precedenti per la incredibile difficoltà d'una rassegnazione in apparenza contraria alla ragione medesima, perché contraria di verità a desiderj più fervidi, alle speranze e più certe, e da disegni più vasti di nuova gloria di Dio, e di nuove conquiste e maggiori delle passate. A ben comprendere la malagevolezza di questa rassegnazione considerate per un momento, o Signori, d'onde movevano i desiderj del Santo; a che s'appoggiavano le sue speranze, e da ultimo che fatto aveva per maturarne i disegni. Non furono tai desiderj eccitati non furono solamente dall'inzaziabil suo zelo; ma Dio medesimo con interne voci sensibili gli avea destati, chiamandolo alla conversione della Cina; e ciò più e più volte, e ciò con tale chiarezza, che dubitar non poteva di vocazione divina. Le sue speranze poi si appoggiavano [f. 195]a quel Signore che confortandolo già in addietro all'acquisto prima dell'India, poi del Giappone haveva fatto esultare di tante palme: quindi come ardentissimamente desiderava, così fermissimamente sperava di conquistare la Cina; anzi sicuro tenevasi della vittoria né le speranze del santo si racchiudeano tra i confini della Cina, benché si vesti. Ma dalla Cina già convertita innoltrando nella Tartaria, quindi spingendosi nell'Etiopia, e internandosi in tutta l'Africa, e al fin tornando nell'Asia, sperava nel solo svolgersi d'altri dieci anni d'aggiungnere tutta quanta l'Africa e l'Asia alla Chiesa di Gesù Cristo. Queste erano le speranze, e questi erano insieme i disegni del suo gran cuore. Osservate da ultimo, che fa il Saverio per maturare e condurre ad effetto questi disegni, e quante cure, quanti disagi gli costano, quante pene. Io

77 In interlinear word.

dirò poche parole, e voi intenderete, gran cose, abbandona il suo diletto Giappone; risolca gli stessi mari infiniti dal Giappone a Malacca, da Malacca a Goa. Ottiene e prepara in Goa con inespicabil travaglio un'ambasceria all'Imperador della Cina, onde agevolar per tal mezzo l'adito all'Evangelio. Rinaviga nuovamente a Malacca, e qui sostiene per colmo de' superati travagli l'insuperabile persecuzione di chi per ambizione frastona l'ambasceria; persecuzione sì fiera che il santo stesso [f. 195v] affermò ad un amico di non averne provata maggiore neppure tra barbari. Ma non rallentato da tutto questo, tanto adoprassi, che impetrò per se almeno l'imbarco all'Isola di Sanciano. Eccovi, Signori miei, quali erano i desiderj, quai le speranze di convertire la Cina, e quando patir dovette per adempiere i disegni. Pensate or voi con qual gioia con qual esaltazione, con qual impeto uguale a fervidi desiderj, alle certe speranze, a patimenti sofferti parte il Saverio dalla Cina di Malacca? Vedetelo tutto giulivo e contento far vela verso Sanciano; e dopo molti pericoli da lui vinti con più prodigi, vedetelo scendere sull'Isola sospirata; vedetelo più che mai lieto e impaziente salutar la sua Cina, da cui lo divide sol breve spazio di mare; vedetelo cercar tragitto; vedetelo, ohimé qual veder lo dovete! Addio desiderj, speranze e disegni addio: addio Cina, addio Tartaria, addio Etiopia, addio Africa tutta, Asia tutta. Il Saverio ascolta nel più profondo dell'anima un'altra voce ascolta di Dio, la qual parole gli porla[sic!] di pronta morte. Quest'è il cimento, il contrasto è questo, questo l'ostacolo a cui Dio mette talora la santità de' gran santi. Che dice dunque il Saverio, e come regge a un ostacolo sì repentino e sì forte? Ostacolo che opponendosi in certo modo alla ragione, la quale non sa ben intendere, come Dio possa volere ciò che distrugge [f. 196] i desiderj, e le speranze, e[78] i disegni, che vennero da Lui stesso, e che costarono tanto, e che son per tornare a tanta gloria di Lui, opponesi perciò medesimo fortissimamente si oppone alla santità, che ha mestieri per vincerlo della più forte e più pronta e più cieca e più profonda rassegnazione. Lagnasi forse il Saverio, si duole inquietasi delle disposizioni di Dio, esita a crederla voce di Dio, chiede indugio? Egli con occhio amoroso e languente mira la Cina, poi volgesi al Crocefisso, che strigne in mano, e gli dice: cotesta dunque è la vittima, il sagrificio è cotesto che voi volete? Ah mio Dio! qui torna uno sguardo alla Cina, e poi risponde al suo Dio: accettate la vittima, il sagrificio accettate, che vittima né sagrificio non ho maggiore. Oh rassegnazione che compie e manifesta nel tempo stesso una santità superior d'ogni ostacolo, d'ogni cimento. Poiché riflettete meco, o Signori: che accettasser la morte senza rincrescimento, senza querela gli Appostoli primitivi nell'atto anch'essi di mietere novella messe, ben io l'intendo. Motivan'essi tra i provocati supplici degl'infedeli a confermazione ed a gloria dell'annunciata lor Fede; e morivano colla certezza ch'il sangue loro sarebbe un'ubertosa semente di novelli Cristiani. Ma che il nostro Appostolo la morte accetti con rassegnazione sì

---

78 E interlinear word.

eroica, e l'accetti non dalle punte e dal taglio [f. 196v] di barbario ferro, come bramò e sperò sempre mai, e l'accetti non a testimonianza della sua Fede, e senza alcuna speranza che la sua morte sia per la Cina uno stimolo ad abbracciare la Fede, e l'accetti in fine nell'atto quasi di convertirla quest'è ch'io non arrivo a comprendere, e che mi colma d'un indicibile meraviglia. È ver che il Santo oppresso da crudo morbo gioisce al sentirsi da Dio chiamare al riposo, al premio, alla palma di Paradiso: è ver, che placido, e sereno in volto mostra la contentezza del cuore: è ver ch'affissandosi nel Crocefisso prorompe in un soavissimo pianto d'esultazione nulla dimeno, o Signori, questa inalterabile tranquillità non palesa diminuzione di malagevolezza e di pena nel sagrificio, poiché i santi antepongono la promulgazion della Fede, la dilatazione della Gloria di Dio, la conversione dell'anime affrettamento de beni stessi[79] del Paradiso; palesa bensì la grandezza, e la forza della santità, la qual offre tal sagrificio e l'offre con rassegnazion sì perfetta che non arriva a turbarsene pur[80] lievemente la serenità del sembiante, la contentezza del cuore. Consumata in tal modo la sua santità, in un perfettissimo assoggettamento a Dio di tutto se stesso a fronte del triplice ostacolo, che grande opporre doveva la qualità dell' [f.197] Appostolato; più grande il successo dell'Appostolato; grandissimo il termine dell'appostolato, andò il Saverio coll'anima avventurosa a ricevere la mercé preparata alla sua santità e al suo Appostolato lassù nel cielo; e restò in terra coll'incorrotto Cadavero a continuare le maraviglie e i prodigi a favor de' mortali, e a far fede visibile della sua santità.

Permettetemi, Signori miei, che io v'interroghi finalmente che giudichiate voi della santità del Saverio. Dite s'io avea ragion d'affermare sin da principio, che fra tante cose mirabili d'un tal genere d'appostolato, la più mirabile è il Saverio santo, e un gran santo in questo suo sì mirabile Appostolato? Dite s'io avea ragion di pretendere, che niente più manifesti la santità, e la gran santità del Saverio, ch'il considerare l'Appostolato come triplice ostacolo di Santità? Dite se non doveva essere ostacolo grande veramente ed insolito; e dite infine, ma questo dir non potrete né intendere, quanto fu grande la santità vincitrice di tant'ostacolo. Santità per la quale il Saverio assoggettando a Dio le proprie passioni, la propria eccellenza, la ragion propria resse a sì grandi travagli, a sì grande gloria, a sacrificio sì grande.

Deh ammirabile santo dal seggio di vostra gloria inchinate lo sguardo su tutti [f. 197v] noi, e veggendo quai son gli ostacoli, che tutto giorno si oppongono a quell'assoggettamento di noi, che Dio pretende da noi, impetrateci una vittoria, se non ammirabile e gloriosa come la vostra, almeno tal che ci salvi e ci conduca nel Cielo a goder con voi l'immarcescibil mercede. Così sia.

---

79 Affrettamento de' ben stessi interlinear word.

80 Pur interlinear word.

Section 4
Martyrs of Japan: Models, Emotions, and the Causes for Beatification and Canonization

Carla Tronu Montané

From 'Martyrs of Japan' to 'Japanese Martyrs'

Models of Sanctity and Diversity in the Canonization Causes for Martyrs of Japan[1]

Introduction

The martyrs of Japan have been present in the media in the past decade not only because of the popularity of the 2016 feature movie by Scorsese *Silence*, but also because of the beatification in 2017 of a Japanese lay Christian, Takayama Ukon. This is the first individual cause for a Japanese martyr and stands out among martyrs the of Japan because he was a high rank warlord who was expelled from Japan in 1614 and died of illness in Manila. Thus, he is the first recognized 'white martyr', as opposed to the thousands of 'red martyrs' or 'blood martyrs' who were executed or died in prison or during torture. His profile differs considerably from that of the earliest martyrs of Japan recognized by the Catholic Church, Pedro Bautista OFM and companions and Paulo Miki SJ and companions, also known as the protomartyrs of Japan, the 26 Saints of Japan, or the 26 martyrs of Nagasaki (d. 1597). They were six foreign (mainly Spanish) Franciscan missionaries and 20 lay Japanese Christians, most of whom helped the missionaries take care of hospitals.

The 26 Martyr Saints of Japan have also recently been in the media. Original documents found in the inventory of the church of the Monastery of Our Lady of Loreto in Espartinas, Seville (Spain) confirm that the relics kept in the old church belong to Pedro Bautista and his companions. Luis Sotelo personally donated them in 1615 when he visited Seville with the Japanese embassy sent by Lord Date Masamune.[2] Up to the present the Vatican has accepted 6 canonization causes for martyrs died in Japan, most of them collective. In total the Catholic Church has beatified 437 martyrs and has canonized 42 of them as saints. This is but a small portion, approximately 10% of all those reported to have lost their lives for

1 This research was funded by the Japanese Society for the Promotion of Science (Grant-in-Aid for Early Career Scientists 20K13157 'Laity in the Early Modern Japanese Mission: Confraternities and Missionary Rivalry').

2 This finding by Prof José Caño, from the University of Cadiz, was reported in the Andalusian edition of the Spanish public television news. RTVE, Noticias Andalucía, on 16 August 2022.

the Christian faith in early modern Japan, estimated around 4.045.[3] For many of them, especially for the Japanese lay commoners, it is extremely difficult to find reliable historical data (sometimes not even their name being traceable). However, new causes for martyrs of Japan might be opened if and when enough historical evidence becomes available.

These are the six canonisation causes accepted by the Sacred Congregation of the Rites concerning martyrs of Japan (closed causes as of 2022 are underlined):

a. 26 Martyr Saints of Japan (d. 1597) beatified in 1627 (Roma) and canonized in 1862 (Roma)
b. 205 Blessed Martyrs of Japan (d. 1617–1632) beatified in 1867 (Roma)
c. 16 Japan Martyr Saints (d. 1633–1637) beatified in 1981 (Manila) and canonized in 1987 (Roma)
d. 2 Augustinian Blessed Martyrs (d. 1632) beatified in 1989 (Roma)
e. 188 Japanese Blessed Martyrs (d. 1603–1639) beatified in 2008 (Nagasaki)
f. (1) Blessed Martyr Takayama Ukon (d. 1615) beatified in 2017 (Osaka)

There are many modern hagiographies of the martyrs of Japan, often published on the occasion of the opening of the cause or after their beatification or canonization.[4] Besides these, the martyrs of Japan have mainly been the object of hagiographic works and academic-style historiography by Catholic male historians, often belonging to the missionary orders involved or to the Catholic Church.[5] Recently,

---

3 F.J. Schütte, *Introductio ad Historiam Societatis Jesu in Japonia, 1549–1650* (Roma: Institutum historicum Soc. Jesu, 1968) 435–446.

4 G. Boero SJ, *Relazione della gloriosa morte di ducento e cinque beati martiri nel Giappone* (Roma: Civiltà Cattolica, 1867); G. Boero SJ *The Jesuit Martyrs of Japan: A History of the Lives and Martyrdom of Paul Michi, James Chisai, and John Soan De Goto, of the Society of Jesus* (Dublin: James Duffy, 1862); M. Jimenez OSA *Mártires Agustinos del Japón: o sea vida y martirio de los Beatos Fr. Fernando de San José, Fr. Pedro de Zúniga y demás compañeros Mártires, beatificados en 7 de Julio del presente año por N. Santísimo Padre Pío IX* (Valladolid: Juan de la Cuesta, 1867); J. Boero, *Los Doscientos Cinco Mártires del Japón. Relación de la Gloriosa Muerte de los Mártires, Beatificados por el Sumo Pontífice Pío IX, el día 7 de Julio de 1867* (México: J.M. Lara, 1869); Villarroel, F. *Lorenzo Ruiz the Protomartyr of the Philippines and his companions* (Pasay City: Saint Paul, 1979); J.M. Luengo/ P.R. Mamot, *Lorenzo Ruiz, the Filipino protomartyr in Nagasaki: the first Filipino beatified by Pope John Paul II* (Indianapolis: Philippine Heritage Endowment, 1984).

5 F. Robles Dégano OFM, *Vida y martirio de San Pedro Bautista: religioso descalzo de la Orden de San Francisco y embajador de España en Japón* (Roma: Moderna, 1927); A. Cermeño, SJ, *Corona de Daimyos, Don Justo Takayama* (Bilbao: El Siglo de las Misiones, 1950); R. Rodrigo, *Mártires en el Japón. Martín de S. Nicolás y Melchor de S. Agustín, agustinos recoletos* (Granada: Augustinus Monachil, 1988); J. Delgado García/P. González Tejero OP "Martyrs of Japan" in C. Puebla Pedrosa OP, *Witnesses of the faith in the Orient: Dominican martyrs of Japan, China and Vietnam* (Hong Kong: Provincial Secretariat of Missions Dominican Province of Our Lady of the Rosary, 1989) 13–150; J.I. Tellechea

non-confessional female academic historians have conducted research on the 26 Martyr Saints of Japan, either focusing on contemporary Franciscan narratives or on the image that the Jesuits constructed and disseminated in Europe through hagiography, visual iconography and theatre.[6] However, the rest of the groups remain under researched, and there are no comprehensive studies in western languages considering all the groups of martyrs of Japan recognized by the Vatican.[7]

This chapter tackles the question of to what extent the profiles of the martyrs of Japan provide diverse models of sanctity. First, I elucidate the historical context in which the six canonization causes started and how they developed in time, then I present a comparative analysis on the profiles of the two groups of sanctified martyrs of Japan (the 26 Martyrs of Nagasaki and the 16 Dominican Martyrs), focusing on nationality, gender, as well as religious status and affiliation. Finally, I look at the variations, trends and *lacunae* that emerge when including the profiles of the blessed martyrs of Japan, who have not yet been canonized, into the comparative analysis.

The canonization processes for martyrs of Japan in context

The mission frontier was attractive to zealous missionaries for the potential chances to face martyrdom. However, since Catholic missionaries arrived at Japan in a period of political decentralisation and internal wars, the chances of losing one's life were higher than they could imagine, both for foreigners and Japanese. Since martyrdom is defined as the testimony of one's faith by choosing to suffer or die rather than to renounce the Christian faith and morals, not all Christians who lost their life in the Japanese mission can be consider martyrs. As Cieslik pointed out, the conditions for martyrdom are the sacrifice of one's life, either by execution or

---

Nagasaki. Gesta martirial en Japón (1597) (Salamanca: Universidad Pontificia de Salamanca, 1998); J. Ruiz de Medina, SJ, *El martirologio del Japón 1558–1873* (Roma: Institutum Historicum Societatis Iesu, 1999); P. Panedas Galindo OAR, *Letras de Fuego: epistolario de los mártires agustinos de Japón* (Madrid: Agustinus, 2018); A. Muñoz Martín OFM & M. Prieto Prieto OFM, *Primeros mártires en Japón, Nagasaki. Historia e iconografía* (Madrid: Anaquel de Historia, 2021).

6 H. Vu Thanh, "The Glorious Martyrdom of the Cross. The Franciscans and the Japanese Persecutions of 1597", *Culture & History Digital Journal*, 6/1 (2017) 5–2253; H. Omata Rappo, "How to make 'Colored' Japanese Counter-Reformation Saints – A Study of an Iconographic Anomaly" *Journal of Early Modern Christianity* 4/2 (2017), 195–225; H. Omata Rappo, *Des Indes lointaines aux scènes des collèges: les reflets des martyrs de la mission japonaise en Europe (XVIe – XVIIIe siècle)* (Münster: Aschendorff, 2020).

7 See my preliminary study in Japanese in C. Tronu, "Nihon no junkyōsha no rekishiteki kioku to shūkyōteki aidentiti [Historical Memory of the Martyrs of Japan and religious identity]" *Ajia, Kirisutokyō, Tagensei* 17 (2019) 24–32.

by starvation or illness while in prison, during torture or in exile, the acceptance of death without offering resistance, and one's religious beliefs as the reason of death. Therefore, the Christian peasants who were killed in the Shimabara Rebellion cannot be recognised as martyrs because they offered resistance, like the Christian warriors who died in the Crusades. Finally, Japanese Christians who were executed for political reasons like Yukinaga Konishi or Gracia Hosokawa, are not considered martyrs either.[8]

The proof of martyrdom is usually assessed and validated (or not) at the beginning of the process of canonization. The official recognition of martyrdom by the Pope is part of the process, and traditionally, if confirmed, the validation of supernatural signs or miracles are not required for beatification. There is not an independent procedure to solely credit martyrdom. Therefore, only those who are presented for canonization because they died for the Christian faith receive official recognition as martyrs, and those who are not candidates for canonization remain unrecognized and cannot be venerated as martyrs.[9] While the early modern system of canonization by which the 26 Martyrs of Japan were officially recognized involved several inquires to witnesses and the compilation of historical proof of the circumstances and causes of their death, most of the saints in the post-Tridentine Roman Missal and the Roman Breviary did not undergo any administrative process at all. This is because from ancient times to the Middle Ages, Christians considered by their contemporaries as martyrs or saints were venerated as heavenly mediators for the laity, without any official procedures involved. For centuries, only the authorization of the local bishop was necessary to exhume the holy remains and place them in a separate, publicly visible location. A mass was celebrated yearly on the anniversary of the martyr's death and his or her name was recorded in the diocesan calendar and in martyrologies. Initially veneration was local, but the belief that saints responded to prayers with miracles popularized some saints beyond their dioceses and their cult spread to other regions and countries, with no official proclamation of the Holy See and with no verification process for the evidence of the claimed miraculous manifestations.

As the cult of saints expanded, the Holy See felt the need for intervention. From the 10th century the Pope was to be called upon to ratify decisions that had already been taken in practice. Although local veneration continued to grow and, in numerous places, flourished without much interference, from the late medieval

8 H. Cieslik, "Junkyō [Martyrdom]" in *Nihon Kirisutokyō rekishi daijiten* (Tokyo: Kyobunkan, 1988) 667.

9 For a synthesis of the historical development of the canonisation process see C. Renoux "Une source de l'histoire de la mystique moderne revisitée; les procès de canonisation" *Mélanges de l'Ecole françaie de Rome. Italie et Méditerranée*, 105/1 (1993) 177–217.

period Papal assertion was necessary for new canonisations.[10] In the sixteenth century, the Reformation divided European Christianity and the Catholic Church started serious internal reforms. The cult of saints and the canonization process were also regulated. A distinction was made between blessed (*beatus*) and saint (*sanctus*). While the veneration of the blessed, including memorial masses and the display of relics and images, is restricted to specific places or institutions with strong connections to the blessed's life or death, saints are entitled to universal public veneration within the Catholic Church.

In the sixteenth century, the veneration of saints was strongly questioned by the Protestant Reformation and from 1523 to 1587, although several non-universal cults were authorized, no papal canonizations occurred.[11] In 1588 Pope Sixtus V (1521–1590) restarted canonizations and created the Sacred Congregation of Rites and Ceremonies. This new institution oversaw the examination of biographies of saints within the canonization process, that gradually became more rigorous.[12] It became necessary to gather as much reliable information as possible about the life, suffering and death of the martyrs. After that, further revisions on the regulations for canonization were made by his successor Pope Urbanus VIII (1568–1644), and later in the mid eighteenth century by Pope Benedictus XIV (1675–1758). These reforms created the basis for the complex canonization procedures based on the judicial model that prevailed until the beginning of the twentieth century. However, after the revision of Canon Law in 1917, and under the influence of the Second Vatican Council, which took place from 1962 to 1965, in 1969 Pope Paul VI (1897–1978) announced the simplification of the canonization procedures and created a dedicated Congregation for the Causes of Saints, devoted to the assessment of proposals for sainthood, separate from the Congregation of Divine Worship and the Discipline of Sacraments, dedicated exclusively to liturgical matters and the administration and implementation of sacraments. In 1983, a simplified procedure for canonization was established. It should be noted that the first two causes for martyrs of Japan were presented prior to this reform, when the process followed a judicial trial model in which the resolution could take various decades, or even centuries. For the other four causes, however, it took only a few years for

---

10 S. Ditchfield, "Tridentine worship and the cult of saints" *The Cambridge History of Christianity. Reform and Expansion 1500–1660* (Cambridge: Cambridge University, 2012³) 201–260, on p.208.

11 S. Ditchfield, "Tridentine worship", 207.

12 P. Burke, "How to be a Counter-Reformation Saint" in K. von Greyerz (ed.), *Religion and Society in Early Modern Europe 1500–1800* (London: George Allen & Unwin, 1984) 45–55; S. Ditchfield, "Coping with the *Beati Moderni*: Canonisation procedure in the aftermath of the Council of Trent" in T. M. McCoog (ed.), *Ite Inflmmate Omnia* (Roma, Institutum Historicum Societatis Iesu, 2006) 413–439.

beatifications or canonizations to be authorized. Let us have a look at the history of each of the causes for martyrs of Japan.

The first process of canonization for martyrs of Japan was that of the 26 martyrs executed in Nagasaki in 1597. As Hitomi Omata Rappo has compellingly argued, the cause was eagerly put forward by the Franciscans. Not only they started the preparation of necessary documents (for example a translation of Hideyoshi's sentence) and asked the bishops in Manila and Macao to start the ordinary inquiries to the witnesses immediately after the events, but the martyrs' letters and behaviour before the execution seem to have been preparing the ground for a perfect martyrdom.[13] Franciscans, being the main profile for early modern European sainthood, were fully aware and familiarized with the conditions and procedures for canonization. The 26 martyrs of Nagasaki were the very first martyrs after the Reformation and exemplary victims of a non-Christian 'enemy'. This provided a model of sainthood that compensated for the rather controversial Reformation martyrs that resulted from the sixteenth century religion wars, in which Christians of various denominations had been killed by fellow Christians. All the documents produced by the Franciscans concerning the martyrs seemed to be oriented and designed to be of use for the canonization process, and consequently the 26 martyrs were relatively quickly beatified by the Holy See, in 1627, only 30 years after their death.[14]

In contrast, the second canonization process for martyrs of Japan, including 205 martyrs who died in different parts of Kyushu between 1617 and 1632, followed a very different course. The group included Jesuit, Franciscan, Dominican and Augustinian clergy as well as laity. The missionary orders started preparatory regional processes in Madrid, Manila and Macau for some of the candidates as soon as in 1618, but up to 1637, as the number of executions of Christians in Japan increased, more candidates were added gradually. However, new regulations on canonization as well as controversial events in the mission field before the Vatican initiated the apostolic process led to the stagnation of this cause.[15] On the one side, Pope Urbanus VIII (1568–1644) issued a series of decrees *super non cultu* in 1625, 1631 and 1634 banning any kind of public cult or images with symbols of

13 The anticipation of martyrdom by the mendicant orders in the missionary field persisted over the decades. They relied on the theological basis for dissimulation to justify irregular actions and concealment of the truth. Nonetheless, in a seventeenth century publication the fact that Recollect Augustinian Pedro de Zuñiga, one of the 205 blessed, wore merchant clothes instead of their habits and hid his religious condition when interrogated were pointed out as potential obstacles for martyrdom. See Y. Orii, "Disimulación sobre la 'disimulación' en historiografías españolas: mártires del siglo XVII en Japón", in Y. Orii/M. J. Zamora Calvo (ed.), Cruces y Áncoras. La influencia de Japón y España en un Siglo de Oro global (Madrid: Abada, 2020) 59–80 on pages 70–73.

14 H. Omata Rappo, *Des Indes lointaines*, 99, 103.

15 J.S. Cummings, *Jesuit and Friar in the Spanish Expansion to the East* (London: Variorum, 1986).

sainthood before the acceptance of the canonization process. Besides this, in 1634 he established a rule by which no canonization processes would be accepted until at least 50 years had passed since the candidate's death.[16] On the other side, the confusion created by the apostasy of Cristovão Ferreira, the Jesuit Provincial in Japan in 1633 had direct consequences on the Holy See's decisions.

Initially, both in the mission field and Europe, the arrest and imprisonment of Ferreira had been assumed as forecasting a new case of martyrdom, and one that was especially valuable, since he held the highest rank in the Japanese mission. This is why the Jesuits themselves were in shock when they heard that not only had he apostatized under torture, but that he had also been forced to adopt a new Japanese name, marry a local woman and serve as inquisitor for the Japanese government. The Jesuits in Macao sent a group of missionaries with the purpose of finding him, confirm the facts, and help him return to the Christian faith, but they too were arrested and executed, so the Jesuits did not report on such shameful events to Europe.[17] However, in 1636, in the context of the ongoing disputes between the Mendicants and the Jesuits regarding the Japanese and the Chinese missions,[18] the Dominican Diego Collado broke the news to the Congregation of Propaganda Fide, and Jesuits received harsh critiques within and outside the Catholic world.[19] The scandal surrounding the disclosure of Ferreira's apostasy questioned the reliability of the news on the Japan mission that missionary orders were disseminating in Europe, and the Vatican did not admit any candidates who died in or after 1632 in the second canonization cause for martyrs of Japan.[20] In spite of this setback, not all the martyrs of Japan were discredited, and the cause for the 205 followed its course, although very slowly.

In 1675 Pope Clement X called a preparatory congregation to discuss whether miracle validation was necessary, or the 205 Martyrs of Japan could be exempted of that condition, as had traditionally been the case for verified martyrs. He seemed inclined to proceed with the beatification without requiring the verification of

16 E. Serrano Martin, "La Santidad en la Edad Moderna: límites, normativa y modelos para la sociedad", *Historia Social*, 91, 2018, 149–166, on pp. 156–157.

17 H. Cieslik, "The case of Christovao Ferreira", *Monumenta Nipponica* 29/1 (1974) 1–54, on p. 46.

18 C. Tronu, "The rivalry between the Jesuits and the Mendicant orders in Nagasaki at the end of the sixteenth century and the beginning of the seventeenth century", *Agora* 12 (2015) 25–39.

19 Letter of Diego Collado dated 31 May 1636. APF SOCG col. 107, f.50r–50v cited in H. Omata Rappo, *Des Indes lointaines*, 173. To appease their enemies, after 1652 Jesuits claimed Ferreira had retracted his apostasy and had consequently been tortured until death. He was included in hagiographies by Philippe Alegambe in 1657 and by Matthias Tanner in 1675, but after 1680, as anti-Jesuit literature increased, Ferreira's martyrdom was considered a construed lie to hide his scandalous apostasy. H. Omata Rappo, *Des Indes lointaines*, 175–176.

20 F. Villaroel, *Lorenzo Ruiz*, 155. H. Omata Rappo, *Des Indes lointaines*, 177.

miracles, but he died of illness the following year before doing so.[21] Under his successor, Innocent XI, a list recognizing the martyrs of Japan (excluding Ferreira) was published in 1687, but no beatification followed.[22] No further advances are reported during the eighteenth century. The Church had to face the crisis caused by the Enlightenment and the French Revolution, and missionary work in Japan was discontinued until the mid-nineteenth century. In 1858, although the ban on Christianity in Japan had not yet been lifted, Catholic missionaries were allowed to reside in Japan as chaplains of the incipient foreign community. This prompted a renewed interest in Japan and its martyrs, and within a few years, in 1862, the 26 Martyrs of Japan were made saints.[23] After their canonization, the Postulators of the four religious orders with candidates in the 205 martyrs' cause asked Pope Pius IX to restart the cause. The Spinola family, cardinals and bishops from Europe and apostolic vicars in Asia also send their petitions and the cause was finally opened.

The third and fourth causes for martyrs of Japan were Dominican and Augustinian enterprises to recognize martyrs of Japan died after 1632, who had been excluded of the second cause because of the Ferreira controversy. The second cause was initially for 17 martyrs executed in three different occasions, between 1633 and 1637, including four Dominican priests and their entourage of local clergy and laity. In this case two local inquiries were carried out soon after their death, in Macau (1636) and Manila (1637), but only for Dominicans.[24] Lay members were added later in an inquiry held in Macao in 1639. This third enquiry was submitted to Rome in 1663, and although a congregation met in 1575 to discuss the need of validation of the miracles, no request for an apostolic inquiry was issued by the Vatican, and in 1687 this cause too was stopped.[25] Although in the nineteenth century, after the 1867 beatification of the 205, the Dominicans renewed the bid for the third cause of martyrs of Japan, there were no further advances because at the time the Dominican Postulator was busy with several open canonization processes related to other group causes for East Asian martyrs. After five causes of martyrs of China and Vietnam were successfully closed in 1951, things started to move forward for the third cause for martyrs of Japan and in 1959 a canonical inquiry was carried out in Nagasaki to testify about the continuation of their fame of martyrdom.[26] Along the process, the Spanish Dominican priest Juan de los Ángeles Rueda OP was left out of the group because there was not satisfactory historical information

21 J. Boero, *Relación de la Gloriosa Muerte*, 177.

22 H. Omata Rappo, *Des Indes lointaines*, 181–182.

23 J. Boero, *Los Doscientos Cinco Mártires del Japón*, 168.

24 F. Villaroel, *Lorenzo Ruiz*, 128–129.

25 F. Villaroel, *Lorenzo Ruiz*, 156.

26 F. Villaroel, *Lorenzo Ruiz*, 158.

on the circumstances of his death,[27] but in 1981, only two years after the historical study (*positio*) had been submitted, the rest of the members were beatified. In 1987, after a miracle by the 16 Martyr Blessed of Japan in the Philippines was validated by the Vatican, they were canonized.[28] Together with the 26 martyrs of the first cause, these are the only sanctified martyrs of Japan at present. The fourth cause was put forward by the Augustinians for 2 Augustinian priests died in 1632 in Nagasaki. They were beatified in Rome in 1989, two years after the canonization of the 16 saints. With these four causes all the foreign missionaries executed in Japan for whom enough historical data were available had been canonized. The following causes would focus on the Japanese laity and clergy.

The fifth and sixth causes, started in the twentieth century were presented in the early twenty-first century, in 2004 for 188 Japanese martyrs died between 1603 and 1639, and in 2008 for Takayama Ukon, who died in 1615. The 188 Japanese martyrs were beatified in 2008, and Takayama Ukon in 2017. Changes in the canonization procedures after the Second Vatican Council made the process simpler and required local dioceses to assume the leadership. Therefore, this causes were not the enterprise of missionary orders anymore, but of several Japanese dioceses, although Jesuit priests and Immaculate Heart of Mary's nuns were part of the historical committee that prepared the cause documents, and the postulators in charge were Augustinian and Jesuit respectively.[29] Having said that, and with no intention to diminish the role and efforts of the Japanese bishops and the local commissions to disseminate and gather funds for the beatification causes, the history of the cause starts in 1981, when the Vatican prompted the Japanese Council of Bishops to start preparing the cause for the many unrecognized lay martyrs, on the occasion of the visit of Pope Jean Paul II to the Philippines and Japan for the

---

27 His companions were arrested, exiled, imprisoned, and executed after a judicial sentence by Japanese magistrates, but Juan de los Ángeles Rueda OP, after being arrested, while being taken away into exile by ship by Japanese officials, must have been thrown into the sea. Therefore, he died by drowning, without a previous sentence, trial, or imprisonment, which are usually requirements for the recognition of martyrdom. J. Delgado García (ed.), *Fr Juan de los Ángeles Rueda, O.P. Misionero itinerante en el Japón del siglo XVII. Cartas y Relaciones* (Madrid: Institutos de Filosofía y Teología Santo Tomás, 1999) 35.

28 Holy See, Canonizations during the Pontificate of His Holiness John Paul II, The Holy See Website https://www.vatican.va/news_services/liturgy/saints/ns_lit_doc_19871018_ruiz-compagni_en.html last retrieved 10 July 2022.

29 Congregatione de Causis Sanctorum, *Beatificationis seu declarationis martyrii servorum Dei Petri Kibe Kasui, sacerdotis professi Societatis Iesu et CLXXXVII sociorum sacerdotum, religiosorum, et Christifidelium laicorum in odium fidei, uti fertur, interfectorum, annis 1603–1639: positio super martyrio* (Roma: Nova Res, 2004) 19; Congregatione de Causis Sanctorum, *Tokiensis beatificationis seu declarationis martyrii servi Dei Iusti Takayama Ukon viri laici in odium fidei, uti fertur, interfecti (†3 februarii 1615): positio super martyrio* (Roma: Nova Res, 2015) 153–154.

beatification of the 16 Martyrs of Japan.[30] Among the 188 candidates, three Japanese priests had been included in seventeenth century inquiries, when clergy was the main target of missionary orders' canonization efforts, but they had been excluded from the second cause because they had been executed after 1632.

The cause for Takayama Ukon, who died in exile in 1615, only 40 days after arriving to Manila. was not open until after the second world war, but his sainthood was envisioned by Jesuits in Manila already in 1634. They organized a local inquiry in Manila to gather data for his canonization, but the plan did not go forward, because the prohibition of Christianity and the closure of the Japanese ports to Spanish and Portuguese ships made impossible a local inquiry in Japan, where Ukon had lived most of his life. In 1930 the Japanese Church decided to promote the cause, but canonization procedures established that the cause should be presented by the diocese in which the martyrs had died. Since he had spent most of his life in Japan, in 1940 the Catholic Bishop's Conference of Japan requested a transfer of competence for this cause from the Archdiocese of Manila to the Diocese of Osaka, which was formalized in 1964.[31] This cause was different from the previous causes related to Japan, because it was presented *per viam virtutem* (not *per viam martyrium*) since the candidate's cause of death was illness. Nevertheless, in 1995 another transfer was petitioned to the Tokyo diocese, with the intention to demonstrate Ukon's formal and material martyrdom. In 2011 the cause was officially changed into a martyr's cause and three years later in 2017 he was beatified in Osaka.[32]

At present, the only cause that has been thoroughly examined from an academic and multidisciplinary approach is that of the 26 martyrs. The monograph by Hitomi Omata Rappo is a pioneer work, that examines not only the canonization process, but also the historiography and iconography of the 26 martyrs, and their image in European theatre plays. Monographic academic studies are desirable for all of the causes, but while causes are still open, this is, for those who have not yet been recognized as saints, the documentation is kept at the archive of the Congregation for the Cause of Saints and is not easy to access. An in-depth study for each cause is beyond the scope of this paper, which only aims at a preliminary comparative analysis of the profiles of the saints and the blessed of Japan.

---

30 Congregatione de Causis Sanctorum, *Beatificationis seu declarationis martyri*, 41–44.

31 Congregatione de Causis Sanctorum, *Tokiensis beatificationis*, VII–VIII.

32 Congregatione de Causis Sanctorum, *Tokiensis beatificationis*, VIII–IX.

Profiles of the Martyr Saints of Japan

Profiling the martyrs of Japan is a challenging task, because of the high number of data (42 saints and 473 blessed) and because collective causes for martyrs often include individuals for whom detailed data and not available.[33] In the search for specificities and trends in the profile of the martyrs of Japan and aiming for an overarching survey that considers not only the saints, but also the blessed martyrs of Japan recognized to the present day, I will present succinctly their profiles looking mainly at gender, country of origin or ethnicity, religious status (clergy *vs.* laity) and religious affiliation (diocesan *vs.* the four missionary orders active in Japan). I mention age (adults *vs.* children) and social class only occasionally, since data are scarce. Demographic data for the first two causes have been collected from the lists in the beatification and canonization bulls,[34] and for the rest of causes from the Vatican website.[35]

Previous scholarship on early modern saints in Europe provides as the most common profile a male Italian or Spanish aristocratic cleric, more specifically a Franciscan friar.[36] Among the 26 Martyr Saints of Japan, we can identify four male Spanish Franciscans, whose profile coincides with that of the Europe saints, living aside the aristocratic origin, which is not obvious for all cases. Pedro Bautista was the Superior of the Franciscans in Japan at the time of his execution, as well as the ambassador of the Spanish Governor in the Philippines, so that it can be undoubtedly considered a member of the elite within the Franciscan mission and in the Philippine colonial community. There are, however, other profiles in this group, that show certain diversity in terms of ethnicity and religious status (see table 1 below). On the one side, there are two male Franciscan friars who came to Japan with the Spanish friars but are not Spanish. One is Felipe de Jesús, a Mexican *criollo* (born in Mexico of Spanish parents) and the other one is Gonzalo Garcia, a mestizo born to a Portuguese man and an Indian woman. On the other, there are 20 Japanese laymen in the group. They were not initially meant to be executed, since only foreign missionaries were the target of the expulsion edict banning evangelization

33 Previous studies on sainthood profiles do not take into account the groups of martyrs. M.J. Walsh, "Pope John Paul II and His Canonisations", in P. Clarke and T. Claydon (ed.), *Saints and Sanctity* (Woodbridge: Boydell, 2011) 415–437 on pp. 424, 433.

34 L. Magnino, *Pontificia Nipponica. Le Relazioni tra la Santa Sede e il Giappone attraverso i documenti pontificii. Parte Prima (secc. XVI-XVIII)* (Roma: Officium Libri Catholici, 1947); L. Magnino, *Pontificia Nipponica. Le Relazioni tra la Santa Sede e il Giappone attraverso i documenti pontificii. Parte Seconda (secc. XIX–XX)* (Roma: Officium Libri Catholici, 1948).

35 Holy See, Canonisations during the Pontificate of His Holiness John Paul II, The Holy See Website https://www.vatican.va/news_services/liturgy/saints/ns_lit_doc_19871018_ruiz-compagni_en.html last retrieved on 10 July 2022.

36 P. Burke, "How to be a Counter-Reformation Saint".

on which basis they were arrested. However, they were finally executed together with the missionaries, as an example, to dissuade the Japanese commoners from supporting missionary activity. In early modern Europe they were exoticized as the first 'coloured' saints from the mission field.[37] Among them, the most abundant profile is that of the fourteen male Japanese commoner laymen collaborators of the Franciscans in Kyoto and Osaka. There are also three male Japanese commoner lay children, who were the sons of three of the Japanese lay collaborators,[38] and three male Japanese Jesuit clerics. The later were in fact Jesuit collaborators who were not formally accepted as members of the Society of Jesus until after they were arrested. Some even consider they were arrested by mistake, since they were not helping the public evangelization activities of the Franciscans, and therefore did not overrule Hideyoshi's edic, but they were given the same treatment as the Franciscan collaborators anyway. There are also one male Mexican *criollo* Franciscan cleric, and one male Indo-Portuguese *mestizo* Franciscan cleric.

The fact that this group includes not only local Japanese, but also a Mexican *criollo* Franciscan cleric, and an Indo-Portuguese, speaks of the connections of the Japanese mission with the Portuguese and Spanish imperial expansion. The Jesuits had approached Japan from India, through the Indic Ocean route under Portuguese patronage. In contrast, the Franciscans had just started to approach Japan from the Philippines, through the Atlantic-Pacific route under Spanish patronage. While there was no agreement regarding the official acceptance of local Japanese into the Society of Jesus and the clergy, in practice, the Jesuits listed many Japanese or mixed-race close collaborators as *dojuku* as dependents in their catalogues. The Indo-Portuguese Gonzalo Garcia had in fact come to Japan with the Jesuits, but joined the Franciscans later. The Mexican criollo Felipe de Jesús, had entered the Franciscan order in Mexico, but later left it and moved to the Philippines. There he wished to join the order again and even prepared to be ordained. On his way to Spain to be ordained as priest because there was no bishop in Manila at the time, his ship was stranded to Japan, where he was executed.[39] Therefore, he died before being ordained, but as a Franciscan friar. It must be noted that in the documentation

37 H. Omata Rappo, "How to make 'Colored' Japanese Counter-Reformation Saints".

38 There are precedents of beatification of children in early modern Europe. In 1588 Urban VII authorized the local cult of the Child 'martyr' Simonino of Trent (d. 1475). Ditchfield, 'Tridentine Worship and the Cult of Saints', p. 208 n. 17.

39 R. Kawata, "Mekishiko 'Sei Feriipe de Hesusu' nikansuru ichi kōsatsu [Investigation about Mexico's 'St Felipe de Jesús']" *Laten America Kenkyū Nenpō* 16 (1996) 60–96. R. J. Morgan, *Spanish American Saints and the Rhetoric of Identity 1600–1810* (Tucson: University of Arizona, 2002); C. Conover, "Saintly Biography and the Cult of San Felipe De Jesús in Mexico City, 1597–1697" *The Americas* 67/4 (2011) 441–466.

for this cause, affiliation to a specific religious order is provided for all the Japanese martyrs, both laymen and clerics.

Table 1: Profiles of the Japan Martyr Saints

a. 26 OFM & SJ Martyr Saints	**c. 16 OP Martyr Saints**
14 male Japanese Franciscan laity	4 male Japanese Dominican clergy
4 male Spanish Franciscan clergy	4 male Spanish Dominican clergy
3 male Japanese Jesuit clergy	3 male Japanese Dominican laity
3 male underage Japanese Franciscan laity	2 female Japanese Dominican laity
1 male Mexican *criollo* Franciscan clergy	1 male Italian Dominican clergy
1 male Indo-Portuguese *mestizo* Franciscan clergy	1 male French Dominican clergy
	1 male Filipino laity (Rosario)

If we look at the profiles of the 16 Martyr Saints, executed in three groups between 1633 and 1637, and canonized in 1987 (table 1), the two dominant profiles are four male Spanish Dominican clergy and four male Japanese Dominican clergy followed by three Japanese lay men (Dominican catechists or tertiaries) and two Japanese lay women (Dominican tertiaries Magdalena of Nagasaki and Marina of Ōmura, both of noble origin).[40] There were no women among the Japanese laity in the 26 Martyr Saints, so this group is more diverse in terms of gender. We also find diverse nationalities or ethnic origins: nine Japanese men and women, four Spaniards, one Frenchman, one Italian and a Filipino *mestizo*, the son to a Tagalog mother and a Chinese father (Lorenzo Ruiz). The Dominicans emphasized him as the protomartyr of the Philippines, and his cult is bigger in the Philippines than Japan. Saint Lorenzo Ruiz is especially popular within the Chinese community in Manila.[41] As for religious status, in this case all the members are affiliated to the Dominican Order in a way or another. The 10 clerics are all male friars, and all the lay are affiliated to the third Dominican Order. Two of the lay men were Dominican catechists, and the other one was an interpreter and guide for the Dominicans. The two women are Dominican tertiaries, members of the third Orde of St Francis, which in Japan often overlapped with members of the two

40 H. Nawata Ward, "Women in the Eyes of a Jesuit Between the East Indies, New Spain, and Early Modern Europe" in C.H. Lee (ed.), *Western Visions of the Far East in a Transpacific Age, 1522–1657* (London/New York: Routledge, 2017) 117–138 on p. 125.

41 Personal communication from C. H. Lee to the author, who asked her about the survey of popular religiosity of the Chinese community in Manila which she conducted for the preparation of one of the chapters in the book C. H. Lee, *Saints of Resistance. Devotions in the Philippines under early Spanish rule* (New York, Oxford University, 2021).

confraternities founded by the Dominicans. If we look at their ethnic background or country of origin, of the nine Dominican priest, four of them Spanish (Dominic Ibáñez de Erquicia, Lucas Alonso del Espíritu Santo, Anthony González, and Michel de Aozaraza), three Japanese priests (James Kyushei Tomonaga, Thomas Hioli and Vincent Shiwozuka), one Italian priest (Hyacinth Jordan Ansalone) and one French priest (William Courtet). Together with a Japanese Dominican co-operator brother (Francis Shoyemon), friars make for more than half of the members of the group. Laity is not the dominant profile, and also in this cause all the lay members are affiliated to a specific order, so that all the members are connected to the Dominicans.

The first non-European saints can be seen as a result of the transposition to the mission field of the Franciscan Order efforts to produce saints in the European context. Their zeal for having their members recognized as saints also explains why Franciscans consider Pedro Bautista the main martyr of the group. Bautista has exactly the same profile of most of the early modern Europe saints a Spanish male Franciscan cleric. While Jesuits are represented, the three Japanese Jesuits were officially accepted into the Society of Jesus after they were arrested and just before their execution. The belonging to the order of the 3 Japanese collaborator brothers, was therefore somewhat controversial, since it brought attention to the Jesuits' reticence and lack of consensus regarding official acceptance of natives into the Society. Initially, Jesuits had no intention to collaborate or provide any support for the cause, even doubting that these deaths could be considered martyrdom. This was partly due to the antagonism between Jesuits and Franciscans, and partly because the Society of Jesus prioritized the causes of Ignatius of Loyola, its founder, and Francis Xavier, one of the founding members and leader of the Jesuit Asian missions. However, after the beatification of Loyola and Xavier, the Jesuits joined forces with the mendicants for the cause for the 205 martyrs of Japan, which included 33 of the Society members.

In sum, the profile of the 42 Japanese Martyr Saints is diverse in ethnicity, gender, age, religious status and religious affiliation. Such diversity reflects the historical background of the Japanese mission, in which 4 religious orders were active, and the structure of Japanese society and its laws, that not only condemned the foreign missionaries but also their local collaborators and their family members. Also, the inclusion of lay female martyrs in the 16 Dominican Martyr Saints of Japan, speak of the Catholic Church emphasis and interest in the laity in the second half of the twentieth century. In this two causes the Franciscans and the Dominicans took the initiative, and the canonization of members of their order and their companions was the main incentive. The canonization of the 26 Martyr Saints and the 16 Martyr Saints can be considered, borrowing Espinoza Rúa's expression, a means for 'corporative promotion', that Espinoza identifies as an important objective of early modern hagiographies of potential lay native saints written by missionary orders with the objective to promote role models for the local population.[42] Although clergy was prioritized by the religious orders who put forward the causes, some of the lay martyr saints of Japan have played an important role outside Japan. On the one side, Felipe de Jesús was given a central role in Mexican criollo identity and later as the patron saint of Mexico, and Lorenzo Ruiz, as the Filipino protomartyr, has been given a central role in the Filipino Church, as suggested by the fact that his canonization was confirmed on the 400th anniversary of the establishment of the archbishopric of Manila. On the other side, the Recollect Augustinians have made Saint Magdalena of Nagasaki the patron saint of the Augustinian Third Order all over the world. Although we have not been able to deepen into the personalities of each of the Saints of Japan, we have presented their dominant and minoritarian profiles. Will different profiles, objectives and phenomena emerge if we consider the profiles of martyrs of Japan that are not yet sains, but have been beatified?

Profiles of the Martyr Blessed of Japan

When looking into the country of origin (or ethnic origin), like among the saints, also among the blessed the number of Japanese is higher than the number of European and other minority ethnic groups. While in the 205 Blessed, the proportion of Japanese is 75%, all the martyrs in the 188 are Japanese. While this could be seen as a decrease in ethnic diversity, it shows a clear trend towards prioritizing the representation of the local Japanese Church. The emphasis in the cause of the 188 Blessed Japanese Martyrs is not anymore on affiliation to religious orders or confraternities, but on regional inclusivity. They martyrs are grouped according to their execution places, representing nine of the current sixteen Catholic dioceses of Japan. I want to mention that there are at seven male Koreans among the 205 blessed, four of them affiliated to the Dominicans, one to the Franciscans and one to the Jesuits. They were the first Korean ever blessed, but Korean martyrs who died in Korea in the nineteenth century are more popular in Korea.[43] Nevertheless, the presence of Koreans among the 205 Japanese Martyr Blessed accounts for the Korean communities in early modern Japan, especially among the Christian communities in Kyushu.[44]

---

42 C. A. Espinoza Rúa, "Un indio camino a los altares: santidad e influencia inquisitorial en el caso del «siervo de Dios» Nicolás de Ayllón" *Historica* 36/1 (2012) 135–180, on p. 141.

43 Pope Pius XI beatified 103 Korean martyrs in 1926. They were canonized in 1984 by Pope John Paul II, and one of them, Andrew Kim Taegon, became the patron Saint of Korea. In 2014 Pope Francis beatified a group of 124 Korean martyrs.

44 In Nagasaki, for example, the Korean community had its own church and confraternity. C. Tronu, "Anti-Christian Measures in Nagasaki during the Early Edo Period (1914–44)", in S. Kock/B.Pickl-

The proportion of women among the blessed, is around 10% in the 205 Blessed Martyrs and the 16 Saints, but it reaches 33% in the 188 Blessed Martyrs. Of course, part of the female blessed were allegedly executed because they were related to male martyrs as spouses, widows, mothers, or daughters, but both causes include women that were not executed as relatives of male Christians, but because of their own religious beliefs and their refusal to recant. As is the case of the two Japanese female saints mentioned above, their role within their Christian community as catechists, tertiaries of the mendicant orders, or members of lay confraternities is emphasized. We can say that the increase of female martyrs is a consequence of the increase of lay martyrs since there was no recognized female clergy in the Japanese mission, which leads us to the discussion on religious status and affiliation.

The 205 Blessed include martyrs from 32 different execution episodes, in which all the four missionary orders are represented both among the clergy (33 Jesuits, 21 Dominicans, 18 Franciscans and 5 Augustinians) and the laity (24 Dominicans, 11 Franciscans, 7 Jesuits and 6 Augustinians). There are many cases in which it is difficult to provide a single affiliation for the laity, since belonging to more than one confraternity or third order (either simultaneously or at different moments in life), was not unusual at the time, especially among the mendicant lay organizations.[45] In contrast, in the cause for the 188 Blessed, the emphasis is not anymore on affiliation to religious orders or confraternities, but in regional inclusivity regarding the site of martyrdom, gender, social class, profession and age.[46] A shift in focus can be seen, from the missionary orders (foreign clergy) and their acolytes (affiliated Japanese laity) to the local secular Church (Japanese laity and diocesan clergy).

In general, laity is higher than clergy in almost all the causes. Only in the case of the 16 saints the proportion of laity is less than half. For the 26 Saints and the 205 Blessed, the proportion of laity is close to two thirds. But the 188 Blessed are mainly lay men and women, a striking 98%, and the only individual cause so far is for a layman (Takayama Ukon). Therefore, the general trend is a clear increase of the proportion of laity over clergy. Here it should be noted that in the early modern missionary context in Japan, the incipient local Church depended on royal patronage and missionary orders were in charge not only of evangelization in the frontier but also of pastoral care of the established communities, and even in charge of parishes.[47] In this context, religious orders were eager to provide lay martyrs with an affiliation, even if only formalized after their arrest or imprisonment. This

---

Kolaczia/B. Scheid (ed.), *Religion, Power, and the Rise of Shinto in Early Modern Japan* (London: Bloomsbury, 2021) 47–60, on p. 49.

45 J. Boero, *Relación de la gloriosa muerte*, 166.

46 Congregatione de Causis Sanctorum, *Beatificationis seu declarationis*, 43.

47 On the missionary orders' function in and disputes about the parish system in early modern Nagasaki see C. Tronu, "The Post-Tridentine parish system in the port city of Nagasaki" in N. Amsler/A. Badea/

can be understood as a way for the orders to demonstrate local support, which was an asset in the constant rivalries and disputes between Jesuits and mendicants in early modern Japan. In contrast, in causes started in modern times that is not the case anymore. On the contrary, nowadays, in a very different context, in which the Japanese Church Hierarchy is well-established, the Japanese dioceses claim lay men and women as martyrs on their own right. Thus, the increase of recognized lay martyrs points at bigger questions such as the importance given to the laity after the Second Vatican Council, both in the mission field and in the Catholic Church in general.

Conclusion

The overview of the demographic data of the 42 Japan Martyr Saints (26 canonized in 1867 and 16 in 1989) reveals that the most common profiles among canonized martyrs of Japan are male Japanese laity affiliated to a mendicant order and European (mainly Spanish) male mendicant clerics. However, a few minority profiles stand out because of their significance outside Japan. These are, first, San Felipe de Jesús, a Mexico-born Spanish criollo saint, the first Latin-American saint, made patron saint of Mexico. Second, Gonçalo García, an India-born Indo-Portuguese *mestizo*, first Indian-born saint, as well as the first mixed-race saint. Third, Lorenzo Ruiz, the first Filipino saint, and a mixed-race Tagalog Chinese *mestizo*. And finally, the first Asian female saints, Saint Magdalena de Nagasaki and Saint Marina of Omura, both canonized in 1989, who are also the first Japanese female saints. Saint Magdalena of Nagasaki has been made the patron saint of the Third Order of the Recollect Augustinians, quite popular in Latin America. When looking at the six causes for martyrs of Japan, including the blessed, the trend is an increasing proportion of Japanese martyrs, which implies the increase of lay martyrs and female martyrs.

Among the blessed martyrs of Japan, we can see a shift from foreign regular clergy of the four religious orders who were active in early modern Japan (Jesuits, Franciscans, Dominicans, and Augustinians) and their Japanese collaborators or affiliated laity, into local (Japanese) laity and diocesan clergy. A geographical shift is also evident, from a focus on Kyushu to an interest in representing as many as possible regions and present-day dioceses of Japan. In other words, we see a shift from 'martyrs of Japan' to 'Japanese martyrs.' This can be explained partly by the changes in the leadership of the canonization processes. The first fourth causes were put forward by Europe-based religious orders. In the case of the second cause for

B. Heyberger/C. Windler (ed.), *Catholic Missionaries in Early Modern Asia. Patterns of Localization* (2020) 83–95.

the 205 Martyr Blessed of Japan, the orders enjoyed the support of noble relatives of martyrs like the Dominican Alonso Navarrete or the Jesuit Carlo Spinola, and secular authorities such as the Spanish and Portuguese kings, the Austrian emperor and the Genoa city council.[48] In contrast, for the fifth and sixth causes opened after the Second Vatican Council, where the importance of the local Church was recognised, the canonization process was put forward by local (Japanese) Catholic bishops and dioceses. Thus, we can conclude that the profiles of the martyrs reflect both the structures of the early modern Church and the early modern Japanese society, but the trends seen in the diachronic analysis of the profiles of the Japan saints and blessed recognized across five centuries reflect the changes in the Catholic Church and society at large.

The Congregation of Propaganda Fide in charge of the missions, in the Jesuit experiences in Asia, envisioned the emphasis on local diocesan clergy already in the seventeenth century, inspired. It was also a way to gain direct authority in the mission field and the new dioceses and put an end to the model of Iberian royal patronage of religious missionary orders, which had proven inefficient in territories outside the colonial sphere.[49] This shift in the missionary paradigm encountered resistance, for example in India, where the Portuguese empire perdured, but in Japan resistance was not possible because of the clear cut between the early modern and the modern missions. Due to the systematic ban on Christianity by the Japanese government from 1614, missionary work by religious orders was discontinued in the mid seventeenth century and when Japan was forced to allow Catholic missions again in the mid nineteenth century, the Vatican put the diocesan missionary clergy (Missions Etrangères de Paris) in charge. In 1890 the Japanese Hierarchy was established, and the Catholic religious orders approached Japan already in the twentieth century, finding new motivation and opportunities for reactivating the early modern canonization processes for their members.

The profiles of the Japanese martyrs resonate with the growing concern to acknowledge diversity and compensate for ethnocentrism, sexism, and classism. The shift from European male clergy to Japanese male clergy and both male and female laity shows the concern of the Church for an inclusive and naturalized sainthood. However, the absence of female clergy is striking. In her study of female models of sainthood in the Japanese translation of Lives of Saints published by the Jesuit Press in the late sixteenth century, Haruko Nawata Ward brings attention to the Japanese female Christian congregation in Kyoto referred in Jesuit sources as the 'Miyako *bikuni*', this is, the nuns of Kyoto, since *bikuni* is the Japanese word for (Buddhist) 'nuns'. She argues that by self-organizing a nunnery, Japanese women

---

48 J. Boero, *Relación de la gloriosa muerte*, 176.

49 H. Rzepkowski, "Asia" in H. Burkle (ed.) *La Misión de la Iglesia* (Valencia: Edicep, 2022), 243–304.

overcame the ban on female members in in the Society of Jesus. While Jesuits did not create a female branch, they supported and trained this informal community of Japanese Christian nuns.[50] Julia Naito, a former Buddhist nun, was their leader, and might as well have inspired the character of the learned Christian nun in the *Myotei Mondo*, a manuscript refutation in Japanese language of Buddhism, Shintoism and Confucianism in the form of a dialog between a Christian nun and a Buddhist nun.[51] Like Takayama Ukon, the 'Miyako *bikuni*' were expelled to Manila in 1614, where they continued their religious way of life. Like Takayama Ukon, Julia Naito was considered by contemporary sources in the Philippines as an example of virtue and 'sanctity'.[52] Whether Julia Naito provides the missing profile of Japanese female clergy might be controversial, since neither the Jesuits nor the bishop ever formalized her status as a Catholic nun. Nevertheless, her case raises questions on the role and status of female clergy within the Catholic Church, which as of today rejects the petitions to allow female priesthood and condemns the grass-roots initiatives in that direction.[53]

---

50 H. Nawata Ward, "Translating Christian martyrdom in Buddhist Japan in the early modern Jesuit mission" in N. Terpstra (ed.), *Global Reformations. Transforming Early Modern Religions, Societies, and Cultures* (London/New York: Routledge, 2019) 33–51, on p. 42.

51 J. Baskind/R. Bowring (ed.), *The Myōtei Dialogues: A Japanese Christian Critique of Native Traditions* (Leiden: Brill, 2015).

52 H. Nawata Ward, "Translating Christian martyrdom", 42.

53 J. Ratzinger, *Decree on the Attempted Ordination of Some Catholic Women*, December 21, 2002, in *Acta Apostolicae Sedis* 95 (2003) 271–273.

Linda Zampol D'Ortia

Emotional Practices of Catholic Martyrdom in Early Modern Japan

> He showed so much happiness that, as the path was uneven and the night very dark[1] … most [of the guards] stumbled, but [Arakawa Adán][2] walked with such levity that he was nearly dragging them after himself. Kneeling, he prayed devoutly; with two strikes they cut his head: because it was night, the first hit a shoulder and the holy man, without swaying, waited for the second, calling out loud: "Iesus, Iesus." The Gentiles said that after his head had fallen, it called twice the holy name of Jesus, so loud that it was heard throughout the valley: frightened by this, they said that it was sufficient to see the perseverance and happiness he showed when dying, to make one Christian; nor was it possible that a person who died like this would not be saved.[3]

This text fragment is part of a narrative of martyrdom that was written in Japan by a Jesuit missionary and then sent to Europe as a letter. It belongs to a vast corpus of Jesuit documents that strove to present the persecutions suffered by the Catholic communities of Japan under the Tokugawa shogunate. The letters that were sent to Europe and other Catholic centres in Asia and the Americas certainly represent the most extensive output in terms of overall production of martyrdom narratives in Japan: printed editions were translated into different languages and were widely disseminated across the Catholic world.[4]

---

1 The research for this paper has received funding from the European Union's Horizon 2020 Research and Innovation Programme under the Marie Skłodowska-Curie grant agreement No 101028277.

2 Arakawa Adán (approx. 1554–1614; beatified 2008) had been a lay helper of the Jesuit mission of Shiki (Amakusa). Being a pious and experienced old man, he was chosen to be the spiritual leader and catechist of the Christian community after the expulsion of the missionaries to Nagasaki. He was arrested, tortured, and then executed on the 5th of June 1614 (J. Ruiz de Medina, *El martirologio del Japón, 1558–1873* (Rome: Institutum Historicum Societatis Iesu, 1999), 332.)

3 *Relacion de la persecucion que huuo estos años contra la Iglesia de Japon y los ministros della* (Zaragoza: Juan de Larumbe, 1617), 102.

4 For instance, in the first half of the seventeenth century, more than 430 titles were printed in Europe on the topic of the persecutions in Japan (A. Fernandes Pinto, *Tragédia mais gloriosa que dolorosa. O discurso missionário sobre a perseguição aos cristãos no regime Tokugawa na imprensa europeia (1598–1650)*, Universidade Nova de Lisboa, 2014). Doctoral dissertation.) For publications in Spanish, see R. Roldán-Figueroa, *The Martyrs of Japan. Publication History and Catholic Missions in the Spanish World (Spain, New Spain, and the Philippines, 1597–1700)* (Leiden, Boston: Brill, 2021).

However, missionary correspondence is not the only source of information about the model of sanctity and martyrdom that developed in Japan. The *Kirishitan-ban* corpus, comprised of the titles printed in Japan by the Jesuit press, also offers important details.[5] In addition, as will be considered below, some of the documents that belonged to the depository of the so-called hidden Christians (*kakure* or *senpuku kirishitan*) survived in manuscript copies and also offer insights into the development of this model of martyr.

This paper will analyse this varied collection of written documents to identify the model of sanctity achieved through martyrdom that developed in Japan, with a focus on the emotional practices that were attributed to it. The emotional practices of Jesuits and Japanese Christians will be investigated by following the approach proposed by Monique Scheer, which is to consider the bodily practices that aim to mobilise, regulate, communicate emotions, passions, feelings, etc.[6] The fact that Jesuits and Japanese Christians could recognise these emotions in others, through these practices, says more about their shared values about emotions than what was "really" felt in that moment. This paper will show that this model was widely disseminated throughout a Catholic community consisting of Japanese laity and Jesuit missionaries of both European and Japanese origins. Finally, it will illustrate how this exemplar depictions were fundamentally marked by their emotional practices, as suggested by the above quotation: together with their blood, the emotions displayed by the martyrs, too, could become "the seed of the Church", as the famous expression by Tertullian goes.

The Origins of the Model

The Catholic mission in Japan was founded in 1549 by Jesuit Francis Xavier under the patronage of the Portuguese Crown.[7] The missionaries immediately identified the Japanese people as an excellent target for evangelisation, describing them as rational and curious about religious matters. After a challenging start, partly due to instability caused by the civil war that had been fragmenting Japan since 1464, the mission began to thrive in the 1570s, thanks to the financial and political support of the Portuguese silk trade with Macao. At the beginning of this decade, the Christian

5 On the Kirishitan-ban corpus, see Y. Orii, "The Dispersion of Jesuit Books Printed in Japan: Trends in Bibliographical Research and in Intellectual History", *Journal of Jesuit Studies* 2 (2015) 189–207.

6 M. Scheer, "Are Emotions a Kind of Practice (and Is That What Makes Them Have a History)? A Bourdieuian Approach to Understanding Emotion", *History and Theory* 51 (2012) 193–220. The term "emotion" is thus used in this paper as an umbrella term.

7 For an overview of the history of the mission, see M. Cooper, "A Mission Interrupted: Japan", in R. Po-chia Hsia (ed.), *A Companion to the Reformation World* (Oxford: Blackwell, 2004) 393–407.

port city of Nagasaki was founded in southern Japan and soon became the heart of the Christian presence in the country. This first period of missionary work was characterised by the intense support of Japanese helpers, most of whom had informal roles. The years after 1579, under Visitor Alessandro Valignano's policy of adaptation to Japanese culture and etiquette, were marked by a growth in the production of religious literature in the form of theological treatises, catechisms, and similar texts to guide and assist the Catholic community. During this period, more Japanese men acquired formal roles, and by the end of the century, they represented half of the members of the Society of Jesus in Japan. In addition, the daily activities of Christian communities were guided by lay leaders and members of confraternities, such as the Misericórdia.[8]

The seemingly positive relationship with the Japanese authorities suddenly came to an end when Toyotomi Hideyoshi, on his way to becoming the unifier of the country, banned the missionaries' evangelisation in 1587. The first phase of the persecutions, mostly sporadic and local, ended in 1597. The crucifixion of twenty-six missionaries and their Japanese lay helpers in Nagasaki marked the beginning of the second phase, which was characterised by a limited number of deaths and the growth of the Christian communities due to the arrival of mendicant preachers. The numerous mass executions in the following stage were initiated by the shogunate's complete ban on Christianity in 1612. Finally, between 1624 and 1650, the Japanese Christians were nearly annihilated, although further persecutions did happen as late as in the nineteenth century, targeting communities that had survived in hiding. The population was strictly controlled, with annual ceremonies of *fumi-e* (stepping on Christian icons) and mandatory Buddhist parish enrolment. The Sakoku edicts of 1633–1639 cut ties with all European nations except the local Dutch merchants, who were secluded on a small island in Nagasaki Bay. An estimate puts the number of martyrs at the height of the persecution, between 1614 and 1640, at around 4,000 out of a Christian population of approximately 300,000–400,000.[9]

Examples of martyrdom, as elaborated and communicated through the Catholic tradition, had been presented to the Japanese Christians by various didactic means. A significant educational tool was the rich literature on the lives of many martyrs of the early Christian period. While oral narrations of the lives of martyrs had been

8 See M.A. Üçerler, *The Samurai and the Cross. The Jesuit Enterprise in Early Modern Japan* (Oxford: Oxford University Press, 2022). J.F. Moran, *The Japanese and the Jesuits: Alessandro Valignano in Sixteenth-Century Japan* (London; New York: Routledge, 1993). On the confraternities, see J.P. Oliveira e Costa, "The Misericórdias Among Japanese Christian Communities in the 16th and 17th centuries", *Bulletin of Portuguese-Japanese Studies* 5 (2002) 67–79.

9 H. Nawata Ward, "Women Martyrs in Passion and Paradise", *Journal of World Christianity* 3, No. 1 (2010) 47–66.

circulating in the mission since its founding,[10] the most comprehensive example in this sense was *Sanctos no gosagueo no uchi nuqigaqi* (*Compendium of the Acts of the Saints*, Kazusa, 1591), the first text printed in Japan by the Jesuit press.[11] The final section of this publication was dedicated to the persecutions and resulting martyrdoms under Roman emperors, with an explanation of their importance in demonstrating the righteousness of the Christian faith. The narrations presented in this collection were translated, abridged, and re-elaborated from various textual sources, including Jacopo da Varazze's renowned thirteenth-century collection of saints' lives, *Legenda Aurea*, and *Introducción al Símbolo de la Fe* by Luis de Granada. Some elements that were present in the European stories were adapted or eliminated, arguably to adhere to Japanese sensibilities. The final product was the result of a collaboration between European missionaries and Japanese laypeople to create a text that would best suit the needs of the Christian community in Japan.[12] Printed explanations on the matter of martyrdom can also be found in Alessandro Valignano's *Catechismus Christianae Fidei*, published in 1586 for the use of missionaries, whose sixth *concio* elaborated on the point of the martyrs' importance as witnesses of the Christian faith.[13] The later *Fides no doxi* (*Guide to the Faith*, Amakusa, 1592), a partial translation of Granada's *Introducción*, exhorts the faithful to follow the examples of the ancient martyrs, while the martyrdom model par excellence, Jesus Christ, is presented in the Japanese translation of *Imitatio Christi*, or *Contemptus Mundi* (1581, earliest print in 1596 in Amakusa).[14] These texts offered representations of a martyrdom model that was not necessarily to be imitated to the point of death. While dying for the faith was a possibility, in the years in which the texts were translated and adapted, it was rather a remote one. Instead, the narratives aimed to depict these holy people as examples of religious perfection and were to be seen as sources of inspiration more than direct models.[15]

---

10 T. Gonoi, "*Kirishitan*: les chemins qui mènent au martyre. Pour une histoire des martyrs chrétiens du Japon", *Karthala* 11 (2009), 48.

11 E.M. Satow, *The Jesuit Mission Press in Japan, 1591–1610* (Privately printed, 1888), 1–12. For a complete list of texts on martyrdom composed in Japan see M. Anesaki, "Writings on Martyrdom in Kirishitan Literature", *Transactions of the Asiatic Society of Japan*, 2nd series, 8 (1931) 21–65, on pp. 21–22.

12 On the complex process of translating the *Sanctos*, see P. Jolliffe/A. Bianchi, "Jesuit Translation Practices in Sixteenth-Century Japan. *Sanctos no gosagueo no uchi nuqigaqi* and Luis de Granada", in J. Kiaer et al (ed.), *Missionary Translators. Translations of Christian Texts in East Asia* (London: Routledge, 2021) 29–51.

13 A. Valignano, *Catechismus Christianae Fidei* (Tokyo: Tenri Central Library, 1972 [facsimile of the 1586 edition]) 53–54.

14 Gonoi, "*Kirishitan*", 46–48.

15 As martyrdom as a complete fulfilment of a Christian life, see P.A. Fabre, "Conclusion: The Narrow Road to Martyrdom", *Journal of Jesuit Studies* 9, no. 1 (2022) 125–135, on p. 131.

With the beginning of the first organised persecutions, written Jesuit texts became, unsurprisingly, more focused on martyrdom and its mechanisms.[16] In 1597, as an answer to the twenty-six executions in Nagasaki, mission Vice-Provincial and theologian Pedro Gómez compiled a short treatise on the theme of dying for the faith, returning to some points he had already raised in his *Compendium*, which he had written for the local Jesuit college in Funai just a few years earlier. While this treatise is lost, its contents can be found in a later composition, conventionally titled *Exhortations to Martyrdom* (*Maruchiriyo no Susume*).[17] This latter text circulated among the hidden Christian communities at least until the end of the eighteenth century, when a copy was seized by the authorities in Urakami (Nagasaki). While its structure suggests that active persecutions were affecting the Christian community it was composed for, the general lack of urgency in its language points to a composition prior to their exacerbation, putting its creation around 1615. Another text relevant to the topic at hand, which was also confiscated in Urakami, is *Instructions on Martyrdom* (*Maruchiriyo no Kokoroe*); this shorter treatise was probably written at a later date than *Exhortations*, as it focuses on more practical aspects of martyrdom and contains repetitions that hint at the author's haste.[18] The last text on martyrdom found in Urakami was a compilation of three *vitae* of virgin female martyrs, *Mirror of Martyrdom* (*Maruchiriyo no Kagami*).[19]

These didactic texts of various kinds strove to present a model of sanctity that did not concede to violence in its proclamation of the faith. Unsurprisingly, central to the emotional state of the martyrdom model, as presented by this literature, is hope. For instance, explicit references to this theological virtue, which has strong roots in feelings,[20] can be found in *Sanctos no Gosagyou, Fides no Doxi* and *Instructions*.[21] *Instructions* and *Exhortations*, composed during the heat of persecution, were more inclined to mention emotional states and sometimes even emotional practices to

---

16 Anesaki, "Writings", 23–25.

17 Üçerler, *The Samurai*, 61–62; Gonoi, "*Kirishitan*", 51.

18 A Japanese critical edition of *Exhortations* is in A. Ebisawa (ed.), *Kirishitansho, Haiyasho* (Tokyo: Iwanami Shoten, 1970); *Instructions* is available in a partially critical edition in M. Anesaki, *Kirishitan shūmon no hakugai to senpuku*, (Tokyo: Dōbunkan, 1925). For this article, I have used the English translations taken from Anesaki, "Writings", except when indicated.

19 When compared to the narration of the same martyrdoms in the *Sanctos*, the style of the *Mirror* is more colloquial (H. Nawata Ward, "Images of the Incarnation in the Jesuit Japan Mission's Kirishitanban Story of Virgin Martyr St. Catherine of Alexandria", in W. Melion/L.P. Wandel (Ed.), *Image and incarnation: The early modern doctrine of the pictorial image* (Leiden: Brill, 2015) 489–509, on p. 495).

20 On the historically close connection between virtues and feelings developed in the Middle Ages, see B. Rosenwein, *Generations of Feeling. A History of Emotions, 600–1700* (Cambridge: Cambridge University Press, 2015), 67–87.

21 Anesaki, "Writings", 26; 28; 65.

guide future martyrs. The complete definition of hope in the context of martyrdom is indeed found in *Exhortations*: it is described as the "virtue of holding the hope that the afterlife is saved", i. e. hope to be saved after death.[22] *Exhortations* declared that hope would allow the faithful to endure the tortures they would suffer.[23] *Instructions*, with its more practical slant, suggested practices to mobilise this emotion: "While being tortured visualize the Passion of Jesus … the [angels] awaiting the coming of you [soul] … Hope and confidence should occupy your mind."[24] Far from being the only emotion mentioned in these treatises, hope often appears in emotional sequences[25] or, at least, in causal relation to other feelings: fortitude and joy are frequently mentioned, as is humility.

In addition to literary texts, Jesuit correspondence contains references to other didactic means, such as oral narrations of the lives of martyrs and saints, and mystery plays. Theatrical pieces often accompanied Christmas festivities: "Christmas is celebrated here with much happiness … [the Japanese Christians] performed many stories of the Holy Scriptures, containing much doctrine; chants and couplets are composed in the [Japanese] manner about these stories, and they sing them continuously."[26] During the celebrations of 1561 in Funai (Ōita), various religious stories were staged for the faithful: the fall of Adam and Eve, the hope of future salvation offered by the angel, the judgement of Solomon, and other scenes until the birth of Jesus. At Easter, the Christians portrayed the "past sorrows of the Passion", putting them into perspective with the subsequent "cheerfulness of the Resurrection",[27] two key elements also found in the martyrdom narrative. The main objective of these plays was didactic in a broader sense, aimed to console and edify the audience. Nevertheless, they represented examples of sacrifice whose perceptibility by and engagement of the senses could facilitate the assimilation of its underlining precepts by the faithful and even modify their attitude towards emotions.[28]

---

22 My translation from Ebisawa, *Kirishitansho*, 335.

23 Anesaki, "Writings", 47.

24 Anesaki, "Writings", 26.

25 Sequences are concatenations of emotions and their practices that put them in relation chronologically, allowing a better interpretation of their specifics (Rosenwein, *Generations*, 8).

26 Luis De Almeida to Antonio de Quadros, Japan, 1st October 1561, in J. Ruiz de Medina (ed.), *Documentos del Japón* (Rome: Instituto histórico de la Compañia de Jesús, 1995) vol. 2, 378.

27 This example refers to the 1562 Easter festivities of Funai (Aires Sanches to the Jesuits in India, Funai, 11th October 1562, in Ruiz de Medina (ed.), *Documentos* vol. 2, 526). On Christian music set to Japanese melodies, see M.H. Takao, "'In Their Own Way': Contrafactal Practices in Japanese Christian Communities during the 16th Century", *Early Music* 47, no. 2, (2019) 183–198.

28 R. Garrod, "Senecan Catharsis in Nicolas Caussin's Felicitas (1620): A Case Study in Jesuit Reconfiguration of Affects", in R. Garrod/Y. Haskell (ed.), *Changing Hearts. Performing Jesuit Emotions between Europe, Asia, and the Americas* (Leiden; Boston: Brill, 2019) 23–42, on p. 24.

The Embodiment of the Model

The previous section showed that an initial model of sanctity centred around martyrdom emerged from the didactic and general examples offered by Jesuit literature. This section will consider what forms this model took when it was embodied by the Japanese Christian community. The sources that facilitate this consideration are mainly Jesuit correspondence, from which it is also possible to track and describe which correct emotional practices were attributed to the model and how the latter circulated within the Japanese Christian community.

Persecutions represented fraught moments for the Christians in Japan, who faced uncertainty and fear of exile and death for themselves and their loved ones. Previously used as general models of sanctity to follow in everyday life,[29] the martyrdom narratives found in the literary canon provided the community with the tools to face this threat, suddenly more concrete, by renewing and resignifying them within the changing historical context. The models offered by the ancient martyrs assumed a new relevance because of the similar circumstances of persecution from which the models had emerged. Negative emotions, such as fear, were resisted by recuperating from this repository the understanding of persecution as both God's gift to Christians to provide them with an occasion to earn salvation, and as a call to arms against Evil.[30] *Exhortations* states: "[Christians] are persecuted seem[ingly] against reason, yet it is the device of [God], its beneficial effects being profound and infinite."[31] As it happened in other exceptional situations, the believers were assured that God would grant them a special grace to sustain them during their future trials as long as they kept their faith: "[the gifts of Grace and baptism] are given for your service in exalting the glories of Jesus in the battles to rage in a reign of persecution."[32] Emotional practices of daily life were held to be even more effective in mobilising and regulating feelings: extraordinary grace, thus, allowed for extraordinary effects. For example, fortitude born from hope (as defined above) was one of the most common forms that this emotional resilience took. Another emotion that frequently poured from the hope of future salvation, signalling the bestowal of this special grace, was joy. This is a typical example from the beginning of the description of the martyrdom of Takeda Giovanna and Takeda Agnese, who died on the 9th of December 1603 in Yatsushiro (Kumamoto, Kyūshū):

---

29 Consider, for instance, the examples of the Virgin Martyrs, who were primarily used to exhort Japanese women to avoid premarital and extramarital sexual relations.

30 This framing is present, for example, in the *Fides no Doxi* (Anesaki, "Writings", 28).

31 Anesaki, "Writings", 37.

32 Anesaki, "Writings", 47. See also B.S. Gregory, *Salvation at Stake. Christian Martyrdom in Early Modern Europe* (Cambridge: Harvard University Press, 1999) 286–87.

> "Ladies, be in good spirits, because I heard that … you will receive the same death [of Takeda Simone]."[33] … Giovanna and Agnese dried their tears at once and, full of joy as if they had received a very happy news, said: "What are you saying, sir, that we too must die? So, there is no reason to be sad, thinking that we sinners were not deserving of this favour."[34]

As this example illustrates, the practices that communicated and named the emotions felt by future martyrs signposted the beginning of the narrative of martyrdom proper. The two women in question were then recognised by the witnesses as receivers of the martyr's special grace through the emotional practices they were displaying:

> Their happiness was so extraordinary, so devout and wonderful the words that came out of their mouths … that the Holy Spirit was clearly visible harbouring in their breasts … The three [*jihiyakusha*[35] saw that] the Holy Spirit harboured in the hearts of these women, as, there by themselves, they showed a calm demeanour (*animo riposato*).[36]

If the emotional sequence present here is considered, it appears that the martyrdom model paired hope and fortitude with joy and interior peace. The practices of joy and fortitude thus imparted a certain composure and "calm demeaneour", too.

The Circulation of the Model

The process of embodiment and resignification of the model was sustained by the circulation of the same throughout the Christian community. The stories contained in *Kirishitan-ban* literature were, undoubtedly, used by many Christians as a precedent to imitate before and during the trials, as this episode illustrates:

> In the meantime, Agnese took a devotional book of holy Martyrs, written in Japanese, and gave it to [the *jihiyakusha*] Michele, to read [out loud] … She [then] said … "Oh,

33 Simone Takeda Gohyoe, Giovanna's son and Agnese's husband, was a Christian nobleman, who had been decapitated just before his family was condemned to death. On this group, see Ruiz de Medina, *El martirologio*, 298–300.

34 *Relatione della gloriosa morte, Patita da sei Christiani Giaponesi per la fede di Christo alli 25. di Genaro 1608* (Fermo: appresso Giovanni Bonibello, 1609), 57.

35 The *jihiyakusha* were representatives of the brotherhood of the Misericórdia dedicated to charity works (Costa, "The Misericórdias"), who gave spiritual support to fellow Christians during the trials of martyrdom, for which they also had the role of witness.

36 *Relatione della gloriosa morte, Patita da sei Christiani Giaponesi*, 59–60.

> I feel so much consolation in myself. So, if we die in this manner, we will be martyrs? Oh my God, why do you delay so much our death?"[37]

Therefore, the initial martyrdom model circulated in the form of written narratives and provided antecedents that could be emulated. Quickly, however, the community started proposing its own examples, which were integrated into the model and either circulated in turn or rejected.

Japanese martyrs soon became objects of imitation themselves. Testimonies can be found of exhortations by Christians to relatives and friends to also follow the examples of those who had died just before them and not only the examples of the Roman martyrs distant in space and time.[38] Letters from prison were another kind of medium through which Japanese Christians could circulate their beliefs about the correct forms and emotional practices of martyrdom; some of them still exist in translations embedded in Jesuit correspondence to Europe.[39] Before being burnt at the stake in 1614 in Takeda (eastern Kyūshū), in his request for prayers to his friends, Tarōemon Lino wrote: "I place all my hope in the mercy of the Lord … I am very spirited, and ready to persevere until death."[40] Uchibori Paolo Sakuemon, martyrised in 1627 on Mount Unzen,[41] wrote at least three letters during his incarceration: one to his confessor, one to his fellows in the Company of Saint Ignatius, and one to his wife. He addresses his fellows in this manner:

> I beg you to help me with your prayers: because, even if the spirit is ready, the flesh is disgusted, and it is right to do so, as it has been treated too well, like a fattened horse, who fights the bit. I nevertheless hope that God will give me the grace to obtain a victory, so that I will happily reach Heaven: to attain which, I pray you again to help me.[42]

Letter-writing becomes, in this case, another practice of hope for deliverance and an attempt to rebuild the feeling of belonging to a community that can no longer be physically joined. Paolo's pleas remind his fellows of their role in his salvation

---

37 *Relatione della gloriosa morte, Patita da sei Christiani Giaponesi*, 60.

38 See for example, *Relacion de la persecucion que huuo estos años*, 76.

39 On this kind of correspondence, see R. H. Hesselink, "A Letter from Jail: Christian Culture in Seventeenth-Century Nagasaki", *The Journal of World Christianity* 7, No. 2 (2017) 166–186. Fragments of numerous letters are collected in L. Pagés, *Histoire de la religion chrétienne au Japon, depuis 1598 jusqu'à 1651* (Paris: Charles Douniol, 1869), vol. 2.

40 *Relacion de la persecucion que huuo estos años*, 73. On the death of Lino, his brother Miguel and his sister-in-law Maxencia, see Ruiz de Medina, *El martirologio*, 332–34.

41 Ruiz de Medina, *El martirologio*, 567–68.

42 *Lettere annue del Giappone de gl'anni MDCXXV, MDCXXVI, MDCXXVII* (Rome/Milan: Filippo Ghisolfi, 1632) 217.

and the correct practices they, too, need to follow to help him obtain fortitude and, therefore, happiness.

The centrality of emotional practices was an aspect that endured in the model and was often expressed by Christian convicts: "Look at us carefully", two of them are reported to have said, communicating their emotions verbally and bodily to their tormentors, "and understand that suffering what we suffer willingly, and with the joy you can see, is a clear sign that our [religion] leads to salvation".[43] On the occasion of the exile of Takayama Ukon,[44] his group was (incorrectly) informed that they would be executed: they began to pray "with much happiness, without showing sadness, nor resistance".[45] If the communication of certain emotions was a crucial practice, equally important were bodily demonstrations that other, specific emotions were not present.

While internal Jesuit mission letters promoted the dissemination of the model in the various local communities, these texts also show that witness accounts of many martyrdoms circulated through the dispersed community in other ways. This is particularly evident following the 1614 ban issued by Shogun Tokugawa Ieyasu. The Jesuit missionaries were forcibly gathered in Nagasaki to be expelled and left the faithful to be guided and helped by local lay leaders. The presence of these spiritual authorities, who was deemed necessary both socially and spiritually during the trials, was sanctioned specifically in regards to women, as they were generally executed after their male relatives and therefore lacked paterfamilias.[46] Children, too, were given this particular support, although it was often the mother who had the primary role of instructing them.[47] In any case, the missionaries were always careful to mention the people to whom their information could be attributed, even if they were not necessarily called witnesses in an explicit manner. On some occasions, a sort of preliminary process for canonisation was organised to establish the trustworthiness of some specific aspects of witness reports, as happened with Shichirōbyōe Mathias's case.[48] Jesuit correspondence sometimes copied letters from eyewitnesses, such as a letter sent by an anonymous "trustworthy Japanese Christian" who had been sent to spiritually support a group exiled from Miyako

43 *Relacion de la persecucion que huuo estos años*, 60–61.

44 Takayama Ukon (1552–1615), baptised with the name of Dom Justo in 1563 and beatified in 2017, was one of the most important Christian daimyō (warlords); he was exiled to Manila, where he died, when he refused to abandon Christianity. See J. Laures, "Takayama Ukon. A Critical Essay", *Monumenta Nipponica* 5, no. 1 (1942) 86–112.

45 *Relacion de la persecucion que huuo estos años*, 64.

46 See for example the *Exhortations* (Anesaki, "Writings", 58).

47 See, for instance, the martyrdom of Luigino in *Relatione della gloriosa morte, Patita da sei Christiani Giaponesi*, 74.

48 *Relacion de la persecucion que huuo estos años*, 86. On Mathias, who died in Akizuki on the 15th of March 1614, see Ruiz de Medina, *El martirologio*, 330.

(Kyoto); he testified to the group's fortitude and declared that "they are happy to be able to somewhat imitate the martyrs, of whose struggles they discussed among themselves."[49]

The narratives that related to a specific martyr also followed the latter's relics. The practice of collecting and worshipping relics from those condemned to death was very popular in Japan,[50] to the point that the shogunate implemented various strategies (such as using secret executions and hiding the remains or throwing them in the sea) to prevent it.[51] Envisioning a similarly glorious future, the blood collected in handkerchiefs from the martyrs' wounds in 1597 was explicitly equated to that of the martyrs of primitive Christianity, which had made Christendom grow.[52] Between the missionaries' banishment to Nagasaki in January 1614 and their expulsion from the country in November of the same year, numerous accounts of martyrdom in their correspondence concluded with a paragraph to the effect that the holy remains had been taken to the priests confined in the city, to be treasured in the Jesuit church of Todos os Santos. For example, it is stated that the body of Shichirōbyōe Mathias, whose head was reputed to have cried out the name of Jesus three times after being severed, was taken there to lie with the remains of other martyrs.[53] These relics necessarily arrived in Nagasaki accompanied and marked by the accounts of the eyewitnesses to the death of their respective martyrs. These narratives and the relics they observed circulated their own interpretation of the model of the martyr as it had been embodied and interpreted by the witnesses, in that specific historical moment. Relics were also emotionally charged and often

---

49 *Relacion de la persecucion que huuo estos años*, 56.

50 An example offered by *Kirishitan-ban* literature is found in the life of Saint Polycarp, included the *Sactos* (Gonoi, "*Kirishitan*", 46), but it was a practice that predated the diffusion of this specific narrative and had deep roots into the connection Christian practices had to healing in Japan (see for example I. Higashibaba, *Christianity in Early Modern Japan. Kirishitan Belief and Practice* (Leiden; Boston; Köln: Brill, 2001), 32–33.)

51 Japanese polemical texts against Christianity comment on this practice: the *Kirishito-ki* notes that sometimes remains were even shipped overseas (see George Elison, *Deus Destroyed: The Image of Christianity in Early Modern Japan* (Cambridge: Harvard University Press, 1988), 206); the *Taiji Jashū-ron* denounces the preservation of remains of criminals as relics (H. Omata Rappō, "La quête des reliques dans la mission du Japon (xvie-xviiie siècle)", *Archives de sciences sociales des religions* 177 (2017) 257–282, on p. 264–65.) Some instances of destruction of bodies to prevent relic collection are mentioned in Stephen Turnbull, "The Veneration of the Martyrs of Ikitsuki (1609–1645) by the Japanese 'Hidden Christians,'" *Studies in Church History* 30 (1993) 295–310, on p. 303. Arakawa Adán suffered the same fate (*Lettera Annua del Giappone del M. DC. XIV.* (Rome: Bartolomeo Zannetti, 1617), 151–152.)

52 *Breue relatione della gloriosa morte di Paolo Michi, Giovanni Goto, e Giacomo Ghisai martiri giapponesi della Compagnia di Giesu* (Rome: per l'erede di Zannetti, 1628), 13.

53 *Relacion de la persecucion que huuo estos años*, 86. The finger of Mathias was later taken by future martyr Pedro Kibe to Rome as a relic (Gonoi, "*Kirishitan*", 46).

promoted emotional practices. Giovanna and Agnese both caressed and expressed their love for the severed head of Simone, and prayed to him to intercede for them with God.[54]

Jesuit correspondence also gives examples of debates among the condemned, their friends, and their relatives about the correct practices of martyrdom. Debates on the admissibility of specific actions or emotions also developed from the Christians' habit of meeting to pray together when under threat. The Christians of Arima considered the value of allowing the authorities to drag their female members to be exposed in the streets naked as a practice of humility (both for the exposed women and for the men, who would not take arms to defend them), against framing it as a risk of losing the women's chastity, which was to be avoided even at the cost of fighting. They solved the problem by asking authorities to use more traditional punishments instead of exposure that, they asserted, would have met the censure of the Court.[55] The literary canon was often evoked during discussions to identify correct practices: Simone Takeda Gohyoe referred to the imitation of the Passion of Jesus Christ to further his martyrdom bid when his Christian friends wanted him to save himself instead.[56] Arakawa Adán, imprisoned in a private house, was often visited by other Christians. However, he spent all his free time praying and reading devotional literature, especially *Contemptus Mundi*, "of which he was very fond".[57] When an old Christian visited him to confess that he was afraid of apostatising if his wife and young children were tortured, Adán told him not to be perturbed by his own imagination because God would give him the strength to face such a trial, too.[58] Fear was not an emotion that a prospective martyr was supposed to entertain and, thus, did not belong in the model. The old Christian's expression of fear contrasts with the emotional practices of Adán and highlights the perfection of the latter's embodiment of the model.

Another, less explicit, contrast among future martyrs on the correct emotional practices that characterised the model can be found in the account of the preparation for the death of Agnese and Giovanna. They invited to their house a third woman, Maddalena, and her young son Luigino, likewise condemned, to spend some time together before going to their executions together.[59] While this decision was supported by the *jihiyakusha* as Maddalena did not have a male relative to over-

54 *Relatione della gloriosa morte, Patita da sei Christiani Giaponesi*, 54–55.

55 *Relacion de la persecucion que huuo estos años*, 88.

56 *Relatione della gloriosa morte, Patita da sei Christiani Giaponesi*, 47.

57 *Lettera Annua del Giappone del M. DC. XIV.*, 143–44.

58 *Lettera Annua del Giappone del M. DC. XIV.*, 154.

59 On Maddalena and Luigino, see Ruiz de Medina, *El martirologio*, 299; they, too, are among the martyrs beatified in 2008.

see her in this fraught moment, it might still have suggested a lingering attachment to earthly connections:

> At night, they saw Maddalena arriving with her Luigino … Giovanna and Agnese went out to greet her, and their meeting was of the greatest consolation for all of them … "Oh, how happy we are, to see here our companion, together we'll go to heaven from here." "I too", answered Maddalena, "am happy, that we'll go together from here, even if it didn't matter much, to see each other in this world, because we were together in the spirit in Christ; and at home I was praying and preparing for death. But I appreciate much that you remembered and thought of me, making it possible for me to come here."[60]

The meeting, even if it gives the three women "great consolation", is stated to be of minor importance when compared to the joy that is generated by the imminent prospect of going to heaven. This passage underlines the lessened potency of the distribution of emotional practices on fellow humans when it comes to martyrdom: earthly connections, including those fostered by love, become secondary if compared to future divine relations. Maddalena (or her three witnesses) redresses the correctness of the emotional practice, and the diminished value of earthly consolation with it, by marginalising the latter in the model of martyrdom she has chosen to embody.

The correctness of the model and its emotional practices as proof of the salvation brought by the Christian God was, unsurprisingly, debated with non-Christians and lapsed Christians, too. Debates and arguments with guards, jailors, persecutors, judges, and other figures were common, as they are in the narratives on the ancient martyrs. Martyr Paolo Miki displayed his fortitude by preaching to the spectators about the righteousness of his faith while he was being crucified.[61] Numerous instances of Christians converting fellow prisoners were recorded.[62] From these interactions, the perception of the martyrdom model as presented in Japanese anti-Christian literature emerges, where it, unsurprisingly, takes the form of caricature. The chapbook *Kirishitan monogatari* presents a comical depiction of the emotional practices common in the martyr model: the communication of the emotion of joy and the use of imagination and visualisation of heaven to foster hope. Tied up in rough straw sacks and piled on one another, the condemned

60 *Relatione della gloriosa morte, Patita da sei Christiani Giaponesi*, 63.

61 *Breue relatione della gloriosa morte di Paolo Michi*, 11. On Paolo Miki, see Ruiz de Medina, *El martirologio*, 289–90.

62 See, for example, the three martyrs charged with preaching while in prison, in *Relationi della gloriosa morte di nove Christiani Giaponesi* (Rome: Bartolomeo Zannetti, 1611), 7.

> kept telling one to the other: "Well, now, how fortunate! Just us, and us alone—meeting with the final extremity, we'll obtain salvation from [God] and be born in [Heaven], where no want will disturb our life of ease, where we'll have jewels dangled from our necks. Every [Sunday] we hear this in the sermon. Quick, let them go ahead and kill us!" Thus they kept whispering to each other.[63]

Unsurprisingly, the model of the "martyr"[64] presented in this polemical text did not have the same qualities of heroism and fortitude as those presented in Jesuit correspondence. After receiving threats of being burnt alive, the condemned recant among the laughs of the crowd: their emotional practices are revealed to be empty and ineffective, aimed only at trying to save their honour. Thus, while on a superficial level, such practices resemble those of the Christian martyrdom model, indicating that some echo of it had reached the Japanese population at large, they are resignified, attributed to different emotions, and perceived as demonstrating the convicts' less noble dispositions.

Debating the Model

As the emotional practices considered above suggest, the model of sanctity via martyrdom that emerged in Japan was capacious. If its resilience allowed it to survive through the difficult periods of persecution, succumbing only at the end, it also meant that various elements it originally did not entertain could be recognised as coherent (or not), and accepted (or rejected) in subsequent embodiments, resulting in a changed model. Emotions that could compromise the model were outright rejected, together with their practices: fear of torture and death, if not temporary and overcome, was a common emotion that characterised failed martyrs; in other words, Christians who expressed fear could not be martyrs, as they were not recognised as embodying the model correctly.[65]

Statements in support of the correctness of the model against misunderstandings or attempts to obtain renunciations are numerous. Two examples can be found in the martyrdom narrative of Masuda Maddalena of Arie (south-east of Nagasaki). Taken to the sea to be killed, she was told to jump into the water. This offer from

63 Elison, *Deus Destroyed*, 359.

64 It is not possible to speak of "martyrs" when considering the point of view of the shogunate; in this sense, the one presented in the *Kirishitan Monogatari* is the model of a criminal. See H. Omata Rappō, "De l'universalité du 'martyre' à l'histoire 'globale': repenser l'écriture de l'histoire du christianisme au Japon", *Diogène* 4, no. 256 (2016) 67–86. K. Paramore, *Ideology and Christianity in Japan* (London, New York: Routledge, 2009).

65 An example is provided in *Lettere annue del Giappone de gl'anni MDCXXV*, 314.

her guards would have allowed her to maintain her honour; it is not clear from the text if they knew that it would also make her lose her martyr status. However, she refused, stating that "they're free to throw her in", but she would not do it herself.[66] She was then tortured by continuous submersions, and, by the end, she seemed to be making some sort of sound. Two different interpretations by the people present are reported in the text. Her guards believed she was crying and interpreted it as an expression of fear or despair. The witness who reported the events to the missionaries instead stated that she was singing the hymn *Laudate Dominum omnes gentes*, which is explicitly identified as a practise of joy.[67] The suggestion by the guards that Maddalena was afraid imperiled the embodiment of the model and, therefore, the recognition of her as a martyr, and it is not surprising that her witness (probably her brother) felt the need to correct it. The practice of singing to mobilise happiness and, arguably, to help control unwanted feelings, such as fear, had been adopted by Japanese martyrs since the 1597 executions in Nagasaki: Paolo Miki sang from his cross before being killed.[68]

With such a widely encompassing model, individuals were at liberty to choose the practices they preferred among those that their circumstances allowed, and still be recognised as embodying it. For example, *Relationi della gloriosa morte di nove Christiani Giaponesi* presents the different preparatory practices enacted by two future martyrs: the text informs the readers that Giovanni, although sick and forced to go without food and personal slaves, never rested during the day, never stopped his devotions, and never stopped performing the many spiritual exercises in which he was engaged. He "trust[ed] completely the divine Providence, refusing all human help and comfort"[69] (such as the medicines to treat his illness), interpreting this as part of his trials for God. His fellow prisoner, Michele, was "of a different spirit", believing it best to accept the treatment and recover to then be stronger to "suffer more and bleed for Christ".[70] The text confirms that they were "both walking on the path of suffering for Christ and for the greater glory of God", thereby validating their practices.[71]

A special role in the authorisation of the emotional practices of the martyrdom model was given to the Japanese community leaders that accompanied the convicted to their deaths; as the above-mentioned *jihiyakusha*, these figures assumed

66 Cristóvão Ferreira's letter of the 14th September 1627 (printed with the title of "Relatione della persecutione sollevata nel Tacacu contro la S. Fede, nell'anno 1627"), in *Lettere annue del Giappone de gl'anni MDCXXV*, 237. On Maddalena's martyrdom, see Ruiz de Medina, *El martirologio*, 572.

67 *Lettere annue del Giappone degl'anni MDCXXV*, 237.

68 *Breue relatione della gloriosa morte di Paolo Michi*, 10.

69 *Relationi della gloriosa morte di nove Christiani*, 37.

70 *Relationi della gloriosa morte di nove Christiani*, 41.

71 *Relationi della gloriosa morte di nove Christiani*, 37.

a particular relevance, reflected in the texts, in the cases of female martyrs without surviving adult Christian male relatives. Doubling as witnesses, they are often shown debating with the women about the appropriateness of certain practices and correcting their behaviour or, most often, approving it and lending it their authority. Naturally, the practical conditions of the martyrs did not generally allow for a perfect imitation of the theoretical model offered by the literature, especially that provided by the narratives of the Passion. Still, the latter provided an example of the practice of humility in Jesus' walking up Calvary and Japanese Christians strove to imitate him, as the correspondence always notes to highlight their piety.[72]

This, however, was not always possible or considered appropriate in Japanese culture, especially for noble women. The group of Giovanna and Agnese was taken to their execution place in litters, as was deemed proper for the group's status. This perturbed Agnese, who discussed how permissible it was with Giovanni of the Misericórdia:

> Giovanni said to Agnese: "Please remember now, lady, how our Lord Jesus Christ, at the time of his very holy Passion, was dragged through the streets of Jerusalem, and meditate on this passage." To which she replied, "You reminded it to me just at the right moment. And since our Redeemer, when he went to die, went barefoot, it is not appropriate that I go in a litter." And she started asking to be let off the litter. But Giovanni stopped her, saying that any way of dying was the same, especially if the guards were not allowed to [let her off]; and she appeared to be satisfied of this.[73]

Some emotional practices were, indeed, integrated into the martyr model from Japanese culture. In Jesuit correspondence, these new elements were generally discussed and excused for the benefit of European readers. As the example of the litter above illustrates, the acts' legitimacy was often debated among the convicts and their spiritual advisers, especially if there was the risk of contradicting the model inherited from the written canon. In other cases, the Japanese did not appear to doubt the validity of their practices: Mine Sukedayū Gioachino bowed in front of the ashes of those executed before him, in one such example. Later, while walking to the gallows, he took a moment to compose a poem. The letter informs us that it was a typical emotional practice in Japan:

> It is common for the Japanese, in situations of great joy, to compose verses… Gioachino, staring at the sky, wrote… "I believed it was far from me and apart, now I see that heaven

72 See the example of Paolo Miki in *Breue relatione della gloriosa morte di Paolo Michi*, 10.

73 *Relatione della gloriosa morte, Patita da sei Christiani Giaponesi*, 69–70.

> is close." This shows their desire for heaven, and how deep was peace in their hearts; because being so close to death, they could think of composing poems.[74]

New practices of this kind mainly came from everyday habits and were recontextualised to mobilise emotions that were believed compatible with the martyrdom model: in this case, joy, in a sequence with peace and hope to reach heaven.

Subject to correction were, in particular, practices of neighbourly and familial love. In early modern plays about martyrs, the scripts highlighted the thematic importance of the tension between the love felt for fellow human beings and the spiritual love for God. The first, considered positively in the broader Christian tradition, in martyrdom narratives became an obstacle that needed to be overcome to achieve complete dedication to God.[75] The aspect of rejection of human connections is present in martyrdom narratives from Japan, too. *Exhortations* presents the figure of the devil who, disguised as a friend, attempts to convince the condemned to avoid martyrdom.[76] Attempting to save the life of a fellow Christian was no longer understood as behaviour associated with neighbourly love, but was instead seen as an attempt to disguise more sinister feelings and earthly attachments. The convict was, therefore, to refuse any help or would otherwise be accused of deserting God. Maddalena showing disregard for earthly connections when talking with Agnese and Giovanna is another example of this re-evaluation of the practices of love. If the common death sentence could unite the convicts, the earthly connection they shared paled in contrast with the future, heavenly one they would recreate after martyrdom. The model of martyr presented instead, as the correct practice of love towards convicts, exhortation to fortify them in the face of suffering. As mentioned, with regards to children, the mother instructed them until the moment of death, since the male relatives had generally already been executed. For example, Maddalena is depicted encouraging her son Luigino to repeat after her the names of Jesus and Mary, "like a very devout echo", as they die.[77]

This warning doubled as an admonition for the friends and relatives of the martyr and even the spectators of their death. An imploring wife could become an obstacle to martyrdom, as she did not adhere to the correct practices that dictated that she should support her husband during his trial:

> Giovanni was tempted … as another saintly Job, by his young [non-Christian] wife, who was foreigner, immoral, and deprived by the Court of all her belongings; she often

74 Lettere annue del Giappone degl'anni MDCXXV, 241. On Gioachino, who was martyrised in Unzen in 1627, see Ruiz de Medina, *El martirologio*, 576.

75 Raphaële Garrod, "Senecan Catharsis."

76 Anesaki, "Writings", 45.

77 *Relatione della gloriosa morte, Patita da sei Christiani Giaponesi*, 74.

> presented tearfully to her husband her misery and the continuous insults that she had to put up with for his choice of lifestyle.... Even if there were other paths to reach salvation; but he, without losing himself, exhorted her, with words and letters, to be patient and persevere...[78]

In times of martyrdom, the correct practice that fostered familial love became acceptance and obedience, as martyrdom could only be ordered by God's will[79] and opposing it was, therefore, to negate Providence. This change in the practices of familial and neighbourly love was significant, considering that love and concordance among Japanese Christians had been one of the central tenets of Jesuit teachings.

In some cases, the friends of the martyr could be given the benefit of the doubt when they tried to have the execution suspended by highlighting the fact that their love still had positive elements. This process was particularly evident during the 1597 trials in Nagasaki when various practices of love were condemned explicitly by the Jesuits because they did not adhere to the model of martyrdom. When the three future Jesuit martyrs of Nagasaki were incarcerated, their friends expressed a wish to free them through political pressure; however, Father Organtino Gnecchi-Soldo, superior of the house of Miyako, explained that it would be a sin to hinder their progress towards martyrdom, because it had been ordered by God. An attempt was carried out all the same, but it was unsuccessful; this prompted Organtino to commend the martyrs' friends for showing such great love for the Society of Jesus.[80] This example highlights how older emotional practices could still be evoked to spin a positive interpretation of the actions of the Christian and, at the same time, encourage the behaviour held as most correct in times of persecution.

Conclusion

Before 1597, the model of sanctity through martyrdom of the Japanese Christian community, that had been imported into the country by the Jesuit missionaries since 1549, represented mostly a distant ideal that supported various religious practices in daily life. After the first mass crucifixion of that year, this model started to undergo changes to adapt to the new lives of the community under the pressure of the shogunate. A major element that had marked the model of the martyr since its arrival in the country were its emotional practices. Indeed, a martyr would not

78 *Relationi della gloriosa morte di nove Christiani*, 35–36.

79 For example: "this matter [of martyrdom] non currentis, neque volentis, sed miserentis est Dei" (*Relationi della gloriosa morte di nove Christiani Giaponesi*, 12); this is a reference to Rom. 9:16: "So it depends not on human will or exertion, but on God who shows mercy" (NRSE-CE).

80 Archivum Romanum Societatis Iesu, *Japonica-Sinica* 53, on fs. 24v–25r.

be recognised as such if they did not foster and communicate the correct emotions. Practices that facilitated arousing and controlling emotions were thus used to achieve with more surety a successful martyrdom. The specific historical reality of persecutions in Japan contributed to the changes that the model underwent on the emotional level, as the communities openly debated to identify compatibility with the original ideal, and thus with Christian life. The model's resilience allowed it to incorporate new practices (from Japanese culture, for instance), even if they modified the embodiment of key emotions of martyrdom, such as hope and joy. In other cases, leaders and missionaries reiterated the restrictions expressed by the original model, especially in cases when they curbed ordinary practices that had been at the core of the community before the persecutions. This is the case of familial and neighbourly love, that assumed a diminished importance in comparison with love for God, also through the modification of the practices that expressed it. Thus, the model of martyr assumed various expressions as it circulated in the community, thanks to eyewitnesses, relics, letters, and various media that carried the narratives of martyrdom.

Hitomi Omata Rappo

Profiling the Japanese Martyrs

The Beatification Process of the Twenty-Six Martyrs of Nagasaki (1597–1627)

In 1627, the twenty-six martyrs of Japan—crucified in Nagasaki in 1597—were the first to be beatified after the reform of the system during the early 17th century. This event was a milestone in the history of sainthood, especially as this group contained many non-Europeans. The twenty-six martyrs consist of two distinct groups: twenty-three people related to the Franciscans (among them six friars and seventeen Japanese converts) and three Japanese Jesuits. Throughout the 17th century, the martyrs of both Franciscan and Jesuit sides would be represented in various forms, including lives of saints, illustrations, iconography, and theater, generating a literary and symbolic typology that spread widely in Europe and in the Catholic world.

The beatification happened quickly, within a mere thirty years of their death. While similar procedures for other people "of color," such as Benedetto il Moro, were started before them, they were completed later.[1] In fact, they can be considered as a sort of exception, as the general mood of the Holy See was moving towards more strict control. This culminated in 1625, with a papal decision that severely tightened the conditions of access to holiness for recent cases.[2] In 1628, a decree from Pope Urban VIII even forbade proceeding with any canonization, beatification, or declaration of martyrdom until fifty years had passed since the person's death.[3]

This speed was thus remarkable, and an examination of this process will illustrate what was expected of the Post-Tridentine conception of martyrdom. However, the twenty-six martyrs were also probably an exception. In fact, the manner of their crucifixion served as a striking emulation of Jesus's—which had a deep impact in the Catholic world—and it is explicitly stated as the main reason for the final decision.[4]

---

1 H. Omata Rappo, "How to Make "Colored" Japanese Counter-Reformation Saints – A Study of an Iconographic Anomaly", *Journal of Early Modern Christianity* 4 no. 2 (2017) 195–225.

2 M. Gotor, *I beati del papa : santità, Inquisizione e obbedienza in età moderna* (Firenze: L.S. Olschki, 2002), 290–93.

3 Gotor, *I beati del papa : santità, Inquisizione e obbedienza in età moderna*, 325.

4 On the impact of this symbol, see H. Omata Rappo, "Death on the Cross; the Beatification of the Twenty-Six Martyrs of Nagasaki (1627) and the Iconography of the Crucifixion", in F. Quiles García, *et al.* (ed.), *A la luz de Roma: Santos y santidad en el barroco iberoamericano. Volumen III. Tierra de santidad* (Sevilla; Roma: Enredars, Roma Tre-Press, 2020) 129–50.

Despite, this success, the whole process was characterized by one major factor: the rivalry between the Jesuits and the mendicant orders. In fact, such rivalry had already started during the events that lead to the tragedy, and both groups blamed each other for the outcome.[5] This animosity also created a certain climate even among the faithful, which had extremely concrete consequences on the procedure itself.

The Franciscans, who constituted the majority of the victims, wanted to advance their beatification as quickly as possible, so they began working towards this goal immediately after their deaths. They succeeded with a very organized campaign—which still stagnated until the mid 1610s—that focused on showing how the twenty-six martyrs were perfect illustrations of the contemporary models of sanctity.[6]

On the other hand, the Jesuits were not inclined to promote the concept of martyrdom in their missionary activities in Asia.[7] Regarding the twenty-six martyrs, they saw the events as a consequence of a lack of precaution from the friars, and they did not participate directly to the cause.

Another major factor was that the main priority at the time for the Society of Jesus was dealing with the problem of the beatification and later canonization of Ignatius Loyola, the founder of the Society. To a lesser extent, they focused on the same for Francis Xavier, although these priorities did not really fit with the image of sanctity encouraged by the Vatican during the early 17th century, which focused heavily—as the martyrs of Japan partly illustrate—on martyrdom and miracles.[8] The Society, which advocated caution in missionary activities, was thus not necessarily eager to promote martyrdom. These particular martyrs of Japan were not a priority—contrary to later figures such as Carlo Spinola —especially due to doubts regarding the status of the three allegedly Jesuit victims.[9]

In fact, for the Society, the beatification was an almost unintended outcome,[10] as they did not participate at all in the trials organized for the recognition of their

5 See H. Omata Rappo, *Des Indes lointaines aux scènes des collèges : les reflets des martyrs de la mission japonaise en Europe (XVIe-XVIIIe siècle)* (Münster: Aschendorff, 2020), 102–15.

6 On the Franciscans conception of martyrdom in general, also see C. H. MacEvitt, *The martyrdom of the Franciscans : Islam, the papacy, and an order in conflict* (Philadelphia: University of Pennsylvania Press, 2020).

7 See Omata Rappo, *op. cit.*, *ibid.*

8 On this issue of competing images of sanctity in the Society, see S. Mostaccio, "Au carrefour des regards: le théologien et la mystique. Virgilio Cepari sj et Maria Maddalena de' Pazzi", in R. Dekoninck, É. Granjon, and A. Guiderdoni (ed.), *Fiction sacrée. Spiritualité et esthétique durant le premier âge moderne* (Leuven: Peeters, 2013) 319–35.

9 On Spinola, see Omata Rappo, *Des Indes lointaines aux scènes des collèges*, 179–81.

10 As Dominique Bouix puts it, the Jesuits in great part owe these Japanese saints to the friars. D. Bouix, *Histoire des vingt-six martyrs du Japon crucifiés à Nangasaqui, le 5 février 1597 : avec un aperçu*

sanctity. As you will see, their reluctance even had a negative impact on the process, through their influence on some of the local converts.

The Trials for the Beatification of the Twenty-Six Martyrs

The Official Process

Right after the execution, the Franciscans and Dominicans conducted a series of auditions designed to reassemble evidence of their martyrdom. The trials, organized in Manila and Macao, produced various questions that would become the basis for the official beatification procedure. The Jesuits were more circumspect and held a hearing in Nagasaki in order to gather arguments supporting their more cautious—or even negative—view of the victims, and, above all, of their status as true martyrs.[11]

However, despite their efforts,[12] the Franciscans were not able to concretely advance their cause in Rome before the famous Hasekura embassy, a Japanese delegation which arrived in Rome in 1615. Their presence led to an increased interest in the beatification of Japanese martyrs at the Holy See.

This would bear fruit in the next year. Pope Paul V asked three members of the Rota to initiate the process: Giovanni Battista Coccini, dean of the Rota, Alfonso Manzanedo de Quiñones, patriarch of Jerusalem, and the auditor, Filippo Pirovano. This commission then appointed the secretary of the Rota, Quirino Farina, to take care of the case.

Franciscan Alfonso Muñoz of the province of St. Gregory of the Philippines became "promoter" of the cause following an official letter dated June 30, 1616. However, he fell ill, and was eventually replaced by his successor, Pedro Bautista Porres Tamayo (to be distinguished from the martyr of the same name). This friar would then lead the entire beatification process.[13]

After his nomination, Tamayo organized a series of trials that would take place between 1621 and 1622 in Puebla, Mexico, Macao, Manila, and Nagasaki. Each of them had to deliver a report to Rome, which would be used for the decision.

The localization of the trials, spread all over the Catholic world, demonstrates the global stature of the Japanese martyrs at the time, and also mirrors the structure

---

historique sur les chrétientés du Japon depuis cette époque jusqu'à nos jours (Lyon; Paris: Librairie Catholique de Perisse Frères, Régis Ruffet, 1862), 183.

11 Omata Rappo, *Des Indes lointaines aux scènes des collèges*, 131–38.

12 Including a petition by Japanese Christians in 1604. See Omata Rappo, *Des Indes lointaines aux scènes des collèges*, 138–40.

13 Omata Rappo, *Des Indes lointaines aux scènes des collèges*, 150–52.

of the whole missionary enterprise. Given that all the trial questions were identical, this article will focus on the most peculiar, and probably relevant trial of them all—Nagasaki—which took place in September 1622.

The Nagasaki Trial

The trial in Nagasaki began in 1621, the year of the Vatican's letter of appointment (litterae remissoriales).[14] It was initially entrusted to three Dominicans, Diego Collado (1589–1641), Juan de Rueda, and Jacinto Orfanel, a friar famous for his extensive history of the Japanese mission.[15]

However, Juan de Rueda had left Japan in 1620 for Manila,[16] and Orfanel had been captured in 1621.[17] It was therefore Diego Collado who would take charge of the whole procedure. Diego Collado was a major figure during the Dominican mission in Japan, where he officiated under difficult conditions.

Diego Collado is a fascinating character, who took a deep role in both the beatification process and also the disputes between the friars and the Jesuits. Interestingly, he left Japan right after the trial with the documents,[18] first to the Philippines. Then, he went back to Rome, after a perilous journey.[19]

The trial was in fact conducted in September 1622, a year after the emission of the initial remissory letter. The context was extremely tense. Diego Collado himself was probably partly responsible for the intensification of persecutions in Nagasaki, when, in March of the same year, he tried to save his colleague, Luis Flores, from

---

14 The proceedings can be analysed in detail thanks to the handwritten report, in Latin, kept in the Vatican Apostolic Archives, formerly known as the Secret Archives. See ASV. Arch. Congr. SS. Rituum, Processus 1222.

15 Omata Rappo, *Des Indes lointaines aux scènes des collèges*, 153–54.

16 See J. D. García (ed.), *Fr. Juan de Los Angeles Rueda, O.P. Misionero itinerante en el Japón del siglo XVII, Cartas y Relaciones* (Madrid: Institutos de Filosofía y Teología "Santo Tomás", 1999), 28.

17 J. D. García, and M. G. Pola (ed.), *Beato Jacinto Orfanell, O.P. Mártir del Japón (s. XVII), Cartas y Relaciones. Segunda Edición* (Madrid: Institutos de Filosofía y Teología "Santo Tomás", 1989), 47–49.

18 Collado is the main signatory of the letter closing the procedure (see ASV. Arch. Congr. SS. Rituum, Processus 1222, f. 1v).

19 A biography of Collado can be found in H. O. OP, and E. N. OP, *Misioneros Dominicos en el Extremo Oriente 1587–1835, vol. 1. Edición corregida y actualizada de la obra del P. Hilario Ocio OP: "Compendio de la Reseña Biográfica de los Religiosos de la Provincia de Nuestra Señora del Rosario de la Orden de Predicadores" Manila, Filipinas, 1895* (Manilla: Life Today Publications, 2000), 109–10. For more details on Diego Collado's impact, especially on the editorial side, see R. Roldán-Figueroa, *The Martyrs of Japan: Publication History and Catholic Missions in the Spanish World (Spain, New Spain, and the Philippines, 1597–1700)* (Leiden; Boston: Brill, 2021), 101, and J.-N. Robert, "La langue japonaise au crible de la grammaire latine : L'*Ars grammaticae linguae japonicae* de Diego Collado (Didacus Colladus)", in D. Couto, and F. Lachaud (ed.), *Empires éloignés : l'Europe et le Japon (XVIe -XIXe siècle)* (Paris: École française d'Éxtrême-Orient, 2010) 39–49.

prison, with the active help of the local Christians. The coup failed and was severely repressed by the authorities. A price was even put on his head, and it was in this condition of fugitive that he initiated the trial.[20]

During September of 1622, Christianity in Japan was thus suffering from an intense persecution by the Tokugawa regime. In fact, September 1622 is also the date of the great Genna martyrdom. Fifty-five Christians and missionaries were executed, either by beheading or burning. This included major figures, such as the Jesuit Carlo Spinola and Iacinto Orfanel himself.

The Procedure of the Trial

While there were procedural differences of course, the trial was fairly similar to its modern equivalent, with witnesses summoned to answer questions from the judges. Held from September 5th through 28th, 1622, it was presided by Diego Collado and assisted by his fellow Dominican, Domingo Castellet (1592–1628), the latter of whom had arrived in Nagasaki clandestinely inside a merchant ship in July of the previous year.[21] The friars Pedro Vasquez, the apostolic notary, and Antonio de San Bonaventura, who was tasked with choosing the witnesses, also took part in the trial. There were no Jesuits present.

An interesting characteristic of the Nagasaki trial is that its report describes not only the contents of the testimonies involved, but also how the witnesses were called to testify. Such precision was most certainly unnecessary in normal circumstances—such as in Mexico—but their presence clearly suggests a very difficult situation.

In fact, the location of the trial changed almost regularly, probably in order to avoid being discovered by the authorities. Sometimes it was held aboard a ship, and the designated area was not specified in writing, but was communicated verbally.

The judges were able to summon eighteen witnesses. Each time, they sent one of two envoys to their houses—a most certainly dangerous task. The first was a man named Pedro de la Rosa, on whom little information is available. The second was a Japanese convert, Thomas Rokuzaemon. This is probably Thomas Hioji Nishi

---

20 P. Humbertclaude, "Le *Spiritual Shugyô no Manual* ou la presse jésuite au Japon et l'*Index*", in C. Marquet (ed.), *Présences occidentales au Japondu "siècle chrétien" à la réouverture du XIXe siècle* (Paris: Cerf, 2011) , 276. However, another view of this event is that Collado merely gave his blessing to the converts. See J. D. García, ""El Salmantino" Fr. Diego Collado, O.P. (1587–1641)", *Ciencia Tomista* 115 (1988) , 248–49.

21 For details on Castellet, see J. D. García, *Dos hijos de la Provincia Dominicana de Aragón, misioneros en Japón: Fr. Juan de la Badía y el beato Domingo Castellet* (Madrid: Instituto pontificio de teologia/misionologia, 1986), 23–24. On the context, see J. S. Cummins, *Jesuit and Friar in the Spanish Expansion to the East* (London: Variorum repr., 1986), 23–24.

Rokuzaemon, also called Thomas of Saint Hyacinth, who was born in 1590 in Hirado.[22] A *dōjuku* as the moment of the events, he later left Japan for Manila, and, in 1624, he officially became a Dominican—the first Japanese to do so. He traveled to Taiwan in 1627,[23] and returned to Japan, where he died a martyr in 1634, on the Nishizaka slope.[24]

The envoys brought a juramentum, which was handed to the witnesses, and told them that they were summoned to a trial, which would be held at a given time and place.

The Interrogations

The interrogation was the same in all the trials. It was based on a list of six factual confirmations, and thirty-one articles containing questions for the witnesses, which were made to either confirm the general or deal with more specific details. The contents closely resembled the articles of the Macao trial of 1597, but they were more detailed and dealt with later events as well. They are also based on the various reports and letter produced at the time of the events, or a little later. The function of these hearings was therefore to have the witnesses confirm that they saw or heard the things stated in each article.

The content is very specific, and deals with many aspects of their martyrdom, the circumstances in which it took place, and its consequences. They can be divided into several groups based on their subjects. The first one (1 to 4) describes their arrival, status in Japan, and the fact that they had a good reputation and were not illegally there, or considered as criminals. The first article not only aims at proving that Bautista and his companions were present in Japan and preached the Gospel there, but it also insists on the fact that the friar had felt great pain upon his arrival in Nagasaki, insisting on his perseverance and the prestige he gained from it.[25] The second asks to confirm that this missionary and his companions were legally resident in Japan, as that they had come as ambassadors of the governor of the Philippines, bearers of a peace treaty, and that they had received safe conduct from the authorities. The third takes up the argument of the hospitals held by Bautista and his companions, while the fourth asks about the church they built in the capital.

---

22 The name Rokuzaemon can be seen in the official list of the 16 martyrs of Japan (Saint Thomas Nishi and 15 martyrs) established by the Vatican.

23 J. E. Borao Mateo, "La colonia de japoneses en Manila en el marco de las relaciones de Filipinas y Japón en los siglos XVI y XVII", *Cuadernos CANELA* 17(2005) , 50, note 75.

24 His biography can be found in Katorikku chūōkyōgikai (ed.), *Sei Thomas Nishi to 15 junkyō-sha* (Tokyo: Katorikku chūōkyōgikai, 1988).

25 For a summary, see Omata Rappo, *Des Indes lointaines aux scènes des collèges*, 155–57.

The second group (article 5 to 9) clearly show the Rota has integrated the providential scenario contained in the hagiographic accounts of the martyrdom. The fifth article describes a comet that appeared, according to the editor, as soon as they were arrested. The sixth is about their arrest, their march from the capital to Nagasaki. It also insists on the fact that the friars could have fled, but decided to stay and suffer martyrdom for their faith. Articles seven and eight refer respectively to an earthquake and a flood that happened close to the execution.[26] We also learn that an image of St. Francis kept in the Japanese capital purportedly bled at the same time (9).

The articles in the next group (12 to 14) deal with the prodigies that occurred at the time of the crucifixion. The tenth describes a flaming pillar that appeared the night after the execution of the twenty-six martyrs. The eleventh explains that a dying "Indian" woman, who had lived for a long time in Nagasaki, was cured of her illnesses by placing a piece of the cross of Bautista in her mouth. We then return to the treatment of the martyrs' remains, which were considered relics. Their popularity was so great that the crowd rushed to them (12), while a believer purportedly went as far as biting off Bautista's heel to make a precious relic (13). After that comes the oft-mentioned issue of the miraculous preservation of the bodies. Article 14 verifies that blood continued to flow from Bautista's body three or four days after his crucifixion. The seventeenth article asks to confirm that despite the abundance of scavengers in Japan, none of them touched the bodies of the twenty-six martyrs, while they immediately devoured those of the gentiles.

The fifteenth is fundamental, because it explains why the Franciscans had taken such care to obtain a "reliable" copy of the sentence. It was important to prove that the martyrs had been killed because of "hatred of the faith." The sixteenth article returns to an argument that the friars of the minors had already emphasized in the testimony commissioned from Pedro Martins, and which will be recurring in all the accounts of the Japanese martyrs thereafter: the constancy and dignity of the twenty-six in the torture. Article 18 even states that Bautista continued to sing and give mass while being crucified. His body even raised several times during his torture, disappearing from his cross to the great surprise of the guards.

Another common argument in the accounts of these martyrs is the idea that their deaths greatly increased the number of converts, an element of crucial importance in the trials (19). We learn, moreover (20), that the location where they were executed was transformed by this event in the following article: indeed, whereas it had been a sinister site of execution, it had turned to a sort of holy site after the death of the

26 On such issues, see C. Jacquelard, "Une catastrophe glorieuse : le martyre des premiers chrétiens du Japon, Nagasaki, 1597", *e-Spania [En ligne]* 12(2011) 2–15. These events are also attested in Japanese sources, such as the Daigoji monk Gien. See Gien jugō nikki v. 1, Shiryō sanshū 15–1 (48), (Tokyo: Zoku gunsho ruijū kanseikai 1976), 41.

twenty-six martyrs. The converts planted trees where the crosses once stood, and it became a popular location. The following article (21) even goes so far as to say that these trees were venerated by the entire population.

The site was also linked to various prodigies. Thus, article 22 evokes a lamp that would appear every Wednesday in this same place, only to disappear the following morning. Green lights would also regularly shine near the trees mentioned above (23). Bautista even sometimes was said to have disappeared from his cross, only to reappear, like a blinking spirit (24).

After these prodigies, the next two articles propose to confirm the firmness of their faith (25), as well as their moral qualities (26–27). The twenty-eighth point deals with more prosaic verifications. First of all, it presents a complete list of the names of the twenty-six martyrs, which would thus be submitted to each of the witnesses. After that came the content of the sentence, which is exactly the same as that of the pre-inquiry of 1597. The second part emphasizes the torments undergone by the martyrs, their constancy in the faith, and the mode of their execution, by crucifixion then transpiercing by spears, still following scrupulously the previous sources. The question even adds that Bautista asked for iron nails to be used to crucify him, in order to imitate the model of Christ (29).

The penultimate article discusses the impact of the event, asking more specifically if everyone recognized the twenty-six men as martyrs. The interrogation is concluded by telling the witnesses to confirm that the articles as a whole include facts known to all.

In general, these articles are manifestly based on the pre-inquiries conducted in 1597. However, they put even more emphasis on the miracles brought about by the twenty-six martyrs, and sook to make them correspond to the criteria necessary to attain sainthood. The questions also directly reference the Manila and Macao trials of 1597 and 1598. As a whole, they "profiled" the martyrs, by having them clear all the prerequisites for beatification. Thus, while a good part of the facts mentioned above cannot be corroborated by Japanese sources, the existence of these specifications is a historical fact in itself. Further, its content, which will moreover be mostly confirmed by the official decision, would largely determine the perception of the Nagasaki martyrs as well as the cult to them after their beatification.

The Nagasaki Trial: From Factual Confirmations to Micro-History

As seen above, in the case of the Nagasaki trial, there was first a description of how and where each witness was called, and who went looking for him. Then came the six factual confirmations. The first aimed at confirming that the witness knew how severe perjury would be, and that he would answer truthfully. The second asked for his surname, given name, occupation, origin, and the identities of his parents. The third dealt with whether he had properly confessed or not, while the fourth queried about an eventual excommunication. The fifth questioned whether the contents of his testimony were influenced by anyone else. The sixth, and last, asked if their testimony—especially on miracles, was affected by some kind of a drug.

Out of these, while the issue of excommunication would prove an acute problem later in the trial, the first factual confirmation, combined with the description of the circumstances of the subpoena, provides the most concrete historical information. In fact, the answers, while trivial in appearance, contain precious detail on the people directly involved in the process, and also on the state of the Christian community in Nagasaki at the time.

The first actual witness, on September 14, was Georgius Bastian, age 50, a man born to Sebastianus Georgius and of Catharina Biena of Kyoto. He was thus 25 at the time of the incident, In 1597. He was, like many other witnesses, a merchant who traveled between Japan and India. In his case, there was no specific mention of where the testimony took place or the circumstances.[27] This would change quickly.

The next testimony that proceeded normally was on September 17, with Michael Inoue, another merchant, whom the Westerner Pedro de la Rosa went looking for. The report also says that due to the persecutions, it was impossible to find a large place, so the trial was held on a small boat (navilio).[28]

In fact, two days later, on September 19, Pedro de la Rosa was replaced by the Japanese Thomas Rokuzaemon. It seems he was tasked with fetching the Japanese witnesses, while Pedro de la Rosa was in charge of the Westerners (or maybe half-Westerners). The first witness that day, the carpenter Johannes Araqui, also testified on a small boat.[29] The same can be said of two witnesses on September 22 (the merchant Koyobashi Loday Johannes[30] and the soldier Kondo Bastian), who too were brought by Thomas Rokuzaemon to a similar place.[31]

However, the next day, it was Pedro de la Rosa who went looking for the witness, Simon Rodrigues, a merchant born in Goa. This time, it is only recorded that he testified "at a given place and at a given time," which suggests that this was decided at the last moment.[32] In fact, on the same day, Thomas Rokuzaemon brought a man called Antonius Matzuda, who was asked to join them at a designated place in the evening.[33]

---

27 Arch. Congr. SS. Rituum, Processus 1222, f. 23r.

28 "quia ex causa persecutionis non adfuit alius locus magis ad propositum". Arch. Congr. SS. Rituum, Processus 1222, f. 27v.

29 Arch. Congr. SS. Rituum, Processus 1222, f. 31v.

30 Arch. Congr. SS. Rituum, Processus 1222, f. 35v.

31 Arch. Congr. SS. Rituum, Processus 1222, f. 40r.

32 Arch. Congr. SS. Rituum, Processus 1222, f. 44v.

33 Arch. Congr. SS. Rituum, Processus 1222, f. 48r.

On September 24, Itō Johannes, another soldier, was told by Thomas Rokuzaemon to come to a small boat later that day, at 7:00 P.M.[34] He thus did not take him directly to the trial, but probably went separate ways. A similar pattern, albeit with the boat replaced by a "designated place," was repeated with Cagi Laurentius, a blacksmith,[35] and Mori Xembioe Martinus, a merchant, on September 26,[36] as well as with Jifiyacus Michaelis[37] and Yamada Yafiyoe Leo,[38] a merchant and a carpenter, the following day.

In all, the missionaries spent considerable time and resources in a dangerous situation in order to hold an apostolic trial in Nagasaki. The fact that it took place in Nagasaki suggests that finding actual witnesses would be easy. On the contrary, since being a Christian was required, the friars had to look for people who were able to live in Nagasaki and to keep their faith for twenty-five years, despite increasing persecutions.

Testifying also implied meeting several Western European priests, with a high probably of being caught. The missionaries were clearly aware of this issue, and some consideration was given to the danger to the person who would be the witness, such as switching the times, places, and the emissaries. This shows that the very act of testifying at this particular trial had become its own kind of ordeal in demonstration of the witness' faith.

The Testimonies

The testimonies themselves, as in the other trails were made in such a manner that they clearly emphasized the fact that the twenty-six martyrs met the criteria for beatification. The geographic proximity with the actual events allowed for more relevant testimonies in some cases, but most witnesses replied that they did not know the answers to a large number of questions. For example, Georgius Bastian responds in this way to all the queries, except five (6, 12, 15, 20 and 21). Even then, he rarely provides new information of interesting detail.[39]

As the following chart shows,[40] the witnesses were most eloquent when mentioning—logically—things that happened after the execution such as the relics (13–14), the causes of their execution (15), the miracles surrounding their bodies

34 Arch. Congr. SS. Rituum, Processus 1222, f. 52r.
35 Arch. Congr. SS. Rituum, Processus 1222, f. 55v.
36 Arch. Congr. SS. Rituum, Processus 1222, f. 59v.
37 Arch. Congr. SS. Rituum, Processus 1222, f. 62v.
38 Arch. Congr. SS. Rituum, Processus 1222, f. 66v.
39 Arch. Congr. SS. Rituum, Processus 1222, f. 23v–24r.
40 The chart divides the answers provided to each article into five types. Since all the replies are the same, the last question, which confirms that the witness said the truth, is classified as confirm.

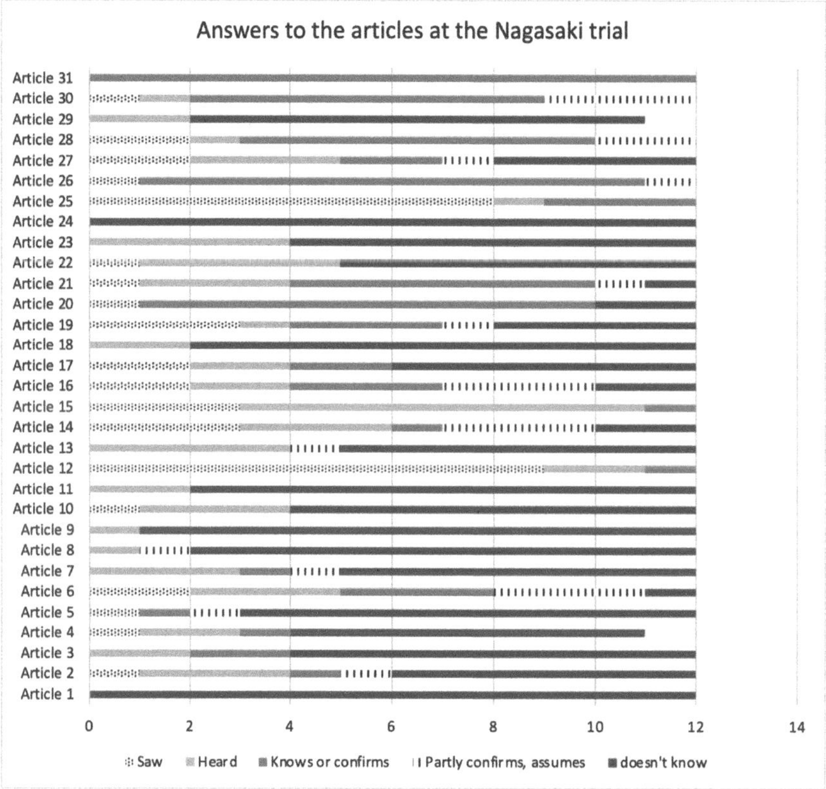

(16–18), the fact that this event greatly increased the number of Christians (19) and the beginning of their cult and supernatural prodigies related to the place of their deaths (20–23). The witnesses also confirmed the qualities of the martyrs, such as the firmness of their faith (25–26, and the factual confirmations in 29), and some testified about the story of Antonio, a child who chose to die, crucified like his heroes (27). Some articles, such as 24 (as well as the first one, on the illness Bautista recovered from when he arrived in Japan), were impossible to verify.

Cobayaxi Loday Johannes thus affirms, for example, that he saw many miracles when the martyrs were put on the cross, including the columns of lights mentioned in question 10. He also says that he had witnessed people collected their blood (12), and had heard that someone did bite one of Bautista's fingers off (13).[41] While he does not answer question 18, Bastian Kondo does, confirming he had heard that

41 Arch. Congr. SS. Rituum, Processus 1222, f. 37r.

Bautista did descend from his cross to give mass.[42] Mori Xembioe Martinus is even the only one to affirm that he had heard about the image of St. Francis bleeding, mentioned in article 9.[43] This shows that efforts were made to obtain testimony on all the topics found in the original list.

Given the new definition of sanctity, insisting on miracles established at the time,[44] it was fundamental to gather more information about the miracles that happened after the events, which could not be all properly investigated during the trials of 1597 and 1598. However, some witnesses also provided accounts that offered a different viewpoint. Johannes Araki, whose testimony as a whole seems to have cast doubt on some of the details the judges were expecting (such as the fact that the birds did not eat their bodies), still confirms crucial points regarding the miracles, such as the lights seen after their deaths or the blood flowing from Bautista for days. He even says that he received some of the blood of the martyrs from people present at the execution scene.[45]

The 30th question could at first appear as a routine confirmation on whether everyone at the time recognized their deaths as martyrdom. However, a few of the answers suggest a deeper issue lying within the wording. Johannes Araki replies that everyone did recognize them, and adds that only the Jesuits declared they were not martyrs, despite the fact that they now claim not to know whether such words were ever spoken.[46] Replying to the same question, even the 80-year-old Cagi Laurentius, in a hearing where his memory often failed him, said he had heard some Jesuits say that the twenty Japanese were true martyrs, but not the six Franciscan brothers.[47] The last two people who testified, Jifiyacus Michaelis and Yamada Yafioye Leo do not go into detail. However, they do make reference to some doubts on their nature as martyrs.[48]

As shall be demonstrated in the next section, this general animosity towards the Jesuits from certain local Christians was not a simple one-sided affair.

---

42 Arch. Congr. SS. Rituum, Processus 1222, f. 42r.

43 Arch. Congr. SS. Rituum, Processus 1222, f. 61r.

44 See . Also, Mostaccio, "Au carrefour des regards," 332–33.

45 Arch. Congr. SS. Rituum, Processus 1222, f. 33r.

46 Arch. Congr. SS. Rituum, Processus 1222, f. 35r : (…) "respondit quod omnes tenuerunt mortem divorum patrorum et sociorum pro gloriosis martryribus solum modo societas Jesus dixit pro tunc quod non erant martyres attamen nunc ignorant quod tale dicant et hoc respondet."

47 Arch. Congr. SS. Rituum, Processus 1222, f. 59r : "(…) audivisse quod ex parte Societatis dicebatur quod ex dicti viginti sex solum viginti Japones erant martyres ceteri autem sex religiosi non. (…)"

48 Arch. Congr. SS. Rituum, Processus 1222, f. 66r and f. 69v.

Those Who Did Not Testify

Indeed, some people summoned to testify refused to do so. By examining the account given in the final report, it is possible to determine the reasons for this—reasons that are related to what Johannes Araki explained. On September 13, Pedro de la Rosa visited two witnesses, Balthazar and Aloysius Martinez de Figueredo. However, they declined to appear in court. Balthazar said that he did not know the events well enough, and that he did not want to testify in front of the fathers, while Aloysius gave different various excuses. Pedro de la Rosa finally threatened them with excommunication, but they still refused to listen.[49]

The case of Balthazar de Sosa, first summoned on September 15, is similar. When he was called, he regretted not being able to testify due to traveling. However, he skipped the new trial date and made the judges wait. Pedro de la Rosa tried to persuade him the next day, and he threatened him with excommunication. This still was not enough, and he refused again, pretexting he could not take his religious equipment with him, and that the persecution was too severe.[50]

While they seem to have acted out of fear, the records on the other witnesses who refused to testify paint a different picture. Antonio Silva was the first one to do so. When summoned on September 5, he simply ignored the request. The next day, Pedro de la Rosa went to his home to persuade him with threats of immediate excommunication, but to no avail. When Pedro de la Rosa tried to actually notify him of the excommunication, Silva put his fingers in his ears and insisted that he would not listen.[51]

He also claimed that he had already testified in front of another priest and would give a letter instead of his testimony. The letter, which is quoted by Pedro de la Rosa, can be summarized as follows. After insisting he was a good Christian, he said that he followed Diego Valente, a Jesuit priest, and refused to obey Franciscan and Dominican priests, because he doesn't recognize their authority in Japan. He went even further, blaming the bad relations between Christians as the main cause for the persecutions. His parting line was also quite striking, as he stated that he would obey his prelate, Diego Valente, if he were told to go anywhere—even to hell—thus implying that he would never do so the same for the friars.[52]

Understanding the whole picture requires a look at the last witnesses. Francisco Martinez and Martinus de Lobea were both Portuguese born in Kyoto and living in Nagasaki. Pedro de la Rosa visited their homes on September 21, but they refused

---

49 Arch. Congr. SS. Rituum, Processsus 1222, f. 21v-22r.

50 Arch. Congr. SS. Rituum, Processus 1222, f. 27r-27v.

51 Arch. Congr. SS. Rituum, Processus 1222, f. 26v.

52 Arch. Congr. SS. Rituum, Processus 1222, f. 26v–27r.

to testify. On September 23, Pedro de la Rosa came back, bringing a letter that stated that they would be immediately excommunicated upon refusing to testify.

This led to strong protests from them and from members of their group. The report states that Balthazar Sosa was among them. They affirmed that they would not testify unless the previous excommunications were withdrawn. Then, they showed a letter to Pedro de la Rosa, claiming it to be from the Jesuit Superior General and head of the Church in Japan, which stated that such excommunications were null and void.[53]

The aftermath of these events can be seen in the description of September 25. Here, the report provides a list of several people who were immediately excommunicated due to ignoring their convocation to an apostolic trial: Aloysius Martinez, Balthazar Martinez, Francisco Martinez, Antonio de Silva, Balthazar de Sosa, and Martinus de Lobea.[54]

This demonstrates that this was a group of Westerners—or half-Westerners—who were all related to the Jesuits. More importantly, the reason for their refusal was not really the fear of persecution, but the fact that they did not want to follow the Dominicans. The consequences of their choice were immediate, as they all were excommunicated.

Conclusion

The Jesuits are usually depicted as having been very passive during the actual beatification process of the twenty-six martyrs. However, the documents demonstrate that the general hostility between them and the mendicant orders had demonstrable consequences even in the local communities. While the Society of Jesus as a whole was probably not directly giving orders, this had a major impact on the trial.

These documents also reveal animosity among the local Christians themselves, depending on their allegiance. Thus, the initial reluctance of the Society to recognize the twenty-six martyrs as true martyrs is mentioned in the testimonies—especially of the Japanese—in a clearly critical tone, insisting that everyone saw them as such and venerated them with the exception of the Jesuits.

For their part, the group that refused to testify was manifestly on the side of the Society. Diego Collado and the organizers of the trials were undoubtedly aware of this situation, and yet they clearly insisted on obtaining their testimonies, returning several times to get them if they refused. In fact, for them, it was fundamental to obtain as many depositions as possible, especially since some of the articles

53 Arch. Congr. SS. Rituum, Processus 1222, f. 70r.

54 Arch. Congr. SS. Rituum, Processus 1222, f. 70r.

were hardly, if at all, mentioned by the other witnesses. The sentence of immediate excommunication pronounced against them, which seems to have been disputed by the Jesuits, is another indication of the importance of this trial for the Friars Minor. It was in Nagasaki, more so than in Puebla, for example, that most of the eyewitness accounts were gathered and included in the final report. The Nagasaki trial was thus a crucial step in the process of creating the twenty-six martyrs as true modern saints. The beatification of 1627, which the Jesuits would eventually support afterwards, was in some ways at odds with the major trends in the Holy See, where the files were examined with much greater severity than before.

Although information does not survive regarding how the witnesses were chosen, we can assume that they were selected due to the knowledge of local communities that figures like Collado, or perhaps even more so local *dōjuku* like Thomas Rokuza-emon, had. It was also because they were among the few Christians in Nagasaki still alive who were able to testify about events that had occurred twenty-five years earlier, that the Friars Minor did their utmost to bring them to their court, despite the mortal danger that this could notice in the persecution situation.

This trial was thus the occasion for profiling on two levels. The first was to obtain arguments that would help conform the twenty-six martyrs to the profile of the ideal martyr saint of the modern age. The second was to determine the profiles of witnesses who could provide the fathers with what they needed to fulfill this objective. However, as the comments on the Jesuits given by some of the Japanese Christians show, there was still a wide gap between the friars' vision of the twenty-six martyrs and that of the Society of Jesus.

Section 5
Vocation to Holiness: Three Case Studies from Early Modern Europe

Beatrice Saletti

Lucia Broccadelli da Narni in Ferrara

The Short Season of a Living Saint, the Changing Memories of the Biographers

In Ferrara, corso Giovecca, at no. 179, there is a building, erected in 1646: this was a monastery of Capuchin Poor Clares, who in 1987 moved to the monastery of S. Giovanni Rotondo. The adjoining church, dedicated to St. Clare, was consecrated in 1673, and today it is a reference point for a lively community of parishioners. Inside the church, on a lectern, a hardcover notebook and a pen are available to the faithful, where those who feel the need ask for help from the Clarissa Sister Veronica of the Blessed Sacrament, who died in 1964. I was able to read myself the prayers of the faithful: requests for protection and help for oneself, children, grandchildren, to cope with an illness, a divorce, or economic problems etc.

A group of faithful, organized as an association, collected testimonies and money in order to start a cause for the beatification of the nun, undertaken in 2015 and still ongoing. Devotion to Sister Veronica is a contemporary phenomenon, and as such visible and documentable. Nevertheless, if a scholar wanted to measure the intensity of this devotion, there would be perhaps no adequate tools: even if he or she could obtain from the notebooks the number of devotees who asked for graces to Sister Veronica, which other data could it be related to? Devotion remains, to a large extent, in a private dimension, without visible manifestations.

This essay intends to deepen, through contemporary and subsequent sources, the devotion connected to Lucia Brocadelli in Ferrara, from her arrival in the city in 1499 to her beatification, which took place in 1710. As is known, the figure of Lucia is closely linked both to the Savonarolian phenomenon and to that of the 'living saints'.[1] As a 'saint' she was invested by the duke Hercules d'Este with a political role: the fact of hosting in her capital a saint – not formally declared, but considered such as a bearer of visible stigmata – made the duke a ruler protected by heaven, potentially the recipient of prophecies, and 'manager' of the relics of Lucia, or pieces soaked in the blood that came from her stigmata. The figure of Lucia, who had not had to submit to the cloister as the duke Hercules had obtained for her from the

1 T. Herzig, *Christ transformed into a Virgin woman: Lucia Brocadelli, Heinrich Institoris and the defense of the faith* (Roma: Storia e letteratura, 2013a); Ead, "The Rise and Fall of a Savonarolan Woman: Lucia Brocadelli's Contribution to the Piagnone movement", *Archiv für Reformationgeschichte* 95 (2013c) 36–37.

pontiff ample concessions (revoked shortly after the death of the duke, in 1505), has been studied within this complex both political and religious context, on which there is already an extensive literature.[2] What interests me here is instead to verify what the inhabitants of Ferrara wrote about her, both during the long period of her stay, which lasted until her death in 1544, and after the duke's death.

Several chronicles of Ferrara (many of which are anonymous) lie unpublished in public libraries between Ferrara and Modena. Although there is no reliable overall work that helps to assess their reliability, origin, or even mutual relationships,[3] I have tried to recover as many as possible sources to look for references to Lucia Brocadelli and her stigmata, miracles, prophecies, or pious deeds. Let's start with three contemporary chroniclers of Lucia: the anonymous writer of the *Diario Ferrarese*; the jurist Bernardino Zambotti; the master at the ducal mint Paolo Zerbinati (whose chronicle as was transcribed almost a century later by his descendant Giovanni Maria). Contemporaries of Lucia, at least for a certain period, were also Giuliano and Giacomo Antigini, who wrote a diary ending in 1514;[4] Alessandro Sardi (died in 1551);[5] and Filippo Rodi, active during the last decade of Lucia's life, and particularly devoted to another nun: Beatrice d'Este, who appears very often as a promoter of miracles and visions in Rodi's chronicle.[6]

Let's read the few lines that they dedicate to Lucia:

> The duke himself, drawn from the great fame that flew everywhere of the holiness of a nun of Viterbo named Sister Lucia, who led a very austere and very religious life and was

---

2 I only quote O. Niccoli, *Profeti e popolo nell'Italia del Rinascimento* (Roma: Laterza, 1987); G. Zarri, *Le sante vive: profezie di corte e devozione femminile tra '400 e '500* (Torino: Rosenberg & Sellier, 1990); L. Polizzotto, "When Saints Fall Out: Women and the Savonarolan Reform in Early Sixteenth-Century Florence", *Renaissance Quarterly* 46/3 (1993) 486–525; Id., *The elect nation. The Savonarolan movement in Florence 1494–1545* (Oxford: Clarendon press, 1994); D. Weinstein, *Savonarola. The rise and fall of a Renaissance prophet* (New Haven-London: Yale University Press, 2011). The autograph visions of Lucia are edited in E. A. Matter/A. Maggi/M. Lehmijoki-Gardner (ed.), ""Le rivelazioni" of Lucia Brocadelli da Narni", Archivum Fratrum Praedicatorum 71 (2001) 311–344.

3 B. Saletti, *Un notaio nella Ferrara del secondo Quattrocento: Ugo Caleffini e le sue cronache. Con un'edizione della Storia della città di Ferrara* (Milano: Mimesis, 2021, 53–59.

4 G. Antigini/G. Antigini, *Annali di Ferrara dal 1384 al 1514*, Biblioteca Comunale Ariostea di Ferrara (henceforward: BCAFe), ms. Cl. I 757. Giuliano died in 1505 while Giacomo – of whom his father writes that he was born on 1467, August 31 (ibid., 30r) – is not known the date of death. In their memoirs the Antigini pay attention mainly to family events, and to very few external events. For this reason their silence on Lucia is not strange.

5 A. Sardi, *Chronici libri duo*, Biblioteca BCAFe, ms. Cl. I 474, 189–191, lists only rare national and European political events, so it is not surprising the lack of data on Lucia.

6 F. Rodi, *Annali di Ferrara*, BCAFe, ms. Cl. I 645.

a great example, arranged with the pope to have her in Ferrara... [7]
And up to the fifth of August [1501] Sister Lucia, who they say to be a saint, for whom the duke Hercules had built [a monastery] near the church of the friars of the Angels in Ferrara, with a great procession entered the said monastery with some companions, to stay there continuously.[8]
On day 5 [June 1501]. Sister Lucia da Viterbo, a young woman who has Christ's stigmata in her hands, and according to what I heard from a friar in the pulpit preaching in the dome, and from many religious people who saw them, she was conducted by commission of our duke, in the new monastery de Sancta Catharina, endowed by His Excellency, near the church of the Angels. And she took twenty-two sisters with her. Of which monastery she will be abbess, and [sisters] are under the government of the Anzoli friars, and our duke makes this monastery entirely at his expense.[9]

The aforementioned year [1502] the lord duke adopted the monastery of the Sisters of Santa Caterina da Siena in Terra Nova and gave him annuities which pay them 1500 lire each year and the half of the tithe of San Martina which gives them annually in his part, going well, cans 100 of wheat, without the other large fodder and legumes; not happy with this, he has determined that he wants to give them so much that they can reach the entrance of a thousand scudi a year. This monastery was commissioned in 1501 by the said duke Hercules to give it to Sister Lucia of Viterbo and her companions as he did. On August 5, the feast of Saint Dominic, in 1501 the said Sister Lucia entered with about 12 sisters of ours from Ferrara, accompanied by the same lord duke who dressed them all, and by the court; and this Sister Lucia, with 4 of her companions of the Third Order, the duke sent them to Ferrara with mules and with 24 crossbowmen on horseback twice,

7 "Il duca medesimo tratto dalla fama grande che per tutto vollava della gran santità di una monacha di Viterbo nominata suor Lucia, la quale conduceva vitta austerissima et religiosissima et di grande esempio et edifficatione, procurò con il papa di haverla in Ferrara...": Ibid. 451v.

8 "Et insino a dì v de Agosto [1501] Suor Lucia, che se dice santa, per cui il duca Hercole facto fare [un monestero] apreso la giesia di frati di Angeli in Ferrara, cum grande processione intròe in dicto monestero cum alcune sue compagne, per starli continue": G. Pardi, (ed.), "Diario ferrarese dal 1409 sino al 1502 di autori incerti", in: *Rerum Italicarum Scriptores*[2], XXIV/7 (Bologna: Zanichelli, 1933), 1–289: 273.

9 "A dì 5 [giugno 1501]. Sore Lucia da Viterbo, zovene che ha le stigmate de Christo a le mano, e segondo lo ho intexo da uno frate in pergolo predicando in domo, e da molte persone religioxe le hanno viste, fu conducta de commissione del duca nostro, in lo monastero de Sancta Catharina novo, dotato per la Excellentia Soa, aprovo la chiesia di Anzoli. E menò con sieco vintedoe sore. Del quale monastero essa ne serà abbadessa, et sonno sotto il governo di frati d'i Anzoli, e lo duca nostro fa tale monestero tuto a soe spexe.": G. Pardi (ed.), Bernardino Zambotti, "Diario ferrarese dall' anno 1476 sino al 1504", in: *Rerum Italicarum Scriptores*[2], XXIV/7 (Bologna: Zanichelli 1937), 1–359: 307.

the first time the people of Viterbo forbade it, but the second time came to rescue for the grace of God, and arrived in Ferrara on May 7, 1499, at the age of 26.[10]

On the day 23 [January 1502]. Our illustrious duke went with Sister Lucia from Viterbo, who is in the monastery of S. Caterina degli Angeli, out over the bridge of S. Giorgio, on horseback (and she was in a closed caretta with two sisters); and they took Sister Beatrice da Narni with 13 nuns on the Po, at the pillar of S. Giorgio, in caretta, whom our duke sent to take up to Rome and accompanied them to the monastery of S. Nicolò dal Cortile, made in Tera Nova. They say they are all very holy nuns, they all have crucifixes in their hands.[11]

On Friday, which was the 4th of February [1502], in the morning, the most illustrious lord duke with a large party came to the palace of the prefate lord orator [*sc.* of France] and together they went to Santa Caterina, monastery of the nuns of s. Dominic, where they listened to Mass, then saw and talked with her, a holy woman named Sor Lucia da Viterbo, to whom apparently stigmata appeared in five places of her body, such as Jesus Christ had them, and every Friday she suffers great passion and they bleeds, where with tissues and some gloves some touched those places, and she gave to the lord orator some cloths that she keeps above the said stigmata. And then together they went to the Castle to see it and the very dignified artillery that is inside it in huge numbers.[12]

---

10 "L'anno sudetto [1502] il signor duca adottò il monasterio delle sure de Santa Caterina da Siena in Terra Nova et gli diede d'entrata usi che li pagano ogn'anno lire 1500 et la mettà della decima della san Martina che li dà all'anno in sua parte, andando bene, moggia 100 di frumento, senza le altre biade grosse e legumi, né contento di questo, ha determinato di volerli dare tanto che assenda all'entrata di mille scudi l'anno il qual monasterio fu fatto fare del 1501 dal detto signor duca Ercole per darlo a suor Lucia da Viterbo e compagne come fece. Adì 5 agosto festa di San Domenico del 1501 vi entrò dentro detta suor Lucia con circa 12 suore delle nostre di Ferrara, accompagnate dal'istesso signor duca che le havea vestite tutte, e dalla corte; la qual suor Lucia, con 4 sue compagne del Terzo Ordine, il duca le mandò a condure a Ferrara con mulli e con 24 balestriri a cavallo due volte, la prima volta il populo di Viterbo lo vietò, ma la seconda volta vene a salvamento per la gratia de Dio, et arrivò a Ferrara adì 7 maggio 1499 d'età d'anni 26.": M. G. Muzzarelli (ed.), Giovanni Maria Zerbinati, *Croniche di Ferrara quali comenzano del anno 1500 sino al 1527* (Ferrara: Deputazione Provinciale Ferrarese di Storia Patria, 1989), 44.

11 "A dì 23 [gennaio 1502]. Lo illustrissimo duca nostro andò con sore Lucia da Viterbo, che sta in lo monesterio de Sancta Katharina dali Anzoli, fora per il ponte de San Zorzo, a cavalo (e lei con doe sore herano in una caretta aserate); e tolseno a Po, al pilastro de San Zorzo, in caretta, sore Beatrixe da Narni con 13 sore, le quali il duca nostro ha manda' a tuore insino a Roma e le acompagnò in lo monasterio de San Nicolò dal Cortile, facto in Tera Nova. Dicesse essere tute sore sanctissime, haveano crucifixi in mano tute.": Pardi, "Diario Ferrarese", 312.

12 "Vegneridì, che fu a 4 de febraro [1502], la matina, lo illustrissimo signore duca con gran comitiva venne al palazo del prefato signore oratore [*sc.* di Francia] e insieme andorno a Sancta Catharina, monastero de monache de San Domenico, dove oldeteno Messa, poi vedeteno, e con lei parlorno, una

> Thursday, which was the 10th of February [1502], the illustrious duke came with a large group to take the aforesaid lord orator from home and together they went to visit the aforementioned Sister Lucia, who has the stigmata, and then they came to the dome to hear the Mass, where the said lord orator was followed by the Venetian ambassadors, and they took leave from His Lordship with many words and utterances. And after lunch the aforesaid lord duke returned to the said lord orator and together they went to accompany the referred to above cardinal de Libreth, who began his journey towards Rome.[13]
> On the 24th [April 1503], the day of s. George. The race of the gold brocade race was not run by the Berber horses following the usual, but on that day our duke donated the said race to the monastery of the Sisters of Santa Caterina, where Sister Lucia, the one with the stigmata, is staying, because the Lord Messer Rainald, his brother, had died a few days ago.[14]
> Saturday 14 said [July 1509] the church of S. Caterina da Siena was consecrated by Messer Miliaduse d'Este bishop of Comacchio, and the whole monastery inside, in which everyone could enter and see it all this day, since the nuns were retired and could not be seen.[15]
> And I was in that monastery and I saw it all, which is a great monastery, and is as beautiful as any other in Ferrara, indeed perhaps more beautiful than all the others.[16]

We can note, without fear of over-interpreting the sources, that the references to Lucia focus on the moment of her arrival in the city, on the conclusion of the construction works of the new monastery to house her and on the actions of

---

sancta donna nomine sor Lucia da Viterbo, che evidentemente nel corpo suo ze appariva le stigmate in li cinque lochi, como hebbe Jesù Christo, e ogni veneridì patisse gran passione e gè sanguinano, dove con panici e guanti alchuni tocorno quelli loci, e lei donòe al signore oratore alchune pezole che tene sopra dicte stigmate. E poi insieme andorno al Castello a vederlo e le artelarie dignissime gè sono dentro a numero grandissimo.": Ibid., 326.

13 "Zobia, che fu a dì 10 de febraro [1502], lo illustrissimo duca venne pur con gran comitiva a levare de caxa lo prefato signore oratore e insieme andorno a vixitare la soprannominata sore Lucia, che patisse le stigmate, e poi venero al domo ad odire la Messa, dove da li ambasatori veneti fu seguitato il dicto signore oratore e da Soa Segnoria pilgiorno licentia con molte parole e proferte. Et da poi il dexenare ritornò el prefato signore duca dal dicto signore oratore e insieme andorno ad acompagnare el soprascripto cardinale de Libreth, qual pilg[i]òe il suo camino verso Roma": Ibid., 332.

14 "A dì 24 [aprile 1503], il dì de San Zorzo. El palio de brochà d'oro non se corse con li barbari segondo il consueto, ma in tal zorno il duca nostro donnò dicto palio al monastero de le sore de Sancta Catarina, dove stà sore Lucia da le stigmate, perchè l'hera morto pochi zorni fa il signore messer Raynaldo suo fratello.": Ibid., 349.

15 "Sabbato 14 detto [luglio 1509] la chiesa di S. Caterina da Siena fu consecrata da messer Miliaduse d'Este vescovo di Comachio, e tutto il monasterio di dentro, nel quale ha potuto ognuno entrare e vederlo tutto questo dì, essendo le suore retirate che non si poteano vedere.": Muzzarelli, *Croniche di Ferrara*, 82.

16 "Et io fui in detto monasterio et lo vidi tutto, il quale è un magno monasterio, et è così bello com'ogn'altro che sia in Ferrara, anzi forsi più bello de tutti gli altri.": Ibid., 45.

the duke towards the nun and her entourage of nuns. The only reference to her supernatural conditions is in relation to an external visit, namely the presence of the orator of the king of France, who had gathered in Ferrara on the occasion of the wedding of duke Hercules's son, Alfonso, with Lucrezia Borgia. Although the court was besieged in those days by ambassadors from numerous Italian powers, Hercules decided to bring only the king's ambassador to the new Dominican monastery, twice. The young woman is exhibited to impress the ambassador, and cloths and gloves are applied to the points of the stigmata. Lucia gives the diplomat some cloths that she had placed on the stigmata. The episode has an obvious public significance. However, apart from it, no chronicler spends a word to inform the reader of a prophecy, a miracle, a devotional event connected to Lucia. Nor of Lucia's visits to citizens of Ferrara, or vice versa of citizens (or foreign visitors) to Lucia. None of them refers to a devotion practiced by the citizens of Ferrara towards the nun.

It should be noted that, for the first half of the century, the only chronicler who dwells on city events beyond 1504 is Zerbinati. He writes about a nun who gets to have herself bricked up in a room built next to the bishop's palace on Thursday 7 October 1507.[17] He also reports that in the same year the Franciscan Giacomo Ungarelli founded the brotherhood of Jesus, and that the people of Ferrara enrolled in it in mass.[18] Two years later, on April 7, 1509, Zerbinati wrote that he adored the cross of Christ in the palace of San Francesco that Isabella del Balzo, the widow of Frederick of Aragon, had brought with her from the Neapolitan exile.[19] Although the information is concise, it is likely that the relic was exhibited for the veneration of the faithful – if not of all the people without distinction, at least of selected courtiers. The chronicler notes that, in 1511, an event considered to be miraculous aroused the attention of many people from Ferrara: an image of the Virgin became an object of prayer and donations, and in the following decades it remained a destination of pilgrimage and devotion, so much so that it needed an administrative apparatus to manage alms.[20] Zerbinati himself claims to have been elected, in 1513, from among the 32 members of the commission, among the purposes of which was the erection of a church on the site of the miracle built in 1526 (from the late sixteenth century and until today, the church is called in Ferrara the church 'della Madonnina', but it was erected under the title of Santa Maria della Visitazione).[21]

17 Ibid., 72.

18 Ibid.

19 Ibid., 78.

20 Ibid., 117.

21 Ibid., 133. On the documentation relating to the church: E. Peverada, "Il fondo archivistico cinquecentesco del santuario ferrarese della Madonnina", in: Enrico Angiolini (ed.), *Le vie della devozione: gli archivi dei santuari in Emilia Romagna* (Ravenna: Mucchi, 2000), 149–191.

The fact that contemporary chroniclers inform their readers of news concerning the religious life of the city but not of Lucia cannot be considered a proof of the fact that any form of devotion towards Lucia was absent. However, it is noteworthy that not even Zerbinati, the only contemporary witness who was also so sensitive to ecclesiastical and spiritual events as to describe a Marian miracle that took place well outside the local borders (i. e. in Prato),[22] testifies to any interest in Lucia.

It would certainly help to sift on a large scale the bequests and testamentary dispositions of the sixteenth century, in order to recover any traces of attachment in life or in death to Lucia on the part of the citizens of Ferrara; at present, however, the entire Ancient Notary Archive is closed since years, and it is not yet known until when. It is therefore elsewhere, for the moment, that clues can be sought. For example, we may look at the documentation of the monastery erected to put Lucia Brocadelli at its head. An important document is the manuscript containing "by order the sisters who are entered and who will enter, and the time of their profession, their names, parentage, death",[23] partially written by Benedetto of Mantua. In reality, the first intention declared by Benedetto, confessor of the nuns from February 20, 1505 to October 18 of the following year,[24] is to transmit "the origin and principle and the cause together with the way of the construction" of the building, but to such a purpose he devotes just one page. However, I find it useful to transcribe the passage back here.

> During the years of our health 1499, in perpetual memory, the illustrious duke Hercules d'Este, second duke of the noble city of Ferrara, knowing the public fame of a woman sister of the third habit of the Order of our father St. Dominic, called Sister Lucia, from the city of Narni, who *tunc temporis* lived in the city of Viterbo – who was said to have and carry openly in her hands, feet and side the stigmata of our Lord Messer Jesus Christ – sought the aforementioned illustrious gentleman, due to the devotion caused by her fame, to lead and transfer the said Sister Lucia to the city of Ferrara, with the intention and promises of building a monastery for her. And giving work to this in a few days, *Deo dante*, obtained his intent, *licet cum* some difficulty, because it was *furtive* and against the will of many citizens of Viterbo; I omit the way because it would be long and of little use. In the said year 1499, on the 7th of May, the said Sister Lucia arrived in Ferrara and had in her company her mother, a widow in secular dress called Madonna Anna, and a cousin of hers in the third habit of S. Dominic, aged 15, called Sister Ursula, and her confessor,

22 Pardi, "Diario Ferrarese", 129.

23 Benedetto da Mantova OP, *Cronaca*, Archivio Storico Diocesano di Ferrara (henceforward: ASDFe), Santa Caterina da Siena, B. 3/22 1r. The following sentence, "the dowries given by their relatives to the monastery [le dotte date per li lor parenti al monasterio]", is quashed.

24 A. Samaritani, *Lucia da Narni ed Ercole I d'Este a Ferrara tra Caterina da Siena, Girolamo Savonarola e i Piagnoni: fonti e letteratura* (Ferrara: Edizioni Cartografica 2006), 26.

called Fra Cristoforo da Viterbo. And she was received and lived in a place called the Ca' Bianca, near S. Vito from the back door. This place was then given to the Servite nuns. In this place she lived until the 24th of July which followed. *Item* died in this place the said Sister Ursula, cousin of the said Sister Lucia, and this was on the third day of her arrival, that is, on the 9th of May 1499. And she was buried in S. Domenico *sub deposito*. Then her bones were transferred to our monastery in the tombs of the nuns, and so she was the first to be buried there on the 25th of October 1502.[25]

The text continues alternating the lists of nuns who entered the monastery with bishops' decrees or edicts of Hercules on the monastery. Unfortunately, however, it does not describe any devotional phenomena, miracles, or notable events relating to Lucia. We cannot therefore draw useful data from it, and this is extremely frustrating. Except for the miraculous stigmata seen by those present on the occasion of her death, our information on Lucia's life, including her autobiography which, however, has come down to us in a much later copy (and therefore may have been manipulated even to defame her image),[26] refers to internal disagreements in the community of the monastery which led to the loss, by Lucia, of the role of abbess and to her isolation by the sisters, as Lucia lived in the monastery of Santa Caterina da Siena without interruption until her death in 1544.

We continue to expose the information in order. After the death of duke Hercules (m. January 1505) the monastery lost the importance that had been attributed to it by the duke. His successor, Alfonso I, was much more interested in international politics (or perhaps he was forced to take an interest in it because of the wars of Italy), and there are no interventions of his regarding religious groups or community reform projects, unlike the father.[27] While we are following the traces of devotion to Lucia between 1504 and 1544, it is perhaps useful to remember some events that took place in Europe and caused the already present aura of suspicion towards

25 Benedetto da Mantova OP, *Cronaca*, 1r.

26 The question is of extreme importance and has been debated for a long time, until a generally agreed conclusion on the authenticity of the text: G. Zarri, "La scrittura mistica e un testo controverso: l'autobiografia di Lucia da Narni", in: M. Fumagalli Beonio Brocchieri/R. Frigeni (ed.), *Donne e scrittura dal XII al XVI secolo* (Bergamo: Lubrina Editore 2009a), 163–182; E. A Matter/G. Zarri, *Una mistica contestata. La vita di Lucia da Narni (1476–1544) tra agiografia e autobiografia. Con l'edizione del testo* (Roma: Edizioni di Storia e Letteratura, 2011), xxv–xli; G. Zarri, "Memoria individuale e memoria collettiva. Gli scritti di Lucia da Narni († 1544) e la loro conservazione", in: G. Zarri/N. Baranda Leturio (ed.), Memoria e comunità femminili Spagna e Italia, secc. XV–XVII (Firenze: Firenze University Press – UNED, 2011), 73–86. On the physical experience of Lucia as a mystic see N. Nerbano, "Estasi, performance e ricreazione del corpo nell'esperienza delle «sante vive». Il caso di Lucia Brocadelli da Narni", Annali online UniFE – Sezione di Lettere 10 (2015) 1–3.

27 M. Folin, "Sul "buon uso della religione" in alcune lettere di Ercole d'Este e Felino Sandei: finte stigmate, monache e ossa di morti", *Archivio Italiano per la Storia della Pietà* 11 (1998) 181–244.

mystical phenomena to intensify.[28] All in all, the picture looks like this: once her main benefactor dies in 1505, a woman endowed with controversial mystical powers remains unprotected and the members of her community can retaliate against her for the much inferior treatment they had previously received.[29] She then withdraws into silence and nothing leaks from the monastery until her death. This phase of Lucia's life, from 1505 to her death, appears to be an empty space, full of only questions.

Even the immediately following phase is a sort of black hole: from 1544 to 1616, the year in which Lucia's first biography appears, I have not found any vague clues about any Ferrarese devotion to her. Giovanni Maria di Massa, who wrote a chronicle in the 1580s, did not even mention Lucia, neither on the occasion of her arrival in the city, nor in relation to the erection of the new monastery, and not at the time of her death.[30]

Another chronicler, Girolamo Merenda, writes as follows:

> Monastery of St. Caterina da Siena
> Having refused all the marriages given to him by her brother to marry, she resolved to take the third dress of S. Domenico and this was revoked by S. Caterina da Siena one day later the received habits, to be a person of holy life, she deserved to feel the very stiff pains of our Lord's passion, and the sacred stigmata were impressed on her. Nevertheless because it was thought that it was a diabolical illusion she was called to Rome in the time of Pope Alexander V (*recte*: Alexander VI, died 1503) and then, His Holiness certified by

---

28 Although the topic is fundamental for understanding the different positions towards Lucia, there is no space here to deal with it properly. One of the most traumatic events for the Dominican order was the so-called 'Bern scandal', which saw some Dominican friars burn at the stake for simulating mystical events: T. Herzig, "Genuine and Fraudolent Stugmatics in the Sixteenth Century", in: M. Eliav-Feldon/T. Herzig (ed.), *Dissimulation and Deceit in Early Modern Europe* (Houndmills, Basingstoke, Hampshire: Palgrave Macmillan 2015), 142–164. For Italian examples of suspicion towards mystical phenomena: A. Prosperi, "L'elemento storico nelle polemiche sulla santità", in G. Zarri (ed), Finzione e santità tra medioevo ed età moderna (Torino: Rosenberg & Sellier, 1991), 88–1; Matter/Zarri, *Una mistica contestata*, xvii–xxi; T. Herzig, *Le donne di Savonarola: Spiritualità e devozione nell'Italia del Rinascimento* (Roma: Carocci, 2014), 144–164. An extreme synthesis in Samaritani, *Lucia da Narni*, 45–46.

29 As Folin Sul "buon uso", 187, writes, already in 1498 the person in charge of duke Ercole to obtain information on Lucia in Viterbo declared, in a letter dated February 16: "I have searched in various ways if these stigmata of Sister Lucia who is in Viterbo are true, nevertheless with great secret and occultly I have undoubtedly found the truth and I find that it is a fake thing and of great sadness, without any truth [io o cercato per diverse vie se queste stygmate de sor Lucia che è a Viterbo sono vere, tandem con gran secreto et ocultamente ho trovato il vero indubitatamente et trovo che è cosa finta et de gran tristicia, senza alcuna verità]".

30 M. Provasi (ed.), Giovanni Maria di Massa, *Memorie di Ferrara (1582–1585)* (Ferrara: Deputazione Provinciale Ferrarese di Storia Patria, 2004).

> his doctor Bernardo and other doctors having done every diligence to know the truth, it was concluded to be true stigmata and as a sign of the truth the doctor made a brief signature in his hand of this justification, which I have seen in the writings of the said monastery and other writings which speak of this, as I will say later [...]. /151r / But before Sister Lucia entered the monastery, the duke wanted to see the stigmata with his own eyes as the said duke testifies in a brief signed by his hand [...]. / 151v / This Lucia lived in this monastery for 42 years, she died on November 15th, most holy woman, I have seen her holy body of her whole and the sign of the stigmata on her side.[31]
> In the monastery of these reverend mothers the body of the blessed Lucia da Narni, founder of this monastery, is seen, which body is completely intact in a coffin and the sign of the stigmata can still be seen in the side, which she deserved, felt and had for our Lord in the feet and hands and side.[32]

Merenda, rector of the church of S. Biagio and chaplain and ducal cantor since 1577, as well as author of historical works, died in 1603. Nothing else is known about him besides these scant data. However, it is likely that he visited Lucia's remains sometime after her death, unless we hypothesize that he was a teenager at the time (his date of birth is unknown). Zarri affirms that on the occasion of the funeral the city population showed great veneration, so much so as to delay her burial for three days; however, she does not specify where she found this information.[33]

Keeping a stigmatized body, even if in the climate of the Reformation and the European wars, was no small thing for a monastery. Yet, Marc'Antonio Guarini (1570–1638) wrote absolutely nothing about this. Not even the anonymous chronicle owned by Elia Minerbi, and ending in 1607, is about Lucia. Both describe various events concerning spirituality in Ferrara.

They report of a miraculous Madonna near the Porta d'Amore;[34] of the passage of foreign pilgrims who visit the city (but do not go to Lucia's tomb),[35] of the removal of a Madonna from a column next to the portal of the cathedral,[36] of various processions to implore graces or to thank for having received them that take place elsewhere than to the monastery of S. Caterina da Siena,[37] and also of the interest of the duke and foreign visitors in the blood traces on the wall of the

31 G. Merenda, *Storia di Ferrara*, BCAFe, ms. Cl. I 472, 150r–151.

32 Ibid., 177v.

33 Zarri, *Memoria individuale*, 81.

34 M.A. Guarini, *Annali della città di Ferrara dal 1570 a tutto il 1596*, BCAFe, ms. Antonelli 266, 13r.

35 Ibid., 32v.

36 Ibid., 75r; Anonimo Minerbi, *Giornale della casa d'Este dal 1412 al 1607*, BCAFe, ms. Antonelli 759, 114r.

37 Guarini, *Annali*, 79v; Ibid., 82v.

church of S. Maria in Vado, dating back to the Eucharistic miracle of 1171.[38] But of Lucia, and her spoils, or miracles, not even the shadow. Not even the Pope, having triumphantly entered the city just taken from the Este family in 1598, ever visits Lucia's remains, much less her monastery, celebrating instead in the churches of S. Maria in Vado and at the monastery of Corpus Domini.[39] The only mention of the monastery of S. Caterina da Siena concerns the burial of Count Girolamo Montecuccoli in 1588, which took place in that place because five of his daughters were nuns there.[40]

The testimonies from Ferrara do not mention Lucia, nor any form of interest in her remains. Apart from the isolated case of Merenda, the other chroniclers are silent on the subject. It will be in quite a different context that Lucia's life will be presented to the public: by Serafino Razzi, a Florentine Dominican follower of Savonarola, who in 1577 wrote a life of saints and blessed belonging to the order of Preachers. Razzi explains to the reader that the information about Lucia was told to him in the same year in which he finished the work and gave it to the press (1577) by Antonino da Ravenna, a prior in Pesaro. He in turn had received the information from Arcangelo da Viadana, who had known Lucia intimately as he had been her confessor.[41] He in 1577 promotes Lucia's life, and even chooses to omit an important detail (her marriage)[42] to provide her with an image that adheres more to the most widespread ideal of holiness; he is therefore a figure extraneous to the city context.

Serafino Razzi was a great innovator: in addition to spreading the memory of saints and blessed of his own order, a practice of ancient tradition, he recovered the use of *laudes* and wrote poems in *terzine* intended for recitation or singing by the nuns.[43] Razzi was among the protagonists of the Savonarolian reform in the Tridentine period; thus, it is reasonable to suppose that Lucia, like other Dominican nuns, in the pages of Razzi could relaunch the spiritual ingredients which Savonarola had promoted. Samaritani enumerates two texts briefly concerning Lucia, between the few lines of Razzi and the first book totally devoted to the nun written in 1616: the book *De signis Ecclesiae Dei contra omnes haereses* by Tommaso Bozio, published

38 Ibid., 93; Anonimo Minerbi, *Giornale*, 108r.

39 Ibid., 96 and 101v.

40 Ibid., 68v–69r.

41 It is not clear, however, when and for much time father Arcangelo frequented Lucia: Zarri, "Lucia da Narni e il movimento femminile savonaroliano", in: M. Miegge/G. Fragnito (ed.), *Girolamo Savonarola da Ferrara all'Europa* (Firenze: SISMEL Edizioni del Galluzzo, 2001), 112–113.

42 S. Razzi, *Vite dei santi e beati cosi hvomini, come donne del sacro ordine de' frati predicatori* (Firenze: Bartolomeo Sermartelli, 1577), 152.

43 Zarri, *Libri di spirito: Editoria religiosa in volgare nei secoli XV–XVII* (Torino: Rosenberg & Sellier, 2009b), 159–161.

in Rome in 1591, and the book *De stigmatibus Divae Cattarinae senensis* by the Sienese Dominican Gregorio Lombardelli.

In both works Lucia is not the protagonist. She became such only in 1616, thanks to Marcianese, a Dominican. His text becomes the point of reference for all subsequent biographical production but raises great problems. First of all, almost nothing is known about Marcianese. We know only that he was a preacher, and a theology teacher. In the volume's dedication to the bishop of Ferrara (the hated cardinal Leni),[44] he appears to reside in the convent of S. Maria degli Angeli, but for a Dominican friar the information sounds like a tautology. It is also the content of the text that arouses perplexity in the reader.

Beginning his narration from the birth of the nun, Marcianese comes to the monastication of Lucia in Viterbo, and to the numerous miracles that would have made the monastery very popular. However, the only chronicles of Viterbo so far known from the last decade of the fifteenth century are the memories of Francesco and Giacomo Sacchi, who wrote nothing from 1494 to 1520, and nothing even on the occasion of Lucia's burial, which according to the hagiographers would have been accompanied by copious miracles.[45]

This would confirm the severe judgment of Felino Sandeo who on April 6, 1499 wrote from Viterbo to Duke Ercole d'Este: "It is not seen that she performs any miracle nor is there a throng of people to see it, while if the thing were (wanted) by God she would have more faithful than Rome will not have in the year of the Jubilee."[46]

The biography deserves an extensive discussion. Marcianese claims, among other things, that he has consulted three manuscripts of Lucia, of which he does not specify the content, and other handwritten books of which he does not specify the author.[47] We do not know if Lucia's manuscripts that Marcianese consulted differ from the only surviving manuscript known today. Anyway, Marcianese's Lucia is an original but reassuring saint, while in her autobiography many events are peculiar: to name just three, one of her confessors confesses that he had passionately desired to be born a woman, in order to be a nun subject to her; her husband, after becoming

44 The citizens of Ferrara bitterly opposed bishop Leni for his attempt to revoke the Bonifacian bull (a privilege granted to the Este and their subjects in 1391): B. Saletti, *Le visite pastorali del vescovo Giovanni Battista Leni nella diocesi di Ferrara (1616, 1620, 1622, 1624, 1626)*, tesi di laurea, Un. di Ferrara, rel. prof. Massimo Donattini, 1997, 22–29.

45 *Ricordi della casa Sacchi*, in I. Ciampi, *Cronache e statuti della città di Viterbo* (Firenze: Cellini, 1872), 427–428 and 437.

46 Folin, Sul "buon uso", 191.

47 G. Marcianese, *Narratione della nascita, vita, e morte della B. Lucia da Narni dell'ordine di S. Domenico, fondatrice del monastero di S. Caterina da Siena di Ferrara* (Ferrara: presso Vittorio Baldini, 1616), 101–102.

an observant Franciscan friar, obsessed with her memory, follows her to Ferrara, going so far as to perform (or commission) demonic spells to obtain her love; and Jesus himself explains to Lucia that he sent the deceased Pope Alexander VI to hell because of his abominable life.[48]

The detailed lists of Lucia's miracles in life of which Marcianese writes, which would have occurred in Narni, Viterbo and Ferrara, find no confirmation in previous texts. This would perhaps be understandable in the case of unknown miracles, of poor social condition; it is unlikely in the case of the future duke Alfonso d'Este.[49]

Even if the documentation in the diocesan archive is copious, there are no attestations of her miracles before the seventeenth century, and the dated and signed declarations by miraculously saved people reported in the cause of beatification of Lucia, are rare before the eighteenth century. Moreover, the very biography of Marcianese and the subsequent one of the nun of the convent of S. Caterina da Siena Fulvia Aventi[50] date back to a century after the events.[51] Even the documentation of the Estense Archive does not, despite containing Lucia's letters to the duke and various certificates relating to her beatification, refer to any miracles prior to the entire seventeenth century.[52]

We previously mentioned the bishop of Ferrara in office when Lucia's biography was published: Giovanni Battista Leni. It is only the successor of his successor, Francesco Maria Machiavelli, who in 1647 promoted the cause of beatification of Lucia. The first stage foresees the recognition of the cult from immemorial times, and for this reason, having not found any previous attestations on site, I hypothesize that Marcianese's text was considered a highly reliable source.

As I have already mentioned, the chronicles of Ferrara are for the most part unpublished. If this is valid for the fifteenth and sixteenth centuries, the statement becomes peremptory for the period after the devolution of Ferrara to the pope. Historians seem to have lost interest in the city which, after hosting a sumptuous and powerful dynasty, had become the periphery of the papal state. However, it is not due to the scarcity of sources that I avoid citing chronicles about this period: since Vincenzo Bellini (d.1783), Cesare Barotti (d. 1782) and Giuseppe Maria Maffei

---

48 In Matter/Zarri, *Una mistica contestata*, 6, 68 and 126.

49 Marcianese: *Narratione della nascita*, 200.

50 F. A. Aventi, *Memorie della vitta, gratie, e successi occorsi in ordine alla beata Lucia da Narni cavate di libri antichi, dalle memorie delle più anziane del monastero, da persone che anno riceuto le gratie e da quello che o veduto e sentito [1697]*, ASDFe, Santa Caterina da Siena, B. 3/25.

51 The oldest document that I have recovered in the chronicle of Sister Fulvia dates back to 1655, when is collected the testimony of Lucia Antogniola who, after having endured 10 wounds in one leg for 5 months, votes to Blessed Lucia (well before that this definition was legitimate) and in 22 days it was completely restored (ASDFe, B. 3/25, loose sheet, undated).

52 Archivio di Stato di Modena, Giurisdizione Sovrana, b. 430/b, fascicolo 2.

write about events that occurred in the late sixteenth century, or in the seventeenth century and live when devotion to Lucia has been consolidated for decades, I did not consider it wise to resort to their works.[53]

Giovanni Andrea Ciriani, an Augustinian friar, in describing in his chronicle the funeral of a nun of the monastery of St. Catherine of Siena which took place on April 13, 1651, writes that her body was shown "in the usual place the Blessed Lucia da Narni is shown".[54] That Lucia's body was located inside the convent and that it was exposed to the public in the late seventeenth century, is apparent from a book in press by Andrea Faoro, which I was able to read by the courtesy of the author:

> In 1684 Sister Osanna Margherita [Consumati] was elected prioress again, achieving a highly respectable result for those who, like her, were not born a noble. During her assignment, she returned to direct her action towards a goal of the utmost importance: the founder of the convent, the mystic Lucia Broccadelli. According to the testimony of some nuns collected in 1715, Sister Osanna Margherita in 1686 covered the body with a richer hood than the previous one and in the same way replaced the pillow placed under her head with a more ornate one. In this case, the gesture of munificence was appreciable both inside the convent, because the reliquary was kept in the nuns' choir, and outside, as on November 16 of each year (anniversary of death) "everyone is allowed to see this holy relic."[55]

In 1710, Pope Clement XI granted the decree confirming the cult; it was not therefore an effective beatification. It is known that the promoter of Lucia's sanctification – which never took place – was Ferdinando Agostino Bernabei, theologian who took vows in Viterbo and who, in order to better organize the material, was advised by Cardinal Giuseppe Sacripante, born in Narni and an ardent supporter of the canonization of Lucia.[56] It could be inferred from these elements that the cause perhaps interested the citizens of Narni and Viterbo more than the people of Ferrara, with the obvious exception of the nuns of the monastery of St. Catherine of Siena. It should also be remembered at this point that, at the same time as the recognition of the cult, Pope Clement decided that a leg of Lucia was cut off to be delivered to the community of Narni, where it had to be placed in a chapel of the cathedral.

---

53 C. Barotti, *Memoria per servire alla formazione di una storia della Città di Ferrara dall'anno 452 al 1598*, BCAFe, ms. Antonelli 220; V. Bellini, *Breve cronaca di Ferrara dal 1412 al 1597*, BCAFe, ms. Antonelli 211; G.M. Maffei, *Memorie storiche della città di Ferrara, dal 322 al 1635*, BCAFe, ms. Antonelli 483.

54 G. A. Ciriani, *Cronaca di Ferrara dal 1651 al 1673*, BCAFe, ms. Antonelli 269, 11r–v.

55 A. Faoro, *I Consumati: la vera storia di una famiglia del Seicento tra affari, intrighi, monacazioni forzate* (Limena: libreriauniversitaria.it, 2022), 312–313.

56 Matter/Zarri: *Una mistica contestata*, xxv.

To try to clarify at least the times and characteristics of the escalation in the attestations of miracles that occurred in the eighteenth century in Ferrara, it would be necessary to collect, number and analyze their size: to date, these testimonies are unpublished. Perhaps not even by scrupulously investigating the devotional climate of Ferrara and its equilibrium will it be possible to find a reason. Matter and Zarri clearly identify the critical issues that the figure of Lucia contained: in the sixteenth century the simulation of the stigmata,[57] the diabolical suggestion, and heresy; in the late seventeenth century, instead, the dubious virginity of the woman, who had been married for three years before taking her vows.[58] The strategies adopted by Lucia's biographers are extremely interesting, but they inform us above all about the intellectual and cultural tools of those who put them into play; it remains in the shadows if and what they achieved success. For now, it seems evident that the number of Lucia's faithful has increased significantly in years close to the granting of the cult. Previously, even after her death, the attention towards her appears as a phenomenon imposed from above: by the priorcss of the Viterbo monastery of Lucia (according to Felino Sandei) and then, by duke Hercules, by the Dominican theological authorities, by hagiographers of Savonarolian sensitivity (Razzi), etc. In short, I believe that only further and extensive research will help us to fully understand the dynamics that led to promoting the memory of this controversial woman many years (or centuries) after her death. And, perhaps, to understand what a society fears and what approves of within the same concept of holiness.

57 A. Bartolomei Romagnoli, "Un trattatello cinquecentesco in difesa delle stimmate di Caterina da Siena", *Archivio Italiano per la Storia della Pietà* 26 (2013) 177–225; T. Herzig, *Christ transformed into a Virgin woman: Lucia Brocadelli, Heinrich Institoris and the defense of the faith* (Roma: Edizioni di Storia e Letteratura, 2013a).

58 Ibid., xxiv–xxv.

Lucio Biasiori

Holiness and Madness in Early Modern Florence

The disturber

> On the second Sunday of Advent, preaching in the Church of the monastery of San Jacopo Soprarno, the capuchin Friar Agostino of Lucignano, with permission of the superiors, uttered this opinion: no one, while he is in this mortal life, can know for certain that he is in grace except by revelation, quoting the opinions of several theologians and in particular of Saint Bonaventure … . At that moment one of the listeners, who later identified himself as Zanobi Niccolini, rose up and proclaimed: "That's enough! You are preaching heresy." The father answered from the pulpit: "Calm down and let me finish the sermon and then I will answer you."
>
> When the sermon was finished, Zanobi approached him and the Father said: "What did you say?" Zanobi replied: "Father, I did not want to say anything, but the zeal of my soul has prompted me to intermit you." To which Agostino replied: "How did this zeal of the soul move you?" and Zanobi answered: "Father, when you receive absolution, do you then believe that you are discharged?" and the Father replied, "Yes, I believe it," and he added: "You must also hold it certain that you are in grace." Hearing this answer, the father said to him: "Beware that this indeed is heresy. It would be necessary to know your name." And he answered: "My name is Zanobi Niccolini and you should not preach in this way, for you take away the confidence." Then the father said: "This is against the council."
>
> Then I, priest Marcantonio della Rena, confessor of the said nuns, since I was there, quietly said to Zanobi:
>
> "You have used great presumption and could have waited until the end of the sermon," and so I accompanied the preacher outside of the church. Then, returning to warn the nuns and showing them that the Father preached the sound and good doctrine and that they should not put their minds to the words of the said Zanobi nor believe them, I asked the mother abbess if they had been aware of the thing and she answered me that they were, because the said Zanobi, going to the stairs, said in a loud voice turned to the grates: "You are to hold for certain that after the absolution and repentance you are in grace and that the father had preached heresy."[1]

---

1 I warmly thank Thomas Santamaria for his help in translating this text, as well as Elisa Frei and Eleonora Rai for involving me in their book project.

The trial against Zanobi Niccolini is in Archivio della Curia Arcivescovile Firenze (from now on ACAF), *Tribunale dell'Inquisizione* (from now on TIN), 1, 26, cc. 577–632, cc. 603r–v.

The temptation to let Marcantonio della Rena, confessor of the nuns of the convent of San Jacopo Soprarno, continue to speak is strong, so much inside his words seem to lead us to what happened in Florence on that Advent Sunday in 1581. In doing so, however, we would risk not fully realizing how difficult it is to imagine a gesture that more openly challenged the barriers of Counter-Reformation Italian society than that which Zanobi Niccolini dared, abruptly interrupting the sermon of Friar Agostino of Lucignano.

The first barrier was that between the orthodoxy established at the Council of Trent and the believers' confidence that they were in a state of grace and thus saved: from its earliest sessions, the Council of Trent had truncated any possible attempt to come to an agreement with Protestants around this issue and reiterated the necessity of good works for salvation. The second barrier was that between clerics and laity: the Counter-Reformation swept away that intermingling between the shepherds and their flock that – it was thought – had provided arrows to the bow of the Church's critics. Instead, Catholicism was reshaped as a religion administered by men immediately recognizable by their dress and behavior and as such rigidly separated from the rest of the community. The third barrier was that between men and women: custodians of the monopoly on religion, on the one hand; on the other, creatures in need of direction so that their ears might not become aware of heretical ideas, as the first among them had been: Eve, led astray by the serpent.

The solemnity of the occasion had certainly prompted Zanobi Niccolini to speak in public, but he must have cultivated the same idea for a long time in private. A few days after the sermon episode, on December 30, 1581, a certain Gianantonio Sergriffi, his fellow in the brotherhood of the Trinity, appeared before the inquisitor to complain that he had heard Zanobi say that people can know for certain that they have God's grace, that those who have charity cannot lose it, that one must have the love of God inwardly without any outward works, and "that he knows certain to have charity and would stand in the midst of a hundred naked women and not sin." Until then he had hesitated to denounce his acquaintance. He had been held back by the fact that Zanobi "sometimes was not master of one's self, that is, when he reasons about these concepts he becomes so heated that he almost gets out of his mind". Furthermore, he was a "humanist." Whatever that definition meant at the time, Sergriffi probably wanted to allude to the fact that Zanobi was a person with a strong passion for reading books and determined to think deeply about their meaning.[2] That is why, together with a Giovanni Nicolozzi of Prato and

2 A. Campana, "The Origin of the Word 'Humanist'", *Journal of the Warburg and Courtauld Institutes* 9 (1946) 60–73.

a certain Girolamo Leopardi, he had first taken him to the Jesuits to "disabuse" him of his opinions.[3]

It was a predictable move: through the conversation inside and outside the confessional, the Society of Jesus had built a model of religious integration that favored the gentle reentry into the Church of figures who were on the margins of the Christian community, such as heretics, Jews and infidels. The result remained the same, but the means were different: the errant was re-routed through the means of consolation and help rather than those of denunciation and judicial prosecution.[4] As a good Jesuit, then, Giulio Mancinelli with the help of the Scriptures had shown Zanobi his errors, but the latter had remained adamant. Consequently, the Father had advised Sergriffi to speak first to the archiepiscopal vicar and then, in an extreme case, to the inquisitor. When the path of fraternal correction and that of episcopal justice had led nowhere, Sergriffi had therefore decided to denounce him to the Florentine inquisitor, the Franciscan Dionigi Costacciari.

How could it be, Costacciari wondered, that an experienced theologian like Mancinelli had not identified the certainty of grace as a heretical doctrine? It was Zanobi himself, once called upon to exonerate himself, who explained that the Jesuit left the thing "undecided, although I inwardly remained of the idea that he did not understand very well", as Mancinelli spoke "by way of doctrine," while Zanobi meant "that supernatural light given by God in which I always stand."[5]

Mancinelli was actually all too able to understand the effects that the infusion of grace could give. His confrere and biographer Giulio Cellesi tells us how in his youth he had had very similar experiences to those of Zanobi: he shunned sermons in churches "as being of too sublime a style, in regard to his still small understanding," and, since "it did not seem to him to bring forth the desired fruit, he eagerly ran through the streets and squares to hear poor pilgrims and hermits." Moreover, the young Mancinelli "often burst into devout tears; as a reward for which God then granted him throughout his life great confidence in his mercy and never to despair over any sin." The Jesuit and the inquirer thus shared the same trust in divine mercy, which led them to positions of open and explicit defiance of religious ceremonies and even sexual temptations. If Zanobi, as we have seen, was so certain of the steadfastness of his election to grace to remain in the midst of a hundred naked women, also Mancinelli "touching the bones of his body, exhorted himself not to caress it with flattery, and transitory pleasures."[6] Mancinelli's hesitations in the face

3 ACAF, TIN, 1, 26, c. 579v.

4 Most recently see J. M. Dalton, *Between Popes, Inquisitors and Princes: How the First Jesuits Negotiated Religious Crisis in Early Modern Italy* (Leiden: Brill, 2020), esp. ch. 2.

5 ACAF, TIN, 1, 26, c. 578r.

6 These biographical details on Mancinelli come from G. Cellesi, *Vita del servo di Dio padre Giulio Mancinelli della Compagnia di Giesù* (Rome: Varese, 1668) 5, 16.

of Zanobi Niccolini's case were thus also nourished by common experiences. In his case, these practices bordering on mysticism were absorbed within the Society of Jesus, an order that, unlike others, knew how to channel its future members' potentially centrifugal thrusts with respect to the religious hierarchies within a framework of secure orthodoxy.[7]

As we shall see, Zanobi Niccolini's life took a different turn.

"And I adore fra Girolamo"

Unlike what his accuser believed, Niccolini did not come from the tradition of humanism. Not only that, at least. He was a fervent devotee of the disgraced Dominican friar Girolamo Savonarola. The inventory of his books and images taken at the time of his imprisonment clearly indicate his preference. No fewer than twelve of his forty-five volumes were written by Savonarola. Furthermore, alongside those of the Madonna, Saint Jerome, Saint Catherine of Siena and Saint Francis (both with the stigmata) and a crucifix, he owned

> above the door of his room the image of three hanged men with fire below and with a sign saying 'in igne sicut aurum probati sunt' (they were tried in fire like gold) and with halos in the manner of a diadem and with their names saying 'Beatus Dominicus, Beatus Hyeronimus Savonarola, Beatus Silvester'[8] .... Then, the portrait of Savonarola in paper with these words written around it 'Beatus Hyeronimus Savonarola Ferrariensis' ... written with two verses in this form: 'Salve o precellens vates, salve inclite martir et noster doctor fidei morisque magister (Hail o highest prophet, hail o glorious martyr, our doctor of the faith and master of morality).[9]

Among those "many very inconvenient paintings," were busts of Savonarola, and his two condemned brethren, in addition to "a petty crucifix with its head turned upside down and its feet up," according to the testimony of the Pisan Franciscan Francesco di Jacopo Franceschi. Someone also saw the inscription "il mondo alla roverscia"

---

7 On the ability on the part of the Society of Jesus to absorb the psychological and familial tensions of its members see A. Prosperi, *La vocazione. Storie di gesuiti tra Cinquecento e Seicento* (Turin: Einaudi, 2016). For a case similar to Mancinelli's, pp. 165ff.

8 Domenico and Silvestro were the two confreres who were burnt at the stake together with Savonarola.

9 ACAF, TIN, 1, 26, c. 578r. On the evolution of Savonarola's iconographic model, cf. L. Sebregondi, *Iconografia di Girolamo Savonarola 1495–1998* (Florence: SISMEL-Edizioni del Galluzzo, 2004) 92–3, 122–3, 428–32, which shows the long duration (until the eighteenth century) of images similar to those owned by Zanobi and the texts that accompanied them.

(the world turned upside down).[10] Even if we did not have this explanation, the meaning of the arrangement of the sacred furnishings in Zanobi's room would be quite clear: that where the saints were led to the gallows, was a wrong world; those who had carried out that condemnation were responsible for shedding the blood of martyrs.

What was particularly serious was that Zanobi expressly set out to imitate these martyrs: to those who admonished him not to reveal such opinions lest he be imprisoned and burnt, he replied that it would be a supreme grace to die to tell the truth.[11] The *imitatio Christi* gave way to the *imitatio Savonarolae*: to a cobbler named Domenico, who did not want to worship saints not approved by the Church but only God, Zanobi gave a dry reply: "and I adore fra Girolamo."[12]

He would be asked to account for these words at his trial: why, they asked, did he adore Savonarola and the brethren who had followed him to the stake? Why did he call them martyrs if they had been damned by the Apostolic Church? Zanobi answered evasively, correcting himself and saying that he did not know "whether the Church as Church has condemned them." Indeed, it had been a pope who had excommunicated Savonarola, but a pope infamous for dubious or outright lecherous conduct like Alexander VI Borgia. Then, at the trial that had led to Savonarola's execution, the two ecclesiastical commissioners had taken part only in the last of three interrogations. Finally, even after Savonarola's death, the Church held throughout the sixteenth century an undecided attitude toward his veneration and adherence to his ideas of profound reform of the Church and society. While Julius II and Clement VIII even considered his canonization, other popes, such as Leo X and Paul IV fiercely persecuted the memory of Savonarola and his followers. This inconsistency in the Church's attitude toward the friar actually allowed Zanobi to justify his own Savonarolan worship by entrenching himself behind his ignorance: "If I had known, not only would I not have worshipped them, I would not have kept them in the house either."[13]

Of course, provisions against Savonarola worship in convents and private homes had begun long before then. As early as February 1499 – Savonarola had not even been dead for a year – the Dominican order had issued an ordinance forbidding any conversation about that cumbersome confrere and the possession of relics of his body such as bones, hair, fragments of skin or pieces of wood taken from

10 ACAF, TIN, 1, 26, c. 611r.

11 Ivi, c. 580v.

12 The cobbler's direct testimony about his exchange of views with Zanobi was scarcely less serious than that reported by the other witnesses: in fact, it is clear from his words that Zanobi did not set God and Savonarola against each other, but put them on the same plane: "I told him that I wanted to worship God, and he answered that he wanted to worship God too, and fra Girolamo" (Ivi, c. 582v).

13 ACAF, TIN, 1, 26, c. 589r.

the gallows. Fifteen years later, the offensive also extended outside the Florentine convent of San Marco and of the very Dominican order. Giulio de' Medici, vicar of the Florentine archbishop and future pope Clement VII, issued a new ordinance against Savonarolan devotion, according to which all who kept in their houses relics or writings of "the Friar" – as they called him – had to hand them over to the archbishop's vicar. Thirty years later, in 1545, Cosimo I took new measures, accusing the friars of San Marco of idolatrous veneration of Savonarola, and of promoting his worship as that of a saint. The case of Zanobi, however, marked a new stage in this conflict between the Medici family and the ghost of Savonarola. That veritable private cult he had organized in his home, and the underground channels that had fed it, aroused great concern, in a city where Savonarola's religious message, almost a century after the events, continued to be surrounded by suspicion of both a religious and a political nature.

For these reasons, on August 26, 1583, Alessandro de' Medici, Archbishop of Florence and future Pope Leo XI, wrote about it to his cousin, Grand Duke Francesco.[14] Until then the archbishop had always avoided taking up the pen, thinking that he would be able to provide for himself or have someone to help him. But, "seeing that the evil grows, that my strength is not enough and here the affair has been neglected," he had finally made up his mind:

> The case is this: that by the obstinacy of the friars of San Marco the memory of Fra Girolamo Savonarola, which was ten or twelve years ago extinct (having died those who had known him) rises again, teems, and is more in bloom than ever it was. His madness is sown among the friars, among the nuns, among the laity, and the youth does most presumptuous things: they occultly celebrate masses in his honor, as to a martyr; they preserve his relics as if he were a saint; even that gallow where he was hanged, the chains that bound him, the garments, the hoods, the bones that were spared from the fire, the

14 The important letter from Alessandro de' Medici to Grand Duke Francesco, hitherto devoid of its subtext, is cited countless times in Savonarolan studies, beginning with C. Guasti, *L'officio proprio per fra Girolamo Savonarola e i suoi compagni scritto nel secolo XVI* (Prato: Ranieri Guasti, 1863) 27ff and is the starting point for the essay by S. Dall'Aglio, *Domestic Prayers and Miracles in Renaissance Italy: The Case of Savonarola and His Cult*, in M. Corry/M. Faini/A. Meneghin (ed.), *Domestic Devotions in Early Modern Italy* (Leiden: Brill, 2018) 375–88. Dall'Aglio, whom I thank for taking the time to read an early version of this work, notes how even if "it is more difficult to find direct testimonies of private and intimate devotions than of cults openly performed in public places in front of hundreds of people … , the very existence of these concerns is itself a demonstration that the cult existed and was largely practiced, or nobody would have felt the need to intervene" (p. 379). The Zanobi affair thus gives us a rare chance to shine a direct light on one of the many cases of Savonarola's intimate and private cult, on which, from another perspective, see also D. Rosenthal, *The Tailor's Song: Notes from the Savonarolan Underground in Grand-Ducal Florence*, in P.F. Howard/C. Hewlett (ed.) *Studies on Florence and the Italian Renaissance in Honour of F.W. Kent* (Turnhout: Brepols, 2016) 359–72.

> ashes, the cilice; they keep wine blessed by him, they give it to the sick, they count his miracles; his images they make in bronze, in gold, in cameos, in print; and, what is worse, they make him inscriptions of martyr, prophet, virgin and doctor.

Up to that point the archbishop had done what he could: he had ordered the destruction of the prints and the relocation to Viterbo of their author – a certain Friar Bernardo da Castiglione; he had then prevented Savonarola's image from being painted in the cloister of Santa Maria Novella among the saints of the Dominican order and the summary of his life and miracles from being given to printers; he had finally "scared the friars," making them "reprimand, admonish and punish by their superiors." Now, however, having lacked the support of an influential Dominican cardinal like Vincenzo Giustiniani, he had nowhere to turn. Therefore, "because of the much practice of the moods of this city" that the grand duke had, he urged him to intervene to prevent "two bad, indeed very bad effects" of devotion to Savonarola: the first is that those who believe him "alienate themselves from the Apostolic See, and if they do not become heretics, they do not have a good opinion of the secular clergy and prelates, and obey them unwillingly"; the second, "which concerns Your Highness, is that they alienate themselves from your present happy state and conceive a certain intrinsic hatred, even if power and fear keep them in their place ... but because they fear to speak of the Prince, they speak of his ministers and orders."

On October 12, Grand Duke Francis responded to the almost Machiavellian analysis with which the future pope dissected the ways in which religion can contribute to the stability or instability of a state. He showed that he understood the seriousness of the situation and informed him that the inquisitor Dionigi Costacciari had also set out to verify and set straight all that he wrote to him about Fra Girolamo. "But" – he added – "before moving anything, the inquisitor would like to have some light on the matter": therefore, the archbishop had to notify the grand duke of all the information in his possession, so that Costacciari could instruct the process and uncover the ambition and superstition of those friars. The inquisitor had probably realized that the archbishop's complaints and all his protests of being left alone were aimed at him, and in fact the words he addressed to the grand duke and which the latter reported to the archbishop brought the confrontation around Savonarola to a different terrain: if the Savonarolan movement was to be finally cleared, all available evidence and information had to be gathered and formal trials had to be instituted against its sympathizers. This was impervious ground, too impervious for the archbishop, who stepped back. Of course, he would have given the Grand Duke all the news in his possession, but it was one thing to alert the political power about the damage that the Savonarolan cult was doing to the political and religious stability of Florence, and quite another to institute a trial, putting the matter in the hands of the Inquisition. Costacciari's words had, in short, cornered the bishop:

It is well true that, when I wrote, I did not think that my warnings should be turned into a trial. Otherwise, I would have gone more cautiously and left out everything of which I could not have entire findings. ... In spite of this, if the inquisitor knows how to proceed, it is not possible that he will not discover the whole matter, because it is in many people.

And here came a final blow to Costacciari and the overly surrendering behavior he had held during the trial of Zanobi Niccolini:

I have no esteem for him; above all because I see that he does not remember the images he found in the hands of Zanobi Niccolini, who was at the Holy Office for telling a preacher that he was speaking falsely while he was preaching, and although he was acquitted because of insanity, the images had not been made by himself and had come out either from the friars or from the nuns of the convent of San Vincenzo in Prato, from where all things of the Friar spring.[15]

The letter ended with the archbishop begging the Grand Duke not to mention his own name to the inquisitor. It was better that everything take place without him being discovered: Alessandro de' Medici knew how little Costacciari loved him, "and the hatred of the friars is a bad thing," something that risks turning someone "from judge to witness". Even if one had no skeletons in the closet, it was still better not to play with fire too much or one risked that one's testimony at trial could be overturned and become, if not into complicity, at least into suspicion of delicate contiguity with the accused. For one who, even if for less than a month, was destined to bring the Medici family back to Saint Peter's throne it was not an advisable move.

"My certainty is a light and a taste of God"

More than the inquisitor, the outright adoration Zanobi had for Savonarola seemed to worry the archbishop – and the latter more as a member of the house of Medici than as the city's highest religious authority. Instead, at the heart of the inquisitorial proceedings against Zanobi was a different matter altogether, one that we can summarize with the statement he made before the inquisitor on January 15, 1582:

those who are in the grace of God and have Jesus in their heart enlightened by him, when they holds certain that they are and stay in the grace of God, cannot be in mortal sin

15 On the importance of the convent of San Vincenzo for the late-sixteenth-century Savonarolan movement see S. Dall'Aglio, *Savonarola and Savonarolism* (Toronto: Centre for Reformation and Renaissance Studies, 2010).

> nor excommunicated because grace does not stand together with sin, and where there is excommunication and sin there is no grace, and where there is grace there cannot be excommunication.[16]

As we can see, here Savonarola is only a distant memory, resurfacing just behind that reference to the ineffectiveness of excommunications against the power of divine grace. Instead, in the foreground is the problem of the certainty of grace, a problem that, however present in the writings of the Dominican and his followers such as Girolamo Benivieni, went beyond the ranks of the Savonarolan movement and transcended even Zanobi's case.[17] Therefore, it is here that we touch upon the point from which this research illuminates the more general problem of the ways in which the profile of a saint was constructed during the Counter-Reformation: who certifies the possession of grace? How do we sanction those who boast of possessing it, if it is above the excommunications issued by the Church as an institution? How to control the behavior of those who believe they are enlightened by it? How can people distinguish these people who claim to have achieved perfection from the saints canonized by the Church?

These were familiar questions in Florence. The certainty of grace was an issue of concern to Florentine religious authorities at least as early as 1543, when the Franciscan Benedetto of Locarno had preached that doctrine in Santa Croce, followed seven years later by the Augustinian Giuliano Brigantino of Colle Val D'Elsa, author of a lost *Tractatus de certitudine gratiae Dei* (Treatise on the Certainty of God's Grace). Above all, stirring up trouble in the city had been a sermon delivered on January 20, 1544, on the subject of grace and works by another Augustinian: Andrea Ghetti. In his words, the death on the cross of Jesus for the salvation of all should not instill in the faithful fear for the insufficiency of their works, but confidence in the salvation of their soul. The sermon earned Ghetti a denunciation to the Roman Inquisition by the Catholic theologian Ambrogio Catarino Politi, but it was so successful that it was immediately published by the Florentine printer Bernardo Giunta under the title of *Trattato utile del reverendo frate Andrea da Volterra sopra la disputa della grazia e delle opere* (Useful treatise of Friar Andrea of Volterra about the dispute of the grace and of the works). More importantly, the book came out with a dedication to Duke Cosimo and under the patronage of the future commissioner against heresy Alessandro Strozzi, but evidently fourty years

---

16 ACAF, TIN, 1, 26, c. 584v.

17 For the presence of the theme of *certitudo gratiae* in the Savonarolan movement see D. Benivieni, *Trattato in difesa di Girolamo Savonarola*, ed. by G. C. Garfagnini (Florence: SISMEL-Edizioni del Galluzzo, 2000), XVII–XXXVI.

later it no longer enjoyed political and religious favor and in fact was among those seized from Zanobi.[18]

Although his words had gotten him into trouble, Zanobi always protested his innocence and perfect orthodoxy. In his view, his ideas had been misrepresented by the inquisitor, who claimed to measure by the yardstick of theological definitions a sentiment that instead had no certification other than itself: "I said as you have said, but I added, and if I did not add it I meant it, that I was speaking of those who had the living faith, a gift of God, supernatural, which is a light that illuminates the mind and pacifies the heart and makes it certain that it is in the grace of God, which light is the holy spirit."[19]

As well as in his dialogue with the Jesuit Mancinelli, before the inquisitor Zanobi expressed the same clear distrust of "doctrine" and his certainty in a state of mind of inner enlightenment, of which, ultimately, the guarantor remained the individual: "I hold certain that I have the grace of God by the higher light given me by God." How do you know this? – The inquisitor then asks him. And Zanobi: "I know it by this foundation: by the abundance of the holy spirit which I feel in me, and by the abundance of light by which I am often visited, in which lights I then feel a certainty." And again, "I have no particular expression according to these doctrinal distinctions, but my certainty is a light and taste of God, … which I cannot express in any better word than by revelation."[20]

The claim to have the certainty of divine grace in the name of the inner revelation provided by the illumination of the Holy Spirit was more insidious than disagreement on individual doctrinal points: to put the charisma of the individual against the authority of the institution paved the way to a radical and potentially uncontrollable subjectivism, in which it was no longer the Church but the enlightened conscience of the individual that decided what was holy and what was unholy.

The danger behind these positions would only become clear decades later with the repression of quietism, a doctrine that promised to achieve Christian perfection and impeccability by trustingly surrendering to God and not following the religious practices prescribed by the hierarchies.[21] But even in the 1580s, the Inquisition could not turn its glance to the other side: at the meeting of the cardinals of the

---

18 On Ghetti see G. Dall'Olio, "Ghetti Andrea", in *Dizionario Biografico degli Italiani* 53 (2000), *online*. For the general topic G. Caravale, *Preaching and Inquisition in Renaissance Italy: Words on Trial* (Leiden: Brill, 2016) and, for the Florentine context, M. Firpo, *Pontormo's Frescos in San Lorenzo. Heresy, Politics and Culture in the Florence of Cosimo I* (Rome: Viella, 2020) 352 and ff.

19 ACAF, TIN, 1, 26, c. 591r.

20 Ivi, c. 591r.

21 For a recent analysis of this phenomenon, see A. Malena, *The So-Called Italian Quietism: Siena in the 1680s*, in L. Laborie/A. Hessayon (ed.), *Early Modern Prophecies in Transnational, National and Regional Contexts*, (Leiden: Brill, 2020) 201–45.

Holy Office and their consultants held in the apostolic palaces in the presence of Pope Gregory XIII on March 16, 1582, Timoteo Bottoni, vicar general of the Dominican order expressed a relatively mild opinion about Zanobi[22]. Yes, he was mildly suspected of heresy but not stubbornly so and, as such, he was to abjure without too much fuss and clamor – at the next meeting, on March 29, Bottoni even said that Zanobi was not a heretic but merely ignorant ("ignarus"). However, another Dominican, that Sisto Fabri who a few years later would be in the forefront of erasing Savonarola's memory within the Order, was harsher: Zanobi may not have had the stubbornness typical of heretics, but that did not excuse him from error and indeed it was necessary to continue examining, questioning and instructing him with greater diligence.[23] The Roman order of Sisto Fabri was followed in Florence, and the trial against Zanobi was far from being closed.[24]

All Apologies

When Zanobi Niccolini had interrupted the preacher, he had done so cautiously, taking off his hat, and even when the mass was over and he went to meet the preacher in the aisle, he always maintained a reverent tone. Nevertheless, the monastery's confessor, Marcantonio della Rena, had admonished him for having "used great presumption," but above all he had admonished the nuns, "showing them that the father preached sound and good doctrine and that they should not listen to the words of Zanobi nor believe them"[25]. In fact, as will be recalled, the man had explicitly attempted to communicate with the nuns, advising them to consider themselves in a state of grace after receiving absolution.

Since this public display of dissent threatened to infect the nuns, Zanobi had to officially apologize in a public ceremony of repentance before them on August 5, 1582. Dressed in a white robe, with his head uncovered, his feet bare and a large

22 This is not all that surprising, since Bottoni in 1566 had rewritten, passing it off as his own, the biography of Savonarola attributed to another follower of Savonarola, the Lucchese Pacifico Burlamacchi. See *La vita del Beato Ieronimo Savonarola scritta da un anonimo del sec. XVI e già attribuita a fra Pacifico Burlamacchi*, ed. P. Ginori Conti (Florence: Olschki, 1937).

23 The role of the Dominican general Sisto Fabri in the offensive against Savonarola's memory is known thanks to an ordinance dated April 5, 1585 and published by A. Gherardi, *Nuovi documenti e studi intorno a Girolamo Savonarola* (Florence: Sansoni, 1887) 351.

24 The opinions that emerged during the meeting of the Roman commission of the Holy Office on March 16 can be read in Archivio della Congregazione per la Dottrina della Fede, *Decreta*, 16, f. 205r, those of the meeting on the 29th of the same month in ivi, f. 230v. The Roman Holy Office also examined Zanobi's case at its meetings on May 31 and November 25, deciding to summon him to Rome, which, as we will see, never took place.

25 ACAF, TIN, 1, 26, c. 602r.

crucifix in his hand, he placed himself on his knees at the feet of the main altar and remained so until the nuns finished saying their office. Della Rena, however, was vigilant, as he had seen a folded paper in his hand.[26] Zanobi dryly replied that he had noticed on the paper what he had to say and so, lying prostrate on the ground, he turned toward the people and the nuns, asking forgiveness. As Della Rena feared, however, that paper was more than just a memory aid. His plea for repentance before the nuns was actually a renewed profession of faith in the certainty of grace and, above all, it became an indictment against those who were trying to convince him and them that that position was heretical:

> Reverend Mothers and in particular Reverend Prioress in Jesus Christ, I want to obey the Reverend Inquisitor, not only because if I did not I would pay 500 scudi which I pledged to him as collateral and induce myself into his hands to be tormented at his discretion, but also out of humility and in order not to be to others an example of pride. Therefore, I have come to ask forgiveness from all of you. But avert that in this request of forgiveness I do not intend to affirm their heresy that those who believe for certain that they are in the grace of God are excommunicated. Therefore, without prejudice of the honor of God and the health of the soul and out of humility, to you nuns and to all I ask forgiveness of all the scandal I have given: but, have I given you scandal, Mother? In charity answer, Mother Prioress.[27]

With ingenious reversal, Zanobi turned his recantation into an accusation against the orthodox theologians, transformed into the true heretics, and against the inquisitor himself, whom he was forced to obey under threat of having his possessions seized and his body tormented.[28] Zanobi knew how to take advantage of this with timing and skill, circumventing the scrutiny he had been subjected to. Who did he think he was?

Successful and unsuccessful models of sanctity on the gender line

When the inquisitors asked him from whom he had learned the doctrine of the certainty of grace, Zanobi initially replied that the spirit of God had taught it to him, but then he slowly let emerge the responsibilities of his confessor, Bastiano Carleschi, a native of Monterchi, a village near Arezzo. "Before I confessed to Friar

---

26 Ivi, c. 603r.

27 Ivi, c. 603v.

28 For similar episodes see Dall'Aglio, "Voices under Trial. Inquisition, Abjuration, and Preachers' Orality in Sixteenth-Century Italy" *Renaissance Studies* 31 (2015) 25–42.

Bastiano," – he told the inquisitor on January 23, 1582 – "I was a worldly, carnal man, and then I became another man, who no longer cares for the things of the world."[29] It was, no more and no less, than an accuse of complicity.

The inquisitor thus diligently began to gather information about Bastiano's account as well. Jacopa de Cortis, abbess of the monastery of San Girolamo delle poverine ingesuate, knew Bastiano from having been confessor there for a decade. Then he had been removed by Jacopo Serguidi, vicar of the archbishop of Florence and at that time bishop of Volterra. If Mother Jacopa speculated that this had happened because he had "come to bore some nuns because he had been there so long," her successor, Zanobia de Gherardi, was more precise: "the vicar told me that he had discharged him because he gave communion to one side more often than the other." When interrogated, the vicar Guido Serguidi could no longer remember well, apologizing with the fact that more than ten years had passed and pointing to possible ways to understand more: looking in the archives of the Apostolic Nuncio, compulsing the papers of the notaries of the archbishopric, questioning the nuns. A certain Francesco di Jacopo Franceschi, a Pisan Franciscan who had been deputy inquisitor at the time of Don Bastiano's trial, remembered better than did Vicar Serguidi, by then distracted by his new commitments as bishop of Volterra. Franceschi immediately identified the reason why Bastiano had been removed. The problem was always that of the certainty of grace: while preaching, he had been aware of the fact that Bastiano often used to reason about the grace by showing that he was certain of it. Therefore, the nuns had been questioned and their confessor, though judged more a simple man than a dangerous tempter, had been removed.[30]

Before arriving in Florence to sow the insidious doctrine of the certainty of grace, we know that don Bastiano had been a companion of Bartolomeo Garosi, better known as Brandano da Petroio. A popular prophet,[31] Brandano is often remembered for his heated invectives against Pope Clement VII, whom he blamed for causing the Sack of Rome, which he infallibly predicted. And indeed the extreme tones of his preaching, while attracting him many followers admired by his asceticism and mysticism, often put him at odds with the authorities. He was imprisoned and exiled on several occasions, both in Rome and Siena, but each time popular favor brought him back to the center of political and religious life. This was because his preaching was characterized by intense attention to the problems of the poor and excluded, who evidently rewarded with their support Brandano's activities on their behalf, like caring for the sick in the Hospital of Santa Maria della Scala, creating

29 ACAF, TIN, 1, 26, c. 589v.

30 Ivi, c. 617.

31 On popular prophetism in early sixteenth-century Italy see O. Niccoli, *Prophecy and People in Renaissance Italy* (Princeton: Princeton University Press, 1990).

an elementary school for abandoned children and improving the living standards of beggars.

This mixture of admiration on the part of the people and distrust on the part of power earned Brandano an eloquent nickname: "the fool of Christ." It is a label that must be read carefully if one is to understand the true nature of the religious experience from which he came and which, through Bastiano of Monterchi, influenced Zanobi. Too often reduced to a mere itinerant hermit, Brandano had in fact gone through a radical change of life, transforming himself from "a great blasphemer, disobedient to divine precepts, a great gambler, full of every vice," to a devout preacher, whose mission was to "take up and call to penance the wretched and obstinate sinner by announcing to him great pestilence and famine." This turning point had stemmed from listening to a sermon by the observant minor Serafino of Pistoia, but his "conversion" – it is a word he uses in the autobiography he dictated to his disciple Giovanni Battista Fonteblanda – was admittedly prepared by his awareness of the disproportion between God's infinite mercy and man's sin, great but nevertheless finite: "I do not want to despair," – he wrote again in his autobiography – "because the mercy of God and benignity of the loving Jesus is greater than my sins."[32] The result was a real certainty in salvation through Christ, of which the man offered public proof through the renunciation of material goods and the consequent commitment to good works – without this, of course, implying any closeness to the views of the Lutherans, against whom Brandano indeed polemicized bitterly. The origins of Brandano's pauperism are thus rooted in his desire to imitate Christ because of his confidence in the liberating significance of his death and resurrection for believers. In short, Brandano's social commitment had behind it the theological option in favor of the certainty of grace.[33]

When Bastiano da Monterchi was summoned to court on April 28, 1582, all this belonged to a time long gone: his master had died in 1554 and four years later we find Bastiano in Florence. At first he confessed and administered the sacraments to the cloistered nuns of San Felice, then also to the Augustinian nuns of the convent of Santa Maria della Neve al Portico and to the Jesuate nuns of the convent of San Girolamo.[34] He had then left the assignments because – according to him – they

---

32 The passages from his autobiography quoted above can be read in the truly pioneering essay by G. Tognetti, "Sul 'romito' e profeta Brandano da Petroio" *Rivista storia italiana* 72 (1960) 20–44, 29.

33 Credit for emphasizing the importance of the certainty of grace and its consequences for Brandano goes to V. Marchetti, *Gruppi ereticali senesi del Cinquecento* (Florence: La Nuova Italia 1975) 40–2. For his Sienese period, in which Bastiano of Monterchi was linked to him, see P. Nardi/P. Turrini/ A. Valboni (ed.) *Brandano da Petroio. L'uomo, il mistico, il profeta e il confratello* (Monteriggioni: Edizioni Il Leccio, 2015).

34 On the church of San Felice in Piazza, the location of the school of Saint Peter Martyr, a shelter for women and widows retired from the world, see M. G. Bianchi, *Le zitelle povere a Firenze e in Toscana. La condizione femminile sotto il governo di Pietro Leopoldo di Lorena* (Florence: Semper, 2005), 33 ff.

were too burdensome to fulfill all three well. Actually, he had continued to hear the confessions of the nuns of San Felice and give them a few sermons, but the archbishop's vicar had warned him off.

Did he have a license to give these sermons? – the inquisitor asked him. Did he need a license? – he retorted, citing the fact that they were more exhortations than sermons. Were they, by any chance, exhortations to have some particular opinion on matters of grace? He did not remember: he preached according to what the Gospel of the day said, and on grace he always believed what the Church believed. Don Bastiano fashions himself as someone who does not understand philosophy or theology at all, even the Gospel he understands "superficially" and, when he does not understand, he asks those who know more than him. What about Zanobi Niccolini? Did he know him? Yes, he had him as tenant two years at the request of an aunt of his, but then he had kicked him out: "he was sick without keeping himself in check and was also harassed by certain moods ... which were sometimes unbearable: he shouted, screamed, struggled in a way that frightened me." When he was well, however, he read the letters of Saint Catherine of Siena and took communion every day. "Was it good" – the inquisitor asked him again – "to give the body of Christ to a man so many times to taste, all the more so if he was disturbed"?[35]

The question of how often it was permissible to taste the body of Christ was then at the center of the Catholic Church's concerns. Having just concluded the long decades in which it had fought against those reformers who denied the real presence of Christ in the host and went so far as to make it a mere reminder of an event in his life, the hierarchies were increasingly facing a pendulum swinging in the opposite direction. An increasing number of people between the fifteenth and sixteenth centuries began to abandon the tradition that had prevailed in the Middle Ages, which preferred to insist on a respectful distance from the sacrament and actually ordered annual reception of it. Starting in the early decades of the 16th century, the frequency with which the faithful approached the Eucharist instead intensified. Florence had inaugurated this trend thanks to the religious pedagogy of its saintly bishop Antonino Pierozzi and of Savonarola himself, and so it is well possible that its effects were felt more intensely there.[36] It is, of course, difficult to have precise statistics in this regard, but facts speak for themselves: new religious orders such as the Barnabites and the Jesuits support frequent communion – the latter even coming into conflict with the ecclesiastic authorities on the matter; popular books, such as the *Beneficio di Cristo*, advise making remembrance of Holy Communion

---

On the Jesuates see I. Gagliardi (ed.) *Le vestigia dei gesuati: L'eredità culturale del Colombini e dei suoi seguaci* (Florence: Firenze University Press, 2021).

35 The interrogations to Don Bastiano are in ACAF, TIN, 1, 26, cc. 620v–24v.

36 A. D'Addario, *Aspetti della Controriforma a Firenze* (Rome: Pubblicazioni dell'Archivio di Stato, 1972) 17.

as often as possible; and then it is talked about in confraternity oratories, among the ordinary faithful, in monasteries (especially female ones). The Council of Trent softened on that point: In the session of October 11, 1551, it was determined that all the faithful may receive that supernatural bread frequently.[37] The decree sounds like a concession, and it was: for the time being, it was more urgent to sanction the final rupture with those who had rejected, debased, soiled the sacrament of the Eucharist, than to open a new one with those who perhaps abused it, but out of too much love. Sooner or later, however, the Church would have had to deal with them as well: excessive consumption of sacredness undermines the barrier between those who celebrate Christ's sacrifice and and the rest of the Christian flock; a sacrament, then, when abused, becomes a sacrilege; to abandon too hastily the public and liturgical occasion of approaching the Holy Communion once a year there is finally the risk of living the most intimate religious experience in a purely individualized way and according to a rythm increasingly disconnected from the liturgical calendar, like those "many times," that Zanobi had communicated from the hands of don Bastiano.[38]

This is what lay behind inquisitor Costacciari's question to the latter, who replied that he did not know that the matter was so serious. After all, he too – like his disciple Zanobi and his master Brandano – preferred not to deal with too subtle theological issues. At that point, however, the inquisitor showed him the danger that overconfidence with the sacrament of the Eucharist and an overly intimate relationship between a priest and the faithful could bring, and he did so by opening before him a letter from his "most affectionate daughter" Ginevra Niccolini dated August 6, 1581:

> Reverend and dear father, I can no longer be without seeing you. I would like you to come in the morning by all means to dine with us since we both desire to see you, and I would like you to send or bring me that thing by Maddalena about renovation *(quella cosa della Maddarena della renovatione)* which shows how a pope should be and other things, and do not worry that I would not show it to anyone.

Was Zanobi that other one who, like his aunt Ginevra, was waiting so eagerly for Don Bastiano? Above all, who was that Maddalena, who had written a work on the renovation of the Church at a time when everything needed to remain as before? On both questions Bastiano was evasive: he could not remember if the other one

37 G. Alberigo/G. Dossetti/H. Jedin (ed.) *Conciliorum oecumenicorum decreta* (Bologna: Istituto per le scienze religiose, 1973) 693.

38 For the increasing frequency of the act of approaching the Eucharist by the faithful, see the few, very dense pages devoted to the social and cultural implications of that theological problem by Prosperi, *Il Concilio di Trento. Un'introduzione storica* (Turin: Einaudi, 2001) 116–21.

was Zanobi and, as for the work much sought after by Ginevra, it was a "writing that a nun from the monastery of Santo Spirito made, where she foretold the renewal of the church or the pontiff."

It is unfortunately difficult to ascertain whether "quella cosa della Maddarena della renovatione," which Ginevra Niccolini mentioned in her letter to Don Bastiano that ended up in the hands of the inquisitor, was an early draft of the *Renovatione della Chiesa*, the main work of the Florentine mystic Maria Maddalena de' Pazzi. Admittedly, Maddalena composed the letters that make up the work between July and August 1586, and in August 1581 she had not yet taken that name, but she still bore the nickname Lucrezia – although she had been baptized as Caterina. Therefore, it is not permissible to caress too seductive hypotheses. Moreover, we know nothing about her ties to this monastery of the Spirito Santo, which is probably the Church of S. Giorgio alla Costa, where in 1520 Lucrezia de' Medici, daughter of Lorenzo the Magnificent, founded a new convent dedicated to the Holy Spirit and granted it to the Vallombrosian nuns. The reference to the content of the work is then too abrupt to understand whether its content coincides with the *Renovatione della Chiesa*. However, to compare Maddalena de' Pazzi's first steps toward sainthood with those that brought Zanobi and his spiritual father before the inquisitor allows us to better understand the slippery difference between successful and unsuccessful models of sanctity in late-sixteenth century Italy: from 1574 to 1578 the future Maria Maddalena had been a novice in the monastery of San Giovanni delle Cavalieresse di Malta under the spiritual direction of the Jesuit Pietro Blanca, who had directed her toward an assiduous Eucharistic practice, viewed with dislike by the other nuns. It was for this reason that Blanca wanted his spiritual daughter to enter the Carmelite monastery of Santa Maria degli Angeli, where, by the way, the memory of Savonarola was still very much alive. Another Savonarolan bastion to which Maria Maddalena de' Pazzi was attached was the Dominican monastery of S. Vincenzo in Prato, from which the images of Savonarola found in Zanobi's house had come out and where Maddalena's inspirer, Caterina De' Ricci, resided. To her Maddalena asked to become her co-helper in the work of renewing the Church, under the sign of the saint whose name they both bore: Saint Catherine, whose letters, as will be recalled, were among Zanobi's favorite readings between the humoral accesses that harassed him.[39]

Be that as it may, don Bastiano had never seen this writing on the *renovatione* and in any case had not been able to read it, but, if it interested the inquisitor, he could have asked Ginevra or the nun herself who had written it. The inquisitor

39 In the immense bibliography on Maria Maddalena De' Pazzi, I refer to Clare Copeland's recent book: *Maria Maddalena de' Pazzi: The Making of a Counter-Reformation Saint* (Oxford: Oxford University Press, 2017), also very comprehensive from a bibliographical point of view.

objected to him that it was understood that he was the one who had to bring that book to the woman, indeed perhaps he had even written it. As it was, the problem fell away of its own accord: Don Bastiano is now seventy-five years old, too old for prison, and so he is ordered into forced residence under bail of 200 scudi.

But historians can move even where inquisitors stopped, so much as they no longer deal with the life of a defendant, but rather with the progress of our knowledge of the past. Let us then hear what a protagonist of these events says, namely the Jesuit Giulio Mancinelli, before whom, as will be remembered, Zanobi had been brought in order to make him "come to his senses" of his heresies. Chapter XIV of the *Historia della vocatione et peregrinatione* (History of vocation and pilgrimage), a work that recounts his life before 1604, is devoted to the deceptions of the devil under the disguise of sanctity that Mancinelli discovered. Those pages provide us with a portrait of Don Bastiano quite different from the one he gave of himself before the inquisitor. Mancinelli acknowledged that Carleschi was "a spiritual man and of a holy life as to morals" and "commonly held for a holy man." However, when someone questioned his reputation of holiness – such as one of his penitents, who had not given faith to his revelations – the man knew how to make himself respected: "this was diabolical temptation!" – he had said to him – "Don't you believe that now God has his prophets and holy men, as it was for times past?". In short, if we are to give credibility to the profile Mancinelli draws of him, we are dealing with a cleric with a righteous moral life, but one who, "being always ready to speak his mind of things spiritual and perfect and to recommend his visions and revelations, had seduced all the best spirits of Florence." Like another Savonarola, Bastiano had been able to persuade "the best spirits of Florence" of things that Mancinelli found simply ridiculous, such as that "our Lord from his side a cup of blood had given him to drink, and similar other arrogant follies." His great influence could bord on something akin to mythomania, as when, "hearing preaching in the cathedral over a distinguished saint, he said to one of his disciples, that still in that way of him they will one day preach." That is why Mancinelli – a kind of detective in his activity of discovering false saints in the streets of Florence – made sure to approach him:

> At first, he spoke of true humility and annihilation of himself, quoting Johannes Tauler in this and similar too subtle things. He added that this was an easy thing, and that 24 years had already passed, since he had completely annihilated himself and in Christ converted, so that it was no longer he who lived but Christ who lived in him. And he mentioned again the cup of blood and other follies; for which he immediately declared himself not only without humility, but also without brains.

For Bastiano as well as for Brandano, conversion was more than just a metaphor: it was the concrete transformation of self into Christ and vice versa. "Follies" for Mancinelli, who also, as we have seen, had come very close to it; things for people "not only without humility, but also without brains."

Lunatic

From a certain point on, Mancinelli's dialogue with Bastiano overlaps with the one he had with Zanobi:

> Taking information from our own and his devotees, by evident demonstrations he was judged ignorant and insane, and with dexterity this was made known to the vicar. Having already other information of him especially from the monastery, he had him put in prison for legitimate causes; and having his writings taken, he found many books of revelations of several women, and having him examined concerning doctrine, he was found unfit to confess, and he was deservedly forbidden confession and the cure of souls, and discovered to be mad.[40]

Mancinelli believed that Don Bastiano was "discovered to be mad", as well as Archbishop Alessandro de' Medici believed that Zanobi was "acquitted because of insanity". Something does not add up; Let's see what.

Costacciari had sent the entire case file against Zanobi to the Roman tribunal of the Holy Office, which had recognized behind the defendant's "many intricate answers" the audacity and arrogance typical of the heretic, who presumes "to know for certain that he has and is in the grace of God, which thing is immediately repugnant to the holy Catholic faith." However, while expressing themselves in favor of condemnation, the Roman judges believed that his views came more from ignorance than malice.[41]

"To put such heretical opinion out of his mind," Costacciari then subjected Zanobi to a long and very detailed examination of the Tridentine canons on grace, with which he declared to agree. It had to be ascertained, however, that the defendant detested that opinion of the certainty of grace, because certainly ideas are dangerous but if they do not find fertile ground they do not take root: "It is not enough that the fire is willing to burn the straw," – the inquisitor went on with pedantic logic –

---

40 The passages from Mancinelli's life are in Archivum Romanum Societatis Iesu, *Vitae Nostrorum*, Vita 42, ff. 209–210 and were kindly pointed out to me by Silvia Notarfonso, who is conducting a promising research on him.

41 See note 23.

"if the straw were not well arranged, because being wet it could not produce the fire to cause in it its effect, which is combustion." And so it was necessary to throw water on the burning straw that was Zanobi Niccolini's soul and convince him that his thoughts about being in a perpetual state of grace and therefore immune from sin "are called conjectures, but never certainty."[42]

Going through this story, one almost gets the impression that those who judged Zanobi Niccolini were incapable of framing his heresy into clear theological categories and therefore carried the trial forward almost by force of inertia, taking advantage of their own objective superiority to remain calm and drive the accused to an ever-increasing rate of nervousness, which eventually might lead him to unpredictable outcomes.

Starting from January 1583, Zanobi had a month to appear in Rome and defend his position. But he never went to Rome. The coercive force of the family proved to be stronger than that of the Inquisition. On April 2 his brother Andrevolo pleaded with the grand duke for his brother to be released from the Stinche (the Florentine prisons that were also used by the Inquisition) and received in the Florentine asylum, the Ospedale dei pupilli, "come mentecatto" (as a lunatic):

> Seeing that the past few days Zanobi his carnal brother, coming out of feeling, as he says, stripped naked in the piazza and did some other public foolishness to his shame and that of his relatives, giving his clothes and other stuff of his own to various people, he begs Your Most Serene Highness that you deign to grace him that as a lunatic he be put and accepted under the care of your magistrate.[43]

Like Saint Francis, whose image he kept in his chamber above the entrance door as a testimony to the fact that "by light he was certified" of his election to grace; like the master of his spiritual father, Brandano da Petroio, who in Siena deprived himself of his possessions to give refreshment to the poor of the city; so also Zanobi Niccolini stripped himself of his clothes and distributed them among the people. For him, however, neither the gates of sanctity nor those of popular favor opened, but only those of the prison of the Stinche, from which he was translated to an asylum.

So much for "acquitted because of insanity," as the archbishop had written to the grand duke. Of course, madness could be a mitigating factor for heresy, if the persons who had had unseemly thoughts or uttered unseemly propositions had

42 ACAF, TIN, 1, 26, cc. 593v–596r.

43 Portions of Andrevolo Niccolini's plea are quoted for different purposes in E. Mellyn, *Mad Tuscans and Their Families: A History of Mental Disorder in Early Modern Italy* (Ann Arbor: University of Pennsylvania Press, 2014) 95.

done so when they were furious. But that was precisely *furor*, a temporary state in the midst of intervals of lucidity. From ancient times, the *furiosus* had to be clearly distinguished from the *mentecaptus*, he whose mind is perpetually captive and therefore not guilty for the ideas he gives birth to. And if the mind is captive, the body must follow the same fate.[44]

Zanobi Niccolini paid a very harsh personal toll for his pursuit of holiness.[45] In the end, however, he was right about his judges: by agreeing to equate his mysticism with a mental pathology, the Inquisition had to give up seeking a point of disagreement on a doctrinal basis, thus sanctioning the impossibility of judging his ideas. Unknowingly, without meaning to, he had succeeded in checkmating the inquisitor.

---

44 On the links between madness and heresy in the early modern age see L. Roscioni, *Il governo della follia. Ospedali, medici e pazzi nell'età moderna* (Milan: Bruno Mondadori, 2003) especially chapter 8 (*Eretiche follie*) but the whole book is important.

45 Ch. Trinkaus/H. Oberman (ed.), *The Pursuit of Holiness in Late Medieval and Renaissance Religion* (Leiden: Brill, 1974).

Patryk M. Ryczkowski

Like a Phoenix into the Ashes

Christological and Jesuit Profile of Uniate Martyrdom in Andrzej Młodzianowski's Emblematic *Vita* (1675) of Josaphat Kuntsevych (1580–1623)[1]

Introduction: *quid Iosaphat cum phoenice*?

On the one hand, Josaphat Kuntsevych (1580–1623) was proclaimed a Greek Catholic saint in 1867; on the other hand, he appears against the backdrop of the mythological phoenix – and the question, which takes up the topos of controversial complementarity between Christian and non-Christian culture,[2] arises: what can both figures have possibly in common? The narrative of a phoenix illustrates, above all, the multiplication of the life cycle: sensing the end of its time, the bird prepares a fragrant pyre, in which it will burn and be reborn from the ashes.[3] The motif was represented in ancient times in various sources which differ in details and exceed the Mediterranean space.[4] In Latin poetry, the first prolific description of the phoenix was delivered by Ovid (1 BCE/1 CE) in the *Metamorphoses*

---

1 A contribution to the project: *Caelestis Hierusalem Cives*. The Role and Function of the Latin Hagiographic Epic in Early Modern Saint-Making; Austrian Science Fund (FWF): P 33258-G; cf. P.M. Ryczkowski, "*Caelestis Hierusalem Cives*. The Role and Function of the Latin Hagiographic Epic in Early Modern Saint-Making: An Introduction to a New Research Project", *Neulateinisches Jahrbuch* 23 (2021) 292–9.

2 The topos is based on the biblical question *quae conventio Christi ad Belial* (2 Cor 6:15). At the end of the eighth century it was updated by Alcuin through juxtaposition of Christ and a warrior from early English and Norse legends as *quid Hinieldus cum Christo* (epist. 124); cf. M. Garrison, "'Quid Hinieldus cum Christo?'", in K. O'Brien O'Keeffe/A. Orchard (ed.), *Latin Learning and English Lore. Studies in Anglo-Saxon Literature for Michael Lapidge* (Toronto/Buffalo/London: University of Toronto, 2005) 1.237–59; C. Cardelle de Hartmann, "Was ist ein Klassiker? Mittelalterliche Antworten auf eine nicht gestellte Frage (Hrotsvit von Gandersheim, Walter von Châtillon, Alanus von Lille)", in T. Leuker/Ch. Pietsch (ed.), *Klassik als Norm, Norm als Klassik. Kultureller Wandel als Suche nach funktionaler Vollendung* (Münster: Aschendorff, 2016) 135–67, on pp. 141–3.

3 All essential aspects and representations of the motif are discussed in C. Schindler/H. Witte, "Phoenix", in G. Schöllgen/H. Brakmann/S. de Blauuw/T. Führer/H. Leppin/W. Löhr/H.-G. Nesselrath/I. Tanaseanu-Döbler (ed.), *Reallexikon für Antike und Christentum. Sachwörterbuch zur Auseinandersetzung des Christentums mit der antiken Welt* (Stuttgart: Hiersemann, 2016) 27.670–91.

4 For the transcultural development of the motif, see J. Nigg, *The Phoenix. An Unnatural Biography of a Mythical Beast* (Chicago/London: University of Chicago, 2016); cf. R. van den Broek, *The myth of the phoenix according to classical and early Christian traditions* (Leiden: Brill, 1972); M. Walla, *Der*

(15.391–407). In Late Antiquity, Christian culture appropriated the motif to express Christ's sacrifice and resurrection, and so it was shaped by Lactantius (3/4 CE) and Claudian (4/5 CE) in poems construed as Christological allegories.[5] The phoenix was given Christological substance in the *Physiologus*, a didactic presentation of animals displaying Christian morals: the Greek text, going back to the second century, was translated into Latin, among other languages, and was thus widely read in the Middle Ages.

In early modern times, the phoenix enjoyed popularity in various literary genres.[6] It was especially employed in devotional and hagiographical contexts, including the emblems,[7] as exemplified by the case of Kuntsevych.[8] He was born into an orthodox family in 1580 in Volodymyr (today in Ukraine) and destined to continue his education as merchant in Vilnius; however, in 1604 he joined the local community of the Basilians. They belonged to an originally orthodox Order that chose to follow the Union of Brest and consequently evolved into a pillar of the Greek Catholic (Uniate) Church in the Polish-Lithuanian Commonwealth.[9] Kuntsevych pursued a career in his Order and was elected in 1614 as an archimandrite; he became a close

---

Vogel Phoenix in der antiken Literatur und der Dichtung des Laktanz (Vienna: Notring, 1969); M.F. McDonald, "Phoenix Redivivus", *Phoenix* 14.4 (1960) 187–206.

5 On the poems, see W. Richter, "Zwei spätantike Gedichte über den Vogel Phoenix", *Rheinisches Museum für Philologie* [N. F.] 136 (1993) 62–90; M.T. Callejas Berdonés, "Confrontación del *De ave phoenice* de Lactancio y el *Phoenix* de Claudiano", *Cuadernos de filología clásica* 20 (1986–1987) 113–20. On the phoenix in Christian iconography, see J. Kramer, "Phönix", in E. Kirschbaum/G. Bandmann/W. Braunfels/J. Kollwitz/W. Mrazek/A.A. Schmid/H. Schnell (ed.), *Lexikon der christlichen Ikonographie* (Rome/Freiburg/Basel/Vienna: Herder, 1971) 3.430–2.

6 On vernacular poetry, see R. Häfner, "Bild und Tradition. Caspar von Barths *Deutscher Phoenix* (1626)", in A. Aurnhammer, /J.A. Steiger (ed.), *Christus als Held und seine heroische Nachfolge. Zur* imitatio Christi *in der Frühen Neuzeit* (Berlin/Boston: De Gruyter, 2020) 309–20. Especially on Latin poetry, see F. Schnoor, *Das lateinische Tierlobgedicht in Spätantike, Mittelalter und Früher Neuzeit* (Bern et al.: Peter Lang, 2017), 162–3.

7 For general remarks on the emblematics, see P.M. Daly, "Emblem Theory: Modern and Early Modern", in idem (ed.), *Companion to Emblem Studies* (New York: AMS, 2008) 43–78; idem, *Literature in the Light of the Emblem* (Toronto/Buffalo/London: University of Toronto, 1979); K.A.E. Enenkel, "The Neo-Latin Emblem: Humanist Learning, Classical Antiquity, and the Virtual 'Wunderkammer'", in Daly (ed.), *Companion*, 129–53.

8 In the context of the works about Kuntsevych's martyrdom, see J. Liškevičienė (ed.)/A. Mlodzianovskis, *Palaimintojo kankinio Juozapato, Polocko arkivyskupo, gyvenimo ir mirties atvaizdai. Šaltinis, vertimas ir studija* (Vilnius: Vilniaus dailės akademija, 2015), 465; cf. a general overview in A. Henkel/A. Schöne (ed.), *Emblemata. Handbuch zur Sinnbildkunst des XVI. und XVII. Jahrhunderts* (Stuttgart: J.B. Metzler, ^{2}2021), 794–7.

9 The Union of Brest was an act signed in 1596 by the majority of the orthodox bishops in Poland-Lithuania who recognised the primacy of the pope; cf. B. Skinner, *The Western Front of the Eastern Church. Uniate and Orthodox Conflict in 18th-century Poland, Ukraine, Belarus, and Russia* (DeKalb: Northern Illinois University, 2009), 18–41; B. Gudziak, *Crisis and Reform: The Kyivan Metropolitanate,*

collaborator of Hipacy Pociej, an Uniate metropolitan of Kyiv. Under his successor, Józef Welamin Rutski, he was ordained in 1618 as the archbishop of Polotsk and Vitebsk on the Commonwealth's eastern border (today in Belarus). He devoted himself to the consolidation of the Union which was progressing quite weakly in his region. Eventually, trying to take over the orthodox churches in Vitebsk and thus to confirm the presence of the Uniates, he was martyred on 12 November 1623.[10]

The attempts to make Josaphat a saint have been undertaken directly after his death:[11] in a letter about the events in Vitebsk, sent on 23 December 1623 to Rome, metropolitan Rutski named him a martyr for the cause of uniting the eastern Church with the Holy See.[12] A detailed account (*Relatio*) of the martyrdom was addressed in 1624 to Pope Urban VIII.[13] Josaphat Isakowicz developed the *Relatio* into the *Josaphatis*, an epic narrative in which the Pope was asked to make Kuntsevych a saint (1628).[14] The poem was dedicated to Antonio Santa Croce, a nuncio in Poland-Lithuania, in anticipation of his support. All these texts endorsed Josaphat's

---

the Patriarchate of Constantinople, and the Genesis of the Union of Brest (Cambridge: Harvard University, 1998).

10 For an overview of Josaphat's life, his cult, and hagiography, see K.S. Jobst/S. Rohdewald, "Josafat Kuncevyč", in J. Bahlcke/S. Rohdewald/T. Wünsch (ed.), *Religiöse Erinnerungsorte in Ostmitteleuropa. Konstitution und Konkurrenz im nationen- und epochenübergreifenden Zugriff* ([Berlin]: Akademie, 2013) 726–35; R. Gustaw, "Jozafat Jan Kuncewicz (Kuncycz)", in idem (ed.), *Hagiografia Polska. Słownik bio-bibliograficzny* (Poznań/Warsaw/Lublin: Księgarnia Św. Wojciecha, 1971) 1.632–54.

11 On Josaphat's saint-making, see A.G. Welykyj, "Historia beatificationis et canonizationis s. Josaphat", *Analecta OSBM* [Series II. Sectio II] 6 [12] (1967) 1–16; cf. the summary of the documents in idem (ed.), *S. Iosaphat hieromartyr. Documenta Romana beatificationis et canonizationis. Vol. I (1623–1628)* (Rome: Scuola salesiana del libro, 1952), XIII–XXIII.

12 Ibid., 6–8. Roman curia had already been informed about the events in Vitebsk in a letter from 7 December drafted by the nuncio Joannes Baptista Lancelotti (ibid., 5–6): although he recognised the qualities of Kuntsevych, he neither called him a martyr nor presented him as a candidate to sanctity.

13 [J. Morochowski], *De nece reverendissimo patri Iosaphat Kuncewicz, archiepiscopo Połocensi ritus Graeci a schismaticis pro Unione et Sancta Sede Apostolica Romana ... atrociter illata ... vera et compendiosa relatio* (Zamość: Simon Nizolius, 1624).

14 J. Isakowicz, *Iosaphatidos sive de nece Josaphat Kuncewicz, archiepiscopi Polocensis ritus Graeci, pro unione et Sancta Sede Apostolica Romana Vitebsci a schismaticis caesi, libri tres ...* ([s.l.] [s.n.], 1628). The poem, including a passage which employs the phoenix motif, will be discussed in a project monograph (see note 1); an English translation is planned. For general remarks, see A. Fediuk, "Il poema *Josaphatis* di G. Isakowicz, OSBM", *Analecta OSBM* [Series II. Sectio II] 6 [12] (1967) 184–200.

saint-making,[15] as supported by the Jesuits,[16] which was supposed to integrate the hitherto orthodox region into the Latin culture, and so to reinforce Rome's influence. Eventually, Urban VIII issued an indult *In Sede principis Apostolorum* on 16 May 1643:

> … Nobis fuit humiliter supplicatum, ut interim donec ad solemnem canonizationem dicti servi Dei Josaphati deveniatur, idem … beatus nuncupari, atque officium et missa de eo, ut infra, celebrare possit. Nos itaque, … hujusmodi supplicationibus inclinati, … Apostolica auctoritate tenore praesentium licentiam et facultatem concedimus, et impartimur.[17]
> [We were humbly requested that in the meantime, until the solemn canonisation of the mentioned Josaphat, servant of God, is enacted, he is allowed to be called blessed, and that the office and the mass devoted to him, as specified below, may be celebrated. As we are inclined to such supplications, by apostolic authority, in the tenor of the present, we therefore grant and indulge such permission and license].

Considering the dynamic of cultic worship in the post-Tridentine Church, recognising the sanctity of the first Uniate martyr was a remarkable step also in procedural terms. The Pope suspended the regulation of the period of fifty years resting after the death of a candidate to sanctity, which from his time on was required to initiate the procedure. In the end, Josaphat's public veneration was allowed within the Basilian Order and the Ruthenian church metropolis.

The authorisation of the limited cult, which fits the framework of beatification, was a transitional solution: according to the indult, the canonisation, which means recognition of the worship in the entire Church, was the ultimate goal. The local actors and Uniate hierarchy therefore tried to maintain the euphoria:[18] between 1664 and 1666, Jakub Jan Susza, a Basilian bishop of Chełm (in Poland) promoted Josaphat's case in Rome. His *Cursus vitae et certamen martyrii beati Iosaphat Cuncevii* (1665) replaced the *Relatio* as the standard *vita*; it was re-edited in 1865 to

---

15 On the forming of Josaphat's early *fama sanctitatis* in literature, see M. Čiurinskas, "Naujas dangiškasis globėjas: kai kurie opinio sanctitatis aspektai istoriniuose ir literatūriniuose pal. Juozapato gyvenimo šaltiniuose XVII a.", in J. Liškevičienė (ed.), *Dangiškieji globėjai, žemiškieji mecenatai / Celestial Patrons and terrestrial Benefactors* (Vilnius: Vilniaus dailės akademija, 2011 = Acta Academiae Atrium Vilnensis 60) 85–98.

16 On the role of the Jesuits in Josaphat's cult and saint-making, see J. Krajcar, "Saint Josaphat and the Jesuits of Lithuania", *Analecta OSBM* [Series II. Sectio II] 6 [12] (1967) 75–84.

17 J. Martinov (ed.)/J.J. Susza, *Cursus vitae et certamen martyrii beati Iosaphat Cuncevii, archiepiscopi Polocensis* … (Paris: Victor Plamé, 1865), 147. English translation is my own.

18 M. Niendorf (*Das Grossfürstentum Litauen. Studien zur Nationsbildung in der Frühen Neuzeit [1569–1795]* [Wiesbaden: Harrasowitz, ^{2}2010], 157–8) is more sceptical about the popularity of Josaphat's cult, yet he clearly underestimates his vast hagiographical dossier, especially from the 17th and 18th centuries.

contribute to the revived process,[19] which concluded with the proclamation of Josaphat as a saint two years later.[20] Given the course of his saint-making, he might be indeed regarded as a phoenix raised from the tragedy of his death to be reborn as a saint enjoying eternal fame as a martyr. A subtle play on the concept of such a 'saint phoenix' can be observed in his hagiographical dossier.

An image of the phoenix was substituted for Josaphat's figure in his emblematic *vita*:[21] Andrzej Młodzianowski, a Jesuit, published the *Icones symbolicae vitae et mortis beati Iosaphat martyris* in 1675,[22] just a few years after Susza's *Cursus*, and thus still on the wave of the canonisation efforts. The propagandistic angle of the work corresponded with the parenetic function of the Jesuit iconography, which in this case was directed at the religious and political instruction of the dedicatee.[23] It also re-evaluated and updated Josaphat's *vita* in a literary form responding to the Baroque taste of a contemporary audience.[24] Coming from outside the protagonist's background, Młodzianowski assisted the Basilian and Uniate archbishop with the transition from being blessed to being a saint, and so he participated in instrumentalising Josaphat as "... staatspolitisches sowie katholisches Integrationsmedium ..."[25] in the sense of Jesuit inculturation adapted to the premises of an

---

19 J.J. Susza, *Cursus vitae et certamen martyrii beati Iosaphat Cuncevii, archiepiscopi Polocensis ...* (Rome: Varesius, 1665); for the re-edited version, translated into many languages, with a few additions, see Martinov (ed.)/Susza, *Cursus vitae*. The impact of the *Cursus* was not diminished by a new *vita* in French: A. Guépin, *Saint Josaphat, archevêque de Polock, martyr de l'unité catholique et l'église grecque unie en Pologne* (2 vol.; Poitiers: Henri Oudin, 1874).

20 On Josaphat's canonisation, see S. Samerski, *"Wie im Himmel so auf Erden"? Selig- und Heiligsprechung in der Katholischen Kirche 1740 bis 1870* (Stuttgart: Kohlhammer, 2002), 138–56.

21 On Jesuit emblematic *vitae*, see É. Knapp/G. Tüskés, "Emblematische Viten von Jesuitenheiligen im 17./18. Jahrhundert", *Archiv für Kulturgeschichte* 80 (1998) 105–42.

22 A. Młodzianowski, *Icones symbolicae vitae et mortis beati Iosaphat martyris, archiepiscopi Polocensis ...* (Vilnius: Jesuit Academy, 1675); cf. K. Estreicher, *Bibliografia Staropolska* (vol. 23; Cracow: Jagiellonian University, 1908), 451–2. A modern edition of the text (Liškevičienė (ed.)/Mlodzianovskis, *Palaimintojo kankinio Juozapato*) comprises a facsimile of the Latin booklet with an annotated translation and short studies (all in Lithuanian). The current contribution follows the Polish spelling of the poet's name as given on the title page of the *editio princeps* of his work.

23 On the parenetic function of Jesuit iconography, see G.R. Dimler, "The Jesuit Emblem", in Daly (ed.), *Companion*, 99–127, on pp. 101–5; cf. W. Telesko, *In Bildern denken. Die Typologie in der bildenden Kunst der Vormoderne* (Vienna/Cologne/Weimar: Bühlau, 2016), 232–3.

24 M. Čiurinskas, "XVIIa. unitų literatūros bruožai: biografiniai kūriniai Lietuvos didžiojoje kunigaikštystėje", *Senoji Lietuvos literatūra* 26 (2008) 183–212, on pp. 200–1.

25 S. Rohdewald, "Medium unierter konfessioneller Identität oder polnisch-ruthenischer Einigung? Zur Verehrung Josafat Kuncevyčs im 17. Jahrhundert", in Y. Kleinmann (ed.), *Kommunikation durch symbolische Akte. Religiöse Heterogenität und politische Herrschaft in Polen-Litauen* (Stuttgart: Franz Steiner, 2010) 271–90, on p. 284.

encounter between Uniate and Roman Catholicism.[26] He thus drafted a hagiographical typology into an emblem and connected Christ (allegorical phoenix) with his martyr according to the Jesuit pattern.[27] The emblem unites three conventions: firstly, it employs the Christological symbol of a phoenix in the hagiographical setting indebted to the Jesuit commemorative literature and epic poetry. Secondly, it recontextualises the motif with a quotation from Martial, a Late-Antique poet (1/2 BCE), to emphasise the process of dying. The Jesuit and classical frame is provided, thirdly, with a biblical overtone to stress Josaphat's merits of a bishop and martyr.

The Jesuit profile shaped indirectly in the *Icones* evolved shortly thereafter into a direct juxtaposition of Josaphat and Ignatius of Loyola, the founder of the Jesuits and the most exemplary saint of early modern times. In 1693, a drama about the saints Canus and Cantianus was performed at the Jesuit college in Vitebsk to honour the Ruthenian lesser noble house of Kisiel. In the first choral song, the genius of the family receives the helmet and shield of Ignatius from the genius of the Roman Church; the sword of the blessed Josaphat is given by the genius of the Uniate Church.[28] This equal performance by both figures symbolically concludes the process of profiling Josaphat as a Catholic saint through Jesuit lenses, which was essentially brought forward with Młodzianowski's *Icones*.

Josaphat's emblematic *vita*: Młodzianowski's *Icones*

At first, the *Icones* appear to be a local expression of devotion to Josaphat in the region of his former activity.[29] Młodzianowski, born in 1626, joined in 1642 the Jesuits in Vilnius, where he started to study rhetoric at the local academy; he continued his education in Pinsk. Having taught grammar at the colleges in Kaunas and Orsha, he came back to Vilnius and devoted himself to the study of theology.

---

26 On Jesuit inculturation, see M. Sievernich, "Von der Akkomodation zur Inkulturation. Missionarische Leitideen der Gesellschaft Jesu", *Zeitschrift für Missionswissenschaft und Religionswissenschaft* 86 (2002) 260–76, on pp. 266–70.

27 On hagiographical typology, see Telesko, *In Bildern denken*, 207–19.

28 The playbill summarises G. Lühr, "24 Jesuitendramen der litauischen Ordensprovinz", *Altpreussische Monatsschrift* [N.F.] / *Neue Preussische Provinzial-Blätter* [5. F.] 38.1–2 (1901) 1–61, on pp. 46–8.

29 For general overview of the *Icones*, see J. Liškevičienė, "Images from the Life of the Beatified Josaphat Kuntsevych", in I. Höpel/L.O. Larsson (ed.), *Emblematik im Ostseeraum / Emblematics around the Baltic. Ausgewählte Beiträge zur 10. Internationalen Tagung der Society for Emblem Studies in Kiel, 27. Juli bis 1. August 2014* (Kiel: Ludwig, 2016) 73–84; the biographic details in the current contribution are based on the biography drafted in this article (ibid., 73). On Młodzianowski's *vita* in the resources of the ARSI in Rome, see Liškevičienė (ed.)/Mlodzianovskis, *Palaimintojo kankinio Juozapato*, 525–8.

He took refuge in Moravia during the so-called Deluge, the Swedish invasion of Poland-Lithuania (1655–1660), and was ordained there as a priest. After his return to Lithuania in 1660 he taught in colleges, including in Polotsk (1672–1676), and published the *Icones*.[30] Slightly earlier, in 1671, he created the *Suppetiae militares*, a collection of the emblems and prose eulogies devoted to the patrons of Poland-Lithuania and other military saints, which he dedicated to Michał Kazimierz Pac, voivode of Vilnius and Grand Hetman of Lithuania.[31] Apart from the emblems, Młodzianowski is said to have authored two occasional works for prominent figures in Lithuania, although the prints are signed by the communities of the Jesuit schools in Kražiai (1668) and Polotsk (1673).[32]

The *Icones* were published after 9 December 1675 (the date of the *imprimatur*)[33] in the Jesuit printing house in Vilnius. The booklet consists of four parts: first, the intention of the work is explained in a dedicatory foreword. Secondly, a summary (*compendium*) highlights standard components of Josaphat's *vita*: symbolical moments (like the vocation to sanctity) interfere with realistic details (like the death through the head blows).[34] The main part constitutes, thirdly, a cycle of forty units devoted to the themes from Kuntsevych's life. Each unit contains one emblem and one prose eulogy, both with references to further texts and explanatory notes. All standard elements can be distinguished in each emblem. An *imago*, a graphic depiction enclosed in an ornamental framework, illustrates the title; in some cases, it draws on Athanasius Kircher's work on China (1667).[35] A *lemma*, a motto in

30 On Młodzianowski's output, see B. Milewska-Waźbińska, "The Literary Heritage of Jesuits of the Polish-Lithuanian Commonwealth", *Journal of Jesuit Studies* 5 (2018) 421–40, on pp. 439–40. J. Pelc ("The Emblem in Poland", in Daly [ed.], *Companion*, 291–307) associates the popularity of the emblematics in Poland-Lithuania with the Jesuit circles and especially with Vilnius, yet does not draw any attention to the *Icones*.

31 A. Młodzianowski, *Suppetiae militares ex divis Poloniae Lituanaeque gentis tutelaribus nec non sanctis militibus … domino Michaeli Pac palatino Vilnensis supremo Magni Ducatus Lituaniae exercituum duci* … ([Vilnius: Jesuit Academy], 1671).

32 Estreicher (*Bibliografia*, 451) specifies both pieces under Młodzianowski's name without any justification. The Jesuits in Kražiai prepared for Kazimierz Pac, instituted as the bishop of Samogitia, the eulogies of his predecessors and of his diocese ([A. Młodzianowski], *Domestica Samogitiae Ducatus ornamenta in venerationem amplissimorum decorum … domini Casimiri Pac episcopi Samogitiae dum auspicato suam ingreditur dioecesim obviam* … [Jelgava: Michał Karnall, 1668]). The *Auguria spei publicae*, a collection of good wishes for Jan Sapieha, who took over the voivodship of Polotsk, were published by the Polotsk Jesuits ([A. Młodzianowski], *Auguria spei publicae … Casimiro Ioanni Sapieha palatino Polocensi … dum palatinus sui fasces capesseret* … [Vilnius: Jesuit Academy, 1673]).

33 Młodzianowski, *Icones*, fol. Q4^{r}.

34 On the simple and chronological composition of the *Icones*, see O. Daukšienė, "Šventasis kankinys kaip šventųjų pirmavaizdžio ir globėjo Kristaus atspindys XVII a. poezijoje: 'Krauju tapytas' Juozapato Kuncevičiaus paveikslas", in Liškevičienė (ed.), *Dangiškieji*, 99–111, on pp. 102–3.

35 Liškevičienė, "Images", 78–9.

a few words inscribed on the banner in the *imago*, points out the interpretative angle, which is elaborated in an epigram in six elegiac couplets placed beneath each graphic. The *Icones* close, fourthly, with an ode in Sapphic strophe directed at Josaphat.

The foreword and the ode associate Josaphat's figure with the Sapieha noble house, a powerful family closely involved in his martyrdom and cult. The work is dedicated to Jerzy Stanisław Sapieha (1668–1732), the son of Kazimierz Jan Sapieha, the voivode of Polotsk and castellan of Borysaw. At this time, the dedicatee was about seven years old – in the conclusion, he is expected to grow up to the credit of his ancestors ("Adolesce in eam, quam augur bonorum omnium pollicetur animus, felicitatis maturitatem inter palmas …").[36] A connection between the protagonist and the Sapiehas is established at the beginning, however: the work is focused on the special affection they showed Josaphat ("… Sapiehanae pietatis in divum … exempla")[37] and implicitly demanded from the dedicatee. The splendour of the house, and its engagement in public and church matters, is outlined with a quotation from a poem by Maciej Kazimierz Sarbiewski (1595–1640): "Grandinat gemmis riguoque caelum / Depluit auro" (lyr. I 1, 10–11; 'the sky hails jewels and casts liquid gold').[38] It is derived from programmatic praise of Urban VIII: the time of peace, a new golden age, is expected to come under Urban, since the victory over the Turks was achieved in the battle of Khotin (1621), shortly before the start of his pontificate (1623) and the poem's publication (1625).[39] Sarbiewski, a Jesuit and teacher at schools in Poland-Lithuania and Rome, earned his fame across Europe with a collection of odes and epigrams.[40] The reference to his poem underlines the poetical value of the *Icones* and opens an intertextual discourse, as it engages the Sapieha house and Josaphat's cult in the international discussion of the Turkish threat, which is indeed discussed in the latter part of the dedication.

A short ancestry line, adjusted to the subject of Kuntsevych's veneration, commences with Lew Sapieha (1577–1633), Grand Chancellor of Lithuania. He was on the side of the lay administration, and cooperated with Josaphat in consolidating the Union; after the events in Vitebsk, he was entrusted with conducting the trial

36 Młodzianowski, *Icones*, fol. II2^v. All quotes from the *Icones* are taken from the *editio princeps* and slightly modernised. English translations are my own.

37 Ibid., fol. I2^r.

38 Ibid., fol. I^v; cf. M.K. Sarbiewski, *Lyricorum libri tres* (Cologne: Bernhard Gualter, 1625), 2.

39 Młodzianowski acted exactly in a manner of Sarbiewski who made the Turkish threat the leitmotif of his work. In this context, on the battle at Khotin in 1621, see P.M. Ryczkowski, "A Farmer Who Does Not Want to Be a Poet: The Motif of *recusatio* in the Compositional Structure of Sarbiewski's Ode IV 4", in A. Brzozowska/M. Plago (ed.), Ars recusandi. *Odmowa jako zabieg literacki w tekstach greckich i łacińskich od starożytności do końca XVIII wieku* (Warsaw: DiG, 2022) 159–74.

40 On Sarbiewski, see Milewska-Waźbińska, "The Literary Heritage", 428–38.

of the assassins. The interconnection of these figures is indicated in the foreword (Lew was *vindex immanissimi sceleris*)[41] and in addition becomes the theme of the last emblem and eulogy: the title presents the Chancellor in similar words as the avenger of Josaphat's death (*vindex sceleris et mortis*).[42] Next, the speaker turns to Kazimierz Lew Sapieha (1609–1656), Lew's son, who founded a silver sarcophagus in Polotsk cathedral to serve as Josaphat's main reliquary (1646–1650).[43] A rhetoric question ("Sed quid vetera commemoro?") marks the change to other figures: it creates a contrast between Lew and his son, who belong to the past, and the younger Sapiehas, who emulate their devotion in a metaphorical 'contest of piety' ("... eximio cum virtute certamine de pietate in Iosaphat cum illiustrissimis maioribus certant posteri").[44] Among them is to be found the dedicatee's father, Kazimierz Jan Sapieha (ca. 1642–1720), who was voivode of Polotsk from 1671, and not a direct descendant of Lew. He demonstrated the ancestral virtue and followed in the footsteps of his father, Paweł Sapieha (1609–1665), when he fought the Turks at Khotin in 1673 and stayed loyal to Michał Korybut Wiśniowiecki, King of Poland and Grand Duke of Lithuania (1669–1673). His bravery was apparently a sign of Josaphat's favour to whom he previously entrusted himself and his people during a votive mass held in Polotsk. He was not the only Sapieha who went to the war, however: his brother, Franciszek Stefan (ca. 1647–1686) is also mentioned.

The victory of 1673 did not remove the Turkish threat, only temporarily moved it away: it still jeopardises the peace of the Christian world and of its eye of focus, Poland ("Lacessitus, non deletus hostis est. ... Feralis illa luna ... plenum orbem acuit in cornua; ... confinem pupillam veluti orbis Christiani impetit Poloniam").[45] The speaker alludes to the initial quotation borrowed from Sarbiewski and describing the dedicatee's family: since the fate of the Sapiehas, who were experienced in the Turkish combat, is essentially bound with Kuntsevych, it seemed right to offer the *Icones* to Jerzy Stanisław as a legacy (*haereditario cum iure*). He was to be encouraged at a young age to pursue comparable achievements both in public life and in Josaphat's worship – his ancestors show him the proper way ("... haec [memoria] tibi tritum ad augusta monstrat callem ...").[46] The parenetic argument

41 Młodzianowski, *Icones*, fol. I2^{r}.

42 Ibid., fol. P4^{v}.

43 On the sarcophagus, see P. Krasny, "Relikwiarz św. Jozafata Kuncewicza w katedrze połockiej. Przyczynek do badań nad srebrnymi trumnami relikwiarzowymi w Rzeczypospolitej w XVII wieku", in J. Lileyko (ed.), *Studia nad sztuką renesansu i baroku 4* (Lublin: Towarzystwo Naukowe Katolickiego Uniwersytetu Lubelskiego, 2000) 121–40; T. Račiūnaitė, "Globojant šventą kankinio kūną: Juozapato Kuncevičiaus kultas loca sancta aspektu", in Liškevičienė (ed.), *Dangiškieji*, 127–47, on pp. 134–7.

44 Młodzianowski, *Icones*, fol. I3^{v}.

45 Ibid., fol. II2^{r}–II2^{v}.

46 Ibid., fol. II2^{v}.

is ornamented with a citation from a political poem by Claudian and speaking about the value of an example passing from a father through son and grandson to further descendants.[47] As a persuasive tool, it differs from Sarbiewski's verses, which are a programmatic link between Josaphat, militarised in the context of the Turkish threat,[48] and the Sapieha house, always concerned about the current political, confessional, and military issues.

Josaphat as a phoenix in Młodzianowski's *Icones*

The fifth unit of the *Icones* describes Josaphat's vocation to sanctity: as explained in the title, a spark of fire descended on his chest from the depiction of the crucified Jesus that he was admiring ("Scintilla ignis in sinum Iosaphat e crucifixi imagine descendit").[49] The vocation came to him in early life, when he still lived in Volodymyr with his parents, who brought him to the church; once, he asked his father about the meaning of the crucifix icon and learnt that it depicts the Saviour. The story, taken to the *Icones* from Susza's *Cursus*, constitutes a part of tradition developed in the local investigation. In Młodzianowski's work, the story is adjusted to a short summary: when the spark struck Josaphat's chest, it caused him to devote himself to pious activities and to explore divine matters.[50] Susza reports the moment similarly, but focuses on the internal change:[51] the spark inflamed Josaphat's heart with devotion and zeal for the faith.[52] The narrative is given exactly in this form in the testimony

47 Ibid., fol. II2^{v}; cf. Claud. *Mall.* 336–7.

48 A *Militarisierung der Heiligen* was a common practice (also) in early modern cult of saints; cf. L. Berezhnaya, "Soldaten und Märtyrer: Zum Prozess der Militarisierung der Heiligen im östlichen und westlichen Christentum", in eadem (ed.), *Die Militarisierung der Heiligen in Vormoderne und Moderne* (Berlin: Duncker & Humboldt, 2020) 9–56. The *Icones* follow the pattern established at the time of the local investigation and pursued thereafter (cf. Rohdewald, "Medium", 277; 283–5), including in Młodzianowski, *Suppetiae militares*, fol. K7^{v}–K9^{r}; cf. J. Liškevičienė, "Ankstyvieji palaimintojo Juozapato Kuncevičiaus portretiniai atvaizdai", in eadem (ed.), *Dangiškieji*, 113–25, on pp. 117–18.

49 Młodzianowski, *Icones*, fol. B3^{r}.

50 Ibid., fol. [III^{r}]: "Cum puer admodum in ecclesia s. martyris Parasceves, in qua Christianis initiatus fuerat mysteriis, pendentis de cruce Salvatoris conspexisset effigiem didicissetque parentum magisterio Dei hominis extremo pro salute mundi affecti supplicio hanc esse iconem, repente e latere Crucifixi erumpens scintilla ad intimos tenerrimi spectatoris penetravit sinus. Nec sub operosi elementi imagine gratia Dei in Iosaphat vacua fuit, nam exinde pietatis studia ardentius colere, familiarum consortio ereptas horas Deo divinisque rebus impendere, puerile nihil praeter aetatem agere visus est".

51 Cf. Guépin, *Saint Josaphat*, 1.6–7.

52 Susza, *Cursus vitae*, 2–3: "A parentibus in timore divino ab uberibus nutritus et ad eam quondam, in qua Christianis initiatus erat mysteriis, illatus ecclesiam effigiem Redemptoris nostri de cruce suspensi advertit et, quid rei foret, rogavit. Cui ipsi appositis ad tenellae aetatis cognitionem verbis esse

of Gennady Chmielnicki, a Jesuit in Polotsk and confessor of Kuntsevych, who claimed during the second *processus in partibus* in 1637 that Josaphat himself told him about this moment;[53] however, it is missing in his first testimony given in 1628.[54]

Older sources also retell the story: in the *Josaphatis*, God stabbed Josaphat's chest with a ray of light to inspire him with the task of fighting the Orthodoxy; at this time he was already a Basilian and an archbishop.[55] Although the poem dwells on the *Relatio*, the report does not make any use of the spark narrative; it simply adds that during his training as merchant Josaphat occupied himself with pious books, and as a result decided to join the Basilians.[56] Nevertheless, the vocation to sanctity, according to the details given by Młodzianowski and Susza, was treated in the Old Polish poem *Tryumph duchowny* by Walenty Szlachtowicz, published in 1628 and alluding to the first local process in the same year:[57] the spark descended on young Josaphat as he was visiting the church with his father, who explained to him the meaning of the crucifix.[58] It can thus only be speculated that the story had already circulated during the first *processus in partibus*, even if it was not recorded in the preserved protocol. The *Relatio*, missing the story, was written directly after Josaphat's death in order to serve as a reliable account for the

---

Dei hominisque imaginem pro asserendo in libertatem et in salutem homine enecti propalaverunt. Mutatus exinde puellus sensit e latere appensi Domini igneam erumpentem scintillam in cor suum cecidisse. Quae illum ad devotionis ardorem, corporis macerationem, fidei sanctae zelum ab hinc usque ad extremum inflammaret spiritum".

53 A.G. Welykyj (ed.), *S. Iosaphat hieromartyr. Documenta Romana beatificationis et canonizationis. Vol. II (1628–1637)* (Rome: Scuola salesiana del libro, 1955), 217.

54 A.G. Welykyj (ed.), *S. Iosaphat hieromartyr* (1952), 174–85.

55 Isakowicz, *Iosaphatidos*, 12–13: "… Caelituum Genitor Cuncevii conscia sacro / Pectora percussit radio caelique sequacem / Excivit mentem … / … Nec plura, ambrosio perfusum pectora motu / Liquit et agnovit praesul …".

56 [Morochowski], *De nece*, fol. A4^{v}: "… cum intermissione suorum negotiorum, quibus distinebatur, inserviens cuidam civi Wilnensi, non tantum domi, sed etiam foris lectioni librorum spiritualium intentus erat magis quam quibusvis aliis occupationibus. Inde secutum est, ut anno MDCIV, viginti et aliquot annos natus, monasticam vitam sub regula sancti patris Basilii in ritu Graeco Catholico Wilnae, ad ecclesiam S. Trinitatis, amplecteretur".

57 Towards the end of the poem, the investigation of Josaphat's tomb is treated briefly; W.A. Szlachtowicz, *Tryumph duchowny wielebnego ojca Iosaphata Kuncewicza, episkopa witebskiego, życiem duchownym i śmiercią męczęńską oświecony* … (Lviv: Jan Szeliga, 1628), fol. 21–4. The description tallies with the protocol preserved in the materials of the first *processus in partibus* in 1628 (Welykyj [ed.], *S. Iosaphat hieromartyr* [1952], 191–3).

58 Szlachtowicz, *Tryumph*, 6–7; cf. R. Radyszewśkyj, (ed.), *Roksolański Parnas. Polskojęzyczna poezja ukraińska od końca XVI do początku XVIII wieku. Część II: Antologia* (Cracow: Wydawnictwo Oddziału PAN, 1998), 117–18. On the poem, see idem, *Polskojęzyczna poezja ukraińska od końca XVI do początku XVIII wieku. Część I: Monografia* (Cracow: Wydawnictwo Oddziału PAN, 1996), 104–7.

Roman curia; conversely, the *Josaphatis* and all later texts, including the *Tryumph* and the *Cursus*, mainly adapted the report and the investigation materials to the conventions of each hagiographical genre, and so amplified the *vita* with the usual topos of vocation.

Such a hagiographical adaptation affected Młodzianowski's *Icones*: he accommodated the partial, or rather early, version of the spark story to his hagiographical agenda. The adoration of the crucifix is depicted separately from the vocation moment in the fourth unit ("Singulari affectu Jesum crucifixum contemplatur").[59] The *imago* shows Josaphat with a rosary in his hands, which are folded for prayer, kneeling before an altar on which lies an opened book – a Bible. Behind the altar stands an angel holding a board in the form of a diptych with a crucifix in the middle. The Greek letters alpha and omega on both sides refer to Christ's self-presentation as beginning and ending (Rev 22:13). Accordingly, the lemma introduces him as *vitae mortisque magister*, the teacher of life and death. The theme is explained in the epigram:

> Alpha notat vitam, tristem notat omega mortem:
>   Iosaphat in Christo spectat utrumque libro
> Et nova dum mortis vitaeque duella revolvit,
>   Vivendi discit commoriendo modum.
> O, quam grande mori lucrum censebitur illi,
>   Artem vivendi qui moriendo sciet?
> [Alpha signifies life, omega stands for a sad death – Josaphat observes both in Christ like in a book and, while he contemplates the new struggles of death and life, he simultaneously learns the way of living through dying. O, how valuable profit will death seem to be to the one who knows the art of living by dying?].

The book, the word of God and an account of Christ's sacrifice, is the object of meditation and teachings received by Josaphat. Given his hagiographical dossier, however, it is an addition – the readings of the Bible and other scriptures are not described in Młodzianowski's *compendium*; Susza does not speak about the books in the context of vocation, but a few lines later, when he discusses Josaphat's education. Conversely, the *Relatio* suggests that the readings were a turning point in Josaphat's life, although it does not mention the spark. The emblem, which emphasises the role of the pious book in Josaphat's vocation to sanctity, is strikingly redolent of a decisive moment in the life of Ignatius of Loyola (1491–1556), a model Catholic saint inspired to pious life by the books containing Christ's life story and hagiographical

---

59 Młodzianowski, *Icones*, fol. B^{v}; cf. a commentary in Liškevičienė (ed.)/Mlodzianovskis, *Palaimintojo kankinio Juozapato*, 463–4.

legends.[60] Apparently, Młodzianowski shifted the profile of his protagonist slightly towards the image of the founder of his Order, who was meant to be imitated,[61] and thus contributed to the universal narrative of Ignatius as a converter.[62]

Having internalised the example of Christ, who lived and died to be resurrected, Kuntsevych approaches death already in his lifetime. Death is therefore a greater profit – the conclusion reveals his readiness to sacrifice himself for the cause of faith even at the cost of life, which correlates with the vocation topos. Hence, an epigram in one further emblem about the moment of the martyr's death can announce: "Unica martyrii namque est victoria vinci / Et sunt ipsa salus vulnera, vita mori" ('For a martyr, a victory means in fact only to be defeated and also the wounds are salvation, life is death').[63]

Following the conclusion of the fourth epigram, the fifth emblem, depicting the moment when Josaphat realised his vocation to sanctity, places the emphasis on death.[64] The Christological framework consists in the *imago*: a phoenix rises towards the sun from a fire consuming a nest on a rock; the sunrays are reminiscent of the spark of fire. While the image seems to suggest rebirth, the epigram emphasises the process of dying:

> Candidus aestivi phoenix, Hyperionis ales,
> Urget odoratum per flabra bina rogum.
> Empyrei flammam phoenix en noster amoris
> De cruce ceu geminis excitat ipse flabris.
> Cum sit odor Christi bonus, ustus Iosaphat isto
> Igne suo gratum fit thymiama Deo.[65]
>
> [The phoenix, a radiant bird of glowing Hyperion, stimulates the fragrant pyre with two blasts of his wings. Here, our phoenix similarly incites a fiery flame of celestial love from the cross with two blasts. Since he is a pleasant aroma of Christ, Josaphat, having been burnt in this fire, becomes an agreeable incense for his God].

60 For this standard element of Ignatius's *vita* in prose, see P. Ribadeneira, *Vita Ignatii Loiolae …* (Antwerp: Christophorus Plantinus, 1587), 22. For an emblematic *vita*, see I. Querck, *Acta S. Ignatii de Lojola, Societatis Jesu fundatoris, iconibus, symbolis, ac versibus exornata …* (Vienna: Leopold Voigt, 1698), VII; on the work, see Telesko, *In Bildern denken*, 233–5. On the conversion narrative, see M. Leone, *Saints and Signs. A Semotic Reading of Conversion in Early Modern Catholicism* (Berlin/New York: De Gruyter, 2010), 23–105.

61 Cf. E. Levy, *Propaganda and the Jesuit Baroque* (Berkeley/Los Angeles/London: University of California, 2004), 118–20.

62 On the model, see Leone, *Saints and Signs*, 105–67.

63 Młodzianowski, *Icones*, fol. O^{v}.

64 Conversely, a standard interpretation of the motif, focusing on the resurrection, offers a commentary in Liškevičienė (ed.)/Mlodzianovskis, *Palaimintojo kankinio Juozapato*, 464–5.

65 Młodzianowski, *Icones*, fol. B3^{r}.

The entire emblem shifts to the death theme in three subtle ways. Firstly, the epigram employs several meanings of the phoenix, but it is always in the context of death. In the first couplet the phoenix is described in its general meaning as a bird which lights the pyre; in the next one, it turns out to be Christ who sets the pyre on fire from the cross. The metaphor is uncovered in the last couplet: Josaphat, burnt like a phoenix, offers himself voluntarily to God as an aroma of Christ. Secondly, the resurrection is not mentioned at all, and thus it needs to be interpreted from the motif represented in the *imago* and explained in a note below ("Phoenicem senescentem ex casiae thurisque surculis construere rogum, quo accenso a sole ipsum superemori tradit Manilius").[66] The note is quoted, without any direct reference, from the *Naturalis historia* (X 2) by Pliny the Elder (1 CE) with two significant changes. The neutral *nidus* ('nest'), attested in the contemporary text edition,[67] is replaced with the funeral pyre (*rogus*); information about the sun igniting the pyre is added, which goes well with the sunrays depicted in the image.

Thirdly, the focus on death is indicated by the lemma *nobiliore rogo* which implies that the phoenix dies on a more noble pyre. Taken from the *Icones*, it was included in the *Apelles symbolicus*, a lexicon of symbols published by Johannes Michael von der Ketten in 1699, where it distinguishes itself from other mottos devoted to the rebirth of the phoenix instead.[68] The phrase is borrowed from Martial's epigram about Festus who became suddenly ill and decided to commit suicide:[69]

Nec tamen obscuro pia polluit ora veneno
 Aut torsit lenta tristia fata fame,
Sanctam Romana vitam sed morte peregit
 imisitque animam nobiliore rogo (Mart. I 78, 5–8).

[And neither did he soil his righteous face with a secret poison nor did he torment his sad fate with clinging fame, but he ended his life in the sacred death of Romans: he dismissed his soul on a more noble pyre].

---

66 The poem does not make any lexical use of the phoenix poems by Lactantius and Claudian. The passage in Pliny's work, used to explain the motif, speaks about the cult of light, but does not mention Hyperion explicitly. A certain influence of Ovid's narrative could therefore be recognised in the quite typical phrase *Hyperionis ales*, which links the phoenix to the cult of Hyperion, the mythological Titan of light (cf. Ov. *Metam.* 15.406–7).

67 Plinius Secundus, *Naturalis Historiae tomus primus …* (Leiden/Rotterdam: Hack, 1699), 656.

68 J.M. von der Ketten, *Apelles symbolicus exhibens seriem amplissimam symbolorum poetisque, oratoribus ac verbi Dei praedicatoribus conceptus subministrans varios …* (2 vol.; Amsterdam/Ghent: Gillis Janssonius van Waesberge, 1699), 1.582 (the *Icones* are mentioned with the title, but without the author's name).

69 The facsimile edition does not recognise the source of the lemma; Liškevičienė (ed.)/Mlodzianovskis, *Palaimintojo kankinio Juozapato*, 211.

Festus chose the 'Roman death': the comparative *nobiliore* suggests that death by a sword was a more appropriate way for a Roman citizen to end life than poison or starvation.[70] The metrics of the verse (dactylic pentameter) stress the first syllable of the adjective (*nobiliore*) and the last of the noun (*rogo*), and thus the whole phrase appears as a coherent item.

The focus on death in the emblem is in a contrast with the fifth eulogy,[71] which makes only imagistic use of the phoenix:[72] the bird's name is a keyword designation for Josaphat (*noster phoenix*). According to the conclusion, divine fire turns everything into something better ("Ignis quippe divinus, qui omnia consummat in melius ..."). The fire, a leading theme of the eulogy, is a Christological metonymy created in the initial allusion, explained in a footnote, to Christ's self-presentation as the one who brings fire (Luke 12:49) and juxtaposed with a general reference to Rome founded by the exiles from Trojan flames. The conclusion complements the phoenix motif with four symbols of endurance in fire (clarified in a footnote). The unburnt bush stems from a biblical context (*rubus*; Exod 3:2); further authorities include Pliny the Elder (*asbestos*, a kind of incombustible linen),[73] Aristotle (salamander living in fire),[74] and the historian Florus (narrative about the Vestals cultivating the sacred fire). Młodzianowski's strategy thus presupposes a separation of both components of the phoenix motif: although the usual meaning is implied in the *imago*, the emblem is coherently limited to the theme of death, or rather martyrdom, due to the lemma and epigram. Conversely, the eulogy is concerned with the rebirth; the phoenix is mentioned simply as one of the many programmatic keywords.

---

70 Cf. P. Howell, *A Commentary on the Book One of the Epigrams of Martial* (London: The Athlone, 1980), 283; M. Citroni (ed.), *M. Valerii Martialis Epigrammaton liber primus. Introduzione, testo, apparato critico e commento* (Florence: La nuova Italia, 1975), 254.

71 Młodzianowski, *Icones*, fol. B3^{v}–B4^{r}.

72 On the imagistic use of words in the emblems, see Daly, *Literature*, 69.

73 On asbestos, see M.C. Biederbick, "Tradition and Empirical Observation – Nature in Giovio's and Symeoni's *Dialogo Dell' Imprese* from 1574", in K.A.E. Enenkel/P.J. Smith (ed.), *Emblems and the Natural World* (Leiden/Boston: Brill, 2017) 271–318, on p. 300. However, Pliny seems to have invented this incombustable plant; cf. J.F. Healy, *Pliny the Elder on Science and Technology* (Oxford et al.: Oxford University, 1999), 196–7.

74 On salamander emblems, see A. Henkel/A.Schöne (ed.), *Emblemata*, 738–42; Biederbick, "Tradition", 294–303.

Jesuit commemorative literature as inspiration for Młodzianowski's phoenix emblem

Młodzianowski's approach differs from the concept of a phoenix emblem in the *Imago primi saeculi Societatis Iesu*, a widely disseminated work published in 1640 to celebrate the first century of the Society of Jesus,[75] which might have served him as a source of inspiration. As suggested by the title, the emblem illustrates the precious death of martyrs (*martyrum pretiosa mors*),[76] and so it is a proper closure to the fourth book concerned with the travails, inclusive of martyrdom, encountered by the Jesuits in different mission lands (*Societas patiens*).[77] The *imago* is arranged in the same way as the image in the *Icones*: a phoenix nests on a rock and burns while illuminated by the sun. A similarly phrased lemma, also speaking about death (*non poterat fato nobiliore mori*), is taken from another piece by Martial: "Nec queror infernas quamvis cito rapta sub umbras. / Non potui fato nobiliore mori" (XI 69, 11–12; 'I am not complaining, although I was quickly whisked away to the shadows of the underworld. I could not have died by a nobler fate'). Martial's phrase, modified to a third person narrative (*poterat* instead of *potui*), fits the context perfectly: just as his speaker does not complain about death, the martyrs are eager to sacrifice their lives to testify for Christ. Although the Late-Antique epigram is composed as an animal's self-epitaph, of a hunting dog killed by a boar,[78] the conclusion is recontextualised as a religious motto. The quotations derived from ancient authors and separated from the context, as in the lemmas,[79] were commonly exploited in post-antique poetry; Martial's phrase *nobiliore rogo* is found in the contemporary handbooks of poetry.[80]

According to the epigram, death grants the martyrs, followers of Christ, access to heaven (*merito gens addita caelo*). The praise of martyrdom fills the whole of the poem up to the concluding simile with the phoenix:

---

75 On the work, see J.W. O'Malley, "The *Imago*: Context, Contents, and Controversy", in idem (ed.), *Art, Controversy, and the Jesuits: The* Imago Primi Saeculi *(1640)* (Philadelphia: Saint Joseph's University, 2015) 11–49 (a contribution in the facsimile edition with several studies and an extensive bibliography); cf. Dimler, "The Jesuit Emblem", 100.

76 *Imago primi saeculi Societatis Iesu a provincia Flandro-Belgica eiusdem Societatis repraesentata* (Antwerp: Balthasar Moretus, 1640), 580.

77 O'Malley, "The *Imago*", 37–8.

78 On Martial's epigram, see N. Mindt, "Rede toter Tiere. Tierrede in antiken Epigrammen und im *Culex*", in H. Schmalzgruber (ed.), *Speaking Animals in Ancient Literature* (Heidelberg: Winter, 2020) 207–51, on pp. 228–31. On the context of dog encomium, see F. Schnoor, *Das lateinische Tierlobgedicht*, 204–39; cf. 324–36.

79 Enenkel, "The Neo-Latin Emblem", 131.

80 Cf. *Gradus ad Parnassum sive novus synonymorum, epithetorum, phrasium poeticarum ac versuum thesaurus* … (Cologne: Wilhelm und Franz Metternich, 1691), 238.

Unica sic ales sibi post sua fata superstes,
  Muneris hoc instar, quod moriatur, habet.
Nempe ubi felici posuit cum morte senectam,
  A leto melior, quam fuit ante, redit.
[Thus the unique bird that survives for / itself after its decease has this as the reward that it dies. / When for sure it has forgone old age with a happy death, / it returns from its demise better than it was before].[81]

Even if the lemma, being somewhat a longer version of Młodzianowski's motto, increases the value of death, the poem elaborates on rebirth, a proper reward for martyrs. The emblem in the *Imago* thus employs, on the contrary to the *Icones*, the conventional meaning of the phoenix: it turns the bird into a gentle symbol of martyrdom and diminishes the cruelty of its bloody price.[82] It advertises the benefits of death suffered for faith as a desirable solution, free from drawbacks, for all recipients.[83] This partly propagandistic and partly panegyrical approach rests on the Jesuit programme outlined in the frontispiece of the *Imago*: the phoenix, decorating one of the columns which hold up the whole ensemble of symbols, rises towards the sun from the flames consuming the nest.[84] According to the motto (*et benepatientes erunt*; Ps 91:15), death does not concern the Jesuits, many of whom are willing to endure the travails.[85]

Considering the year of the Jesuit celebrations which produced the *Imago*, the choice of motto for the fifth emblem in the *Icones* might have had another motive. The *Primum saeculum Societatis Jesu Deiparae Virgini sacrum*, a collection of Marian elegies compiled and authored in part by Pierre Pennequin, a French Jesuit, was published in 1640.[86] Diego Alvarez de Pas, a Spanish mystic and preacher,

81 English translation by Michael C. J. Putnam in O'Malley (ed.), *Art*, 625.

82 M. Fumaroli, "Classicism and the Baroque. The *Imago primi saeculi* and Its Detractors", in O'Malley (ed.), *Art*, 57–88, on p. 79.

83 On the Jesuit martyrdom, see C. Russell, "Early Modern Martyrdom and the Society of Jesus in the Sixteenth and Seventeenth Centuries", in L. Cohen (ed.), *Narratives and Representations of Suffering, Failure, and Martyrdom. Early Modern Catholicism Confronting the Adversities of History* (Lisbon: Centro de Estudos de História Religiosa – Universidade Católica Portuguesa, 2020) 67–99.

84 On the programmatic, or structural, significance of the phoenix motif, see P.J. Smith, "Joachim Camerarius's Emblem Book on Birds (1596), with an Excursus on America's Great Seal", in Enenkel/ Smith (ed.), *Emblems*, 149–83, on pp. 157–65.

85 Cf. M.C.J. Putnam, "The frontispiece and opening emblem of the *Imago*: a translation", in O'Malley (ed.), *Art*, 50–55, on p. 54; Fumaroli, "Classicism", 66.

86 On the collection, in context of the genre of the heroides, see J. Eickmeyer, *Der jesuitische Heroidenbrief. Zur Christianisierung und Kontextualisierung einer antiken Gattung in der Frühen Neuzeit* (Berlin/Boston: De Gruyter, 2011), 423–65; H. Dörrie, *Der heroische Brief: Bestandsaufnahme, Geschichte, Kritik einer humanistisch-barocken Literaturgattung* (Berlin: De Gruyter, 1968), 394–5.

contributed a piece on his educational incident:[87] he recalls learning Latin with the help of the Virgin who inspired him to write books under her command. The writing became a mystical experience, as the poet finds himself in front of the teacher.[88] At the end of the poem the speaker recommends his own works which originate from the Virgin:

Si rapiunt flammae, dedit illas fibra Mariae,
  Hinc urunt animos nobiliore rogo.
Suggerit e superis et digerit omnia Virgo:
  Non opus hoc hominis, Virginis esse puta.[89]
[If the flames are erupting, Mary's seed induced them, hence they burn the souls on a more noble pyre. The Virgin excites and carries out all things from heaven, thus you need to think that this is not the work of a man, but of the Virgin].

The conclusion uses Martial's phrase, found in the *Icones*, in the context of releasing of the soul, although through burning rather than by sword. It legitimises Alvarez' own work: the ecstatic process of writing compares to the internal fire inspired by the Virgin. The comparative *nobiliore* makes it clear that it is not just an ordinary fire, but a more noble one for the souls devoted to divine work. Młodzianowski's lemma therefore needs to be read as an expression of ecstatic elation which, as an edifying experience, comes close to the vocation to sanctity and contributes to the Christological meaning of the phoenix.

Epic context of the phoenix emblem in Młodzianowski's *Icones*

The Christological substance of the phoenix motif can furthermore be traced in the epic poetry regarded in early modern times as the finest form of verse composition; it was especially used to celebrate prominent figures and important events.[90] The *Christias*, penned by the Italian humanist Marco Girolamo Vida on the wish of Pope Leon X (published in 1535), enjoyed great popularity and became a contemporary

87 P. Pennequin (ed.), *Primum Societatis Jesu saeculum Deiparae Virgini Mariae sacrum* (Arras: Gerard de Raisme, 1640), 43–5.

88 This iconic 'educational ecstasy' allowed to include Alvarez among prominent Jesuits scholars in Jean Vincart's *Sacrum Heroidum Epistolae* (1675) III 8, 85–6; Eickmeyer, *Der jesuitische Heroidenbrief*, 750–1.

89 Pennequin (ed.), *Primum Societatis Jesu saeculum*, 45. English translation is my own.

90 F. Schaffenrath, "Narrative Structures in Neo-Latin Epic: 16th–19th Century", in Ch. Reitz/S. Finkmann (ed.), *Structures of Epic Poetry. Volume III: Continuity* (Berlin/Boston: De Gruyter, 2019) 301–29, on p. 302.

model of Christian poetry.[91] It displays a poetical version of the Salvation in six books; the matters of the Old Testament are merged into the dominant Passion narrative, although the biblical typology is not always strictly obeyed. The last book embraces the events from the descent from the Cross until the apostles are sent out. Before the narrator describes Mary Magdalene setting off to anoint Christ (VI 313–348), he draws a parallel between the resurrection and the beginning of a new day (VI 292–305), which develops into a simile involving the phoenix:

> Talis, ubi turpe irrepsit senium, unicus ales
> Congessitque sibi ramis felicibus altum
> Summo in colle rogum posuitque in morte senectam,
> Continuo novus exoritur nitidusque iuventa
> Effulget cristis et versicoloribus alis.
> Innumerae circum volucres mirantur euntem;
> Ille suos adit Aethiopas Indosque revisit (Vid. *Christ.* 6.306–12).
> [Similarly, after unsightly old age has crept in and an unique bird has built for himself a vast funeral pyre of auspicious branches on the top of a hill, having deposited its senility in death, it immediately rises reborn and sparkling with young age, shining with a tuft and colourful wings. Countless birds, floating along, admire it on its way: it approaches its own Ethiopians and visits the Indians].

The verses, which draw on the details in Pliny's *Naturalis historia*,[92] seek a balance between life and death giving rise to a new life, and thus they focus on the resurrection. The pleasant odour of the branches used to build the funeral pyre is not mentioned, since it was already explored at the beginning of the poem.

The first book comprises the time from the arrival in Jerusalem until the judgement of Pilatus. After the resurrection of Lazarus (I 236–299), Jesus visits Simon and meets Mary Magdalene, who converts herself under his influence (I 300–375). As a sign of appreciation, she embalms Christ:

> Tum de marmoreis varios deprompsit odores
> Thesauris: casias et nardi mollis aristas
> Aut thuris lacrimam atque auram fragrantis amomi,
> Pronaque permulsit nudas liquido unguine plantas;
> Suavis in aereas diffugit spiritus auras.

91 On the poem, see E. von Contzen/R.F. Glei/W. Polleichtner/M. Schulze Rober (ed.)/M.H. Vida, Christias. *Band. 1: Einleitung, Edition, Übersetzung. Band 2: Kommentar* (Trier: WVT Wissenschaftlicher Verlag, 2013), 1.9–66; Schaffenrath, "Narrative Structures", 318–19.

92 von Contzen/ Glei/Polleichtner/Schulze Rober (ed.)/Vida, Christias, 2.373.

Cuncta Deus placida quae mente accepit et illam
Dignatus venia monitis implevit amicis (Vid. *Christ.* 1.361–7).
[Then she took out from marble jewel boxes various fragrances: wild cinnamon, the fruit of the soft nard, a drop of incense and a touch of fragrant balsam – leaning forward, she rubbed the smooth oil on his bare feet; a sweet aroma spread through the air. God calmly accepted all this, found her worthy of forgiveness and gave her many kind instructions].

The phoenix does not occur in the passage directly, but is alluded to through the combination of aromas that refers to Ovid's poem.[93] Consequently, the phoenix motif is split into two parts in the *Christias*, which indicates its symmetrical composition, and marks the crucial moments of the Passion story, in its first (arrival in Jerusalem) and last stage (crucifixion). Therefore, it suits the heroic image of Christ constructed through, on the one hand, the epic and biblical models and, on the other hand, the Christian topoi and symbols.[94]

The inclusion of the Christological motif of the phoenix in the reservoir of early modern epic poetry, as demonstrated by Vida's poem, proved to be fertile in hagiographical poems, cultivated in the Society of Jesus as well: since saints and martyrs are Christ's followers, the motif was applied to describe their imitative devotion. The first example concerns Francisco Pacheco, a Portuguese man who joined the Jesuits in 1585, and was a teacher at the college in Coimbra. He was sent on a mission in 1592, first to India and then to Japan; eventually, he was burnt to death in Nagasaki on 20 June 1626 during the persecutions of Christians. Bartolomeu Pereira, a teacher in Coimbra, treated his martyrdom in the twelve books of the *Paciecis*,[95] published in 1640 to promote his saint-making; a beatification followed,

93 Ibid., 2.40–1.

94 On Christ's heroic image in the *Christias*, see D. Pulina, "Christus als epischer Held in Marco Girolamo Vidas *Christias*", in Aurnhammer/Steiger (ed.), *Christus*, 219–36.

95 On the poem, see C.M. Urbano, "The *Paciecidos* by Bartolomeu Pereira S.J. – an epic interpretation of the evangelisation and martyrdom in 17th century Japan", *Bulletin of Portuguese-Japanese Studies* 10–11 (2005) 61–95. On classical models, see E. Klecker, "Ein Missionar in Japan auf den Spuren des Aeneas: die *Paciecis* des Bartholomaeus Pereira, S.J. (Coimbra, 1640)", in D. Briesemeister/ A. Schoenberger (ed.), *De litteris neolatinis in America Meridionali, Portugallia, Hispania, Italia cultis* (Frankfurt a. M.: Valentia, 2002) 99–112; on Jesuit models, see Y. Haskell, "The tears in things: How the Jesuits "ripped up" Virgil. Revised from a paper given to the Virgil Society on 20 January 2019", *Proceedings of the Virgil Society* 30 (2020) 61–75, on pp. 69–70. On intercultural background of the poem, see A. Watanabe, "*Mirum videri non debet, si Iapones Romano nonnumquam vestitu induantur* – Romanization of the Japanese in Jesuit Neo-Latin", *Bulletin of Portuguese-Japanese Studies* [2nd series] 4 (2018) 107–22, on pp. 116–19.

although this was as late as 1867.[96] The narrative starts with Pacheco and other Jesuits seeking support in Macao after they had been exiled from Japan (book I), where they return to continue the mission in secret (book II). Soon Pacheco is betrayed by one of his companions and taken prisoner (book III): the incarceration causes an extensive retardation in the development of the frame narrative, and so the protagonist presents his earlier life in a retrospective inset speech (book IV–IX). The transfer to Nagasaki and mystical, or allegorical, preparation for death (books X–XI) precede his martyrdom (book XII).

While waiting for his pyre to be lit, Pacheco provokes the fire with his last words, which are compared to a swan's song:[97] he claims his willingness to sacrifice the life in order to be rewarded in heaven. Only after he had addressed his flock and the land of Japan (*sponsa Dei*, 'God's bride'), was he submitted to the fire:

> Ah, phoenix, quam laetus abis? Quam despicis iras
> Vulcani gaudesque tuis pubescere flammis?
> Quam flavus quantoque volas formosior? Ipsam
> Lunam ultra solemque subis: iamque aurea pennis
> Sidera, iam vitreos axes transcendis et ipsi
> Non te acie possunt oculi servare sequentum.
> I, felix, partoque diu laetare triumpho.[98]
> [Ah, phoenix, how happy are you leaving? How much do you despise the anger of Vulcan and how much do you rejoice over maturing in your own flames? How sparkling are you with flaming gold and how much more beautiful when you fly away? You pass by the moon and the sun as well, you cross now the golden stars, now you cross the clear sky on your wings – and the eyes of your followers cannot keep you in sight. Go, you blessed, to rejoice long in triumph that you have deserved].

The narrator does not create a direct simile with the phoenix, but uses the name of the bird as a keyword which is supposed to evoke in the recipients associations with the motif: the phoenix's story describes Pacheco's fate. The protagonist is glad to be burnt: reborn in a more beautiful form, he will enjoy a triumph in heaven, a festive reception which is an allegory for the canonisation pursued with the *Paciecis*. Indeed, in the following verses Pacheco is welcomed by the leader of Jesuit missions in Asia, Francis Xavier, who demands all due honours for him from

96 On the contextualisation and (vernacular) sources of the poem, see C.M. Urbano, "The *Paciecidos* of Pereira SJ (Coimbra 1640): A Neo-Latin Epic Paraphrasing a *Vita*", in V. Milazzo/F. Scorza Barcellona (ed.), *Bilinguismo e scritture agiografiche. Raccolta di studi* (Rome: Viella, 2018) 207–21.

97 B. Pereira, *Paciecidos libri duodecim. Decantatur clarissimus P. Franciscus Paciecus ... pro Christi fide lento igne concrematus anno 1626 ...* (Coimbra: Emmanuel de Carvalho, 1640), 205.

98 Ibid., 207. English translation is my own.

Ignatius of Loyola: the phrase *parto triumpho* in the quoted passage points out that such a festive reception has been deserved through the martyr's death.

The second example of the phoenix motif in the Jesuit epic poetry shows the devotion of Ignatius of Loyola, who was made an epic hero owing to his function as a model saint.[99] Laurent Le Brun, a French Jesuit, published the *Ignatius sive Societas Jesu fundata*,[100] the youngest of Ignatian poems in Latin, in 1661.[101] It concentrates on the early stage of Ignatius's life and so on his internal maturation to pious life and to founding the Society of Jesus. The poem starts shortly after his conversion: in an ecstatic vision God induces Ignatius to undertake a pilgrimage to the Holy Land (book I). The dominant description of the journey (books I–VIII) closes with the return to Europe (book IX): having visited Rome (book X), Ignatius continues on his way and arrives at Montmartre in Paris (book XI). There, he experiences another vision: the *gloria divina* teaches him about the dissemination of faith and about work that he and his companions will conduct in Europe, Asia, Africa, and America (book XII). Encouraged by this revelation, Ignatius devotes himself to the task of the Order's foundation, which concludes the poem.

In the sixth book, the protagonist explores Jerusalem and contemplates the Passion through the stations of the Cross. When he reaches Calvary, his chest is suddenly inflamed by the *amor divinus*. Obsessed with this divine ardour, a sign of God's influence, Ignatius releases his emotions in a short speech, on which the narrator comments:

> Mors illi votum est, sola est in morte voluptas –
> Haud aliter quam cum vivax sua funera phoenix
> Nobiliore rogo reducisque exordia flammae
> Praeparat et tumulum foliis et thure sabaeo
> Componit, laeta senium positurus in herba.
> At simul accessit Titan faecundaque praebet
> Flamma faces – radiis proprior, nihil ille moratus,
> Parturiente rogo Phoebaeos concipit ignes,
> Ut pereat, gaudetque mori festinus in ortum.

---

99 On the heroisation of Ignatius, see Leone, *Saints and Signs*, 167–203.

100 For a content overview, see L. Braun, Ancilla Calliopeae. *Ein Repertorium der neulateinischen Epik Frankreichs (1500–1700)* (Leiden/Boston: Brill, 2007), 551–73. On the classical models, see T. Gärtner, "Die *Ignatias* des Laurentius Le Brun. Ein Jesuitenepos über den Ordensgründer Ignatius von Loyola", *Neulateinisches Jahrbuch* 6 (2004) 17–49.

101 On Ignatian epic poems, see F. Schaffenrath, "Unedierte lateinische Jesuitenepik aus dem *Fondo Gesuitico* der Biblioteca Nazionale Centrale di Roma", *Neulateinisches Jahrbuch* 9 (2007) 328–42, on pp. 340–1 (does not mention the poem *De raptu Manresano S. Ignatii de Loiola … libri IV* published in 1647 by Carolus Warpaeus); cf. idem, "Narrative Structures", 323–4.

Sic et Loiolides blanditur imagine mortis,
Totus inardescit nec frustra nomen ab ipso
Igne trahit, rapidis flagrant praecordia flammis.[102]
[Death is his wish, only in death does he find pleasure – just like the phoenix which, being still alive, prepares the burial for itself on a more noble pyre, arranges the seed of the recurrent flame and forms the tomb from the leaves and Sabean incense – it will deposit its senility in the agreeable herbs. Then, the Titan came up, and so the fertile flame induces the fire: close to the sunrays and on the rebirth pyre, the phoenix catches, without delay, fires of Phoebus in order to pass away; in a hurry to be reborn, it rejoices to die. Similarly, the son of Loyola is also urged by the vision of death and is entirely glowing: his name truly stems from the fire not without reason – his heart burns in rapid flames].

The *Ignatius* pursues with this passage a different strategy than the *Paciecis* – a phoenix is not just a keyword, but the object of a proper simile. Martial's phrase, emphasising death (*nobiliore rogo*), is combined with the juncture from Claudian's phoenix poem and expressing the rebirth (*parturiente rogo*).[103] Both phrases together, varying the context of the pyre and stages of rebirth process, comply with Ignatius's mindset: death is his wish and pleasure. Delighted by such a prospect, he feels a 'devotional fire' running through his body and soul. Consequently, even if Ignatius was not a martyr, he followed God's inspiration and showed the same devotion and willingness to sacrifice his life for faith which was further to inflame other souls.

Josaphat – phoenix – as *odor Christi* in Młodzianowski's *Icones*: biblical context

The conclusion of Młodzianowski's epigram in the last couplet provides the phoenix motif with biblical connotations which substantiate its Christological meaning. Josaphat burns on the fragrant pyre, and thus turns into an aroma pleasing to God. The odour is, however, spread not only by the pyre, but also by Josaphat himself.

---

102 L. Le Brun, *Ignatius sive Societas Jesu fundata*, in idem, *Virgilius Christianus* (Paris: Simeon Piget, 1661) 5–380, on pp. 170–1.

103 Claud. carm. min. 27.62; the phrase can be found in the poetical handbooks, also under the keyword 'phoenix' (cf. *Gradus*, 565–6). Le Brun reused Claudian's poem more extensively – the verse *ut pereat, gaudetque mori festinus in ortum* repeats carm. min. 27.58, but changes *redeat* to *pereat*, and so it emphasises Ignatius's sacrifice. However, there is a trace of Lactantius's poem: the key verse *mors illi votum est, sola est in morte voluptas* goes back to his poem *De ave phoenice* 165: the *votum*, instead of the original *venus*, shows Ignatius's wish for death.

This thought is repeated in the fifth eulogy in an address to the protagonist and, indirectly, to the recipients:

> … cum flagrando fragrabis, bonus odor Christi in omni loco aut novus novae legis Noe. Post expiatum Dominici sanguinis diluvio mundum offer holocaustum Domino.[104]
> [While you will be burning, you will spread to every place the fragrance, being a pleasant aroma of Christ, or, being a new Noah, the aroma of a new law. After the world has been cleansed through the deluge of the Lord's blood, offer a sacrifice to Him].

A biblical dimension is revealed in a footnote by the reference to the second chapter of Paul's Second Epistle to the Corinthians:

> Deo autem gratias qui semper triumphat nos in Christo Iesu et odorem notitiae suae manifestat per nos in omni loco quia Christi bonus odor sumus Deo … ad haec quis tam idoneus (2 Cor 2:14–16).[105]
> [Therefore, thanks to God who always makes us triumph for Jesus Christ and manifests through us the savour of his knowledge at every place, because we are the pleasant aroma of Christ for God – and who is more appropriate for this?].

In Paul's words, the dissemination of faith by the apostles compares to the Roman custom of appreciating the leaders who return successful from military campaigns.[106] As the *Paciecis* has demonstrated, the triumph motif was adapted in early modern hagiography to illustrate sanctity and its recognition. The saints and martyrs, heroes fighting against vices and evil on behalf of Christ and the Church, deserved a triumphant reception in heaven; moreover, the triumph was a common staging of the festivities celebrated in their honour.

Although Paul speaks explicitly about the apostles in his letter, early modern emblematics applied the motif to every Christian. In the vast collection of the *Emblemata sacra*, published in 1622 by Daniel Cramer, the eighth emblem of the first decade has a quotation from Paul's letter for the title ("Christi bonus odor sumus Deo"; 2 Cor 2:15).[107] The *imago* picks up a Baroque motif of a flaming hart:

---

104 Młodzianowski, *Icones*, fol. B4^{r}.

105 All quotations from the Bible follow R. Weber/R. Gryson (ed.), *Biblia sacra iuxta Vulgatam versionem* (Stuttgart: Deutsche Bibelgesellschaft, ^{5}2007). English translations are my own.

106 Cf. P. Müller, "Wer is geeignet und würdig? 2 Kor 2,14–17 und der römische Triumph", in D. Sänger (ed.), *Der zweite Korintherbrief: literarische Gestalt, historische Situation, theologische Argumentation. Festschrift zum 70. Geburtstag von Dietrich-Alex Koch* (Göttingen: Vandenhoeck & Ruprecht, 2012) 224–39; P. Arzt-Grabner, *2. Korinther* (Göttingen: Vandenhoeck & Ruprecht, 2014), 262–7.

107 D. Cramer, *Emblemata Sacra, das ist: fünfftzig geistliche in Kupffer gestochene emblemata oder Deutungsbilder aus der Heiligen Schrifft* … (Frankfurt a. M.: Hartmann Palthenius, 1622), 45.

it burns on a grate under which a censer emits smoke.[108] God's hand emerges from the clouds and spreads myrrh on the heart, so that even more fragrant smoke wafts to heaven. Neither the lemma (*suspiro*) nor an elegiac couplet below the image, about the pleasant aroma, alludes to the phoenix. Similar proof for the extended meaning of the *odor Christi* delivers the contemporary exegesis. Cardinal Roberto Bellarmino used Paul's words to explain the psalm verse: "murra et gutta et cassia a vestimentis tuis ..." (Ps 44:9). All these fragrances are linked to the divine ointment of Christ (Ps 44:8) who spread pleasant aromas construed as virtues during the Passion.[109] Still, Młodzianowski engages in the intertextual discourse with Paul's words exactly, and answers his question at the end of the relevant passage: Kuntsevych, an archbishop and successor of the apostles, was the appropriate one (*idoneus*) for the task of disseminating the true faith. As he propagated the Union, he diffused Christ's fragrance just as the apostles, his predecessors, did.

The eulogy makes it clear that the odour is to be understood specifically in the context of the encounter, through the Union, of two separated Christian rites. Within the same sentence, the *odor Christi* is juxtaposed with the story of Noah, not specified in a footnote. Considering the deluge narrative, the speaker typologically links two motifs: the deluge which purified the world is turned into a stream of divine blood, meaning Christ's sacrifice on the Cross, a sign of the New Covenant. Similarly, a new bond between God and the people was established after the deluge, as Noah made an offering of the animals, including birds relating to the phoenix – its sweet aroma pleased God ("odoratusque est Dominus odorem suavitatis ..."; Gen 8:21).[110] In Młodzianowski's eulogy, it is Josaphat, the phoenix, who acts as a new Noah and contributes to the New Covenant: the Old one, requiring purification, obviously stands for the Orthodoxy, a deviation from the true faith, which Noah-Kuntsevych tried to restore through his bishopric activity, and, above all, consolidated through martyrdom. In this way, the *imago* of the fourth emblem reveals another aspect: the diptych represents two rites of Christianity reunited through Josaphat's working and sacrifice.

---

108 On the motive, see P. Davidson, *The universal Baroque* (Manchester: Manchester University, 2018), 166–82.

109 R. Bellarmino, *Explanatio in psalmos* ... (Lyon: Horace Cardon, 1612), 318–19. The work was a standard book in the Jesuit curriculum; Bellarmino's oeuvre was widely represented in the library of the Academy in Vilnius; cf. P. Urbański, "Roberto Bellarmino (1542–1621) i wpływ jego myśli na rozwój kulturowych oraz religijnych idei w Rzeczypospolitej", in J. Dąbkowska-Kujko (ed.), *Formowanie kultury katolickiej w dobie potrydenckiej. Tom VI: Powszechność i narodowość katolicyzmu polskiego* (Warsaw: University of Warsaw, 2016) 181–222.

110 On the context of the story, see L. Ruppert, *Genesis. Ein kritischer und theologischer Kommentar. 1. Teilband: Gen 1,1–11,26* (Würzburg: Echter, ^{2}2003), 266–374; J.A. Soggin, *Das Buch Genesis: Kommentar* (Darmstadt: Wissenschaftliche Buchgesellschaft, 1997), 132–51.

Conclusion: *noster phoenix* Josaphat in Młodzianowski's *Icones*

In order to make Ruthenia more visible on the political and cultic map of early modern Europe, Josaphat Kuntsevych was to be forged as a confessional symbol through canonisation. He entered the scene of saint-making as a Basilian and the first Greek Catholic martyr: he came from an interconfessional background which oscillated between the Orthodox and Latin culture. Josaphat's figure and environment therefore needed to be integrated into the approved matrix of Latinity thriving in the Roman Church. One step was taken by Josaphat Isakowicz with the *Josaphatis* at the time of the first canonisation investigation which resulted, however, in beatification. Later on, in the crucial phase of the transition from being blessed to being a saint, Andrzej Młodzianowski took another step and applied the Jesuit pattern of martyrdom and sanctity to the hagiographical profile of Kuntsevych. He used the phoenix as the symbol established in the *Imago primi saeculi Societatis Iesu* and employed in the Jesuit epic poetry, including the poem about Ignatius of Loyola, an exemplary saint of early modern times. Both the lemma and epigram of his emblem accentuate Josaphat's death and sacrifice, while the recipient is expected to keep in mind the prospect of the reward. As a result, Młodzianowski presented the martyrdom of the Uniate as an achievement matching the Catholic standards embodied by the Jesuits, so that Josaphat could confidently emulate other (epic) heroes of Catholicism. At the same time, the inclusion worked the other way around: presented by the Jesuit poet and according to the Jesuit conventions, Josaphat, a Basilian, was introduced to the Jesuit audience as an example of martyrdom and sanctity on equal terms with the Order's members. In addition, Młodzianowski developed the hagiographical motif of the phoenix by adding the biblical context of the apostolic work and of a bond established after the deluge. The reference to Noah in particular highlights the significance of Josaphat's martyrdom fitting the political and cultural needs of his hagiographical profile.

Sabina Pavone

Sanctity in a Global World

Continuity and Discontinuity in the Early Modern Age. Conclusions to *Profiling Saints*

For some decades now studies of sainthood have moved beyond the confines of anatomising hagiographies to embrace new interpretive approaches exploring by turn different specific aspects of the process; from reconstructing the beatification and canonization procedures pursued by the curia at the time of the Counter-Reformation (an operation that has been described happily if a little too glibly as a "saints' conveyor belt"[1]), to the examination of female sanctity in its various manifestations, whether accepted or rejected by the Catholic Church,[2] to the repudiation of sanctity by the Protestant Churches, or to a recent preoccupation with the history of the emotions. Then again, as Franco Motta and Eleonora Rai wrote in their introduction to an issue of the "Journal of Jesuit Studies" devoted to the subject, "the symbolic system of sanctity is to be decoded through registers that are tied to specific epochs, geographical areas, and social needs".[3]

The volume we are dealing with here takes on board the ongoing debate on this complex theme and provides further insights, paying particular attention to a new historiographical season linked above all to the global dimension which has also conditioned the idea of sanctity since early modern times. An indubitable merit is that of having assembled an international team composed not only of historians but also of theological, legal and art historical scholars, so as to encompass the numerous facets of the global politics of saintliness in the modern age. This collection of essays investigates how the phenomenon of holiness, initially tied to a European perspective, began from the evangelisations of the 16th century onwards to acquire

---

1 See M. Gotor, "La fabbrica dei santi: la riforma urbaniana e il modello tridentino", in L. Fiorani, A. Prosperi (ed.), *Storia d'Italia. Annali 16. Roma. La città del papa. Vita civile e religiosa dal Giubileo di Bonifacio VIII al Giubileo di Papa Wojtyla* (Torino: Einaudi, 2000), 657–727 and many subsequent epigones who have recycled the phrase.

2 On female sanctity and in particular on still-living saints see the groundbreaking studies by G. Zarri, such as *Le sante vive. Profezie di corte e devozione femminile tra '400 e '500* (Milano: Rosenberg & Sellier, 1990); L. Scaraffia, G. Zarri (ed.), *Donne e fede. Santità e vita religiosa in Italia* (Roma: Laterza, 2009); but see also A. Jacobson Schutte, *Aspiring Saints. Pretense of Holiness, Inquisition, and Gender in the Republic of Venice, 1618–1750* (Baltimore: John Hopkins UP, 2001).

3 F. Motta, E. Rai, "Jesuit Sanctity: Hypothesizing the Continuity of a Hagiographic Narrative of the Modern Age", in *Journal of Jesuit Studies* 9 (2022/1) 1–14, here 2.

a worldwide projection, functional to the strengthening of the Catholic Church in the "four corners of the world".

At the same time it provides useful material to reinforce the paradigm according to which the Church of Rome used the ceremonies for the beatification and canonization of new saints as a tool to consolidate its image in Europe and beyond.[4] This sort of 'making theatre' out of sanctity, which was a common element in the celebrations around the great Jubilees (those of 1625 and 1650 in particular),[5] was not enough however to paper over the very real crisis in which the institution of the papacy found itself, having to steer a course between the different European powers, themselves well able to utilise evangelisation to wholly colonial ends. In this context, despite the actually quite exiguous number of canonisations,[6] – perhaps precisely as a push-back against the overweening power of the Iberian empires (as exemplified, for example, by the *patronato real* in the Iberian overseas possessions) – the Counter-Reformation Church made wide use of martyrs' hagiographies, which represented a substantial symbolic capital to be exploited, both in Europe in relation to the Protestant world, and in the extra-European sphere.[7] The tie-in between martyrs and saints became from this point of view a central one, assuming new global connotations even if the actual number of formal canonisations remained low. To the martyrs produced 'at home', as it were, by inter-confessional Christian clashes (I am thinking here in particular of the English Jesuit martyrs),[8] a good number of missionary martyrs were added, on occasion by stretching a point, as in the case of the "40 Brazil martyrs of Brazil", known as such but actually killed by

4 P. Giovannucci, *Canonizzazioni e infallibilità pontificia in età moderna* (Brescia: Morcelliana, 2008); R. Saccenti, "Reforming Canonization after the Council of Trent: Saints and Martyrs as Models of a Pure Christian Life," in N. Terpstra (ed.), *Reframing Reformation: Understanding Religious Difference in Early Modern Europe* (Toronto: Centre for Reformation and Renaissance Studies, 2020), 51–68.

5 See M. A. Visceglia, *La città rituale. Roma e le sue cerimonie in età moderna* (Roma: Viella, 2002).

6 Between 1540 and 1770, 27 men and 5 women were canonized and six more beatified, see R. Po-cha Hsia, *The World of Catholic Renewal (1540–1770)* (Cambridge: Cambridge University Press, 1998) ch. 8 (*Counter-Reformation Saints*) on p. 127. On Counter-Reformation sanctity see too P. Burke, "How to be a Counter-Reformation Saint," in Id. *The Historical Anthropology of Early Modern Italy: Essays on Perception and Communication* (New York: Cambridge University Press, 1987), 48–62.

7 See B. S. Gregory, *Salvation at Stake: Christian Martyrdom in Early Modern Europe* (Cambridge, Cambridge University Press, 1999).

8 It should be remembered that the theme of martyrdom also excited Protestant breasts: one need only think of the enormous success of John Foxe's *Acts and Monuments* (1563), popularly known as *Foxe's Book of Martyrs*, which was for English Protestants second in importance only to the Bible itself (see J. R. Knott, *Discourses of Martyrdom in English Literature, 1563–1694* (Cambridge: Cambridge University Press, 1993); but see also R. Kolb, *For All the Saints: Changing Perception of Martyrdom and Sainthood in the Lutheran Reformation* (Macon: Mercer University Press, 1987); D. Nicholls, "The Theatre of Martyrdom in the French Reformation", *Past and Present* 121 (1988) 49–73.

Calvinist pirates while sailing to South America.[9] New persecutions at the hands of pagans were juxtaposed with those of the early Christians in a continuum that was not only experiential but also textual in situations like that in Japan where the lives of the ancient martyrs were circulated as *exempla.*[10] These last represented, in the brave new modern age, an example and a guide, not only for missionaries but for all those neophytes who, although coming from cultures and traditions far from the Christian-European one, approached the Catholic faith in the conviction that they might die for it .

It should not go unmentioned that the mere suggestion of a confusion between evangelization and colonization slowed down several beatification processes in the 17th century – that of Antonio Criminali is an obvious example[11] – due to suspicions that those struck down by pagans might well have been killed because they were identified with the colonisers rather because of their faith. Many of these procedures were reopened in the 19th century, with the advent of a new season of evangelisation which required a strengthening of the idea of missionary holiness, embracing not only the priests who died as martyrs in distant lands but also local converts who in Japan most notably, following the de-Christianisation launched by the shogunate, had played a substitute role in the Christian communities which had over the intervening centuries been all but erased from memory.[12]

There appears to have been an actual policy of sanctification capable of creating unexpected connections, acting not only through the diffusion of a Eurocentric imagery but also through the promotion of cults better lending themselves to hybridization such as that, for example, of Saint Rose of Lima,[13] among the few 'local'

---

9 See P.-A. Fabre, "*Les quarante «martyrs du Brésil» (1570) et leur procès en béatification (1854): historiographie et hagiographie dans la longue Compagnie de Jésus*", *Rivista di storia del cristianesimo*, 2 (2018) 321–340; M.C. Osswald, Maria-Cristina Osswald, "O martírio de Inácio de Azevedo e dos seus trinta e nove companheiros (1570) na hagiografia da Companhia de Jesus entre os séculos XVI e XIX", *Cultura* 27 (2010) 163–186.

10 See M. Harris Takao, *"In what storms of blood from Christ's flock is Japan swimming": Gratia Hosokawa and the Performative Representation of Japan Martyrdom in* Mulier fortis *(1698)*, in Y. Haskell, R. Garrod (ed.), *Changing Hearts. Performing Jesuit Emotions between Europe, Asia, and the Americas* (Leiden-Boston, Brill, 2018) 87–113.

11 See E. Rai, "La legge e il martirio: Morte e normativa nel processo di canonizzazione del 'protomartire' gesuita Antonio Criminali (xvi–xx secolo)", *Lexia* 31 (2019) 205–44.

12 Allow me here to refer to the case of the lyre player Damiano the blind which I investigated in C. Petrolini, V. Lavenia, S. Pavone *Sacre metamorfosi. Racconti di conversione tra Roma e il mondo in età moderna* (Roma: Viella, 2022) 362–369. As regards the Society of Jesus under Pius IX, between 1846 and 1872, 26 Jesuits were beatified and 2 were canonised. Many of these processes had been initiated prior to the suppression of the order (1773).

13 See T. Weddigen, "Materiality and Idolatry: Roman Imaginations of Saint Rose of Lima", in C. Göttler, M. Mochizuki (ed.), *The Nomadic Object. The Challenge of World for Early Modern Religious Art* (Leiden-Boston: Brill, 2018) 103–148 (but more generally the whole volume on the global dimension

saints to be in due course accepted by Rome, again through a process of negotiation between the Vatican and her community of origin, which – as Alessandra Anselmi notes in an article cited from the GLOBECOSAL project – ends up reflecting diplomatic relations between the papacy and the Iberian empires, as well as being a barometer of the faithfulness of different geopolitical areas.[14] In terms of sanctity, the relationship between cults with a global projection and cults relegated to a peripheral context is clearly relevant to the failure of many local examples, a failure which would become more common following the restrictions of Urban VIII which imposed a much stricter control over beatification processes, dependent on a previous non-cult (*non culto*) status: where in fact the existence of local veneration seemed to be an element in favour of beatification, such a factor was viewed with suspicion by Rome and could be interpreted in a negative light, bringing the worship of the saint within the sphere of possible idolatry. No doubt Rome's firm post-Tridentine grip was to some extent a reaction to the attacks repeatedly mounted by the Protestant churches throughout the 16th century, but it also reflected a distinct distrust of processes that could not be governed from the centre and which were viewed as a kind of legitimisation of local elites through the promotion of certain cults. The options were then to try to control faraway situations by appropriating the cult in question or, alternatively, to deny its validity and condemn it entirely. In the case of the 'living saint' Rose of Lima (whose circle was closely examined by the Inquisition)[15] Rome chose the first option and the process of beatification became 'official', whereas in those of the *creoles* Mariana de Jésus Paredes y Flores and Nicolás Ayllón, we see a failure owing to the 'hybrid' identity of the persons proposed for canonisation, who incurred the suspicion of Rome because not conforming with the dominant colonial paradigm, and in Ayllón's case suspected by the Inquisition to boot. We should not forget, when tracing these processes, that some saintly figures canonised in the course of the 17th century had murky areas in their biographies which hagiographies were at pains to 'reinterpret'. The obvious example is Ignatius of Loyola, the subject of no fewer than seven Inquisitorial trials which the best known *Lives* of the saint (starting with Pedro de Ribadeneyra's[16]) would frame as

---

of relics). For the Indian context, see also the reception of some Jesuit martyrs' cults such as that focused on João de Brito by communities of local converts, cf. G. Mosse, *The Saint in the Banyan Tree. Christianity and Caste Society in India* (Berkely-Los Angeles-London: University of California Press, 2012); M. Trento, *Writing Tamil Catholicism. Literature, Persuasion and Devotion in the Eighteenth Century* (Leiden-Boston: Brill, 2022).

14 A. Anselmi, "Theaters for the Canonization of Saints", in W. Tronzo (ed.), *St. Peter's in the Vatican* (New York: Cambridge University Press, 2005) 244–69.

15 For a summary of the case of Rose of Lima and her circle of (female) devotees, see Hsia, *The World of Catholic Renewal (1540–1770)*, ch. 9 (*Holy women, beatas, demoniacs*) 144–158.

16 P. de Ribadeneyra, *Vita Ignatii Loiolæ Societatis Iesu fundatoris, libris quinque comprehensa* (Neapoli: Iosephum Cacchium, 1572).

persecuciónes of the Society of Jesus and therefore, to be read only as such.[17] Ignatius' case allows us to consider another important aspect – that related to beatifications and canonizations linked to religious congregations: in fact, in the early modern age it is evident how sanctity is often structurally linked to the new orders. If Franco Motta and Eleonora Rai have recently drawn attention to the specific phenomenon of 'Jesuit sanctity', within which considerable space is reserved for the founder, this volume investigates another key figure in Roman Catholic religious life, Saint Filippo Neri (founder of the Oratorians), an expression – argues Thomas Santa Maria – of a new interpretative aspect of the Counter-Reformation, fluctuating between a recovery of the dimension of the senses in devotion and the need, or desire, to fight temptation even through forms of self-torture.

The Council of Trent did, to be sure, represent a key turning point with regard to saintliness, as we have noted, and for this reason the case study contributed by Lucio Biasiori tracing the vicissitudes of the Florentine Zanobi Niccolini is interesting from a comparative viewpoint: through his biography and the inquisitorial proceedings undergone by Niccolini we are not only given an insight into devotion to such a controversial figure as Girolamo Savonarola, but also enabled to reconstruct that subtle distinction between sanctity and mental illness which, despite everything, would continue to persist even after the advent of the Counter-Reformation. This principally concerned a female sanctity that had to deal with the hostility of the church towards a religiousness which sought to escape from established authority above all through phenomena such as mysticism and living female saints (censored by the Inquisition) – studied here by Beatrice Saletti in relation to the case of Lucia Broccadelli from Narni.

A different instance again, not in fact investigated in the volume, but which is worth mentioning, is that of saints who, from a global perspective, are today the object of real differences of opinion linked to post-colonial studies, such as the case of Pedro Claver, canonised for his self-sacrifice in frequenting the docks and converting black slaves arriving in Cartagena de Indias. While Longaro degli Oddi's biography of Claver,[18] which paved the way to the opening of the beatification procedure, provides a hagiographical portrait of the saint, one of the few to look on black slaves as human beings and to concern himself with their spiritual wellbeing, more recent studies have emphasised how the conversion of black slaves was a significant factor in destroying the African traditions and culture of those arriving

---

17 On Ignatius' trials see S. Pavone, "A Saint under Trial: Ignatius of Loyola between Alcalà and Rome", in R. A. Maryks (ed.), *A Companion to Ignatius of Loyola: Life, Writings, Spirituality, Influence* (Leiden: Brill, 2014) 45–65.

18 L. degli Oddi, *Vita del venerabil servo di Dio padre Pietro Claver della Compagnia di Gesù, detto l'Apostolo degli Etiopi* (Rome: Salomoni, 1748).

in the New World,[19] The latter reading has led to Claver's canonisation (again a late one: 1888, following on beatification in 1850) being contested as the glorification of a 'racial hero' who ought instead to be vilified.[20]

In the Far East too the problems we have observed in relation to the Latin American situation also arose, albeit in a profoundly different context, one, that is, of empires where European evangelisation was only partly linked to the colonisation of the territories in question. While the Portuguese *Estado da India* did in fact have a territorial foothold in India and Macau, the same cannot be said for China and Japan. The missionary vocation had in these cases to be exercised in an alien context in which the European powers perforce acted as a minority and had to negotiate their presence with the relevant governments. Without entering here into the detail of the Christianisation and subsequent de-Christianisation of Japan, it is worth observing that the case of the 26 Japanese martyrs turns out to be the most studied in this volume. No less than three essays – those of Hitomi Omata Rappo, Carla Tronu and Linda Zampol D'Ortia – specifically focusing on it, and another two (GLOBECOSAL, Rachel Miller) dealing with it at least tangentially. From the perspective of the attempted evangelization of all the four corners of the world, Japan does, it is true, represent an emblematic case for Asia both in quantitative terms and in relation to the bloody failure of Christianization there from the 1630s onwards. Papal policy, determined to sustain at all costs the Oriental missions, favoured the early beatification of the Japanese martyrs in order to tend the flames of a willingness, even desire, to die for Christ as an essential characteristic of the missionary spirit, but canonisations would, as we have said, only come much later.

Regarding the Society of Jesus, which was, after an initial phase of equivocation, the most disposed of the religious orders to exploit martyrdom as a road to possible

19 W. Chamberlain, "Silencing Genocide: The Jesuit Ministry in Colonial Cartagena de Indias and its Legacy", *Journal of Black Studies* 49/7 (2018) 672–693. A more nuanced position is that of H. Vignaux, "Le rôle primordial des Jésuites dans l'évangélisation des Noirs de Nouvelle Grenade", in Ead., *L'église et les noirs dans l'audience du Nouveau Royaume de Grenade* (Monpellier: Presses Universitaires de la Méditerranée, 2009) 327–504.

20 See K. M. Grimes, "Racialized Humility: the White Supremacist Sainthood of Peter Claver, SJ", *Horizons* 42 (2015) 295–316. Franco Motta and Eleonora Rai have instead highlighted how the figure of Claver is a typical example of the canonization strategy of the Society of Jesus relating to "hegemony over certain geographical areas and social identities." ("Strategie di santità. La politica delle canonizzazioni dei gesuiti fra antica e nuova Compagnia (XVII-XX secolo)", in F. Quiles Garcia *et al.* (ed.), *A la luz de Roma. Santos y santidad en el barroco iberoamericano*, vol. 1, *La capital pontificia en la construcción de la santidad* (Sevilla-Roma: Universidad Pablo de Olavide-Roma Tre-Press, 2020) 91–106, on p. 96. See also G. Neveu, "La fabrique d'un saint missionnaire jésuite dans la longue durée (XVIIe, XVIIIe et XIXe siècles): Pedro Claver (1580–1654) entre rhétorique, théologie et histoire", in *Les dossier du Grhil* 2015 (https://journals.openedition.org/dossiersgrihl/6405). On Claver's slave conversions see now Petrolini, Lavenia, Pavone, *Sacre metamorfosi*, 522–532.

canonisation, worth signalling are volumes by Philippe Alegambe[21] and Matthias Tanner, the latter defining the canon of martyr accounts in strict relation to the evangelisation of the four corners of the world.[22] Both published in the second half of the 17th century, they also contributed iconographically to the promotion of Jesuit sanctity in line with a programme that was later returned to with the *Lettres édifiantes et curieuses* [23] in which Jesuit missionaries are often presented as eager for martyrdom. Also in the same line are the *indipetæ* letters written by young Jesuits requesting to leave for the missions, in which martyrdom is again a frequently recurring theme.[24]

One of the key recurring words in this volume is certainly 'negotiation': promotion of the worship of new saints is understood, in fact, as an aspect of the Catholic Church's broader policy in the aftermath of the Council of Trent of strengthening and defining its own role both from a political perspective, most obviously in its relations with the Iberian empires – a theme central to the ERC GLOBECOSAL project which is investigating the construction of sanctity through the promotion of local works of art – and from a nationalistic perspective in a strategy of promoting 'autochthonous' saints or saints in some other way functional to the political projects of a reigning dynasty.[25] Occasionally a similar strategy could end up involving other Christian Churches as in the case of the Basilian monk Josaphat Kuntsevych studied here by Patryk Michal Ryczkowski, martyred in 1623 and proclaimed blessed in 1643, victim of the unrest following the Union of Brest. There was also an eminently political aspect to sainthood highlighted by Stefan Samerski in his essay, which places due emphasis on the justifications for beatification promoted by the Catholic Church after 1789 in the light of a general disavowal of revolutionary events.

---

21 P. d'Alegambe, *Mortes illustres et gesta eorum de Societate Iesu qui in odium fidei pietatis, aut cuiuqunque virtutis, occasionum Missionum, Sacramentorum administratorum, fidei, aut virtutis propugnata* (Romæ, Varchi, 1657). Martyrdom episodes involving fathers of the Society relating to conversion are recounted in various holdings of the Archivum Romanum Societatis Jesu: *F.G.* (vol. 682: *De Sanctis et martyribus*), *Vitæ*, *Opera nostrorum*. On martyrdom and sanctity see P.-A. Fabre, "Conclusion: The Narrow Road to Martyrdom", *Journal of Jesuit Studies* 9 (2022/1) 125–135.

22 M. Tanner, *Societas Jesu usque ad sanguinis et vitæ profusionem militans* (Pragæ: typis Universitatis Carolo-Ferdinandeæ, 1675); Id. *Societas Jesu apostolorum imitatrix, sive Gesta praeclara et virtutes eorum* (Pragæ: typis Universitatis Carlo-Ferdinandeæ, 1694). Volume one of this second work dealt with Europe, while the second volume, which was to have covered the New World, never saw the light of day.

23 J.-B. Du Halde, *Lettres édifiantes et curieuses, écrites des Missions Étrangères, par quelques Missionnaires de la Compagnie de Jésus* (Paris: Nicolas Le Clerc, 1703–1776).

24 See P.-A. Fabre, G. Mongini G. Imbruglia, *Cinque secoli di Litterae Indipetae. Il desiderio delle missioni nella Compagnia di Gesù* (Roma: Institutum Historicum Societatis Iesu).

25 On the role of Jesuit sanctity in the dialectic between the Society and the Austrian Habsburgs see M.-E. Ducreux, "Patronage, Politics, and Devotion: The Habsburgs of Central Europe and Jesuit Saints", *Journal of Jesuit Studies* 9 (2022/1) 53–75.

Another recurrent theme is the continuous relationship between texts and images. It is hard to imagine the successful promotion of sainthood that did not also rely on a congruent iconography. The value of images in the religious sphere is already a well explored theme both in relation to evangelisation and the promotion of the faith, and as integral to catechisms.[26] It comes as no surprise then to find that many of these essays tackle the theme of sanctity with a due acknowledgement of the iconographic element. If therefore the aforementioned GLOBECOSAL project dwells on the hybridization of Francis Xavier's iconography in a truly global perspective, and on the images and emblems linked to the beatification of Jerónima de la Asunción as well as on the figures of other Andean saints mentioned above, Gerace and Dominici explore the important matching of texts and images through the influence of Johannes Molanus' *De pictura et imaginibus sacris* (1570) on late 16th-century Flemish painting, following in the footsteps to some extent of pioneering works such as that of Paolo Prodi on Gabriele Paleotti's *Discorso intorno alle immagini sacre e profane*, published in Italian in 1582 and two years later in Latin.[27] Also in relation to martyrdom, it should be remembered that re-evocation through images was a much-exploited strategy encouraging the canonization processes and in some contexts such as the Japanese one this might typically involve native painters converted to Catholicism who could bring hybrid styles to the table.[28]

The avenues of enquiry pursued and extended in this volume are many, then, and as with all truly innovative volumes, they raise new questions and point the way to further research.

26 See M. Cattaneo, *Convertire e disciplinare. Chiesa romana e religiosità popolare in età moderna* (Napoli: Federico II University Press, 2022).

27 See P. Prodi, *Arte e pietà nella chiesa tridentina* (Bologna: il Mulino, 2014).

28 See F. Palomo, "Global images for global worship: Narratives, paintings and engravings of the martyrs of Japan in seventeenth-century Iberian worlds", in G. Capriotti, P.-A. Fabre, S. Pavone (ed.), *Eloquent Images. Evangelisation, Conversion and Propaganda in the Global World of the Early Modern Period* (Leuven: Leuven University Press, 2022). On the Japanese converted community (*kirishitan*) cf. K. Miyazaki, "The Kakure Kirishitan Tradition", in M. R. Mullins (ed.), *The Handbook of Christianity in Japan* (Leiden-Boston: Brill, 2003) 19–34.

Notes on Contributors

Lucio Biasiori, University of Padua, Department of Historical and Geographic Sciences and the Ancient World, Padua, Italy

Tamara Dominici, Independent Scholar, Riccione, Italy

Hannah Joy Friedman, University of Zurich, Art History Institute, Zurich, Switzerland

Joris Geldhof, KU Leuven, Faculty of Theology and Religious Studies, Leuven, Belgium

Antonio Gerace, Foundation for Religious Studies, John XXIII, Bologna, Italy; KU Leuven, Leuven, Belgium

Jonathan E. Greenwood, Independent Scholar, Vanier, Ontario, Canada

Wei Jiang, University of Zurich, Art History Institute, Zurich, Switzerland

Rachel Miller, California State University Sacramento, Sacramento, California, United States

Franco Motta, University of Turin, Department of History, Turin, Italy

Sabina Pavone, University of Naples "L'Orientale", Naples, Italy

Carlo Pelliccia, International University of Rome, Rome, Italy; CHAM Centre for the Humanities, Lisbon, Portugal

Raphaèle Preisinger, University of Zurich, Art History Institute, Zurich, Switzerland

Lucia Querejazu Escobari, University of Zurich, Art History Institute, Zurich, Switzerland

Hitomi Omata Rappo, Kyoto University, Hakubi Center, Kyoto, Japan

Shiri Roelofs, KU Leuven, Faculty of Law and Criminology, Leuven, Belgium

Patryk M. Ryczkowski, University of Innsbruck, Institute for Classical Philology and Neo-Latin Studies, Innsbruck, Austria

Beatrice Saletti, University of Ferrara, Department of Humanities, Ferrara, Italy

Stefan Samerski, Ludwig Maximilian University of Munich, Faculty of Catholic Theology, Munich, Germany

Thomas Santa Maria, Yale University, Silliman College, New Haven, Connecticut, United States

Carla Tronu Montané, Kansai University of Foreign Studies, Hirakata, Japan

Linda Zampol D'Ortia, Australian Catholic University, Melbourne, Australia; Ca' Foscari University, Venice, Italy